Esprit Basic Research Series

Edited in cooperation with
the European Commission, Information Society DG

Springer
Berlin
Heidelberg
New York
Barcelona
Hong Kong
London
Milan
Paris
Singapore
Tokyo

Malcolm P. Atkinson
Ray Welland (Eds.)

Fully Integrated Data Environments

Persistent Programming Languages, Object Stores, and Programming Environments

Springer

Editors:

Malcolm P. Atkinson
Ray Welland
University of Glasgow
Department of Computing Science
8-17 Lilybank Gardens, Glasgow, G12 8RZ
United Kingdom
{mpa, ray}@dcs.gla.ac.uk

Library of Congress Cataloging-in-Publication Data

Atkinson, M. P.
Fully integrated data environments: persistent programming languages, object stores, and programming environments / Malcolm P. Atkinson.
p. cm. – (ESPRIT basic research series)
Includes bibliographical references.
ISBN-13: 978-3-642-64055-1 e-ISBN-13: 978-3-642-59623-0
DOI: 10.1007/978-3-642-59623-0
1. Database management. 2. Computer programming. I. Title. II. Series.

QA76.9.D3 A892 2000
005.74–dc21 00-049677

ACM Computing Classification (1998): H.2, D.3.3, D.2.2

ISBN-13: 978-3-642-64055-1 Springer-Verlag Berlin Heidelberg New York

Softcover reprint of the hardcover 1st edition 2000

Cover design: *design & production* GmbH, Heidelberg
Typesetting: Camera-ready by editors
Printed on acid-free paper SPIN 10704038 45/3142PS - 5 4 3 2 1 0

Preface

The research into Fully Integrated Data Environments has the goal of substantially improving the quality of application systems while reducing the cost of building and maintaining them. Application systems invariably involve the long-term storage of data since the human activities that justify their construction and operation have durations of months or years. Much unnecessary complexity obstructs the construction of these systems when conventional databases, file systems, operating systems, communication systems and programming languages are used. This complexity limits the sophistication of the systems that can be built, generates operational and usability problems, and deleteriously impacts both reliability and performance.

The FIDE researchers believe that it is feasible and worthwhile to develop a new integrated environment to support the construction and operation of such persistent application systems. This book reports on the principles which they employed to design such an environment, on the prototypes they built to demonstrate its feasibility and on experience using these prototypes to demonstrate their utility. Overall the potential, viability and utility of Fully Integrated Data Environments has been demonstrated, many detailed design issues have been worked out and an evolutionary path has been devised showing that FIDE systems can inter-work with legacy systems. Although there are many detailed research issues that remain, this approach is now ripe for commercial development.

The consortium that undertook the first three years of FIDE research was formed under the leadership of Dr. François Bancilhon and comprised groups from:

- University of Glasgow, Scotland (Professor Malcolm P. Atkinson)
- Universität Hamburg, Germany (Professor Dr. Joachim W. Schmidt)
- Istituto di l'Elaborazione dell'Informazione del C.N.R (IEI), Pisa, Italy (Professor Costantino Thanos)
- Laboratoire de Recherche en Informatique (LRI) Université Paris XI, France (Professor Nicolas Spyratos)
- GIP Altaïr, INRIA, Rocquencourt, France (Dr. François Bancilhon)
- Universita di Pisa, Italy (Professor Antonio Albano)
- University of St Andrews, Scotland (Professor Ronald Morrison)

The consortium brought together teams who had experience in designing and implementing database programming languages, persistent programming languages, object-oriented languages, conceptual data models, OODBMS and persistent object stores. From the start there was complete commitment to the principle that we need to discover and implement new constructs that would support all aspects of persistent application systems. The transparency gained by using the same coherent set of constructs throughout a system is a powerful simplifying factor. For example, programmers are no longer required to understand the relationship between constructs used in short-lived contexts and those used for long-lived contexts. Furthermore separate processing technology is no longer needed to support the different constructs; and code to translate between them is also eliminated. When incorporated into a well-engineered system this also yields performance gains.

Several criteria are vital for these new constructs. They need to be as simple as possible, they must combine in a uniform manner, their combination must be sufficiently powerful that they satisfy persistent applications builders and they must allow efficient implementation. Furthermore they must be precisely defined.

The consortium found it useful to use the discipline of programming language design and implementation. This forces a rigor of definition, highlights the degree to which regularity and simplicity are being achieved and provides a mechanism for allowing others to use and evaluate the developing model. The demonstrations of the research at this time were three programming languages DBPL, Galileo and PS-algol.

A new consortium was formed by Professor Malcolm Atkinson to continue this line of research, broaden its scope and develop the engineering necessary for its application. This consortium, $FIDE_2$, comprised:

- University of Glasgow, Scotland (Professor Malcolm P. Atkinson)
- Universität Hamburg, Germany (Professor Dr. Joachim W. Schmidt)
- Istituto di l'Elaborazione dell'Informazione del C.N.R (IEI), Pisa, Italy (Dr. Fausto Rabitti)
- INRIA, Rocquencourt, France (Dr. Patrick Valduriez)
- Universita di Pisa, Italy (Professor Antonio Albano)
- University of St Andrews, Scotland (Professor Ronald Morrison)

All the players in this phase of the research agreed in the importance of three guiding principles, which had emerged from the previous work:

- the provision of **orthogonal persistence** is essential, that is *every type of data* should have the same rights to persistence;
- powerful type systems are necessary to fully describe the semantics of data and to provide safety; and
- reflection can be exploited effectively in both the construction and evolution of persistent applications.

New engineering approaches were pioneered, including techniques for implementing caches and transactions on client/server object systems, models for organising queries over object stores, persistent and mobile threads and improved persistent language implementation techniques. The applicability of FIDE technology was seen to depend on adequate techniques to integrate it with legacy systems and on support for programmers building and maintaining a persistent application.

The researchers who developed the $FIDE_2$ results continue to pursue the goal of fundamental improvements to the way in which we build applications for our commerce, industry and society depend on the quality of those applications. Some have gone into industry to develop products based on the FIDE concepts and principles. Others have been joined in their research by workers intent on developing this new model of application development. This book is intended as essential reading for all those who join this effort in industry or academia.

The editors are extremely grateful to Tony Printezis who did a great deal of hard work to impose a uniform format on the contributions.

Glasgow, September 1999

Malcolm P Atkinson
Ray Welland

Table of Contents

Introduction

Malcolm P. Atkinson

Department of Computing Science, University of Glasgow, Glasgow, G12 8QQ, Scotland

This book cannot encompass all the achievements of the FIDE consortia and so it focuses on a selection of highlights that represent the major achievement in the final years. There are references to or synopses of FIDE work that has been published elsewhere. Although there are many publications generated by the FIDE consortia, the majority of this book is new material.

The book is divided into three parts:

Part 1 introduces the languages designed for programming applications in a Fully Integrated Data Environment, that also show the integration and culmination of the FIDE designs and provide a vehicle for the subsequent discussion.

Part 2 presents good engineering techniques that implement a Fully Integrated Data Environment; and

Part 3 shows how programmers working in a Fully Integrated Data Environment may be supported.

Each part of the book commences with an overview that also sets the work in context. Each of the following sections contains a sequence of chapters preceded by a more specific overview and orientation, relating the FIDE research to contemporary systems and research.

Part 1

Part 1 starts with a major section presenting the three programming languages developed during $FIDE_2$: Napier88, Fibonacci and Tycoon. These acted as research vehicles and driving forces during the research and they now capture and introduce most of the important concepts. The languages are used in examples later in the book.

Tycoon is a development of Cardelli's language Quest and explores the potential of richly polymorphic type systems in combination with orthogonal persistence. Fibonacci is derived from the orthogonally persistent language Galileo and develops the conceptual model further by combining relational and role constructs with the object model. Napier88 is developed from PS-algol and explores the balance between dynamic and static binding, has constructs to manipulate linguistic environments, pioneers a form of strongly typed linguistic reflection and explores the interplay between two forms of polymorphism and universal types.

The section on linguistic reflection describes the principles which underlie this powerful technique for building self-adaptive systems and shows its practical realisation and use. Self adaptation is essential for long-lived applications as it allows them to adapt to their changing environments. The power of the technique presented here is that the safety offered by strong typing is still available while extending the system.

A general tenet of the FIDE work is that there is an equivalence in role between types and schemata as set out in the following table.

Databases	**Programming Languages**
Data Model	type system
Schema	type
Database	variable
Data Extent	value

The powerful type systems of the three FIDE languages all show the ability to describe regularity in data needed for large-scale and long-lived data. They also allow sophisticated structures and precise operational controls to be applied. Two major issues arise with these type systems, the ease with which programmers can use them and the tractability of their precise enforcement. The principal chapter of Section 3 in Part 1 presents a major formal result concerning tractability, and the subsequent synopses expose two programming issues.

The success of relational systems is based on exploiting the regularity of just one bulk data type. The object-oriented databases typically build-in several bulk data types. The type systems of the FIDE languages allow an open-ended set of such bulk types to be defined in the language. This allows new regularities in data to be identified, described and exploited typically by library builders rather than every application programmer. The merits of doing this compared with building in system providers' choices are explained in the three chapters of Section 4, Part 1.

Large-scale persistent applications require concurrency control and transactions. The linguistic issues that their requirements raise are briefly summarised in the final section of Part 1.

Part 2

Part 2 is concerned with implementation issues. There are, of course, a huge number of implementation strategies and techniques to be explored in the development of Fully Integrated Data Environments. The essential opportunity is that significant optimisation becomes possible when you set out to support all application requirements with one underlying system designed as a coherent whole. This contrasts with the tug-of-love situation that presently pertains, where operating systems, database management systems and programming language runtime systems fight each other for resources to provide to the self same applications they wish to succour. But developing a single support platform is by no means easy as the issues dealt with separately in conventional systems have now to be comprehended as a unity and because all of our experimental systems are heavily influenced by, and dependent upon, the existing infrastructure.

The first section of Part 2 begins exploring this issue by outlining an architecture for a universal infrastructure. Three example architectures are then presented that concern experimental approximations to this ideal. The first is a synopsis of an integration of two existing systems, a relational storage scheme with a modular language. The second is the kernel of the current implementation of Napier88 and explores the integration between programming language implementation and persistent object stores. The third presents the foundations of the Tycoon system and shows how an open system approach can simplify implementation and interfacing to existing technology with compiled language performance.

In a FIDE system all new data eventually resides in a persistent object store. Section 2 addresses the design issues for such stores. It begins with a synopsis describing a store technology that was widely used in the early FIDE consortium. An approach to object store design, PIOS, which seeks to exploit more semantic knowledge about the structures over objects appears in the next chapter. The three synoptic chapters that conclude this section report on: garbage collection for client/server architectures, unifying interfaces to existing store technology and the measurement of the performance of persistent object stores.

The third section of Part 2 presents implementations of particular parts of a FIDE infrastructure. Though these have not been integrated into one subsystem within the FIDE project we believe they illustrate well, important components of a FIDE platform. Such components need refinement and integration to form an effective FIDE platform just as individual aspects of relational support have been refined and integrated to deliver the high performance RDBMS of today. We consider the components presented here as several significant steps from our starting point on a research journey that is still in progress.

The first chapter of this section provides a synopsis of a recovery mechanism used to ensure atomicity and durability in persistent stores. The next chapter describes an efficient automation of object locking. The optimisation of queries over object stores are presented in the next two chapters. The fifth chapter of this section considers the integration of query optimisation with method code optimisation. The final chapter refers to an efficient technique for implementing the parametric polymorphisms found in FIDE languages.

Part 3

The final part of this book is concerned with demonstrations of how a developed FIDE can be used in contemporary computational environments. Section 1 is concerned with support for programmers developing and maintaining applications in a FIDE. Section 2 is concerned with the data modelling aspects of designing such applications and Section 3 shows how they may interwork with the legacy components around them.

The first three chapters of Section 1 report on developments using hyper-programming in Napier88. Hyper-programming exploits the FIDE's uniform integration during program construction and maintenance. While editing a program a programmer may refer to an object in the store directly, e.g. by identifying it with a browser or query. The source representation then includes a direct reference to this object in contrast to a name or query that would be bound to an object during some later execution. These direct references are then exploitable for many of the activities of a programming life-cycle.

The fourth Chapter presents the persistent programming workshop. Two aspects of this work are important:

- it is implemented using the Napier88 system as a Fully Integrated Data Environment and it therefore illustrates how a persistent application may be built and maintained in such a context exploiting its coherence and integration, and
- it provides a set of tools to help programmers with program construction, software re-use and build management based on a putative persistent programming methodology.

It also gives examples of a trend towards further integration. The tools and development environments can also be considered part of the whole FIDE. The library of components described in chapter 5 is held in the Napier88 FIDE and is a source of the re-usable components described in chapter 4. It's organisation permits tools to use information retrieval techniques and to automatically insert selected interfaces, required types and binding information into a programmer's code.

Experience shows that programmers maintaining a large and long-lived application have difficulty acquiring and maintaining an understanding of the existing components and data in the system. The final chapter of this section describes initial work on tools to help them acquire an understanding of the contents of a persistent programming environment.

The section on data modelling commences with a demonstration of how traditional data models and data model design methods can be supported by all three FIDE languages. The workbench in chapter 2 shows a more detailed development of design tools for applications in the Tycoon language. In Section 4 of Part 1 the definition of bulk types in a polymorphic language was described. A possible drawback to this approach is inadequate syntactic support. The third chapter of this section shows how extensible syntax provides such syntactic support. The final section is concerned with interoperability. The first two chapters open the way to efficiently extracting information from and inserting it into formatted data files. The processes of parsing and selection can be efficiently combined with the transformation to the target type system. The final chapter shows how a simple kernel language, consistent abstract interfaces and dynamic binding can be used to integrate legacy components.

Summary

Where does the FIDE research lead? It has shown that strongly-typed, orthogonally-persistent systems, combined with reflection and dynamic binding, allow sophisticated and long-lived applications to be built and maintained in Fully Integrated Data Environments that are dramatically simpler for application programming than the present conventional environments. It has shown that reasonably efficient realisations of a FIDE can be built and has opened up the territory for improving their engineering and exploring their use.

Part 1

Persistent Languages: Introduction and Overview

Ron Morrison

School of Mathematical and Computational Sciences, University of St Andrews,
North Haugh, St Andrews KY16 9SS, Scotland

1 Introduction

Persistent programming languages are designed to support the construction of persistent application systems which have the potential to be long-lived, concurrently accessed and consist of large bodies of data and programs. Well designed programming languages have two important effects: they provide better notations enhancing and accelerating descriptions, for example definition of schemata via data definition languages or definition of process via programming languages, and they demand the development of clean and precise understanding of the underlying concepts. FIDE therefore paid particular attention to the integration of databases and programming languages focusing on those issues peculiar to persistent application systems.

The implication of orthogonal persistence is that the user need never write code to move or convert data for long or short term storage [1]. There are three design principles of persistence. They are:

The Principle of Persistence Independence

> The form of a program is independent of the longevity of the data that it manipulates. Programs look the same whether they manipulate short-term or long-term data.

The Principle of Data Type Orthogonality

> All data objects should be allowed the full range of persistence irrespective of their type. There are no special cases where objects are not allowed to be long-lived or are not allowed to be transient.

The Principle of Persistence Identification

> The choice of how to identify and provide persistent objects is orthogonal to the universe of discourse of the system. The mechanism for identifying persistent objects is not related to the type system.

The application of these three principles yields ***Orthogonal Persistence***. The advantages of orthogonal persistence have been described elsewhere; they can be summarised as:

- improving programming productivity from simpler semantics;
- avoiding *ad hoc* arrangements for data translation and long-term data storage;
- providing protection mechanisms over the whole environment;
- supporting incremental evolution; and
- automatically preserving referential integrity over the entire computational environment for the whole life-time of a PAS.

By following these design principles, languages that provide orthogonal persistence as a basic abstraction have been developed.

The major achievements in persistent programming language design are summarised in Table 1 which is taken from [2].

1977	Pascal/R [3]
1980	SmallTalk [4], PS-algol [1], Plain [5], Taxis [6]
1981	Daplex [7], Adaplex [8, 9]
1983	Galileo [10], Modula/R [11], Persistent procedures [12]
1984	Amber [13], Persistent Prolog [14]
1985	CPS-algol experiment [15], Poly [16], OPAL [17]
1986	DBPL [18], RAPP [19]
1987	Quest [20], E [21], *X* [22]
1988	DPS-algol [23], Napier88 [24]
1991	P-Quest [25], Staple [26], P-Galileo [27], O_2 [28]
1992	Hyper-programming [29], Commercial Persistent C^{++}
1993	Tycoon [30], Fibonacci [31]
1994	Napier88 version 2 [32]
1996	PJava [33]

Table 1. Milestones in Persistent and Database Programming Languages.

2 The FIDE Challenges for Persistent Languages

The provision of an environmental model of computation does have an influence upon certain language features to support its holistic view of information. Most notably it must pay attention to the following aspects of language design :

- ***Name Space Control*** – to uniquely identify objects and provide name spaces tailored to individual applications

- ***Type Systems*** – to provide a standard type system with parameterised type constructors to take over the role of conceptual data models
- ***Scale*** – to express computations on large bodies of data
- ***Data Evolution*** – to control change including schema evolution
- ***Sharing*** – to avoid re-invention of wheels
- ***Protection*** – to ensure the integrity of valuable data
- ***Concurrent Execution*** – to provide linguistic support for transactions, concurrency, distribution and recovery
- ***Complexity Control*** – to avoid the failures of inconsistent design

The papers in this section give an insight into the FIDE approach to each of these problems.

References

1. Atkinson MP, Bailey PJ, Chisholm KJ, Cockshott WP, Morrison R. An Approach to Persistent Programming. Computer Journal 1983; 26,4:360-365
2. Atkinson MP, Morrison R. Orthogonally Persistent Object Systems. VLDB Journal 1995; 4,3:319-401
3. Schmidt JW. Some High Level Language Constructs for Data of Type Relation. ACM Transactions on Database Systems 1977; 2,3:247-261
4. Goldberg A, Robson D. Smalltalk-80: The Language and its Implementation. Addison Wesley, Reading, Massachusetts, 1983
5. Wasserman AI, Shertz DD, Kersten ML, Reit RP, van de Dippe MD. Revised Report on the Programming Language PLAIN. ACM SIGPLAN Notices 1981; 5,16
6. Mylopoulos J, Bernstein PA, Wong HKT. A Language Facility for Designing Database-Intensive Applications. ACM Transactions on Database Systems 1980; 5,2:185-207
7. Shipman D. The Functional Data Model and the Data Language DAPLEX. ACM Transactions on Database Systems 1981; 6,1:140-173
8. Smith JM, Fox S, Landers T. Reference Manual for ADAPLEX. Computer Corporation of America Report CCA-81-02, 1981
9. Chan A, Dayal U, Fox S. An Ada-Compatible Distributed Database Management System. In: Proceedings of the IEEE, Special Issue on Distributed Databases. IEEE, 1987, pp 674-694
10. Albano A, Cardelli L, Orsini R. Galileo: a Strongly Typed, Interactive Conceptual Language. ACM Transactions on Database Systems 1985; 10,2:230-260
11. Koch J, Mall M, Putfarken P, Reimer M, Schmidt JW, Zehnder CA. Modula/R Report Lilith Version. ETH Zürich, 1983
12. Atkinson MP, Morrison R. Procedures as Persistent Data Objects. ACM Transactions on Programming Languages and Systems 1985; 7,4:539-559
13. Cardelli L. Amber. In: Lecture Notes in Computer Science 242. Springer-Verlag, 1986, pp 21-47
14. Bocca J, Bailey PJ. Logic Languages and Relational DBMSs—the Point of Convergence. In: Proc. 2nd International Workshop on Persistent Object Systems, Appin, Scotland, 1987, pp 346-362

15. Krablin GL. Transactions and Concurrency. Universities of Glasgow and St Andrews Report PPRR-46-87, 1987
16. Matthews DCJ. Poly Report. University of Cambridge Report 28, 1982
17. ServioLogic Ltd. Programming in OPAL, 1987
18. Matthes F, Schmidt JW. The Type System of DBPL. In: Hull R, Morrison R, Stemple D (ed) Database Programming Languages, Proc. 2nd International Workshop on Database Programming Languages, Salishan Lodge, Gleneden Beach, Oregon. Morgan Kaufmann, 1989, pp 219-225
19. Hughes JG, Connolly M. Data Abstraction and Transaction Processing in the Database Programming Language RAPP. In: Bancilhon F, Buneman OP (ed) Advances in Database Programming Languages. Addison-Wesley and ACM Press, 1990, pp 177-186
20. Cardelli L. Typeful Programming. DEC Systems Research Center Report 45, 1989
21. Richardson J, Carey M. Persistence in the E Language: Issues and Implementation. Software—Practice and Experience 1989; 19,12:1115-1150
22. Hurst AJ, Sajeev ASM. A Capability Based Language for Persistent Programming. In: Rosenberg J, Koch DM (ed) Persistent Object Systems. Springer-Verlag, 1990, pp 186-201
23. Wai F. Distributed Concurrent Persistent Languages: an Experimental Design and Implementation. Universities of Glasgow and St Andrews Report PPRR-76-89, 1989
24. Morrison R, Brown AL, Connor RCH, Dearle A. The Napier88 Reference Manual. Universities of Glasgow and St Andrews Report PPRR-77-89, 1989
25. Matthes F, Müller R, Schmidt JW. Object Stores as Servers in Persistent Programming Environments—The P-Quest Experience. ESPRIT BRA Project 3070 FIDE Report FIDE/92/48, 1992
26. Davie AJT, McNally DJ. Statically Typed Applicative Persistent Language Environment (STAPLE) Reference Manual. University of St Andrews Report CS/90/14, 1990
27. Brown AL, Mainetto G, Matthes F, Müller R, McNally DJ. An Open System Architecture for a Persistent Object Store. In: Proc. 25th International Conference on Systems Sciences, Hawaii, 1992, pp 766-776
28. Deux O. The Story of O_2. IEEE Transactions on Knowledge and Data Engineering 1990; 2,1
29. Kirby GNC, Connor RCH, Cutts QI, Dearle A, Farkas AM, Morrison R. Persistent Hyper-Programs. In: Albano A, Morrison R (ed) Persistent Object Systems, Proc. 5th International Workshop on Persistent Object Systems, San Miniato, Italy. Springer-Verlag, 1992, pp 86-106
30. Matthes F, Müßig S. The Tycoon Language TL: An Introduction. University of Hamburg Report DBIS 112-93, 1993
31. Albano A, Bergamini R, Ghelli G, Orsini R. An Introduction to the Database Programming Language Fibonacci. Journal of Very Large Databases 1995; 4,3
32. Morrison R, Brown AL, Connor RCH et al. The Napier88 Reference Manual (Release 2.0). University of St Andrews Report CS/94/8, 1994
33. Atkinson MP, Jordan MJ, Daynès L, Spence S. Design Issues for Persistent Java: a Type-Safe, Object-Oriented, Orthogonally Persistent System. In: Proc. 7th International Workshop on Persistent Object Systems, Cape May, NJ, USA, 1996.

Section 1.1

Language Design: Introduction and State of the Art

Antonio Albano

Dipartimento di Informatica, Università di Pisa, Corso Italia 40, 56125 Pisa, Italy

Three approaches to the design of a persistent programming language have been investigated during the $FIDE_2$ project. The approaches share a common assumption but differ in some basic goals. The common assumption has been that a persistent language should be statically and strongly typed, and based on a type system with parametric polymorphism, recursive types, and functions as first class values. This assumption is motivated by the fact that the reliability of code which is part of long-lived and evolving systems must be automatically checked as far as possible. Static and strong type systems are one of the most effective partial correctness checking tool currently available. On the other side, static type system can be a hindrance for evolution unless they exhibit sophisticated polymorphic features which allow changes to be accommodated.

The $FIDE_2$ languages also pursue different design goals, which can be described as follows:

a) direct support for an innovative data model: the language should support a data model which is more expressive than current data models, specifically in the field of object databases with mechanisms to deal directly and naturally with evolving databases;

b) complete support for persistent programming activities: the language should not be biased toward a specific data model, but it should be supported by a complete environment specifically tailored towards the support of the management of long-lasting and evolving data and applications; the language should provide adequate mechanisms so that the environment can be programmed using the language itself, to gain the maximum flexibility and integration between data and programming environments;

c) support for software integration activities. The language should not be biased towards a specific data model, and it should provide adequate mechanisms to develop large and possibly distributed applications which use both data managed by pre-existing external systems or by the system itself, and mechanisms to communicate with independent software systems.

The first line of investigation has been explored through the languages Fibonacci and Galileo95 at the University of Pisa. The main contributions are:

a) three orthogonal mechanisms to model object databases in terms of objects, classes and associations;

b) a mechanism to model objects which can dynamically acquire and lose new types;

c) a view mechanism for objects which generalizes the view mechanism of relational systems.

The second line of investigation has been explored with the language Napier88 at the University of St. Andrews. The main contributions are:

a) a reflection mechanism to give the system the capability to generate and then to execute Napier88 code;

b) two mechanisms, environments and existential types, to face the different aspects of the modularization and composition problem, with regards to aspects of persistent data, and code, evolution and structuring;

c) a mechanism called "hyper-programming" which extends the traditional textual style of programming by allowing code to contain direct links to the data itself as well as the more traditional referencing of data through textual identifiers.

The third line of investigation has been explored with the language Tycoon at the University of Hamburg. The main contributions are:

a) a full higher-order type system with universal type quantification, subtyping, and a limited form of dependent types. Other polymorphic languages restrict quantification and subtyping to the level of types or tothe level of kinds (types of types);

b) a mechanism to dynamically extend the Tycoon syntax with domain-specific language constructs like SQL-style queries or workflow scripting idioms;

c) language constructs for module and library management to control the evolution of large-scale persistent systems;

d) mechanisms to dynamically establish first-class bindings to functions written in external languages and to seamlessly integrate Tycoon code into external languages.

Although the different design goals have led to languages with complementary features, the experience gained with these experiments has clarified the benefits of each feature and has improved our understanding of their impact on the development of a system supporting a persistent language.

A database programming languages is a single language for data definition, data manipulation and general computation to avoid the so called ``impedance mismatch" problem between the programming language used for doing computations on data and the query language, such as SQL, provided by the database management system to retrieve data.

Several approach have been tried to the design of database programming languages.

The first approach, pioneered by the language Pascal/R [15], has been the integration of the relational data model into the programming language Pascal. Other examples are the languages Rigel [14] and Plain [17].

Another approach has been the design of persistent languages in which any value may persist irrespective of their type. The first examples of these language was PS-algol [3], and a survey of this approach is given in [4].

The third approach has been the design of object-oriented database programming languages to support a more expressive data model to overcome the modelling limitations of other data models. Examples of these languages have been supported by research prototypes of object-oriented databases (TAXIS [13], Galileo [2], FAD [5], ORION [9], IRIS [7], Trellis/Owl [11], ODE [1]) or by commercial products, which started to appear in the mid-80s (G-Base, GemStone, O2 [6], Ontos, Statice, SIM). The approaches can be further classified according to whether they are based on the design of a specific object-oriented database language, on the extension of an object-oriented language with database features, or on the integration of the relational and object paradigm (SQL3, Illustra, UniSQL). Reviews of these approaches are given in [10], [8].

Another aspect which distinguishes among these approaches is the adoption of statically and strongly typed languages. This issue has been considered by the designers of research prototypes such as Galileo [2], Napier88 (Chapter 1.1.3), DBPL (Chapter 2.1.2), Tycoon [12], Cocoon [16], and is now becoming common among commercial systems too. The most evident result in this direction is the effort of designing the SQL3 standard in US. This result also confirms that the trend of database language technology is toward extensible type systems based on the object paradigm, possibly integrated with the relational paradigm.

References

1. Agrawal R., Gehani N. ODE: The Language and the Data Model, Proc. ACM SIGMOD Conf., Portland, OR, 1989.
2. Albano A., Cardelli L., Orsini R. Galileo: A Strongly Typed, Interactive Conceptual Language, ACM Transactions on Database Systems, 10(2), 230-260, 1985. Also in: Readings in Object-Oriented Database Systems, S.B. Zdonik and D. Maier (eds), Morgan Kaufmann, San Mateo, California, 147-161, 1990.
3. Atkinson M.P., Bailey P.J., Chisholm K.J., Cockshott W.P., Morrison R. An Approach to Persistent Programming, Computer Journal 26(4), 360-365, 1983.
4. Atkinson M.P., Buneman O.P. Types and Persistence in Database Programming Languages, ACM Computing Surveys 19(2), 105-190, 1987.
5. Bancilhon F., Briggs T., Khoshafian S.N., Valduriez P. FAD, A Powerful and Simple Database Language, Proc. XIII. Int'l Conf. Very Large Data Bases, Brighton, England, 1987.
6. Bancilhon F., Delobel C., Kanellakis P. (eds), Building an Object-Oriented Database System, the Story of O2. Morgan Kaufmann, 1992.
7. Fishman D.H. et al. Iris: An Object-Oriented Database Management System, ACM Transactions on Office Information Systems 5(1), 48-69,1987.
8. Hughes J.G. Object-Oriented Databases, Prentice Hall, New York, 1991.
9. Kim W., Ballou N., Chou H.T., Garza J.F., Woelk D. Features of the ORION Object-Oriented Database System, in: Object-Oriented Concepts, Database and Applications (eds W. Kim and F.H. Lochovsky), Addison-Wesley, Reading, MA, 1989.
10. Koshafian S., Abnous R. Object Orientation: Concepts, Languages, Databases, User Interfaces, John Wiley & Sons Inc, New York, 1990.
11. O'Brien P., Bullis B., Schaffert C. Persistent and Shared Objects in Trellis/Owl, Proc. Int'l Workshop Object-Oriented Database Systems (eds K. Dittrich and U. Dayal), Pacific Grove, CA, 1986.
12. Matthes F., Müßing S., Schmidt J. W., Persistent Polymorphic Programming in Tycoon: An Introduction, $FIDE_2$ Technical Reports, FIDE/94/106, 1994.

13. Mylopoulos J., Bernstein P.A., Wong H.K.T. A Language Facility for Designing Interactive Database-Intensive Systems, ACM Transactions on Database Systems 5(2), 185-207, 1980.
14. Rowe L. A., Shoens K.A. Data Abstraction, Views and Updates in RIGEL, Proc. ACM SIGMOD Conf., Boston, Mass., 71-81, 1979.
15. Schmidt J.W. Some High Level Language Constructs for Data of Type Relation, ACM Transactions on Database Systems 2(3), 247-261, 1977.
16. Scholl M.H., Laasch C., Rich C., Schek H.J., Tresch M. The COCOON Object Model, Departement Informatik, Technical Report 211, ETH Zurich, 1994.
17. Wasserman A. I. et al. Revised Report on the Programming Language PLAIN, ACM SIGPLAN Notices 16, 59-80, 1981.

Chapter 1.1.1

Higher-Order Persistent Polymorphic Programming in Tycoon

Florian Matthes

Technical University Hamburg-Harburg, Harburger Schloßstraße 20, D-21071 Hamburg, Germany

Abstract. This text provides an introduction to Tycoon[1], an open persistent polymorphic programming environment. The Tycoon language TL is based on expressive and orthogonal naming, typing and binding concepts as they are required, for example, in advanced data-intensive applications. The characteristic language mechanisms of TL are first-class functions and modules, parametric and subtype polymorphism extended to a fully higher-order type system. Tycoon programs are statically typed but may include explicit dynamic type variables which can be inspected at run-time.

1 Introduction and Motivation

The Tycoon system is an open persistent polymorphic programming environment based on higher-order language concepts . It is designed as a robust linguistic and architectural framework for the definition, integration and interoperation of generic services represented as polymorphically-typed libraries. The architecture of the Tycoon system is described in Chapter 2.1.4.

The Tycoon language TL[2] described in this paper is used for the following two activities in database application programming (see also [18]):

Strongly typed, high-level application programming: TL is used by application programmers to implement the full functionality of data-intensive applications which require a tight and controlled interaction between objects on the screen, objects in main memory, objects on disk, and objects on the wire. For example, a value from a screen form may be passed as a parameter to a transaction, be stored in a database and finally be transmitted to a remote log server. TL supports such programming tasks by providing uniform and generalized naming, typing and binding concepts that abstract from the specifics of the underlying object servers like GUI toolkits, programming languages, database systems and RPC services. In particular, Tycoon's type system statically detects any attempt to apply an inappropriate operation from one server to an object from another server. This should be seen in contrast to the current practice in data-intensive applications where there is virtually

[1] Tycoon: Typed Communicating Objects in Open Environments

[2] TL: Tycoon Language

no inter-server consistency checking due to the lack of an integrated type system model.

Generic server integration: Different from fourth-generation languages, high-level application programming in the Tycoon system is not restricted to *built-in* object types like tables, forms and reports. By virtue of Tycoon's polymorphic (higher-order) type system it is possible to also integrate pre-existing, independently developed *generic* servers (like object-oriented databases, C++ GUI libraries or RPC communication services) as strongly typed parametric libraries into the Tycoon programming environment. Therefore, systems developed in TL fit smoothly into open system architectures.

The idea of an open, library-based approach to system construction is currently being pursued in several system frameworks that are based on C++ or distributed object models of similar expressiveness. Tycoon aims at a higher system development productivity in a language framework with the following characteristics:

Improved language orthogonality: All language entities in TL (like values, functions, modules and types) have first class status. For example, it is possible to write a TL function that receives a type as its argument and returns a module which aggregates a set of dynamically constructed functions for a fresh abstract data type. Such *higher-order* language concepts are particularly helpful to factor-out repetitive programming tasks from individual applications into shared, reusable library code.

Increased type system expressiveness: TL combines subtype and parametric polymorphism. Furthermore, both forms of polymorphism are generalized to (higher-order) type operators supporting the type-safe definition of highly polymorphic system libraries.

Orthogonal persistence abstraction: TL programmers don't have to distinguish between local volatile data and shared global and persistent data. As a consequence, programmers can fully abstract from store properties (size of main memory, garbage collection, transfer between primary and secondary store, data format conversion between nodes in heterogeneous networks, etc.).

Reflective programming support: Some system tasks in data-intensive applications (e.g. query optimization, transaction scheduling, GUI generation) are based on run-time reflective programming techniques. Run-time linguistic reflection denotes the ability of a system to inspect parts of the system (e.g. query expressions, transaction instruction sequences, type structures) at run-time and to dynamically extend or modify the system based on the outcome of this inspection [25]. For example, the TL programming environment exports a (strongly-typed) function *reflect.optimize* that takes a TL function value, re-invokes the TL compiler back-end on this function, and returns an optimized version of the function. Contrary to static code optimizations which are based on a limited static context (a single function or a single module), such dynamic code optimizations can exploit run-time information available for the dynamic context of a function (e.g. external function implementations or values of abstract data types).

A more detailed discussion of the rationale behind Tycoon is given in [14] and [18]. Readers interested in the formal definition of the TL semantics are referred to [17].

This text is organized as follows: Section 2 gives a quick overview of the Tycoon language in comparison with other modern (persistent) programming languages. The subsequent sections (Section 3–8) provide a step-by-step introduction to Tycoon's language concepts in a functional setting (values, types, bindings, signatures, predefined type and value constructors, user-defined types and type operators, subtype and parametric polymorphism). Section 9 explains how these concepts interact with the imperative concepts of Tycoon, namely mutable variables, destructive assignment, sequential execution and exception handling. Section 10 and 11 discuss alternative approaches to the structuring of large Tycoon software systems into interfaces, modules and libraries. Section 12 and 13 present some important system-oriented aspects of Tycoon like its transparent persistence management and bindings from and to external C libraries.

2 Language Classification

This section is intended primarily for readers who are familiar with the state of the art in programming language research and who are interested in a rough TL language classification.

The programming language TL evolved from the experimental languages Quest[3] [5,6] and P-Quest[4] [21,15]. All semantic concepts of these languages are supported in TL (in a slightly varied syntactic from). TL eliminates some ad-hoc restrictions of Quest's language orthogonality. Furthermore, it introduces new language concepts such as subtyping between type operators, recursive type operators, extensible record values, and libraries as scopes for modules and interfaces.

The syntactic structure and the module concept of TL are similar to those of the languages of the Modula family (Modula-2 [12], Oberon [26], Modula-2+ [23], Modula-3 [22], and Ada [11]). Regarding its semantics, TL is more closely related to the polymorphic functional languages of the ML language family [5,6,19,8,10]. The semantic concepts of TL are derived from the language $F_{\leq}$ [7], a widely accepted formal basis for the study of modern type systems.

Like C [13] TL is intended for application programming and for system programming tasks. By virtue of its polymorphic type system TL can also be utilized as a data modeling language. In this respect, TL resembles Lisp development systems [3] and commercial object-oriented languages like Smalltalk [9]. From integrated database programming languages like PS-Algol [2], Napier88 (see Chapter 1.1.3), Amber [4], and P-Quest, mentioned before, *Tycoon* inherits the orthogonality of elementary kernel concepts for persistence abstraction, type-complete data structuring, and iteration abstraction [1,24].

[3] Quest: Quantifiers and Subtypes

[4] P-Quest is a Quest System extended by an orthogonal persistence concept.

Motivated by an analysis of the conceptual and technological foundations of existing database languages (see Chapter 1.4.2), the *Tycoon* system pursues the idea of a strictly reduced kernel language supporting naming, binding and typing of predefined semantic objects (variables, functions, type variables, type operators). On the other hand, it is possible to extend the language kernel with external semantic objects (integers, floating-point numbers, strings, arrays, relations, views, files, windows, etc.) and generic functions associated with these objects in a completely type-safe way (*add-on* vs. *built-in*) [16].

TL enables the programmer to use different modelling styles. *Functional* and *imperative* programming are supported directly. Due to the linguistic neutrality several variants of the *object-oriented* programming style are supported by TL. *Relational* and *logic-based* programming [20] are not supported directly, since unification-based evaluation models and declarative approaches deviate strongly from functional and imperative structures.

The *Tycoon* system offers an interactive programming environment. Such environments are known from functional systems (ML, Lisp). This distinguishes the *Tycoon* system from conventional translation systems like, for example, C, Modula-2, or Ada compilers. Due to the interactive environment, ad-hoc TL database queries are possible in addition to the use of TL as a database programming language. The persistence concept enables the user to perform incremental system development spanning several sessions. At the same time, the library concept of TL supports the controlled use of shared data and programs by several users.

3 Lexical and Syntactical Rules

This section introduces the most important lexical and syntactical rules of TL for the construction of symbols, reserved identifiers, and productions.

3.1 Symbols

The character set predefined on a given system is partitioned into the disjoint classes of letters, digits, delimiters, printable special symbols, and non-printable formatting characters. On the basis of this classification a sequence of characters is divided into atomic symbols (e.g. numbers and identifiers).

TL distinguishes *alphanumeric identifiers* and *infix symbols*. Alphanumeric identifiers consist of a character followed by a sequence of characters and digits whereas infix symbols are composed solely of special symbols. A space is only required between two alphanumeric identifiers or two infix symbols that appear in direct succession.

3.2 Reserved Keywords

Reserved keywords and infix symbols of must not be used as user-defined identifiers or infix symbols.

The reserved keywords are written in **bold face** in the programming examples. This facilitates the distinction from the rest of the symbols in the examples which are presented in *italics*.

Keywords associated with types start with a capital letter whereas all other keywords begin with lower case characters. It is advisable to adopt this rule as a convention for all other identifiers to improve the readability of programs.

3.3 Comments

In TL, comments are enclosed between *(** and **)*. Arbitrary nesting of comments is possible. Comments may include arbitrary (printable and non-printable) characters and can span several lines.

```
(* This is a comment. *)
```

3.4 Factoring of Expressions

Operators represented by infix symbols are left-associative and of equal precedence. The parsing of type and value expressions containing infix symbols can be controlled by the use of curly brackets. Consequently, the following expressions are equivalent.

```
3 – 7 * 4
{3 – 7} * 4
{*(–(3 7) 4)}
int.mul(int.sub(3 7) 4)
⇒ –16 :Int
```

Infix symbols starting with a colon (e.g. := and :+) have a weaker precedence than the other infix symbols. These operators are also left-associative. The bracketed expressions in the following examples show the factoring of the corresponding expressions without brackets.

```
x := a + b
x := {a + b}

x := y := z
{x := y} := z
```

3.5 Coercion and Overloading

Automatic coercions, e.g. of integers to real numbers, are not performed in TL. For example, a type error is caused by the following expression.

```
3.0 + 4
⇒ Argument type mismatch: '_builtin.Int' expected, 'Real' found
  [while checking function argument '<anonymous>']
```

Neither symbolic nor alphanumeric identifiers may be overloaded. For this reason it is, for example, necessary to have different operators (infix symbols) for the addition of integers and real numbers, respectively.

2 + 7
⇒ 9 :Int
2.4 ++ 3.8
⇒ 6.2 :Real

4 Predefined Values and Functions

This section presents the basic semantic rules of TL.

4.1 Naming, Binding, and Typing

Contrary to many traditional programming languages, neither the base types, nor their constants, nor the functions defined on them are predefined in TL. The identifiers of the base types (e.g. *bool.T*), the constants of the base types (e.g. *bool.true* and *bool.false*), and the functions defined on the base types can be imported explicitly from modules of the standard *Tycoon* library. They obey the same syntax, typing, and evaluation rules as user-defined types, values, and functions. The rationale behind this approach is to give predefined and user-defined data types equal status in the language.

In order to avoid the notational disadvantages resulting from this approach, the base types and many functions defined on the base types are bound to symbolic identifiers and infix symbols, respectively, in an initial context that is defined when the system is started. Thereby, the identifiers appear to be built into the *Tycoon* system environment without including them into the language TL. In the following sections we, therefore, use the phrases 'predefined base types' and 'predefined functions'.

4.2 Literals

The following enumeration lists examples of literal values of the base types *Int*, *Real*, *Char*, *String*, and *Bool*, respectively, from left to right.

~3 3.0 'c' "string" true

Note that TL avoids overloading. For this purpose negative integer numbers are marked by an prefix "~". The symbol "−" is reserved for integer subtraction.

5 User-defined Values and Functions

The *binding* of a user-defined *identifier* to a semantic object and the repeated use of this identifier in *expressions* denoting the bound object is a basic concept in TL.

Furthermore, a *signature* assigns static type information in the form of a *type expression* to an identifier. A signature restricts the set of possible semantic objects that can be bound to an identifier. This makes it possible to control the correct use of identifiers in expressions [14].

In this section, the discussion of naming and scoping concepts is restricted to value bindings. The orthogonal extension of these concepts to type bindings, presented in section 6, gives rise to much of the expressive power of TL.

5.1 Static Bindings

Static value bindings in TL are defined as follows.

let n = *10*

After evaluating the term, the variable *n* is statically bound to the value *10*. Every subsequent use of the identifier *n* in an expression evaluates to the bound value.

let x = *1* + {*2* * n}
⇒ *21 :Int*

Sequences of bindings are interpreted as *sequential* bindings in TL.

let n = *10*
let x = *1* + {*2* * n}

The identifier *n* used in the second binding, therefore, refers to the binding *n=10* established in the first line of the example above. In order to achieve a *simultaneous* binding, the single bindings have to be connected by the keyword **and**.

let a = *4*
let a = *123 / 3* **and** b = a + *2* **and** c = *true*

The variable *b* is bound to the value *6* in this expression. The associated binding for an expression is determined by static *scoping rules* in TL.

let a = *1.0*
begin let a = 'x' **let** b = a **end**
let c = a

The scope of the local identifiers *a* and *b* is restricted to the block delimited by the keywords **begin** and **end** (see section 9.3.1). For this reason, the identifier *c* is bound to the value *1.0* denoted by the global identifier *a*, whereas the local identifier *b* is bound to the value 'x' denoted by the local identifier *a*.

The bindings described above are determined by two basic scoping rules: local declarations have precedence over global declarations and an identifier in an expression always refers to the last binding established for this identifier.

A block in TL evaluates to the value of its last binding. This is illustrated by the following example.

begin let *a* = *3* **let** *b* = *true* **end**
begin let *a* = *3* *true* **end**
begin *3* *true* **end**
begin end

Evaluation of the first three blocks yields the value *true* whereas the result of evaluating the last block is the canonical value **ok** of type **Ok**. The second and third example contain so-called *anonymous* bindings, i.e. bindings without an identifier.

Signatures assign static type information to bindings; they are ordered sequences of pairs each consisting of an identifier and a type. The signatures of the bindings established by the previous example are considered as illustrative examples.

a :Int b :Bool
a :Int :Bool
:Int :Bool
(empty signature *)*

It is possible to declare the type of the bound value in a binding explicitly. This declaration is optional. If the type specification is omitted, it is inferred by the compiler from the expression given in the binding.

let *a :Int* = *3*
let *b :Bool* = *true*

Recursive bindings are used for the construction of *recursive* and *cyclic* data structures. In TL, pointer types are not necessary for this purpose. Recursive bindings are introduced by the keyword **rec**. Examples of recursive value bindings are given in section 5.2.2 and section 6.4 since they have to be used in combination with functions and recursive data types.

The problem of uninitialized identifiers is avoided completely in TL, since identifiers can only be introduced in bindings and, furthermore, recursive bindings are subject to static constraints that avoid access to uninitialized variables [14].

5.2 Dynamic Bindings

Dynamic bindings are established by passing parameters to functions. In addition to *simple* and *recursive* functions known from other programming languages, TL supports *higher-order* functions and *polymorphic* functions. Simple and recursive functions as well as higher-order functions are presented in the following sections. The description of the polymorphic functions is postponed until section 8.1 for didactical reasons.

5.2.1 Simple Functions

Functions are introduced by the keyword **fun**. In TL, functions can be defined without binding them to an identifier. Such a *function abstraction* consists of an ordered, possibly empty list of formal parameters (signatures) and an expression defining the body of the function.

```
fun(x :Int) x + 1
```

The body of the function (here *x + 1*) can refer to identifiers of different scopes. The formal parameters introduced by the signature of the function, the global identifiers present in the static scope of the function, and the identifiers defined locally inside the function are all visible in the function body.

```
let global = 1
fun(x :Int) begin let local = 3  x + global – local end
```

A function defined by a function abstraction can be bound to an identifier.

```
let succ = fun(x :Int) x + 1
let add = fun(x :Real  y :Real) x ++ y
let succ2 = succ
```

The first function (*succ*) expects a parameter of type *Int* and returns a value of type *Int* as its result. It computes the successor of an integer value passed as a parameter. The second function (*add*) adds two real numbers. It takes two parameters of type *Real* and returns a value of type *Real*. The third identifier (*succ2*) is bound to the function denoted by *succ*. The syntax of TL also supports the following abbreviated notation.

```
let succ(x :Int) = x + 1
let add(x, y :Real) = x ++ y
```

The type of the result can be made explicit, improving the readability of the program; if omitted it is inferred by the compiler.

```
let succ(x :Int) :Int = x + 1
let add(x, y :Real) :Real = x ++ y
```

Infix symbols can be chosen as names for functions that can be used as binary infix operators. In the following example, the function concatenating two strings (*string.concat*) is bound to the infix symbol <>.

```
let <> = string.concat
```

A function bound to an infix symbol can be applied in two different ways, either using the standard prefix notation or the infix notation:

```
<>("concat" "enation")
"concat" <> "enation"
```

As shown in the next example, the use of the infix symbol in the prefix notation can lead to unexpected results because of the factoring rules for expressions.

```
begin
  let a = 3
  <>("concat" "enation")
end
```

The above expression causes a syntax error since the compiler recognizes an expression of the form *3 <> ("concat" "enation")*. As usual, such problems can be avoided by the use of brackets to control the parsing of expressions.

```
begin
  let a = 3
  {<>}("concat" "enation")
end
```

5.2.2 Recursive Functions

TL supports the definition of recursive functions. Recursive bindings introduced by the keyword **rec** are used for this purpose. In contrast to normal bindings where the types of the bound values can be inferred by the compiler they have to be specified explicitly for recursive bindings. The well-known computation of the factorial function is an example of a recursive function binding.

```
let rec fac(n :Int) :Int = if n == 0 then 1 else n * fac(n - 1) end
```

As mentioned above, TL does not support the overloading of operators. The operator for an equality test, therefore, is the doubled equality sign (==) and not the simple equality sign (=) used in **let**-bindings. The polymorphic operator == tests simple values like numbers and booleans for equality whereas it checks structured values like tuples and arrays for identity, i.e. the equality of the values of the tuple and array components is not tested.

Mutually recursive functions have to be defined in *parallel*. In TL the bindings are connected by the keyword **and** for this purpose. A parity test is given as an illustrative example.

```
let rec even(x :Int) :Bool =
  if x == 0 then true else odd(x - 1) end
and odd(x :Int) :Bool =
  if x == 0 then false else even(x - 1) end
```

5.2.3 Function Types

Since function types are a prerequisite for the definition of higher-order functions, they are introduced here in anticipation of the discussion in section 6. A function type defines the signature of a function value, i.e. the names and types of its formal parameters and the function result type. Function types are introduced by the keyword **Fun**. The types of the previously defined functions *succ*, *add*, and *succ2* are given as examples.

succ :**Fun**(*x :Int*) *:Int*
add :**Fun**(*x :Real y :Real*) *:Real*
succ2 :**Fun**(*x :Int*) *:Int*

The following abbreviating notation is also supported in TL.

succ(x :Int) :Int
add(x :Real y :Real) :Real

5.2.4 Higher-Order Functions

Higher-order functions are functions accepting functions as parameters or returning functions as a result.

The functions *twice* and *newInc* are examples of higher-order functions.

let *twice* = **fun**(*f* :**Fun**(*:Int*) *:Int a :Int*) *:Int f(f(a))*
let *newInc* = **fun**(*x :Int*) :**Fun**(*:Int*) *:Int* **fun**(*y :Int*) *:Int x + y*

Again, the functions can be written down more concisely.

let *twice(f(:Int) :Int a :Int) = f(f(a))*
let *newInc(x :Int)(y :Int) = x + y*

The function *twice* receives two parameters. The first parameter is a function mapping an integer value to an integer value, and the second parameter is an integer. In the function body (*f(f(a))*) of *twice*, the function passed as a parameter is applied twice to the second parameter.

twice(succ 3)
⇒ *5 :Int*
*twice(***fun***(x :Int) x * x 3)*
⇒ *81 :Int*

The function *newInc* is an example of a function with a function result. An application of *newInc* returns an anonymous function whose application finally computes the addition.

let *add2 = newInc(2)*
add2(5)
⇒ *7 :Int*
newInc(3)(5)
⇒ *8 :Int*

As illustrated by the example, the application of the function can be performed in a single step or in two steps (currying).

6 Predefined Value and Type Constructors

The predefined type constructors of TL, tuple, tuple with variants, and record are presented in this section. Function types have already been introduced in section 5.2.3.

6.1 Tuple Types

The tuple types of TL resemble records in Pascal and in Modula-2 as well as structures in C. A tuple type is a labelled Cartesian product type. The fields of a tuple are described by an ordered, possibly empty, sequence of signatures. The signatures may contain anonymous identifiers.

Let *Person* = **Tuple** *name :String age :Int* **end**
Let *IntPair* = **Tuple** *:Int :Int* **end**

Tuple values are ordered lists of bindings.

let *peter* = **tuple let** *name* = *"Peter"* **let** *age* = *3* **end**
let *paul* = **tuple** *"Paul" 5* **end**
let *pair* = **tuple** *12 21* **end**

The scope of the field names *name* and *age* is restricted to the block limited by the keywords **tuple** and **end**. Components of tuples are referenced using the dot notation.

peter.age
⇒ *3 :Int*

The rules for type compatibility of TL make an α-conversion between anonymous and non-anonymous field names possible. This conversion takes the order of the fields defined by the binding into account.

let *p :Person* = *paul*
p.name
⇒ *"Paul" :String*

let *namedPair* :**Tuple** *x, y :Int* **end** = *pair*
namedPair.x
⇒ *12 :Int*

In TL it is possible to include functions as fields in tuples. Combining this concept with recursive bindings makes it possible to capture the concept of methods known from object-oriented programming. Illustrative examples are presented in the sections 8.4 and 9.1 and in [14].

6.2 Variant Types

Tuples with variants resemble variant records in Pascal and in Modula-2. Like tuples, tuples with variants represent ordered sequences of signatures.

```
Let Address =
  Tuple
    case national with street, city :String  zip :Int
    case international with street, city, state :String  zip :String
  end
```

The two variants *national* and *international* in the example have a common prefix. This prefix can be extracted from the variants and placed in front of them.

```
Let Address1 =
  Tuple
    street, city :String
    case national with zip :Int
    case international with state :String  zip :String
  end
```

If all signatures of the variants are empty, the tuple type with variants degenerates to an enumeration type.

```
Let Day = Tuple case mon, tue, wed, thu, fri, sat, sun end
```

The definition of a value of a tuple type with variants consists of the choice of a variant and the definition of the corresponding bindings.

```
let address1 =
  tuple case national of Address1 with
    let street = "Johnsallee 21"
    let city = "Hamburg"
    let zip = 21234
  end
```

The keyword **with** in the definition of *address1* is optional. It is also possible to use anonymous bindings in tuples with variants.

```
let address2 =
  tuple case national of Address1
    "Johnsallee 21" "Hamburg" 21234
  end
```

A value of type *Day* can be defined as follows.

```
let today = tuple case mon of Day end
```

The projection on fields in the prefix and on fields of the variants requires two distinct notations. Fields of the prefix can be accessed using the dot notation as in the case of simple tuple fields.

address1.street
⇒ *"Johnsallee 21" :String*

For the fields of the variants a complete (**case of**) or an incomplete case analysis (**case**) is necessary.

case of *address1*
  when *national* **with** *n* **then** *fmt.int(n.zip)*
  when *international* **with** *i* **then** *i.zip*
end

The use of the complete case analysis avoids unexpected runtime errors by ensuring that later extensions of a tuple type with new variants are accompanied by corresponding extensions of the case analysis. The incomplete case analysis has the following form.

case *address1*
  when *national* **with** *n* **then** *fmt.int(n.zip)*
end

Since an incomplete case analysis can lead to runtime errors, an **else**-branch can (and should) be specified in this situation.

case *address1*
  when *national* **with** *n* **then** *fmt.int(n.zip)*
  else *"not national"*
end

Finally, two abbreviating notations for the simple test of variants and for the projection of variants are presented.

address1?national
address1!national

These two examples are equivalent to the following expressions.

case *address1*
  when *national* **then** *true* **else** *false*
end

case *address1*
  when *national* **with** *n*
  then *n*
  else raise *tupleProjectError* **with** *line column "national" 1* **end**
end

The variant projection opens the scope of the selected variant.

address1 !national.zip
⇒ *21234 :Int*

6.3 Record Types

In contrast to tuple types, record types represent *unordered*, possibly empty sets of *non-anonymous* signatures in TL. The names of all fields have to be different.

Let *Person* = **Record** *name :String age :Int* **end**

Record values are unordered sets of non-anonymous bindings.

let *peter* = **record let** *age* = *3* **let** *name* = *"Peter"* **end**

As for tuple values, the scope of the field names *name* and *age* is restricted to the block enclosed by **record** and **end**. The fields of a record are accessed using the dot notation.

peter.age
⇒ *3 :Int*

In contrast with tuple values, record values can be extended dynamically by non-anonymous bindings without losing their identity. The keyword **extend** is provided for this purpose. In the process of extending a record, the uniqueness of the field names has to be ensured.

let *peterAsStudent* = **extend** *peter* **with let** *semester* = *1* **end**

The infix operator == checks the identity of two values.

peter == peterAsStudent
⇒ *true :Bool*

The record value *peterAsStudent* fulfills the following type specifications, amongst others (see also sec. 7.3)

Record *name :String age :Int semester :Int* **end**
Record *age :Int name :String semester :Int* **end**
Record *semester :Int name :String age :Int* **end**
Record *name :String age :Int* **end**

6.4 Recursive Data Types

Recursively defined data structures like lists, sets, and trees play a central role in computing science. TL provides means for the definition of recursive data types enabling a straightforward realisation of recursively defined data structures.

A recursive type definition is introduced by the keyword **Rec** in TL. A supertype (e.g. *IntegerList* <:**Ok**) has to be specified when defining a recursive type. The definition of a list of integer values is presented as an example.

```
Let Rec IntegerList <:Ok =
  Tuple
    case nil
    case cons with car :Int  cdr :IntegerList
  end
```

The following expressions show the construction of an empty list and the construction of a new list from an existing (possibly empty) list by appending a new element.

```
let emptyList =
  tuple case nil of IntegerList end

let singleList =
  tuple case cons of IntegerList with
    let car = 7
    let cdr = emptyList
  end
```

The next example shows the definition of a recursive value. As in the case of recursive functions, the type of the value has to be given explicitly.

```
let rec circularList :IntegerList =
  tuple case cons of IntegerList
    7  circularList
  end
```

6.5 Dynamic Data Types

In data-intensive applications there are programming situations where a context has to use a value generated by another context although the two context do not share common type information supporting static checking. In such situations it is desirable to defer the type checking to well-defined points during program evaluation. In TL, the keywords **Dyn** and **typecase** are provided for this purpose. Their application is illustrated by the following example.

```
Let Auto = Tuple Dyn T <:Ok  x :T end
let a1 = tuple Let Dyn T = Int  let x = 3 end
let a2 = tuple Let Dyn T = String  let x = "Hello" end
```

```
let asString(a :Auto) :String =
  typecase a.T
    when Int then fmt.int(a.x)
    when String then a.x
    when Tuple name :String end then a.x.name
    when Tuple end then "Tuple"
    else "???"
  end
```

As discussed in [14] and in [22] structural equivalence is a prerequisite for dynamic type checking in persistent, distributed systems.

7 Subtype Relationships and Subtype Polymorphism

In TL, a signature of the form *x :A* is considered a partial specification. A value bound to the variable *x* has to fulfil at least the specification defined by the type *A*. The underlying partial order on types (*B* is more precise than *A*) is described explicitly by an inductively defined subtype relationship (*B <:A*, *B* is subtype of *A*).

The supertype of all non-parameterized types is **Ok** [14]. It represents the trivial specification that is fulfilled by all values. The following example illustrates the use of the type **Ok**. The functions *fst* and *snd* both discard one of their parameters. The type of this parameter needs just a trivial specification.

```
let fst(a :Int  b :Ok) :Int = a
let snd(a :Ok  b :Int) :Int = b
fst(3 4)  fst(3 true)  snd(3 4)  snd(true 4)
⇒ 3 :Int  3 :Int  4 :Int  4 :Int
```

The kind of polymorphism represented by the functions *fst* and *snd* is called *subtype polymorphism*. According to the subsumption principle the dynamic binding of formal parameters of a static type *A* to values of an arbitrary subtype *B <:A* is possible.

7.1 Subtyping on Predefined Types

All predefined base types fulfil the trivial specification (<:**Ok**), e.g.

```
Int <:Ok
Real <:Ok
Fun(:Int) :Int <:Ok
Tuple :Int end <:Ok
```

Non-trivial subtype relationships, e.g. of the form $\mathit{Int} <: \mathit{Real}$ do not exist between the base types of *Tycoon*. It is, however, possible to define subtypes of these types in the *Tycoon* libraries as, for example, $\mathit{directory.T} <: \mathit{String}$. Values of the type *directory.T* represent syntactically correct path names within the file system and thereby are also strings. The reverse is not true.

7.2 Subtyping on Tuple Types

In TL, subtyping on tuple types is based on structural compatibility. Subtype relationships are not only defined between two tuple types without variants and two tuple types with variants, but also between a tuple type without and a tuple type with variants.

A tuple type *B* without variants is a subtype of a tuple type *A* without variants if the signatures of *B* are a prefix of the signatures of *A*, e.g. for

Let *Student* = **Tuple** *name :String age :Int semester :Int* **end**
Let *Person* = **Tuple** *name :String age :Int* **end**
Let *Car* = **Tuple** *name :String age :Int* **end**
Let *Machine* = **Tuple** *name :String fuel :String* **end**
Let *NamedThing* = **Tuple** *name :String* **end**

the following subtype relationships hold

$\mathit{Student} <: \mathit{Person}$ $\mathit{Person} <: \mathit{NamedThing}$
$\mathit{Car} <: \mathit{NamedThing}$ $\mathit{Machine} <: \mathit{NamedThing}$

but also

$\mathit{Car} <: \mathit{Person}$ $\mathit{Person} <: \mathit{Car}$

On the other hand, it is described in [14] how the *Tycoon* subtype relationship can be restricted systematically to explicitly defined *subclasses* ensuring, for example, that $\mathit{car.T} \not<: \mathit{person.T}$ holds.

A subtype of a tuple type can also be defined by specializing the types of tuple fields. For example, the definition

Let *Student2* = **Tuple** *name* :**Ok** *age :Int semester :Int* **end**

implies the following subtype relationship.

$\mathit{Student} <: \mathit{Student2}$

In TL, a subtype can be defined without repeating explicitly all the components of the supertype. The keyword **Repeat** is used for this purpose. A definition of the type *Student* on the basis of the type *Person* may look as follows.

Let *Student* = **Tuple** **Repeat** *Person semester :Int* **end**

This notation is applicable wherever signatures are expected, e.g. in function signatures. A corresponding construct exists on the value level. The keyword **open** supports the repetition of existing bindings. The value *peter* defined in section 6.1, for example, can be extended by specifying its semester.

let *peterAsStudent :Student* = **tuple open** *peter* **let** *semester = 6* **end**

The major advantage of subtyping is the fact that functions working on a type also accept values of arbitrary subtypes of this type. Thereby, subtyping facilitates a later extension of programs, in particular, the extension of data structures with new components. Functions written for the original type are also applicable to values of the new type. These values are recognized as instances of the old type. A function expecting two parameters of type *NamedThing* also works on values of the types *Student*, *Car*, or *Machine*.

let *sameName(x, y :NamedThing) :Bool* =
  string.equal(x.name y.name)

let *fiat :Machine* = **tuple let** *name = "Uno"* **let** *fuel = "unleaded"* **end**

sameName(peter fiat)
⇒ *false :Bool*

A tuple type B with variants is a subtype of a tuple type A with variants, if the ordered sequence of variant names of B is a prefix of the sequence of variant names of A and the signatures S_i of each variant of B are tuple subsignatures of the corresponding variant signatures S_i' of A. For example, the relationship *RGBColor* <:*Color* holds for

Let *RGBColor* = **Tuple case** *red, green, blue* **end**
Let *Color* = **Tuple case** *red, green, blue, cyan, yellow* **end**

and the relationship *Address* <:*Address2* holds for the type *Address* declared in section 6.2 if *Address2* is defined as follows:

Let *Address2* =
  Tuple
    case *national* **with** *street, city :String zip :Int*
    case *international* **with** *street, city, state :String zip :String*
    case *unknown*
  end

Finally, a tuple type without variants having signatures S is a subtype of a tuple type A with variants if the signatures S are tuple subsignatures of the signatures S' of the first variant of A. The relationship *AddressTuple* <:*Address2*, therefore, holds for

Let *AddressTuple* = **Tuple** *street, city :String zip :Int* **end**

7.3 Subtyping on Record Types

As in the case of tuple types, subtypes of record types can be constructed by specialization of types of existing components as well as by extension with new components. Additionally, the fact that the signatures of record types are not ordered is taken into account by the subtyping rules. A record type B with signatures S is a subtype of a record type A with signatures S' if the signatures S contain a subset of signatures S'' which are subsignatures of S'.

Let *Person* = **Record** *name :String age :Int* **end**
Let *Student* = **Record** *name :String semester :Int* **end**
Let *Employee* = **Record** *ssno :String salary :Real* **end**
Let *Tutor* = **Record** *name, ssno :String age, semester :Int salary :Real* **end**

For these types the following subtype relationships hold in TL,

Tutor <:Person Tutor <:Student Tutor <:Employee

enabling the application of functions which are defined for arguments of the types *Person*, *Student*, or *Employee* to values of the type *Tutor*. Furthermore, it becomes possible to construct heterogeneous data structures consisting, for example, of values of the types *Person*, and *Tutor*. Subtyping hierarchies over record types are not restricted to tree structures as in the case of tuple types. Other directed acyclic graphs are also possible, thus making the representation of multiple inheritance hierarchies possible.

7.4 Subtyping on Function Types

The interpretation of types and signatures as partial specifications and of subtypes and subsignatures as specification refinements implies the well-known *contravariance rule* for the subtyping on function types. According to this rule a function type with signatures S for its formal parameters and result type B is a subtype of a function type with signatures S' and result type A iff $B <:A$ and S' are subsignatures of S. In other words, a function F_1 is a specialization of a function F_2, if under the assumption, that the preconditions of F_2 hold, the postconditions of F_1 fulfil at least the postconditions of F_2 and the preconditions of F_1 are not more restrictive than the preconditions of F_2 [14].

For example, assuming the relationship *Student <:Person* the relationship *GetRichestStudent <:GetRichestPerson* holds for the following function types because the result types of the function types are in covariance relationship.

Let *GetRichestPerson* = **Fun**() *:Person*
Let *GetRichestStudent* = **Fun**() *:Student*

However, for the function types

Let *HirePerson* = **Fun**(*:Person*) *:***Ok**
Let *HireStudent* = **Fun**(*:Student*) *:***Ok**

the relationship *HirePerson <:HireStudent* holds because the types of the function parameters are contravariant.

8 Parametric Polymorphism

The type system of TL supports two kinds of polymorphism: subtype polymorphism and parametric polymorphism. Subtype polymorphism is presented in the previous section. Parametric polymorphism is the topic of this section. It makes the introduction of explicit type parameters into function and type definitions possible.

Function definitions with parameters describe *polymorphic* functions, whereas the introduction of type parameters into type definitions results in *type operators*. Type operators are functions mapping types to types. They introduce parametrization into type declarations.

If a type is restricted explicitly to a subtype of a given type, this kind of polymorphism is called *bounded parametric polymorphism*.

8.1 Polymorphic Functions

A function is made polymorphic (generic) by extending its signature by one or more type parameters. The type parameters are instantiated with type expressions when the function is applied.

The polymorphic identity function is a simple example of a polymorphic function.

let *id(A <:***Ok** *a :A) :A = a*

Such a function is called with a type (e.g. *:Int*) and a value (e.g. 7) of this type as actual parameters.

id(:Int 7)
⇒ *7 :Int*
id(:String "Peter")
⇒ *"Peter" :String*

The specification of the type argument can be omitted in most cases because it can be inferred by the system from the value passed as parameter.

id(7)
⇒ *7 :Int*
id("Peter")
⇒ *"Peter" :String*

The instantiation of type parameters is not restricted to base types. Arbitrary user-defined types (e.g. the type *Person* with the value *peter*) can be chosen as parameter for a polymorphic function

id(peter)
⇒ **tuple** *name = "Peter" age = 3* **end** *:Person*

Parametric polymorphism makes it possible to write functions which work uniformly for arbitrary types. Polymorphic functions, therefore, can be used to describe type-independent behaviour. Separate functions for each considered parameter type would be necessary for this purpose in languages like C or Modula-2.

Much of the power of TL results from the possibility of combining the concepts of polymorphic and higher-order functions with each other. This is illustrated by a polymorphic sorting function. The pure sorting process, i.e. the permutation of the elements, is type-independent. Therefore, it can be described by a polymorphic function. On the other hand, the comparison of the elements during the sorting process is type-dependent. This task can be solved by passing a function whose application compares two elements as a parameter to the polymorphic sorting function. The signature of a polymorphic function sorting arrays of an arbitrary element type follows.

let *sort(A <:***Ok** *a :***Array***(A) order(a, b :A) :Bool) :***Array***(A)* = ...

In order to sort an array of a specific type, it is sufficient to write a function for the element comparison of this array. The sorting of persons by ascending age is considered as an example.

let *older(a, b :Person) :Bool = a.age >= b.age*

The following call of the function *sort* sorts an array of persons according to their age.

sort(:Person personArray older)

Again, the type parameter can be omitted.

sort(personArray older)

Further examples of polymorphic functions can be found in the sections 8.3 and 8.4.

8.2 Bounded Parametric Polymorphism

Bounded parametric polymorphism, a restricted form of parametric polymorphism, is introduced into polymorphic functions by specifying a type as a bound for the formal type parameter in the signature. Only subtypes of the given type can be passed as parameters to such functions. Employing subtype polymorphism, a function comparing the component *age* of two values of an arbitrary subtype of the type *Person* can be defined in the following way.

let *chooseOlder(p1, p2 :Person) :Person =*
  if *p1.age > p2.age* **then** *p1* **else** *p2* **end**

let *peter :Student =*
  tuple let *name = "Peter"* **let** *age = 24* **let** *semester = 3* **end**

let *paul :Student* =
  tuple let *name* = *"Paul"* **let** *age* = *29* **let** *semester* = *6* **end**

chooseOlder(peter paul)
⇒ **tuple let** *name* = *"Paul"* **let** *age* = *29* **end** *:Person*

Considering the function result displayed by the system, it can be seen that the attribute *semester* of *paul* is missing. This is a consequence of the fact that type information is lost at compile time. In order to avoid the loss of attributes of subtypes, *chooseOlder* has to be defined as a polymorphic function.

let *chooseOlder(P <:Person p1, p2 :P) :P* =
  if *p1.age > p2.age* **then** *p1* **else** *p2* **end**

chooseOlder(peter paul)
⇒ **tuple** *name* = *"Paul" age* = *29 semester* = *7* **end** *:Student*

As a result of integrating enough type information into the function definition, all attributes are taken into account. By introducing the specification *P <:Person*, the function *chooseOlder* is made polymorphic, but in contrast to the unrestricted parametric polymorphism, the polymorphism is restricted to subtypes of the type *Person*. The type variable *P* makes the intended relationship between the type of the formal parameters and the type of the result of the function explicit.

8.3 Type Operators

Polymorphic functions support the description of type-independent behaviour. Similarly, type-independent patterns on the type level lead to generic type expressions in the form of type operators, which can be instantiated with concrete types.

8.3.1 Simple Type Operators

A simple example of a type operator is an identity function on the type level corresponding to the polymorphic identity function presented above.

Let *Id* = **Oper**(*A* <:**Ok**) *A*

Similar to the function definition, the following abbreviated notation is also possible.

Let *Id(A* <:**Ok**) = *A*

The operator *Id* maps the type passed as parameter to itself.

:Id(Int)
⇒ *:Int*
:Id(Id(Bool))
⇒ *:Bool*

A more practical application of the type operators is the description of optional values.

```
Let Opt(A <:Ok) =
  Tuple
    case nil
    case notNil with val :A
  end
```

The syntax for the application of a type operator is equivalent to the syntax for the function application.

```
Opt(Person)
Id(Opt(Id(Person)))
```

Symbolic identifiers bound to type operators can be used in infix notation. These infix operators on the type level are all left-associative and of the same precedence. The classical binary type operators of functional programming languages can be introduced into TL in the following way.

```
Let ->(X, Y <:Ok) = Fun(:X) :Y
Let *(X, Y <:Ok) = Tuple fst :X  snd :Y end
Let +(X, Y <:Ok) = Tuple case fst with x :X  case snd with y :Y end
```

The preceding examples are restricted to first-order type operators. TL also supports the definition of higher-order type operators. Higher-order type operators are, for example, type operators accepting a type operator as parameter and applying it to different types in the body. Other examples are type operators generating type operators as result based on non-parametrised types passed as parameters. The coding of case selections on the type level is considered as an illustrative example.

```
Let Boolean(Then, Else <:Ok) = Ok
Let True(Then, Else <:Ok) = Then
Let False(Then, Else <:Ok) = Else
Let Cond(If <:Boolean  Then, Else <:Ok) = If(Then Else)

let i :Cond(True Int String) = 3
let s :Cond(False Int String) = "Peter"
```

8.3.2 Recursive Type Operators

In addition to recursive types TL supports recursive type operators. The type operator *List* maps a type E to the type of a list with elements of type E. For this purpose a type parameter is introduced into the definition of lists presented in section 6.4.

```
Let Rec List(A <:Ok) <:Ok =
  Tuple
    case nil
    case cons with car :A  cdr :List(A)
  end
```

The corresponding list operations can be implemented by polymorphic functions.

```
let new(A <:Ok) :List(A) =
  tuple case nil of List(A) end

let cons(A <:Ok  head :A  tail :List(A)) :List(A) =
  tuple case cons of List(A) with head tail end
```

The polymorphic functions *new* generates empty lists with elements of an arbitrary but specific type. Elements can be added at the beginning of the list by the function *cons*.

In contrast to commercial programming languages, generic list, set, and tree types and polymorphic operations on these types can be defined in TL reducing the number of functions that have to be implemented.

The concepts of polymorphic functions and type operators complement each other. Generic code can be used for the description of structures as well as of behaviour.

8.4 Abstract Data Types

An abstract data type (ADT) consists of a data type and a set of operations defined over this data type. Only the name of the type and the names and signatures of the operations are visible to programs that use the ADT. The implementation of the type and of the operations are hidden by the ADT. The operations provided by the ADT are the only possible and legal ones on the ADT. This protects the values of the ADT against undesired manipulations.

Since the implementation is hidden, it can be changed locally without invalidating programs that use the ADT. If different implementations exist for an ADT, these implementations can be exchanged dynamically.

A general functional stack is presented as an example. The stack is declared employing a polymorphic abstract data type.

```
Let Stack =
  Tuple
    T(E <:Ok) <:Ok
    new(E <:Ok) :T(E)
    empty(E <:Ok stack :T(E)) :Bool
    push(E <:Ok element :E stack :T(E)) :T(E)
    pop(E <:Ok stack :T(E)) :T(E)
    top(E <:Ok stack :T(E)) :E
  end
```

In the following an implementation of this interface based on the module *list*[5] is presented.

```
let listStack :Stack =
  tuple
    Let T(E <:Ok) <:Ok = list.T(E)
    let new(E <:Ok) :T(E) = list.new(:E)
    let empty(E <:Ok stack :T(E)) :Bool = list.empty(stack)
    let push(E <:Ok element :E stack :T(E)) :T(E) =
      list.cons(element stack)
    let pop(E <:Ok stack :T(E)) :T(E) = list.tail(stack)
    let top(E <:Ok stack :T(E)) :E = list.head(stack)
  end
```

In this example, *T* is defined as a type operator and the operations *new*, *empty*, *push*, *pop*, and *top* are implemented as polymorphic functions. Therefore, stacks for arbitrary data types can be generated.

ADTs are based on the concept of type signatures in tuple types. This leads to the concept of *semi-abstract* data types in TL. As an example, the signature of the type operator in the ADT *Stack* above can be modified in order to exhibit more information about the implementation of the ADT.

```
Let Stack2 =
  Tuple
    T <:list.T
    ...
  end

let listStack2 :Stack2 =
  tuple
    ...
  end
```

Users of the ADT *Stack2* can apply operations that expect values of the type *list.T* on the values of type *listStack2.T* in addition to the functions defined for the stack. On the other hand, a value of type *list.T* is incompatible with functions defined by *listStack*.

In TL, a subsignature relationship between signatures of ADTs is defined:

Stack2 <:Stack

Finally, a tuple signature can make a local type binding visible globally.

[5] *list* is a module of the standard library implementing polymorphic lists and the associated operations.

Let *Stack3* =
  Tuple
    Let *T* = *list.T*
    ...
  end

Such type definitions are particularly useful in interfaces of modules when programming libraries (see section 11.1).

9 Imperative Programming

The discussions in the previous sections are restricted to the functional concepts underlying the language TL. The imperative programming features are described in this section.

Imperative programming is based on *mutable* variables in a global (possibly *persistent*) store. The flow of control between operations as allocation, inspection, and destructive update of objects in the store is determined by constructs for sequences and loops.

9.1 Mutable Variables

Binding a value to an identifier by the **let**-construct is equivalent to the definition of a *constant* because no update of the value bound to the identifier is possible. A further binding of an existing identifier to a new value employing the **let**-construct establishes a new constant.

In TL, bindings of identifiers to mutable variables are marked by the keyword **var**. Subsequently, an existing mutable variable can be updated with new values employing the *destructive* assignment :=.

let var *x* = *3*
let var *y* = *4*
x y
⇒ *3 :Int 4 :Int*

x := *y*
⇒ **ok** :**Ok**
x y
⇒ *4 :Int 4 :Int*

y := *5*
⇒ **ok** :**Ok**
x y
⇒ *4 :Int 5 :Int*

For anonymous variables, e.g. inside of tuple values, the keyword **var** precedes the value used to initialize the variable.

tuple var "*text*" **var** *3* **end**

The destructive assignment is a globally defined function with the following signature.

:=(A <:**Ok** **var** *lValue :A rValue :A)* :**Ok**

The signature of the function defines that the assignment evaluates to the trivial value **ok** of type **Ok** as it is the case for the empty block. Note that the infix symbol := is not a keyword. Therefore, it can be bound locally to a user-defined polymorphic function.

TL realizes two parameter passing mechanisms for functions, namely the concept of value parameters (*call by value*) presented in section 5.2.1 and the concept of variable parameters (*call by reference*). The latter concept is illustrated by the following example.

```
let swap(A <:Ok var x, y :A) =
  begin let tmp = x  x := y  y := tmp end

let var a = 3 and var b = 5
swap(:Int a b)
a b
⇒ 5 :Int  3 :Int
```

When applied, the function *swap* references the L-values of the mutable variables a and *b* through the formal parameters in the signature. On return from the function, the values of the mutable variables are swapped.

The concept of higher-order functions presented in section 5.2.4 supports the dynamic generation of encapsulated state variables, which can be shared by several functions (*shared variables*). In the following example, the variable *state* can be updated and inspected, respectively, by the three defined functions only.

```
let newCounter() =
  begin
    let var state = 0
    tuple
      let reset() :Ok =  state := 0
      let inc() :Ok =  state := state + 1
      let value() :Int =  state
    end
  end

let cntr1 = newCounter() and cntr2 = newCounter()
cntr1.inc()  cntr1.value()  cntr2.value()
⇒ ok :Ok  1 :Int  0 :Int
```

Mutable function bindings enable the programmer to *override* functions.

```
let var f(x :Int) = x + 1
f(3)
⇒ 4 :Int
f := fun(x :Int) x - 1
f(3)
⇒ 2 :Int
```

9.2 Subtyping Rules for Mutable Bindings

The details of the interaction between the subtyping rules and the destructive assignment are very important for the type-safety of polymorphic programming languages. TL follows the example of the language Quest (and loosely related concepts in C++) and disallows the application of the subsumption rule to mutable variables. For this reason

```
Fun(x :Person  y :Person) :Ok <:Fun(x :Student  y :Student) :Ok
Tuple x :Int end <:Tuple x :Ok end
```

holds, but the following subtyping relationships do not hold in TL [14]:

```
Fun(var x :Person  y :Person) :Ok <:Fun(var x :Student  y :Student) :Ok
Tuple var x :Int end <:Tuple var x :Ok end
```

However, the concept of the bounded parametric polymorphism supported in TL makes the definition of a type-safe polymorphic function *update* working uniformly for arbitrary subtypes of type *Person* possible.

```
let update(P <:Person  var a, b :P) = a:= b
```

Finally, it is possible in TL to type a mutable variable in an aggregate as a non-mutable value. As a consequence, the more liberal subtyping rules can be applied for the read-only access to value variables, e.g.

```
Tuple var x :Int end <:Tuple x :Int end <:Tuple x :Ok end
```

9.3 Control Structures

In addition to *sequences*, TL offers control structures for *conditional expressions*, three kinds of *loops* and structured *exception handling* supporting a flexible imperative programming style. For the sake of completeness, concepts already introduced in previous sections are mentioned again.

9.3.1 Sequences

A sequence describes the sequential execution of expressions. As mentioned in section 5.1, expressions are enclosed by the keywords **begin** and **end** in order to form a block. The type of a sequence is determined by the type of the last expression or binding in the block.

```
begin
  let s = "text"
  let x = 1
end
⇒ 1 :Int
```

9.3.2 Conditional Expressions

The simplest form of a conditional expression is described by an **if**-expression in TL. The result types of all **then**-branches and the **else**-branch have to be compatible.

```
if x == 0 then
  0
elsif x < 0 then
  -1
else
  1
end
```

Several conditions can be conjoined by **andif** and **orif** operators in TL.

```
if x == 0 andif y == 0 orif x != 0 andif y != 0 then
  0
else
  x
end
```

Since **andif** and **orif** have the same precedence and are evaluated from left to right the above expression is equivalent to the following more complex expression:

```
if x == 0 then
  if y == 0 then
    0
  else
    if x != 0 then
      if y != 0 then
        0
      else
        x
      end
```

```
      else
        x
      end
    else
      x
    end
  else
    x
  end
```

Two further constructs for conditional expressions are provided in TL (see sections 6.2 and 6.5).

```
let weekDay(d :Day) :Bool =
  case d
    when mon, tue, wed, thu, fri then true
    else false
  end

let asString(Dyn A <:Ok  a :A) :String =
  typecase A
    when Int then fmt.int(a)
    when String then a
    else "???"
  end
```

9.3.3 Loops

Loops enclose sequences of expressions for the purpose of iteration. The most general kind of loop is introduced by the keyword **loop**. The result type of loops of this kind is **Ok**.

```
loop
  x := x + 2
  if x > 100 then exit end
  x := x - 1
end
```

Furthermore, there are two more special forms of loops, the prechecking **while**-loops and the enumerating **for**-loops. The function computing the greatest common divisor of two integers is considered as an example of a prechecking loop.

```
let gcd(n, m :Int) :Int =
  begin
    let var vn = n  and var vm = m
    while vn != vm do
```

```
        if vn > vm then vn := vn % vm end
        if vn < vm then vm := vm % vn end
    end
    vn
end
```

Two versions of enumerating loops are distinguished in TL, one counting upwards (**upto**) and the other counting downwards (**downto**).

```
let var x = 0
for i = 50 downto 1 do
  x := x + i
end
x
⇒ 1275 :Int
```

Note, that it is not necessary to declare the loop variable *i* which has local scope. In section 9.4, an example of a loop counting upwards is presented.

9.3.4 Exception Handling

Exception handling is a further important structuring facility. In TL, it is also integrated smoothly into the type system. Exceptional situations that have to be handled can be caused by partially defined functions as, for example, *int.div* (division by zero), and also by an overflow of a partially represented domain. Furthermore, the projection on variants described in section 6.2 can raise exceptions in TL.

Each exception returns an exception package containing a string which supports the identification of the exception at the outermost level.

```
3 / 0
⇒ Exception: "Int error"
```

If an exception occurs inside a composite expression, the further evaluation is aborted and the exception package is propagated.

```
let safeDiv(x, y :Int) :Int =
  try x / y else int.maxValue end
```

In this example, the further propagation of an exception is stopped by the **try**-construct. As in the case of the **if**-construct, the result types of both blocks have to match.

In addition to the standard exceptions, TL also supports user-defined exceptions. The definition of an exception includes the identifier of the exception and, optionally, a signature for exception arguments. The definition is introduced by the keyword **exception**.

```
let noCredit = exception "No Credit" with overdrawn :Int end
```

The type of an exception defines only its signature not its identity.

```
noCredit :Exception with overdrawn :Int end
```

A **raise**-expression returns an exception package as its result, which encapsulates the identity of the exception. Depending on the exception signature it can contain further bindings.

```
let withdraw(var account :Int  amount :Int) =
  if amount <= account then
    account := account - amount
  else
    raise noCredit with let overdrawn = amount - account end
  end
```

Exception packages propagate through nested expressions along the dynamic call hierarchy until an exception block enclosed by **try** and **end** or the main program is reached.

```
try
  withdraw(petersAccount  300)
  print.string("Transfer succeeded")
when noCredit with exc then
  print.string("Overdrawn by " <> fmt.int(exc.overdrawn))
else
  print.string("Unexpected exception occurred")
end
```

Similar to the **case**-expressions a local value variable (here *exc*) in a **when**-branch of the **try**-construct can be used to access the bindings of the exception package in a type-safe way.

A handled exception can be propagated explicitly by reraising it (**reraise**). The following example also shows that exceptions raised by functions exported from *Tycoon*-libraries are bound to exported identifiers enabling the user to define handlers for these exceptions.

```
try x / y
when int.overflow then int.maxValue
when int.error then print.string("Division by zero")  reraise
end
```

Types in TL only specify the values of terminating computations. For this reason an *arbitrary* type can be assigned to terms containing **raise**, **reraise**, or **exit** (see section 9.3.3), e.g.

```
if a then 3 else raise int.overflow end  :Int
if a then "String" else raise int.overflow end  :String
```

This fact is reflected by the type rules **raise** ... **end** **:Nok**, **reraise** **:Nok**, and **exit** **:Nok**, where **Nok** denotes the subtype of all non-parametrised types in TL, i.e.

$A <: \mathbf{Ok} \rightarrow \mathbf{Nok} <: A$

This property of the type **Nok** is frequently used for the definition of polymorphic *null elements*.

```
Let Rec AnyStream <:Ok =
  Tuple empty() :Bool  get() :Nok  rest() :AnyStream end
let emptyExc = exception "Empty Stream"

let emptyStream :AnyStream =
  tuple
    let empty() :Bool = true
    let get() :Nok = raise emptyExc
    let rest() :AnyStream = raise emptyExc
  end
```

9.4 Arrays and Array Indexing

An array is an ordered, possibly empty sequence of anonymous bindings to mutable variables of a common supertype indexed by non-negative integers ($i >= 0$). The size of an array is fixed statically when it is generated. The size cannot be modified dynamically, whereas the elements of an array can be updated dynamically by destructive assignments. A check of the index bounds is performed at runtime only.

In TL, array types are defined using the constructor *Array(A)* and array values are initialized enumerating their elements inside of an **array-end**-block. The elements of an array are accessed by indexing. The indices are expressions of type *Int* enclosed in square brackets.

```
let a :Array(Int) = array 0 1 2 3 4 5 end
a[0] := a[1] + 7
```

Using the **for**-loop it is possible to define, for example, a summation function accepting arrays of an arbitrary size.

```
let sum(arr :Array(Int)) :Int =
  begin
    let var result = 0
    for i = 0 upto extent(arr) do
      result := result + arr[i]
    end
    result
  end
```

Finally, examples for the application of the function *sum* are presented illustrating the *listfix* notation that can be used for functions on arrays in TL.

*sum(***array** *1 2 3 4* **end***)*
sum **of** *1 2 3 4* **end**

10 Multi-Paradigm Programming in Tycoon

It has been one of the design goals of the Tycoon system to support generic, model-independent naming, binding, and typing schemata providing an environment that is open for external services. TL can be used to support programming styles, which differ substantially from each other (see [14]). This is illustrated here by the realisation of two concepts: abstract data types and object-oriented encapsulation.

The different programming styles and concepts are not supported by special language constructs but are realised using the TL primitives for naming, binding, and typing.

In order to implement the concept of abstract data types the primitives of TL can be combined in three different ways. It is possible to aggregate an opaque type together with the functions working on this type.[6] This approach can be implemented purely functionally or state-based resulting in the first two realisation variants. The third variant aggregates methods that work on a hidden, internal state. The different realisation alternatives are called

- *functional* encapsulation,
- *imperative* encapsulation, and
- *method-based* encapsulation.

A generic stack implementation is used to compare the three different realisation alternatives. Each of them provides a type operator that maps the element type of the stack to a tuple type. In the first two cases this tuple type aggregates the opaque stack type *T*, the common stack operations *empty, push, pop, top*, and a parameterless function *new* for the creation of new empty stacks. For the third alternative, the tuple type aggregates only the stack operations. It represents the type of a stack. The function *new* has to be defined outside this type signature.

Functional Encapsulation In the functional realisation the modified stack is returned by the the update operations. Therefore, the result type of these functions is the opaque type *T*:

Let *FunStack (E* <:**Ok***)* =
  Tuple
    T <:**Ok**
    new() :T

[6] This is comparable to an implementation of abstract types in Modula-2 using the module concept of that language.

```
    empty(stack :T) :Bool
    push(element :E stack :T) :T
    pop(stack :T) :T
    top(stack :T) :E
  end
```

The data type is implemented by a parametrised variable. It provides a tuple value consisting of a definition of the representation type and of the functions of this type. The generic service (*list*) providing the list type and the operations on this type is also based on a functional implementation.

```
let listStack (E <:Ok) : FunStack(E) =
  tuple
    Let T <:Ok = list.T(E)
    let new() :T = list.new(:E)
    let empty(stack :T) :Bool = list.empty(stack)
    let push(element :E stack :T) :T = list.cons(element stack)
    let pop(stack :T) :T = list.tail(stack)
    let top(stack :T) :E = list.head(stack)
  end
```

Using this realisation a new stack with elements of type *Int* containing the element 4 can be created by the following function calls:

```
 let intStack = listStack(:Int)
 let myStack = intStack.push(4 intStack.new())
```

Imperative Encapsulation In the imperative realisation the update operations change the state of the stack passed as parameter via side-effects. In contrast to the functional solution, the modified stacks are not returned as function results. For this reason the result type of these operations is **Ok**.

```
Let ImpStack (E <: Ok) =
  Tuple
    T <: Ok
    new() : T
    empty(stack :T) :Bool
    push(element :E stack :T) :Ok
    pop(stack :T) :Ok
    top(stack :T) :E
  end
```

The representation type of the implementation is defined as a tuple type with a mutable component. The update operations are implemented using assignments.

```
let listStack (E <:Ok) : ImpStack(E) =
  tuple
```

```
    Let T <:Ok = Tuple var l :list.T(E) end
    let new() :T = tuple let var l = list.new(:E) end
    let empty(stack :T) :Bool = list.empty(stack.l)
    let push(element :E stack :T) :Ok= stack.l := list.cons(element stack.l)
    let pop(stack :T) :T = stack.l := list.tail(stack.l)
    let top(stack :T) :E = list.head(stack.l)
end
```

In this case a new stack containing the integer 4 can be created by the following function calls:

```
let intStack = listStack(:Int)
let myStack = intStack.new()
intStack.push(4 myStack)
```

Method-Based Encapsulation The third encapsulation technique binds functions to an internal, shared, mutable variable. The function signatures are defined by a tuple type. This type represents the type of a stack object.

```
Let StackObject (E <:Ok) =
  Tuple
    empty() :Bool
    push(element :E) :Ok
    pop() :Ok
    top() :E
  end
```

An implementation of the stack functions is provided by a *new*-function that can be used to create "objects" of this type. The implementation of their methods are value components of these objects. In this implementation framework, method overwriting for subtype objects can also be realised (see [14]). For this reason this encapsulation method is called object-oriented in [14]. It avoids an opaque type and input parameters of this type.[7]

```
let newStackObject(E <:Ok) :StackObject(E) =
  begin
    let var state = list.new(:E)
    tuple
      let empty() :Bool = list.empty(state)
      let push(element :E) :Ok = state := list.cons(element state)
      let pop() :Ok = state := list.tail(state)
      let top() :E = list.head(state)
    end
end
```

[7] Operations expecting more than one input parameter of the opaque type lead to recursive type definitions when this implementation style is used [14].

For this realisation variant the creation of an integer stack with the element 4 looks as follows:

```
let myStack = newStackObject(:Int)
myStack.push(4)
```

11 Programming in the Large

Besides function abstraction, modularization is the most important structuring facility in modern programming languages. Large programs can be split into *interfaces* and *modules* in TL. Moreover, it is possible to group interfaces and modules into *libraries*.

These structuring mechanisms do not introduce new concepts for naming, binding, or typing. They just deliberately restrict existing concepts of TL [14].

11.1 Modules and Interfaces

Interfaces define the signatures of exported values, functions, types, and type operators. Interfaces, therefore, can be viewed as named tuple types containing references to explicitly imported modules (e.g. *bool*) and interfaces visible in the global scope.

```
interface List
import bool
export
  T(E <:Ok) <:Ok
  Let AnyT = T(Nok)
  error :Exception
  nil :AnyT
  cons, ::(E <:Ok  hd :E  tl :T(E)) :T(E)
  empty(E <:Ok  l :T(E)) :bool.T
  car(E <:Ok  l :T(E)) :E
  cdr(E <:Ok  l :T(E)) :T(E)
end
```

Interfaces can include type bindings (*AnyT*). The definition of these types is visible to all users of the interface. If such types are imported by other modules, the name of the interface as well as the name of the module can be employed as qualifying identifiers.

A module defines a tuple value aggregating bindings according to its interface. In TL, an arbitrary number of modules can exist for a single interface.

```
module list
import bool
export
  Let Rec T(E <:Ok) <:Ok =
```

```
    Tuple case nil case cons with hd :E tl :T(E) end
  Let AnyT = T(Nok)
  let error = exception "Empty list"
  let nil = tuple case nil of AnyT end
  let cons(E <:Ok hd :E tl :T(E)) :T(E) =
    tuple case cons of T(E) hd tl end
  let :: = cons
  let empty(E <:Ok l :T(E)) :bool.T = l?nil
  let car(E <:Ok l :T(E)) :E =
    try l!cons.hd else raise error end
  let cdr(E <:Ok l :T(E)) :T(E) =
    try l!cons.tl else raise error end
end
```

Type bindings established in the interface (here *AnyT*) have to be repeated in the module. Modules and interfaces are *first-class* objects of the language. They can be bound to identifiers and passed as parameters to functions. Modules and interfaces can be imported by other modules and interfaces employing the **import**-clause. In the library a unique interface is assigned to every module name.

Interfaces and modules are definable at the *top level* of the interactive programming environment. Their definition implicitly generates persistent data structures describing the types of interfaces and the values of modules, respectively.

After importing a module its components are referenced by the dot notation.

```
module main
import list print
export
  let l = list.cons(3 list.nil)
  let l2 :list.AnyT = list.nil
  if not(list.empty(l)) then
    print.int(list.car(l))
  end
end
```

11.2 Libraries

The rapidly growing number of modules in real systems and the necessity for tools supporting consistent system restructuring in persistent systems makes it necessary to organize modules and interfaces into libraries and suggests the introduction of a library concept into the language TL.

A library defines the scope of the names of its local modules and interfaces and supports the definition of subsystems encapsulating hidden modules and interfaces.

The definition of the standard library(*StdLib*) is presented as a simple example.

```
library StdLib
with
```

```
  interface
    Bool Int Char Real ArrayOp
  module
    bool :Bool  int :Int  char :Char  real :Real  arrayOp :ArrayOp
  interface
    List
  module
    list :List
end
```

The order in which the names of the modules and interfaces are listed matters. A module or interface can only import interfaces or modules that are declared before this module or interface in the library, e.g. *bool* cannot import *list*.As a consequence, cyclic dependencies are ruled out. The modules of the standard library introduced in the previous example can be imported into a further library (*BulkLib*).

```
library BulkLib
import arrayOp :ArrayOp  list :List  iter :Iter
with
  interface
    Set Bag Assoc Dictionary VarList
  module
    linkedSet :Set  bitSet :Set  hashedSet :Set
  module
    bag :Bag  assoc :Assoc  dictionary :Dictionary
  hide
    varList :VarList
end
```

For this purpose, the libraries *StdLib* and *BulkLib* have to be defined in the following order as parts of an enclosing library.

```
library Root
with
  library
    StdLib BulkLib
  interface
    Test
  module
    test :Test
end
```

The example of the library *BulkLib* illustrates two further facilities of the library concept of TL. Modules and interfaces can be hidden in the library employing the **hide**-clause. Furthermore, it is possible to specify different modules (*linkedSet*, *bitSet*, and *hashedSet*) for a single interface (*Set*).

TL supports hierarchic library structures, but the names of all modules, interfaces and libraries inside of a library have to be unique. This is also true for components defined as hidden.

12 Persistence and Garbage Collection

In *Tycoon* no linguistic difference between *persistent* and *temporary* data is made. Every object can be made persistent. Persistence is defined by *reachability* either from a linked library module or from a local name space of a user (*top level*). This persistence concept works for values, functions, and (dynamic) type bindings.

Consistent states of the object store are marked by explicitly stabilising the object store. The module *store* provides the function *stabilise* for this purpose. A call of this function stabilises the actual state of the object store.

```
import store;
store.stabilise();
```

The operation *store.stabilise* generates a *checkpoint*. If a user quits the session with the command **do exit** or if a system crash occurs, all changes of objects in the persistent store performed after the checkpoint are undone (*rollback*). At the beginning of the next session the object store is in the state of the last checkpoint. Furthermore, it is possible to rollback explicitly to the state of the last checkpoint without leaving the system. This is accomplished by the function *restart* which is also exported by the module *store*. The effect of the functions *stabilise* and *restart* is illustrated by the following example.

```
import store list;
let var l = list.nil
l := list.cons(1 l)
l := list.cons(2 l)
store.stabilise();
(* object store with list l containing elements 1 and 2 is stabilised *)

l := list.cons(3 l)
store.restart();
(* rollback to last checkpoint; insertion of 3 into l is undone *)

list.car(l);
⇒ 2
```

Objects that are no longer reachable are automatically deleted from the object store by a *garbage collector*.

13 External C Libraries

Tycoon provides a bidirectional programming interface between TL and C that features a seamless integration of both languages' function paradigms. External C functions can be integrated into TL as ordinary function values. TL functions can be wrapped in a way that makes it possible to use them directly as C function pointers.

13.1 Function Calls from Tycoon to External C Libraries

Tycoon provides a generic mechanism to use system functionality implemented in external languages. The binding of TL identifiers to external function values is achieved by the predefined function *bind*. This function has the following signature:

*bind(Function <:***Ok** *library, label, format :String) :Function*

The parameters of the *bind* function have the following meaning: *Function* describes the type of the resulting TL function. It has to be of the form **Fun**(...) :A. The *library* parameter is a string that identifies the library file that contains the required external C function. This can either be the full path name[8] of a dynamic library or the string result of one of the functions exported by the module *runtimeCore* (see the following table) belonging to the *Tycoon* library *stdenv*.

Function	Description
library	identifies the core of the *Tycoon* runtime system
cLibrary	identifies the standard C library
dynamicLibrary	identifies dynamically bound libraries
staticLibrary	identifies statically bound libraries

The *label* parameter is a string that contains the original C source text name of the C function. The *format* parameter is a string that specifies the assumed parameter format of the C function. Every single character of this string corresponds to one parameter. It specifies the conversions between tagged and untagged data representations to happen before and after a call. The parameter order is *from left to right* as in C, except for the function result type. It is given by the last character which is mandatory. The following table contains the set of characters that denote parameter formats.

[8] If the same shared library is referenced several times the path should always be exactly the same. Otherwise the dynamic linker loads several instances of the shared object. This means not only consuming more process memory than necessary, but leads to subtle bugs when global C variables are defined multiple times in the same process.

Format	TL type	C type	Description
i	*Int*	**long**	integer number
r	*Real*	**double**	floating point number
c	*Char*	**char**	ASCII character
b	*Bool*	**long**	boolean value (see text)
s	*String*	**char ***	zero-terminated string
v	**Ok**	**void**	return value only
=	<:**Ok**	**void ***	*Tycoon* value, no conversion
w	*word.T*	**void ***	32-bit word

There is no predefined type for boolean values in C. Boolean TL values are converted to C long values as follows.

true → *1*
false → *0*

A C value x produces the following TL boolean values:

x != 0 → *true*
x == 0 → *false*

When *s* is used as a format character for a string parameter, every call is enclosed by automatic fix and unfix operations for the argument. The result of the fix operation, a main memory pointer is passed to C. The latter refers to a valid C string, because all *Tycoon* strings are represented with zero-termination.

Used in return value position the format character *s* causes strings returned from C to be copied into newly created store objects (*copy-out*).

Suppose a library */usr/lib/libexample.so* contains a function *example* that takes a string argument and returns a 32 bit integer number. Thus, *example* is assumed to match the following declaration:

extern long *example(***char** **s);*

An appropriate binding for *example* in TL is:

let *cCallExample =*
*bind(:***Fun***(:String) :Int "/usr/lib/libexample.so" "example" "si")*

The value *cCallExample* has the type **Fun***(:String) :Int*. Therefore, the C function can be called as follows.

let *result :Int = cCallExample("My favorite String")*

Note that external bindings are persistent and portable across host architectures. For example, if the value *cCallExample* is transferred with *dynamic.extern/intern*, the C binding would be re-established automatically.

13.2 Function Calls from External C Libraries to Tycoon

The programming interface between TL and C is bidirectional. It is not only possible to call C functions from TL, but also to *call back* from C to TL.

In order to minimize the programming effort for callbacks on the C side, it is desirable to make TL functions appear like ordinary C function pointers. Moreover, this is indispensable in situations where an external software component requires C callbacks but cannot be changed.

The module *cCallback* exports an abstract type *cCallback.T* which represents C function pointers that refer to callbacks. The creation function for values of type *cCallback.T* has the following signature:

*new(Function <:***Ok** *function :Function format :String) :callback.T(Function)*

The first value argument (*function*) of *new* must always be a function, although this restriction is not checked. Nevertheless, the function's signature has to be mirrored in the *format* string that specifies how C arguments of the resulting callback are converted into TL values. Every single character of the string corresponds to one parameter. The parameter order is *from left to right* as in C, except for the function result type which is given by the last character. The latter is mandatory. The format characters are shown in the table in section 13.1.

If the format character *s* is used for a parameter, a C string argument will be copied into a newly created store object (*copy-in*). In case of a return value, a C string is copied into a chunk of memory allocated by *malloc*. Hence the parameter passing semantics are *copy-out* instead of *by reference* which apply for strings within C only.

The format character *v* specifies a function result value of **ok** irrespective of the actual C value returned by C.

For parameters with format code *w* a TL type that is equivalent to *word.T* or to an instance of *word.Handle* must be used. In particular callbacks conform to *word Handle*, because *cCallback.T* <: *word.Handle*.

A simple example follows:

```
import cCallback fmt

let myMessage(n :Int  r :Real) :String =
  fmt.int(n) <> " = " <> fmt.real(r)

let myMessageCallback =
  cCallback.new(myMessage "irs")

let test =
  bind(:Fun(n :Int  messageCallback :cCallback.T) :Ok
    ".../example.so.1.0" "test" "iwv")

test(2 myMessageCallback)
```

The resulting console output would be

```
"pi * 2 = 6.28"
ok
```

assuming that the corresponding C program .../*example.c* looks like this:

```
#include <stdio.h>

void test(long n, char *message(long n, double r))
{
 printf("pi * %s\n", message(n, n * 3.14));
}
```

As callbacks can be transferred to address spaces which are not under control of the *Tycoon* system, there is in general no way to determine their temporal extent automatically. Callbacks are never persistent. Callbacks occupy some memory resources that can only be released explicitly:

```
cCallback.free(myMessageCallback)
```

After freeing a callback it is invalid. Any subsequent usage is most likely to cause strange system behaviour (e.g. crashes). Attentive readers may have noticed some more problems in the example: In what manner does the result string of the function *message* get allocated on the C side before it is passed to *printf*, who is in charge of releasing its memory and how can this be done?

The current solution is that the format character *s* in a return value position causes the allocation of an appropriate memory block by calling *malloc*. This block has to be released by the C programmer by a call to *free*. Thus, the C program in the example should be written as follows:

```
#include <stdio.h>
#include <malloc.h>

void test(long n, char *message(long n, double r))
{
 char *p;

 p = message(n, n * 3.14);
 printf("pi * %s\n", p);
 free(p);
}
```

Acknowledgements. This research was supported by ESPRIT Basic Research, Project FIDE, #6309. The Tycoon system described in this paper was developed by Andreas Gawecki, Bernd Mathiske, Florian Matthes and Rainer Müller. Section 13 of this text was written by Bernd Mathiske who also developed Tycoon's external language bindings. The author would also like to thank Claudia Niederée, Gerald Schröder, Petra Münnix, Andreas Rudloff and Dominic Juhász for their careful reviewing of this paper and numerous hints which helped to improve the presentation of the material.

References

1. M.P. Atkinson and P. Buneman. Types and persistence in database programming languages. *ACM Computing Surveys*, 19(2), June 1987.
2. M.P. Atkinson, K.J. Chisholm, and W.P. Cockshott. PS-algol: An algol with a persistent heap. *ACM SIGPLAN Notices*, 17(7), July 1981.
3. D.G. Bobrow, L.G. De Michiel, R.P. Gabriel, S.E. Keene, G. Kiczales, and D.A. Moon. Common Lisp object system specification. *ACM SIGPLAN Notices*, 23, September 1988.
4. L. Cardelli. Amber. In *Combinators and Functional Programming Languages*, volume 242 of *Lecture Notes in Computer Science*. Springer-Verlag, 1986.
5. L. Cardelli. Typeful programming. Technical Report 45, Digital Equipment Corporation, Systems Research Center, Palo Alto, California, May 1989.
6. L. Cardelli. The Quest language and system (tracking draft). Technical report, Digital Equipment Corporation, Systems Research Center, Palo Alto, California, 1990. (Shipped as part of the Quest V.12 system distribution.)
7. L. Cardelli, S. Martini, J.C. Mitchell, and A. Scedrov. An extension of system F with subtyping. In T. Ito and A.R. Meyer, editors, *Theoretical Aspects of Computer Software, TACS'91*, volume 526 of *Lecture Notes in Computer Science*, pages 750–770. Springer-Verlag, 1991.
8. A.J. Field and P.G. Harrison. *Functional Programming*. Addison-Wesley Publishing Company. 1988.
9. A. Goldberg and D. Robson. *Smalltalk-80: The Language and its Implementation*. Addison-Wesley Publishing Company, 1983.
10. P. Hudak. Conception, evolution, and application of functional programming languages. *ACM Computing Surveys*, 21(3):359–411, September 1989.
11. Ichbiah et al. The programming language Ada: Reference manual. Technical Report MIL-STD-1815A-1983, ANSI, 1983.
12. ISO/IEC JTC1/SC22/WG13. *Interim Version of the 4th Working Draft Modula-2 Standard*. 1991.
13. B.W. Kernighan and D.M. Ritchie. *The C Programming Language*. Prentice Hall, Englewood Cliffs, New Jersey, 1977.
14. F. Matthes. *Persistente Objektsysteme: Integrierte Datenbankentwicklung und Programmerstellung*. Springer-Verlag, 1993. (In German.)
15. F. Matthes, R. Müller, and J.W. Schmidt. Object stores as servers in persistent programming environments – the P-Quest experience. FIDE Technical Report Series FIDE/92/48, FIDE Project Coordinator, Department of Computing Sciences, University of Glasgow, Glasgow G128QQ, July 1992.
16. F. Matthes and J.W. Schmidt. Towards database application systems: Types, kinds and other open invitations. In *Proceedings of the Kiev East/West Workshop on Next Generation Database Technology*, volume 504 of *Lecture Notes in Computer Science*. Springer-Verlag, April 1991. (Also appeared as TR FIDE/91/14.)

17. F. Matthes and J.W. Schmidt. Definition of the Tycoon language TL – a preliminary report. Informatik Fachbericht FBI-HH-B-160/92, Fachbereich Informatik, Universität Hamburg, Germany, November 1992.
18. F. Matthes and J.W. Schmidt. System construction in the Tycoon environment: Architectures, interfaces and gateways. In P.P. Spies, editor, *Proceedings of Euro-Arch'93 Congress*, pages 301–317. Springer-Verlag, October 1993.
19. M. Mauny. Functional programming using CAML. Technical report, INRIA, Domaine de Voluceau, Rocquencourt 78153 Le Chesnay Cedex, France, September 1991.
20. J. Minker. *Foundations of Deductive Databases and Logic Programming*. Morgan Kaufmann Publishers, 1988.
21. R. Müller. Language processors and object stores: Interface design and implementation. Master's thesis, Fachbereich Informatik, Johann Wolfgang Goethe-Universität, Frankfurt, Germany, November 1991. (In German).
22. G. Nelson, editor. *Systems programming with Modula-3*. Series in innovative technology. Prentice Hall, Englewood Cliffs, New Jersey, 1991.
23. P. Rovner, R. Levin, and J. Wick. On extending Modula-2 for building large, integrated systems. Technical Report 3, Digital Equipment Corporation, Systems Research Center, Palo Alto, California, January 1985.
24. J.W. Schmidt and F. Matthes. Language technology for post-relational data systems. In A. Blaser, editor, *Database Systems of the 90s*, volume 466 of *Lecture Notes in Computer Science*, pages 81–114. Springer-Verlag, November 1990.
25. D. Stemple, R.B. Stanton, T. Sheard, P. Philbrow, R. Morrison, G.N.C. Kirby, L. Fegaras, R.L. Cooper, R.C.H. Connor, M.P. Atkinson, and S. Alagic. Type-safe linguistic reflection: A generator technology. Research Report CS/92/6, University of St. Andrews, Department of Computing Science, July 1992.
26. N. Wirth. The programming language Oberon. Technical report, Department Informatik, ETH Zürich, Switzerland, 1987.

Chapter 1.1.2

Fibonacci: A Programming Language for Object Databases

Antonio Albano, Giorgio Ghelli and Renzo Orsini*

Dipartimento di Informatica, Università di Pisa, Corso Italia 40, 56125 Pisa, Italy

Abstract. Fibonacci is an object-oriented database programming language characterized by static and strong typing and by new mechanisms for modelling databases in terms of objects with roles, classes and associations. A brief introduction to the language is provided to present those features which are particularly suited to modelling complex databases. Examples of the use of Fibonacci are given with reference to the prototype implementation of the language.

1 Introduction

Fibonacci is an object-oriented database programming language characterized by static and strong typing and by new mechanisms for modelling databases in terms of objects with roles, classes and associations.

Fibonacci[1] was conceived in an effort to integrate features for naturally modelling object-oriented database applications in a general purpose programming language which is statically and strongly typed. The design of the language has drawn heavily from experience with the Galileo language, which was also developed at the University of Pisa. Since 1985 Galileo has been used extensively for teaching database programming using a strongly typed language. The language has proved to be useful for modelling complex databases in terms of objects grouped into classes which are organized in hierarchies, and it has shown the importance of static type checking in implementing database applications. However, this experience also highlighted that the techniques used by object-oriented languages for modelling objects and associations between sets of objects are not satisfactory. Overcoming these limitations has been one of our major goals in the design of Fibonacci.

This paper presents Fibonacci, and is organized as follows. Section 2 outlines our language design choices. Section 3 surveys the main features of Fibonacci. Section 4 presents the constructs of the language to define objects with roles. Section 5 presents the constructs to model sets of objects and associations between them. Section 6 describes the architecture of the current Fibonacci implementation. Section 7 compares the proposed solution with related works. In the conclusions, we comment on our future plans.

---

* Present address: Corso di Laurea in Scienze dell'Informazione, Università di Venezia, Via Torino 153, 30170, Mestre.

[1] Originally the language was called Nuovo Galileo because it borrows heavily from the Galileo language, but as the new language evolved it was given its own name, Fibonacci, in honour of the medieval mathematician Leonardo Pisano (Leonardo of Pisa), also known as Leonardo Fibonacci.

2 Background

In this section we will briefly discuss the requirements on which the design of the language was based.

2.1 Why a database language?

Database languages integrate the abstraction mechanisms of a data model within a programming language. The result is an integrated programming language where data stored in the database are manipulated in the same way as any data structure of the language.

Database languages have been proposed to overcome the limitations of the traditional approach, where applications using the database are programmed by languages which host the data model operators, using *ad hoc* mechanisms to exchange information between a program and the DBMS. This traditional programming environment is not suitable for the growing complexity of applications, due to the limited integration of the data model into the programming language.

From the latter half of the 1970s, attention was initially focused on the integration of the relational data model abstraction mechanisms in the type system of a programming language, to construct an integrated programming environment to develop database applications. The term "database programming language" was used to refer to these approaches. Examples of this approach are languages such as Pascal/R [39], RIGEL [37], PLAIN [44] and DBPL [40]. A different approach to integrate the relational data model in a complete programming language is exemplified by the Datalog language, which allows relational database applications to be written in a Prolog-like logic programming language. At the end of the 1970s new database programming languages were proposed to support a more expressive data model, named "semantic data model", in order to overcome the modelling limitations of the traditional data models. This resulted in the development of so-called conceptual languages such as ADAPLEX [41], Taxis [32] and Galileo [2]. More recently, new database programming languages have been proposed which are based on the object-oriented programming paradigm [3, 45, 15], which seems the best suited to satisfy the needs of complex database applications. The same phenomenon is taking place in the world of commercial database systems, where most of the new systems support some features of the object-oriented data model, and offer a language which is not just a DDL-DML but is a complete language supporting application development. This trend suggests that database programming languages may become one of the basic tools to write database applications.

2.2 Why a persistent language?

Persistent programming languages are characterized by the following properties:

- any value, irrespective of its type, has the same rights to persistence (orthogonal persistence);
- programs are written in a way which does not depend on the persistence of data on which they operate (persistence independence).

As a consequence the programmer uses the same operators on data whatever their lifetime, and does not need read and write operators to control data movement. Examples of such languages are PS-Algol [9], Napier88 (Chapter 1.1.3), [33], Galileo [2], and Tycoon (Chapter 1.1.1), [31].

Orthogonal persistence is especially important in those applications where complex data types are manipulated or where the number of different types is similar to the number of different values manipulated. In these applications, orthogonal persistence allows the types of persistent data to be defined by using any type constructor of the language, and the programmer is freed from the task of finding a way to represent any persistent data structure by using only the abstraction mechanism of a specific data model [10, 11, 13].

It is a matter of debate whether database application development would be better supported by a persistent programming language which offers a set of built-in data definition and manipulation operations, offering direct support for a fixed data model (*built-in approach*), or by a persistent programming language which gives programmers the possibility of defining their own data model (*add-on approach*) [30]. Fibonacci follows the built-in approach, while Napier88 and Tycoon are two examples of the add-on approach.

2.3 Why a statically and strongly typed language?

A language is strongly typed if all computations are checked for type errors. A language is statically checked if all type errors are discovered through textual analysis. Static typing is essential for languages used in the final encoding of applications, in particular for complex applications, which evolve in time, as happens with database applications. Software systems are always evolving due to the constant evolution of requirements and to the continuous discovery of bugs, and a statically typed language provides one way to control change, and thus helps to produce and maintain reliable software systems, since it ensures that no evolutionary step introduces run-time type errors.

Static and strong typing, however, can also be a hindrance to software evolution when it is unduly restrictive. For example, a function *gimmeJohns* which takes a set of persons and returns only those whose name is John, need not be modified, in a dynamically typed system, when the definition of type *Person* is modified, if the *name* field is not affected. However, in most typed languages (e.g. in Pascal), *gimmeJohns* should at least be re-checked, if not modified, whenever type Person is modified. This problem essentially disappears in polymorphic languages, such as Fibonacci, where it is possible to describe that *gimmeJohns* just needs a *name* field and returns values of the same type as its input type. In this situation, the function must be modified and re-checked only when the *name* field of Person is changed. Such modification would also be required in an untyped language, but there the programmer would not be notified of the need for a change by the type checker.

Other benefits achieved by a static and strong typing discipline are:

1) programs and data definitions are more readable, hence they can be more easily maintained;

2) debugging is greatly eased by the controls made by the type checker: it is typical of database applications that once the program is well-typed very few errors (or none at all) remain in the code;

3) programs are more efficient since they do not perform run-time type checking [20].

2.4 Why an object-oriented language?

The object-oriented data model is the best suited to represent complex data types, especially when the data base is a graph of interconnected entities with a structure which is not so homogeneous and regular as in traditional business applications. Other important features of this data model are the possibility of describing procedural information (methods) within the schema, and the encapsulation of object state. This allows a stricter maintenance of some classes of constraints. These features make object-oriented database languages well suited to applications which use complex data of different types, such as those in office information systems, computer-aided design and manufacturing systems, computer-aided software engineering, multimedia and hypermedia information systems, and knowledge-based systems.

In the field of programming languages, the object-oriented paradigm is characterized by the fact that the combination of encapsulation, inheritance, and late binding allows the functionalities of data types to be extended without knowing their implementation. This feature of object-oriented languages explains the high level of modifiability and reusability which characterizes object-oriented software [12, 23, 28, 45].

2.5 Why objects and roles?

The standard object-oriented data model is not satisfactory when entities need to be modelled which change the class they belong to and their behaviour during their life. When an object is allowed to acquire new object types, the problem arises that different and inconsistent behaviours may have been defined for these different object types. This problem can be solved by preventing these inconsistent behaviours from "mixing up". In this approach, an object has a context dependent behaviour, and in each context it exploits only a consistent subset of its possible behaviours, and this subset depends on the "role" that the object is playing in that context. A role mechanism faces this problem, and, more generally, allows one to model entities which can play several roles and behave according to the role being played [5, 36].

2.6 Why an object-association data model?

The object-association data model extends the object-oriented data model with a specific construct to model associations. Usually, in object-oriented data models, objects model entities of the domain of discourse, classes[2] model sets of homogeneous entities, and an association between two objects is represented by having a method in each of them which returns the other one; one-to-many associations are modelled by methods which return collections of objects. The

---

[2] The term *class* is used with different meanings in the literature. In object-oriented languages, a class is like a type in conventional programming languages and it is used to define the structure and behaviour of a set of possible objects. Often in object-oriented database languages a class is also used to refer the set of all existing instances of a class. In this paper a class is used with the meaning of a collection of homogeneous values of any type.

advantage of this traditional approach is that cardinality constraints on the associations can be enforced using types, and associations are dealt with exactly like object attributes. Nevertheless, this approach has a number of drawbacks, namely:

- associations are conceptually a higher-level, abstract notion, whose implementation should be decided by the DBMS, while attributes force the programmer to choose a specific implementation for them;
- an association is a single conceptual entity whose semantics, in the object model, is split among several objects;
- the enforcement of the inverse relation constraint, i.e. the fact that the two methods modelling the associations are the inverse of each other, is left to the programmer;
- associations relate objects which exist independently, and it should be possible to define them incrementally without redefining the structure of existing objects;
- associations are not necessarily binary, and can have their own attributes; these aspects can only be modelled indirectly by means of attributes;
- operations on relationships as a whole are not possible in a straightforward way.

To overcome these problems, an extension of the object-oriented data model with an *association* construct was proposed [4]. The *association* is a first class type constructor. An *association* is a modifiable set of tuples which is used to represent the existence of associations between classes of objects, in a way which resembles how n-m associations are represented in relational schemas: to represent the fact that two objects are associated, a tuple containing the two objects is inserted into the association. When an association is defined, some constraints can be defined on its extensions, such as referential and cardinality constraints, as described in Section 5.

This approach solves the problems listed above. Specifically, in the object-association data model, an association is defined in a purely declarative way, its description doesn't depend on the description of the types of the associated objects, and the system is free to represent, internally, the association in the most convenient way.

3 Overview of Fibonacci

Here we present an overview of the main features of Fibonacci.

Fibonacci is an expression-based language. Each construct is applied to values and returns a value.

Fibonacci is a persistent language. All data transitively accessible from the global environment (top-level), survive automatically between different work-sessions, irrespective of their type. Data are removed by a garbage collector when they are no longer reachable from any identifier in the global environment.

Fibonacci is an interactive language. The system repeatedly prompts for input and reports the result of the computation; this interaction is said to happen at the top-level of evaluation. At the top-level one can evaluate expressions or perform declarations. Stand-alone applications interacting with the top-level environment can also be written.

Fibonacci is a higher order language. Functions are denotable and expressible values of the language. Therefore, a function can be embedded in data structures, passed as a parameter and returned as a value.

Fibonacci is a safe language. Each legal expression has at least one type, which is statically checked. Each type is related to a set of operators which can be applied to values of this type (e.g. the field selectors of a tuple type). The basic types are `None, Null, Bool, String, Int, Real, Any`. The instances of basic types are all disjoint, with one notable exception: the value `unknown` (of type `None`), which belongs to any type whatsoever. Besides these types, type constructors exist to define new types, from basic or previously defined types. They are divided into two categories, *concrete* type constructors (tuple, sequence, discriminated union, function, class and association types) and *generative* type constructors (object and role types). Type constructors take types as parameters, and produce other types. Type equality is structural for concrete types (i.e. two types are equal if they are built with the same constructor applied to types recursively equal), while it is by name (more precisely by definition time) with generative types.[3]

Fibonacci types are first class. All Fibonacci values have an equal possibility to be stored in persistent or temporary data structures and to be parameters or results of functions independently of their type. Any type operator can be applied to any other type.

Fibonacci assignment has sharing semantics. Values of any type are always used *directly*, and not by copying them, when they are passed as parameters to functions, bound to identifiers in declarations, and used in constructing complex values.

Fibonacci has subtyping. A subtype relation is defined on concrete types. This relation allows the so called *inclusion polymorphism* to be exploited: if T1 is a *subtype* of T2 (also, T2 is a *supertype* of T1), then a value of T1 is also a value of T2, consequently, it can be used in every context where a value of T2 is expected. A subtype relation with this property exists among role types too, which must be explicitly declared when a new role type is defined.[4]

Fibonacci supports inheritance. Inheritance is the ability to define a new object type and a new object type implementation by extending a previous type or implementation definition. In Fibonacci, as in most object-oriented languages, inheritance can be used to define object subtypes and their implementations, starting from the corresponding definitions for object supertypes.

Fibonacci has objects with roles. Objects are entities with an immutable identity and a mutable state. The state is encapsulated and can only be queried and updated by sending messages to the object. An object is internally organized as an acyclic graph of *roles*. A role is also an entry to access the object it belongs to: an object can only be accessed through one of its roles, and its behaviour depends on this role. An object could be considered as simply being a container for its roles, since messages are handled and cooperatively answered by these roles. Fibonacci distinguishes between object and role operations. Object operations allow one to test for the existence of

---

[3] While in some object-oriented languages the term "value" is used to refer to values of concrete types only, in our terminology it refers to values of every type, including objects.

[4] Subtyping between types with modifiable fields creates some well-known problems [1], [2], [22], which are solved in Fibonacci by having a specific type constructor **`Var`** for modifiable data, such that no subtyping relation exists between different **`Var`** types.

certain roles in the object and to gain a reference to one of these roles, and to *extend* objects by giving them new roles (for example, adding the *Employee* role to a *Person*). The basic role operation is message passing. The Fibonacci role-based approach is a conservative extension of the classical object-based approach: if the special object operations are not used, and objects are never extended, then message passing behaves as in traditional object-oriented languages, and Fibonacci role types can be used as if they were traditional object types. Finally, in Fibonacci the implementation of a role type is defined separately from the type itself, and the same type can have several implementations.

Fibonacci has polymorphic functions. A function is polymorphic when its type does not prescribe a single input type, but describes the set of all acceptable input types and how the output type depends on the current input type. Fibonacci supports both inclusion polymorphism (subtyping), and parametric polymorphism, since functions can be defined with types as parameters, and these types can then be used to give the types of the other parameters and of the result.

Fibonacci has an exception-trap mechanism. Exceptions can be raised and selectively trapped, and exception handlers can be specified.

Fibonacci has a nested transaction mechanism. When a transaction fails, all its side-effects, both on persistent and transient values, are undone; transactions may be nested.

4 Objects and Roles

4.1 Overview

An object is the computer representation of certain facts about a real-world entity. An object is a software entity which has an internal state equipped with a set of local operations (*methods*) to manipulate that state. The request for an object to execute an operation is called a *message* to which the object can reply. The state of an object can only be accessed and modified through operations associated with that object. Each object can send messages to itself (*self-reference*). Message interpretation, i.e. the choice of the method used to reply to a message, always depends on the object that receives that message. This means that different objects may use different methods to reply to the same message. Each object is distinct from all other objects and has an identity that persists over time, independently of changes to its state. All these features of object oriented languages are retained in Fibonacci, and are extended as follows.

Suppose that a *Person-Student* hierarchy has been defined in any object-oriented language. When a *Student* "*john*" receives a message it may either answer as a *Person*, if the corresponding method has been inherited (e.g., *Age*) or as a *Student*, if the method has been added or redefined (e.g., *StudentNumber*), or finally, it may ask itself "how would I answer if I were just a *Person*?" before composing its answer as a *Student* (the *super* mechanism). In Fibonacci terminology we describe this situation by saying that *john* contains both a *Person* and a *Student* role. From the outer world, every message is addressed to its *Student* role, but, internally, the two roles cooperate to build up the answer, in two different ways:

- by inheritance: when the *Student* role does not have a method, it looks for a method in its super-role *Person* (*method lookup*);
- by message passing (the *super* mechanism): a method of the *Student* role can send a message to the *Person* role.

The essential assumption underlying the classical model is that every object has one most specialized role, and this role is the one which receives any message sent to the object and starts the method lookup mechanism. Fibonacci extends the classical model in two directions. First of all, due to object extendibility, a single object may have different most specialized roles. For example, if *Employee* is a second subtype of *Person*, by extending *john* with the *Employee* role, we obtain an object with two unrelated most specialized roles, *Student* and *Employee*. Second, messages are not sent to objects, but they are always directed to a specific role of the object. The operations which build and extend an object in fact return, as a result, a reference to a specific role of the object; the most specific role in the first case, and the new role in the second case. Hence, in Fibonacci we never manipulate objects directly, but we always manipulate roles of objects; and a role is implicitly cast to its object only when an object operation, such as equality or extension, is applied. When we want to send a message to john we must either send it to the value, say *johnAsStudent*, returned when john as been created as a student; or to the value, say *johnAsEmployee*, returned by the object extension operator. In the first case *johnAsStudent* will answer as a *Student*, i.e. it will look for the method starting from its *Student* role and then will try to inherit it from its *Person* role. In the second case, method lookup will start from the *Employee* role, and then will go up to its only ancestor *Person*.

The role mechanism was introduced in Fibonacci to preserve *cousin independence*. We say that two object types are *cousin types* when no one type is a subtype of the other one, but they are subtypes of a common ancestor. Cousin independence means that when programmers are defining an object type (a *role* type in Fibonacci) they only have to know the definition of its supertypes, and don't have to be aware of the existence of other cousin types. This principle implies that no relationship can be assumed to exist between two methods defined for two cousin types for the same message. Hence, any method lookup mechanism must ensure that no message addressed to an object of type *T* is answered by a method which has been designed for a cousin type *S*. Cousin independence holds for the standard object-oriented languages since an object is created with a type and cannot acquire new types.

Now, suppose that two different subtypes *Employee* and *Student* are defined for type *Person*, and that in both types a *Code* field is defined, with a different meaning and even a different type, e.g. *String* and *Int* respectively. If *Employee* and *Student* have no common subtype, then this situation must be legitimate, due to the cousin independence principle. This situation is not a problem in traditional object-oriented languages, where no object can be an *Employee* and a *Student* at the same time. In Fibonacci, however, such an object may exist, and this object must answer a *Code* request in a way which is related to the "role" it is playing. This was the main reason behind the design of Fibonacci role mechanism.

This mechanism, whose primary purpose is to deal with object extendibility, also enables Fibonacci to model those real world situations where a single entity can play several roles and behaves differently according to the role it is playing. In traditional object-oriented languages, where every object is always accessed through its most specialized role, it is not easy to model such situations.

Note that a Fibonacci object which is built directly in its most specialized role, and which never acquires new roles, behaves exactly like an object in other object-oriented languages. Hence Fibonacci programmers can ignore the object-roles mechanism with all its subtleties until they actually need it.

To emphasize the distinction between object and role operations, Fibonacci distinguishes between *object types* and *role types*. A typical hierarchy of role and object types is depicted in Figure 1.

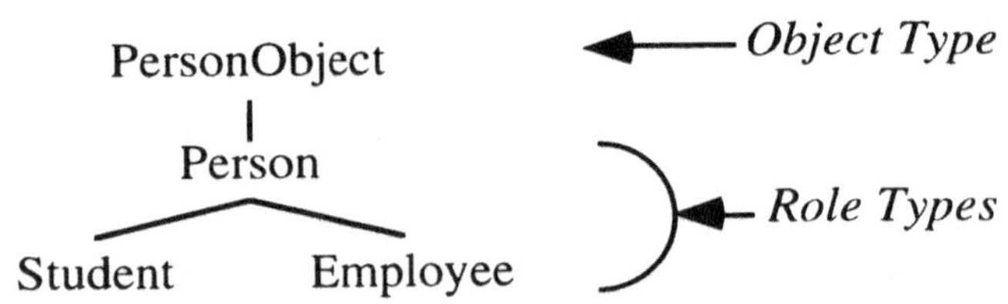

Fig. 1. An object-role type hierarchy

A role type is characterized by the messages it accepts, hence it is very similar to an object type in a traditional object-oriented language. An object is simply a set of roles, hence an object type specifies the set of roles which *may* be part of an object of that type: referring to the figure, an object of type *PersonObject* may contain a *Person*, a *Student* and an *Employee* role. This set of role types is open-ended, since new sub-role types can be added to any object type at any moment, and is called the *role type family* of the object type. Since the object type is a supertype of its role type family, object operations, such as equality and tests for the existence of a specific role, can be applied to values which denote a role.

4.2 Objects and Roles: Type Operators

NewObject is the constructor for a new object type which is needed to begin the construction of a role type family. Since objects cannot be manipulated independently of their roles, this operator introduces a new type without giving any information about the messages managed by its values: this information is specified in the definition of its role type family. For example, a definition of a new object type *PersonObject* is:

```
Let PersonObject = NewObject;
```

A role type is defined with the constructor **IsA** ... **With** ... **End** as a subtype of an object type or as a subtype of other role types. In both cases a role type always belongs to the role family of one object type, called its *object supertype*. A value belonging to a role type is called *a role value* (or simply a *role*). By subtyping, a role value also belongs to the object supertype of its role type, so that both object operations (equality, role casting, role inspection, extension) and role operations (message passing) can be applied to a role value. The messages which can be sent to a role are those specified by its role type, either by listing them in the role type definition or by inheriting them from the role supertypes.

A role type is defined by a set of *properties*, i.e. by giving the signature of the methods of that role. **NewObject** and **IsA** are *generative* type constructors, i.e. each object type and role type definition produces a new type, different from any other type previously defined. Figure 2 shows the definition of the role type *Person*.

```
Let Person = IsA PersonObject With
             Name: String;
             BirthYear: Int;
             Age: Int;
             Address: String;
             modAddress (newAddress: String): Null;
             Introduce: String;
           End;
```

Fig. 2. A Person role type definition

The **Let** keyword precedes a type declaration. Fibonacci adopts the lexical convention in which lower-case keywords and identifiers relate to values, while capitalized keywords and identifiers relate to types. **IsA** `<ObjectType>` **With** `<properties list>` **End** is the type constructor for role types. The semicolon terminates a phrase (declaration or expression).

A role type family can be extended dynamically by defining a new role type T as a *subtype* of others, called its *supertypes*. The subtype *inherits* all the properties of its supertypes, unless they are explicitly redefined in the subtype (*overriding*). In the case of multiple inheritance, if a property is present in more than one supertype, and there is not an explicit redefinition in the subtype, then the property of the *last specified supertype* is inherited (but its type must specialize all the types of all the other inherited versions; see below). Multiple inheritance of a property is allowed only if that property has been defined in a common ancestor. This rule is enforced to prevent two methods with the same name but different meanings from being accidentally merged in a subtype. Thus, when two methods have the same name and the same meaning, this rule forces the programmer to define a common supertype where such a method is introduced. Figure 3 shows the definition of the subtypes `Student` and `Employee` of the type `Person`.

In a subtype definition *S*, for any property *p* of *S* (inherited, redefined or added), if *p* is also defined in the supertype *T* then the following conditions hold:

- the signature of *p* in *T* is a subsignature of the one in *S* (*contravariance*); [1]
- the output type of *p* in *S* is subtype of the one in *T* (*covariance*).

```
Let Student = IsA Person With
          Faculty: String;
          StudentNumber: Int;
          Introduce: String;
          End;
Let Employee = IsA Person With
          Department: String;
          EmployeeNumber: Int;
```

```
    Introduce: String;
    End;
```

Fig. 3. Role subtype definitions

4.3 Object construction

A role type T defines the interface of the objects with such a type, but doesn't give any information about their internal structure. An object of type T is created with the construct **role** T <implementation> **end**, where the implementation specifies the private state of the object and the body for all the methods specified in the interface; to be more precise, the **role** operator builds an object with one role, and returns a reference to that role of the object. Figure 4 shows an expression which creates a new object and returns a value (john) of type Person, which denotes both the new object and its only role.

```
let john = role Person
     private
          let address = var ("Darwin road, 123 - London");[5]
          methods
               Name = "John Daniels";
               BirthYear = 1967;
               Age = currentYear() - me.BirthYear;
               Address = at (address);
               modAddress (newAddress: String) =
                         if stringLength(newAddress) <= 0
                         then failwith "incorrect address"
                         else address := newAddress
               Introduce = "My name is " & me.Name &
                           " and I was born in " &
                           intToString(me.BirthYear);
          end;
```

Fig. 4. An example of object construction

The **private** section of the **role** construct specifies a private environment which can only be accessed by the role methods. The **method** section specifies the methods of the role which, in a database example, can be as simple as a method which just returns a constant value, thus making an object very similar to a record. Once an object is created, its methods can be selected with the dot notation (e.g. john.Address). A method call causes the evaluation of an expression in the private environment with possible side-effects; this is the only way to ask an object to modify its internal state.

To create many instances of a role type, with the same internal structure and the same methods, a constructor can be defined, which is a function that returns objects of a certain type. An example of a constructor for objects of type Person is shown in Figure 5.

[5] In Fibonacci, a modifiable cell is introduced with an expression **var** expr, and its value is read with the expression **at** expr.

```
let createPerson =
      fun (name, address: String; birthyear: Int) : Person is
      role Person
      private
            assert stringLength(address) <= 0
            elsefail "incorrect address";
            let address = var (address);
      methods
            Name = name;
            BirthYear = birthyear;
            Age = currentYear() - me.BirthYear;
            Address = at (address);
            modAddress (newAddress: String) =
               if stringLength(newAddress) <= 0
               then failwith "incorrect address"
               else address := newAddress
            Introduce = "My name is " & me.Name &
                  " and I was born in " &
                  intToString(me.BirthYear);
      end;
```

Fig. 5. An example of a constructor for objects

The expression `fun (<arguments>): <type> is <exp>` defines a function with type `Fun (<arguments>): <type>` and body `<exp>`.[6] When the function is applied, a new instance of *Person* is created. While the private data are generally different for each instance, method bodies are shared by all the instances.

In the body of the `Introduce` method the special identifier **`me`** denotes the constructed object. The *static type* of **`me`** is always the type of the expression role where **`me`** is written (in this example `Person`), but when the method is executed by a role which inherits it, then **`me`** denotes the role which inherited the method (working as *self* in other object-oriented languages). **`me`** can only be used in the method bodies. `intToString` is a predefined function to convert an integer into a string. The infix operator **&** is the concatenation operator on strings.

By separating object implementation from object types, Fibonacci allows objects with different implementations but with the same type to coexist safely. This is especially useful in evolving environments, where the best implementation of an object type may change over time, and is also useful in accommodating objects with a different nature but a unique interface.

4.4 Dynamic object extension and inheritance

To model the possibility of real world entities to acquire new roles, Fibonacci provides an *extension operator*, which allows an object to be extended with new

---

[6] A function definition has a different syntax from that of a method. This is to reflect the fact there are differences between functions and methods. A function is a first class value, and so can be passed as a parameter or returned as a value by a function. A method is not a value by itself, but is a part of a role definition, and it can only be evaluated by sending a message to the object which it belongs to.

subroles. A new role provides the object with a new piece of private environment and a new set of methods, which override previously defined ones (more details will be given when method lookup is defined). Figure 6 shows how the **ext-to-private-methods-end** operator can be used to extend `john` from `Person` to `Student`.

```
let johnAsStudent = ext john to Student
      private
            let studentNumber = newStudentNumber();
      methods
            Faculty = "Science";
            StudentNumber = studentNumber;
            Introduce = (me as Person)!Introduce
                        & ". I am a Science student";
      end;

john = johnAsStudent; (* returns true *)
```

Fig. 6. An example of an object extension

The object acquires the new role without changing its identity. After the extension in Figure 6, `john` and `johnAsStudent` are two different roles of the same object; the test `john = johnAsStudent` returns `true` since equality is an object operation. The semantics of the expression `(me as Person)!Introduce` used in the definition of the method `Introduce` will be explained in the next section. Informally, it executes the method `Introduce` defined in `Person`.

```
let createStudent = fun (name, address, faculty: String;
                         birthyear, studentNumber: Int): Student is
      ext createPerson(name, address, birthyear) to Student
      private
            let studentNumber = newStudentNumber();
      methods
            Faculty = faculty;
            StudentNumber =  studentNumber;
            Introduce = (me as Person)!Introduce &
                    ". I am a student of " & faculty;
      end;
```

Fig. 7. Defining a constructor by inheritance

Figure 7 shows how the **ext** operator can be used to define a constructor for students by inheritance, i.e. by extending the person constructor `createPerson`. Note however that, in Fibonacci, a constructor for a role type with a super-role can be defined either by inheritance, using the **ext** operator, or directly, using the **role** operator.

Figure 8 shows how the **ext** operator can be used to define an extension constructor, i.e. a function to transform a `Person` into an `Employee`.

```
let toEmployee =
fun (aPerson: Person; dept: String) : Employee is
     ext aPerson to Employee
     private
          let employeeNumber = newEmployeeNumber();
     methods
          Department = dept;
          EmployeeNumber = employeeNumber;
          Introduce = (me as Person)!Introduce
                     & ". I am an employee";
     end;
```

Fig. 8. An example of an extension constructor

4.5 Method lookup

In traditional object-oriented languages every message is directed to only the most specialized role, which either has a method for the message, or looks for a method in its ancestors. The same happens in Fibonacci when a message is sent to one of the most specialized roles of an object. However, when a message is sent to a role which has several descendants, two different extensions of the standard mechanism are possible:

- *upward lookup*: the method is looked up first in the receiving role and then in its ancestor roles;
- *double lookup*: the method is first looked for in all the descendants of the receiving role, then in the receiving role, and finally in its ancestor roles.

Upward lookup emphasizes the difference of behaviour between different roles, while the double lookup results in a more uniform behaviour. Both rules, however, ensure that if *T* and *S* are two cousin roles, then no message sent to *S* will be answered by a method in *T*. Since both rules can be useful in some situations, Fibonacci gives both possibilities. Upward lookup is achieved by `object!message` and double lookup by `object.message`; upward and double lookup coincide, and also coincide with the traditional lookup technique, when a message is sent to a most specialized role of an object.

The following example illustrates the mechanism. Recall that the object *John* has two roles `johnAsStudent` and `john`, of type `Student` and `Person`. Upward and double lookup coincide for `johnAsStudent`, which has no descendant, while they may behave differently for `john`:

```
johnAsStudent.Introduce     =>
              "My name is John Daniels and I was born in 1967.
              I am a Science student"
johnAsStudent!Introduce     =>
              "My name is John Daniels ... Science student"
john.Introduce         =>
              "My name is John Daniels ... Science student"
john!Introduce         =>
              "My name is John Daniels and I was born in 1967"
```

Once `john` is extended to an employee, its double lookup behaviour changes, since the last acquired subrole is the first to be looked for:

```
toEmployee(john; "Quality Management");

john.Introduce          =>
                  "My name is John Daniels and I was born in 1967.
                  I am an employee"
```

However, neither the upward lookup behaviour of `john` nor the behaviour of `john` as a `Student` are affected:

```
john!Introduce          =>
                "My name is John Daniels and I was born in 1967"
johnAsStudent.Introduce     =>
                "My name is John Daniels ...  Science student"
johnAsStudent!Introduce     =>
                "My name is John Daniels ...  Science student".
```

Both upward and double lookup are two forms of *late binding* (or *dynamic binding*, or *dynamic lookup*). In object-oriented terminology, *late binding of methods to messages* means that the method executed to answer a message does not depend on the static type of the receiver (i.e. on its compile-time type), but on its run-time type, or, in languages where different implementations are allowed for the same type, on its run-time value. For example, *late binding* means that if a `Student` is bound to a variable of type `Person`, or is passed to a function expecting a `Person` parameter, it still behaves like a `Student`.

```
let aPerson: Person = johnAsStudent;
aPerson!Introduce       =>
                  "My name is John Daniels ...  Science student"
```

4.6 Object comparison, role inspection, role casting

Since an object in Fibonacci is a modifiable collection of roles, the language provides the following operators on objects:

- the equality operator (=) to test whether two objects are the same, independently of the role used to access them; for example

  johnAsStudent = john; (* returns true *)

- the infix predicate **isAlso** to test whether an object has a certain role; for example:

  john **isAlso** Employee; (* after extension, returns true *)

- the infix operator **as** to coerce an object to one of its possible roles (*role casting*). The operator fails if the object does not have the specified role:

  let johnAsEmployee = john **as** Employee;

The expressions x **as/isAlso** T are well typed if T and the type of x belong to the same role type family.

The combination of casting with strict lookup (e.g. (X **as** T)!P) allows the simulation of the traditional *send-to-super* mechanism of object-oriented languages, as shown in Figure 6 above. The same combination also allows simulating static binding, as shown below, where anotherPerson behaves like a Person:

```
let anotherPerson: Person = johnAsStudent as Person;
anotherPerson!Introduce  =>
            "My name is John Daniels and I was born in 1967."
```

Finally, the **isExactly** operator is available on role values, to test their run-time role type. For example:

```
johnAsEmployee isExactly Employee;      (* returns true *)
john isExactly Employee;                (* returns false *)
aPerson isExactly Student;              (* returns true *)
anotherPerson isExactly Student;        (* returns false *)
```

5 Bulk Types: Class, Association, Sequence Types

Bulk types describe collections of values with common properties. Fibonacci supports three kinds of bulk types: class, association, and sequence type.

Classes are modifiable ordered sets of homogeneous values, used to model sets of entities in the domain of discourse. Associations are modifiable ordered sets of tuples, used to model associations between entities. Sequences are constant collections of homogeneous values of any type.

Fibonacci query algebra is defined on sequences; since a class or an association type is a subtype of a sequence type, Fibonacci's algebraic operators can be applied in the same way to the three kinds of data structure. On the other hand, operators to insert and remove data, and to declare integrity constraints, are only available on the updatable bulk types: classes and associations.

Classes, associations and sequences are first-class types of the language, hence it is possible to apply these type constructors to any other type of the language, at any nesting depth.

5.1 Class and association types

Class ElemType is a type of homogeneous ordered sets of elements of type ElemType. Classes differ from sequences since they can be updated (while sequences are constant), no repeated element is allowed in a class, and it is possible to define constraints on classes, such as inclusion or mutual disjointness, as described below.

Assoc TupleType is a type of homogeneous sets of tuples of type TupleType. Tuples are ordered associations of values with identifiers; the notation [Ide_1: Type_1; ... ; Ide_n: Type_n] denotes a tuple type while the notation [**let** Ide_1 = v_1; ... ; **let** Ide_n = v_n] denotes a tuple value. Associations behave like classes of tuples: they can be updated, no repeated tuple is allowed, and it is possible to define constraints on them, mainly to connect association fields with classes.

5.1.1 Operations

A new empty class and a new empty association are created by the **emptyClass of** and **emptyAssoc of** operations, as in the example below, where `Student` and `Class` are previously defined types:

```
let students   = emptyClass of Student end;
let classes    = emptyClass of Class end;
let enrolled   = emptyAssoc of
                  [student: Student; class: Class] end;
```

Elements and tuples are inserted and removed from classes and associations using the **insert** and **remove** operators:

```
insert Expr into Expr
remove Identifier from Expr where BoolExpr
```

In the **insert** operations, the type of the value or tuple inserted must be a subtype of the element type of the class or association. **remove** removes all values, or tuples, which satisfy `BoolExpr`, from the specified class or association, but the removed elements are not deleted while an access path exists for them. When a value is inserted into a class or into an association, a check is made to establish whether the value is already there. In this case the insertion is a no-operation. Removal and insertion are executed atomically: if the operation cannot be completed (typically due to some constraint violation) every side effect is undone.

Besides these operators, all the operations on sequences defined below can be applied to classes and associations, since, as already discussed, the following type inclusions hold, where {T} is the type of sequences of elements of type T:

```
Class ElType     ≤   { ElType }
Assoc TupleType ≤   { TupleType }
```

5.1.2 Integrity constraints on classes and associations

The following integrity constraints can be specified when a class or an association is defined:

- Inclusion constraints
- Referential constraints
- Surjectivity constraints
- Uniqueness constraints
- Constancy constraints
- General triggers on insertion and removal

A detailed description of these constraints is reported in [4]. Hereafter the discussion will be limited to the inclusion constraint on classes, to the referential and surjectivity constraints on associations, and to general triggers on insertion and removal.

Inclusion constraints

Classes can be organized into an inclusion hierarchy, which means that the elements of a class are a subset of those of its superclasses (inclusion constraint). Moreover, subsets of the same class can be defined as disjoint.

To this aim, the **are** inclusion constraint is used, which means that elements inserted into a class are also automatically inserted into their superclasses; whereas elements removed from a superclass are also automatically removed from their subclasses. Here is an example of three subclass definitions:

```
let foreignStudents =
          emptyClass of ForeignStudent are students end;
let femaleStudents = emptyClass of Student are students end;
let femaleForeignStudents =
          emptyClass of ForeignStudent are
               foreignStudents, femaleStudents end;
```

The **butNot** disjointness constraint means that the insertion of an element in a subclass fails if the element is already present in another subclass. Here is an example:

```
let femaleStudents =
          emptyClass of Student are students;
let maleStudents = emptyClass of Student are students
                   butNot femaleStudents end;
```

Referential constraints

The *referential constraint* specifies the fact that a component of an association must belong to a given class C. In general, the referential constraint may be violated either because (*a*) the associated object is not a "valid" (in some sense) object, or (*b*) the associated object does not belong to C. For example, in relational databases, where the mechanism of *external keys* is used to model associations, problem (*a*) is the main concern: the external key may not be associated with any tuple in the database. In Fibonacci, every object found inside an association (or everywhere else) is a valid object, but it may not belong to the intended class; hence problem (*b*) is our main concern.

More generally, the kind of referential constraint problem to be dealt with in an object-oriented database system depends essentially on how objects are removed from classes and deleted. *Deleting* an object means that the object ceases to exists, i.e. any reference to it becomes invalid, or becomes a reference to a "tombstone". Removing an object from a class just means that the object does not belong to the class any more, but is still a valid object. Object-oriented database systems take two different approaches to deletion and removal:

- A deletion operation is provided, which both removes an object from every class and deletes it.
- No deletion operation is provided. Removing an object from a class does not imply its deletion; the object is deleted behind the scenes by the system only when no more references exist to the object (garbage collection).

When deletion is provided, problem (*a*) (invalid object references) arises: how can it be verified that no method, used to model an association, returns a reference to a deleted object? When class removal is provided, problem (*b*) (objects not belonging to classes) arises: how can it be verified that no method, used to model an association with class A, returns a reference to an object which has been removed from class A? If any procedure can form the body of a method, it is impossible for the system, in both cases above, to decide which kind of object a general procedure would return.

In Fibonacci, however, the referential constraint can be enforced, because associations are not represented by methods but by a specialized mechanism, associations, and the system is fully aware of association semantics. The fact that the referential constraint can be maintained in the presence of removals is an important accomplishments of the object-association data model.

Referential constraints in Fibonacci are associated with some fields of the tuples of an association. We call these fields, submitted to a *referential constraint* and so constrained to belong to a specified class, *association components*; and we call the other attributes *association attributes* (or just *components* and *attributes*, for short). The constraint is specified in the **emptyAssoc** expression which creates the association, by writing:

```
emptyAssoc of [...
     label: Type in/are/owned by class;
     ... ]
end
```

in, **are** and **owned by** class specify the same referential constraint (the field value must belong to *class*), to be maintained with different styles, i.e. either by raising failures or by modifying the database to force its satisfaction.

A referential constraint may be violated either when a new tuple is inserted into the association, if the component does not belong to the class, or when an element is removed from a class, if it is a component in a tuple in the association. The `label: Type` **in** `class` constraint raises a failure in both cases.

`label: Type` **owned by** `class` forces a "cascade deletion" of the tuple when the element is removed from the class (the association is "owned" by the class), but raises a failure when a tuple is inserted in the association. So **owned by** codifies a dependency constraint, more precisely a dependency of the association on the class, where *dependency* means cascade removal.

`label: Type` **are** `class` means that the projection of the association on `label` behaves like a subclass of `class`: a removal from the class forces a removal from the association (as in the **owned by** case); and an insertion in the association of a component which does not belong to the class forces an insertion in the class (instead of raising a failure as happens with **in** and **owned by**).

For a summary, see Tables 1 and 2.

Surjectivity constraints

While the referential constraint specifies that the existence of a tuple in an association implies the existence of a value in a class, the *surjectivity* (or *totality*) constraint enforces the converse implication: the existence of elements in a class necessitates the existence of a tuple involving them in the association. The constraint is specified in the `emptyAssoc` expression by writing:

```
label: Type onto/owns class
```

A surjectivity constraint may be violated either when a new element is inserted into the class, if it is not a component of any tuple in the association; or when a tuple is removed from an association, if it was the last which involves an element in the class.

The **onto** clause corresponds to the **in** clause: it fails in both cases. Suppose that both a referential and a surjectivity constraint are being defined for a component of an association with respect to the same class (which is quite common, see e.g. field `composite` of association `assembly` in the example in Appendix A). Then a class element and the first tuple referring to it should be created "at the same time", since each insertion should come before the other one (see Table 1). The same is true for class and association removals. For this reason, the surjectivity constraint is not checked immediately after a class insertion or an association removal, but at the end of the smallest transaction which encloses the operation execution. Since the language supports nested transactions, this smallest transaction can be made as short as required; the language also supports a general mechanism to define an expression to be executed at the end of the current smallest enclosing transaction (the **defer** operator). Note that a similar problem occurs when a couple of classes are associated by an association which is surjective (total) on both of them. In this case, two related elements have to be inserted in the two classes "at the same time". This is impossible in many languages which support the object-oriented data model, while it is possible in Fibonacci, thanks to the delayed checking of surjectivity.

The **owns** clause is the surjectivity counterpart of the referential **owned by** clause: like **onto**, when an element is inserted into the class, then the operator fails if in the same transaction a tuple referring to that element has not been inserted into the association. However, when the last tuple referring to an element is removed from an association, then that element is automatically removed from the class, at the end of the transaction. So **owns** codifies a dependency constraint, more precisely the dependency of a class on an association. Dependency of a class B on a class A through an association AB can be expressed, in this language, by saying that AB **owns** B and that AB is **owned by** A.

The following tables summarized the precise relationships between the above constraints.

Table 1. Conditions enforced and operations monitored by the constraints.

Constraint	*Enforced condition*	*Monitored operations*
referential	$x \in$ assoc.label $\Rightarrow x \in$ class	**insert in** assoc, **remove from** class
surjectivity	$x \in$ class $\Rightarrow x \in$ assoc.label	**insert in** class, **remove from** assoc

Table 2. Action requested by a referential constraint, before an insertion/removal operation.

Constraint	*when* [**let** label=x...] *is inserted into* assoc if $x \notin$ *class*	*when* x *is removed from* class if [**let** label=x...] $\in$ assoc
in	**fail**	**fail**
owned by	**fail**	**remove** assoc **where** label=x
are	**insert** (x) **in** class	**remove** assoc **where** label=x

Table 3. Action requested at commit time by a surjectivity constraint.

Constraint	*when* x *is inserted into* class if (**let** label=x...) $\notin$ assoc	*when* [**let** label=x...] *is removed from* assoc if $x \in$ class
onto	**fail**	**fail**
owns	**fail**	**remove** y **from** class **where** y=x

General triggers on insertion and removal

Triggers are the most popular mechanism to give a database the capability of reacting to events. In Fibonacci it is possible to associate an unlimited number of triggers with a class or an association, through the constructs **`beforeInsert`** `Expr` and **`beforeRemove`** `Expr`. The action `Expr` may be any expression of the language, which is then executed every time an element is inserted from (or removed into) the class or association. `Expr` can access the inserted (or removed) element and the class, or association, through the predefined identifiers `thisElement`, `thisClass` and `thisAssociation`, as in the example below, where triggers are used to check a key constraint and to maintain a count of class elements.

```
let femaleStudentsCount = var 0;
let femaleStudents =
   emptyClass of Student are students
    beforeInsert
      assert no x in thisClass have x.Name = thisElement.Name
    beforeInsert
      femaleStudentsCount := at femaleStudentsCount + 1
    beforeRemove
      femaleStudentsCount := at femaleStudentsCount - 1
end;
```

Triggers can also be added to previously defined classes and associations. In [4] it is shown that all the constraints (inclusion, referential, etc.) which can be declared for classes and associations may be defined using the trigger mechanism; in the current Fibonacci implementation, class and associations constraints are actually implemented in this way.

The behaviour of triggers can be presented using the dimensions suggested in [25] to characterize active database semantics.

- *Granularity*: Triggers are activated for each insertion or removal operation.
- *Coupling modes*: Usually the action defined in a trigger is executed as soon as an insertion or removal operation is executed (immediate coupling). However, by exploiting the language construct **defer** Expr, it is also possible to specify that the action must be executed at the end of the smallest transaction containing the operation that has activated the trigger (deferred coupling).
- *Atomicity of rule execution*: The action of a trigger may generate new events which trigger other actions. When a new event is generated, the current action is suspended, and is resumed when the triggered actions have been completed.
- *Relationship to transactions*: The action of a trigger is executed in the same transaction as that where the triggering event arises.
- *Conflict resolution*: If an event activates several triggers, they are executed serially in the order in which they are defined.
- *Event consumption*: The triggered event no longer activates the processed rule, but may still trigger different rules.
- *Transaction history inspection*: In the action part of a trigger, the state of data before the execution of the action can be inspected with the construct **old**.

5.2 Sequence type

Sequences are ordered collections of homogeneous values with duplicates. Fibonacci query algebra operators are defined on sequences, and may be applied to classes and associations too, thanks to subtyping.

Fibonacci query algebra is characterized by the following features:

- Although it may be used in an SQL fashion, it is not based on a select-from-where operator (as happens with O_2, for example [14]), but on a set of atomic algebraic operators which may be combined in many different ways, which gives more flexibility to the algebra.

- No attention has been paid to minimality. Although it is well known that essentially all of the algebraic operators may be defined in terms of the fold (also called pump) operator typical of functional languages with lists [17], in Fibonacci product, projection, selection and iteration are defined as different operators. This improves both language usability and optimizability.

The notation $\{T\}$ denotes the type of a sequence of elements of type T, and $\{E_1;\ldots;E_n\}$ denotes the sequence containing $E_1,\ldots,E_n$. Several operators are defined on sequences, and the presentation will be focused on those that constitute the Fibonacci query algebra.

A typical Fibonacci query has the following form:

```
for   (ide1 in SeqExpr1 times ...  times iden in SeqExprn)
where BoolExpr(ide1,... ,iden)
do    Expr(ide1,... ,iden)
```

which essentially evaluates `Expr(ide1,... ,iden)` for all the tuples `ide1,... ,iden` of values from `SeqExpr1 ... SeqExprn` which satisfy the condition `BoolExpr(ide1,... ,iden)`. However, **`for-in-times-where-do`** is not a single construct but just a typical way of combining different atomic operators, and each of these operators has its own elementary semantics. We now give the semantics and examples for each of these operators, using the sequences `employees` and `departments` with elements of the following tuple types:

```
Let Employee =
      [empNo: Int;
       deptNo: Int;
       name: [name, surname: String];
       birthYear: Int;
       dependents: { [name: String;
                      birthYear: Int; relationship: String]}  ];

Let Department =
      [deptNo: Int;
       deptName: String;
       deptBudget: Int;
       mgrNo: Int];
```

Note that classes of objects and associations would be queried exactly in the same way; a nested-relational-like schema has been used since it may be more familiar to the reader.

The query operators are defined as follows.

```
Label in Sequence
```

This returns a sequence of tuples with a unique field named `Label`, associated with the value of the corresponding element in Sequence.

```
L-TupleSequence times R-TupleSequence
L-TupleSequence join R-TupleSequence
```

Both return a sequence of tuples obtained by concatenating each tuple in `L-TupleSequence` with every tuple in `R-TupleSequence`. If the tuples in `L-TupleSequence` and `R-TupleSequence` have attributes with the same name, **`times`** fails, while **`join`** only concatenates in the result those tuples with the same value in these attributes (*natural join*). The tuples in `R-TupleSequence` to be concatenated with each tuple *t* in `L-TupleSequence` can be defined in terms of *t* (*dependent product* and *dependent natural join*). For example:

```
(emp in Employees) times (dep in emp.dependents)
```

creates a sequence of two-field tuples, containing one tuple for each employee-dependent pair. This is possible since in `R-TupleSequence` the labels of the tuples in `TupleSequence` (emp is the only such label, in this example) can be used to denote the corresponding field.

More generally, the expression which is the second operand of the operators on sequence of tuples (such as **`times`**, **`join`**, **`where`**, **`for-do`**, **`group by`**, **`all`**, **`some`**), can always directly access the fields of the tuples in the first operand.

```
TupleSequence where BoolExpr
e.g.: employees where birthYear = 1960
      (e in employees) where e.birthYear = 1960
```

This returns the sequence of the tuples in `TupleSequence` which satisfy the condition `BoolExpr`.

```
for TupleSequence do Expr
e.g.: for employees do name
      for e in employees do e.name
```

This returns the sequence obtaines by evaluating `Expr` once for each element of `TupleSequence`.

```
the SeqExpr
e.g.: the (employees where empNo=132)
```

This returns the only element of the singleton `SeqExpr` and fails if `count(Sequence)` is different from one.

```
setof Sequence
e.g.: setof (for employees do name.name)
```

This eliminates duplicates from `Sequence`.

```
all Sequence have BoolExpr
some Sequence have BoolExpr
e.g.:        all employees have birthYear > 1900
     some e in employees have isEmpty(e.dependents)
```

all and **some** verify whether a condition holds for all elements, or respectively for at least one element, of a sequence of tuples.

```
TupleSequence group by (Expr)
pick Sequence
```

group by returns a partition of the elements in *TupleSequence* in subsequences; two tuples are put in the same partition whenever the expression *Expr* has the same value for both of them. **pick** returns one element of *Sequence*, chosen non deterministically. It is usually used in conjunction with **group by**. For example, the query:

```
for empGroup in (employees group by birthYear)
do [ let year := pick(empGroup).birthYear;
     let count := count(empGroup);
     let employees := empGroup]
```

partitions the employees according to the birth year and, for every birth year, returns a tuple containing the birth year, the number of employees with that birth year, and the sequence of those employees. The **where** operator allows us to restrict both the employees and the employee groups to be considered, as in the following example:

```
for empGroup in( employees
                 where isEmpty(dependents)
                 group by birthYear)
where count(empGroup)>2
do ...
```

6 The Architecture of the Fibonacci System

The first implementation of Fibonacci is currently being completed. The current implementation is a single-user system with a minimal programming environment, and is used to experiment with the language.

The system is organized into three layers, the Compiler, the Persistent Hierarchical Abstract Machine and the Persistent Store, described in the next three sections.

6.1 The compiler

The main tasks of the compiler are to typecheck Fibonacci expressions and to generate the corresponding PHAM code, which is then executed by the PHAM.

The compiler is written in Modula-3 and is structured in an object-oriented way. For any syntactic construct of the language, a corresponding object type exists. Hence, any node in an abstract syntax tree is represented by an object, which refers to the objects representing its children in the tree. Each object class has its own Parse, Type-Check and Code-Generate methods, which typically use the corresponding methods of the children: for example, an object modelling an "**if** b **then** e1

else e2" node refers to the objects modelling b, e1 and e2, and uses their Code-Generate methods to generate the code for the whole construct. This structure makes it easier to add and remove new constructs to and from the language, since all the code which is related to a construct is collected in the corresponding object class.

In Fibonacci all information is persistent, not only data, but the environment (i.e. the current associations of identifiers to values and types) and the types are persistent too. For this reason, the compiler does not use Modula-3 variables to store this information, but they are encoded as PHAM data structures and stored inside the persistent store. The availability of this information inside the persistent store means that browsing tools can be written which access this information by connecting themselves directly to the store, with no need to interact with the compiler; one such tool, which allows browsing data, sending messages to objects, and browsing the environment and the types, is already part of the current system. We plan to re-implement the system, in a future version, using Fibonacci itself. The compiler information would thus be stored inside the persistent store without having to rely on any interface to manipulate them.

6.2 The Persistent Hierarchical Abstract Machine

The PHAM has two main tasks. First of all it builds, on top of the primitive and general purpose data structure supported by the persistent store, the more complex and specialized Fibonacci data structures. Moreover, it executes the compiled Fibonacci code, and stores it as first class data.

The PHAM is a stack machine which manipulates data and closures (i.e. compiled functions). The PHAM derives from Landin's SECD (Stack-Environment-Code-Dump) machine, and more directly from Cardelli's FAM [29, 19]. A piece of PHAM code is a linear sequence of zero-address operations which take their arguments from, and put their results to, the stack. The PHAM is characterised, with respect to other similar persistent SECD-machines used to implement persistent or volatile functional programming languages, by features which concern its interface and its implementation.

Most SECD-machines are designed to offer a minimal set of operations and a minimal set of very general data types[7], so that the machine is general and small. PHAM, on the other hand, offers higher-level data types and much more complex operations, which closely correspond to Fibonacci. This difference is due to a change in perspective about optimization. In non-persistent functional languages optimization is a compiler task, hence the compiler emits a low-level code. In persistent systems, some kinds of optimization decisions, such as access plan generation for queries, have to be dealt with at run time, hence a query must not be transformed into a sequential program by the compiler, but a query construct must be part of the abstract machine language.

PHAM is characterised by its architecture and by the fact that it does not have any local store, but completely relies on the persistent store for this. The internal architecture of PHAM is represented in Figure 9.

---

[7] Landin's SECD only has one data type, the closure, and three operations: stack access, λ-abstraction, and application.

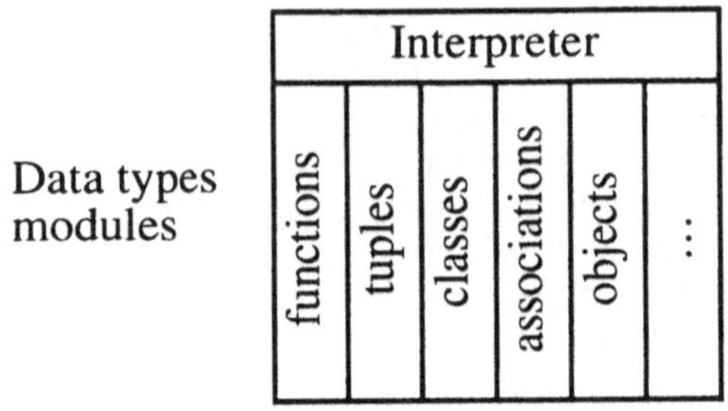

Fig. 9. PHAM architecture.

The PHAM is divided in two layers. The higher layer is a PHAM interpreter, whose task is to execute the PHAM code. More precisely, the PHAM interpreter directly executes control-flow operations and stack manipulation, and, when it recognizes an operation which is specific to a data type, it invokes the corresponding module. This approach was chosen to make it easier to define new data types and to test various implementations for them. Furthermore, this means that we still have a small general purpose abstract machine (the interpreter) with a manageable complexity, plus a set of data type modules which are "external" with respect to this kernel.

6.3 The Persistent Store

The persistent store manages a persistent collection of data items, where a data item is a string of uninterpreted bytes and of references to other data items. The store also offers a mechanism for atomically saving a frozen version of its state and for restoring the last frozen state in case of failure. This mechanism is used by the PHAM to realize the outer level of nested transactions.

Since the PHAM directly stores all its data inside the persistent store, without trying any kind of caching or special treatment of volatile data, the persistent store must be able to manage temporary data with an efficiency which is comparable to that of the central memory. This is a very strong requirement. However, the alternative choice of having the PHAM realizing a buffering scheme on top of the persistent store was discarded to avoid the risk of having two different and contrasting buffering schemes built on top of the other, with the consequent well known problems.

Another design choice is that the persistent store will not be built as part of the Fibonacci project, but is based on a component built elsewhere, to avoid duplicating efforts in a field which is currently being widely investigated. For this reason, the operation set required from the persistent store is minimal, to allow tests and comparisons involving different persistent stores. This minimality choice clearly has drawbacks, since it does not allow us to exploit the more advanced features of the available stores. Our current implementation relies on the Napier88 store described in [18]. We are currently experimenting with the O_2 engine too.

7 Related Work

7.1 Object-oriented database languages

Like other database languages, Fibonacci has been designed to overcome the limitations of traditional systems due to the lack of integration of the data model with the programming language (impedance mismatch) and the unsuitable modelling capability of the data model. Examples of these languages are Taxis [32], Galileo [2], Statice [42], O_2 [15], Orion [28, 16], Gemstone [26], Vbase and Ontos [34, 35]. Below is a brief comparison of Fibonacci with two other well known object-oriented database programming languages, O_2 and ORION, to show the different solutions offered to model the following aspects: objects, object types, classes, associations between sets of objects, type hierarchies, and class hierarchies.

Objects. The languages all support the notion of objects with identity. The state encapsulation is provided only in O_2 and Fibonacci. In Fibonacci and O_2 all the language values can either be temporary or persistent, as persistence is an orthogonal property of the type system, while in ORION only objects can become persistent, and management of versions is provided. In Fibonacci objects can have roles and an operator is provided to change the role of an object without affecting its identity. A similar mechanism has been proposed in other languages (Galileo [2], Iris [24], Aspects [36], Views [38], and Clovers [43]). A detailed analysis of these proposals is made in [5]. The conclusion is that the proposals which support late-binding (Galileo and Iris), always assume the existence of a most specialized type in order to resolve the message dispatching ambiguities that can arise from type multiplicity. On the other hand, when the previous assumption is abandoned and objects are allowed to have multiple minimal types (Clovers, Views and Aspects), late-binding is never provided. A novel aspect of Fibonacci is thus the coexistence of late-binding and multiple inheritance with role multiplicity and dynamic object extension, in a framework with strong type-checking and subtyping.

Object types. The languages all support a construct to define object types, with associated methods. Only ORION has the restriction that the state of an object can have components of the following types only: elementary, object, and set of objects. The other languages have a collection of type constructors (e.g., tuple, set) that can be used without restrictions to define a component of the object state. In Fibonacci only a single object type can have many implementations. Only the Fibonacci type system provides a constructor to distinguish constant values from modifiable ones, and this has important consequences on the possibility of statically typechecking definitions and applications.

ORION allows the definition of composite objects, i.e. objects that have other objects as components with the possibility of enforcing (*a*) the constraint that an object is a part of only one object, and (*b*) that the existence of an object depends on the existence of its parent object. Fibonacci can express the same constraints by exploiting the association mechanism.

Methods are defined differently in the three languages. In ORION and O_2 the method signature is specified in an object type definition, and the body of a method is specified separately as a Common LISP or O_2C function with the object type to which the method belongs is the type of the first parameter. In Fibonacci the body of a method is specified with the object constructor. Only Fibonacci is a statically and strongly typed, polymorphic language.

Classes. Fibonacci and O_2 provide two separate mechanisms to deal with objects and sets of objects, here called classes; objects are explicitly inserted and removed from a class. As in most object-oriented database languages, in ORION an object type definition entails automatically defining a variable with the same name to denote all the objects of that type.

Associations. In O_2 and ORION, associations between objects are only modelled by aggregation, i.e. by the definition of objects which have other objects as components. In Fibonacci, associations relate objects which exist independently, and they can be defined incrementally without redefining the structure of existing objects.

Type hierarchies. In all these languages, object types can be organised into hierarchies and the benefits of the inheritance mechanism can be exploited. However, only the Fibonacci type system has been designed for a statically and strongly typed language.

Class hierarchies. Classes can potentially be organised into a subset hierarchy with the following properties: (*a*) the type of the subclass elements is a subtype of the type of the superclass elements, and (*b*) the extension of a subclass is a subset of the extension of the superclass. A subclass can be defined from a single superclass, or from several superclasses, and can be populated by creating new elements, and also by moving objects from a superclass into the subclass. Class hierarchies are treated differently in object-oriented database languages. O_2 does not provide this mechanism. ORION provides disjoint subclasses, except when a class is defined by multiple inheritance, and subclasses cannot be populated by moving objects from a superclass into the subclass. A construct is provided to access the element of a class without considering those elements which also belong to a subclass. Fibonacci provides subclasses in the most general form with the option of moving objects from a superclass into a subclass.

7.2 Persistent languages

Persistent languages are languages where persistence is a property which is orthogonal to types. Fibonacci is a persistent language, but differs from some of them such as PS-algol, Napier88 and Tycoon since it is also a database language, meaning that Fibonacci directly supports a specific data model. The scope of Fibonacci research is currently twofold: in the field of data modelling, to design a data model which is richer than current object-oriented data models, and in the field of type systems, to extend the expressivity of the type system of current languages.

The design goal of the Napier88 and Tycoon persistent languages is slightly different. Both support the add-on approach for data modelling, i.e. they do not provide direct support for a specific data model but provide programmers with the tools they need to define their own data model. The main tools provided by the Tycoon language (Chapter 1.1.1) for this aim are:

- a rich type system, which is indeed very similar to the Fibonacci type system, in that both derive directly from the Quest type system [21];
- a rich sublanguage for module and library management;
- a mechanism to extend Tycoon syntax;

- a linguistic mechanism and an implementation style which allow Tycoon to be used as a gateway to operate on different systems; a similar mechanism was developed for the Galileo system and is present in Fibonacci too, but the Tycoon project gives this aspect more attention.

The Napier88 project has a yet another aim. While Tycoon focuses on openness, i.e. extendibility and interoperability, the Napier88 project tries to define a complete Napier88 based environment, where the persistent Napier88 store becomes the repository of all the data, and even the file system, and every tool is written in Napier88 itself, taking the maximum advantage from the persistence of the language and from the integration of the environment. The main mechanisms which are offered by the Napier88 language (Chapter 1.1.3) to fulfill this project are:

- a rich type system. It lacks inclusion polymorphism, however it has an environment construct which provides for a form of controlled dynamic typechecking which is very useful for dealing with database evolution;
- a reflection mechanism, which gives the system the ability to generate and then evaluate the Napier88 code.

8 Conclusions

This paper is an introduction to the Fibonacci database programming language. We have presented the most important language features for modelling databases but we have omitted general language features as well as several details on the concepts discussed. Further information on the object mechanism may be found in [5], on the class mechanism in [27, 4], and on the association mechanism in [4]. The informal definition of the language may be found in [6].

The implementation of the language is in progress. The language is implemented as an interactive compiler written in Modula-3 and running on Sun workstations and on Windows machines. The present implementation does not support concurrent access to persistent data. The persistence of data is achieved using the persistent object store of the Napier88 language developed at St Andrews University. A description of the Fibonacci system and the features of the programming environment may be found in [7].

The research in progress on the Fibonacci language addresses the following aspects: a modularization mechanism, constructs for viewing and schema evolution, mechanisms to connect Fibonacci with other languages.

A modularization mechanism is needed to be able to partition big software projects into manageable units (modules) with an interface which only indicates the types of the values which are exported by each unit. The Fibonacci proposal will be based on the idea that modules are first-class values and module interfaces are first-class types. In this way, it is possible to define a very flexible module mechanism by adding a small number of new constructs to the language.

Viewing and schema evolution mechanisms, such as the **`view`** and **`alter table`** constructs of SQL, must be present in every database programming language, to manage the fact that the same piece of information may be best viewed in different ways in different contexts, and the fact that the structure of a database naturally evolves with time. The traditional SQL approach cannot be directly transposed into a persistent language such as Fibonacci for many different reasons. The most important is that in a persistent language there is not an exact equivalent to the notion of a "database schema" which only describes the structure of classes. The "environment" of a persistent language merges the definition of types, classes, functions and simple variables. Hence, a schema evolution mechanism must manage, in a linguistically consistent way, the coherent evolution of all these pieces of information. Moreover, in a statically and strongly typed language, it is important that the viewing and evolution mechanisms do not break the strong typing of the system. First steps in this research direction have been taken in [8], where a view mechanism for objects is described.

Finally, mechanisms to connect Fibonacci to other languages are needed in order to allow Fibonacci programmers to access software packages written in different languages and data managed by different systems. The current Fibonacci system contains a mechanism which allows any package with a C language interface to be dynamically linked to the Fibonacci system and its constants, variables, and functions to be accessed as if they were predefined Fibonacci functions. The mechanism will be generalized, mainly to allow more languages to be accessed, more parameter passing techniques to be exploited, and to allow Fibonacci functions to be passed as call-back parameters.

Acknowledgements. The design and implementation of Fibonacci was carried out jointly by the University of Pisa and Engineering S.p.A. In addition to the authors, other project members were R. Bergamini, M. Diotallevi, A. Marrara, C. Brasini, R. Rossi, M. Pieragnoli, and L. Vinciotti. D. Blakeman gave an essential contribution to the success of the implementation. This work has been supported in part by grants from the C.E.C. under ESPRIT BRA No.6309 (FIDE2: Fully Integrated Data Environment), the Progetto finalizzato "Sistemi informatici e calcolo parallelo" of C.N.R. under grant No. 93.1502.PF69, and by Ministero dell'Università e della Ricerca Scientifica e Tecnologica.

References

1. A. Albano, "Type Hierarchies and Semantic Data Models", *ACM SIGPLAN '83: Symposium on Programming Languages Issues in Software Systems*, San Francisco, pp. 178-186, 1983.
2. A. Albano, L. Cardelli and R. Orsini, "Galileo: A Strongly Typed, Interactive Conceptual Language", *ACM Transactions on Database Systems*, Vol. 10, No. 2, pp. 230-260, 1985. Also in: Readings in Object-Oriented Database Systems, S.B. Zdonik and D. Maier (eds), Morgan Kaufmann, San Mateo, California, pp.147-161, 1990.
3. A. Albano, G. Ghelli, "Object-Oriented Data Base Programming Languages", invited paper, *IEEE EuroComp Conference*, Bologna, 1991, pp. 726-734.
4. A. Albano, G. Ghelli, R. Orsini, "A Relationship Mechanism for a Strongly Type Object-Oriented Database Programming Language", *Proc. of 17th Int. Conf. on VLDB*, Barcelona, 1991, pp. 565-575.
5. A. Albano, R. Bergamini, G. Ghelli, R. Orsini, "An Object Data Model with Roles", *Proc. of 19th Int. Conf. on VLDB*, Dublin, 1993, pp.39-51.
6. A. Albano, G. Ghelli, R. Orsini, "*Fibonacci Reference Manual: A Preliminary Version*", FIDE2 Technical Reports, FIDE/94/102.
7. A. Albano, C. Brasini, M. Diotallevi, G. Ghelli, R. Orsini, and R. Rossi, "*A Guided Tour of the Fibonacci System*", FIDE2 Technical Reports, FIDE/94/103.

8. A. Albano, G. Antognoni, and G. Ghelli, "*View Operations on Objects with Roles*", FIDE2 Technical Reports, FIDE/95/129.
9. M.P. Atkinson, K.J. Chisholm, and W.P. Cockshott, "PS-algol: An Algol with a Persistent Heap", *ACM SIGPLAN Notices*, vol. 17, n.7, pp. 24-31, 1981.
10. M.P. Atkinson, P.J. Bailey, K.J. Chisholm, W.P. Cockshott and R. Morrison, "An Approach to Persistent Programming", *Computer Journal*, vol. 26, n.4, pp. 360-365, 1983.
11. M.P. Atkinson, and O.P. Buneman, "Types and Persistence in Database Programming Languages", *ACM Computing Surveys*, Vol. 19, N. 2, pp. 105-190, 1987.
12. M.P. Atkinson, F. Bancilhon, D. DeWitt, K. Dittrich, D. Maier, and S.B. Zdonik, "The Object-oriented Database Manifesto", *Proc. DOOD 89*, Kyoto, Japan, December 1989.
13. M.P. Atkinson. "A vision of persistent systems". *Proceedings of the International Conference on Deductive and Object-Oriented Databases*, Munich, December 1991. Invited paper.
14. F. Bancilhon, S. Cluet and C. Delobel, A Query Language for the O_2 Object-Oriented Database System, in *Proc. of the Second Intl. Workshop on Database Programming Languages*, Salishan Lodge, Oregon, 1989.
15. F. Bancilhon, C. Delobel, and P. Kanellakis (eds), *Building an Object-Oriented Database System, the Story of O_2*. Morgan Kaufmann, 1992.
16. J. Banerjee, H. Chou, J. F. Garza, W. Kim, D. Woelk, and N. Ballou, "Data Model Issues for Object-Oriented Applications", *ACM Trans. on Office Information Systems*, Vol. 5, N. 1, pp. 3-26, 1987.
17. V. Breazu-Tannen, P. Buneman and S. Naqvi, Structural Recursion as a Query Language, *Proc. of the third Intl. Workshop on Data Base Programming Languages*, Nafplion, Greece, P. Kanellakis, and J. W. Schmidt (eds), Morgan Kaufmann, San Mateo, California, pp. 9-19, 1991.
18. A.L. Brown, "*Persistent Object Store*", Persistent programming, Research Report 71-89, Department of Computer Science, University of Glasgow and St. Andrews, Scotland, 1989.
19. L. Cardelli, "*The Functional Abstract Machine*", AT&T Bell Labs Technical Report N. 107, Murray Hill, NJ, 1983.
20. L. Cardelli and P. Wegner, "On understanding types, data abstraction and polymorphism", *ACM Computing Surveys*. 17(4):471--523, December 1985.
21. L. Cardelli, "*The Quest Language and System (Tracking Draft)*", Technical Report, Digital Equipment Corporation, Systems Research Center, Palo-Alto, California, 1990.
22. R. Connor, D. McNally and R. Morrison, "Subtyping and Assignement in Database Programming Languages", *Proc. of the third Intl. Workshop on Data Base Programming Languages*, Nafplion, Greece, P. Kanellakis, and J. W. Schmidt (eds), Morgan Kaufmann, San Mateo, California, pp.363-382, 1991.
23. K. Dittrich, "Object-Oriented Database Systems: The Next Miles of the Marathon", *Information Systems*, Vol. 15, N. 1, pp. 161-167, 1990.
24. D.H. Fishman, D.Beech, H.P. Cate, E.C. Chow, T. Connors, J.D. Davis, N. Derrett, C.G. Hoch, W. Kent, P. Lyngbaek, B. Mahbod, M A. Neimat, T.A. Ryan, and M.C. Shan, "Iris: An Object-Oriented Database Management System", *ACM Trans. on Office Information Systems*, vol. 5, n. 1, pp. 48-69, Jan. 1987.
25. P. Fraternali, and L. Tanca, "*A Structured Approach for the Definition of the Semantics of Active Databases*", Politecnico di Milano, Dipartimento di Elettronica e Informazione, Report n. 94-073, 1994.
26. "*Gemstone Product Overview, GemStone Version 1.0*", Servio Logic Development Corporation, March 1986.

27. G. Ghelli, "A Class Abstraction for a Hierarchical Type System", in: *Third Intl. Conf. on Database Theory*, Paris, S. Abiteboul (ed.), Springer-Verlag LNCS 470, 1990, pp. 56-71.
28. W. Kim, *Introduction to Object-Oriented Databases*, The MIT Press, Cambridge, MA, 1990.
29. P. Landin, "The Mechanical Evaluation of Expressions", *Computer Journal*, Vol. 6, pp. 308-320, 1964.
30. F. Matthes and J. W Schmidt, "Bulk-Types: Built-In or Add-On", *Proc. of the third Intl. Workshop on Data Base Programming Languages*, Nafplion, Greece, P. Kanellakis, and J. W. Schmidt (eds), Morgan Kaufmann, San Mateo, California, pp.33-54, 1991.
31. F. Matthes and J.W. Schmidt, "*Persistent Polymorphic Programming in Tycoon: An Introduction*", FIDE2 Technical Reports, FIDE/94/106.
32. J. Mylopoulos, P.A. Bernestein and H.K.T. Wong, "A Language Facility for designing Interactive Database-Intensive Systems", *ACM Trans. on Database Systems*, vol. 5, n. 2, pp. 185-207, 1980.
33. R. Morrison, A. L. Brown, R. C. H. Connor, Q. I. Cutts, A. Dearle, G. N. C. Kirby, and D. S. Munro, "*The Napier88 Reference Manual (Release 2.0)*", FIDE2 Technical Reports, FIDE/94/104.
34. Ontologic Inc., *VBASE System Documentation*, Billerica, MA., 1987.
35. Ontologic Inc., "*ONTOS Object Database Documentation, Release 1.5*", Burlington, MA, 1989.
36. J. Richardson and P. Schwartz, "Aspects: Extending objects to support multiple, independent roles", *Proceedings of the Int. Conf. on Management of Data*, ACM SIGMOD Record, vol. 20, pp. 298-307, May 1991.
37. L.A. Rowe and K.A. Shoens, "Data abstraction, views and updates in RIGEL", *Proceedings ACM SIGMOD Conference*, Boston, MA. pp 71-81, 1979.
38. J.J. Shilling and P.F. Sweeney "Three Steps to View: Extending the Object-Oriented Paradigm", *OOPSLA '89*, ACM SIGPLAN Notices, vol. 24, n. 10, pp. 353-361, Oct. 1989.
39. J. W. Schmidt, "Some High Level Language Constructs for Data of Type Relation", *ACM Trans. on Database Systems*, 2 (3), pp.247-261, 1977.
40. J.W. Schmidt and F. Matthes, "Language technology for post-relational data systems", In *Database Systems of the 90s*, volume 466 of Lecture Notes in Computer Science, Berlin, Germany, November 1990. Springer-Verlag.
41. J.M. Smith, S. Fox and T. Landers, "*Reference Manual for ADAPLEX*", CCA-81-02, Computer Corp. of America, January, 1981.
42. Symbolics Inc., "*Statice™* ", Cambridge, MA 02142, USA, 1988.
43. L.A. Stein and S.B. Zdonik, "*Clovers: The Dynamic Behavior of Type and Instances*", Brown University Technical Report No. CS-89-42, Nov. 1989.
44. A. I. Wasserman, "The data management facilities of PLAIN", *Proceedings ACM SIGMOD Conference*, Boston, MA. pp 60-70, 1979.
45. S.B. Zdonik, and Maier D., "Fundamentals of Object-Oriented Databases", in *Readings in Object-Oriented Database Systems*, S.B. Zdonik, and D. Maier (eds), Morgan Kaufmann, San Mateo, California, 1990.

Appendix A

A database example

Let us consider the classical example of parts and suppliers, with parts defined recursively by other parts, either composite or base. The scheme is shown in Figure 10.

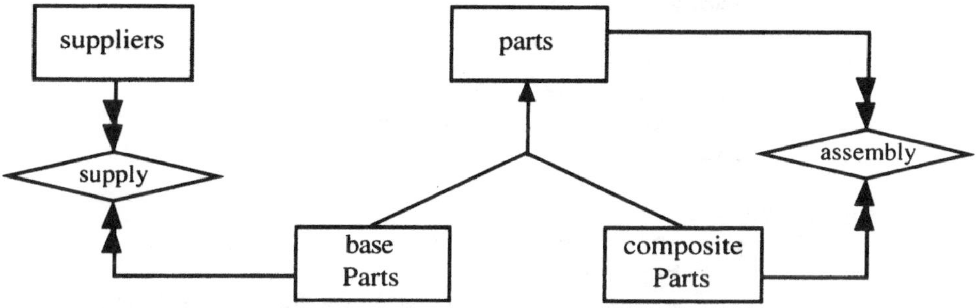

Fig. 10. The Parts example

Here is the Fibonacci scheme:

```
(* object and role type definitions *)

Let PartObject = NewObject;
Let SupplierObject = NewObject;

(* role types *)

Let Part =
            IsA PartObject With
                Name: String;
                Cost: Int;
                Mass: Int
            End;
Let BasePart =
            IsA Part With End;

Let CompositePart =
            IsA Part With
                AssemblyCost: Int
            End;

Let Supplier =
            IsA SupplierObject With
                Name: String;
                Address: String
```

```
            End;

(* classes *)
let parts =
            emptyClass of Part
                key   Name
                elsefail "parts key: duplicated Name"
            end;

let baseParts =
            emptyClass of BasePart are parts end;

let compositeParts =
            emptyClass of CompositePart
                are parts butNot baseParts
            end;

let suppliers =
            emptyClass of Supplier
                key   Name
                elsefail "suppliers key: duplicated Name"
            end;

(* associations *)
(* a base part cannot exist without a supplier for it  *)

let supply =
            emptyAssoc  of
                [ basePart :BasePart are baseParts
                            onto baseParts
                            elsefail
                            "supply: basePart onto baseParts";
                 supplier :Supplier in suppliers ]
            end;

let assembly =
            emptyAssoc  of
            [ composite :CompositePart are compositeParts
                        onto compositeParts
                        elsefail "assembly:
                        composite onto compositeParts";
             component :Part in parts
                        elsefail "assembly:
                        component in parts";
             quantity :Int ]
                key composite, component
                elsefail "assembly key:
                duplicate pair composite component"
            end;
```

```
(* auxiliary constructors used to create values *)

let createBasePart =
            fun(aName :String; aCost, aMass :Int) :BasePart is
            begin
            assert not (isUnknown aName)
            elsefail "createBasePart: Name cannot be unknown";
            role BasePart
                methods
                Name = aName;
                Cost = aCost;
                Mass = aMass
                end;
            end;

let createCompositePart =
            fun(aName :String;
                anAssemblyCost :Int) :CompositePart is
            begin
            assert not (isUnknown aName)
            elsefail "createCompositePart:
                        Name cannot be unknown";
                role CompositePart
                    methods
                    Name = aName;
                    AssemblyCost = anAssemblyCost;
                    Cost = anAssemblyCost +
                            sum(for assembly
                                where composite = me
                                do component.Cost*quantity);
                    Mass = sum(for assembly
                            where composite = me
                                do component.Mass*quantity)
                end;
            end;

let createSupplier =
            fun(aName, anAddress :String) :Supplier is
            begin
            assert not (isUnknown aName)
            elsefail "createSupplier: Name cannot be unknown";
                role Supplier
                    methods
                        Name = aName;
                        Address = anAddress
                    end
            end;

(* functions to insert elements in classes which are not domain
of surjective associations *)
```

```
let insertIntoSuppliers =
            fun(aName, anAddress :String) :Supplier is
            begin
                let newSupplier =
                    createSupplier(aName; anAddress);
                insert newSupplier into suppliers;
                newSupplier
                end;

(* functions to insert elements in classes which are  domain of
surjective associations *)

let insertIntoBasePartsAddSuppliers =
            fun(suppliers: { Supplier} ;
                aName :String; aCost, aMass: Int)
:BasePart is
            atomic
                let bp = createBasePart(aName; aCost; aMass);
                loop s in suppliers do
                    insert [bp; s.  into supply
                end;
                bp;
            end;

let insertIntoCompositePartsAddComponents =
            fun(someComponents :{ [component: Part;
                                   quantity: Int]} ;
                aName :String; anAssemblyCost :Int)
                : CompositePart is
            atomic
                let newCompositePart =
                    createCompositePart(aName;anAssemblyCost);
                loop someComponents do
                    insert [newCompositePart;
                            component; quantity]
            into assembly
                end;
                newCompositePart
            end;

(* function to add a new supplier for a base part *)

let addSupply =
            fun(aBasePart :BasePart; aSupplier :Supplier)
            : Null is
            insert [aBasePart; aSupplier. into supply;

(* query examples *)
```

```
(* find the base parts which cost more than 100.000 *)

baseParts where Cost > 100000;
(* result type :{ BasePart}  *)

(* find Name, Cost and Mass of the base parts which cost more
than 100.000 *)

for baseParts
where Cost > 100000
do [let Name = Name; let Cost = Cost; let Mass = Mass];
(* result type :{ [Name :String; Cost :Int; Mass :Int]}  *);

(* find the cost of part "FunBike" *)

(the (parts where Name = "CityBike")).Cost;
(* result type :Int *);

(* find the names of base parts supplied by Alfred *)

for supply
where supplier.Name = "Alfred"
do basePart.Name;
(* result type :{ String}  *)

(* a recursive function to find all the base parts composing a
part *)
rec let findBaseComponents =
            fun(aPart: Part): { BasePart } is
                if aPart isAlso BasePart
                then {  aPart as BasePart}
                else setOf(
                    flatten(
                        for assembly
                        where composite = aPart
                        do findBaseComponents(component) ))
end;

(* find the base parts of the part named "FunBike" *)
findBaseComponents(the (parts where name = "FunBike"));
```

Chapter 1.1.3

The Napier88 Persistent Programming Language and Environment

Ron Morrison[1], Richard Connor[1]*, Graham Kirby[1], David Munro[1], Malcolm P. Atkinson[2], Quintin Cutts[1]*, Fred Brown[3] and Alan Dearle[4]

[1] School of Mathematical and Computational Sciences, University of St Andrews, North Haugh, St Andrews KY16 9SS, Scotland
[2] Department of Computer Science, University of Glasgow, Glasgow G12 8QQ, Scotland
[3] Department of Computer Science, University of Adelaide, Adelaide 5005, Australia
[4] Department of Computing Science, University of Stirling, Stirling FK9 4LA, Scotland

Abstract. Persistent programming systems are designed as an implementation technology for long lived, concurrently accessed and potentially large bodies of data and programs, known here as persistent application systems (PASs). Within a PAS the persistence concept is used to abstract over the physical properties of data such as where it is kept, how long it is kept and in what form it is kept. As such it is seen as having a number of benefits in simplifying the task of PAS programming. Here, we describe the integrated design of the Napier88 persistent programming system and how Napier88 may be used to develop PASs.

1 Introduction

The Napier88 persistent programming system was originally planned as part of the PISA project [1] with the major goal of constructing a self contained, orthogonally persistent system. The system was also intended as, or turned out to be, a testbed for experiments in: type systems for data modelling [2-7], bulk data [8, 9] and protection [10, 11]; programming language implementation [12, 13]; binding mechanisms [14-17]; programming environments [17-20]; system evolution [21-24]; concurrency control and transactions [25-28]; object stores [27, 29-36] and software engineering tools [37-40].

The Napier88 system consists of the Napier88 language [41] and its persistent environment [42]. The persistent store comes pre-populated, rather like the SMALLTALK Virtual Image [43], and indeed the system uses values within the persistent store to support itself. The user is able to operate entirely within the persistent environment which provides editors, window managers, compilers etc.

Unlike its predecessor, PS-algol [44], which took the approach of extending an existing programming language, S-algol [45], with persistence, Napier88 was designed as an integrated persistent programming system [46]. As such some of the decisions as to what is built into the language and what is supported by the environment would justify re-evaluation in future designs. For example, bulk types and concurrency control are supported by values and procedures in the environment whereas graphics facilities, both raster [47] and line drawing [48], are supported in the base language. In particular, there was no attempt to define a minimal language

---

* Present address: Department of Computer Science, University of Glasgow, Glasgow G12 8QQ, Scotland

with support facilities being supplied by the persistent environment; rather the design attempted to separate the concepts required for persistent programming and to provide a powerful composition mechanism that allowed these concepts to be freely combined.

The Napier88 system is designed as a layered architecture [35] as shown in Figure 1.1. All the architectural layers are virtual in that, in any implementation, they may be implemented separately or together as efficiency dictates. Thus, they are definitional rather than concrete. The details of the architecture are given in [35] and the specification of the layers in [49]. By replacing any of the layers, a different implementation of Napier88 may be formed with different performance characteristics. For example, there are implementations of the stable storage layer using logging [50], shadow paging [27, 31] and a variation of the DBcache [51]. By experimentation and measurement the most efficient implementation for a given workload may be found and used in the choice of the components of the Napier88 architecture.

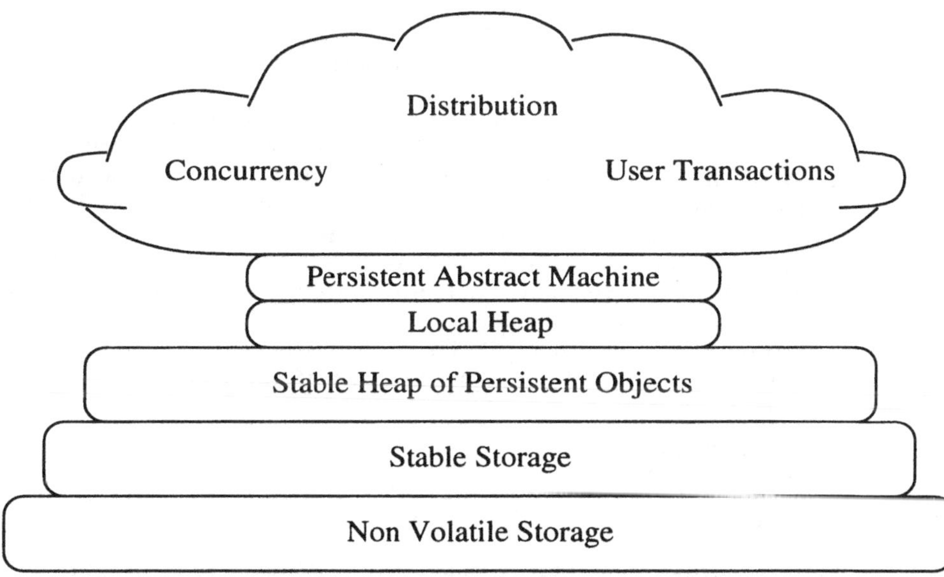

Fig. 1.1. The Napier88 layered architecture.

The success of the Napier88 architecture is highlighted by the fact that it was used in the implementations of P-Galileo [52], P-Quest [53], PIOS [54] and Staple [55].

The Flask architecture [27] was developed from the above to accommodate concurrency control and distribution. This architecture is shown in Figure 1.2 as a "V-shaped" layered architecture to signify the minimal functionality built-in at the lower layers. At the top layer the specifications of the model are independent of the algorithms used to enforce them and can take advantage of the semantics of these algorithms to exploit potential concurrency [56]. The information gleaned from the specifications is fed down to the lower layers to aid efficient implementation. Thus specifications are mapped onto programs which can access the subsets of data that are visible to them. Again the form of these layers may be different in different implementations allowing the architecture the flexibility to accommodate different models of concurrency control and distribution. This is just one example of how the closed persistent world can use its high-level semantics to guide the execution of systems.

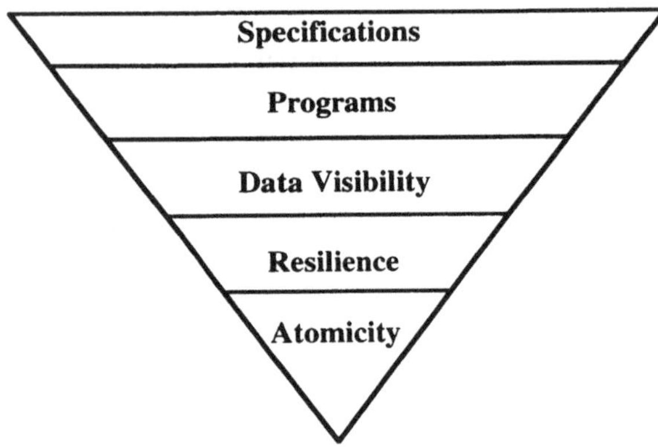

Fig. 1.2. The Flask architecture.

A large body of technology such as compilers, browsers, object stores, abstract machines, garbage collectors and hyper-programming facilities underlies the implementation of the Napier88 system. Here we concentrate on the design philosophy of the system and the techniques for persistent programming. This is done through the following areas: controlling complexity, the provision of orthogonal persistence, data modelling, the protection of data, controlled system evolution, concurrency control and transactions, and programming within the persistent environment, including hyper-programming.

The justification of the persistence design decisions is given in [57] and the advantages of the abstraction is outlined in [4, 11, 15, 18, 35, 58-67].

2 Controlling Complexity

2.1 Language Design

McCarthy [68], van Wijngaarden [69], Strachey [70] and Tennent [71] all observed that expressive power in programming languages could be gained by separating the underlying concepts and allowing them to be combined by general composition rules. Strachey and later Tennent distilled these ideas into three principles for use in the design of programming languages:

- the principle of correspondence,
- the principle of abstraction and
- the principle of data type completeness.

The principle of correspondence states that the rules governing the use of names and bindings in a programming language should be consistent. In particular the rules for introducing names and bindings in declarations should have a corresponding mechanism for abstraction parameters. This ensures that formal parameters behave consistently with local declarations. In Napier88 there is only one parameter passing technique, call by value, and there is a 1-1 correspondence between declarations and parameter passing modes.

The principle of abstraction states that for all significant syntactic categories in the language there should be an abstraction mechanism. This allows inessential details to be ignored by concentrating on the general structure. An abstraction consists of naming the syntactic category and allowing it to be parameterised. The Napier88 abstractions are procedures in the value space, polymorphic procedures and abstract data types in the type space and type operators in the type algebra.

The principle of data type completeness states that any combination or construction of data should be allowed for all types. As a consequence all data objects in a language should have the same "civil rights".

The overall goal of the above principles is to design languages that are both simple and powerful. They are simple in that there are a minimum of defining rules with no exceptions, since for every exception to a rule the language becomes more complicated in terms of understandability and implementation. The minimisation of defining rules without exceptions also contributes to the power of the language since every exception makes the language less powerful, in that it introduces a restriction. The expressive power therefore comes from ensuring that the composition rules are complete and minimal with no exceptions.

As an example of the application of the above principles, we highlight the design of the Napier88 type system which defines the Universe of Discourse of the language.

The Napier88 type system is based on the notion of types as a set structure imposed over the value space. Membership of the type sets is defined in terms of common attributes possessed by values, such as the operations defined over them. In the absence of polymorphism these sets or types partition the value space; polymorphic forms, which in Napier88 are polymorphic procedures and abstract data types, allow values to belong to more than a single type [72]. The sets may be predefined, like *integer*, or they may be formed by using one of the predefined type constructors, like *structure*. The Universe of Discourse of Napier88 is defined by the following rules:

1. The scalar data types are *int*, *real*, *bool*, *pixel*, *file* and *null*.

2. Type *string* is the type of a sequence of characters; this type embraces the empty string and single characters.

3. Type *pic* is the type of a conceptual line drawing, modelled in an infinite 2-D real space; this type embraces single points.

4. Type *image* is the type of a value consisting of a rectangular matrix of pixels.

5. Type *env* is the type of an environment; a value of this type consists of a collection of bindings.

6. Type *any* is an infinite union type.

The following type constructors are defined in Napier88:

7. For any type t, $*t$ is the type of a vector with elements of type t.

8. For labels $I_1,...,I_n$ and types $t_1,...,t_n$, *structure* $(I_1: t_1,...,I_n: t_n)$ is the type of a structure with fields I_i and corresponding types t_i, for i = 1..n and n ≥ 0.

9. For labels $I_1,...,I_n$ and types $t_1,...,t_n$, *variant* $(I_1: t_1,...,I_n: t_n)$ is the type of a variant with labels I_i and corresponding types t_i, for i = 1..n and n ≥ 0.

10. For any types $t_1,...,t_n$ and t, *proc* $(t_1,...,t_n \rightarrow t)$ is the type of a procedure with parameter types t_i, for i = 1..n, where n ≥ 0, and result type t. The type of a resultless procedure is *proc* $(t_1,...,t_n)$.

11. *proc* $[T_1,...,T_m]$ $(t_1,...,t_n \rightarrow t)$, where the definitions of types $t_1,...,t_n$ and t may include the use of the type variables $T_1,...,T_m$, is the type of a procedure which is universally quantified over these type variables for m > 0 and n ≥ 0. These are polymorphic procedures. The type of a resultless polymorphic procedure is *proc* $[T_1,...,T_m]$ $(t_1,...,t_n)$.

12. *abstype* $[W_1,..., W_m]$ $(I_1: t_1,...,I_n: t_n)$, where the definitions of types $t_1,...,t_n$ may include the use of the type variables $W_1,...,W_m$, is the type of a structure which is existentially quantified over these type variables for m > 0 and n ≥ 0. These are abstract data types.

The world of data values is defined by the closure of rules 1 to 6 under the recursive application of rules 7 to 12.

An essential element for controlling complexity is that there should be a high degree of abstraction. Thus, in the above type rules, vectors and structures are regarded as store abstractions over all data types, procedures as abstractions over expressions and statements, polymorphic procedures and abstract data types as abstractions over types, and type operators as abstractions in the type algebra. The infinite unions **env** and **any** are used to support persistence, as well as being a general modelling technique; they are dynamically type checked.

The type constructors of Napier88 obey the *Principle of Data Type Completeness*, in that, where a type may be used in a constructor, any type is legal without exception. Thus all data values are first class.

2.2 Orthogonal Persistence

The implication of orthogonal persistence is that the user need never write code to move or convert data for long or short term storage [57]. There are three design principles that may be used to achieve orthogonal persistence. They are:

The Principle of Persistence Independence

The form of a program is independent of the longevity of the data that it manipulates. Programs look the same whether they manipulate short-term or long-term data.

The Principle of Data Type Orthogonality

All data objects should be allowed the full range of persistence irrespective of their type. There are no special cases where objects are not allowed to be long-lived or are not allowed to be transient.

The Principle of Persistence Identification

The choice of how to identify and provide persistent objects is orthogonal to the universe of discourse of the system. The mechanism for identifying persistent objects is not related to the type system.

The application of these three principles yields ***Orthogonal Persistence***.

Persistence independence frees the programmer from the burden of having to explicitly program the movement of data among the hierarchy of storage devices and from coding translations between long-term and short-term representations; this is performed automatically by the system. The mechanical cost of performing the movement of data does not disappear but the intellectual cost does. That is, the programmer need not specifically write code for it, making the application code smaller and more intellectually manageable. However, the implementor of the support system now has the challenge of automating that data movement and any translation efficiently.

Data type orthogonality is an aid to data modelling in that it ensures that the data model can be complete and independent of the persistence of the data being modelled. For example, bulk data types abstract over size and are used in persistent programming languages to aid the manipulation of massive collections of data such as scanned data from satellites or insurance policies sold by a company. In traditional systems, where such data is only considered long-term, then the data model has to allow explicit conversion between long and short-term forms to facilitate creation of new bulk data and the manipulation of extracts from the long-term bulk data as short-term data. Such conversions are a distraction when the PAS programmer has to code them.

Persistence identification may be satisfied by identifying the persistent data automatically. In a natural extension of the garbage collection technique, where only useful data survives, the persistent data of a program can be found by computing the transitive closure of all the data from a number of distinguished roots. This technique is called *identification by reachability* and is the one now most commonly used in orthogonally persistent systems.

The Napier88 system obeys all three of the above principles of persistence. Programs operate on long and short term data identically, all data types may persist and the useful data is identified by reachability.

3 Using Persistent Data

Napier88 programs may access their home persistent environment by calling the only pre-defined procedure in the language, *PS*. Other persistent stores may also be accessed and values from those stores copied into the home environment. Each persistent store is organised as a graph of objects but the topology of the graphs may vary from store to store. The *PS* procedure is specified as follows:

```
PS: proc (→ any)
```

That is, *PS* is a procedure that takes no parameters and yields a value, the root of persistence, of type **any**. The root of persistence is constant and may not be altered after the store has been created. However the values reachable from the root may be updated if they are variable.

Type **any** is the infinite union of all types into which values may be injected (coerced) dynamically. Stores are initialised by a standard procedure that takes a parameter of type **any** which will have the initial store value injected into it. The mechanism for creating stores is contained in [42].

To retrieve values from the persistent store, a projection operation (coercion), from type **any**, is required. So, for example, if a persistent store consists of one value which is a structure with a *name* and *address* in it, both of type **string**, then the following program fragment can be used to retrieve the value:

```
type person is structure (name, address : string)
! This declares a type, person, as a structure (labelled cross product)
! with two fields (name and address) of type string

let ps = PS () ! Calling the PS predefined procedure yields
                 ! the root of persistence.
                 ! It is then declared as the constant ps.
                 ! Constancy is denoted by the =
                 ! variables are declared using :=
project ps as X onto
person :       ! The value X may be used here with type person
default:       { } ! This is the catch all and X has type any here
```

Fig. 3.1. Using persistent data.

The **project** clause takes a value, *ps* in this case, and either coerces the type to one in the list of types that follows or executes the **default** option. The value is also given a constant identifier, *X* in this case, to avoid side effects. This identifier is in scope on the right hand side of the colon and has the type on the left hand side. In practice, the persistent stores are much more complicated, often forming large structured graphs.

The movement of data for execution is hidden from the user. When the program accesses a value it is automatically made available, thus the user may abstract over this physical property of the store. To change values in the persistent store, they must first be accessed and then updated. At the end of the program execution the transitive closure of the values from the original root of persistence is calculated and these values preserved in the persistent store. This action may change the topology of the store but not the original root which is constant once created.

```
type person is structure (name, address : string)

let ps = PS ()
project ps as X onto
person :        begin
                X (name) := "Ronald Morrison"
                X (address) := "St Andrews"
        end
default :       { } ! This is the catch all and X has type any here
```

Fig. 3.2. Changing persistent values.

In Figure 3.2, the value contained in the persistent store is a structure. Its fields have been updated to record the information on a very nice person. At the end of the program, all the information reachable from the original root is preserved.

Figure 3.3 outlines the initial structure of the Napier88 standard release system 2.2 [42]. Most of the names represent environment (**env**) objects which are collections of bindings. The type **env** is the infinite union of all labelled cross products but environments differ from structures in that bindings may be added and removed dynamically. This requires an existence check and a dynamic type check on the first use of an environment object to ensure that it contains the bindings assumed in the programs.

Figure 3.4 stores a procedure in the *User* environment for later use. The procedure is part of a complex number package which may be used or added to later. The **in** clause places the value that is declared, *add*, into the environment, *User*. At the end of the program this value is reachable from the persistent root, via *User*, and is therefore preserved. The binding that is placed in the environment is an *L-value* binding in that it contains a location [73].

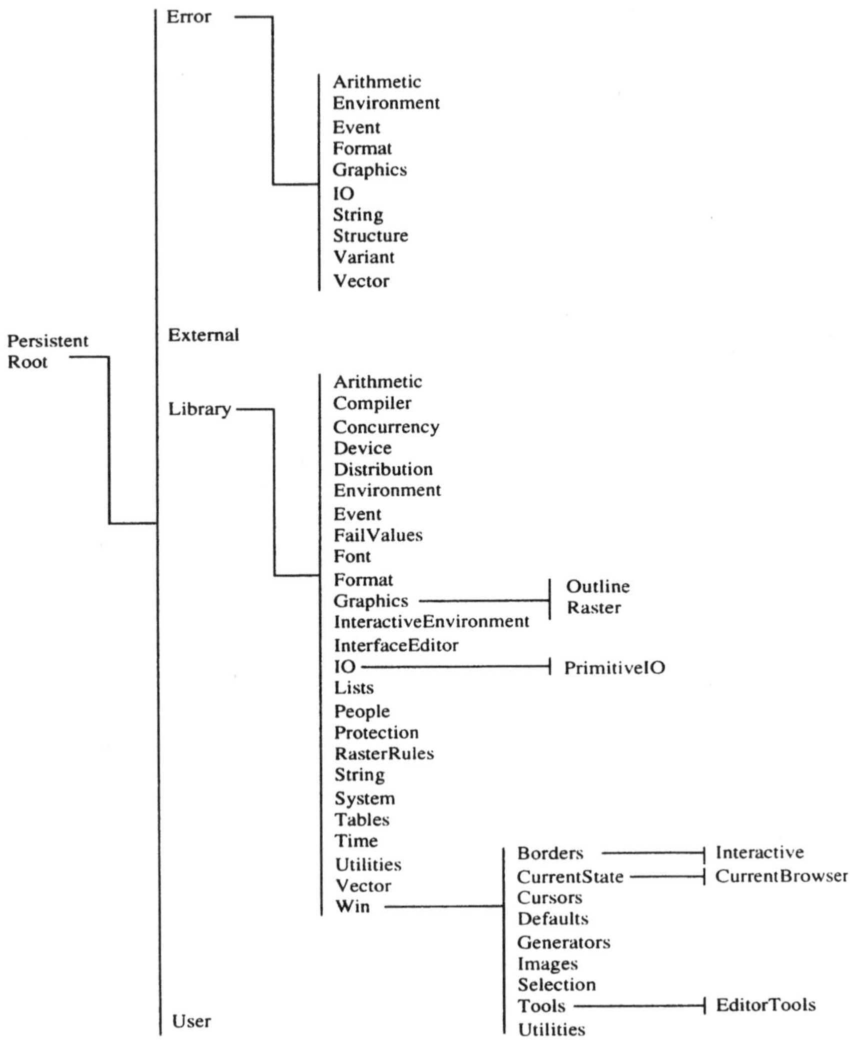

Fig. 3.3. The standard release persistent store structure.

Figure 3.5 shows how a second procedure may be placed in the same, *User*, environment. In this way the package can be built up incrementally.

```
let ps = PS ()

project ps as X onto
env :   use X with User : env in
        begin
             type complex is structure (rpart, ipart : real)
             in User let add := proc (a, b : complex → complex)
                  complex (a (rpart) + b (rpart), a (ipart) + b (ipart))
        end
default : { } ! This is executed if the projection fails
```

Fig. 3.4. Placing a procedure in the persistent store.

```
let ps = PS ()

project ps as X onto
env :   use X with User : env in
        begin
             type complex is structure (rpart, ipart : real)
             in User let subtract := proc (a, b : complex → complex)
                  complex (a (rpart) - b (rpart), a (ipart) - b (ipart))
        end
default : { } ! This is executed if the projection fails
```

Fig. 3.5. Adding a procedure to the *User* environment.

```
type complex is structure (rpart, ipart : real)

let ps = PS ()

project ps as X onto
env :   use X with User : env in
        use User with add, subtract : proc (a, b : complex → complex) in
        begin
             let one = complex (1.0, 1.0) ; let two = complex (2.0, 2.0)
             let three = add (one, two)
             let minusOne = subtract (one, two)
        end
default : { } ! This is executed if the projection fails
```

Fig. 3.6. Using the procedures in the *User* environment.

Figure 3.6 demonstrates how these procedures may now be accessed in a program. Notice that the values *one*, *two*, *three*, and *minusOne* are not preserved when the program terminates since they are not reachable from the root of persistence.

The second **use** clause projects two procedure values, *add* and *subtract*, into the current scope. The semantics of the clause is the same as declaring these values within the block except that they are reachable from the root of persistence.

The need for dynamic type checking should now be apparent. The dynamic check is required to ensure that the given environment contains the values of the correct type. If it does then the values are placed in scope and may be used like any other value. Otherwise an error condition is raised. Programs that use the values may be statically type checked since the compiler can compile the code against the static assumption that the dynamic check will succeed.

The environment mechanism [73] provides a contextual naming scheme that can be composed dynamically. All values in Napier88 are anonymous. However, the same value may be contained in more than one environment and have different names in each of these environments. This allows different name spaces to be placed over the value space enabling applications to use their own private persistent name space while sharing values in the persistent store.

The syntactic noise involved in using the persistent store, through **project** and **use** clauses, may be reduced by hyper-programming [20] which allows values to be directly linked to source code at composition time. Thus the navigational code and type specifications need not always be included in the program.

4 Data Modelling

Type systems provide two important facilities within both databases and programming languages, namely data modelling and data protection. Data modelling is performed in databases using data models, which have types to describe the form of the data, and in programming languages by using a classical type system. In both cases the universe of discourse of the system is defined by the set of allowable types which in turn are denoted by the set of legal expressions in the language. Data protection is provided by enforcing explicit and implicit integrity constraints in databases and by type checking in programming languages. A goal of persistent programming language design is to develop a type system that will accommodate the structures required for both modelling and protection in novel database applications such as scientific programming, engineering applications and office automation, whilst also capturing the type description of more conventional database systems [74].

As a first step in the unification of data models and type systems some approximate equivalences can be recognised. These are summarised in Table 1.

Table 1. Equivalences between data models and type systems.

Databases	Programming Languages
data models	type systems
schema	type expression
database	variable
database extent	value

The issue of type checking is central to a type system that will provide data modelling and protection for persistent systems. Generally, data models in databases are concerned with the manipulation of the data that is consistent with the constraints imposed by the data model. In some cases these constraints may depend upon values calculated during the computation. As such they can be dynamic in nature and require dynamic integrity constraint checking for enforcement. By contrast classical type systems for programming languages are concerned with static checking which allows assertions to be made and even proved about a computation before it is executed. Static checking therefore provides a level of safety within the system. It also allows more efficient code since type checking code is not required at run-time.

At first the dichotomy between the checking times in databases and programming languages appears to be beyond resolution. The Napier88 approach is to ensure that the type system is mostly statically checkable. However, some dynamic checking on projection out of unions for types **any** and **env**, as well as variant selection, allows the dynamic binding required for orthogonal persistence [57] and system evolution [23].

For data modelling, Napier88 provides the types described earlier including polymorphic procedures and the existentially quantified types of Mitchell & Plotkin [5, 75] for abstract data types. There is deliberately no type inference to allow polymorphic forms to be stored in the persistent store and, when accessed, specialised with their specialising type. A unique design feature of the implementation of the typed objects is that their storage format may be non-uniform [12] even in the presence of polymorphism.

The type equivalence rule in Napier88 is by structure to allow separately prepared programs and data to be composed without reference to a common scheme. To accommodate expressive power, type parameterisation is provided and both recursive and parameterised types are allowed in the type algebra.

An illustration of a typical data model being defined in Napier88 is given in [46].

4.1 User Defined Types

Napier88 provides the user with the ability to assign names to type constructions. For example,

```
type complex is structure (rpart, ipart : real)
```

declares a structure (labelled cross product) with two fields *rpart* and *ipart* both of type **real**. The structure type is given the local name *complex* which may now be used as a shorthand for the type expression.

Napier88 provides recursive types which yield the ability to define repeating and cyclic data structures. Consider, for example, a binary tree in which each node has a *key* field of type **int** and a *value* field of type **string**. Each node of the binary tree also has a *left* and a *right* field of the tree type, to point to the descendent sub-trees. The nodes of the tree are represented by a structure type and the tree itself, and all its sub-trees, can be either a node or an empty tree represented by the **null** type. The declaration of the type name, *intStrBTree*, defines such a binary tree.

```
rec type intStrBTree is variant (node : Node ; tip : null)
& Node is structure (key : int ; value : string ; left, right : intStrBTree)
```

Expressive power is further increased by type operators which allow types to be parameterised by others. For example

```
type Pair [t] is structure (first, second : t)
```

Pair is not strictly a type but a type operator which defines an infinite class of types. It may be parameterised by a type to produce a specific type definition. For example:

```
type intPair is Pair [int]          ! This is equivalent to
                                    ! structure (first, second : int)
type imagePair is Pair [image]      ! This is equivalent to
                                    ! structure (first, second : image)
```

The combination of recursive definition and type parameterisation yields further expressive power. For example, the following type operator defines an infinite class of binary trees.

```
rec type binaryTree [Key, Value] is variant (node : Node [Key, Value] ;
                                             tip : null)
& Node [Key, Value] is structure (key : Key ; value : Value ;
                                  left, right : binaryTree [Key, Value])
```

These may be used as before to define specific binary trees.

```
type intStringBinaryTree is binaryTree [int, string]

type stringImageBinaryTree is binaryTree [string, image]
```

The uncontrolled introduction of recursive type operators leads to the ability to describe types over which no decidable structural equivalence algorithm is known. Napier88 therefore restricts these definitions by the following rule in order to retain decidable type checking [4]:

> The specialisation of a recursive operator on the right hand side of its own definition may not include any types which are constructed over its own formal parameters.

The importance of type declarations is that they allow the programmer to introduce new and succinct notations and to assign them names that are meaningful within the application being constructed. It therefore aids the traditional role of Data Description Languages by allowing data to be accurately described.

4.2 Polymorphism

In [76] and its companion papers, an analysis of what constitutes a persistent type system is given. For modelling purposes, it is generally agreed that some form of polymorphism is required to capture the expressiveness of data models and to increase component re-use [18].

Napier88 provides polymorphism in the form of universally quantified procedures and existentially quantified types (abstract data types). The utility of these mechanisms will be illustrated with the aid of an example that implements an index. Initially the index will use integer keys and store string values.

Each instance of the index is produced by evaluating a generator procedure that returns a structure containing the index, together with a procedure to enter values into the index, and another procedure to lookup values in the index. The generator procedure and the index instances will be stored in the persistent store in two new environments, *indexGenerators* and *indexInstances*.

Creating the new environments entails using the standard procedure *environment*. This, itself, is kept in the *Library* environment in the persistent store and must be located and called. This is illustrated in Figure 4.1. Notice that the new environments are made reachable from the persistent root by placing them in the *User* environment.

```
project PS () as X onto
env :   use X with User, Library : env in
        use Library with Environment : env in
        use Environment with environment : proc (→ env) in
        begin
                in User let indexGenerators = environment ()
                ! This places the new environment in the User environment
                ! with the name indexGenerators

                in User let indexInstances = environment ()
        end
default : { } ! This is executed if the projection fails
```

Fig. 4.1. Creating the environments to hold index generators and instance.

Figure 4.2 defines a procedure that generates the index by returning a structure, of type *indexShell*, containing the index, together with a procedure to enter values into the index, and another procedure to lookup values in the index. The generating procedure takes as a parameter a fail value which is returned by the *lookup* procedure if the key is not valid. The index is implemented as a binary tree. The generator procedure is placed in the persistent store.

```
rec type index is variant (node : Node ; tip : null)
& Node is structure (key : int ; value : string ; left, right : index)

type indexShell is structure (i : index;
                 enter :    proc (int, string, index → index);
                 lookup :   proc (int, index → string))

project PS () as X onto
env : use X with User : env in
use User with indexGenerators : env in
in indexGenerators
let generateIntStringIndex = proc (failValue : string → indexShell)
begin
   let nullIndex = index (tip : nil)
   ! Construct the empty index by injecting the nil value into the variant

   rec let enter = proc (k : int ; v : string ; i : index → index)
   ! Enter the value into the binary tree indexed by key 'k'
   if i is tip then index (node : Node (k, v, nullIndex, nullIndex)) else
   case true of
   k < i'node (key)       : {i'node (left) := enter (k, v, i'node (left)) ; i}
   k = i'node (key)       : i                    ! do nothing
   default                : {i'node (right) := enter (k, v, i'node (right)) ; i}

   let lookup = proc (k : int ; i : index → string)
   ! Look up the value in the binary tree
   begin
        let head := i
        while head is node and k ≠ head'node (key) do
              head :=     if k < head'node (key)
                          then head'node (left) else head'node (right)
        if head is node then head'node (value) else failValue
   end
   indexShell (nullIndex, enter, lookup)
end
default : { } ! This is executed if the projection fails
```

Fig. 4.2. The procedure to generate the index.

To create an index, the generator procedure is located in the persistent store and called. The resulting structure is subsequently stored in the persistent store in the *indexInstances* environment. All of this is contained in Figure 4.3.

Figure 4.4 demonstrates how the index may now be accessed in the persistent store and subsequently used. Notice that the new entry in the index will be preserved in the persistent store after the program terminates since it is reachable from the root of persistence.

```
rec type index is variant (node : Node ; tip : null)
& Node is structure (key : int ; value : string ; left, right : index)

type indexShell is structure (i : index;
            enter :     proc (int, string, index → index);
            lookup :    proc (int, index → string))

project PS () as X onto
env :   use X with User: env in
        use User with indexGenerators, indexInstances : env in
        use indexGenerators with
            generateIntStringIndex : proc (string → indexShell) in
        begin
            in indexInstances
            let intStringIndex1 = generateIntStringIndex ("This is a failure")
            ! This places the index instance in the indexInstances
            ! environment with the name intStringIndex1
        end
default : { } ! This is executed if the projection fails
```

Fig. 4.3. Placing the index in the persistent store.

```
rec type index is variant (node : Node ; tip : null)
& Node is structure (key : int ; value : string ; left, right : index)

type indexShell is structure (i : index;
            enter :     proc (int, string, index → index);
            lookup :    proc (int, index → string))

project PS () as X onto
env :   use X with User: env in
        use User with indexInstances : env in
        use indexInstances with intStringIndex1 : indexShell in
        begin
            let Y = intStringIndex1
            Y (i) := Y (enter) (49, "Ron", Y (i))
        end
default : { } ! This is executed if the projection fails
```

Fig. 4.4. Using the index.

Thus an index from integers to strings has been created and used. If a second index, say from strings to integers, is required a new set of programs has to be written. Alternatively the power of polymorphism can be used to define a generic procedure that will produce the correct index on application. The polymorphic procedure abstracts over the types of the index key and stored value but requires an extra parameter to provide an ordering on the keys.

```
rec type Index [Key, Value] is variant (node : Node [Key, Value] ; tip : null)
& Node [Key, Value] is structure (key : Key ; value : Value ;
                                  left, right : Index [Key, Value])
type IndexShell [Key, Value] is structure ( i : Index [Key, Value];
    enter :   proc (Key, Value, Index [Key, Value] → Index [Key, Value]);
    lookup :  proc (Key, Index [Key, Value] → Value))

project PS () as X onto
env : use X with User : env in
use User with indexGenerators : env in
in indexGenerators
let generateGeneralIndex = proc [Key, Value] (
        lessThan : proc (Key, Key → bool); failValue : Value
                              → IndexShell [Key, Value])
begin
    type index is Index [Key, Value]
    type node is Node [Key, Value]
    let nullIndex = index (tip : nil)
    ! Construct the empty index by injecting the nil value into the variant
    rec let enter = proc (k : Key ; v : Value ; i : index → index)
    ! Enter the value into the binary tree indexed by key 'k'
    if i is tip then index (node : node (k, v, nullIndex, nullIndex)) else
    case true of
    lessThan (k, i'node (key))
                        : {i'node (left) := enter (k, v, i'node (left)) ; i}
    k = i'node (key)    : i
    default             : {i'node (right) := enter (k, v, i'node (right)) ; i}

    let lookup = proc (k : Key ; i : index → Value)
    ! Look up the value in the binary tree
    begin
        let head := i
        while head is node and k ≠ head'node (key) do
               head :=  if lessThan (k, head'node (key))
                        then head'node (left) else head'node (right)
        if head is node then head'node (value) else failValue
    end
    IndexShell [Key, Value] (nullIndex, enter, lookup)
end
default : { } ! This is executed if the projection fails
```

Fig. 4.5. A polymorphic generation procedure.

Figure 4.5 defines the polymorphic procedure *generateGeneralIndex* which will generate a given index on application. The extra parameter, *lessThan*, is a procedure that compares two keys. Note that equality is defined over all types in Napier88.

Notice also the use of the type operators and their specialisations within the polymorphic procedure.

It should be noticed how little the polymorphic code changes from the monomorphic form. This means that there is little extra cost in producing such code. Figure 4.6 illustrates how the *generateGeneralIndex* procedure may be used to create a specific index.

```
rec type Index [Key, Value] is variant (node : Node [Key, Value] ; tip : null)
& Node [Key, Value] is structure (key : Key ; value : Value ;
                                   left, right : Index [Key, Value])

type IndexShell [Key, Value] is structure ( i : Index [Key, Value];
    enter :    proc (Key, Value, Index [Key, Value] → Index [Key, Value]);
    lookup :   proc (Key, Index [Key, Value] → Value))

project PS () as X onto
env :   use X with User: env in
        use User with indexGenerators, indexInstances : env in
        use indexGenerators with
             generateGeneralIndex : proc [Key, Value] (
                        proc (Key, Key → bool), Value
                              → IndexShell [Key, Value]) in
begin
        let stringLT = proc (a, b : string → bool) ; a < b

        in indexInstances let stringIntIndex2 =
             generateGeneralIndex [string, int] (stringLT , -999)
end
default : { } ! This is executed if the projection fails
```

Fig. 4.6. Creating an index from strings to integers.

Figure 4.7 illustrates the final step in using the new index. Notice again that a type operator is used to generate the correct type and that the code is almost identical to Figure 4.4.

The advantage of the polymorphic abstraction should be obvious in the context of software re-use. By using the polymorphism in Napier88, one procedure for all types may be written instead of a different one for each pair of types. This polymorphic generating procedure may then be used to generate many instances of the index which can vary by type. Thus the major advantage of the combination of polymorphism and persistence is that it greatly reduces the amount of code that has to be written. In the above examples the indexes and generating procedures are stored in environments in the persistent store. All the other code fragments may also be stored for later re-use in the persistent store but such details have been omitted here.

There is a second type of abstraction that may be required over indexes. In the above examples all of the indexes are implemented by binary trees and the data structure implementing these has to be known for correct use. Further abstraction can be had by hiding the implementation while still allowing the user to construct programs that will work for indexes of all implementations. For this, the power of abstract data types is required.

```
rec type Index [Key, Value] is variant (node : Node [Key, Value] ; tip : null)
& Node [Key, Value] is structure (key : Key ; value : Value ;
                                  left, right : Index [Key, Value])

type IndexShell [Key, Value] is structure ( i : Index [Key, Value];
    enter :   proc (Key, Value, Index [Key, Value] → Index [Key, Value]);
    lookup :  proc (Key, Index [Key, Value] → Value))

type indexShell is IndexShell [string, int]

project PS () as X onto
env :   use X with User: env in
        use User with indexInstances : env in
        use indexInstances with stringIntIndex2 : indexShell in
        begin
                let Y = stringIntIndex2
                Y (i) := Y (enter) ("Richard", 35, Y (i))
        end
default : { } ! This is executed if the projection fails
```

Fig. 4.7. Using the string to integer index.

The implementation of the index may be a binary tree, a B-tree, a B^+-tree or a list, etc. The essential element is that they all have the same abstract interface of an index value, a procedure that will take a key, a value and an index as parameters and return an index, and another procedure that will take a key and an index as parameters and return a value. Such an interface may be defined in Napier88 using abstract data types. For example, the type of all integer to string indexes irrespective of their implementation can be written as:

```
type intStringAbsIndex is abstype [index] (
                Index       : index;
                Enter       : proc (int, string, index → index);
                Lookup      : proc (int, index → string))
```

The witness type, *index*, is hidden to the outside of this interface. This is the implementation type. Thus all values of type *intStringAbsIndex* have the same type, no matter which implementation type is used to construct the abstract data type.

Figure 4.8 illustrates how both kinds of polymorphic abstraction can be combined. The *generateGeneralAbsBtreeIndex* procedure is polymorphic in the key and value types allowing any ordered type to be used as an index key for any other type. The procedure returns an abstract data type which has the implementation of the index encapsulated within it.

```
rec type Index [Key, Value] is variant (node : Node [Key, Value] ; tip : null)
& Node [Key, Value] is structure (key : Key ; value : Value ;
                                  left, right : Index [Key, Value])

type absIndex [KEY, VALUE] is abstype [index] (
            Index    : index;
            Enter    : proc (KEY, VALUE, index → index);
            Lookup   : proc (KEY, index → VALUE))

project PS () as X onto
env :   use X with User : env in
use User with indexGenerators : env in
in indexGenerators let generateGeneralAbsBtreeIndex = proc [Key, Value] (
            lessThan : proc (Key, Key → bool); failValue : Value
            → absIndex [Key, Value])
begin
   type index is Index [Key, Value]
   type node is Node [Key, Value]

   let nullIndex = index (tip : nil)
   ! Construct the empty index by injecting the nil value into the variant

   rec let enter = proc (k : Key ; v : Value ; i : index → index)
   ! Enter the value into the binary tree indexed by key 'k'
   if i is tip then index (node : node (k, v, nullIndex, nullIndex)) else
   case true of
   lessThan (k, i'node (key)) : {i'node (left) := enter (k, v, i'node (left)) ; i}
   k = i'node (key)       : i
   default                : {i'node (right) := enter (k, v, i'node (right)) ; i}

   let lookup = proc (k : Key ; i : index → Value)
   ! lookup the value in the binary tree
   begin
      let head := i
      while head is node and k ≠ head'node (key) do
            head :=  if lessThan (k, head'node (key))
                     then head'node (left) else head'node (right)
      if head is node then head'node (value) else failValue
   end
   absIndex [Key, Value] [index] (nullIndex, enter, lookup)
end
default : { } ! This is executed if the projection fails
```

Fig. 4.8. Combining universal and existential quantification.

Figure 4.9 creates two abstract index instances with different key and value types, and stores them in the persistent store. Two abstract data types are created one using the binary tree implementation generator and the other using an unspecified list implementation generator.

```
rec type Index [Key, Value] is variant (node : Node [Key, Value] ; tip : null)
& Node [Key, Value] is structure (key : Key ; value : Value ;
                                  left, right : Index [Key, Value])

type absIndex [KEY, VALUE] is abstype [index] (
            Index       : index;
            Enter       : proc (KEY, VALUE, index → index);
            Lookup      : proc (KEY, index → VALUE))

let ps = PS ()

project ps as X onto
env :   use X with User: env in
        use User with indexGenerators, indexInstances : env in
        use indexGenerators with
            generateGeneralAbsBtreeIndex : proc [Key, Value] (
                     proc (Key, Key → bool), Value
                                  → absIndex [Key, Value])
begin
        let intLessThan = proc (a, b → bool) ; a < b
        let stringLessThan = proc (a, b → string) ; a < b

        in indexInstances let intStringAbsIndex1 =
            generateGeneralAbsBtreeIndex [int, string] (intLessThan , "")

        in indexInstances let stringIntAbsIndex1 =
        generateGeneralAbsListIndex [string, int] (stringLessThan , -99)
end
default : { } ! This is executed if the projection fails
```

Fig. 4.9. Creating an index from strings to integers.

Figure 4.10 illustrates how the abstract data types may be used. Notice that while the implementations of the abstract data types are incompatible, as are the operations over them, a procedure that will operate over both of them may be constructed. The example is a little contrived in that a similar effect could be obtained by first-order information hiding by encapsulating the index in the closures of the two procedures. However, it is now possible to manipulate the index as a separate abstract entity.

The abstype **use** clause is a scoping and renaming device. The abstract data value is renamed as *Y* in the clause following the **in**. By giving the object a constant name, *Y*, the application of the interface procedures can be statically checked. This ensures that the interface procedures will only be applied to objects of the same representation. Indeed the rule is even stronger than this since objects named by fields can only operate on other fields of the same *Y* as they are the only ones that are known to be compatible.

```
type absIndex [KEY, VALUE] is abstype [index] (
            Index      : index;
            Enter      : proc (KEY, VALUE, index → index);
            Lookup     : proc (KEY, index → VALUE))

let updateIndex = proc [T, S] (adt : absIndex [T, S] ; k : T ; v : S)
use adt as Y in
        Y (Index) := Y (Enter) (k, v, Y (Index))

project PS () as X onto
env : use X with User: env in
    use User with indexInstances : env in
    use indexInstances with
            stringIntAbsIndex1 : absIndex [string, int];
            intStringAbsIndex1 : absIndex [int, string] in
    begin
        updateIndex [string, int] (stringIntAbsIndex1, "Graham", 29)
        updateIndex [int, string] (intStringAbsIndex1, 49, "Ron")
    end
default : { } ! This is executed if the projection fails
```

Fig. 4.10. Using abstract data types.

The difference in application between universal and existential quantification is that in universal quantification, abstract polymorphic forms can be written from which special cases can be generated, whereas with existential quantification existing objects are described by a more general type thereby allowing more general abstraction over that type.

In summary, the power of the Napier88 type system in the context of data modelling is dependent on the following: the base types and type constructors; the ability to have user defined types that may be parameterised and recursive; and the polymorphism facilities, both universal and existential. These facilities combined with the persistent environment provide for traditional data modelling but can also cater for new applications which require concurrency control, protection and schema evolution within the modelling framework.

5 Protection of Data

Persistent object systems, such as Napier88, support large collections of data that have often been constructed incrementally by a community of users [61, 77]. The data is inherently valuable and requires protection from: system malfunction, such as hardware failure; misuse of common facilities, such as the operating system; and finally from users themselves [11]. Hardware malfunction has little to do with software protection and is best dealt with by techniques such as incremental dumping or stability strategies [78, 79]. Here the focus is on software methods designed for the protection of persistent data. Information hiding is one such software technique in which the access to the data, or the type interface to it, is restricted. By varying the restriction, a variable degree of protection may be obtained.

There are three well-known mechanisms which support information hiding within a strongly typed system. These are subtyping, procedural encapsulation (first-order information hiding) and existential data types (second-order information hiding). Subtyping achieves protection by removing type information, causing the static failure of programs which try to perform undesirable accesses. First-order information hiding prevents the protected data from being named by untrusted programs allowing access only through a procedural interface. Second-order information hiding is somewhere between these two, allowing access mainly through procedures, but also allowing the protected data to be named. The data is viewed through a mechanism which causes type information loss thus ensuring that only a limited set of operations may be performed on the hidden data.

The current version of Napier88 does not provide subtyping and therefore the focus here is on first and second-order information hiding as well as on the use of second-order information hiding to implement database viewing mechanisms.

5.1 First-Order Information Hiding

First-order information hiding is achieved by allowing access only to a procedural interface that operates over the hidden data. In Napier88, which has first-class procedure values and block-style scoping, access to the data may be removed simply by its name becoming unavailable (out of scope).

As an introductory example consider a random number generator for which the Napier88 code is given in Figure 5.1. This is written as a generator procedure, *randomGenerator*, which takes an integer seed, *seed*, and returns a procedure value that will yield a sequence of random numbers when repeatedly called. The returned procedure uses a value, *hiddenValue*, that is encapsulated in its closure. This value is out of scope at the outermost level but still available for use within the inner procedure. Thus the value is hidden, protected and only available for use through the procedural interface. That means that it can only be manipulated through that interface and not in unintended ways. The typing of Napier88 ensures that pointers to internal values cannot be constructed, thereby preventing disallowed operations.

```
let randomGenerator = proc (seed : int → proc (→ int))
begin
let hiddenValue := seed
proc (→ int)
begin
    hiddenValue := (519 * hiddenValue) rem 8192
    hiddenValue
end
end
let random = randomGenerator (2111)
let firstRandomNumber = random ()
let secondRandomNumber = random ()
```

Fig. 5.1. A random number generator.

A more sophisticated example of first-order information hiding is that of a bounded buffer into which users may place and obtain messages. The bounded buffer is intended to be used by concurrent threads and therefore access to the buffer is synchronised.

```
type boundedBuffer [t] is structure (get : proc (→ t) ; put : proc (t))

type Semaphore is structure (wait, signal : proc ())

project PS() as X onto
env :   use X with Library, User : env in
        use Library with Concurrency : env in
        use Concurrency with semaphoreGen : proc (int → Semaphore) in
begin
        in User
        let bBGen = proc [t] (bufferSize : int ; initV : t → boundedBuffer [t])
        begin
                let ringBuffer = vector 1 to bufferSize of initV
                let avail = semaphoreGen (bufferSize)
                let mutex = semaphoreGen (1)
                let empty = semaphoreGen (0)
                let getPtr := 1 ; let putPtr := 1

                let Get = proc (→ t)
                begin
                        empty (wait) () ; mutex (wait) ()
                        let result := ringBuffer (getPtr)
                        getPtr := getPtr rem bufferSize + 1
                        mutex (signal) ()
                        avail (signal) ()
                        result
                end

                let Put = proc (message : t)
                begin
                        avail (wait) () ; mutex (wait) ()
                        ringBuffer (putPtr) := message
                        putPtr := putPtr rem bufferSize + 1
                        mutex (signal) ()
                        empty (signal) ()
                end
                boundedBuffer [t] (Get, Put)
        end
end
default : { }
```

Fig. 5.2. A synchronised polymorphic ring buffer generator.

Concurrency control in Napier88 will be covered later and it is sufficient here to use semaphores, which are provided by standard procedures in the environment, for synchronisation. Figure 5.2 illustrates how the bounded buffer may be implemented in Napier88. The example is polymorphic in that the generating procedure, *bBGen*, will produce buffers of any type. The implementation of the buffer (a vector), the semaphores and the buffer pointers are hidden in the closures of the generated procedures. The result of the generating procedure is a structure which contains one procedure to obtain a value from the buffer, *get*, and one procedure, *put*, to place a value in the buffer. The generating procedure is placed in the *User* environment in the persistent store.

Figure 5.3 demonstrates how the polymorphic bounded buffer generator may be used. First it is identified in the persistent store and then initialised to operate on strings. The buffer is initialised to 500 elements in size, each containing the null string. The procedures in the structure are renamed locally for succinctness. Notice that all the details of the implementation are hidden behind the procedural interface and not even mentioned in this code.

```
type boundedBuffer [t] is structure (get : proc (→ t) ; put : proc (t))

project PS () as X onto
env :   use X with User : env in
        use User with bBGen : proc [t] (int, t → boundedBuffer [t]) in
begin
        let thisBuffer = bBGen [string] (500, "")
        let get = thisBuffer (get) ; let put = thisBuffer (put)
        put ("Ron Morrison") ; put ("Richard Connor")
        let first = get () ; ...
end
default : { }
```

Fig. 5.3. Using the ring buffer.

The bounded buffer is designed to provide concurrent access. This has not been shown here as it requires threads which are the subject of a later section.

5.2 Second-order Information Hiding

Second-order information hiding differs from first-order information hiding in that it does not restrict access to the protected values, but instead abstracts over the type in order to restrict the operations allowed on the values. Thus the protected values may be manipulated by some basic operations, such as assignment and equality, but their full set of operations are not allowed due to the abstracted type view. This allows the implementation values to be safely placed in the interface with their abstracted type along with the procedures which manipulate them.

Napier88 provides existentially quantified types (abstract data types) to implement second-order information hiding. To illustrate their utility, we will use the example of a banking system, taken from [10], in which customers have access to their accounts through autoteller machines. The autoteller machines have different styles of access to accounts. A customer's own bank may have full access to an account whereas another bank may not access the customer's account balance, but must know if a withdrawal can be made. The purpose of using second-order information hiding is to allow the autotellers to manipulate the account through its abstract interface without knowing its concrete implementation.

The local autoteller machine is accessed through the following abstract interface:

failAc	is the value returned by *getAc* if a password check fails
getAc	is a procedure which takes as input an account number, and a password and provided that the password is correct, returns the account, otherwise it returns the fail value *failAc*
withdraw	is a procedure which removes the amount specified from the account. If there are insufficient funds, the procedure returns **false** otherwise it returns **true**
balance	is a procedure which returns the balance in the account
olimit	is a procedure which returns the account overdraft limit
transfer	is a procedure that transfers an amount from one account to another

This interface is captured in the declaration of the type to represent the local teller.

```
type localTeller is abstype [absAc](
        failAc      : absAc;
        getAc: proc (int, string → absAc);
        withdraw    : proc (int, absAc → bool);
        balance     : proc (absAc → int);
        olimit: proc (absAc → int);
        transfer    : proc (int, absAc, absAc))
```

Notice that an instance of the hidden type, *absAc*, sometimes referred to as the witness type, is available in the interface of the abstract data type. However all that is known about the type is that it exists, not how it is implemented.

Figure 5.4 defines a procedure that returns a value of the *localTeller* abstract type. This procedure, *createLocalAutoTeller*, has to define a concrete representation for the account and also to define the procedures that operate over the account. The representation of the account needs to hold the balance, the overdraft limit and the pin number (password) for the account. This is done using a structure type, *account*, with obvious field names. Once the procedures have been defined then the values are made into the abstract data type to hide the implementation details. For simplicity, details of synchronisation for concurrent access are omitted.

The *getAc* procedure uses a data structure, *lookup*, which when indexed by the account number yields the account. For brevity the definition of this data structure has not been defined here but may be implemented by any standard technique such as B-trees, hashing, etc. This data structure may also be protected by defining it within the closure of the *createLocalAutoTeller* procedure. This would, however, restrict its use to that procedure and a more general solution would be to encapsulate the data structure in a procedure that requires a password in order to obtain it. The technique is demonstrated later.

```
let createLocalAutoTeller = proc (→ localTeller)
begin
    type account is structure (Balance, Limit : int ; Pin : string)

    let failAc = account (0, 0,"")              ! This is a fail value.

    let getAc = proc (accNumber : int ; passwd : string → account)
    ! Look up the account number, check user password and if the
    ! password matches the password in the database return the account,
    ! otherwise return a fail value.
    begin
        let new = lookup (accNumber)
        if new (Pin) = passwd then new else failAc
    end

    let withdraw = proc (debit : int ; ac : account → bool)
    ! Withdraw debit pounds from ac.
    begin
        let result = ac (Balance) - debit
        if result > ac (Limit) and debit > 0 then
        begin
            ac (Balance) := result
            true
        end else false
    end

    let balance = proc (ac : account → int) ; ac (Balance)
    ! Return the balance of account ac.

    let olimit = proc (ac : account → int) ; ac (Limit)
    ! Return the credit limit of account ac.

    let transfer = proc (amount : int ; from, to : account)
    if amount > 0 and from (Balance) - amount > from (Limit) do
    begin
        from (Balance) := from (Balance) - amount
        to (Balance) := to (Balance) + amount
    end

    ! Make the abstract data type
    localTeller [account] (failAc, getAc, withdraw, balance, olimit, transfer)
end
```

Fig. 5.4. Creating the local autoteller abstract data type.

Figure 5.5 shows how the abstract data type may be used to retire with one million pounds.

```
use createLocalAutoTeller () as X in
begin
        let this = X (getAc) (45, "Ronald")
        if this ≠ X (failAc) then
        begin
                let getMoney = X (withdraw) (1000000, this)
                ! Run off and retire.
        end else ...
        ...
end
```

Fig. 5.5. Using the auto teller.

The interface also contains a procedure which allows a customer with two accounts to transfer money from one to the other via the local autoteller. Figure 5.6 illustrates how this might be done.

```
use createLocalAutoTeller () as X in
begin
        let mine = X (getAc) (45, "Ronald")
        let myOther = X (getAc) (46, "Ann")
        if this ≠ X (failAc) and myOther ≠ X (failAc) then
        begin
                X (transfer) (1000000, myOther, mine)
                ! Get the wife's money
        end else ...
        ...
end
```

Fig. 5.6. Using the auto teller *transfer* procedure.

An important difference between the procedure, *transfer*, and the others is that it is defined over more than one object of the witness type. Although the witness type is abstracted over, the values are bound to the same definition, and so are restricted to being the same implementation type. The procedure is written over two values of the same type. If it were not, a type checking error would be detected in the attempt to create the abstract type.

The *transfer* procedure illustrates a major difference in power between first-order and second-order information hiding. With second-order, a type is abstracted over, and procedures may be defined over this type. With first-order hiding, it is the object itself which is hidden within its procedural interface. Procedures which operate over more than one such object may not be defined sensibly within this interface. Therefore any operations defined over two instances must be written at a higher level, using the interface. At best this creates syntactic noise and is inefficient at execution time forcing the encapsulation to export more primitive operations—a well known problem with object models. It also means that such operations are defined in the module which uses the abstract objects, rather than the module which creates them. Some examples, such as the autoteller, are not possible to write without changing the original interface.

5.3 Viewing mechanisms

Viewing mechanisms are traditionally used to provide security and information hiding. Indeed, in some relational database systems, such as INGRES [80], a relational viewing mechanism is the only security mechanism available. A view relation is one which is defined over others to provide a subset of the database, usually at the same level of abstraction. A slightly higher level may be achieved by allowing relations to include derived data, for example, an age field in a view might abstract over a date of birth field in the schema.

```
let createAutoTellerEnv = proc (envir : env)
begin
        type account is structure (Balance, Limit : int ; Pin : string)

        let failAc = account (0, 0,"")
        in envir let failAc = failAc

        in envir
        let getAc = proc (accNumber : int ; passwd : string → account)
        begin
                ... ! as before
        end

        in envir let withdraw = proc (debit : int ; ac : account → bool)
        begin
                ... ! as before
        end

        in envir let balance = proc (ac : account → int) ; ac (Balance)

        in envir let olimit = proc (ac : account → int) ; ac (Limit)

        in envir let transfer = proc (amount : int ; from, to : account)
                ... ! as before

        in envir let sufficient = proc (debit : int ; ac : account → bool)
        ! Return whether or not debit pounds
        ! may be withdrawn from account ac.
        ac (Balance) - debit > ac (Limit)
end
```

Fig. 5.7. Placing the auto teller values in an environment.

Protection provided by view relations is often restricted to simple information hiding by means of projection and selection. For example, if a clerk is not permitted to access a date of birth field, then the projected data may contain all the attributes with the exception of this one. If the clerk may not access any data about people under the age of twenty-one, then the view relation will be that formed by the appropriate selection.

Read-only security may be obtained in some database systems by restricting updates on view relations. Although this restriction is normally due to conceptual and implementation problems, rather than being a deliberate feature of a database system design, it may be used to some effect for this purpose. Some systems, for example IMS [81], go further than this, and the database programmer can allow or disallow insertions, deletions, or modifications of data in view relations. This allows a fine grain of control for data protection purposes.

Views on persistent data may be constructed using abstract data types in Napier88. The technique involves storing the raw data in the persistent environment and allows access by two mechanisms. The first kind of access is by password where the database administrator may gain access to the raw data on presenting the correct password. The second kind of access is through an abstract data type. The database administrator prepares these abstract data types by placing the raw data and the procedures that operate over it in the interface of an abstract data type. These views may then be stored in the persistent environment for others to use. Data may appear in more than one view and indeed in bulk data types, such as images, overlapping views on the same values are possible.

```
let makeProtectedBank = proc (password : string)
begin
        let ps = PS ()

        project ps as X onto
        env : use X with User, Library : env in
            use Library with Environment : env in
            use Environment with environment : proc (→ env) in
            begin
                    let new = environment () ; let fail = environment ()

                    createAutoTellerEnv (new)

                    in User let protectedBank =
                            proc (attempt : string → env)
                            if attempt = password then new else fail
            end
        default : { } ! This is executed if the projection fails
end
```

Fig. 5.8. Placing the protected data in the persistent store.

The first step in constructing views is placing the raw data and operations in an environment. Figure 5.7 shows how this may be done through the *createAutoTellerEnv* procedure which takes an environment as a parameter and places the interface procedures in that environment. The *lookup* data structure could also be safely placed in this environment. A new procedure *sufficient* determines whether an account contains sufficient funds to allow a withdrawal.

The second step in creating views is to place the raw data environment in the persistent store. This is done by creating a new environment, using the *createAutoTellerEnv* procedure to place the raw data in it, and encapsulating it in a procedure that will only yield the data on the presentation of the correct password. This final procedure is placed in the *User* environment. The technique is demonstrated in Figure 5.8.

To construct a view, the database administrator (the person with the correct password), accesses the raw data and places it in an abstract data type. Figure 5.9 shows how this may be done for the local teller view. It leaves the view in the *User* environment under the name *localTView*.

```
type localTeller is abstype [absAc](
        failAc: absAc;
        getAc : proc (int, string → absAc);
        withdraw    : proc (int, absAc → bool);
        balance     : proc (absAc → int);
        olimit : proc (absAc → int);
        transfer    : proc (int, absAc, absAc))

type account is structure (Balance, Limit : int ; Pin : string)

let createLocalAutoTeller = proc ()
    project PS () as X onto
    env : use X with User : env in
        use User with protectedBank : proc (string → env) in
        begin
            let bank = protectedBank ("Correct Password")
            use bank with failAc :      account;
                          getAc :       proc (int, string → account);
                          withdraw :    proc (int, account → bool);
                          balance :     proc (account → int);
                          olimit :      proc (account → int);
                          transfer :    proc (int, account, account) in
            begin
                in User let localTView = localTeller [account]
                (failAc, getAc, withdraw, balance, olimit, transfer)
            end
        end
    default : {} ! This is executed if the projection fails
```

Fig. 5.9. Constructing the local teller abstract view.

Other views may be created by the same mechanism. Figure 5.10 shows how a remote teller view might be created. Remember that the remote teller cannot transfer money from one account to another and cannot inspect the balance or overdraft limit of the account. However it can find out if there are sufficient funds to make a withdrawal through the *sufficient* procedure in its interface.

```
type remoteTeller is abstype [absAc](
          failAc        : absAc;
          getAc         : proc (int, string → absAc);
          withdraw      : proc (int, absAc→ bool);
          sufficient    : proc (int, absAc→ bool))

type account is structure (Balance, Limit : int ; Pin : string)

let createRemoteAutoTeller = proc ()
      project PS () as X onto
      env : use X with User : env in
          use User with protectedBank : proc (string → env) in
          begin
               let bank = protectedBank ("Correct Password")
               use bank with failAc :      account;
                             getAc :       proc (int, string → account);
                             withdraw :    proc (int, account → bool);
                             sufficient :  proc (int, account → bool) in
               begin
                     in User let remoteTView = remoteTeller [account]
                             (failAc, getAc, withdraw, sufficient)
               end
          end
      default : { } ! This is executed if the projection fails
```

Fig. 5.10. Constructing the remote teller view.

Figure 5.11 illustrates the overall software technique for creating views of data. The raw data and the procedures that operate over the data are stored in the persistent environment and used to construct views as they are required by applications. The view construction is performed by the database administrator who has access to the data through a procedure closure protected by password. Components of the views may be used to construct other views and thus views of views may be constructed to any level of abstraction. Tools to aid the Database Administrator that use a high-level notation and automatically construct the abstract data type corresponding to a view may be built in Napier88 using reflection.

It is interesting to compare this style of encapsulation and information hiding with that of object oriented database systems. In the latter the raw data may only be viewed through one interface and the information is essentially trapped in the object once instantiated. In this technique, the data is placed in an object (view) dynamically when the data modelling requires it. Thus the encapsulation technique is compliant with, and may respond to, the differing and evolving needs of different applications and not with some fixed data model defined *a priori*.

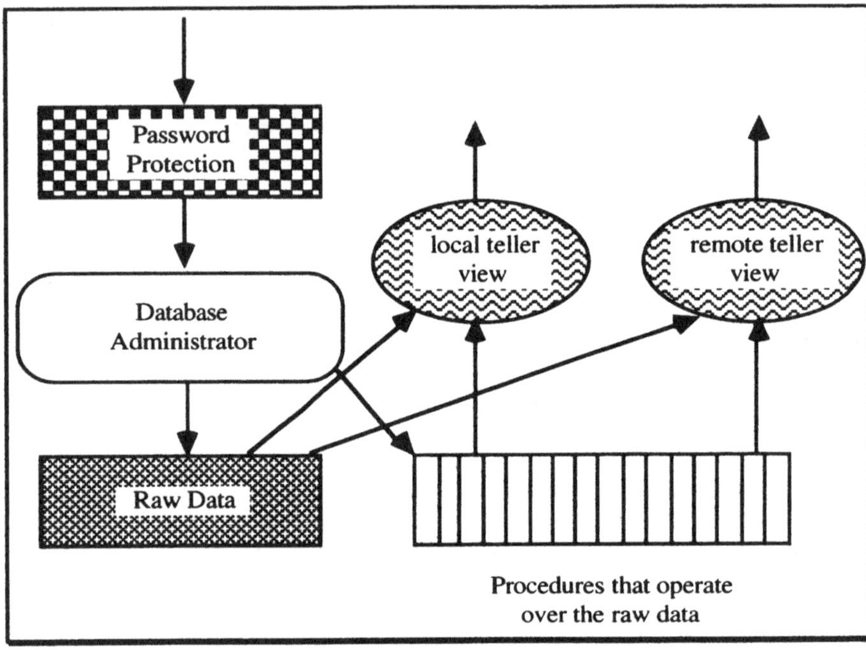

Fig. 5.11. Views over the persistent store.

The diagram signifies that the database administrator may gain access to the raw data through the correct use of a password and may then use this data to provide abstract views for the user. The final advantage of this style of viewing is that it is statically type checked once the views have been constructed.

A further example of protection is that used in the Napier88 programming environment, as outlined in Section 8.4. This utilises the dynamic witness types of Napier88 to provide the power of capabilities [11].

6 Controlled System Evolution

Evolution is inevitable in persistent systems since the people who use the data, the data itself and the uses to which the data is put, all change with time. Systems which cannot accommodate evolution become obsolete as they can no longer meet the changing needs of the applications and user community that they support. A requirement of a persistent system, like Napier88, which contains data, programs and meta-data, is that the evolution should be controllable from within the system. Most importantly, any alteration to the system should not necessarily require total rebuilding. That is, evolution should be incremental since the cost of rebuilding may be prohibitive.

System evolution is caused by changes to the data, the programs which use the data and the meta-data. Changes to program and data with the invariant of fixed meta-data are normally handled by updates to the persistent store. This, however, requires the preparation of new programs, compilation and binding into existing data before updating the persistent store. This non-trivial task is accommodated in Napier88 by a technique called Linguistic Reflection [82] which is described later in this section. A more difficult problem is changes to the meta-data while keeping all the existing programs and data consistent with the semantics of the change [21]. Napier88 provides a number of mechanisms for controlling the evolution of data, programs and meta-data. These include structural type equivalence, the infinite union types **any** and **env**, and linguistic reflection.

6.1 Typing Issues

Separately prepared data and programs require a common mechanism for ensuring that the manner in which they operate is consistent with one another. In a strongly typed system the mechanism is that of type equivalence checking. Two models of type equivalence are in common use: name equivalence and structural equivalence [76]. In name equivalence, the types have the same name defined in a common schema. In structural equivalence, the types have the same structure when compared by an equivalence algorithm. The commonality in this case is the equivalence algorithm. It is shown in [3] that while name equivalence is easier to implement and more efficient it still has to use structural checks to provide important facilities such as schema merging. On the other hand structural equivalence, generally more flexible and less efficient, can often achieve the same performance as name equivalence. Napier88 uses structural equivalence which means that programs and data may evolve without reference to a common schema. Thus data or programs in one store may be copied and used in another as long as a specification of their type can be found. This functionality replaces the requirement for a global schema. Different stores may now evolve separately and still have the ability to be used compatibly.

The infinite union types **any** and **env** may also be used to control system evolution. Remember that the persistent store has a most general dynamically checked type, **any**. To use the values within the store, the dynamic type must be projected onto the specific type for the store. This specific type may in turn contain further instances of **any**. Descriptive changes to the store may be performed by injecting new values into these further instances of **any**. Subsequent use requires the new type descriptions.

This mechanism occurs implicitly in standard database interfaces. When a program opens a database it specifies a schema. During the opening operation the schema used during the program's compilation is compared with the database's current schema. Arbitrary changes may have been made to the database using a schema editor between the compilation and this execution. If the schema no longer matches the expectations established at compilation-time then an error is signalled. Thus, internally the run-time system is able to treat the database as having a dynamic type and to perform a dynamic verification that the expected and actual types match.

In general the persistent store is a graph of objects that has one root of type **any**. Values of type **any** are first class and may also be constituent parts of any other type. Before they can be used with their specific type they also have to be projected onto that type. This allows programs to specify only the part of the schema that they require up to a point of dynamic checking. As a consequence a schema, which is represented by an arbitrarily large collection of mutually referencing types, may scale well since each independently checkable partition of the schema specification is bounded by the dynamic types. Incremental schema changes inject new values into an **any** and the type of the rest of the specification remains unchanged. In addition, where an **any** encapsulates the type, type checking is postponed until required. Hence excessive type checking costs on start-up are avoided. This is illustrated in Figure 6.1.

```
type Address is structure (name : string ; ... ; extra : any)

project PS () as X onto
Address :       ...
default :       ...
```

Fig. 6.1. A partial use of types.

In Figure 6.1, the *extra* field is not used and the specification of its exact type is unnecessary. In figure 6.2, the *extra* field is required and has the type *extraInfo*. Where programs do not use the *extra* field the type *extraInfo* does not have to be declared. Thus only part of the type structure need be specified, the part of interest to the program, as shown in Figure 6.1.

```
type Address is structure (name : string ; ... ; extra : any)

project PS () as X onto
Address :
        begin
                let this = X (extra)                ! this is of type any
                type extraInfo is structure (idNo : int ; spouse : Address)
                ! Programs not using the extra field do not need to specify
                ! extraInfo
                project this as Y onto
                        ! Type check using extraInfo
                extraInfo : ...
                ...
                default :       ...
        end
default :       ...
```

Fig. 6.2. After an incremental schema change.

The use of dynamic types allows the data model to evolve without recompiling all the programs that refer to the data. For example, if the *extraInfo* type is altered, then only programs that use that type need be altered. Thus, explicit dynamic types allow partial specification of the overall structure of the data (schema) and facilitate the evolution of the data, without having to alter programs that do not make use of the evolutionary changes.

The data type **env** is also dynamically typed and may be use in the same manner as type **any** above. In addition the **project** clause permits a partial specification of the bindings thereby allowing programmers to ignore bindings that are not used by them. Programs may therefore remain constant under evolution of bindings which they do not use. This is a very powerful generalisation of the data independence mechanisms pioneered as relational view mechanisms.

6.2 Type Safe Linguistic Reflection

Type safe linguistic reflection is defined in [82] as the ability of a running program to generate new program fragments and to integrate these into its own execution. This is the basis for system evolution in the Napier88 system.

Napier88 uses run-time linguistic reflection [83-85] which is concerned with the construction and binding of new components with existing components. The technique involves the use of a compiler that can be called dynamically to compile newly generated program fragments, and a linking mechanism to bind these new program fragments into the running program. Type checking occurs during both compilation and binding.

Type safe linguistic reflection has been used to attain high levels of genericity [86, 87], accommodate changes in systems [83, 88]. implement data models [66, 67, 89], optimise implementations [90-92] and validate specifications [93, 94]. The importance of the technique is that it provides a uniform mechanism for software production and evolution. A formal description of linguistic reflection is given in [82].

The example in Figure 6.3 shows a simple generator which produces code to write out the value of a named string field of a given record. Although somewhat contrived in order to keep the example small, this does demonstrate a problem which requires reflection.

The difficulty for non-reflective solutions is that the record field name is not known until run-time, while for the record dereference operation the field name must be known at compile-time to allow static type checking. The reflective approach gets around this by performing compilation once the field name is input, so that the field name is known statically with respect to that compilation. The compiler itself is a value in the persistent store and may be called as a procedure by any program.

The program starts by defining representations for code fragments and for type representations within the language. For simplicity here string code representations are used; another possibility would be to use parse trees. Details of the type representations are omitted.

The generator *writeFieldGen* is then defined. It is a procedure that takes as parameters a record, injected into the infinite union type **any**, and a representation of a field name. The result is the representation of a code fragment. The infinite union type is used for the record parameter so that the generator can accept records of any type.

Inside the generator the first step is to obtain a representation of the type of the record, using the standard procedure *getTypeRep*. The generator then performs a series of checks: that the first parameter is indeed of a record type; that the record type contains the required field name; and finally that the field has type **string**. If any of these checks fails an error is reported and an empty code fragment returned, otherwise the result code is formed by concatenating together a number of components. The result represents a procedure which takes a structure of the appropriate type as its parameter and writes out the field. The first part of the result code is a local definition of the record type so that it can be used in the procedure header. This involves transforming the type representation into a code fragment, performed by the procedure *typeRepToString*. The rest of the result contains the procedure header and the body which simply dereferences the record and writes out the field.

```
type CodeRep is string ! For simplicity.
type TypeRep is ...

let nilCodeRep = "" ; let newline = "'n"

project PS () as X onto
env :    use X with User, Library : env in
         use Library with IO, Reflection : env in
         use IO with writeString : proc (string) in
         use Reflection with getTypeRep : proc (any → TypeRep);
                 isRecord : proc (TypeRep → bool);
                 containsField :      proc (TypeRep, CodeRep → bool);
                 fieldType :          proc (TypeRep, string → TypeRep);
                 isString :           proc (TypeRep → bool);
                 typeRepToString :    proc (TypeRep → string) in

in User
let writeFieldGen = proc (aRecord : any; fieldName : CodeRep → CodeRep)
begin
    ! Get representation of type.
    let t = getTypeRep (aRecord)

    ! Check that the any contains a record.
    if isRecord (t) then
        ! Check that the record type contains the given field.
        if containsField (t, fieldName) then
            ! Check that the field has type string.
            if isString (fieldType (t, fieldName)) then
                ! The source code produced.
                "type RecordType is " ++ typeRepToString (t) ++ newline ++
                "proc (instance : RecordType)" ++ newline ++
                "writeString (instance (" ++ fieldName ++ "))"
            else{ writeString ("field is not of type string"); nilCodeRep}
        else{ writeString ("type does not contain given field") ; nilCodeRep}
    else{ writeString ("not a record type") ; nilCodeRep}
end
default : { }
```

Fig. 6.3. A reflective generator.

Figure 6.4 shows an example use of the generator. A particular record type, *Person*, and an instance, *ron*, are defined. The user is then prompted to enter a field name as a string. The generator is then called, passing it the record instance and the field name representation. If no errors occur during generation, the generated code is then compiled with the standard procedure *compile*. Since the type of the result of a compilation is not known in advance, *compile* returns an *any*. This is then projected onto the expected type which is a procedure that takes a single parameter of type *Person*. If the projection matches, the compiled procedure is then available for use as *writeAddress*. Otherwise the compilation has either failed or returned a result of a different type: this implies an error in the definition of the generator.

To save space a number of simplifications have been made in this example. The most significant of these is the omission of details of binding to undefined identifiers in the generated code, in this case *writeString*. In reality the generated code fragment would also contain a specification of its location and type in the store.

```
type Person is structure (name, address : string ; age : int)
type CodeRep is string

let ps = PS ()

project ps as X onto
env : use X with Library, User : env in
        use Library with Compiler, IO : env in
        use Compiler with compile : proc (CodeRep → any) in
        use IO with readString : proc (→ string);
                    writeString : proc (string) in
        use User with writeFieldGen : proc (any, CodeRep → CodeRep) in
begin
    let ron = Person ("ron", "8 Trinity Place", 42)

    writeString ("which field?")
    let theFieldName = readString ()

    let writeAddressSource = writeFieldGen (any (ron), theFieldName)

    if writeAddressSource ≠ nilCodeRep do
    begin
        project compile (writeAddressSource) as writeAddress onto
            proc (Person)  : writeAddress (ron)
        default            : writeString ("error in generated code")
    end
end
default : { }
```

Fig. 6.4. Use of a generator.

Binding to existing values in the persistent store is a particular case of the more general problem of specifying a program's execution environment. For example, some application code which generates the new code might need to equip that code with a value over which it can compute. One approach is to generate code which constructs the value each time the general code is run. This makes the generated code more complex and less efficient. An alternative is to construct that value at generation time and leave it in the persistent store for use when the generated code is executed. This could be achieved by generating code to extract the value from the persistent store every time the generated code is executed but can be simplified and made more efficient where the generator can produce hyper-programs [84].

The detection and reporting of errors in both generators and generated code poses many challenges, in particular giving the user intelligible reports about errors which occur in generated code, the existence of which the user may be unaware.

The example shows the definition and use of a generator within a single program. A generator may also be defined and made available in the persistent store, from where it is used many times in different environments. In addition, the compiled result obtained from a particular use of the generator may itself be stored and used repeatedly. In this way the costs of generation and compilation are amortised over many uses.

7 Concurrency Control and Transactions

Traditionally the database and programming language communities have taken different approaches to concurrency control. In programming languages, concurrency control is based upon the concept of the co-ordination of a set of co-operating processes by synchronisation. Language constructs such as semaphores [95], monitors [96], mutual exclusion [97], path expressions [98] and message passing [99] have been provided to support this concept. By contrast, in databases, concurrency is viewed as a system efficiency activity which allows parallel execution and parallel access to the data. However, each database process may have to suffer abortion in order to sustain the illusion of non-interference. The key concept in databases is that of serialisability [100] which has led to the notion of atomic transactions [100, 101] supported by locking [100] or optimistic concurrency control methods [101].

In both cases the user must attempt to understand the computations in terms of some global cohesion. In programming languages the emphasis is on synchronisation and the overall cohesion is understood in terms of the conflation of all the synchronisations. In database systems, global cohesion is understood in terms of the concept of serialisability [100] but includes failure semantics such as aborting transactions with rollback. Apart from some AI languages, rollback to an earlier state has not been provided in programming languages.

Figure 7.1, taken from [27], illustrates a spectrum of understandability from the points of view of programming language and database users. This represents the fact that databases tend to use atomic transactions to enforce isolation rather than co-ordinated sharing. Programming languages promote co-operation. Thus in integrating databases and programming languages, the designer must unify these established and provenly useful positions. The impetus does not altogether come from persistence however, since languages that support atomic transactions and databases that require non-serialisable and designer transactions [102-104] have been identified as necessary by their respective communities.

Concurrency control facilities have not been built into the Napier88 language. Instead they are provided by a number of mechanisms in the persistent environment. This design decision is in line with the V-shape architecture described earlier in which concurrency control is provided at the highest possible level in order to promote flexibility. To facilitate co-operative concurrency a thread abstract data type is provided for concurrent execution and a semaphore package for synchronisation. For competitive and designer transactions, the Napier88 system will use CACS specifications [28, 105] which map onto different store implementations. Thus the implementation technology will be tailored to the application. It is beyond the scope of this paper to describe the CACS specification method and therefore we concentrate on the use of threads and semaphores.

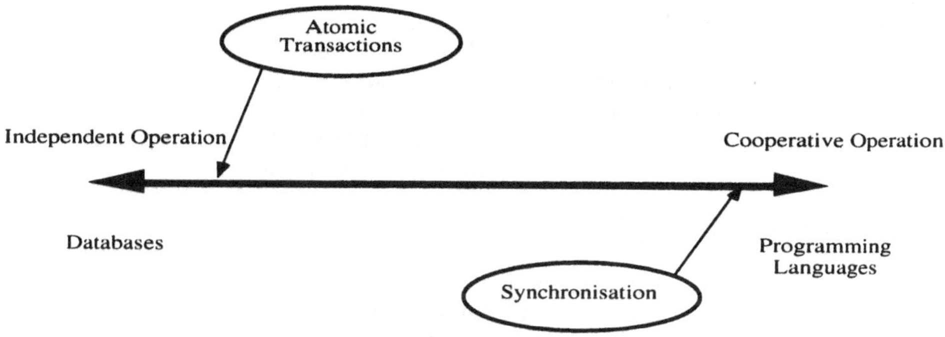

Fig. 7.1. A spectrum of understandability.

The thread package is contained in the *Concurrency* environment and has the following type.

```
type ThreadPack is abstype [thread] (
        start : proc (proc () → thread) ;
        getCurrentThread : proc (→ thread);
        getAllThreads : proc (→ *thread);
        kill, restart, suspend : proc (thread);
        getStatus : proc (thread → string);
        getParent : proc (thread → variant (present : thread ; absent : nil))
```

The package contains procedures to start a thread, to find the identity of the executing thread, to kill, restart and suspend threads, to get the status of a thread and to find the parent of a thread. To start a thread, the start procedure is given as a parameter a second procedure that will execute as the thread. The start procedure returns the identity of the started thread. Control of the thread may be performed through this identity.

The *Concurrency* environment also provides a procedure that takes an integer parameter which is the initial value of the semaphore and returns two procedures, *wait* and *signal*, within a structure that operate over the semaphore.

The use of threads and semaphores is illustrated by a solution to the Dining Philosophers' problem [97]. The solution, shown in Figure 7.2, uses a number of formatting and I/O procedures from the persistent environment.

There are five philosophers each requiring two forks to eat but there are only five forks. The action of obtaining a fork is atomic and therefore protected by a binary semaphore. To avoid deadlock a philosopher must first enter the dining room which is protected by a semaphore with an initial value of four, thereby ensuring that no more than four philosophers may enter at the same time. This is the Butler solution.

```
type ThreadPack is abstype [thread] ...
type Semaphore is structure (wait, signal : proc ())

project PS() as X onto
env :   use X with Library : env in
        use Library with Concurrency, Format, IO : env in
        use Format with iformat : proc (int → string) in
        use IO with writeString : proc (string) in
        use Concurrency with threadPackage : ThreadPack;
                semaphoreGen : proc (int → Semaphore) in
begin
    use threadPackage as Y [thread] in
    begin
        let room = semaphoreGen (4)
        let forkSemaphore = proc (i : int → Semaphore) ; semaphoreGen (1)
        let forks = vector 0 to 4 using forkSemaphore
        let philosopherGenerator = proc (i : int → thread)
        begin
            let this = "Philosopher " ++ iformat (i)
            let philosopher = proc ()
            while true do
            begin
                writeString (this ++ " is thinking'n") ! Think
                room (wait) () ; writeString (this++ " has entered the room'n")

                forks (i, wait) () ; writeString (this ++ " has one fork'n")
                forks ((i + 1) rem 5, wait) ()
                writeString (this ++ " has two forks and is eating'n")

                forks (i, signal) ()
                writeString (this ++ " has put down one fork'n")
                forks ((i + 1) rem 5, signal) ()
                writeString (this ++ " has put down the second fork'n")

                room (signal) () ; writeString (this ++ " has left the room'n")
            end
            X (start) (philosopher) ; writeString (this ++ " is born'n")
        end
        let philosophers = vector 0 to 4 using philosopherGenerator
    end
end
default : { }
```

Fig. 7.2. The dining philosophers with annotation.

The forks are modelled by a vector of semaphore packages where each element of a vector contains a structure containing two synchronisation procedures. The vector is initialised using the *forkSemaphore* procedure. For each element of the vector the procedure is called with the index of the element as a parameter. The result of the procedure activation is used to initialise the element. Thus the following code segment would initialise each element of the *forks* procedure to a structure containing two procedures implementing a binary semaphore.

```
type Semaphore is structure (wait, signal : proc ())

let forkSemaphore = proc (i : int → Semaphore)
                        semaphoreGen (1)

let forks = vector 0 to 4 using forkSemaphore
```

The method of storing threads in the persistent store is the same as for any other data value. That is, to persist the thread must be reachable from the root of persistence.

8 Programming within the Persistent Environment

Napier88 is a complete self-contained persistent programming system. and as such it supports the use of software throughout its life cycle. For this the system provides an interactive programming environment which is implemented in Napier88 itself, together with facilities for composing, executing and storing persistent programs.

8.1 The Standard Library

In common with many programming systems, Napier88 is supplied with a library of pre-written code and values. Since it is an orthogonally persistent system, this library is supplied as a populated persistent store, as a collection of persistent procedures and values [42]. The programmer uses the library facilities by writing programs which bind to the appropriate components. Some components in the populated store are used by the system to support its own activities and are not accessible by users.

Table 2. Standard store contents.

name	environment contents
Error	error handling procedures which are called when errors occur during the execution of Napier88 programs
External	facilities provided by other sites
Library	standard procedures and other data which may be used in Napier88 programs
User	available for user data

The persistent store may be accessed from Napier88 programs by calling the procedure *PS* as described in Section 3. In the standard release store the persistent root is an environment initially containing the following environments:

The initial structure of *Error* and *Library* is standardised, whereas the contents of *User* and *External* are specific to a particular installation and other bindings may be added to this standard environment, for example [77]. The items in the library include procedures for:

- compiling Napier88 programs;
- browsing the persistent store;
- performing I/O and arithmetic;
- constructing graphical user interfaces;
- controlling concurrent threads;
- accessing other Napier88 stores; and
- other utilities.

The library also includes data values which may be updated in order to modify the default behaviour of certain procedures. The initial environment structure of the standard library was shown in Figure 3.3. The names of most of the environments in the standard library should be self-explanatory. Some of the more significant are:

Compiler: this environment contains procedures which provide various interfaces to the Napier88 compiler. The simplest is a procedure which takes a string representing a Napier88 program and returns either an error message or a procedure which will execute that program.

Concurrency: this environment contains procedures to manipulate light-weight threads and semaphores [36].

Distribution: this environment contains procedures which can be used to scan the contents of other Napier88 stores and to copy values from them to the local store. A low-level socket based communication protocol between stores is also supported [36].

InteractiveEnvironment: this environment contains procedures which provide the interactive programming system described in Section 8.3.

Win: this environment contains procedures for building user interfaces, including window managers, text editors and standard user-interface widgets.

8.2 Hyper-Programming

One way for a Napier88 program to use a library component is for the program to contain a textual specification of the component's expected type and location in the persistent store, as described in Section 3. This specification is then checked against the actual state of the store when the program is executed; a run-time error occurs if the two do not match. The activities required of the programmer are thus firstly to discover the type and location of the required library component, and secondly to write down textual descriptions of these in the program.

Since program representations may be held in the persistent store together with the rest of the persistent data, an alternative programming style called *hyper-programming* is possible. With this style the textual descriptions of library components are replaced by direct links to the components themselves embedded within the program representations [20]. The example in Figure 8.1 shows the code of Figure 5.8 as a hyper-program.

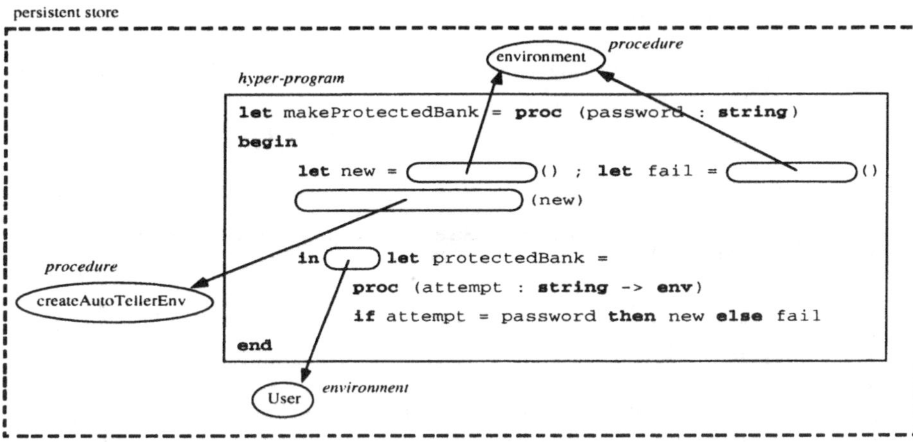

Fig. 8.1. A hyper-program.

The links embedded in the hyper-program are represented by non-textual tokens to allow them to be distinguished from the surrounding text. Note that names for the linked components are no longer necessary. For clarity the components are labelled in the diagram, but these names are not part of the semantics of the hyper-program.

Hyper-programming facilities are used in the persistent programming environment to reduce the need for the programmer to supply textual descriptions of library components. Instead the programmer identifies a component, by means to be described, and then links it into the program under construction. This can lead to a significant reduction in the amount of code written. A hyper-program editor which displays links as light-buttons embedded in the text is supplied.

The hyper-program notation also provides a convenient user-interface representation for procedure values which contain free variables: each free variable is denoted by a light-button in the same way as a linked library component. This enables the system to display the source code of any procedure, even if it has encapsulated state. A flag in the Napier88 compiler specifies whether to retain the source code for a procedure being compiled: if so, the hyper-program source representation is linked to the procedure object, from which it may be later retrieved and displayed. By default this flag is on, so all the library components have their source code attached automatically.

8.3 The Napier88 Programming Environment

The programming environment provides several varieties of window:

- hyper-program editor windows;
- a compilation error display window;
- a browser window; and
- declaration set windows.

8.3.1 Editing Hyper-Programs

Hyper-program windows are created by selecting *New Editor* from the background menu. Each window contains a hyper-program text editing area, a scroll bar and a row of light-buttons. A hyper-program window is shown in Figure 8.2.

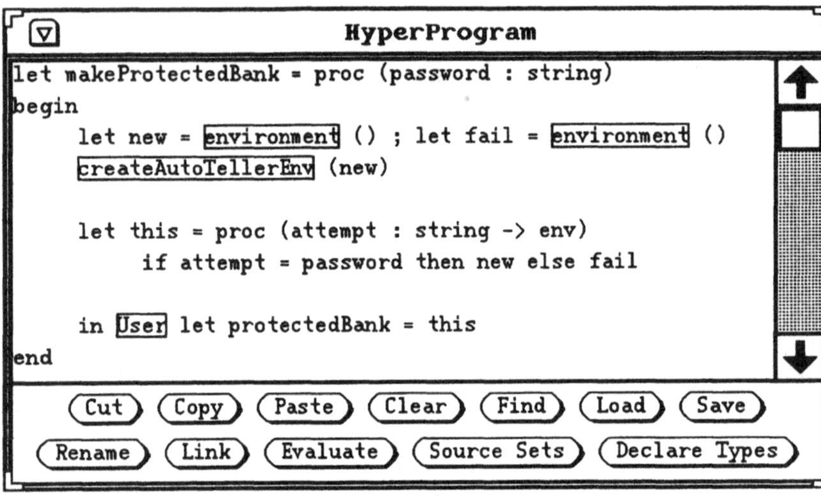

Fig. 8.2. A hyper-program window.

Table 3. Light-button operations in hyper-program window.

operation	action
Link	This inserts a hyper-program link to the currently selected value, location or type. A light-button representing it is inserted into the hyper-program text. The label is the name, if any, associated with the selection. The value, location or type associated with a button can be displayed in the browser window by clicking on the button.
Evaluate	This attempts to compile the currently selected hyper-program text, executes the result if successful, and displays any result in the browser window. If a compilation error occurs the compilation error window is displayed.
Source Sets	This displays a dialogue allowing the source declaration sets to be specified.
Declare Types	This attempts to compile the currently selected hyper-program text and adds any type declarations in scope at the end of the compilation to a selected declaration set.

The editor operations include the usual editing functions together with those described in Table 3.

Components to be linked into a hyper-program are identified by traversing links in the browser window, to be described more fully in Section 8.3.2. This relies on the programmer having some prior knowledge of the library structure or using tools to assist the programmer in finding components [106, 107].

The compilation error window is displayed when compilation errors are encountered in a hyper-program. One sub-window shows the source code with the region of the first error highlighted. The second sub-window shows a message describing the error. When multiple errors are detected the *Next* and *Previous* buttons are used to scroll through the errors. An example is shown in Figure 8.3.

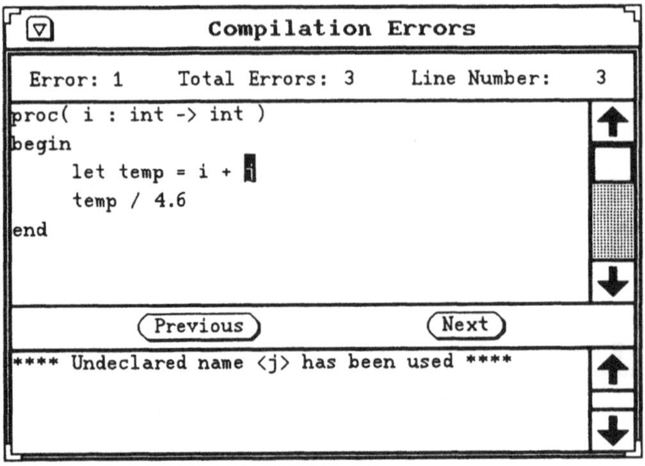

Fig. 8.3. The compilation error window.

8.3.2 The Browser

The browser window is used to display representations of values produced by the evaluation of hyper-programs. The root of the persistent store can be displayed by selecting *Show PS* from the background menu. The form in which a value is represented depends on the type of the value. Integers, reals, strings and booleans are written to the output window.

Each window displayed in the browser window can be selected or deselected by clicking on the border. If the window is not already selected it becomes selected and any other selected windows are deselected. When a window is selected the corresponding value is also considered to be selected: this is of relevance when inserting links into hyper-programs.

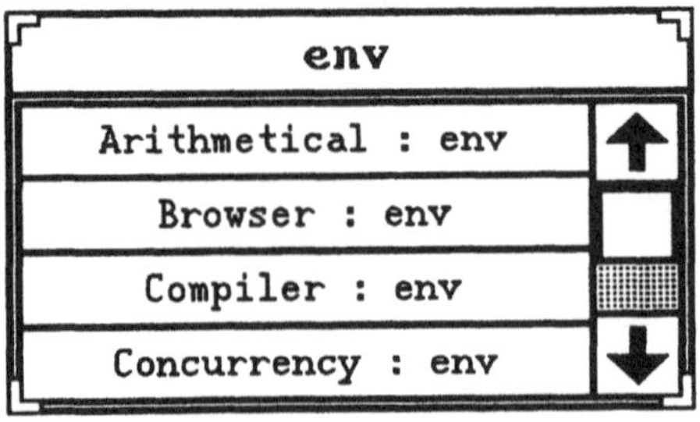

Fig. 8.4. An environment menu.

To show an environment the browser displays a menu window containing an entry for each binding in the environment. For base type values the corresponding entry shows the type while for instances of constructed types only the type constructor is shown. An example is shown in Figure 8.4.

An environment menu entry may be either selected or displayed, depending on the mouse button used to click on it. Displaying an entry results in the value of the corresponding environment binding being displayed in the browser. If the value is of such a type that a new window is displayed for it, an arrow is drawn from the menu entry to the new window as shown in Figure 8.5.

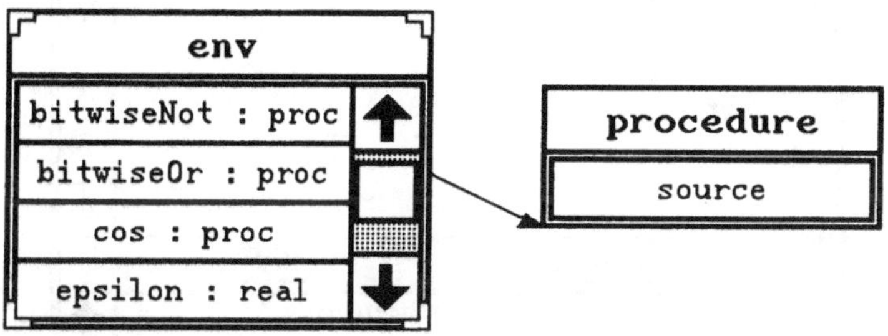

Fig. 8.5. Link from environment location to value.

Structures are displayed in the same way as environments, with a menu entry for each field, as illustrated in Figure 8.6.

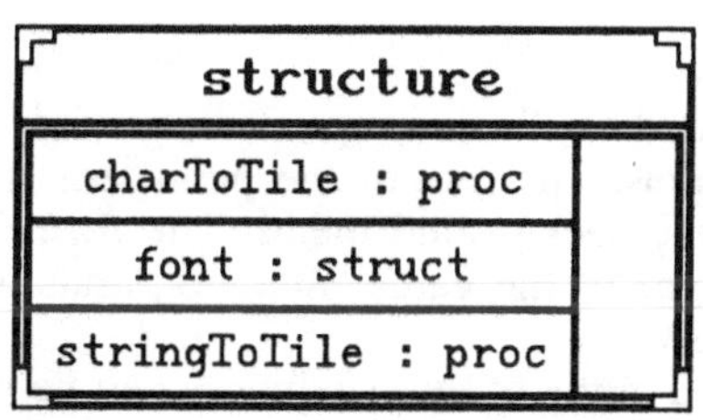

Fig. 8.6. A structure menu.

To show a procedure the browser displays a menu with a single entry *source*. When this entry is clicked on the browser displays a hyper-program window containing the source code for the procedure. The source code may be copied but not altered. An example is shown in Figure 8.7.

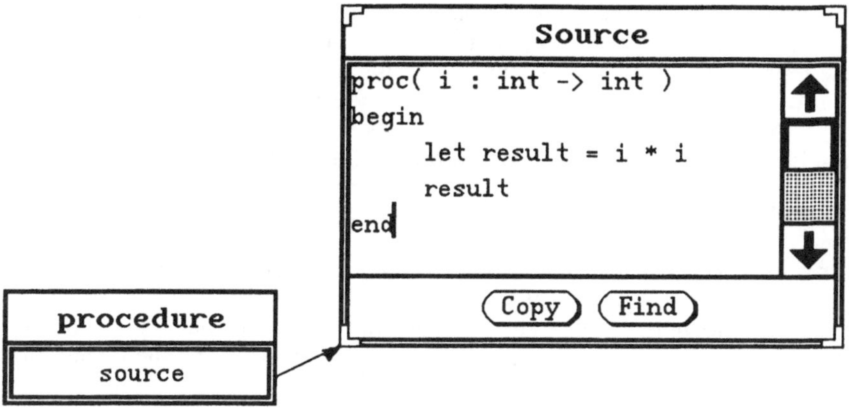

Fig. 8.7. A procedure window.

A representation of the type of a value in the browser window may be obtained by selecting the corresponding window and selecting *Show Type* from the background menu. The browser displays a window containing a canonical string representation of the value's type. An example is shown in Figure 8.8.

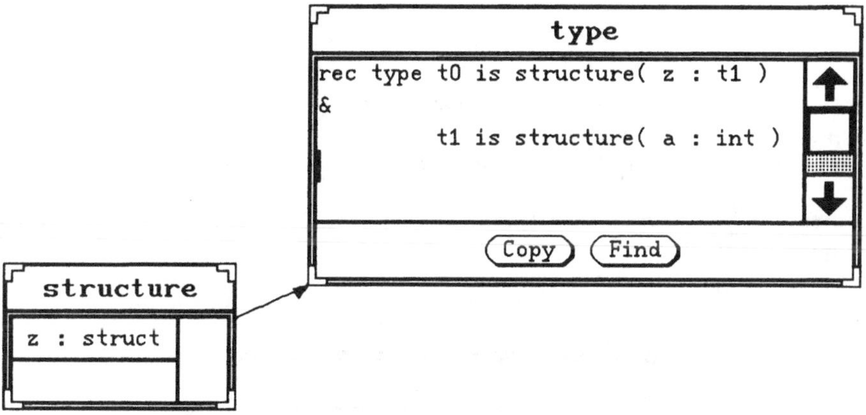

Fig. 8.8. A type representation.

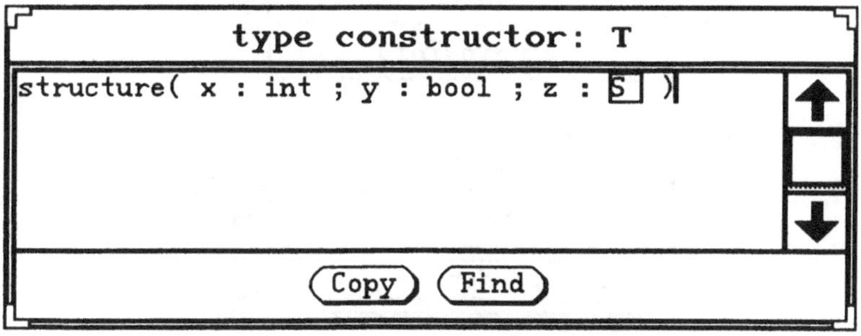

Fig. 8.9. A type constructor representation.

The browser also displays a representation of a type linked into a hyper-program when the corresponding light-button in the hyper-program window is pressed. In this case the representation may be a canonical string as above or, where type constructor information is available, the original source code is displayed as a hyper-program fragment. An example of a type constructor source representation, with a hyper-program link to a component type *S*, is shown in Figure 8.9.

8.3.3 Declaration Sets

For convenience the user may create *declaration sets* containing named values, locations and types to use in future program evaluations. Each declaration set has a unique name and may be thought of as forming an additional outer scope for a program. Free identifiers in a program are resolved by scanning the declaration sets associated with the program.

A type entry in a declaration set may represent either a type only, or a type constructor. Which is obtained depends on the method used to create the entry. Both type and type constructor names may be used as type denotations in programs, but only type constructor names may be used to construct instances of types.

The declaration sets model is based on a number of earlier systems: Napier88 Release 1.0 [108]; ABERDEEN [109]; and a previous version of the Napier88 programming environment [110].

The operations on declaration sets are:

- create a new declaration set;
- delete a declaration set;
- add a value, location or type to a declaration set;
- display the contents of a declaration set; and
- choose an ordered list of declaration sets to use for compilation.

The contents of a particular declaration set may be displayed by pressing the *Show* button in the main declaration sets menu. An example is shown in Figure 8.10.

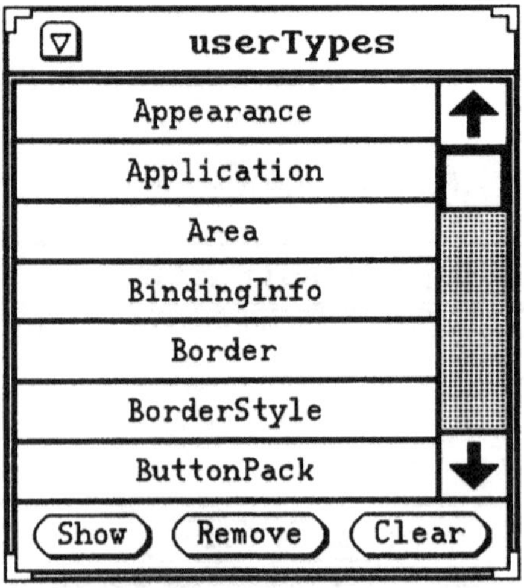

Fig. 8.10. A declaration set menu.

Each menu contains a list of the entries in that declaration set. An entry may be displayed by clicking on *Show* or linked into a hyper-program by selecting it and clicking on *Link* in the editor.

The user may associate a particular combination of declaration sets with a hyper-program editor. These declaration sets are then used in evaluating program fragments in that editor. Declaration sets may be added to an editor's list by clicking on *Source Sets*. This displays a dialogue as shown in Figure 8.11.

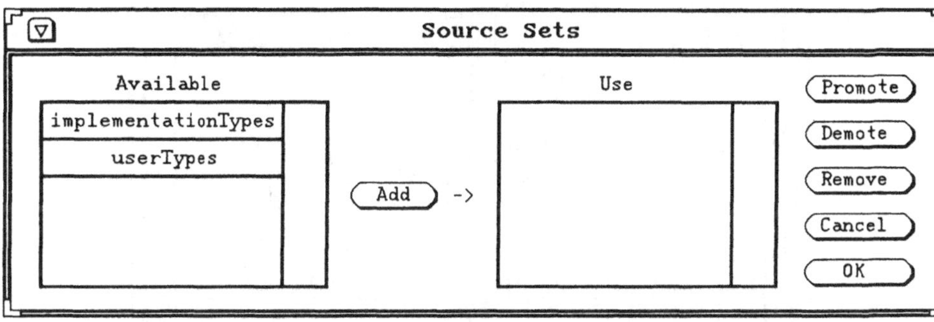

Fig. 8.11. Dialogue for setting source declaration sets.

The *Available* list on the left shows all the existing declaration sets. The *Use* list on the right shows those currently associated with the editor, scope level increasing down the list. If two declaration sets associated with an editor both contain an entry with the same name, the one in the declaration set nearer the top of the list will mask the other. This is analogous to normal scoping rules.

8.3.4 Multiple Users

More than one programming environment session may be active simultaneously. The names of the initial sessions can be specified as parameters to the system startup command allowing multiple users to operate in a given persistent store simultaneously.

Windows persist between sessions of the programming environment. When a session is shut down the positions and sizes of the windows are recorded and restored when it is next started up. Each session contains its own browser, output window, compilation error window, hyper-program windows, etc. No particular concurrency control scheme is enforced: for flexibility this is left to applications as described in Section 7. Thus by default an update to the persistent store by one user is immediately visible to others.

Figure 8.12 shows an example programming environment session. The two windows at the top-left and top-right (when viewed side-on) are hyper-program editors. Currently the editor at the top-right happens to contain only text. The menu between the two hyper-program editors shows the contents of the declaration set *win*: a set of types used for user interface programming. One of the types, *Window*, has been selected and displayed in the browser window in the lower half of the screen. Since this type has source information attached the browser is able to display the original source code from which the type derives. The source contains hyper-program links to other types used in the definition. The user may click on one of the links to display that component type. The menus on the left of the browser window show a series of environments accessible from the persistent root.

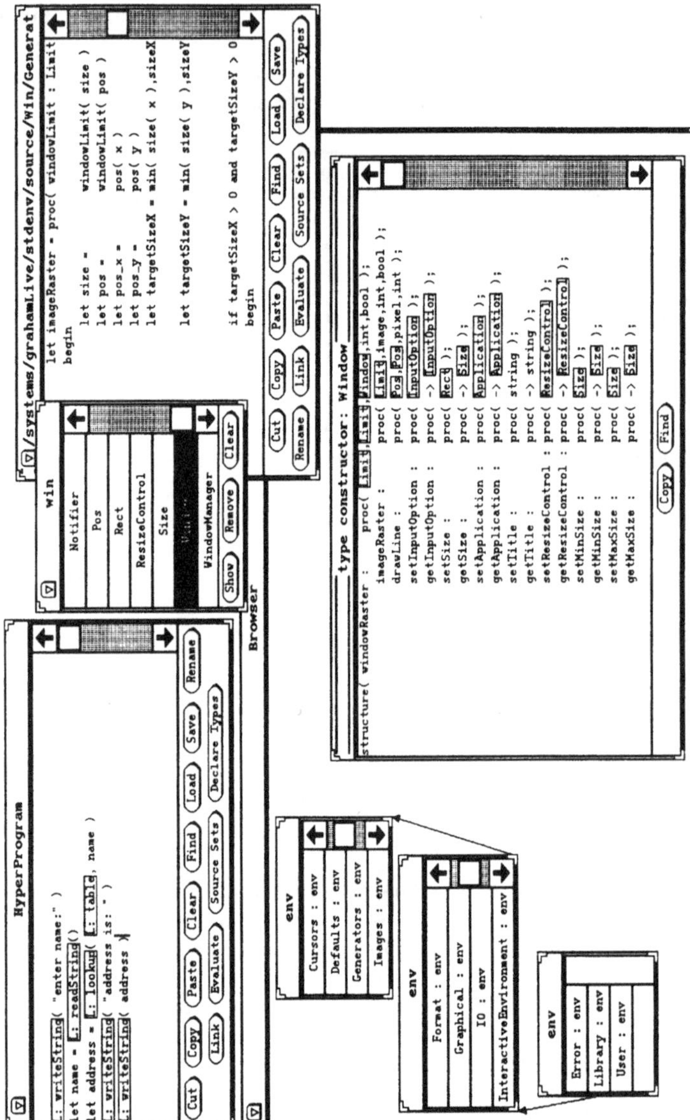

Fig. 8.12. A programming environment session.

8.4 Implementation Issues

The programming environment is entirely implemented in Napier88, except for a very few components (such as parts of the compiler) which need to perform operations below the type system level. The implementation relies heavily on the provision of orthogonal persistence to store the procedure components which make up the system [24]. Much use is also made of the graphics facilities provided by Napier88, which allow the manipulation of graphical data as first class values [47].

Since not all the components present in the standard populated store are designed to be accessible to users, protection mechanisms are necessary. Both first-order and second-order information hiding are used. Some components are hidden in the closures of the procedures which use them, and have no direct access path from the root of persistence. This prevents users from linking to them (although it may be necessary to restrict access to the hyper-program source code of the procedures in which they are encapsulated). second-order information hiding is used to allow users restricted access to components. For example the user may obtain a reference to a representation of the type of a given value in the browser, but is prevented from discovering any information about its internal structure since the representation is a witness of an abstract data type. All the user can do with the representation is pass it to some library procedure which operates on type representations. Password protection is used to restrict access to the raw type representations which can only be accessed by system components.

Acknowledgements. This work was supported by the Alvey funded SERC grant GR/D 43266, a grant from International Computers Ltd (ICL), SERC grants GR/F 02953, GR/G 17578 and GR/J 67611, ESPRIT II Basic Research Action 3070 — $FIDE_1$ and ESPRIT III Basic Research Action 6309 — $FIDE_2$. Richard Connor is supported by EPSRC Advanced Fellowship B/94/AF/1921.

References

1. Atkinson MP, Morrison R, Pratten GD. Designing a Persistent Information Space Architecture. In: Proc. 10th IFIP World Congress, Dublin, 1986, pp 115-120
2. Connor RCH. The Napier Type-Checking Module. Universities of Glasgow and St Andrews Report PPRR-58-88, 1988
3. Connor RCH, Brown AB, Cutts QI, Dearle A, Morrison R, Rosenberg J. Type Equivalence Checking in Persistent Object Systems. In: Dearle A, Shaw GM, Zdonik SB (ed) Implementing Persistent Object Bases, Principles and Practice, Proc. 4th International Workshop on Persistent Object Systems, Martha's Vineyard, USA. Morgan Kaufmann, 1990, pp 151-164
4. Connor RCH. Types and Polymorphism in Persistent Programming Systems. Ph.D. thesis, University of St Andrews, 1990
5. Connor RCH, McNally DJ, Morrison R. Subtyping and Assignment in Database Programming Languages. In: Kanellakis P, Schmidt JW (ed) Database Programming Languages: Bulk Types and Persistent Data, Proc. 3rd International Workshop on Database Programming Languages, Nafplion, Greece. Morgan Kaufmann, 1991, pp 363-382
6. Connor RCH, Morrison R. Subtyping Without Tears. In: Proc. 15th Australian Computer Science Conference, Hobart, Tasmania, 1992, pp 209-225
7. Morrison R, Brown AL, Carrick R, Connor RCH, Dearle A, Atkinson MP. The Napier Type System. In: Rosenberg J, Koch DM (ed) Persistent Object Systems, Proc. 3rd International Workshop on Persistent Object Systems, Newcastle, Australia 1989. Workshops in Computing, Springer-Verlag, 1990, pp 3-18
8. Atkinson MP, Lécluse C, Philbrow P, Richard P. Design Issues in a Map Language. In: Kanellakis P, Schmidt JW (ed) Bulk Types & Persistent Data. Morgan Kaufmann, 1991, pp 20-32

9. Connor RCH, Atkinson MP, Berman S, Cutts QI, Kirby GNC, Morrison R. The Joy of Sets. In: Beeri C, Ohori A, Shasha DE (ed) Database Programming Languages, Proc. 4th International Conference on Database Programming Languages, New York City. Workshops in Computing, Springer-Verlag, 1993, pp 417-433
10. Connor RCH, Dearle A, Morrison R, Brown AL. Existentially Quantified Types as a Database Viewing Mechanism. In: Bancilhon F, Thanos C, Tsichritzis D (ed) Lecture Notes in Computer Science 416, Proc. 2nd International Conference on Extending Database Technology, Venice, Italy. Springer-Verlag, 1990, pp 301-315
11. Morrison R, Brown AL, Connor RCH et al. Protection in Persistent Object Systems. In: Rosenberg J, Keedy JL (ed) Security and Persistence, Proc. International Workshop on Security and Persistence, Bremen, 1990. Springer-Verlag, 1990, pp 48-66
12. Morrison R, Dearle A, Connor RCH, Brown AL. An Ad-Hoc Approach to the Implementation of Polymorphism. ACM Transactions on Programming Languages and Systems 1991; 13,3:342-371
13. Connor RCH, Dearle A, Morrison R, Brown AL. An Object Addressing Mechanism for Statically Typed Languages with Multiple Inheritance. In: Proc. OOPSLA'89, New Orleans, Louisiana, 1989
14. Atkinson MP, Buneman OP, Morrison R. Binding and Type Checking in Database Programming Languages. Computer Journal 1988; 31,2:99-109
15. Atkinson MP, Morrison R. Types, Bindings and Parameters in a Persistent Environment. In: Atkinson MP, Buneman OP, Morrison R (ed) Data Types and Persistence, Proc. 1st International Workshop on Persistent Object Systems, Appin, Scotland. Topics in Information Systems, Springer-Verlag, 1988, pp 3-20
16. Morrison R, Brown AL, Dearle A, Atkinson MP. On the Classification of Binding Mechanisms. Information Processing Letters 1990; 34:51-55
17. Morrison R, Connor RCH, Cutts QI, Dunstan VS, Kirby GNC. Exploiting Persistent Linkage in Software Engineering Environments. Computer Journal 1995; 38,1:1-16
18. Morrison R, Brown AL, Carrick R, Connor RCH, Dearle A, Atkinson MP. Polymorphism, Persistence and Software Reuse in a Strongly Typed Object Oriented Environment. Software Engineering Journal 1987; December:199-204
19. Morrison R, Connor RCH, Cutts QI, Kirby GNC. Persistent Possibilities for Software Environments. In: The Intersection between Databases and Software Engineering, Proc. ICSE-16 Workshop on the Intersection between Databases and Software Engineering, Sorrento, Italy. IEEE Computer Society Press, 1994, pp 78-87
20. Kirby GNC, Connor RCH, Cutts QI, Dearle A, Farkas AM, Morrison R. Persistent Hyper-Programs. In: Albano A, Morrison R (ed) Persistent Object Systems, Proc. 5th International Workshop on Persistent Object Systems, San Miniato, Italy. Workshops in Computing, Springer-Verlag, 1992, pp 86-106
21. Connor RCH, Cutts QI, Kirby GNC, Morrison R. Using Persistence Technology to Control Schema Evolution. In: Proc. 9th ACM Symposium on Applied Computing, Phoenix, Arizona, 1994, pp 441-446
22. Atkinson MP, Sjøberg DIK, Morrison R. Managing Change in Persistent Object Systems. In: Proc. JSSST International Symposium on Object Technologies for Advanced Software, Kanazawa, Japan, 1993, pp 315-338
23. Morrison R, Connor RCH, Cutts QI, Kirby GNC, Stemple D. Mechanisms for Controlling Evolution in Persistent Object Systems. Journal of Microprocessors and Microprogramming 1993; 17,3:173-181
24. Dearle A, Cutts QI, Connor RCH. Using Persistence to Support Incremental System Construction. Journal of Microprocessors and Microprogramming 1993; 17,3:161-171
25. Morrison R, Brown AL, Carrick R, Connor RCH, Dearle A. On the Integration of Object-Oriented and Process-Oriented Computation in Persistent Environments. In: Dittrich KR (ed) Lecture Notes in Computer Science 334, Proc. 2nd International Workshop on Object-Oriented Database Systems, Bad Münster am Stein-Ebernburg, Germany. Springer-Verlag, 1988, pp 334-339

26. Morrison R, Barter CJ, Brown AL et al. Language Design Issues in Supporting Process-Oriented Computation in Persistent Environments. In: Proc. 22nd International Conference on System Sciences, Hawaii, 1989, pp 736-744
27. Munro DS, Connor RCH, Morrison R, Scheuerl S, Stemple D. Concurrent Shadow Paging in the Flask Architecture. In: Atkinson MP, Maier D, Benzaken V (ed) Persistent Object Systems, Tarascon 1994, Proc. 6th International Workshop on Persistent Object Systems, Tarascon, France. Workshops in Computing, Springer-Verlag, 1994, pp 16-42
28. Stemple D, Morrison R. Specifying Flexible Concurrency Control Schemes: An Abstract Operational Approach. In: Proc. 15th Australian Computer Science Conference, Hobart, Tasmania, 1992, pp 873-891
29. Brown AL, Rosenberg J. Persistent Object Stores: An Implementation Technique. In: Dearle A, Shaw GM, Zdonik SB (ed) Implementing Persistent Object Bases, Principles and Practice, Proc. 4th International Workshop on Persistent Object Systems, Martha's Vineyard, USA. Morgan Kaufmann, 1990, pp 199-212
30. Brown AL, Cockshott WP. The CPOMS Persistent Object Management System. Universities of Glasgow and St Andrews Report PPRR-13-85, 1985
31. Brown AL, Morrison R. A Generic Persistent Object Store. Software Engineering Journal 1992; 7,2:161-168
32. Brown AL, Mainetto G, Matthes F, Müller R, McNally DJ. An Open System Architecture for a Persistent Object Store. In: Proc. 25th International Conference on Systems Sciences, Hawaii, 1992, pp 766-776
33. Vaughan F, Schunke T, Koch B, Dearle A, Marlin C, Barter C. A Persistent Distributed Architecture Supported by the Mach Operating System. In: Proc. Proceedings of the 1st USENIX Conference on the Mach Operating System, 1990, pp 123-140
34. Koch B, Schunke T, Dearle A et al. Cache Coherence and Storage Management in a Persistent Object System. In: Dearle A, Shaw G, Zdonik SB (ed) Implementing Persistent Object Bases. Morgan Kaufmann, 1990, pp 103-113
35. Brown AL. Persistent Object Stores. Ph.D. thesis, University of St Andrews, 1989
36. Munro DS. On the Integration of Concurrency, Distribution and Persistence. Ph.D. thesis, University of St Andrews, 1993
37. Sjøberg DIK. Thesaurus-Based Methodologies and Tools for Maintaining Persistent Application Systems. Ph.D. thesis, University of Glasgow, 1993
38. Sjøberg DIK, Atkinson MP, Lopes JC, Trinder PW. Building an Integrated Persistent Application. In: Beeri C, Ohori A, Shasha DE (ed) Database Programming Languages, Proc. 4th International Conference on Database Programming Languages, New York City. Workshops in Computing, Springer-Verlag, 1993, pp 359-375
39. Sjøberg DIK, Cutts QI, Welland R, Atkinson MP. Analysing Persistent Language Applications. In: Atkinson MP, Maier D, Benzaken V (ed) Persistent Object Systems, Tarascon 1994, Proc. 6th International Workshop on Persistent Object Systems, Tarascon, France. Workshops in Computing, Springer-Verlag, 1994, pp 235-255
40. Connor RCH, Cutts QI, Kirby GNC, Moore VS, Morrison R. Unifying Interaction with Persistent Data and Program. In: Sawyer P (ed) Interfaces to Database Systems, Proc. 2nd International Workshop on Interfaces to Databases, Lancaster, 1994. Workshops in Computing, Springer-Verlag, 1994, pp 197-212
41. Morrison R, Brown AL, Connor RCH et al. The Napier88 Reference Manual (Release 2.0). University of St Andrews Report CS/94/8, 1994
42. Kirby GNC, Brown AL, Connor RCH et al. The Napier88 Standard Library Reference Manual (Release 2.0). University of St Andrews Report CS/94/7, 1994
43. Goldberg A, Robson D. Smalltalk-80: The Language and its Implementation. Addison Wesley, Reading, Massachusetts, 1983
44. PS-algol. PS-algol Reference Manual, 4th edition. Universities of Glasgow and St Andrews Report PPRR-12-88, 1988
45. Morrison R. S-algol Language Reference Manual. University of St Andrews Report CS/79/1, 1979

46. Atkinson MP, Morrison R. Orthogonally Persistent Object Systems. VLDB Journal 1995; 4,3:319-401
47. Morrison R, Brown AL, Dearle A, Atkinson MP. An Integrated Graphics Programming Environment. Computer Graphics Forum 1986; 5,2:147-157
48. Morrison R, Brown AL, Bailey PJ, Davie AJT, Dearle A. A Persistent Graphics Facility for the ICL PERQ Computer. Software—Practice and Experience 1986; 16,4:351-367
49. Brown AL, Dearle A, Morrison R, Munro D, Rosenberg J. A Layered Persistent Architecture for Napier88. In: Rosenberg J, Keedy JL (ed) Security and Persistence, Proc. International Workshop on Security and Persistence, Bremen, 1990. Workshops in Computing, Springer-Verlag, 1990, pp 155-172
50. Ruffin M. Kitlog, A Generic Logging Service. In: Proc. 11th IEEE Symposium on Reliable Distributed Systems, Houston, Texas, 1992, pp 139-146
51. Scheuerl SJG, Connor RCH, Morrison R, Munro DS. The DataSafe Failure Recovery Mechanism in the Flask Architecture. In: Proc. 19th Australasian Computer Science Conference, Melbourne, Australia, 1996, pp 573-581
52. Albano A, Cardelli L, Orsini R. Galileo: a Strongly Typed, Interactive Conceptual Language. ACM Transactions on Database Systems 1985; 10,2:230-260
53. Matthes F, Müller R, Schmidt JW. Object Stores as Servers in Persistent Programming Environments—The P-Quest Experience. ESPRIT BRA Project 3070 FIDE Report FIDE/92/48, 1992
54. Rabitti F, Mainetto G, Zezula P et al. Design and Implementation of PIOS: a Physically Independent Object Server. ESPRIT BRA Project 6309 $FIDE_2$ Report FIDE/93/70, 1993
55. Davie AJT, McNally DJ. Statically Typed Applicative Persistent Language Environment (STAPLE) Reference Manual. University of St Andrews Report CS/90/14, 1990
56. Garcia-Molina H. Using Semantic Knowledge for Transaction Processing in a Distributed Database. ACM Transactions on Database Systems 1983; 8,2:186-213
57. Atkinson MP, Bailey PJ, Chisholm KJ, Cockshott WP, Morrison R. An Approach to Persistent Programming. Computer Journal 1983; 26,4:360-365
58. Atkinson MP, Bailey PJ, Chisholm KJ, Cockshott WP, Morrison R. Progress with Persistent Programming. In: Stocker PM, Atkinson MP, Gray PM (ed) Database, Role and Structure. Cambridge University Press, 1984, pp 245-310
59. Atkinson MP, Buneman OP. Types and Persistence in Database Programming Languages. ACM Computing Surveys 1987; 19,2:105-190
60. Atkinson MP, Chisholm KJ, Cockshott WP. PS-algol: An Algol with a Persistent Heap. ACM SIGPLAN Notices 1982; 17,7:24-31
61. Atkinson MP, Morrison R. Procedures as Persistent Data Objects. ACM Transactions on Programming Languages and Systems 1985; 7,4:539-559
62. Atkinson MP, Morrison R, Pratten GD. A Persistent Information Space Architecture. In: Proc. 9th Australian Computing Science Conference, Australia, 1986
63. Dearle A. Constructing Compilers in a Persistent Environment. In: Proc. 2nd International Workshop on Persistent Object Systems, Appin, Scotland, 1987
64. Dearle A. On the Construction of Persistent Programming Environments. Ph.D. thesis, University of St Andrews, 1988
65. Wai F. Distribution and Persistence. In: Proc. 2nd International Workshop on Persistent Object Systems, Appin, Scotland, 1987, pp 207-225
66. Cooper RL. Configurable Data Modelling Systems. In: Proc. 9th International Conference on the Entity Relationship Approach, Lausanne, Switzerland, 1990, pp 35-52
67. Cooper RL. On The Utilisation of Persistent Programming Environments. Ph.D. thesis, University of Glasgow, 1990
68. McCarthy J, Abrahams PW, Edwards DJ, Hart TP, Levin MI. The Lisp Programmers' Manual. M.I.T. Press, Cambridge, Massachusetts, 1962

69. van Wijngaarden A, Mailloux BJ, Peck JEL, Koster CHA. Report on the Algorithmic Language ALGOL 68. Numerische Mathematik 1969; 14:79-218
70. Strachey C. Fundamental Concepts in Programming Languages. Oxford University Press, Oxford, 1967
71. Tennent RD. Language Design Methods Based on Semantic Principles. Acta Informatica 1977; 8:97-112
72. Cardelli L, Wegner P. On Understanding Types, Data Abstraction and Polymorphism. ACM Computing Surveys 1985; 17,4:471-523
73. Dearle A. Environments: A flexible binding mechanism to support system evolution. In: Proc. 22nd International Conference on Systems Sciences, Hawaii, 1989, pp 46-55
74. Atkinson MP, Morrison R. Integrated Persistent Programming Systems. In: Proc. 19th International Conference on Systems Sciences, Hawaii, 1986, pp 842-854
75. Mitchell JC, Plotkin GD. Abstract Types have Existential Type. ACM Transactions on Programming Languages and Systems 1988; 10,3:470-502
76. Albano A, Dearle A, Ghelli G et al. A Framework for Comparing Type Systems for Database Programming Languages. In: Hull R, Morrison R, Stemple D (ed) Database Programming Languages. Morgan Kaufmann, 1989, pp 170-178
77. Atkinson MP, Bailey PJ, Philbrow PC, Welland RC. An Organisation for Napier88 Libraries, 2nd Edition. ESPRIT BRA Project 6309 $FIDE_2$ Report FIDE/94/77, 1994
78. Lorie RA. Physical Integrity in a Large Segmented Database. ACM Transactions on Database Systems 1977; 2,1:91-104
79. Rosenberg J, Henskens F, Brown AL, Morrison R, Munro D. Stability in a Persistent Store Based on a Large Virtual Memory. In: Rosenberg J, Keedy JL (ed) Security and Persistence, Proc. International Workshop on Security and Persistence, Bremen, 1990. Workshops in Computing, Springer-Verlag, 1990, pp 229-245
80. Stonebraker M, Wong E, Kreps P, Held G. The Design and Implementation of INGRES. ACM Transactions on Database Systems 1976; 1,3:189-222
81. Davies CT. Data Processing Spheres of Control. IBM Systems Journal 1978; 17,2:179-198
82. Stemple D, Stanton RB, Sheard T et al. Type-Safe Linguistic Reflection: A Generator Technology. ESPRIT BRA Project 3070 FIDE Report FIDE/92/49, 1992
83. Dearle A, Brown AL. Safe Browsing in a Strongly Typed Persistent Environment. Computer Journal 1988; 31,6:540-544
84. Kirby GNC, Connor RCH, Morrison R. START: A Linguistic Reflection Tool Using Hyper-Program Technology. In: Atkinson MP, Maier D, Benzaken V (ed) Persistent Object Systems, Tarascon 1994, Proc. 6th International Workshop on Persistent Object Systems, Tarascon, France. Workshops in Computing, Springer-Verlag, 1994, pp 355-373
85. Kirby GNC. Persistent Programming with Strongly Typed Linguistic Reflection. In: Proc. 25th International Conference on Systems Sciences, Hawaii, 1992, pp 820-831
86. Stemple D, Fegaras L, Sheard T, Socorro A. Exceeding the Limits of Polymorphism in Database Programming Languages. In: Bancilhon F, Thanos C, Tsichritzis D (ed) Lecture Notes in Computer Science 416 (EDBT '90). Springer-Verlag, 1990, pp 269-285
87. Sheard T. Automatic Generation and Use of Abstract Structure Operators. ACM Transactions on Programming Languages and Systems 1991; 19,4:531-557
88. Dearle A, Cutts QI, Kirby GNC. Browsing, Grazing and Nibbling Persistent Data Structures. In: Rosenberg J, Koch DM (ed) Persistent Object Systems, Proc. 3rd International Workshop on Persistent Object Systems, Newcastle, Australia 1989. Workshops in Computing, Springer-Verlag, 1990, pp 56-69
89. Cooper RL, Qin Z. A Graphical Data Modelling Program With Constraint Specification and Management. In: Proc. 10th British National Conference on Databases, Aberdeen, 1992, pp 192-208

90. Cooper RL, Atkinson MP, Dearle A, Abderrahmane D. Constructing Database Systems in a Persistent Environment. In: Proc. 13th International Conference on Very Large Data Bases, 1987, pp 117-125
91. Fegaras L, Stemple D. Using Type Transformation in Database System Implementation. In: Kanellakis P, Schmidt JW (ed) 3rd International Conference on Database Programming Languages, Proc. 3rd International Workshop on Database Programming Languages, Nafplion, Greece. Morgan Kaufmann, 1991, pp 337-353
92. Cutts QI, Connor RCH, Kirby GNC, Morrison R. An Execution Driven Approach to Code Optimisation. In: Proc. 17th Australasian Computer Science Conference, Christchurch, New Zealand, 1994, pp 83-92
93. Stemple D, Sheard T, Fegaras L. Linguistic Reflection: A Bridge from Programming to Database Languages. In: Proc. 25th International Conference on Systems Sciences, Hawaii, 1992, pp 844-855
94. Fegaras L, Sheard T, Stemple D. Uniform Traversal Combinators: Definition, Use and Properties. In: Proc. 11th International Conference on Automated Deduction (CADE-11), Saratoga Springs, New York, 1992. LNAI 607, pp. 148-162
95. Dijkstra EW. The Structure of the T.H.E. Multiprogramming System. Communications of the ACM 1968; 11,5:341-346
96. Hoare CAR. Monitors: An Operating System Structuring Concept. Communications of the ACM 1974; 17,10:549-557
97. Dijkstra EW. Cooperating Sequential Processes. In: Genuys F (ed) Programming Languages. Academic Press, 1968, pp 43-112
98. Campbell RH, Haberman AN. The Specification of Process Synchronisation by Path Expressions. In: Lecture Notes in Computer Science 16. Springer-Verlag, 1974
99. Brookes SD, Hoare C, Roscoe A. A Theory of Communicating Sequential Processes. Carnegie-Mellon University Report CMU-CS-83-153, 1980
100. Eswaran KP, Gray JN, Lorie RA, Traiger IL. The Notions of Consistency and Predicate Locks in a Database System. Communications of the ACM 1976; 19,11:624-633
101. Kung HT, Robinson JT. On Optimistic Methods for Concurrency Control. ACM Transactions on Database Systems 1982; 6,2:213-226
102. Nodine MH, Zdonik SB. Co-operative Transaction Hierarchies: Transaction Support for Design Applications. VLDB Journal 1992; 1,1:41-80
103. Sutton S. A Flexible Consistency Model for Persistent Data in Software-Process Programming. In: Dearle A, Shaw GM, Zdonik SB (ed) Implementing Persistent Object Bases, Principles and Practice, Proc. 4th International Workshop on Persistent Object Systems, Martha's Vineyard, USA. Morgan Kaufmann, 1990, pp 305-319
104. Ellis CA, Gibbs SJ. Concurrency Control in Groupware Systems. In: Proc. ACM-SIGMOD International Conference on Management of Data, Portland, Oregon, 1989, pp 399-407
105. Morrison R, Barter CJ, Connor RCH et al. Concurrency Control in Process Models. IOPENER 1993; 2,1:11-12
106. Brown JC. A Library Explorer for the Napier88 Glasgow Libraries. M.Sc. thesis, University of Glasgow, 1993
107. Waite CA, Welland RC, Printezis T et al. Glasgow Libraries for Orthogonally Persistent Systems—Philosophy, Organisation and Contents. ESPRIT BRA Project 6309 $FIDE_2$ Report FIDE/95/132, 1995
108. Morrison R, Brown AL, Connor RCH, Dearle A. The Napier88 Reference Manual. Universities of Glasgow and St Andrews Report PPRR-77-89, 1989
109. Farkas AM. ABERDEEN: A Browser allowing intERactive DEclarations and Expressions in Napier88. University of Adelaide, 1991
110. Kirby GNC, Cutts QI, Connor RCH, Dearle A, Morrison R. Programmers' Guide to the Napier88 Standard Library, Edition 2.1. University of St Andrews, 1992

Section 1.2

Linguistic Reflection: Introduction and State of the Art

Ron Morrison

School of Mathematical and Computational Sciences, University of St Andrews, North Haugh, St Andrews KY16 9SS, Scotland

1 Introduction

Linguistic reflection is defined as the ability of a running program to generate new program fragments and to integrate these into its own execution. This is the basis for system evolution which itself is necessary to achieve adequate persistent application system (PAS) longevity. For safety reasons only strongly typed reflection has been investigated in the FIDE project.

Linguistic reflection has the goal of allowing a program's behaviour to adjust dynamically in order to provide flexibility and high productivity. It thus extends the data modelling of the type system and it should not be surprising therefore to find a tension between type systems and reflection. The possibility that a program may significantly change its behaviour decreases the opportunity for static type checking and thus compromises some of the benefits of typing. Thus the reflective facilities are controlled in a manner designed to retain as much static type checking as possible without the control being so severe as to remove all the benefits.

The two techniques for type-safe linguistic reflection that have evolved are: compile-time linguistic reflection and run-time linguistic reflection. Compile-time linguistic reflection [1, 2] allows the user to define generators which produce representations of program fragments. The generators are executed as part of the compilation process. Their results are then viewed as program fragments, type checked and made part of the program being compiled.

Run-time linguistic reflection [3-5] is concerned with the construction and binding of new components with old, in an environment. The technique involves the use of a compiler that can be called dynamically to compile newly generated program fragments, and a linking mechanism to bind these new program fragments into the running program. Type checking occurs in both compilation and binding.

The benefits of linguistic reflection in database and persistent programming mainly consist of two capabilities. The first is the ability to implement highly abstract specifications, such as those used in query languages and data models, within a strongly typed programming language. The second is the ability to accommodate some of the continual changes in data-intensive applications without resorting to *ad hoc* restructuring methods. Both capabilities involve reflective access to the types of a system that is changing itself and both approaches avoid introducing extra levels of interpretation.

Both compile-time and run-time reflection have been provided in previous languages. Compile-time reflection appears in the macro facilities of Scheme [6] and

POP-2 [7]. Run-time reflection appears in the *eval* functions of Lisp [8] and SNOBOL4 [9] and the *popval* function of POP-2 [7].

Type-safe linguistic reflection is different for the following reasons.

- More information is available to the reflective computation, in the form of systematically required types. This information can be used to automatically adjust to implementation details and system evolution. Linguistic reflection without strong typing has little systematic information available about the structures involved in computation.

- The type safety of all newly generated program fragments is checked before they are allowed to be executed. Such type discipline is highly advantageous in a database programming environment in which the integrity of long-lived data must be maintained.

It is somewhat ironic that strong typing, which makes it difficult to integrate reflection with typed programming languages, is what makes linguistic reflection effective as an amplifier of productivity.

Type-safe linguistic reflection has been used to attain high levels of genericity [2, 10] and accommodate changes in systems [11, 12]. It has also been used to implement data models [13, 14], optimise implementations [15, 16] and validate specifications [1, 17]. The importance of the technique is that it provides a uniform mechanism for software production and evolution. A formal description of linguistic reflection is given in the next paper [18].

References

1. Stemple D, Sheard T, Fegaras L. Linguistic Reflection: A Bridge from Programming to Database Languages. In: Proc. 25th International Conference on Systems Sciences, Hawaii, 1992, pp 844-855
2. Stemple D, Fegaras L, Sheard T, Socorro A. Exceeding the Limits of Polymorphism in Database Programming Languages. In: Bancilhon F, Thanos C, Tsichritzis D (ed) Lecture Notes in Computer Science 416 (EDBT '90). Springer-Verlag, 1990, pp 269-285
3. Kirby GNC. Reflection and Hyper-Programming in Persistent Programming Systems. Ph.D. thesis, University of St Andrews, 1992
4. Kirby GNC, Connor RCH, Morrison R. START: A Linguistic Reflection Tool Using Hyper-Program Technology. In: Atkinson MP, Maier D, Benzaken V (ed) Persistent Object Systems, Tarascon 1994, Proc. 6th International Workshop on Persistent Object Systems, Tarascon, France. Workshops in Computing, Springer-Verlag, 1994, pp 355-373
5. Cooper R, Kirby GNC. Type-Safe Linguistic Run-time Reflection—A Practical Perspective. In: Atkinson MP, Maier D, Benzaken V (ed) Persistent Object Systems, Tarascon 1994, Proc. 6th International Workshop on Persistent Object Systems, Tarascon, France. Workshops in Computing, Springer-Verlag, 1994, pp 332-354
6. Rees J, Clinger W. Revised Report on the Algorithmic Language Scheme. ACM SIGPLAN Notices 1986; 21,12:37-43
7. Burstall RM, Collins JS, Popplestone RJ. Programming in POP-2. Edinburgh University Press, Edinburgh, Scotland, 1971
8. McCarthy J, Abrahams PW, Edwards DJ, Hart TP, Levin MI. The Lisp Programmers' Manual. M.I.T. Press, Cambridge, Massachusetts, 1962
9. Griswold RE, Poage JF, Polonsky IP. The SNOBOL4 Programming Language. Prentice-Hall, Englewood Cliffs, New Jersey, 1971

10. Sheard T. Automatic Generation and Use of Abstract Structure Operators. ACM Transactions on Programming Languages and Systems 1991; 19,4:531-557
11. Dearle A, Cutts QI, Kirby GNC. Browsing, Grazing and Nibbling Persistent Data Structures. In: Rosenberg J, Koch DM (ed) Persistent Object Systems, Proc. 3rd International Workshop on Persistent Object Systems, Newcastle, Australia 1989. Springer-Verlag, 1990, pp 56-69
12. Dearle A, Brown AL. Safe Browsing in a Strongly Typed Persistent Environment. Computer Journal 1988; 31,6:540-544
13. Cooper RL. Configurable Data Modelling Systems. In: Proc. 9th International Conference on the Entity Relationship Approach, Lausanne, Switzerland, 1990, pp 35-52
14. Cooper RL. On The Utilisation of Persistent Programming Environments. Ph.D. thesis, University of Glasgow, 1990
15. Cooper RL, Atkinson MP, Dearle A, Abderrahmane D. Constructing Database Systems in a Persistent Environment. In: Proc. 13th International Conference on Very Large Data Bases, 1987, pp 117-125
16. Fegaras L, Stemple D. Using Type Transformation in Database System Implementation. In: Kanelakis P, Schmidt JW (ed) 3rd International Conference on Database Programming Languages, Proc. 3rd International Workshop on Database Programming Languages, Nafplion, Greece. Morgan Kaufmann, 1991, pp 337-353
17. Fegaras L, Sheard T, Stemple D. Uniform Traversal Combinators: Definition, Use and Properties. In: Proc. 11th International Conference on Automated Deduction (CADE-11), Saratoga Springs, New York, 1992. LNAI 607, pp. 148-162
18. Stemple D, Stanton RB, Sheard T et al. Type-Safe Linguistic Reflection: A Generator Technology. ESPRIT BRA Project 3070 FIDE Report FIDE/92/49, 1992

Chapter 1.2.1

Type-Safe Linguistic Reflection: A Generator Technology

David Stemple[1], Leo Fegaras[1*], Robin Stanton[2], Tim Sheard[3], Paul Philbrow[4], Richard Cooper[4], Malcolm P. Atkinson[4], Ron Morrison[5], Graham Kirby[5], Richard Connor[5†] and Suad Alagic[6]

[1] Department of Computer and Information Science, University of Massachusetts, Amherst, MA 01038, USA

[2] Department of Computer Science, Australian National University, Acton, ACT 2601, Australia

[3] Department of Computer Science and Engineering, Oregon Graduate Institute, Beaverton, OR 97006, USA

[4] Department of Computer Science, University of Glasgow, Glasgow G12 8QQ, Scotland

[5] School of Mathematical and Computational Sciences, University of St Andrews, North Haugh, St Andrews KY16 9SS, Scotland

[6] Department of Computer Science and Electrical Engineering, University of Vermont, Burlington, VT 05405, USA

Abstract. Reflective systems allow their own structures to be altered from within. In a programming system reflection can occur in two ways: by a program altering its own interpretation or by it changing itself. Reflection has been used to facilitate the production and evolution of data and programs in database and programming language systems. This paper is concerned with a particular style of reflection, called linguistic reflection, used in compiled, strongly typed languages. Two major techniques for this have evolved: compile-time reflection and run-time reflection. These techniques are described together with a definition and anatomy of reflective systems using them. Two illustrative examples are given and the uses of type-safe reflective techniques in a database programming language context are surveyed. These include attaining high levels of genericity, accommodating changes in systems, implementing data models, optimising implementations and validating specifications.

1 Introduction

Linguistic reflection, which should be carefully distinguished from other uses of "reflection" within the computing literature, is a technique of interest mainly within large, long-lived systems and applications. The importance of the mechanism is that it allows evolutionary change within such systems; it is distinguished from other mechanisms by the fact that no lower-level or external semantics are required to effect the change. The ultimate goal of linguistic reflection is to allow self-supporting, evolving systems: no matter how the system is required to evolve in the

---

* Present address: Department of Computer Science and Engineering, Oregon Graduate Institute, Beaverton, OR 97006, USA

† Present address: Department of Computer Science, University of Glasgow, Glasgow G12 8QQ, Scotland

future, it may always be achieved from within, without stepping out of the system into a different semantic domain.

A rigorous definition of reflection will be given later; in the meantime it is defined rather loosely as the ability for a programming system to change its own behaviour. In general, the behaviour of any system may be captured by a definition of that system with respect to a framework for explaining the definition. For example the behaviour of a program may be captured by the definition of the program itself, and a semantics for the language in which it is written. There are two corresponding mechanisms by which a system can support its own evolution: by changing its own definition, or by changing the interpretation of its definition. These are both potentially dangerous mechanisms, and should be treated with great care. A major motivation for the requirement of type safety with linguistic reflection is to ameliorate the inherent danger of the mechanism.

Figure 1.1 shows a representation of the anatomy of a reflective programming system. The basic structure of the diagram shows a reflective sub-program, part of a larger system, considered with respect to an interpretation. The interpretation itself consists of a number of layers around a kernel.

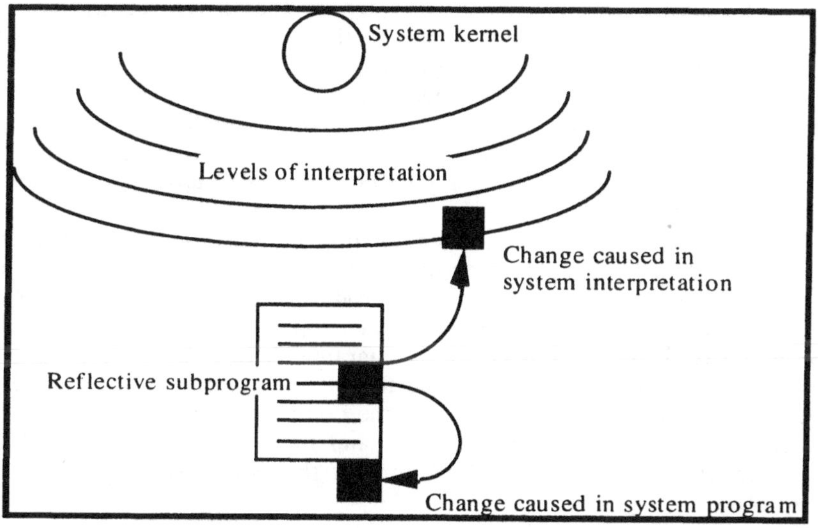

Fig. 1.1. Anatomy of a reflective system.

The kernel represents that part of the system which is not liable to reflective change. To allow some guarantee of behaviour within a reflective system it is essential that such a kernel exists. The layers of interpretation around the kernel consist of levels of abstraction which may be considered as a part of the system interpretation from one perspective, but also as application programs from another. An analogy here is the command structure in the Unix system; at the user level some commands appear to be an intrinsic part of the system, but at the system level they appear as application programs. Thus the notion of whether a reflective program changes the system interpretation, or the system itself, is dependent on the context from which the change is viewed.

The technique studied here, used to effect such changes, is one of program generation. To achieve this, the programming system under consideration must have the capacity to compute the following steps:

1 form a syntactic representation of a program within the same semantic domain as the overall computation

2 cause this syntactic representation to become an executable fragment in its own right

3 allow the executable form produced by this process to be bound into the already executing system

This process of generating new program fragments within the domain of an already executing system, and in particular without resorting to a different semantic domain, is defined as *linguistic reflection.*

To minimise the potential for disaster in systems with reflective mechanisms, there is a requirement for as much protection as possible. The amount of protection which may be attained is clearly compromised by the strong requirement for the almost unbounded flexibility exhibited by reflective systems. The compromise that is taken in the mechanism described here is one of type system protection, thus explaining the term *strongly typed linguistic reflection.* Such systems have the requirement that any new code generated during the execution of reflective subprograms is type correct. Code that is generated may be subsequently manipulated with as much safety as any other typed executable value whose code and closure is not manifest.

Analysis of the reflective generators themselves to determine whether their output is well-typed is an open research issue, and the systems described in this paper do not achieve this; rather, the code produced is tested for type correctness after it is generated. Thus dynamic failure is possible within these systems; however the type integrity of the overall system is guaranteed. In large scale programming systems this is of far greater importance than the elimination of run-time errors within an individual program. In particular, the points at which reflective generation occurs within code are typically well-defined and are generally programmed in such as way as to allow for the possible failure of the generator to produced well-structured code.

2 Definition and Anatomy of Linguistic Reflection

2.1 Linguistic Reflection

Linguistic reflection is defined as the ability of a program to generate new program fragments and to integrate these into its own execution. Given a language, *L*, and a domain of values, *Val*, the nature of execution of a program in *L* will be discussed. The function *eval* is the evaluation function:

$$\text{eval} : L \rightarrow \text{Val}$$

The domain of values, *Val*, differs for different languages. Examples of *Val* include numbers, character strings, final machine states, the state of a persistent object store, and the set of bindings of variables produced by the end of a program's execution.

For linguistic reflection to occur, there must be a subset of *Val*, called Val_L, that can be mapped into L. For example, Val_L could be the set of character strings containing syntactically correct L expressions. Since Val_L is a subset of *Val* that may be translated into the language L it may be thought of as a representation of L.

A subset of L consisting of those language constructs that cause reflective computation is denoted by L_R. L_R is called the reflective sub-language and Val_{L_R} stands for its representation. An evaluation of an expression in L_R invokes a generator. In linguistic reflection the generators, the programs that produce other programs, are written in a subset of the language L which will be denoted by L_{Gen}. L_{Gen} may include all of L but the programs written in L_{Gen} must produce results in Val_L. The major relationships among the language and value sets are:

$$L_R \subset L$$

$$Val_{L_R} \subset Val_L \subseteq Val$$

$$L_{Gen} \subseteq L$$

The significance of the proper subset relationships is explained below. Two functions are required for a full description of linguistic reflection. The first, *drop*, takes a construct in L_R and transforms it into a generator in L_{Gen}. The second, *raise*, takes a value in Val_L and produces an expression in L:

$$\text{drop} : L_R \rightarrow L_{Gen}$$

$$\text{raise} : Val_L \rightarrow L$$

Linguistic reflection is defined as the occurrence of the following pattern of computation, within the *eval* function, in the evaluation of a program in L:

```
procedure eval (e : L) → Val      ! This types e as L and
                                  ! eval as L → Val
        case e of
        ...
        ConstructOfLR => eval (raise (eval (drop (e))))
        ...
```

Fig. 2.1. The linguistic reflective nature of *eval.*

where the ellipses cover all the non-reflective evaluations. The construct *eval (raise (eval (drop (e))))* represents the intuition that during the evaluation of a reflective expression the result of the evaluation is itself evaluated as an expression in the language.

The expression produced by *drop* is a generator that is evaluated by the inner *eval*. The type of a generator g in L_{Gen} is:

$$g : Val \rightarrow Val_L$$

The result of the generator is an expression in Val_L which is then translated into L by *raise*. The result is finally evaluated by the outer *eval*. This is illustrated in Figure 2.2. The whole diagram represents the *eval* function as does the box containing *eval* within the diagram. This structure is a consequence of representing the recursive function *eval* by a flow diagram and will be a feature of other diagrams.

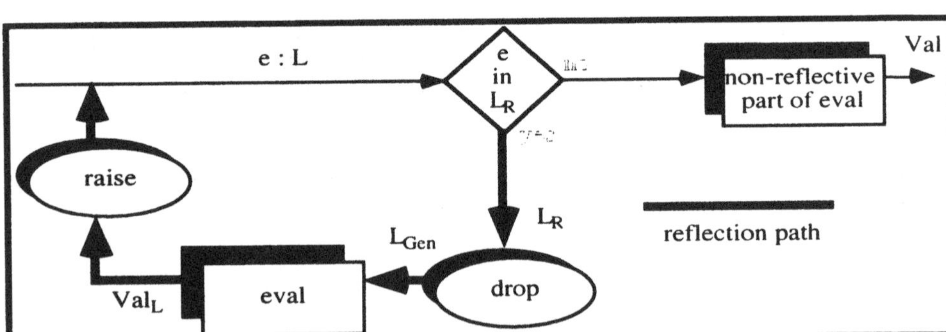

Fig. 2.2. *eval* in linguistic reflection.

In order to make these concepts more concrete an example language is introduced. In this language:

- Val_L is the set of character strings that represent sentences in L;
- L_R contains the single verb **execute** which initiates reflection;
- *drop* presents a string expression to the inner evaluation function;
- *raise* maps a string representation to the corresponding sentence in L;

- L_{Gen} is the set of expressions in L that result in character strings in Val_L.

In this example language, *drop* and *raise* are defined by:

```
drop (execute (stringExpression)) = stringExpression

raise ("expression") = expression
```

Figure 2.3 gives an example of linguistic reflection in this language. The symbol ++ denotes string concatenation. The inner *eval* concatenates the strings to produce the string *"2+3"*, while the outer *eval* evaluates the expression ***execute*** *("2+" ++ "3")* by the following sequence:

```
eval (execute ("2+" ++ "3"))

        ! the reflection is recognised
=> eval (raise (eval (drop (execute ("2+" ++ "3")))))
=> eval (raise (eval ("2+" ++ "3")))
=> eval (raise ("2+3"))
=> eval (2+3)
=> 5
```

Fig. 2.3. An example of linguistic reflection.

The above example shows that some reflective expressions may be evaluated statically, at compile-time, since here all the information to perform the inner *eval* may be found statically. Uses of this style of reflection are described later. This is not always the case however and some reflective computation may have to be delayed until run-time. Figure 2.4 shows such a computation in which run-time input is solicited by the *readString* procedure. The inner *eval* is thus constrained to execute at run-time.

```
execute ("2+" ++ readString ())
```

Fig. 2.4. Example of run-time linguistic reflection.

A reflective computation is well formed if it terminates and the output of each inner *eval* is syntactically correct and typed correctly. Termination requires that the inner *eval* must eventually result in a value in $Val_{L\text{-}L_R}$, the set of values that represent non-reflective program constructs. Syntactic correctness requires that the result of *eval (drop (e))* is in Val_L for all reflective expressions. A generated expression must be internally type consistent as well as typed correctly for its context.

In general, type correctness must be checked for each individually generated expression. Type checking generators for the types of all their possible outputs is a topic for further research but it is thought to be undecidable in general.

2.2 Compilation

This paper is concerned with the mechanisms for linguistic reflection in compiled languages and the anatomy given so far must be further refined to describe these. Figure 2.5 shows the structure of *eval* as a composition of two functions: *compile* and *eval'*. The function *compile* takes an expression in language *L* and produces another in a target language *L'*. The function *eval'* is the evaluation function for *L'*. The types of the functions are defined by:

```
compile : L → L'

eval' : L' → Val
```

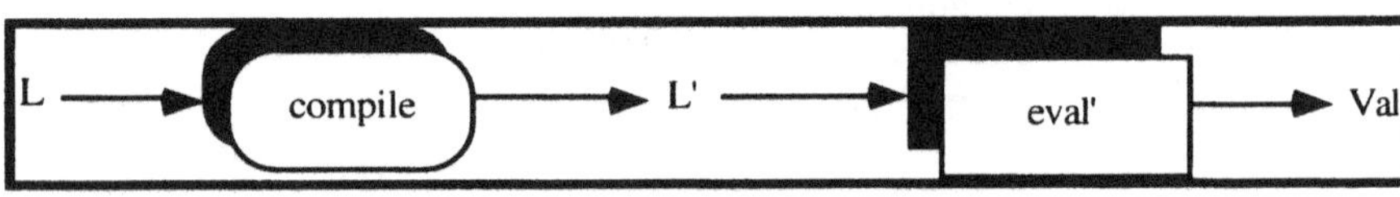

Fig. 2.5. *eval* as function composition.

2.3 Compile-Time Linguistic Reflection

One way in which linguistic reflection can be accomplished in a compilation environment is for reflective constructs to be compiled and executed during the compilation of a program containing them. This is limited to cases where the reflection is over compile-time information and cannot be used for reflection that depends on values that are only available at run-time.

```
procedure eval (e : L) → Val          ! This types e as L and
      eval' (compile (e))             ! eval as L → Val.

procedure compile (e : L) → L'

      case e of
      ConstructOfLR => compile (raise (eval' (compile (drop (e)))))
      notConstructOfLR => translate (e)
```

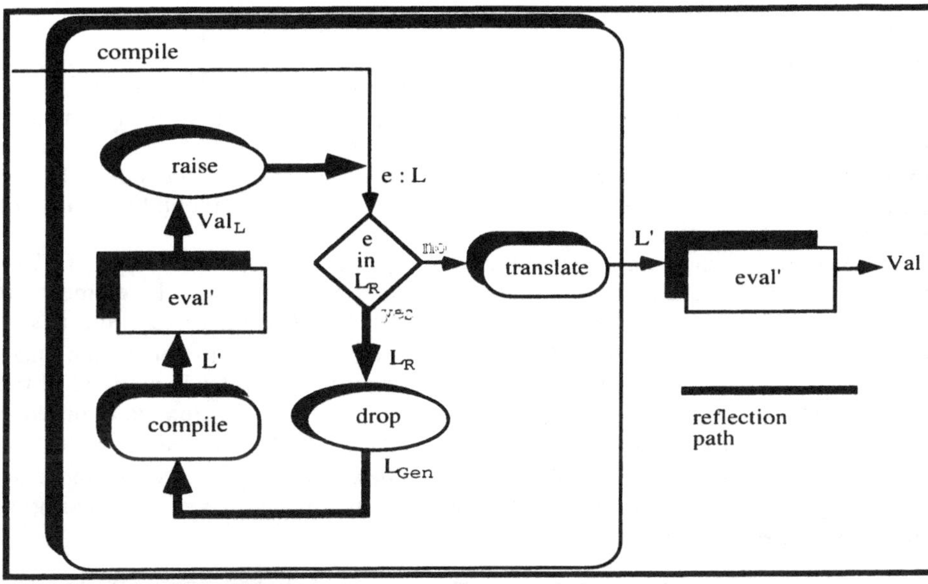

Fig. 2.6. *eval* in compile-time linguistic reflection.

In such a system, generators are used to express computations over the syntactic elements of a program. As in any form of linguistic reflection, the computations are expressed in the subset L_{Gen} of the language L. The reflective sub-language L_R contains the calls to the generators. That is, the pattern of evaluation that defines L_R is only initiated by these reflective calls. A possible *drop* function in this architecture is a function that takes a reflective call, finds its generator definition and uses the definition and the call arguments to form a call to the generator. The inner *eval* executes the call at compile-time to produce a new expression in Val_L. This in turn is transformed to an L expression by *raise* and presented to the outer *eval*. Figure 2.6 illustrates this model. Such a pattern of reflection is called *static* or *compile-time linguistic reflection* since the reflection is performed at compile-time even though the evaluator, *eval'*, is called. The type checking of the generated expressions is performed by the compiler. The pattern of *eval* is given by:

The macro facilities in POP-2 [1] and Scheme [2] contain this style of compile-time reflection without the type checking.

2.3.1 Optimised Compile-Time Linguistic Reflection

An optimised variant of the previous architecture can be produced by having the parser generate abstract syntax as values in *Val*. This choice of Val_L allows the result of the inner *eval* to be passed directly to the post-parse compiler called *postParseCompile*. The *raise* function reduces to the identity function in this optimisation. The *drop* function here produces a compiled version of the generator in the target language generator subset L_{Gen}. This optimised *drop* function is denoted by $drop_{Opt}$. The structure of *eval* in this case is shown in Figure 2.7. Here e_v denotes the parsed form of *e* expressed in Val_L and L_{R_v} the parsed forms of L_R. The pattern of *eval* is given by:

The two versions of the same *eval'* function in both Figure 2.6 and Figure 2.7 highlight some implementation choices. For example, although both *eval'* functions are semantically the same they may be implemented differently. The *eval'* within the compiler could be an interpreter function and the right hand *eval'* could be the machine executing machine code. The details of these implementations are not germane to our description.

An example of such an architecture is the implementation of TRPL [3]. The TRPL reflective constructs are TRPL context sensitive macro calls, the elements of L_R. The $drop_{Opt}$ function takes the parsed arguments of a macro call and passes them to the macro definitions which have been compiled into target language functions (generators) ready for *eval'*. Thus a call of the compiler is avoided in the reflective *eval*. The result of executing the compiled macro definitions is to produce new TRPL code expressed in the parsed form Val_L. This code can contain new function, type and even macro definitions. This new code is presented to the post-parse compiler for compilation and evaluated using *eval'*. Type checking is performed after each inner *eval'*.

```
procedure eval (e : L) → Val                  ! This types e as L and
    eval' (compile (e))                       ! eval as L → Val.

procedure compile (e : L) → L'
    postParseCompile (parse (e))

procedure postParseCompile (eV : ValL) → L'
    case eV of
    ConstructOfLRv => postParseCompile (raiseOpt (eval' (dropOpt (eV))))
    notConstructOfLRv => translate (eV)
```

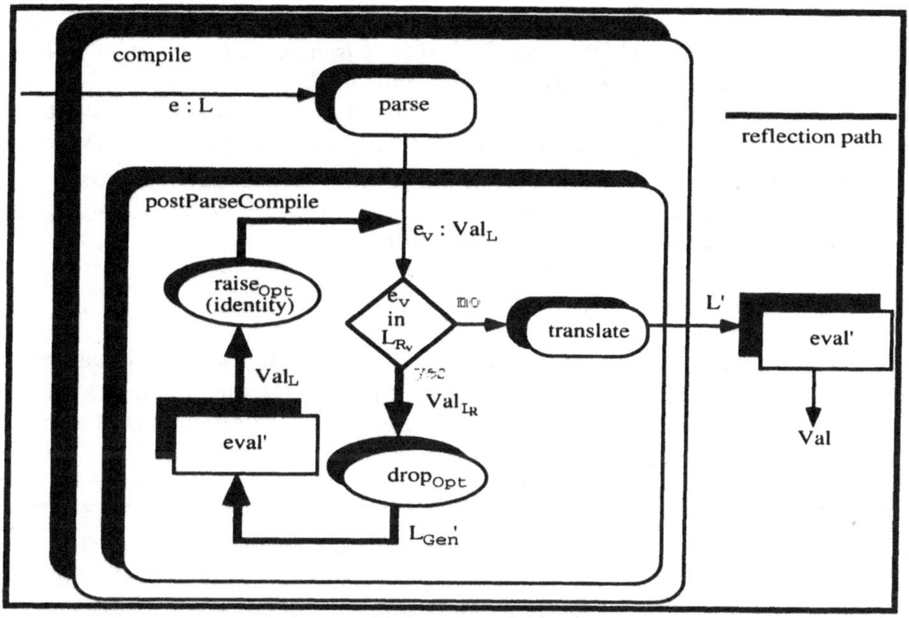

Fig. 2.7. *eval* in optimised compile-time linguistic reflection.

eval (**execute** ("2+" ++ "3"))
=> eval' (compile (**execute** ("2+" ++ "3")))
=> eval' (postParseCompile (parse (**execute** ("2+" ++ "3"))))
=> eval' (postParseCompile ((**execute** ("2+" ++ "3"))$_V$))

! the reflection is recognised
=> eval' (postParseCompile ($raise_{Opt}$ (eval' ($drop_{Opt}$ ((**execute** ("2+" ++ "3"))$_V$)))))

! $drop_{Opt}$ produces $\underline{\text{"2+" ++ "3"}}_{Gen}$ which denotes the compiled
! generator of $(2+3)_V$
=> eval' (postParseCompile ($raise_{Opt}$ (eval' ($\underline{\text{"2+" ++ "3"}}_{Gen}$))))
=> eval' (postParseCompile ($raise_{Opt}$ ((2+3)$_V$)))

! *raise* is the identity function
=> eval' (postParseCompile ((2+3)$_V$))
=> eval' ($\underline{2+3}$)
=> 5

Fig. 2.8. Optimised compile-time linguistic reflection in TRPL.

Figure 2.8 gives an example of optimised compile-time reflection as it occurs in TRPL. e_V denotes the Val_L form of e, while $\underline{e}$ denotes its compiled form.

The original expression, ***execute*** *("2+" ++ "3")*, is parsed and then examined by the post-parse compiler which recognises that it is a parsed form of a reflective construct. A generator previously compiled into its *L'* form from a definition of ***execute*** is produced by $drop_{Opt}$ using the parsed form of ***execute***'s input. This generator, $\underline{"2+" ++ "3"}_{Gen}$, evaluates to the Val_L form of *2 + 3*. The inner *eval'* executes the generator and the parsed form $(2+3)_v$ is produced. This is passed to the post-parser compiler, which completes its compilation. It is eventually evaluated in its compiled form by *eval'* as the completion of the original *eval.*

2.4 Run-Time Linguistic Reflection

Where reflection occurs at run-time the expression in L_R, which causes the reflection, has already been compiled. That is, it is the *eval'* function that recognises the expression in L_R', the compiled form of L_R, to initiate reflection. The original expression *e* is in the process of being evaluated by

```
eval (e)
=> eval' (compile (e))
=> eval' (e̲)                    ! where e̲ is the compiled form of e
```

The pattern of *eval'* in this case is shown by

```
procedure eval' (e̲ : L') → Val     ! This types e̲ as L' and
                                   ! eval' as L' → Val.
        case e̲ of
        ...
        ConstructOfLR' => eval (raiseRun (eval' (dropRun (e̲))))
        ...
```

Notice that the outer evaluation function is *eval* whereas the inner one is *eval'*. The outer *eval* encompasses the compiler since it expands to *eval' (compile (...))*. The $drop_{Run}$ function has the type $L_R' \rightarrow L_{Gen}'$. This is illustrated in Figure 2.9.

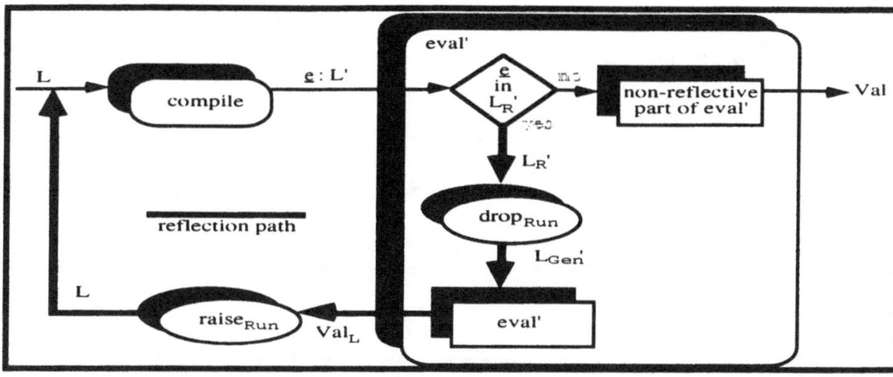

Fig. 2.9. *eval* in run-time linguistic reflection.

An example of this form of reflection is the use of a run-time callable compiler together with the ability to bind and execute newly compiled program fragments within the running program. PS-algol [4] and Napier88 (Chapter 1.1.3), [5] with their callable compilers and incremental loaders are examples of languages that provide run-time linguistic reflection. The function *eval* in Lisp and the function *popval* in POP-2 are early examples of untyped run-time reflection.

Figure 2.10 shows the evaluation of ***execute*** *("2+" ++ readString ())* in run-time reflection:

eval (**execute** ("2+" ++ readString ()))
=> eval' (compile (**execute** ("2+" ++ readString ())))
=> eval' (<u>**execute** ("2+" ++ readString ())</u>)

! now the reflection is recognised
=> eval ($raise_{Run}$ (eval' ($drop_{Run}$ (<u>**execute** ("2+" ++ readString ())</u>))))
=> eval ($raise_{Run}$ (eval' (<u>"2+" ++ readString ()</u>)))

! if "3" is input for the call of *readString*
=> eval ($raise_{Run}$ ("2+3"))

! applying *$raise_{Run}$* and expanding *eval*
=> eval' (compile (2+3))
=> eval' (<u>2+3</u>)
=> 5

Fig. 2.10. Run-time linguistic reflection in Napier88.

The original expression is first compiled and is in the process of being evaluated by *eval'* when the reflection is discovered. The compiled form <u>***execute*** *("2+" ++ readString())*</u> is presented to *$drop_{Run}$* which removes the **execute** verb. The inner *eval'* reads in the string and concatenates it with *"2+"*. If the string read in is *"3"* then the result of the concatenation is *"2+3"*. This expression is in *Val_L* and is transformed into L by $raise_{Run}$. Finally the expression $2+3$ is compiled and evaluated by *compile* and *eval'*.

3 Dimensions of Linguistic Reflection

So far three subtly different forms of linguistic reflection have been described. The pattern:

eval (raise (eval (drop (e))))

within the *eval* function represents the intuition given in the definition of linguistic reflection. With optimised compile-time linguistic reflection the pattern of evaluation is given by:

eval' (postParseCompile ($raise_{Opt}$ (eval' ($drop_{Opt}$ (e_v)))))

with the reflection recognised within the post-parse compiler. The inner evaluation is performed by *eval'* and $drop_{Opt}$ operates on the parsed form of the expression, e_v.

In run-time linguistic reflection the pattern of evaluation is given by:

eval' (compile ($raise_{Run}$ (eval' ($drop_{Run}$ ($\underline{e}$)))))

within the *eval'* function. The *eval'* function operates over the compiled form of the expression $\underline{e}$ and calls *eval* to compile and evaluate the result of the inner *eval'*. Here the reflection is recognised during run-time (target language) evaluation, i.e., in *eval'*, but entails a call of the compiler in performing the outer *eval*. These patterns may be obscured in actual programs, since an intermediate result may be computed at one point in the program and stored for use later in the compilation, execution or, with persistence, later executions.

The inner evaluation characterises linguistic reflection. This we have called generation and as can be seen above the nature of generators can vary. Notice, however, that the generators are always written in the subset L_{Gen} of the language, L. It is the nature of *drop* that differs in that the form of the expression presented to it may be in the language itself (*drop*), its parsed form ($drop_{Opt}$) or its compiled form ($drop_{Run}$).

The dimensions of linguistic reflection can be categorised by the following:

- What initiates linguistic reflection?
- How are the generators written?
- When are the generators executed?
- In what environment are the generators executed?

- How are the generated results bound?

For type-safe linguistic reflection there is one other dimension, namely

- When is the type checking performed?

3.1 What Initiates Linguistic Reflection?

Linguistic reflection is initiated by an expression in the reflective sub-language, L_R, being evaluated. The form of L_R may be a simple verb, such as **execute**, or a more sophisticated function or macro call as will be seen in Section 4.

3.2 How are the Generators Written?

Since the generators are all written in the language subset L_{Gen}, it is the nature of the language forms that they manipulate that distinguishes different linguistic reflective languages. The generators compute over and produce expressions in Val_L. In some systems this may simply be strings.

Where some processing of the expressions has already taken place, there is a possibility of using more structured forms for Val_L. In optimised compile-time linguistic reflection the generators operate over parsed forms of L. Thus Val_L can be the abstract syntax trees constructed by the parser. The generators then have the possibility of computing over these abstract syntax trees forming new ones to construct new program fragments.

3.3 When are the Generators Executed?

In current implementations, type-safe linguistic reflection takes place at fixed points in the evaluation process. To allow the reflective evaluation time to be under the user's control at least two L_R constructs are necessary. Both perform the same function but differ temporally and therefore in the environments in which they operate. They are:

- force which forces the reflective evaluation on the first encounter and replaces the *force* construct with the generated result. It therefore performs the inner *eval* and the *drop*.

- delay which delays reflective evaluation. That is the inner *eval* and *drop* are not performed until the program is executing after the initial compilation phase.

Compile-time linguistic reflection uses *force* implicitly whereas run-time linguistic reflection uses *delay*. Further investigation of the means of bringing the reflective evaluation time under users' control is needed.

3.4 In What Environment are the Generators Executed?

The time of reflective evaluation affects the environment that is available to the generator. There are two environmental issues here. First of all the generators may need access to the details of the compilation such as a symbol table containing type, scoping and identifier definitions. This is trivially available in compile-time linguistic reflection but it is also possible to parameterise the generators, with an environment, and to arrange that the compiler environment is preserved and available at run-time for run-time linguistic reflection.

The second issue is that generators may bind to existing values in a database or persistent store. This may be to R-values, by copy, or L-values, by reference, and may be immediately resolved, by *force*, or delayed until run-time, by *delay*. Means of implementing and exploiting such bindings are under investigation.

3.5 How are the Generated Results Bound?

In compile-time linguistic reflection the result of the generation is bound into the compilation taking place. In run-time linguistic reflection the result of the generation is bound into the executing program. The mechanisms chosen for this in both TRPL and Napier88 are quite simple and only accommodate the binding of generated fragments into the programs containing them. Other aspects involve the binding of free identifiers within both the generated fragment and the original program. The range of binding choices along with their use and implementation are topics for research.

3.6 When is the Type Checking Performed?

In optimised compile-time linguistic reflection the result of the generation is integrated into the program being compiled. The internal type consistency of the new program fragment and its type compatibility with the environment into which it is placed are both checked by the post-parse compiler before execution. In the implementation of TRPL the control of reflection is located in the type checker.

In run-time linguistic reflection the result of the generation is type checked when it is presented to the compiler as part of the outer *eval*. This checks for the fragment's internal consistency. The type compatibility of the fragment with its environment is checked when it is incrementally bound. Thus type checking forms part of the binding phase.

4 Uses of Linguistic Reflection

Here two examples of linguistic reflection are presented in detail. They are examples of:

- abstraction over types, and
- accommodating evolution in strongly typed persistent systems.

Both examples involve reflective access to types in order to achieve the required behaviour. It is somewhat ironic that strong typing, which makes it difficult to integrate reflection with strongly typed programming languages, plays a key role in making linguistic reflection effective in cases exemplified in this section. Linguistic reflection without strong typing, such as in Lisp macro evaluation, has little systematic information available about the structures involved in computation. Types in a strongly typed language constitute systematically required information about all computations. This information can be used in linguistically reflective programming to automatically adjust to specific details such as the names of attributes and to the creation of new types during system evolution.

Following the detailed explanation of the two examples other applications of linguistic reflection are given.

4.1 Abstraction Over Types

4.1.1 The Example

In this section an example of creating an abstraction over types is given using the TRPL style of optimised compile-time linguistic reflection. Abstractions over types are useful when the details of a computation depends significantly on the details of its input types. A generic natural join function provides an example of such abstraction. Here the details of the input types, particularly the names of the tuple components, significantly affect the algorithm and the output type of the function, determining:

- the result type,
- the algorithm to test whether tuples from both input relations match on the overlapping fields, and
- the code to build a relation having tuples with the aggregation of fields from both input relations but with only one copy of the overlapping fields.

The specification of a generic natural join function may be achieved by compile-time linguistic reflection as long as the types of the input relations are known at compile-time. One approach is to generate individual natural join functions for each distinct call. A second approach is to write a generator that produces a call to a parametric polymorphic join function for each unique call to natural join. The reflective ability required for this approach is the same as for the first but the details are simpler. Thus the second approach is chosen to facilitate presentation. A parametric polymorphic join is one in which both the match function and the concatenation function are given as arguments.

The following gives the partial specification of such a join function using TRPL syntax:

```
function (alpha, beta, gamma)
    join( r1        : set (alpha),
          r2        : set (beta),
          match     : [alpha, beta] → boolean,
          concat    : [alpha, beta] → gamma) : set (gamma);
```

This function is polymorphic over types *alpha, beta* and *gamma*. It uses the *match* input function to qualify pairs of tuples for inclusion in the result and the *concat* function to construct elements in the result set. With an arbitrary *match* function this function is a theta-join [6]. By supplying the correct *match* and *concat* functions it can be specialised to a natural join. The point to notice is that all the information necessary for constructing *match* and *concat* for a natural join is obtainable from the types *alpha* and *beta*, which in TRPL are inferred. Linguistic reflection allows the generation of the correct *match* and *concat* functions from the representations of these types.

Consider computing the natural join between variables of types *rtype* and *stype*, defined by the equations

```
rtype = set (struct make_a_b_c (a : integer, b : boolean, c : integer));
stype = set (struct make_a_d (a : integer, d : boolean));
```

The TRPL type equations involving the definition of **struct** types define constructor functions for values (tuples) of the types, in this case *make_a_b_c* and *make_a_d*, and selector functions, e.g., *a, b, c* and *d*. For variables *r* and *s* of types *rtype* and *stype* the following expression for the natural join of *r* and *s* may be written:

```
NATJOIN (r, s)
```

This is a TRPL reflective construct, recognised by virtue of its being fully capitalised, and its inner *eval* generates an appropriate call of the generic join, in its Val_L form. The linguistic reflective process also generates a new type equation to define the type of the join's output and then generates the appropriate *match* and *concat* functions. For example:

```
jointype = set (struct make_a_b_c_d (a : integer, b : boolean,
                                     c : integer, d : boolean));

join(   r, s,
        [x, y] → x.a = y.a,
        [x, y] → make_a_b_c_d (x.a, x.b, x.c, y.d))
```

Forms such as *[x, y] → x.a = y.a* represent lambda functions in TRPL. This example stands for the boolean function of two variables that returns *true* if the *a* components are equal.

4.1.2 Details of TRPL Optimised Compile-Time Reflection

In this section the definition of a natural join context sensitive macro in TRPL is presented in considerable detail and related to the general picture of linguistic reflection presented in Section 2. In TRPL, Val_L comprises values of two types, one for representing types, *type_rep*, and one for expressions, *exp_rep*. Figure 4.1 gives the TRPL type definitions for these. Both are defined as unions of choices for the different types and syntactic categories. The type constructors include *struct*, as described above, *list*, *pair*, and *singleton*, for constructing a type consisting of a single value such as the empty list *nil*. Expression categories are the syntactic categories of the language and include identifier, integer constant, selection of a structure component and function call.

The TRPL reflective sub-language consists of calls of context sensitive macros such as *NATJOIN* above. Calls of these macros initiate linguistic reflection. Macros are called context sensitive since they have access to the types defined at the point of their compilation. The generators invoked by the macro calls are defined in macro definitions and are functions from the parsed input to the macro calls (in Val_L) and types contained in the compiler environment (also in Val_L). They generate in-line expansions as well as new function and type definitions. The new definitions augment the compiler environment at the time of the generation, i. e., at the time of the inner *eval*.

```
type_rep =
union (  int_type : singleton int_rep,

         struct_type : struct struct_rep ( constructor_name : string,
                                struct_components : list (pair (string, type_rep))),

         parametric_type : struct parametric_rep (
                                parametric_constructor_name : string,
                                parameters : list (type_rep)),
         ...)

exp_rep =
union (  identifier :        struct make_identifier (identifier_name : symbol),
         integer_constant :  struct make_integer_constant (integer_value :
                                                               integer),
         selection :         struct make_selection (  structure_value : exp_rep,
                                                      attribute : string),
         function_call :     struct make_function_call (function_name : string,
                                                   parameter_list : list (exp_rep)),
         ...)
```

Fig. 4.1. Types of TRPL Val_L for representing the language.

A TRPL macro definition consists of three parts: the header, the *units* and the inline expansion. The *units* section generates the new function and type definitions. Figure 4.2 shows the outline of a TRPL macro for a natural join function.

```
macro NATJOIN (r, s) ;
1       get and expand types for r and s; generate new names
2       compute the sets of unique and overlapping components of r and s
3       compute the output type definition and add it to environment via units
4       compute the representations of the match and concat functions
5       build the representation of the inline expansion
```

Fig. 4.2. Outline of a TRPL natural join macro definition.

Figure 4.3 shows the header and a segment for accomplishing task 1 in a TRPL macro definition for a natural join function.

```
macro NATJOIN (r, s) ; env e;
let ertype :=  type_of (r, e),              @ get the types of r and s
    estype :=  type_of (s, e),
    rtype :=   expandtype (ertype, e),      @ expand set types to
    stype :=   expandtype (estype, e),      @ remove any type variables

@ build component lists for r and s
    rcomps := case rtype
              {parametric_rep ("set", cons (struct_rep (?, rcompslist), nil))
                           → rcompslist,
                           @ ? indicates tuple constructor name unimportant
              others       → warning ("first argument not a set of tuple", nil)},
    scomps := case stype
              {parametric_rep ("set", cons (struct_rep (?, scompslist), nil))
                           → scompslist,
              others       → warning ("second argument not a set of tuple",
                                      nil)},

@ generate symbols for new type
    tn := genstring ("type$"),

@ and constructor function for output tuples
    constr := genstring ("constr$"),
```

Fig. 4.3. Natural join definition segment for type extraction.

First the types of *r* and *s* are extracted from the current compilation environment *e* using a built-in function *type_of*. This uses an environment variable defined in the header as the current compiler environment. These types are expanded using another built-in function *expandtype*. This expands all type variables contained in a type representation into their structural forms. The next two equations extract the list of component names by using pattern recognition on the representation of the input types. A representation of a legal type for this macro call is of the form *parametric_rep ("set", cons (struct_rep ("constrName", componentList), nil))*. The case statement either matches this for each type representation or returns an error. When a match is made the variables in the pattern are bound to their matched components and the case body is evaluated. Question marks stand for parts of the value to be matched by anything and ignored. The case bodies here are just the extracted list of component name and type pairs. This section ends with the generation of new names for the output type and a constructor function for its tuples.

Figure 4.4 shows tasks 2 and 3: the computation of the unique and overlapping components of the two input relations, along with the *units* section containing the generation of the output type definition.

```
        runique :=
            set_difference (rcomps, scomps, [x & ?, y & ?] → string_eq (x, y)),
        sunique :=
            set_difference (scomps, rcomps, [x & ?, y & ?] → string_eq (x, y)),
        overlap :=
            set_intersection (scomps, rcomps, [x & ?, y & ?] → string_eq (x, y))
in
units
        LIST (  @ the new type definition
                define_type (  tn,
                               parametric_rep ("set", LIST (struct_rep (constr,
                                     append3 (overlap, runique, sunique))))))
```

Fig. 4.4. Computing component overlap and the output type.

This code uses pattern matching lambda expressions, the expressions starting with *[x & ?, y & ?]*. In these functions the input arguments are first matched with the patterns in the brackets. The patterns here are pairs since *&* is the infix pair construction operator. The values are *struct_components* defined as pairs in Figure 4.1. As before, successful pattern matching causes the variables in the patterns to be bound to the matching components of the values. In this case *x* and *y* are bound to the names of the components.

The unique and overlapping components are computed by *set_difference* and *set_intersection* utilising the lambda functions over the component lists. Pattern matching lambda expressions capture the criterion that components are equal when their names represented as strings are equal. If the names are equal but the types are not, the *match* function will produce a type error when it is passed to the compiler. The *units* section contains only the output type definition using another built-in function *define_type*. The first parameter gives the computed type name and the second supplies the representation of the type expression including the tuple constructor function name, bound to *constr*. Note the use of the constructor functions, *parametric_rep* and *struct_rep*, to construct the typed representation of the new type.

Figure 4.5 gives the code for generating the representations of the *match* and *concat* function bodies. The *match* body is an expression of the form *rt.a=st.a && rt.b=st.b && ...* , where *&&* denotes logical *and*. It is to be used in the inline expansion as the body of a lambda function having *rt* and *st* as variables standing for the tuples of the input relations, *r* and *s*.

This portion of the definition uses a macro, *EREP*, to facilitate the generation of expression representations. *EREP* takes as its first argument an expression which gives a pattern for the representation it generates. Optional arguments may follow which give values to be substituted in the representation of the first argument. This allows computed representations to be inserted into constant expressions. A simple example of this is *EREP (f (x), x := s2id ("y"))*, where *s2id* is a function that converts a string value into the representation of an identifier. This evaluates to the representation of *f (y)*. The *match* body is produced by mapping the *eqterm* function over the overlapping component name and type pairs. The *eqterm* function takes a component pair, extracts the component name and constructs an equality expression that compares the named projection of *rt* and *st* tuples. The list of these terms is used to construct a boolean expression *and*ing all the equality terms with *true*. This uses a reduction function over the mapped list. The reduction uses a binary lambda function and *EREP* to build the representation of the *and* expression. Starting the reduction with *true* defines the base case of no common component names to be the cartesian product.

```
@ build bodies of match and concat
@ first a representation for the body of the match lambda
@ expression which looks like rt.a=st.a && rt.b=st.b && ... && true

let   eqterm := [x & ?] → EREP ((rt.field) = (st.field), field := s2id (x)),
      match := listreduce (  listmap( overlap, eqterm),
                             [term, exp] → EREP (t && e, t := term, e := exp),
                             EREP (true)),

@ build a representation for the body of the concat
@ lambda expression which looks like
@ construct (rt.common1, ... rt.unique1, ... st.unique1, ...)

concat := EREP (
      con ( ...args),
      con := s2id (constr),
      args := append3 (  listmap (overlap, [x & ?] → EREP (rt.f, f := s2id (x))),
                         listmap (runique, [x & ?] → EREP (rt.f, f := s2id (x))),
                         listmap (sunique, [x & ?] → EREP (st.f, f := s2id (x)))))
```

Fig. 4.5. Generating the *match* and *concat* representations.

The *concat* body is generated by using *EREP* and *listmap*, together with a feature that allows variable length constructs in the pattern used in *EREP*. The ellipsis before *args* marks it as a parameter that accepts a list for its substitution. The list of representations of component names is produced by the *append3* and *listmap* functions, the former a function that appends three lists. An example of a *concat* body is *make_a_b_c_d (rt.a, rt.b, rt.c, st.d)*.

Figure 4.6 gives the definition of the inline expansion to be generated. It uses *EREP* and the computed bodies of *match* and *concat* to generate the representation of a call to *join*.

```
@ the inline expansion is a call to join with lambda functions
@ for match and concat
in
      EREP ( join (r, s, [rt, st] → mtch, [rt, st] → cnct),
             mtch := match,
             cnct := concat)
```

Fig. 4.6. Defining the inline expansion.

Figure 4.7 shows the evaluation of a call to *NATJOIN*. The types of *r* and *s* are *rtype* and *stype* as given in Section 4.1.1.

```
NATJOIN (r, s)
=> eval (NATJOIN (r, s))
=> eval' (compile (NATJOIN (r, s)))
=> eval' (postParseCompile (parse (NATJOIN (r, s))))
=> eval' (postParseCompile ((NATJOIN (r, s))V))

   ! the reflection is recognised
=> eval' (postParseCompile (raise (eval' (drop ((NATJOIN (r, s))V)))))

   ! drop produces a call to the compiled NATJOIN definition
=> eval' (postParseCompile (raise (eval' (NATJOIN_generator (rV, sV)))))
=> eval' (postParseCompile (raise ((join (r, s,[x, y] → x.a = y.a,
                    [x, y] → make_a_b_c_d (x.a, x.b, x.c, y.d)))V)))

   ! raise is the identity function
=> eval' (postParseCompile ((join (r, s, [x, y] → x.a = y.a,
                      [x, y] → make_a_b_c_d (x.a, x.b, x.c, y.d)))V))
=> eval' (join (r, s, [x, y] → x.a = y.a,
                    [x, y] → make_a_b_c_d (x.a, x.b, x.c, y.d)))
=> natural join of r and s
```

Fig. 4.7. Natural join using optimised compile-time linguistic reflection.

By the time the compilation of *NATJOIN* starts, the definition given in Figures 4.3 through 4.6 has been compiled into a generator comprising the call to *define_type* and the code that constructs the inline expression. *NATJOIN_generator* stands for the compiled form of this generator. *drop* produces a call to this generator with the parsed form of the macro's arguments as input. The output of this generator is bound into the original computation simply by being passed to the post-parse compiler.

While the types of the input of a natural join are inferred by the underlying type system, which is non-reflective, the inference of the output type is beyond the type system's capabilities. Reflection has been, in effect, used to perform this inference. Note however that neither having the programmer provide the output type nor building the ability to do this particular inference into the type system solves the problem. The *match* and *concat* functions would still need to be synthesised and this is beyond the scope of type inference. Natural join is not the only problematical operation in relational database systems. The *nest* and *unnest* operations of nested relational systems make similar demands on a programming language [7].

4.2 Evolution in Strongly Typed Persistent Systems

Another way linguistic reflection may be used is in accommodating the evolution of strongly typed persistent object stores. Characteristics of such stores are that the type system is infinite and that the set of types of existing values in the store evolves independently from any one program. This means that when a program is written or generated some of the values that it may have to manipulate may not yet exist, and their types may not yet be known for inclusion in the program text. For strong typing these values must have a most general type but in some applications their specific types can only be found once they have been created.

An example of such a program is a persistent object store browser [8, 9] which displays a graphical representation of any value presented to it. The browser may encounter values in the persistent store for which it does not have a static type description. This may occur, for example, for values which are added to the store after the time of definition of the browser program. For the program to be able to denote such values, they must belong to an infinite union type, such as Amber's **dynamic** [10], PS-algol's **pntr** [4] or Napier88's **any** (Chapter 1.1.3), [5].

Before any operations may be performed on a value of an infinite union type it must be projected onto another type with more type information. This projection typically takes the form of a dynamic check of the value's type against a static type assertion made in the program that uses it. A projection of a Napier88 **any** value is shown in the example below:

```
proc (val : any)
      project val as specific onto
      int :       writeInt (specific )
      string :    writeString (specific )
      default :   writeString ("not a string or int") ! specific not in scope here
```

This shows a procedure that takes a parameter *val* of type **any**. In the body of the procedure the specific type of *val* is matched against two alternatives. If a match occurs the name *specific*, denoting the value with the specific type, enters scope in the corresponding branch. If the type of *val* does not match either of the statically specified types **int** or **string** then the specific type of *val* is unknown and the default branch is executed.

As stated earlier the browser program takes as parameter an infinite union type to allow it to deal with values whose types were not predicted at the time of implementation. However the program cannot contain static type assertions for all the types that may be encountered as their number is unbounded. There are two possibilities for the construction of such a program: it may either be written in a lower-level technology [11] or else be written using linguistic reflection.

To allow a reflective solution the program must be able to discover dynamically the specific type of a value of the union type. Such functionality may be provided in a strongly typed language without compromising type security by defining representations of types within the value space of the language, i.e., within Val_L. An example of such a representation in TRPL was shown in Figure 4.1. Access to type representations may be provided by a function such as the Napier88 procedure

getTypeRep : **proc** (**any** → TypeRep)

which allows a program to discover type description information by the manipulation of values of the representation type.

4.2.1 Details of Browser Implementation

The linguistic reflective implementation of the browser program has a number of components. First of all the value of the union type passed to the program is interrogated to yield a representation of its specific type. Using this information the browser constructs a representation of some appropriate Napier88 code. The compiler is called dynamically with this code representation as its argument, and returns some executable code which is capable of performing the appropriate projection of the union type, along with the required operations to browse the value. This new code is type-safe since it has been checked by the compiler. A different program will need to be generated for each different type of value which is encountered during the browsing of the persistent store.

An example of the operation of a Napier88 browser program will now be given in the context of the anatomy of run-time reflection defined in Section 2.4. Assume that a value of the following type, injected into the union type **any**, is passed to the browser:

type Person **is structure** (name : **string** ; age : **int**)

To display the value the browser needs to be able to construct and display a menu window such as:

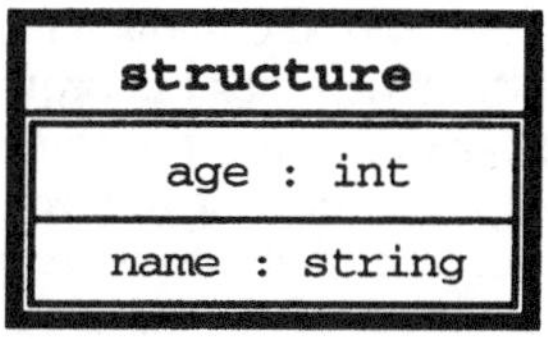

It must also be able to extract the field values for further browsing should the user select one of the menu entries. The browser has built into it methods for displaying instances of the base types such as **string** and **int**. An outline of the browser code is shown in Figure 4.8.

```
let browser = proc (val : any)
begin
    let valTypeRep = getTypeRep (val)

    if valTypeRep denotes a base type then use built-in method else
    begin
        case true of
        valTypeRep denotes a structure type :
        begin
            let new = evaluate (makeCode (valTypeRep))
            ! new is of type any.
            ! makeCode builds up a string program representation through
            ! analysis of valTypeRep.

            ! For the example the result will be
            ! "type T is structure (name : string ; age : int)
            !    proc (x : any)
            !    project x as specificX onto
            !    T : menu2 ('"name : string'", '"age : int'",
            !                proc() ; browser (any (specificX (name))),
            !                proc() ; browser (any (specificX (age))))
            !    default : writeString ('"error'")"

            ! single quote is used as an escape to allow the inclusion
            ! of double quotes in the string.

            project new as newDisplayer onto
            proc (any) :    newDisplayer (val)
            default :       writeString ("error in compilation")
        end
        other cases : use similar methods for other type constructors
    end
end
```

Fig. 4.8. Browsing using run-time linguistic reflection.

When the browser program is called it first obtains a representation of the type of the value passed to it. If it is one of the base types the browser has built-in knowledge of how to display it. Otherwise the type must be an instance of one of a fixed number of type constructors. In the example it is a structure type. The browser displays structures using a generic method. The method involves constructing a program that defines a procedure to display instances of the particular structure type, evaluating it and calling the resulting procedure to display the structure.

For brevity the definitions of the procedures *getTypeRep*, *makeCode*, *menu2* and *writeString* have not been shown. Note that the program produced by the generator itself contains a call to the browser program. This is achieved by binding the browser program into the persistent store where it can be accessed by the generated program. The details of this access have also been omitted.

Figure 4.9 shows the mode of evaluation of the reflective part of the browser program, the call to the *evaluate* procedure.

```
evaluate (makeCode (valTypeRep))
=> eval (evaluate (makeCode (valTypeRep)))
=> eval' (compile (evaluate (makeCode (valTypeRep))))
=> eval' (evaluate (makeCode (valTypeRep)))

    ! now the reflection denoted by the call to evaluate is recognised
=> eval (raiseRun (eval' (dropRun (evaluate (makeCode (valTypeRep))))))
=> eval (raiseRun (eval' (makeCode (valTypeRep))))

=> eval (raiseRun ("type T is ... writeString ('"error"')"))
=> eval' (compile (type T is ... writeString ("error")))
=> eval' (type T is ... writeString ("error"))

    ! the procedure value produced
=> proc( x : any ) ; ...
```

Fig. 4.9. Reflective evaluation within the browser.

The algorithm shown is potentially inefficient as it requires reflection to be performed on every encounter with a structure type. In practice the persistent store is used to cache the results of reflection so that the code generation and reflection need not occur for types encountered previously.

This style of reflection can be analysed in the context of the dimensions of reflection described in Section 3, as follows. The linguistic reflection is initiated at run-time when the evaluator *eval'* encounters the compiled form of the L_R construct *evaluate*. Generators are procedures that produce strings. In the cases that the generators execute without errors the strings represent fragments of Napier88 code, i.e., they are in Val_L. The generators are executed at run-time and may access values in the persistent store but have no direct access to compilation information. In the example type information is passed to the generator as a parameter; this is obtained using a pre-defined procedure that produces a representation of the type of any value injected into an **any** union. The result of the generation is compiled using the run-time callable compiler and the result of executing the new compiled code bound into the original computation using Napier88's **any** projection mechanism. This mechanism supports dynamic incremental binding. Finally, type checking occurs in two stages. In the first the internal type consistency of the generated program fragment is verified during the operation of the compiler at run-time. In the second the type compatibility of the existing program and the value produced by evaluation of the compiled fragment is checked during evaluation of the **any** projection clause. Note that two uses of the infinite union are required. One is to give a type to the *getType* procedure so that it may be statically typed and yet permit type inquiry over values of any type, and the other to give a type to the evaluate procedure so that it can evaluate any expression.

This example illustrates the use of linguistic reflection to define programs that operate over values whose type is not known in advance. These programs potentially perform different operations according to the type of their operands but without endangering the type security of the system. The requirement for such programs is typical of an evolving system where new values and types must be incrementally created without the necessity to re-define or re-compile existing programs.

4.3 Applications of Linguistic Reflection

Applications of reflection in the context of database programming languages have stimulated the development of the technology described above. These applications address the following problems:

- attaining high levels of genericity,
- accommodating changes in systems,
- implementing data models,
- optimising implementations, and
- validating specifications.

4.3.1 Attaining High Levels of Genericity

The examples given in Sections 4.1 and 4.2 both address the problem of attaining a high level of genericity. In each, the type dependent details of instances of a family of functions are generated. Thus the generators can be thought of as highly generic abstractions over the functions. Another example of this approach is a set of four traversal functions over recursive data types [12]. These functions generalise the list map and fold (reduce) functions allowing them to be applied to any recursive data type. Sheard has also used the technique to define a deep equality test for any type [3]. Similarly, forms systems for data entry and access can be automatically generated from type definitions. Cooper has used such a technique to provide a rich repertoire of interaction modes over any structures that may be defined in a range of data models [13]. There is frequently a greater range of type dependent algorithms required than can sensibly be provided by built-in system programs. Linguistic reflection allows programmers to tailor their own style of presentation without requiring them to use a separate language or to penetrate the internal properties of the system. Ease of use of reflective systems remains a significant problem; there have been several attempts to develop more suitable notations for expressing generators and the calls to them [3, 14].

As demonstrated by the examples, the genericity achievable via linguistic reflection has often depended on the ability of a generator to access type details and generate program fragments that are tailored to the types given when the generator is executed. This constitutes a form of *ad hoc* polymorphism [15], but the genericity attained in these examples exceeds the capabilities of current polymorphic type systems [16]. In most polymorphic systems, the behaviour of polymorphic functions must be essentially invariant over the range of input types. The examples listed above have behaviour that varies too much to be accommodated by polymorphic systems.

4.3.2 Accommodating Changes in Systems

The browser described in Section 4.2 illustrates the way in which programs can adjust to system evolution, in this case the creation of values of previously unencountered types. Linguistic reflection can be used to accommodate a wide range of system changes. For example the schema changes of typical database applications become type changes in database programming languages, and reflective programs that are based on type details can regenerate code whenever a schema changes. If algorithms such as joins or form generation are systematically derived from the type information these derivations will be re-computed. With run-time reflection this happens lazily which may save computation since many systems undergo a sequence of changes between runs of many of their applications. In contrast the hand-crafted method of providing the same functionality requires that a programmer locate all the places where changes are necessary, perform all the changes correctly and then re-validate the software. The reflective method gains particularly well in this case as it may avoid the need for re-validation as is discussed below.

4.3.3 Implementing Data Models

A data model is typically defined by a data description language and by one or more data manipulation languages (including query languages). Linguistic reflection allows these languages to be implemented efficiently, avoiding any additional levels of interpretation. Sentences in the data description language introduce new model constructs. The reflective generator translates these sentences into type declarations and declarations of associated procedures and introduces these into the computational context. Sentences in the data manipulation language are then translated into corresponding algorithms against these representational types and executed via reflection. In a persistent language this provides a very rapid means of prototyping and evaluating a data model [13, 17, 18]. With the optimisation strategies discussed below this can be developed into a reasonable quality implementation of a DBMS for the data model.

This use of reflection to implement languages is not confined to data models. The technique is applicable to any language and has been used in a commercial system to develop requirements analysis tools based on process modelling [19-21]. Philbrow has used the same technique to provide polymorphic indexing mechanisms over arbitrary collections [22].

4.3.4 Optimising Implementations

Using linguistic reflection to avoid a level of interpretation is a form of optimisation. In addition to this optimisation, a generator that develops concrete code for high level abstractions can choose from implementation strategies in order to minimise costs [23]. Relational query optimisation, for example, can be integrated directly into the compilation process via linguistic reflection. Run-time reflection allows re-compilation and new optimisation as the statistics of the database change. More general transformations of high level specifications into implementations can also be accomplished using linguistic reflection [24].

4.3.5 Validating Specifications

There are various ways linguistic reflection can be used to support validation of programs. The first derives from the fact that generated program fragments are stereotyped in their form. This stereotyping can be aimed toward producing forms that facilitate verification efforts [25, 26]. Generators themselves can be analysed in order to verify properties of all generated expressions. Though this is a second order problem, there is the possibility of stereotyping the generator programs themselves to produce sub-languages that support the second-order reasoning. Validating generators would be especially useful since it would mean that programs that were regenerated as a result of system evolution such as changes to types would not need to be re-validated.

Theorem proving itself can be integrated with compilation using linguistic reflective capabilities. A version of the Boyer-Moore theorem prover kernel has been implemented in TRPL working over the parsed form of TRPL's functional core language. Using this kernel, validation of properties of TRPL functional programs can be performed as a part of the compilation process. For example, the problem of verifying that database integrity constraints are invariants of transactions can be addressed by this approach [27].

5 Conclusions

A style of reflection appearing in strongly typed programming languages has been identified, defined and described. This style of reflection, termed type-safe linguistic reflection, can extend the class of algorithms that can be written in a type-safe manner. Linguistic reflection is characterised by the ability of a program to generate code in its language that is to be integrated into its own execution. This ability provides a base for generator technology that can be integrated with a programming language in a uniform and type-safe manner. While this capability has been a feature of many interpreter based languages with weak type systems, it is relatively new in compiler based, strongly typed systems. Two styles of linguistic reflection have arisen in database programming languages, compile-time and run-time. Both have been described in detail, allowing a comparison of the mechanisms as currently implemented.

Many uses have been found for linguistic reflection in the database programming area. These uses are characterised by a need for a high level of genericity in specifying data and procedures, a requirement that has proved problematical to meet using programming language type systems alone. Two such uses have been detailed and several more discussed.

Type safety has been achieved in PS-algol, Napier88 and TRPL by type checking each generated program segment, which is necessary when the complete programming language can be used to write generators. Limiting the language subset available for writing generators may allow the generators to be type checked for the type of all output at one time. This is a topic for future research. Other work to be done includes combining the two styles of reflection presented here, finding well engineered means of writing linguistically reflective code, and exploring the relationship of linguistic reflection with other kinds of reflection.

Acknowledgements. This paper was started at a one week workshop on reflection held in St Andrews in January 1991. The work was supported by ESPRIT II Basic Research Action 3070 – FIDE, SERC grants GR/H 15219 and GR/F 02953, and National Science Foundation grants IRI-8606424 and IRI-8822121. Richard Connor was supported by SERC Postdoctoral Fellowship B/91/RFH/9078.

References

1. Burstall RM, Collins JS, Popplestone RJ. Programming in POP-2. Edinburgh University Press, Edinburgh, Scotland, 1971
2. Rees J, Clinger W. Revised Report on the Algorithmic Language Scheme. ACM SIGPLAN Notices 1986; 21,12:37-43
3. Sheard T. A user's Guide to TRPL: A Compile-time Reflective Programming Language. COINS, University of Massachusetts Report 90-109, 1990
4. PS-algol. PS-algol Reference Manual, 4th edition. Universities of Glasgow and St Andrews Report PPRR-12-88, 1988
5. Morrison R, Brown AL, Connor RCH, Dearle A. The Napier88 Reference Manual. Universities of Glasgow and St Andrews Report PPRR-77-89, 1989
6. Codd EF. Extending the Relational Model to Capture More Meaning. ACM Transactions on Database Systems 1979; 4,4:397-434
7. Jaeschke G, Schek HJ. Remarks on the Algebra of Non First Normal Form Relations. In: Proc. 1st Symposium on the Principles of Database Systems, 1982, pp 124-138
8. Dearle A, Brown AL. Safe Browsing in a Strongly Typed Persistent Environment. Computer Journal 1988; 31,6:540-544
9. Dearle A, Cutts QI, Kirby GNC. Browsing, Grazing and Nibbling Persistent Data Structures. In: Rosenberg J, Koch DM (ed) Persistent Object Systems, Proc. 3rd International Workshop on Persistent Object Systems, Newcastle, Australia 1989. Springer-Verlag, 1990, pp 56-69
10. Cardelli L. Amber. In: Lecture Notes in Computer Science 242. Springer-Verlag, 1986, pp 21-47
11. Kirby GNC, Dearle A. An Adaptive Graphical Browser for Napier88. University of St Andrews Report CS/90/16, 1990
12. Sheard T. Automatic Generation and Use of Abstract Structure Operators. ACM Transactions on Programming Languages and Systems 1991; 19,4:531-557
13. Cooper RL. On The Utilisation of Persistent Programming Environments. Ph.D. thesis, University of Glasgow, 1990
14. Kirby GNC. Persistent Programming with Strongly Typed Linguistic Reflection. In: Proc. 25th International Conference on Systems Sciences, Hawaii, 1992, pp 820-831
15. Strachey C. Fundamental Concepts in Programming Languages. Oxford University Press, Oxford, 1967
16. Stemple D, Fegaras L, Sheard T, Socorro A. Exceeding the Limits of Polymorphism in Database Programming Languages. In: Bancilhon F, Thanos C, Tsichritzis D (ed) Lecture Notes in Computer Science 416 (EDBT '90). Springer-Verlag, 1990, pp 269-285
17. Cooper RL. Configurable Data Modelling Systems. In: Proc. 9th International Conference on the Entity Relationship Approach, Lausanne, Switzerland, 1990, pp 35-52
18. Cooper RL, Qin Z. A Graphical Data Modelling Program With Constraint Specification and Management. In: Proc. 10th British National Conference on Databases, Aberdeen, 1992, pp 192-208
19. Bruynooghe RF, Parker JM, Rowles JS. PSS: A System for Process Enactment. In: Proc. 1st International Conference on the Software Process: Manufacturing Complex Systems, 1991
20. Greenwood RM, Guy MR, Robinson DJK. The Use of a Persistent Language in the Implementation of a Process Support System. ICL Technical Journal 1992; 8,1:108-130

21. Warboys B. The IPSE 2.5 Project: Process Modelling as the Basis for a Support Environment. In: Proc. 1st International Conference on System Development Environments and Factories, Berlin, Germany, 1989
22. Philbrow PC. Indexing Strongly Typed Heterogeneous Collections Using Reflection and Persistence. In: Proc. ECOOP/OOPSLA Workshop on Reflection and Metalevel Architectures in Object-Oriented Programming, Ottawa, Canada, 1990
23. Cooper RL, Atkinson MP, Dearle A, Abderrahmane D. Constructing Database Systems in a Persistent Environment. In: Proc. 13th International Conference on Very Large Data Bases, 1987, pp 117-125
24. Fegaras L, Stemple D. Using Type Transformation in Database System Implementation. In: Kanellakis P, Schmidt JW (ed) 3rd International Conference on Database Programming Languages, Proc. 3rd International Workshop on Database Programming Languages, Nafplion, Greece. Morgan Kaufmann, 1991, pp 337-353
25. Fegaras L, Sheard T, Stemple D. Uniform Traversal Combinators: Definition, Use and Properties. In: Proc. 11th International Conference on Automated Deduction (CADE-11), Saratoga Springs, New York, 1992. LNAI 607, pp. 148-162
26. Stemple D, Sheard T, Fegaras L. Linguistic Reflection: A Bridge from Programming to Database Languages. In: Proc. 25th International Conference on Systems Sciences, Hawaii, 1992, pp 844-855
27. Sheard T, Stemple D. Automatic Verification of Database Transaction Safety. ACM Transactions on Database Systems 1989; 12,3:322-368

Chapter 1.2.2

Type-Safe Linguistic Run-time Reflection A Practical Perspective*

Richard Cooper[1] and Graham Kirby[2]

[1] Dept. of Computing Science, University of Glasgow, Glasgow G12 8QQ, Scotland
[2] Division of Computer Science, University of St Andrews, North Haugh, St Andrews, Fife KY16 9SS, Scotland

Abstract. This paper describes the use of reflection to create programs which modify themselves, the difficulties in writing such programs and a practical tool for making reflective programming easier.

1 Introduction

A **reflective language** is one in which it is possible to write programs which can adapt their behaviour to cope with novel data (Chapter 1.2.1). The particular form of reflection with which this paper concerns itself is **type-safe run-time linguistic reflection**. That is, the program modifies itself at run-time, but always through the inclusion of code which is type checked.

The way in which this is usually achieved is by creating the program in such a way that it creates new source code fragments as strings, compiles them and then executes them, as described in detail in the preceding paper in this collection. This is illustrated by the following piece of pseudo-code:

```
let source = "a string containing the source code of a program fragment"
let object = compile( source )
object()
```

As it stands, this is clearly a slow way to execute a procedure, requiring a compilation for every execution. Reflection is of use when the program has accumulated some new data during its run which must be part of the source string and which the programmer could not have known when the program was written. Thus, the pseudo-code should be extended to:

```
let template = "a string containing a program template"
let extraInformation = "a string holding data gathered by the program"
if we already have a version for this value of extraInformation
  then let object = retrieve the stored version
  else begin
      let source = stringManipulate( template, extraInformation )
      let object = compile( source )
      store object for this value of extraInformation
```

---

* The original version of this paper appeared as [1].

```
    end
  object(.....)
```

It is the nature of the extra information which concern this paper, how it is combined with the template and how the resulting code is stored. Section 2 describes where the extra information comes from and some of the difficulties with creating the source string. The third section describes a tool to make this easier.

2 Uses of Reflection

There are two sources of *extraInformation*, which require rather different handling. Firstly, the extra information may come as input from the user during the run of the program. Secondly, the extra information may come from the meta-information about novel types of data being encountered by the program. This can include information about the size, usage patterns and representations of the data types.

The first source is primarily met in those systems which are intended to be **user configurable**. In such systems, the functionality is programmed in the form of a **template**, which the user may then customise. The template contains **placeholders** which are replaced by user choices. The configurable system is supported by a superstructure which permits multiple versions of the configured program to co-exist, by providing a lookup table pairing some part of the user provided information (perhaps a name, for instance) with the compiled version. The Configurable Data Modelling System is one example [2].

The second source of *extraInformation* can be used to build programs which use reflection to **optimise performance**. Such systems can reconfigure the current set of components or construct new compiled versions of components so that the overall system performs better given the current ways of using the data.

Data type representations are used by programs which must support an *ad hoc* style of **polymorphism** in the face of a potentially infinite set of types. In such cases, the basic functionality is again provided as a template, but now the placeholders are automatically filled by meta-information derived from the types encountered. For instance, the field names from records might be embedded in a placeholder reserved for the purpose. Again the parallel versions are stored in a lookup table, but this time the key is the type representation used by the system. This use of reflection is inherently more difficult to manage than the user-configurable form since there is the possibility of recursion added to the process. The PS-algol browser [3] is the first example of an application using reflection in this way.

There are a range of problems encountered with writing a reflective program which are to do with the discontinuous nature of the program. Some of it is the code which will be created (the **internal** program), while some of it is the code which is controlling the creation and storage of this code (the **external** program). The internal code appears in strings and is thus in a subtly different language, since strings inside the code must be escaped and since the source is not one continuous chunk of code, but parts which must be composed. We thus require some support tools to help with this discontinuity.

Polymorphic reflective programs face another problem. While traversing a complex type, the external program must call itself recursively generating an internal program for each component type. Clearly a program which does this will quickly become extremely tricky to write. A set of support tools are therefore required to make the task more tractable.

3. Support Tools for Reflection

The support tools described here are for use with the reflective language Napier88 (Chapter 1.1.3), [5], but the principle of the construction is more general.

The first important technique which has been introduced is the use of a template [4]. A template is a string containing mostly Napier88 code with two exceptions:

- the delimiters and escape characters of strings are replaced by different characters, since, as they need to be embedded in strings they would otherwise perturb the normal compilation of the code;
- at some points where type specific or user supplied detail is required, the code is replaced with a placeholder.

These are supported with procedures which replace placeholders with the actual information and which turn the "nearly Napier" strings into Napier88 code.

The second technique that has been introduced is a keyed lookup table which holds the versions - thus eliminating the need to repeatedly compile code every time the same extra information is encountered. Procedures are provided which maintain the table and so relieve the program of this overhead..

The extra difficulties in managing the polymorphic kind of reflective program requires the generation of code fragments for values of any type. In particular, procedures are provided which, given a value of any type, generate a legal type description for that value and a legal expression for a default value (for instance "int" and "0" for integers). Furthermore, procedures are available which, given a type description, return components such as field names, the type of the components of an array; and so on.

The final tool which is provided is the most important. The motivation for this is the fact that the superstructures of external programs of the infinite *ad hoc* polymorphic type will all be very similar. All will discover the type of the object and then use a case structure based on the kind of type it is (base type, record, array, etc.). For each component of the type system, it will have one piece of code which is to be embedded in the internal program. It is only the contents of these pieces of code which are different between applications.

A support procedure has been created which, given the code to be embedded for each kind as parameters, generates a reflective application. This code takes the following parameters:

a name for the application;

a code fragment for each base type in the type system;

one or more code fragments for each type constructor in the language - in the case of Napier88 this means one fragment for variant types, but three fragments for records and arrays - one before iteration, one for each component; and one after iteration over the components.

Although this work has been carried out in the context of Napier88, there seems no reason why equivalent tools could not be supplied for any language which provides reflection in the same way. This requires creating the kinds of tools described above, in which the basic structure follows the type system. In a language with a sound type system, it should always be possible to write generic procedures which traverse a type representation and allow user-supplied code fragments (one for each construct in the type system) to be embedded systematically. Indeed what has been achieved here is to turn the very difficult task of providing the *ad hoc* form of reflection into the somewhat more tractable user configurable form.

References

1. Cooper R and Kirby GNC. Type-Safe Linguistic Run-time Reflection—A Practical Perspective. In: Atkinson MP, Maier D, Benzaken V (eds) Persistent Object Systems, Tarascon 1994, Proc. 6th International Workshop on Persistent Object Systems, Tarascon, France. Workshops in Computing, Springer-Verlag, 1994, pp 332-354
2. Cooper RL and Qin Z, A Generic Data Model for the Support of Multiple User Interaction Facilities, Proc. International Conference on the Entity Relationship Approach, P. Loucopolous (ed.), Manchester, England, December 1994, Springer Verlag LNCS 881, 351-368.
3. Dearle A, Brown AL. Safe Browsing in a Strongly Typed Persistent Environment. Comp. J. 1988; 31,6:540-544
4. Kirby GNC. Persistent Programming with Strongly Typed Linguistic Reflection. In: Proc. 25th International Conference on Systems Sciences, Hawaii, 1992, pp 820-831
5. Kirby GNC. Reflection and Hyper-Programming in Persistent Programming Systems. Ph.D. thesis, University of St Andrews, 1992

Section 1.3

Type Systems: Introduction and State of the Art

Richard Connor[1]* and Giorgio Ghelli[2]

[1] Department of Mathematical and Computational Science, University of St Andrews, North Haugh, St Andrews, KY16 9SS, Scotland
[2] Dipartimento di Informatica, Università di Pisa, Corso Italia 40, 1-56100, Pisa, Italy

1 Introduction

The most significant difference between persistent and non-persistent programming languages is that, in a persistent language, the long-term data is typed. This results in a major shift in the emphasis of type system protection, from one of a safety mechanism over programs to that of a safety mechanism over the entire software system, including both programs and long-term data. Type systems are normally viewed as providing two aids to the programmer: a modelling framework to aid the task of data abstraction, and a protection mechanism which prevents this modelling framework from being improperly used by a program. The difference in persistent systems is that the integrity of the data modelling is enforced over data which outlive the program invocation in which they are created, and are shareable by other program invocations.

The first problem to be addressed in the design of a persistent type system is how to model type system protection over data which escape from or originate outside the context of a program's text. In a non-persistent language the typechecker is usually invoked during the compilation of each program to check the consistent use of data modelling. Any data accessed externally, for example from a file or database system, are explicitly converted into the type system framework. In a persistent system the program text may contain expressions which externally access values in persistent storage. Before any program statement which uses such data is executed, a check must be made that it will not violate any type system constraints placed on the data from any other context, as well as the current one.

In dynamically checked systems this presents no extra typechecking problem. When values are created their type system attributes are associated with them in such a way that they may be dynamically accessed whenever a check is required. To add persistence to a language with such a type system is relatively easy; the requirements are for an object store implementation which allows values to be stored between program invocations, and a language mechanism which describes a persistent naming protocol so that persistent values may be denoted. The object formats and typechecking mechanisms need not be altered at all. In retrospect, this is perhaps why the earliest successes in the implementation of persistent languages, notably with PS-algol and Smalltalk, occurred in a dynamically typed context.

Dynamically checked type systems however lead to unreliable code as type errors are detected during execution. The economic and social consequences of unreliable

* Present address: Department of Computing Science, University of Glasgow, Glasgow G12 8QQ, Scotland

software systems are well documented and need not be stressed. Statically checked type systems are one established aid to reliability; however all currently available commercial persistent systems are weakly or dynamically typed, giving one cause for concern with their increasing use.

Static type systems are well known to be achievable in non-persistent languages; the challenge is to achieve static typechecking within a persistent system. This seems at first to be an intractable challenge, as persistent programs require the ability to access typed data which is external to the program context. Recent research however has shown how purely static typechecking may be achieved, within a fully integrated persistent programming environment.

2 State of the Art: Static Analysis

In an integrated persistent environment, programs may be constructed and stored in the same environment as that in which they are executed. This means that objects accessed by a program may already be available when the program is composed. In this case links to the objects can be included in the program instead of textual descriptions. By analogy with hyper-text, a program containing both text and links to objects is called a hyper-program.

The contribution hyper-programming makes towards the static typing of persistent applications is to remove the necessity for all bindings to the persistent store to be dynamic. Some dynamic bindings are still required; however, in cases where an application accesses data which exist at the time of its construction, the dynamic binding may occur during composition. This means that normal compile-time static typechecking may occur, and the executable code produced need contain no dynamic type checks. Therefore hyper-programming allows static checking at least as thorough as any non-persistent programming system; in fact it allows much more.

A static scan of hyper-program source yields more information about the way the executing program will access data within the persistent store than any other program form can do. The presence in source code of direct bindings to data has the effect of increasing the knowledge which can be gleaned statically about the way the executable code and data are used in conjunction with each other. This extra knowledge may be divided into two categories:

- extra information about the mapping from program source to the data it accesses when it is executed, and
- by keeping bidirectional links, extra information may also be discovered about the mapping from data to those programs which may access them.

Pre-execution knowledge of the relationship between programs and the data they manipulate is the foundation upon which all aspects of static safety analysis within a programming system is based. The introduction of hyper-programming gives the potential for new and exciting classes of static analysis. Elsewhere in this book two examples of the new static analysis techniques are given; the examples used, those of the static determination of a class of dependent types, and a new mechanism for controlling schema evolution, should give a taste of the potential power of these new mechanisms.

3 State of the Art: Formal Models

No static type system is of any serious use unless its properties are well understood through formal models. As well as the engineering-level work described above, a major part of the FIDE contribution in type systems is at the level of formal models of type systems. One such paper is presented in this section; a taste of some other important results is given now.

The combination of subtyping, type abstraction and recursion is a challenging open problem. During FIDE a first important result in this field was obtained. We studied the following problem: suppose that we add a notion of recursive types to $F_{\leq}$, obtaining a system $\mu F_{\leq}$. Is it true that, if a pair of types T and U do not contain the recursion operator, then T is a subtype of U in $\mu F_{\leq}$ iff T is a subtype of U in $F_{\leq}$? Technically, we are asking whether $\mu F_{\leq}$ is a conservative extension of $F_{\leq}$. If the answer were "yes", this would mean that a $\mu F_{\leq}$ type checker may be written simply by extending an $F_{\leq}$ type checker with some code to deal with the recursive case. If the answer were "no", this would mean that type checking $\mu F_{\leq}$ is very different from type checking $F_{\leq}$, and that results known about $F_{\leq}$ type checking cannot be immediately transferred to $\mu F_{\leq}$. The answer is actually "no", i.e. the mere existence of recursive types changes the subtyping relations between non recursive types.

This result implies that "transitivity elimination" for $F_{\leq}$ is not valid in $\mu F_{\leq}$. Transitivity elimination means, essentially, that every provable subtyping can be proved without using the transitivity rule. The fact that "transitivity elimination" does not hold has vital consequences in terms of type checking implementation, language design and semantics.

To get more insights into the combination of subtyping, type abstraction and recursion we designed and realised an algorithm which checks subtypes in system $\mu F_{\leq}$. We are not able to prove, up to now, whether this algorithm is correct or complete. However it is important to note that it is the first algorithm proposed which is not a conservative extension of the $F_{\leq}$ algorithm, but it is designed on brand new basis, as our theoretical results proved to be necessary. More precisely, it was the design of the algorithm which urged us to devise the theoretical results. The algorithm is based on the idea of representing recursive types as cyclic graphs and type variables as references to an evaluation environment, which remembers, at any stage of the deduction, which is the current bound of any variable. This approach was first used in the Napier88 typechecker to deal with the typechecking of persistent polymorphic procedures and abstract data types. It is interesting to note that, coherently with the theory, the algorithm conservatively extends the known algorithm for the first order case.

Chapter 1.3.1

A Calculus for Overloaded Functions with Subtyping

Giuseppe Castagna[1], Giorgio Ghelli[2], and Giuseppe Longo[1]

[1] LIENS(CNRS)-DMI, 45 rue d'Ulm, Paris, France
[2] Dipartimento di Informatica, Università di Pisa, Corso Italia 40, 56125 Pisa, Italy

Abstract. We present a simple extension of typed λ-calculus where functions can be *overloaded* by putting different "branches of code" together. When the function is applied, the branch to execute is chosen according to a particular selection rule which depends on the type of the argument. The crucial feature of the present approach is that the branch selection depends on the "run-time type" of the argument, which may differ from its compile-time type, because of the existence of a subtyping relation among types. Hence overloading cannot be eliminated by a static analysis of code, but is an essential feature to be dealt with during computation. We obtain in this way a type-dependent calculus, which differs from the various λ-calculi where types do not play any rôle during computation. We prove Confluence and a generalized Subject-Reduction theorem for this calculus. We prove Strong Normalization for a "stratified" subcalculus. The definition of this calculus is guided by the understanding of object-oriented features and the connections between our calculus and object-orientedness are extensively stressed. We show that this calculus provides a foundation for typed object-oriented languages which solves some of the problems of the standard record-based approach.

1 Introduction

An important distinction has been extensively used in language theory for the last two decades, between parametric (or universal) polymorphism and "ad hoc" polymorphism (see [7]). Parametric polymorphism allows one to write a function whose code can work on different types, while using "ad hoc" polymorphism it is possible to write a function which executes different code for each type. Both the Proof Theory and the semantics of the first kind of polymorphism have been widely investigated by many authors (including two of the authors of the present paper), on the grounds of early work of Hindley, Girard, Milner and Reynolds, and developed into robust programming practice. The second kind, usually known as "overloading", has had little theoretical attention, with the notable exception of [35], [26] and [34]; consequently, its wide use has been little affected by any influence comparable to the one exerted by implicit and explicit polymorphism in programming.

This is due, probably, to the fact that the traditional languages offer a very limited form of overloading: in most of them only predefined functions (essentially arithmetic operators defined on integers and reals and input/output operators) are overloaded, while in the relatively few languages where the programmer can define overloaded functions their actual meaning is always decided at compile time. This form of overloading can be easily understood as a form of syntactic abbreviation which does not significantly affect the underlying language.

We believe though that the ability to define new overloaded functions, when combined with subtyping and with late-binding (as defined below), allows a high level of code reusability, and is the main point which distinguishes object-oriented programming from programming with abstract data types.

In this paper we begin a theoretical analysis, and thus a "uniform and general" one, of this richer kind of overloading. It appears that the challenges it poses are non trivial: indeed, this paper is just a preliminary step towards a theoretical universe still to be discovered and which, we claim, may also affect language design.

We design here a formalism where functions can be *overloaded* by adding a different "piece of code". Thus the code of an overloaded function is formed by several branches of code. The branch to execute is chosen when the function is applied, according to a particular selection rule, which depends on the type of the argument. A crucial feature of the present approach is that the branch selection depends on the "run-time type" of the argument, which may differ from its compile-time type (late binding). Hence, branch selection cannot be performed at compile-time, as happens in imperative languages (early binding), but has to be performed during computation, each time the overloaded application is evaluated.

For example, suppose that *Circle* and *Square* are subtypes of *Picture*, and *draw* is an overloaded function defined on all of them; and suppose that x is a formal parameter of a function with type *Picture*. If the compile time type of the argument is used for branch selection (early binding) an overloaded function application (here denoted •) like the following one

$$\lambda x^{Picture} \ldots \text{draw}\bullet\text{x} \ldots$$

is always executed using the *draw* code for *pictures*; with late binding, each time the whole function is applied, the code for *draw* is chosen only when the x parameter has been bound and evaluated. Thus the appropriate code for *draw* is used on the basis of the run-time type of x and according to whether x is bound to a circle or to a square.

We do not present a general treatment for overloaded functions, but we develop a purely functional approach focussed on the study of some features of object-orientedness, namely message-passing, inheritance and subtyping. Since the approach is entirely novel we first felt the need, via this preliminary, proof-theoretic analysis, to develop the non trivial investigation of key functional properties, such as normalization, confluence and "subject-reduction" (i.e. termination and consistency and "how types evolve during computation"), in the setting of a truly type dependent calculus.

Indeed, "type dependency" (the fact that terms and values may depend on types) and the role played by the distinction between run-time and compile-time types are peculiar properties of the calculus. The various (higher order) calculi, such as Girard's System F and its extensions, allow abstraction w.r.t. type variables and the application of terms to types, but the "value" of this application does not truly depend on the argument type, and more generally the semantics of an expression does not depend on the types which appear in it. Indeed, this "parametricity" or "type-erasure" property plays a crucial role in the basic proof-theoretic property of these calculi: the normalization (cut-elimination) theorem. In the semantic interpretations, this essential type independence of computations is understood by the fact that the meaning of polymorphic functions is given by essentially constant functions (we will say more about this in the last section of this paper). On the other hand, it is clear that overloaded functions express computations which truly depend on types, as different branches of code (i.e. possibly unrelated terms) may be applied on the basis of input types.

Our motivation comes from considering overloading as a way to interpret message-passing in object-oriented programming, when methods are viewed as "global" functions. Let us be more specific. In object-oriented languages the computation evolves on objects. Objects are programming items grouped in *classes* and possessing an internal state that may be accessed and modified by sending messages to the object. When an object receives a message it invokes the method (i.e. the code) associated with that message. The association between methods and messages is described by the class the object belongs to.

There are two possible ways to see message-passing: the first is to consider objects as arrays that associate a method with each message. Therefore when a message `m` is passed to an object `obj` then the method associated with `m` in the object `obj` is looked for. In this approach, an object has the form shown in Figure 1.

object	
internal_state	
`message_1`	method_1
⋮	⋮
`message_n`	method_n

Figure 1.
Objects as records.

message_i	
`class_name_1`	method_1
⋮	⋮
`class_name_n`	method_n

Figure 2.
Messages as overloaded functions

This first point of view has been extensively studied and corresponds to the "objects as records" analogy [8]. The second approach to message-passing, as shown in Figure 2, is to consider messages as names of overloaded functions: depending on the class (or more generally, the type) of the object the message is passed to, a different method is chosen (this is the approach of the CLOS language [16]; this approach was introduced, in the context of typed languages, in [19]). In this way, in a sense, we reverse the previous situation: instead of passing messages to objects we now pass objects to messages.

This different approach seems to have some advantages w.r.t. the "objects as records" paradigm, at least in a proof-theoretical study of the typed case.

For example, in the record based approach an object of class A containing a method *binary* of type $A \times A \to B$ is modeled as a record belonging to the following recursive type

$$\mu A.\langle\!\langle \ldots \text{binary: } A \to B \ldots \rangle\!\rangle;$$

since the first argument of the function is the record itself and, thus, it is an internal or *hidden* argument of the method, referred by the keyword *self*. In the same way a recursive type is needed to type an object of class A with a *copy* method of type $A \to A$:

$$\mu A.\langle\!\langle \ldots \text{copy}: A \ldots \rangle\!\rangle.$$

In the model based on overloading there is no need to use recursion to define the type of the *binary* and *copy* methods, and this seems more reasonable, since, intuitively, binary or copying operations generally have nothing to do with fixpoints and do not need the expressive power of recursion.

A similar observation can be made for the first "hidden" parameter *self* of methods, referring to the object receiving the message. In the record model this parameter must be accessed by recursion, while in our model it is just a parameter with the additional feature that it is used for code selection. For other problems regarding inheritance in the record based model see [12,6,27,4,18,19].

Of course other problems arise when overloaded functions are used to define methods, especially to model the dynamic definition of new classes. On the other hand, the full expressiveness of records is recovered, as record types and values are derivable notions in our approach.

In summary, this paper develops a simple extension of the typed λ-calculus meant to formalize the behaviour of overloaded functions with late binding in a type discipline with subtyping. The basic idea is that an overloaded function consists of a finite collection of ordinary functions that are stuck together to form the different branches. Its type will be the set of the types of its branches. Therefore we add, to ordinary λ-terms, new terms such as $(M_1 \& M_2 \& \ldots \& M_n)$, that represent the overloaded function consisting of the n branches M_i.[1] Likewise, we add an operation of overloaded application $M \bullet N$ to the ordinary functional application $M \cdot N$. The types of the overloaded functions are finite lists of arrow types $\{V_1' \to V_1'', \ldots, V_n' \to V_n''\}$ (sometimes denoted by $\{V_i' \to V_i''\}_{i \in I}$), where every arrow corresponds to the type of a branch. Overloaded types must satisfy relevant consistency conditions; among others things, they account for the longstanding debate concerning the use of covariance or contravariance of the arrow type in its left argument. More precisely, the general arrow types will be given by contravariant "$\to$" in the first argument: this is an essential feature of (typed) functional programs, where type assignment (type-checking) helps to avoid run-time errors. On the other hand, the types of overloaded functions are covariant families of arrow types, as explained in detail below.

We stress that the subtyping relation introduced is an essential feature of the calculus: it allows multiple choices, as a type may be a subtype of several types and subtyping is used to choose branches of overloaded terms. The blend of &-terms and subtyping makes our calculus an expressive and original mathematical formalism which shows that "ad hoc" polymorphism may have also theoretical relevance.

In Section 2 we describe the combination of overloading and subtyping and the consequences of their interaction. Section 3 presents the syntax of the system as well

[1] Hereafter we will call a term of the form $(M \& N)$ an "&-term".

as the reduction rules. In Section 4 we show how some other types can be encoded in the primitive system. The next Sections are devoted to the basic properties of the calculus: Section 5 to Subject-Reduction, Section 6 to confluence and Section 7 to the normalization theorem. In Section 8 we give some more intuition on how our calculus fits object-oriented programming, hinting how to implement subtyping and message-passing by the constructs of our calculus. A conclusion suggests further work, in particular the challenging extension to higher order systems.

2 Overloading, Subtyping and "Run-Time Types"

In the introduction we said that overloading is interesting because of its connection with object-oriented languages. However, we think that overloading is worth studying also for its own sake, in spite of the lack of formal studies on this mechanism. This lack may depend on the fact that overloading by itself (i.e. without subtyping), does not increase the expressiveness of the language: an overloaded function can be substituted by the appropriate code, at compile-time; in this case, overloading seems more a notational trick than a programming construct. If combined, though, with subtyping and late-binding, it becomes a flexible and powerful tool.

The idea is that if we have an overloaded function whose n branches have respectively type $U_i \to V_i$ $(i = 1..n)$ and we pass it an argument of type U, the chosen branch j is the one that "best approximates" U, i.e. such that $U_j = \min_{i \in I}\{U_i | U \leq U_i\}$. However, it is known that, when a subtyping relation is defined, the type of a term is no longer the same during computation, but it may decrease (see [15]). This "shrinking of the run-time type" corresponds to the increase of information that characterizes the evolving of computation.[2] The fact that during computation types may get more informative implies that, if one makes the choice of the branch at compile-time (early binding), this choice would be based on rather incomplete information about the "real" type of the argument (see the example with *Picture* in the previous section). Moreover late binding allows, in object-oriented languages, us to write a function whose behaviour may be "extended" by adding new classes. Consider for example a compiler written in object-oriented style, with a class for every syntactic class in the language. Every class implements methods *Parse*, *Type-Check*, *Pretty-Print*, and *Code-Generate*. New syntactic classes may be dynamically added by creating the corresponding class, and every general purpose function which sends, e.g. a *Pretty-Print* message to an object will be able to correctly operate on objects of these new classes too. For this reason, late binding plays an

[2] We think that the increase in information is part of the essence of computation, and is due to the approaching of the result, the normal form, which is the most informative form of the term (informative in the sense of understandability, not in the sense of the theory of information where the computation corresponds to a loss of information). At type level this corresponds to the decrease in the type: the smaller the type, the more informative it is. For instance, think of the real and rational numbers (**Q**≤**R**): if we know that a number is rational then we know that it possesses all the properties of real numbers AND some more (for example, it can be represented as the quotient of two integers).

essential role in the high code reusability which can be attained in object-oriented programming, making it possible to write "graphical editor shells" or "compiler shells" where the general purpose code is written before writing the actual definition of the classes which specify the specific behaviour of the application.

The meaning of terms like "run-time type" and "compile-time type" is reasonably clear in the context of a traditional, eagerly evaluated programming language: in that case, a single term, such as an occurrence of a formal parameter x of a function, is "evaluated" many times, once each time the function is called. Each time x is bound to a value, the run-time type of that value becomes the "run-time type" of x, while in the source code that occurrence of x has a unique compile-time type, the one written by the programmer. However, the "compile-time type" of a term and the "run-time types" of its values are not unrelated: the property holds that all the run-time types of the values will be subtypes of the unique compile-time type of the term.

This distinction may not be intuitive in the context of a rewriting system, such as λ-calculus, where a more formal definition is needed. To follow the different "evaluations" of an occurrence of a term, we may use the notion of *residual* of an occurrence of a term (see [3] where this definition is used only when the term is a redex). Intuitively, a *residual* is what the term has become after a reduction. As happens in traditional languages, in a rewriting system an occurrence of a term has many different residuals with possibly many different types, which are only guaranteed to be subtypes of the original one.

We will adopt the following definition: when a term is closed and normal, we then say that it is "a value",[3] and we mean by this that it cannot evolve anymore. We similarly say that its type is "a run-time type", which means that no more information can be specified about the type of that term. The type of a *value* which is the residual of a given term is a *run-time type* for that term.

Thus the relation between a compile-time type and a run-time type is the same as the relation between a term and a value: a value for a term is any closed normal form obtained by performing reductions and substitutions over that term; a run-time type for that term is the type of any of its values. Note that an open term is bound, during a computation, to many different values, and so it gets many different run-time types. Note also that we did not formally define the notion of "evolution of a term", thought it would be possible. We are now just trying to convey the intuition behind the idea of run-time types, while the formal definition of the reduction rules is given in the next section.

Although the selection of the branches of overloaded functions is based on the run-time types, the static typing of a term is enough to assure that the computation will be type-error free. This is a corollary of Theorem 5.1, which guarantees that types can only decrease during computation (so that the run-time type of any residual of a term is always a subtype of its compile-time type) and thus that well-typed terms rewrite to well typed terms. To guarantee this property a "consistency" condition must be imposed on overloaded types. In short, an overloaded type

[3] For example $\lambda x.\lambda y.x$ and $\lambda x.\lambda y.y$ are the only two values of type $Bool \equiv \alpha \to \alpha \to \alpha$.

$\{U_i \to V_i\}_{i \in I}$ is well-formed if and only if for all $i, j \in I$ it satisfies the following conditions, where $U_i \Downarrow U_j$ means that U_i and U_j are downward compatible, i.e. they have a common lower bound:

$$U_i \leq U_j \Rightarrow V_i \leq V_j \tag{2.1}$$

$$U_i \Downarrow U_j \Rightarrow \text{there exists a unique } h \in I \text{ such that } U_h = \inf\{U_i, U_j\} \tag{2.2}$$

Condition (2.1) is the consistency condition at issue, which assures that during computation the type of a term may only decrease. Informally, in view of our analogy "type–amount of information", it says that, if the input information given to an overloaded function increases, so does the information in the output. More specifically, in our approach, if we have a two-branched overloaded function M of type $\{U_1 \to V_1, U_2 \to V_2\}$ with $U_2 \leq U_1$ and we pass it a term N which has the compile-time type U_1 then the compile-time type of $M \bullet N$ will be (smaller than or equal to) V_1; but if the normal form of N has type U_2 then the run-time type of $M \bullet N$ will be V_2 and therefore $V_2 \leq V_1$ must hold. The second condition concerns the selection of the correct branch: we said before that if we apply an overloaded function of type $\{U_i \to V_i\}_{i \in I}$ to a term of type U then the selected branch has type $U_j \to V_j$ such that $U_j = \min_{i \in I}\{U_i | U \leq U_i\}$; condition (2.2) assures the existence and uniqueness of this branch.

At first sight these restrictions may seem excessively complicated, and may discourage the reader with no experience in object-oriented languages. However, these restrictions are more obvious than they appear; especially with respect to the connection with object-oriented programming where they have a very natural interpretation (see Section 8).

3 The $\lambda\&$-calculus

In this section we define the extension of the typed lambda calculus we study in the rest of the paper. We use the following conventions: A, B denote Atomic Types, $S, T, U, V, W \ldots$ denote (Pre)Types, M, N, P, Q, denote Terms, H, I, J, K denote sets of indexes and h, i, j, k, n indexes. We first define a set of *Pretypes* and then from them we select those that satisfy the conditions above and that constitute the types.

$$\textbf{PreTypes} \quad V ::= A \mid V \to V \mid \{V_1' \to V_1'', \ldots, V_n' \to V_n''\}$$

For technical reasons we consider overloaded types as lists, i.e. possessing an order; the list may also be empty: in this case the type is denoted by $\{\}$.

3.1 Subtyping rules

We define a *subtyping* relation on the set of Pretypes. This relation is used to define the types. The idea is that one may start from a partial order which is predefined on atomic (pre)types and extend it to a preorder on all Pretypes: the relation is obtained by adding the rules of transitive and reflexive closure to the following ones:

$$\frac{U_2 \leq U_1 \quad V_1 \leq V_2}{U_1 \to V_1 \leq U_2 \to V_2}$$

$$\frac{\text{for all } i \in I, \text{ there exists } j \in J \text{ such that } U_i'' \leq U_j' \text{ and } V_j' \leq V_i''}{\{U_j' \to V_j'\}_{j \in J} \leq \{U_i'' \to V_i''\}_{i \in I}}$$

Intuitively, if we consider two overloaded types U and V as sets of functional types then the last rule states that $U \leq V$ if and only if for every type in V there is one in U smaller than it. In contrast to the usual partial order on record types, the cardinality of I and J are unrelated. Note that this is just a preorder, and not a partial order, as $U \leq V$ and $V \leq U$ do not imply $U = V$.

3.2 Types

Our system is an extended strongly typed λ-calculus. Arrow types and overloaded types are defined inductively from atomic types. As mentioned in the introduction, the overloaded types have a well formation rule that allows a consistent application of the reduction rules.

1. $A \in$ **Types**
2. if $V_1, V_2 \in$ **Types** then $V_1 \to V_2 \in$ **Types**
3. if for all $i, j \in I$
   (a) $(U_i, V_i \in$ **Types**$)$ and
   (b) $(U_i \leq U_j \Rightarrow V_i \leq V_j)$ and
   (c) $(U_i \Downarrow U_j \Rightarrow$ there is a unique $h \in I$ such that $U_h = \inf\{U_i, U_j\})$[4]
   then $\{U_i \to V_i\}_{i \in I} \in$ **Types**

In a system with subtyping, if $f: U \to V$, this means that when f is applied to a term u with a run-time type $U' \leq U$, the run-time type of the result will be a type $V' \leq V$. Intuitively, an overloaded type $\{U_i \to V_i\}_{i \in I}$ is inhabited by functions, made out of different pieces of code, such that when they are applied to a term whose run-time type U' is the subtype of some U_i, the run-time type of the result will be a subtype V' of the corresponding V_i. This is assured by condition **(b)** above.

To ensure the existence of an *inf* for any pair of downward compatible types, we require that $\leq$ yields a "partial lattice" on Atomic Types. In accordance with the rules given in the previous section, the whole **Types** inherits this structure.[5] In object-oriented languages this is not always the case. We can distinguish object-oriented languages where Atomic Types have a tree structure (the so called "single

[4] This notation is not very precise; since $\leq$ is just a preorder, a set generally has many equivalent g.l.b.'s; we should then write $U_h \in \inf\{U_i, U_j\}$, or $\{U_h\} = \inf\{U_i, U_j\}$.

[5] More precisely, since $\leq$ is not an order, it is **Types** modulo $\sim$ which inherits the partial lattice structure, where $T \sim U$ when $T \leq U$ and $U \leq T$.

inheritance") and object-oriented languages where Atomic Types have a free order relation and where additional structure is used to solve the problems caused by compatible types without an *inf*. The same kind of technique can be used to extend our approach to this situation, since the partial lattice property is not essential, but is useful for getting a simple branch selection rule, as described in the section on reduction. Likewise, while condition **(b)** above is an essential feature of our approach, condition **(c)** is linked to the branch selection rule, and could easily be modified (see [19]). Furthermore, we suppose that the subtyping relation is decidable on atomic types, which implies that it is decidable on **Types** as well. Note that this poses no problem in the current (simple) approach, as we have fixed atomic types; more work would be needed in order to allow programmer's definable base types.

Henceforth we only deal with **Types** and completely forget **PreTypes**; thus we will intend that all the pretypes which appear in the rest of the paper satisfy the conditions above.

3.3 Terms

Roughly speaking, terms correspond to terms of the classical lambda calculus plus operations to build and apply overloaded functions. Overloaded functions are built as customary with lists, by starting from an empty overloaded function and adding branches with the & operator. We distinguish the usual application $M{\cdot}M$ of lambda-calculus from the application of an overloaded function $M \bullet M$ since they constitute two completely different mechanisms: indeed a notion of variable substitution is associated with the former, while in the latter there is the notion of selection of a branch. This is also stressed by the proof-theoretical viewpoint where these constructors correspond to two different elimination rules. Finally, a further difference, specified in the reduction rules, is that overloaded application is associated with call by value, which is not needed by the ordinary application. For the same reason we must distinguish between the type $U \to V$ and the overloaded function type with just one branch $\{U \to V\}$.

However, in some cases it will be useful to have only one notation to deal with both kinds of application; for this aim the simple juxtaposition will be used.

Variables are indexed by their type, to avoid the use of type environments in the type-checking rules.

$$\textbf{Terms} \quad M ::= x^V \mid c \mid \lambda x^V.M \mid M \cdot M \mid \varepsilon \mid M \&^V M \mid M \bullet M$$

The type which indexes the & is a technical trick to allow the reduction inside overloaded function, as explained later on. c represents generic constants while ε is a distinct constant for the empty overloaded function.

Hereafter, we may use the notation $\lambda x{:}\, V.M$ instead of $\lambda x^V.M$, and we may omit the type indexing of &, when not needed. Also the ε at the beginning of &-terms may be omitted, in examples.

3.4 Type checking

We define here the typing relation ":", a proper subset of **Terms**×**Types**. Therefore, as already pointed out, in the rules below we omit the condition $V \in$ **Types**. This means that, all the *PreTypes* that appear in the following rules are to be considered as well-formed types. Anyway we observe that an algorithm implementing the following type-checking rules should check that the types appearing in the conclusions of the rules [TAUT], [→ INTRO] and [{}INTRO] are well formed.

We use the notation $\vdash M\!:V \leq U$ as a shorthand for the conjunction "$\vdash M\!:V$ and $V \leq U$".

[TAUT] $$\vdash x^V\!:V$$

[→ INTRO] $$\frac{\vdash M\!:V}{\vdash \lambda x^U.M\!:U \to V}$$

[→ ELIM$_{(\leq)}$] $$\frac{\vdash M\!:U \to V \quad \vdash N\!:W \leq U}{\vdash M\cdot N\!:V}$$

[TAUT$_\varepsilon$] $$\vdash \varepsilon\!:\{\}$$

[{}INTRO] $$\frac{\vdash M\!:W_1 \leq \{U_i \to V_i\}_{i\leq(n-1)} \qquad \vdash N\!:W_2 \leq U_n \to V_n}{\vdash (M\&^{\{U_i\to V_i\}_{i\leq n}} N)\!:\{U_i \to V_i\}_{i\leq n}}$$

[{}ELIM] $$\frac{\vdash M\!:\{U_i \to V_i\}_{i\in I} \quad \vdash N\!:U \quad U_j = \min_{i\in I}\{U_i | U \leq U_i\}}{\vdash M\bullet N\!:V_j}$$

In the last rule the premise on U_j as well as the type constraints are indeed *meta-premises*, i.e. they are conditions to the application of the rules but they do not belong to the tree-structure of the deduction. The empty term ε and the empty type $\{\}$ are used to start the formation of overloaded terms and types. We read $M\&N\&P$ as $(M\&N)\&P$.

As the careful reader will have noted, we do not use the *subsumption* rule (see below) in type-checking. We utilized a slightly different type discipline, where the use of subsumption is distributed where needed. The resulting system is equivalent, in the sense explained below, to the subsumption discipline, but every term possesses a unique type, which simplifies the definition of the operational semantics and some proofs.

Consider the functional core of our system, i.e. only the first three typing rules at the beginning of this section and let denote this system by $\vdash_{\leq}$. The subsumption system (denoted by $\vdash_{sub}$) is obtained from this one by replacing $\vdash N\!:W \leq U$ with $\vdash N\!:U$ in [→ ELIM$_{(\leq)}$] and by adding the subsumption rule:

[→ELIM] $$\frac{\vdash_{sub} M\!:U \to V \quad \vdash_{sub} N\!:U}{\vdash_{sub} MN\!:V}$$

[SUBSUMPTION] $$\frac{\vdash_{sub} M\!:U \quad U \leq V}{\vdash_{sub} M\!:V}$$

Now, we can prove the following theorem.

Theorem 3.1. $\vdash_{\leq} M\colon V$ *iff* $V = \min\{U \mid \vdash_{sub} M\colon U\}$ *(which implies that the set* $\{U \mid \vdash_{sub} M\colon U\}$ *is not empty).*

Proof. ($\Rightarrow$) By induction on the proof of $\vdash_{\leq} M\colon V$ and by cases on the last applied rule.

($\Leftarrow$) By induction on the smallest proof that $\vdash_{sub} M\colon V$ and by cases on the last applied rule.

Corollary 3.1. *Every well-typed* $\lambda\&$*-term possesses a unique type*

In conclusion, the theorem states that $\vdash_{\leq}$ is equivalent to $\vdash_{sub}$ in the sense that it always returns the smallest (i.e. most precise) type returned by the subsumption system. This theorem suggests that it is possible to define a subsumption based version $\vdash_{sub}$ for the full system too. We must add subsumption, substitute all judgements $\vdash N : T \leq U$ in the rules with $\vdash N : U$ and finally, in the $[\{\}\text{ELIM}]$ rule, substitute $\vdash N : U$ with "U is the minimum type such that $\vdash_{sub} N : U$".

We can then extend theorem 3.1 to our entire calculus.

Theorem 3.2 (Subsumption Elimination). *For the whole* $\lambda\&$, $\vdash M\colon V$ *iff* $V = \min\{U \mid \vdash_{sub} M\colon U\}$

Since we have chosen the subsumption-free presentation, every term possesses a unique type, because there is a unique derivation for the type of a term.

In our presentation of the subtype rules we implicitly defined a transitivity rule. We can easily prove that this rule is not really needed.

Theorem 3.3 (Transitivity Elimination). $\vdash T \leq U$ *iff* $\vdash^{-} T \leq U$ *where* $\vdash^{-}$ *is defined by the rules of* $\vdash$ *minus transitivity.*

Proof. We first prove that $\vdash^{-} T \leq U$ and $\vdash^{-} U \leq V$ implies $\vdash^{-} T \leq V$. Observe that if $\vdash^{-} T \leq U$ then either T and U are both atomic types, or they are both arrow types or they are both overloaded types. We prove that $\vdash^{-} T \leq U$ and $\vdash^{-} U \leq V$ implies $\vdash^{-} T \leq V$ by induction on the size of T, U, V. If they are all atomic types the thesis is immediate. If $T = \{T_i' \to T_i''\}_{i\in I}$, $U = \{U_j' \to U_j''\}_{j\in J}$ and $V = \{V_l' \to V_l''\}_{l\in L}$, then for all $l \in L$ exists $j \in J$ such that $\vdash^{-} U_j' \to U_j'' \leq V_l' \to V_l''$ and for all $j \in J$ exists $i \in I$ such that $\vdash^{-} T_i' \to T_i'' \leq U_j' \to U_j''$. By induction, for all $l \in L$ exists $i \in I$ such that $\vdash^{-} T_i' \to T_i'' \leq V_l' \to V_l''$, hence $\vdash^{-} \{T_i' \to T_i''\}_{i\in I} \leq \{V_l' \to V_l''\}_{l\in L}$, Q.E.D. The arrow case is similar and simpler. Now the theorem follows by induction on the proof of $\vdash T \leq U$ and by cases on the last applied rule, where the only interesting case is transitivity.

Note that the lack of type variables makes the proof of subsumption elimination and transitivity elimination much easier for this calculus than for $F_{\leq}$ (see [14]).

3.5 Reduction Rules

In order to simplify the definition of the system, we consider the types of overloaded functions as ordered sets, where the order corresponds, more or less, to the order in which branches are added when an overloaded function is built. However the reader may note that this order is completely irrelevant in subtyping and typing rules, with the only exception of [{}INTRO], where we want to be able to distinguish the only arrow type associated with the right hand side of the & from the set of the other ones. Exactly the same information is all that is needed by the reduction rules.

As we mentioned before, the run-time types are used during computation to perform branch selection. Thus, we have to define what the run-time type of a term is. We propose here a simple solution: the deduction system that infers the run-time type of a term is the same as the one used for type-checking. What distinguishes run-time types and compile-time types is thus the time when the deduction is made. In fact, during the computation the type of a term may change since reduction and substitution may decrease the type of a term (as shown in Theorems 5.1 and 5.1).

> We say that the type of a term is its run-time type when that term is a "value", i.e. when it is normal and closed; a run-time type of a residual of a term is also a run-time type of the term. We allow a reduction of the application of an overloaded function only when the argument is a value, i.e. when it is typed by a run-time type.

This is a crucial point. If we allowed selecting the branch of an overloaded function on the basis of the type of an argument whose type could still be decreased (by reduction or by substitution) then the selection would give different results depending on the time when it is applied, and the system would be no longer confluent.

As a matter of fact, this call-by-value constraint is not a limitation if our aim is to model object-oriented languages. In these languages message passing evaluation always requires that the receiving object has been fully evaluated.[6]

We start by defining, in a standard way, substitutions on the terms of our system:

Definition 1 (Substitution) *We define the term $M[x^T := N]$ by induction on the structure of M:*

1. $x^T[x^T := N] \equiv N$
2. $y^S[x^T := N] \equiv y^S$ *if* $y^S \not\equiv x^T$
3. $\varepsilon[x^T := N] \equiv \varepsilon$
4. $(\lambda y^S.P)[x^T := N] \equiv (\lambda y^S.(P[x^T := N]))$ *where y is not free in N*
5. $(P\&^V Q)[x^T := N] \equiv ((P[x^T := N])\&^V(Q[x^T := N]))$
6. $(PQ)[x^T := N] \equiv (P[x^T := N])(Q[x^T := N])$

□

[6] This happens not only for the essential reason we pointed out (the run-time type is generally only known for fully evaluated terms) but also since object oriented languages heavily rely on state and state-updating operations, and programs using updates are much more readable if eagerly evaluated.

Of course, this definition only makes sense when the type of N is a subtype of T. Note that in 5, even if the types of the subterms change, the type of the whole term is always the same, since it is frozen in the index of the &; thus the selection of the branch does not depend on the *grade* of reduction of the &-term. This is a decisive point in our approach, which makes the system type-safe though reductions within an overloaded term are allowed.

We define the one-step reduction relation $\triangleright$ which is a proper subset of **Terms** $\times$ **Terms**. We denote by $\triangleright^*$ its reflexive and transitive closure, under the usual conditions (in β) to avoid free variables being captured:

β) $(\lambda x^S.M)N \triangleright M[x^S{:=}N]$

$\beta_\&$) If $N{:}\,U$ is closed and in normal form and $U_j = min\{U_i | U \leq U_i\}$ then

$$((M_1 \&^{\{U_i \to V_i\}_{i=1..n}} M_2) \bullet N) \triangleright \begin{cases} M_1 \bullet N & \text{for } j < n \\ M_2 \cdot N & \text{for } j = n \end{cases}$$

context) If $M_1 \triangleright M_2$ then

$$(M_1 N) \triangleright (M_2 N) \tag{3.1}$$
$$(N M_1) \triangleright (N M_2) \tag{3.2}$$
$$(\lambda x^U.M_1) \triangleright (\lambda x^U.M_2) \tag{3.3}$$
$$(M_1 \& N) \triangleright (M_2 \& N) \tag{3.4}$$
$$(N \& M_1) \triangleright (N \& M_2) \tag{3.5}$$

The intuitive operational meaning of ($\beta_\&$) is easily understood when looking at the simple case, i.e. when there are as many branches as arrows in the overloaded type. In this case, under the assumptions in the rule:

$$(\varepsilon \& M_1 \& \ldots \& M_n) \bullet N \triangleright^* M_j \cdot N$$

However, in general, the number of branches of the overloaded function may be different from the number of arrows in the overloaded types, both since an overloaded function could begin with an application or with a variable, accounting for an initial segment of the overloaded type (they are just required to possess an overloaded type), and because of the subtyping relation used in the rule of [{}INTRO].

If we allowed ($\beta_\&$) reductions with open or non normal arguments the system would not be confluent, since the type of an open or non normal argument can be different in different phases of the computation. For example, consider a term

$$(\lambda x^V.((P \&^{\{V \to V, U \to U\}} M) \bullet x^V)) \cdot (N^U)$$

with $U \leq V$ (we superscript terms with their types, like in N^U, to increase readability of examples). If the inner $\beta_\&$ reduction were performed with the x argument (which is not closed), the first P branch would be chosen, while if the outer β reduction is performed first then the term becomes:

$$(P \&^{\{V \to V, U \to U\}} M) \bullet N^U$$

and the second branch M is (correctly) chosen. In short, the argument of an overloaded application must be closed and normal to perform the evaluation, since this is the only case where its type cannot decrease anymore, and describes the value as accurately as possible.

Complementary to the idea of freezing the argument of an overloaded application to its normal form, is the use of the type which indexes the &s to freeze the type of &-terms. We outline two short examples to show the problems that arise with reduction and substitution inside &-terms without this index.

We suppose that $U' \leq U$ and $V' \leq V$; consider the term

$$F_1 \equiv (\varepsilon \& M^{U \to V} \& ((\lambda x^{U' \to V'}.x) \cdot N^{U \to V'}))$$

this can be intuitively typed as follows:

$$F_1 \colon \{U \to V, U' \to V'\}$$

Though, if we reduce the right branch, without freezing the index, we are no longer able to recover a type for the contractum, namely for

$$(\varepsilon \& M^{U \to V} \& N^{U \to V'})$$

since both terms possess the same input type. Consider next the term

$$F_2 \equiv \lambda y^{U' \to V'}.(\varepsilon \& (\lambda x^U.M^V) \& (y^{U' \to V'}))$$

again we can intuitively type it as follows.

$$F_2 \colon (U' \to V') \to \{U \to V, U' \to V'\}$$

but if we apply F_2 to $N^{U \to V'}$ and β-reduce, then we are in the same case as above.

Note, finally, that our calculus is truly type-dependent (that is, the type erasure of a term is not enough to forecast its evolution or meaning, see the conclusion) for two different reasons:

- $\beta_\&$ reduction depends on the type of the argument
- $\beta_\&$ reduction depends on the index T of the & in the overloaded term

More specifically, if $\{U_i \to V_i\}_{i=1..n}$ is the index of &, $\beta_\&$ reduction depends on the list $[U_i]_{i=1..n}$ of the *input types* of the overloaded function. For example, if $U' \leq U$, both terms

$$(\varepsilon \& M^{U \to V} \&^{\{U \to V, U' \to V\}} M'^{U \to V})$$

and

$$(\varepsilon \& M^{U \to V} \&^{\{U' \to V, U \to V\}} M'^{U \to V})$$

are well typed, but they behave differently if applied to a normal closed term N^U.

Note that we are here in a different and more flexible situation than in object-oriented languages, since in those languages every branch of an overloaded function (every method) must be understood as a λ-abstraction (when viewing methods as global, overloaded functions in our sense.) In this language, on the other hand, any expression with a functional type (in particular an application) can be concatenated by using &. Thus, when following the object-oriented style, the left hand side U of the type $U \to V$ of an expression $\lambda x^U.M$ does not change when reductions and substitutions are performed inside $\lambda x^U.M$. In our approach, when reducing inside an &, one may obtain a smaller type for the reductum, in particular a larger U in a type $U \to V$. To allow this possibility of "inside" reductions and preserve determinism, we label the &'s with types .

4 Deriving records

In various approaches to object-oriented programming records play an important rôle. In particular, current functional treatments of object-oriented features formalize objects directly as records. Moreover, if records are not included in a calculus, the subtyping relation may be quite trivial. In our system, records can be encoded in a straightforward way.

Let $L_1, L_2, \ldots$ be an infinite list of atomic types. Assume that they are *isolated* (i.e. for any type V, if $L_i \leq V$ or $V \leq L_i$, then $L_i = V$), and introduce for each L_i a *constant* $\ell_i: L_i$. It is now possible to encode record types, record values and record selection, respectively, as follows:

$$\begin{array}{ll}
\langle\!\langle \ell_1: V_1; \ldots; \ell_n: V_n \rangle\!\rangle & \equiv \{L_1 \to V_1, \ldots, L_n \to V_n\} \\
\langle \ell_1 = M_1; \ldots; \ell_n = M_n \rangle & \equiv (\varepsilon \;\&\; \lambda x^{L_1}.M_1 \;\&\ldots\&\; \lambda x^{L_n}.M_n) \\
 & \qquad\qquad\qquad (x^{L_i} \notin FV(M_i)) \\
M.\ell & \equiv M \bullet \ell
\end{array}$$

Since $L_1 \ldots L_n$ are isolated, then the subtyping rule for records is a special case of the rule for overloaded types:

Subtyping-rule

$$\frac{V_1 \leq U_1 \;\ldots V_k \leq U_k}{\langle\!\langle \ell_1: V_1; \ldots; \ell_k: V_k; \ldots; \ell_{k+j}: V_{k+j} \rangle\!\rangle \leq \langle\!\langle \ell_1: U_1; \ldots; \ell_k: U_k \rangle\!\rangle}$$

The type-checking rules are similarly derivable:

Type-checking

$$\text{[RECORD]}\quad \frac{\vdash M_1: V_1 \ldots \vdash M_n: V_n}{\vdash \langle \ell_1 = M_1; \ldots; \ell_n = M_n \rangle: \langle\!\langle \ell_1: V_1; \ldots; \ell_n: V_n \rangle\!\rangle}$$

$$\text{[DOT]}\quad \frac{\vdash M: \langle\!\langle \ell_1: V_1; \ldots; \ell_n: V_n \rangle\!\rangle}{\vdash M.\ell_i: V_i}$$

Finally, the rewriting rules (ρ) and (recd) below are just special cases of ($\beta_{\&}$) and (context) respectively.

ρ) $\langle \ell_1 = M_1; \ldots; \ell_n = M_n \rangle . \ell_i \rhd M_i \quad (0 \leq i \leq n)$
recd) $M \rhd M' \Rightarrow M.\ell \rhd M'.\ell$ and $\langle \ldots \ell = M \ldots \rangle \rhd \langle \ldots \ell = M' \ldots \rangle$

5 The Generalized Subject Reduction Theorem

The Subject Reduction Theorem in classical λ-calculus proves that the type of a term does not change when the term is reduced. In this section, we generalize this theorem for our calculus, since we prove that if a term is typable in our system, then it can only be reduced to typable terms and that these terms have a type smaller than or equal to the type of the redex.

In order to enhance readability, in this and in the following section, we will often omit the turn-style symbol.

Lemma 5.1 (Substitution Lemma). *Let* $x{:}T$, $M{:}U$, $N{:}T'$ *and* $T' \leq T$.
Then $M[x{:=}N]{:}U'$, *where* $U' \leq U$.

Proof. By induction on the structure of M.

$M \equiv \varepsilon$ straightforward
$M \equiv x$ straightforward
$M \equiv y \not\equiv x$ straightforward
$M \equiv \lambda x^V.M'$ straightforward
$M \equiv \lambda y^V.M'$ Then $U = V \to W$ and $M'{:}W$.
By induction hypothesis $M'[x := N]{:}W' \leq W$, therefore $M[x := N] \equiv \lambda y^V.M'[x{:=}N]{:}V \to W' \leq V \to W$
$M \equiv (M_1 \&^T M_2)$ Then $M[x := N] \equiv (M_1[x := N] \&^T M_2[x := N])$; by induction hypothesis and the rule [{}INTRO] $M[x{:=}N]$ is well typed and its type is the same of the one of M that is T.
$M \equiv M_1 \cdot M_2$ where $M_1{:}V \to U$ and $M_2{:}W \leq V$. By induction hypothesis:

$M_1[x{:=}N]{:}V' \to U'$ with $V \leq V'$ and $U' \leq U$
$M_2[x{:=}N]{:}W'$ with $W' \leq W$

Since $W' \leq W \leq V \leq V'$ we can apply the rule [$\to$ELIM$_{(\leq)}$] and thus $M[x{:=}N] \equiv (M_1[x{:=}N]) \cdot (M_2[x{:=}N]){:}U' \leq U$
$M \equiv M_1 \bullet M_2$ where $M_1{:}\{V_i \to W_i\}_{i \in I}$ and $M_2{:}V$.
Let $V_h = \min_{i \in I}\{V_i | V \leq V_i\}$. Thus $U = W_h$.
By induction hypothesis:

$M_1[x{:=}N]{:}\{V'_j \to W'_j\}_{j \in J}$ with $\{V'_j \to W'_j\}_{j \in J} \leq \{V_i \to W_i\}_{i \in I}$
$M_2[x{:=}N]{:}V'$ with $V' \leq V$

Let $V'_k = \min_{j \in J}\{V'_j | V' \leq V'_j\}$. Thus $M[x{:=}N]{:}W'_k$. Therefore we have to prove that $W'_k \leq W_h$
As $\{V'_j \to W'_j\}_{j \in J} \leq \{V_i \to W_i\}_{i \in I}$ then for all $i \in I$ there exists $j \in J$ such that $V'_j \to W'_j \leq V_i \to W_i$. Given $i = h$ we chose an $\tilde{h} \in J$ which satisfies this condition: that is,

$$V'_{\tilde{h}} \to W'_{\tilde{h}} \leq V_h \to W_h \tag{5.1}$$

We now have the following inequalities:

$$V \leq V_h \tag{5.2}$$

by the definition of V_h, as $V_h = \min_{i \in I}\{V_i | V \leq V_i\}$;

$$V_h \leq V'_{\bar{h}} \tag{5.3}$$

which follows from (5.1);

$$V' \leq V'_{\bar{h}} \tag{5.4}$$

which follows from (5.2), (5.3) and $V' \leq V$;

$$W'_{\bar{h}} \leq W_h \tag{5.5}$$

which follows from (5.1).

$$V'_k \leq V'_{\bar{h}} \tag{5.6}$$

which follows from (5.4), as $V'_{\bar{h}}$ belongs to a set with V'_k as least element. Finally,

$$W'_k \leq W'_{\bar{h}} \tag{5.7}$$

follows from (5.6) and from the covariance rule on $\{V'_j \to W'_j\}_{j \in J}$
Thus, by (5.5) and (5.7), $W'_k \leq W_h$

Theorem 5.1 (Generalized Subject Reduction). *Let* $M : U$. *If* $M \rhd^* N$ *then* $N : U'$, *where* $U' \leq U$.

Proof. It suffices to prove the theorem for $\rhd$; the thesis follows from a simple induction on the number of steps of the reduction. Thus, we proceed by induction on the structure of M:

$M \equiv x$ x is in normal form and the thesis is straightforwardly satisfied.
$M \equiv \varepsilon$ as in the previous case.
$M \equiv \lambda x^V.P$. The only case of reduction is that $P \rhd P'$ and $N \equiv \lambda x^V.P'$; but from the induction hypothesis it follows that N is well-typed and the type of the codomain of N will be less than or equal to the one of M; since the domains are the same, the thesis thus holds.
$M \equiv (M_1 \&^T M_2)$. Just note that whenever M is reduced it is still well-typed (apply the induction hypothesis) and its type doesn't change.
$M \equiv M_1 \cdot M_2$ where $M_1 : V \to U$ and $M_2 : W \leq V$. We have three subcases:

1. $M_1 \rhd M'_1$, then by induction hypothesis $M'_1 : V' \to U'$ with $V \leq V'$ and $U' \leq U$. Since $W \leq V \leq V'$, then by rule [$\to$ELIM$_{(\leq)}$] we obtain $M'_1 M_2 : U' \leq U$.
2. $M_2 \rhd M'_2$, then by induction hypothesis $M'_2 : W'$ with $W' \leq W$. Again, $W' \leq W \leq V$ and, thus, by [$\to$ELIM$_{(\leq)}$] we obtain $M_1 M'_2 : U$.
3. $M_1 \equiv \lambda x^V.M_3$ and $M \rhd M_3[x := M_2]$, with $M_3 : U$. Thus, by Lemma 5.1, $M_3[x := M_2] : U'$ with $U' \leq U$.

$M \equiv M_1 \bullet M_2$ where $M_1 : \{V_i \to W_i\}_{i \in I}$ and $M_2 : V$.

Let $V_h = \min_{i \in I}\{V_i | V \leq V_i\}$. Thus $U = W_h$. Again we have three subcases:

1. $M_1 \rhd M_1'$ then by induction $M_1' : \{V_j' \to W_j'\}_{j \in J}$ with $\{V_j' \to W_j'\}_{j \in J} \leq \{V_i \to W_i\}_{i \in I}$. Let $V_k' = \min_{j \in J}\{V_j' | V \leq V_j'\}$. Thus $M_1' \bullet M_2 : W_k'$. Therefore we have to prove that $W_k' \leq W_h$

   Since $\{V_j' \to W_j'\}_{j \in J} \leq \{V_i \to W_i\}_{i \in I}$, then for all $i \in I$ there exists $j \in J$ such that $V_j' \to W_j' \leq V_i \to W_i$. For $i = h$ we choose a certain $\tilde{h} \in J$ which satisfies this condition. That is:

$$V_{\tilde{h}}' \to W_{\tilde{h}}' \leq V_h \to W_h \tag{5.8}$$

   We now have the following inequalities:

$$V \leq V_h \tag{5.9}$$

   by hypothesis, since $V_h = \min_{i \in I}\{V_i | V \leq V_i\}$;

$$V_h \leq V_{\tilde{h}}' \tag{5.10}$$

   follows from (5.8);

$$V \leq V_{\tilde{h}}' \tag{5.11}$$

   follows from (5.9) and (5.10);

$$W_{\tilde{h}}' \leq W_h \tag{5.12}$$

   follows from (5.8);

$$V_k' \leq V_{\tilde{h}}' \tag{5.13}$$

   by (5.11), since $V_{\tilde{h}}'$ belongs to a set with V_k' as least element;

$$W_k' \leq W_{\tilde{h}}' \tag{5.14}$$

   follows from (5.13) and the covariance rule on $\{V_j' \to W_j'\}_{j \in J}$

   Finally, by (5.12) and (5.14), one has that $W_k' \leq W_h$
2. $M_2 \rhd M_2'$ then by induction hypothesis $M_2' : V'$ with $V' \leq V$. Let $V_k = \min_{i \in I}\{V_i | V' \leq V_i\}$. Thus $M_1 \bullet M_2' : W_k$. Since $V' \leq V \leq V_h$ then $V_k \leq V_h$; thus, by the covariance rule in $\{V_i \to W_i\}_{i \in I}$, we obtain $W_k \leq W_h$.
3. $M_1 \equiv (N_1 \& N_2)$ and M_2 is normal. Then we have two cases, that is $M \rhd (N_1 \bullet M_2)$ (case $h < n$) or $M \rhd (N_2 \cdot M_2)$ (case $h = n$). In both cases, by [{}ELIM] or [$\to$ELIM$_{(\leq)}$], according to the case, it is easy to show that the terms have type smaller than or equal to W_h.

6 Church-Rosser

In this section we prove that this system is Church-Rosser (**CR**). The proof is a simple application of a lemma due to Hindley [21] and Rosen [33]:

Lemma 6.1 (Hindley-Rosen). *Let R_1,R_2 be two notions of reduction. If R_1, R_2 are* **CR** *and $\rhd^*_{R_1}$ commutes with $\rhd^*_{R_2}$ then $R_1 \cup R_2$ is* **CR**.

Set now $R_1 \equiv \beta_{\&}$ and $R_2 \equiv \beta$; if we prove that these notions of reduction satisfy the hypotheses of the lemma above, we thus obtain **CR** for our system. It is easy to prove that β and $\beta_{\&}$ are **CR**: indeed, the first one is a well known result while for the other just note that $\beta_{\&}$ satisfies the diamond property.

Thus it remains to prove that the two notions of reduction commute, for which we need two technical lemmas.

Lemma 6.2. *If $N \rhd^*_{\beta_{\&}} N'$ then $M[x := N] \rhd^*_{\beta_{\&}} M[x := N']$*

Proof. The proof is done by induction on the structure of M and consists in a simple diagram chase

M	LHS	RHS	comment
ε	ε	ε	OK
x	N	N'	OK
y	y	y	OK
PQ	$P[\ ]Q[\ ]$	$P[\ ']Q[\ ']$	use the induction hypothesis
$\lambda y.P$	$\lambda y.P[\ ]$	$\lambda y.P[\ ']$	use the induction hypothesis
$(P\&Q)$	$(P[\ ]\&Q[\ ])$	$(P[\ ']\&Q[\ '])$	use the induction hypothesis

Lemma 6.3. *If $M \rhd_{\beta_{\&}} M'$ then $M[x := N] \rhd_{\beta_{\&}} M'[x := N]$*

Proof. We proceed by induction on the structure of $M \rhd M'$ (we omit the index since there is no ambiguity here); we have the following cases:

CASE 1 $\lambda y.P \rhd \lambda y.P'$ the thesis follows from the induction hypothesis on $P \rhd P'$.
CASE 2 $PQ \rhd P'Q$ the thesis follows from the induction hypothesis on $P \rhd P'$.
The same for $QP \rhd QP'$, $P\&Q \rhd P'\&Q$ and $Q\&P \rhd Q\&P'$.
CASE 3 $(P_1\&P_2)Q \rhd P_iQ$ then

$$\begin{aligned} M[x := N] &\equiv (P_1[x := N]\&P_2[x := N])Q[x := N] \\ &\equiv (P_1[x := N]\&P_2[x := N])Q \qquad \text{since } Q \text{ is closed} \end{aligned}$$

Since substitutions do not change the type in $(P_1\&P_2)$ (just recall that the type is fixed on the & and does not change during computation) then the selected branch will be the same for both $(P_1\&P_2)Q$ and $(P_1[x := N]\&P_2[x := N])Q$, thus:

$$\begin{aligned} &\rhd P_i[x := N]Q \\ &\equiv P_i[x := N]Q[x := N] \qquad \text{since } Q \text{ is closed} \\ &\equiv M'[x := N] \end{aligned}$$

The next lemma shows that reductions are not context-sensitive: given a context $C[\ ]$, i.e. a lambda term with a hole, a reduction inside the hole is not affected by the context. This lemma will allow us to reduce the number of the cases in the next theorem:

Lemma 6.4. *Let R denote either β or $\beta_{\&}$; then for all contexts $C[\ ]$ if $M \rhd^*_R N$ then $C[M] \rhd^*_R C[N]$*

Proof. The proof is a simple induction on the context $C[\ ]$

Theorem 6.1 (Weak commutativity). *If $M \rhd_\beta N_1$ and $M \rhd_{\beta_{\&}} N_2$ then there exists N_3 such that $N_1 \rhd^*_{\beta_{\&}} N_3$ and $N_2 \rhd^*_\beta N_3$*

Proof. We proceed by induction on the structure of M. Since M is not in normal form, then $M \not\equiv x$ and $M \not\equiv \varepsilon$. In every induction step we will omit the (sub)cases which are a straightforward consequence of lemma 6.4:

1. $M \equiv \lambda x.P$. This case follows from lemma 6.4 and induction.
2. $M \equiv (M_1 \& M_2)$ then the only subcase which is not resolved by straightforward use of lemma 6.4 is $N_1 \equiv (M_1 \& M_2')$ and $N_2 \equiv (M_1' \& M_2)$ or symmetrically. But then $N_3 \equiv (M_1' \& M_2')$.
3. $M \equiv M_1 \bullet M_2$
   Subcase 1: $N_1 \equiv M_1 \bullet M_2'$ and $N_2 \equiv M_1' \bullet M_2$ or symmetrically. Thus $N_3 \equiv M_1' \bullet M_2'$
   The remaining cases are when $M_1 \equiv (P \& Q)$ and M_2 is closed and in normal form. Then we can have:
   Subcase 2: $N_1 \equiv (P' \& Q) M_2$ and $N_2 \equiv P M_2$ but then $N_3 \equiv P' M_2$
   Subcase 3: $N_1 \equiv (P \& Q') M_2$ and $N_2 \equiv Q M_2$ but then $N_3 \equiv Q' M_2$
   Subcase 4: $N_1 \equiv (P \& Q') M_2$ and $N_2 \equiv P M_2$ but then $N_3 \equiv N_2$
   Subcase 5: $N_1 \equiv (P' \& Q) M_2$ and $N_2 \equiv Q M_2$ but then $N_3 \equiv N_2$
   Note that in the last four cases we have used the property that the type of an &-term doesn't change when we reduce inside it and therefore the selected branch will be the same for the same argument.
4. $M \equiv M_1 \cdot M_2$ then as in the previous case we have:
   Subcase 1: $N_1 \equiv M_1 M_2'$ and $N_2 \equiv M_1' M_2$ or symmetrically. Thus $N_3 \equiv M_1' M_2'$
   The other cases are when M_1 is of the form $\lambda x.P$. Then we can have:
   Subcase 2: $N_1 \equiv P[x := M_2]$ and $N_2 \equiv (\lambda x.P) M_2'$ But $N_1 \rhd^*_{\beta_{\&}} P[x := M_2']$ (by lemma 6.2) and $N_2 \rhd_\beta P[x := M_2']$. Thus $N_3 \equiv P[x := M_2']$.
   Subcase 3: $N_1 \equiv P[x := M_2]$ and $N_2 \equiv (\lambda x.P') M_2$ But $N_1 \rhd^*_{\beta_{\&}} P'[x := M_2]$ (by lemma 6.3) and $N_2 \rhd_\beta P'[x := M_2]$. Thus $N_3 \equiv P'[x := M_2]$

Corollary 6.1. *$\rhd^*_{\beta_{\&}}$ commutes with $\rhd^*_\beta$*

Proof. By lemma 3.3.6 in [3].

Finally, by applying the HINDLEY-ROSEN lemma, we obtain that the calculus is **CR**.

7 Strong Normalization

7.1 The full calculus is not normalizing

The $\lambda\&$ calculus is not normalizing. Consider the following term, where $\emptyset$ is used instead of $\{\}$ to reduce the parenthesis nesting level, and where M stands for any closed term of type $\{\emptyset \to \emptyset\}$, e.g. $M = (\varepsilon \,\&^{\{\emptyset\to\emptyset\}}\, \lambda x^{\emptyset}.\varepsilon)$:

$$\begin{aligned} \mathit{Double} &= (M \,\&^{\{\emptyset\to\emptyset,\{\emptyset\to\emptyset\}\to\emptyset\}}\, (\lambda x^{\{\emptyset\to\emptyset\}}.x\bullet x)) : \mathit{DType} \\ \mathit{DType} &= \{\emptyset \to \emptyset, \{\emptyset \to \emptyset\} \to \emptyset\} \end{aligned}$$

Double is a $\lambda\&$ version of the untyped λ-term $\lambda x.xx$, coerced to a type *DType* such that it is possible to apply *Double* to itself. *Double* is well typed; in particular, $x\bullet x$ is well typed and has type $\emptyset$ as proved below:

$$[\{\}\text{ELIM}] \quad \frac{\vdash x\colon \{\emptyset \to \emptyset\} \quad \vdash x\colon \{\emptyset \to \emptyset\} \quad \emptyset = \min_{U\in\{\emptyset\}}\{U|\{\emptyset \to \emptyset\} \leq U\}}{\vdash x\bullet x\colon \emptyset}$$

It may seem that the possibility to perform self-application is due to the existence of an empty overloaded type which is a maximum element in the set of all the overloaded types. This is not the case; actually, in the following proof of well-typing of *Double* •*Double*, we may substitute $\emptyset$ with any other overloaded type.

$$[\{\}\text{ELIM}] \quad \frac{\begin{array}{l}\vdash \mathit{Double}\colon \mathit{DType} \quad \vdash \mathit{Double}\colon \mathit{DType} \\ \{\emptyset \to \emptyset\} = \min_{U\in\{\emptyset,\{\emptyset\to\emptyset\}\}}\{U|\{\emptyset \to \emptyset, \{\emptyset \to \emptyset\} \to \emptyset\} \leq U\}\end{array}}{\vdash \mathit{Double}\bullet\mathit{Double}\colon \emptyset}$$

Now we can show that *Double* •*Double* has not a normal form as it reduces to itself:

$$\mathit{Double}\bullet\mathit{Double} \quad \rhd_{\beta_\&} \quad (\lambda x^{\{\emptyset\to\emptyset\}}.x\bullet x)\cdot\mathit{Double} \quad \rhd_{\beta} \quad \mathit{Double}\bullet\mathit{Double}$$

Simply typed lambda calculus prevents looping, essentially, by imposing a stratification between a function of type $T \to U$ and its argument, whose type T is "simpler" than the whole type $T \to U$; the same thing happens, in a subtler way, with system F.

When we add subtyping, the type T' of the argument of a function with type $T \to U$ is just a subtype of T, and may be, syntactically, much bigger than the whole $T \to U$: consider the case when T' is a record type with more fields that T. However, the *rank* of T' is still strictly smaller than that of $T \to U$, where the rank of an arrow type is at least the rank of its domain part plus one (for a correct definition see below). This happens, in short, since in $\lambda_{\leq}$ and in $F_{\leq}$ two types can be related by subtyping only when they have the same rank. Hence, $\lambda_{\leq}$ and $F_{\leq}$ are still strongly normalizing [17].

$\lambda\&$ typing does not prevent looping, essentially, since it allows to compare types with a different rank. In our example, we pass a parameter of type $\{\emptyset \to \emptyset, \{\emptyset \to \emptyset\} \to \emptyset\}$ (rank 2) to a function with domain type $\{\emptyset \to \emptyset\}$ (rank 1), and in the $x\bullet x$ case we pass a parameter of type $\{\emptyset \to \emptyset\}$ (rank 1) to a function with domain type $\{\}$ (rank 0). Hence, $\lambda\&$ typing does not prevent looping since it does not stratify functions w.r.t. their arguments.

However, when $\lambda\&$ is used to model object-oriented programming, it is always used in a stratified way. It is then interesting to define a stratified subsystem of $\lambda\&$ which is both strongly normalizing and expressive enough to model object-oriented programming. To this aim, we will prove the following theorem.

Theorem 7.1. *Let $\lambda\&^-$ be any subsystem of $\lambda\&$ closed by reduction and let* rank *be any function associating integers with $\lambda\&^-$ types. Assume also that, if T (syntactically) occurs in U, then* $\text{rank}(T) \leq \text{rank}(U)$. *If in $\lambda\&^-$, for any well typed application $M^T N^U$ one has* $\text{rank}(U) < \text{rank}(T)$, *then $\lambda\&^-$ is Strongly Normalizing.*

Example 7.1. We may obtain a subsystem of $\lambda\&$ with the properties of $\lambda\&^-$ in 7.1 either by restricting the set of types, or by imposing a stricter subtyping relation. We propose here two significant examples based on these restrictions: ($\lambda\&^-_{\mathrm{T}}$) and ($\lambda\&^-_{\leq}$), respectively. In either case, the *rank* function is defined as follows:

$$\begin{aligned}
&\mathit{rank}(\{\}) &&= 0\\
&\mathit{rank}(A) &&= 0\\
&\mathit{rank}(T \to U) &&= \max\{\mathit{rank}(T)+1, \mathit{rank}(U)\}\\
&\mathit{rank}(\{T_i \to U_i\}_{i\in I}) &&= \max_{i\in I}\{\mathit{rank}(T_i \to U_i)\}
\end{aligned}$$

The idea is that, by restricting the set of types or the subtyping relation as described below, the types of a function and of its arguments are "stratified", namely the rank of the functional type is strictly greater than the rank of the input type, as required by theorem 7.1.

- $\lambda\&^-_{\leq}$ is defined by substituting $\leq$ in all $\lambda\&$ rules with a stricter subtyping relation $\leq^-$ defined by adding to any subtyping rule which proves $T \leq U$ the further condition $\mathit{rank}(T) \leq \mathit{rank}(U)$. In any well typed $\lambda\&^-_{\leq}$ application $M^{\{T_i \to U_i\}_{i\in I}} \bullet N^{T'}$, the rank of T' is then smaller than the rank of some T_i, hence is strictly smaller than the rank of $\{T_i \to U_i\}_{i\in I}$; similarly for functional application. The subject reduction proof for $\lambda\&$ works for $\lambda\&^-_{\leq}$ too, thanks to the transitivity of the $\leq^-$ relation.[7]
- $\lambda\&^-_{\mathrm{T}}$ is defined by imposing, on overloaded types $\{T_i \to U_i\}_{i\in I}$, the restriction that the ranks of all the branch types $T_i \to U_i$ are equal, and by stipulating that $\{\}$ is not a supertype of any non-empty overloaded type (see the previous footnote). Then we can prove inductively that, whenever $T \leq U$, then $\mathit{rank}(T) = \mathit{rank}(U)$, and that $\lambda\&^-_{\mathrm{T}}$ is a subsystem of $\lambda\&^-_{\leq}$. To prove the closure under reduction (i.e. that $\lambda\&^-_{\mathrm{T}}$ terms reduce to $\lambda\&^-_{\mathrm{T}}$ terms), observe first that a $\lambda\&$ term is also a $\lambda\&^-_{\mathrm{T}}$ term iff all the overloaded types appearing in the indexes of variables and of &'s are $\lambda\&^-_{\mathrm{T}}$ overloaded types (this is easily shown by induction on typing rules). The closure by reduction follows immediately, since variables and &'s indexes are never created by a reduction step.

Note that $\lambda\&^-_{\mathrm{T}}$ is already expressive enough to model object-oriented programming, where all methods always have the same rank (rank 1), and that $\lambda\&^-_{\leq}$ is even more expressive than $\lambda\&^-_{\mathrm{T}}$.

---

[7] Note that, in this system, $\{\}$ is not a supertype of any non-empty overloaded type; this is not a problem, since the empty overloaded type is only used to type ε, which is only used only to start overloaded function construction. However, we may alternatively define a family of empty types $\{\}_{i\in\omega}$, each being the maximum overloaded type of the corresponding rank, and a correspondent family of empty functions $\varepsilon_{i\in\omega}$.

Theorem 7.1 and the examples show that there exist subsystems of $\lambda\&$ which are strongly normalizing and expressive enough for our purposes. However we preferred to adopt the whole $\lambda\&$ as our target system, since it is easier to establish results such as Subject Reduction and Confluence on the wider system and apply them in subsystems rather than trying to extend restricted versions to more general cases.

In the following subsections we prove Theorem 7.1.

7.2 Typed-inductive properties

As is well known, strong normalization cannot be proved by induction on terms, since β reduction potentially increases the size of the reduced term. For this reason we introduce, along the lines of [28], a different notion of induction on typed terms, called *typed induction*, proving that every typed-inductive property is satisfied by any typed $\lambda\&^-$ term. This notion is shaped over reduction, so that some reduction related properties, such as strong normalization or confluence, can be easily proved to be typed-inductive. Theorem 7.2, which proves that every typed-inductive property is satisfied by any typed $\lambda\&^-$ term, is the kernel of our proof and is related to the normalization proofs due to Tait, Girard, Mitchell and others. We had to avoid, though, the notions of saturated set and of logical relation, which do not seem to generalize easily to our setting. In this section we define a notion of "typed-inductive property" for $\lambda\&^-$ terms and show that every typed-inductive property is satisfied by any (well-typed) $\lambda\&^-$ term. Although many of the results and definitions in this section hold or make sense for $\lambda\&$ too, the reader should remember that all the terms, types and judgments in this section refer to a $\lambda\&^-$ system satisfying the conditions of Theorem 7.1.

Notation 1 *$M \circ N$ will denote $M \cdot N$ if $M{:}T \to U$ and $M\bullet N$ if $M{:}\{M_i \to N_i\}_{i=1\ldots n}$.*

Notation 2 *$\boldsymbol{M}$ denotes a list $[M_i]_{i=1,\ldots,n}$ of terms, possibly empty, and $N{\cdot}\boldsymbol{M}$ means $N \cdot M_1 \circ \ldots \circ M_n$; the same for $N\bullet\boldsymbol{M}$; if $\boldsymbol{M}$ is empty, $N \circ \boldsymbol{M}$ is just N.*

"$\boldsymbol{M}$ is well typed" means "each $M_i \in \boldsymbol{M}$ is well typed"; similarly for other predicates on terms.

Definition 2 *Let $\{\mathcal{S}^T\}_T$ be a family of sets of $\lambda\&^-$ terms, indexed over $\lambda\&^-$ types, such that:*

$$M \in \mathcal{S}^T \Rightarrow\ \vdash M{:}T.$$

$\mathcal{S}$ is typed-inductive *if it satisfies the following conditions[8] (where $M \in \mathcal{S}^{if}$ means "$M \in \mathcal{S}$ if M is well typed"):*

(x/c) $\forall x, \boldsymbol{N} \in \mathcal{S}.\ x \circ \boldsymbol{N} \in \mathcal{S}^{if}$
and similarly for constants and for ε.

[8] We use $\mathcal{S}$ for $\{\mathcal{S}^T\}_T$. Furthermore, since any term M has a unique type T, we will write without ambiguity $M \in \mathcal{S}$ to mean $M \in \mathcal{S}^T$.

($\&_1$) $\forall M_1 \in \mathcal{S}, M_2 \in \mathcal{S}, N \in \mathcal{S}, \boldsymbol{N} \in \mathcal{S}.$
$M_1 \bullet N \circ \boldsymbol{N} \in \mathcal{S}^{if} \wedge M_2 \cdot N \circ \boldsymbol{N} \in \mathcal{S}^{if} \Rightarrow (M_1 \& M_2) \bullet N \circ \boldsymbol{N} \in \mathcal{S}^{if}$
(λ_1) $\forall M \in \mathcal{S}, N \in \mathcal{S}, \boldsymbol{N} \in \mathcal{S}.\ M[x:=N] \circ \boldsymbol{N} \in \mathcal{S}^{if} \Rightarrow (\lambda x{:}T.M) \cdot N \circ \boldsymbol{N} \in \mathcal{S}^{if}$
($\&_2$) $\forall M_1 \in \mathcal{S}, M_2 \in \mathcal{S}.\ M_1 \& M_2 \in \mathcal{S}^{if}$
(λ_2) $\forall M \in \mathcal{S}.\ \lambda x^T.M \in \mathcal{S}^{if}$

The $\mathcal{S}^{if}$ notation means that all the "$\in\mathcal{S}$" predicates in the above implications must only be satisfied only by typed preterms. This is difficult only in case $\&_1$: depending on whether $M_1 \bullet \ldots$ is well-typed, $M_2 \cdot \ldots$ is well-typed or both are well-typed, the first, the second or both are required to be in $\mathcal{S}$; indeed we want to take into account all the branches that could be selected not only the one that will be actually executed. For this reason we used in $\&_1$ a "$\wedge$" rather than a "$\vee$".

We aim to prove, by induction on terms, that every well-typed $\lambda\&^-$ term N belongs to $\mathcal{S}$. The conditions on typed induction allow an inductive proof of this fact for terms like $\lambda x^T.M$ and $M\&N$, but we have no direct proof that $(M \in \mathcal{S} \wedge N \in \mathcal{S}) \Rightarrow (M \circ N \in \mathcal{S})$. For this reason we derive from $\mathcal{S}$ a stronger predicate $\mathcal{S}^*$ which allows term induction through application. We will then prove that $\mathcal{S}^*$ is not actually stronger than $\mathcal{S}$, since for any typed-inductive property $\mathcal{S}$:

$$M \in \mathcal{S}^{*T} \Leftrightarrow M \in \mathcal{S}^T \Leftrightarrow\ \vdash M{:}T.$$

The definition of $\mathcal{S}^*$ is the only part of the proof where we need the stratification by the rank function.

Notation 3 ($\widehat{[T_i]}_{i \in I}$) *For any list of types* $[T_i]_{i \in I}$, $T' \in \widehat{[T_i]}_{i \in I} \Leftrightarrow \exists i \in I. T' \leq T_i$. *Note that if* $\vdash M{:}\{T_i \to U_i\}_{i \in I}$ *and* $\vdash N{:}T'$ *then* $M \bullet N$ *is well typed iff* $T' \in \widehat{[T_i]}_{i \in I}$.

Definition 3 *For any typed-inductive property* $\{\mathcal{S}^T\}_T$ *its application closure on* $\lambda\&^-$ *terms* $\{\mathcal{S}^{*T}\}_T$ *is defined, by lexicographic induction on the rank and then on the size of T, as follows:*

$$
\begin{array}{ll}
(atomic) & M \in \mathcal{S}^{*A} \Leftrightarrow M \in \mathcal{S}^A \\
(\to) & M \in \mathcal{S}^{*T \to U} \Leftrightarrow M \in \mathcal{S}^{T \to U} \wedge \forall T' \leq T. \forall N \in \mathcal{S}^{*T'}.\ M \cdot N \in \mathcal{S}^{*U} \\
(\{\}) & M \in \mathcal{S}^{*\{T_i \to U_i\}_{i=1\ldots n}} \\
 & \Leftrightarrow M \in \mathcal{S}^{\{T_i \to U_i\}_{i=1\ldots n}} \\
 & \quad \wedge \forall T' \in \widehat{[T_i]}_{i=1\ldots n}. \forall N \in \mathcal{S}^{*T'}. \exists i \in [1..n]. M \bullet N \in \mathcal{S}^{*U_i}
\end{array}
$$

In short:

$$M \in \mathcal{S}^* \Leftrightarrow M \in \mathcal{S} \wedge \forall N \in \mathcal{S}^*. M \circ N \in \mathcal{S}^{*if}$$

In the definition of $\mathcal{S}^*$, we say that M belongs to $\mathcal{S}^*$ by giving for granted the definition of $\mathcal{S}^*$ over the types of the N's such that $M \circ N$ is well typed and over the type of $M \circ N$ itself. This is consistent with the inductive hypothesis since:

1. The rank of the type of N is strictly smaller than the rank of the type of M in view of the conditions in Theorem 7.1.

2. Since the type U of $M \circ N$ strictly occurs in the type W of M, then the rank of U is not greater than the rank of W (by the conditions in Theorem 7.1). Hence the definition is well formed either by induction on the rank or, if the ranks of U and W are equal, by secondary induction on the size.

The next lemma shows, informally, that in the condition

$$M \in \mathcal{S}^* \Leftrightarrow \forall N \in \mathcal{S}^*. M \circ N \in \mathcal{S}^{*if}$$

we can trade an $*$ for an , since $\forall N \in \mathcal{S}^*. M \circ N \in \mathcal{S}^{*if} \Leftrightarrow \forall \boldsymbol{N} \in \mathcal{S}^*. M \circ \boldsymbol{N} \in \mathcal{S}^{if}$.

Lemma 7.1. *$M \in \mathcal{S}^* \Leftrightarrow M$ is well typed $\wedge\, \forall \boldsymbol{N} \in \mathcal{S}^*. M \circ \boldsymbol{N} \in \mathcal{S}^{if}$*

Proof.

($\Rightarrow$) "M is well typed" is immediate since $M \in \mathcal{S}^{*T} \Rightarrow M \in \mathcal{S}^{T} \Rightarrow\, \vdash M : T$. $\forall \boldsymbol{N} \in \mathcal{S}^*. M \circ \boldsymbol{N} \in \mathcal{S}^{if}$ is proved by proving the stronger property

$$\forall \boldsymbol{N} \in \mathcal{S}^*. M \circ \boldsymbol{N} \in \mathcal{S}^{*if}$$

by induction on the length of $\boldsymbol{N}$. If $\boldsymbol{N}$ is empty, the thesis is immediate. If $\boldsymbol{N} = N_1 \cup \boldsymbol{N'}$ then $M \circ N_1 \in \mathcal{S}^{*if}$ by definition of $\mathcal{S}^*$, and $(M \circ N_1) \circ \boldsymbol{N'} \in \mathcal{S}^{*if}$ by induction.

($\Leftarrow$) By definition, $M \in \mathcal{S}^* \Leftrightarrow M \in \mathcal{S} \wedge \forall N \in \mathcal{S}^*. M \circ N \in \mathcal{S}^{*if}$. $\forall \boldsymbol{N} \in \mathcal{S}^*. M \bullet \boldsymbol{N} \in \mathcal{S}^{if}$ implies immediately $M \in \mathcal{S}$: just take an empty $\boldsymbol{N}$. $M \circ N \in \mathcal{S}^{*if}$ is proved by induction on the type of M.

(atomic) $\vdash M : A$: $M \circ N$ is never well typed; $M \in \mathcal{S}^{A}$ is enough to conclude $M \in \mathcal{S}^{*A}$.

($\{\}$) $\vdash M : \{\}$: as above.

($\rightarrow$) $\vdash M : T \rightarrow U$: we have to prove that $\forall N \in \mathcal{S}^{*T'}, T' \leq T. M \cdot N \in \mathcal{S}^{*U}$. By hypothesis:

$$\forall \boldsymbol{N} \in \mathcal{S}^*. M \cdot N \circ \boldsymbol{N} \in \mathcal{S}^{if}$$

applying induction to $M \cdot N$, whose type U is smaller than the one of $T \rightarrow U$, we have that $M \cdot N \in \mathcal{S}^{*U}$.

($\{T_i \rightarrow U_i\}$) $\vdash M : \{T_i \rightarrow U_i\}_{i=1 \ldots n+1}$: as in the previous case.

□

Theorem 7.2. *If $\mathcal{S}$ is typed-inductive, then every term $\vdash N : T$ is in $\mathcal{S}^{*T}$.*

Proof. We prove the following stronger property: if N is well-typed and $\sigma \equiv [\boldsymbol{x}^{\boldsymbol{T}} := \mathbf{N}]$ is a well-typed $\mathcal{S}^*$-substitution (i.e. for $i \in [1..n]$. $N_i \in \mathcal{S}^{*T_i'}$ and $T_i' \leq T_i$), then $N\sigma \in \mathcal{S}^*$; $\boldsymbol{x}^{\boldsymbol{T}}$ is called the domain of $\sigma \equiv [\boldsymbol{x}^{\boldsymbol{T}} := \boldsymbol{N}]$, and is denoted as $dom(\sigma)$.

It is proved by induction on the size of N. In any induction step, we prove $\forall\sigma. N\sigma \in \mathcal{S}^*$, supposing that, for any N' smaller than N, $\forall \sigma'. N'\sigma' \in \mathcal{S}^*$ (which implies $N'\sigma' \in \mathcal{S}$ and $N' \in \mathcal{S}$).

(c) $c\sigma \equiv c$. We apply lemma 7.1, and prove that $\forall \boldsymbol{N} \in \mathcal{S}^*. c \circ \boldsymbol{N} \in \mathcal{S}^{if}$. Since $\boldsymbol{N} \in \mathcal{S}^* \Rightarrow \boldsymbol{N} \in \mathcal{S}$ then $c \circ \boldsymbol{N} \in \mathcal{S}^{if}$ follows immediately from property (c) of $\mathcal{S}$.

(x) If $x \in dom(\sigma)$ then $x\sigma \in \mathcal{S}^*$ since σ is an $\mathcal{S}^*$-substitution. Otherwise, reason as in case (c).

($M_1\&M_2$) By applying lemma 7.1 we prove that $\forall \sigma. \forall \boldsymbol{N} \in \mathcal{S}^*. (M_1\&M_2)\sigma \circ \boldsymbol{N} \in \mathcal{S}^{if}$. We have two cases. If $\boldsymbol{N}$ is not empty then $\boldsymbol{N} \equiv N_1 \cup \boldsymbol{N'}$. For any σ, $M_1\sigma \bullet N_1 \circ \boldsymbol{N'} \in \mathcal{S}^{if}$ and $M_2\sigma \cdot N_1 \circ \boldsymbol{N'} \in \mathcal{S}^{if}$ by induction (M_1 and M_2 are smaller than $M_1\&M_2$). Then $(M_1\&M_2)\sigma \bullet N_1 \circ \boldsymbol{N'} \in \mathcal{S}^{if}$ by property ($\&_1$) of $\mathcal{S}$.
If $\boldsymbol{N}$ is empty then $(M_1\&M_2)\sigma \in \mathcal{S}$ follows, by property ($\&_2$) of $\mathcal{S}$, from the inductive hypothesis $M_1\sigma \in \mathcal{S}$ and $M_2\sigma \in \mathcal{S}$.

($\lambda x^T.M$) We will prove that $\forall \sigma. \forall \boldsymbol{N} \in \mathcal{S}^*.\ (\lambda x^T.M)\sigma \circ \boldsymbol{N} \in \mathcal{S}^{if}$, supposing, w.l.o.g., that x is not in $dom(\sigma)$.
We have two cases. If $\boldsymbol{N}$ is not empty and $(\lambda x^T.M)\sigma \circ \boldsymbol{N}$ is well typed then $\boldsymbol{N} \equiv N_1 \cup \boldsymbol{N'}$ and the type of N_1 is a subtype of T. Then for any $\mathcal{S}^*$-substitution σ, $\sigma[x^T := N_1]$ is a well-typed $\mathcal{S}^*$-substitution, since $N_1 \in \mathcal{S}^*$ by hypothesis, and then $M(\sigma[x := N_1]) \circ \boldsymbol{N'} \in \mathcal{S}^{if}$ by induction, which implies $(M\sigma)[x := N_1] \circ \boldsymbol{N'} \in \mathcal{S}^{if}$. Then $(\lambda x^T.M\sigma) \cdot N_1 \circ \boldsymbol{N'} \equiv (\lambda x^T.M)\sigma \circ \boldsymbol{N} \in \mathcal{S}^{if}$ by property (λ_1) of $\mathcal{S}$.
If $\boldsymbol{N}$ is empty, $(\lambda x^T.M)\sigma \in \mathcal{S}$ follows, by property (λ_2), from the inductive hypothesis $M\sigma \in \mathcal{S}$.

($M \circ N$) By induction $M\sigma \in \mathcal{S}^*$ and $N\sigma \in \mathcal{S}^*$; then $(M \circ N)\sigma \in \mathcal{S}^*$ by definition of $\mathcal{S}^*$.

This property implies the theorem since, as can be argued by case (x) of this proof, the identity substitution is a well-typed $\mathcal{S}^*$-substitution. □

Corollary 7.1. *If $\mathcal{S}$ is a typed-inductive property, every well-typed term satisfies $\mathcal{S}$ and its application closure:*

$$M \in \mathcal{S}^{*T} \Leftrightarrow M \in \mathcal{S}^T \Leftrightarrow \vdash M : T$$

Proof.

$M \in \mathcal{S}^{*T}$	$\Rightarrow M \in \mathcal{S}^T$	by definition of $\mathcal{S}^*$.
$M \in \mathcal{S}^T$	$\Rightarrow \vdash M : T$	by definition of typed induction.
$\vdash M : T$	$\Rightarrow M \in \mathcal{S}^{*T}$	by theorem 7.2.

□

7.3 Strong Normalization is typed-inductive

In this section we prove Strong Normalization of $\lambda\&^-$ by proving that Strong Normalization is a typed-inductive property of $\lambda\&^-$ terms.

Consider the following term rewriting system *unconditional-$\beta \cup \beta_\&$*, which differs from $\beta \cup \beta_\&$ since unconditional-$\beta_\&$ reduction steps are allowed even if N is not normal or not closed and the selected branch can be any of those whose input type is compatible with the type of the argument:

β) $(\lambda x^S.M)N \rhd M[x^S := N]$
uncond.-$\beta_\&$) If $N : U \leq U_j$ then

$$((M_1 \&^{\{U_i \to V_i\}_{i=1..n}} M_2) \bullet N) \rhd \begin{cases} M_1 \bullet N & \text{for } j < n \\ M_2 \cdot N & \text{for } j = n \end{cases}$$

Instead of proving Strong Normalization for $\lambda\&^-$ reduction, we prove Strong Normalization for unconditional-$\beta\cup\beta_\&$. Since any $\beta\cup\beta_\&$ reduction is also an unconditional-$\beta\cup\beta_\&$ reduction, Strong Normalization of the unconditional system implies Strong Normalization for the original one. Note that subject reduction still holds and that even if the $\beta_\&$ conditions are not necessary to obtain strong termination, they are still needed to obtain confluence.

Notation 4 *If M is strongly normalizing, $\nu(M)$ is the length of the longest reduction chain starting from M. $\nu(\boldsymbol{M})$ is equal to $\nu(M_1) + \ldots + \nu(M_n)$.*

Theorem 7.3. *$\mathcal{SN}^T$, the property of being strongly normalizing terms of type T (according to the unconditional relation) is typed-inductive.*

Proof.

(x/c) $\forall \boldsymbol{N} \in \mathcal{SN}.\ x^U \circ \boldsymbol{N} \in \mathcal{SN}^{if}$
By induction on $\nu(\boldsymbol{N})$: if $x \circ \boldsymbol{N} \rhd P$ then $P = x \circ N'_1 \circ \ldots \circ N'_n$ where just one of the primed terms is a one-step reduct of the corresponding non-primed one, while the other ones are equal. So $P \in \mathcal{SN}$ by induction on $\nu(\boldsymbol{N})$.

($\&_1$) $\forall M_1 \in \mathcal{SN}, M_2 \in \mathcal{SN}, N \in \mathcal{SN}, \boldsymbol{N} \in \mathcal{SN}$.
$M_1 \bullet N \circ \boldsymbol{N} \in \mathcal{SN}^{if} \wedge M_2 \cdot N \circ \boldsymbol{N} \in \mathcal{SN}^{if} \Rightarrow (M_1 \& M_2) \bullet N \circ \boldsymbol{N} \in \mathcal{SN}^{if}$
By induction on $\nu(M_1) + \nu(M_2) + \nu(N) + \nu(\boldsymbol{N})$.
If $(M_1 \& M_2) \bullet N \circ \boldsymbol{N} \rhd P$ then we have the following cases:
($\beta\&_1$) $P = M_1 \bullet N \circ \boldsymbol{N}$: since P is well-typed by subject-reduction, then $P \in \mathcal{SN}$ by hypothesis.
($\beta\&_2$) $P = M_2 \cdot N \circ \boldsymbol{N}$: as above.
(congr.) $P = (M'_1 \& M'_2) \bullet N' \circ \boldsymbol{N}'$: $P \in \mathcal{SN}$ by induction on ν.
So $(M_1 \& M_2) \bullet N \circ \boldsymbol{N} \in \mathcal{SN}$ since it one-step reduces only to strongly normalizing terms.

(λ_1) $\forall M \in \mathcal{SN}, N \in \mathcal{SN}, \boldsymbol{N} \in \mathcal{SN}.\ M[x := N] \circ \boldsymbol{N} \in \mathcal{SN} \Rightarrow (\lambda x^T.M) \cdot N \circ \boldsymbol{N} \in \mathcal{SN}^{if}$
By induction on $\nu(M) + \nu(N) + \nu(\boldsymbol{N})$. If $(\lambda x^T.M) \cdot N \circ \boldsymbol{N} \rhd P$ we have the following cases:
(β) $P = M[x := N] \circ \boldsymbol{N}$: $P \in \mathcal{SN}$ by hypothesis.
(congr.) $P = (\lambda x^T.M') \cdot N' \circ \boldsymbol{N}'$ where just one of the primed terms is a one-step reduct of the corresponding one, while the other ones are equal: $P \in \mathcal{SN}$ by induction on ν.

($\&_2$) $\forall M_1 \in \mathcal{SN}, M_2 \in \mathcal{SN}.\ M_1 \& M_2 \in \mathcal{SN}^{if}$
By induction on $\nu(M_1) + \nu(M_2)$. If $M_1 \& M_2 \rhd P$ then $P \equiv M'_1 \& M'_2$ where one of the primed terms is a one-step reduct of the corresponding one, while the other one is equal; then $P \in \mathcal{SN}$ by induction.

(λ_2) $\forall M \in \mathcal{SN}. \vdash \lambda x^T.M : T \to U \Rightarrow \lambda x^T.M \in \mathcal{SN}$
If $\lambda x^T.M \rhd \lambda x^T.M'$ then, since $\nu(M') < \nu(M)$, $\lambda x^T.M' \in \mathcal{SN}$ by induction on $\nu(M)$. So $\lambda x^T.M \in \mathcal{SN}$.

□

The last proof can be easily extended to show that the reduction system remains strongly normalizing if we add the following extensionality rules:

(η) $\lambda x^T.M \cdot x \rhd M$ if x is not free in M
($\eta_{\&}$) $M \& (\lambda x^T.M \bullet x) \rhd M$ if x is not free in M

Theorem 7.1 is now a corollary of Theorem 7.3 and of Corollary 7.1.

8 Overloading and Object-Oriented Programming

We already explained in the introduction the relation between object-oriented languages and our investigation of overloading. We discuss this relation here in more depth: by now, it should be clear that we represent class-names as types, and methods as overloaded functions that, depending on the type (class-name) of their argument (the object the message is sent to), execute a certain code.

There are many techniques to represent the internal state of objects in this overloading-based approach to object-oriented programming. Since this is not the main concern of this research, we follow a rather primitive technique: we suppose that a program ($\lambda\&$-term) may be preceded by a declaration of *class types*: a *class type* is an atomic type, which is associated with a unique *representation type*, which is a record type. Two class types are in subtyping relation if this relation has been explicitly declared and it is *feasible*, in the sense that the respective representation types are in subtyping relation too. In other words class types play the role of the atomic types from which we start up, but in addition we can select fields from a value in a class type as if it belonged to its representation record type, and we have an operation $\_^{classType}$ to transform a record value r: R into a class type value $r^{classType}$ of type *classType*, provided that the representation type of *classType* is R. Class types can be represented in our system by generalizing the technique used to represent record types, but we will not show this fact in detail. We use *italics* to distinguish class types from the usual types, and $\doteq$ to declare a class type and to give it a name; we will use $\equiv$ to associate a name with a value (e.g. with a function). Thus for example we can declare the following class types:

2DPoint $\doteq \langle\!\langle x : \text{Int}; y : \text{Int} \rangle\!\rangle$
3DPoint $\doteq \langle\!\langle x : \text{Int}; y : \text{Int}; z : \text{Int} \rangle\!\rangle$

and impose that on the types *3DPoint* and *2DPoint* we have the following relation *3DPoint* $\leq$ *2DPoint* (which is feasible since it respects the ordering of the record types these class types are associated with). A simple example of a method for these class types is *Norm*. This will be implemented by the following overloaded function:

$$\begin{aligned}
\textit{Norm} \equiv (\ & \lambda \textit{self}^{2DPoint}.\sqrt{\textit{self}.x^2 + \textit{self}.y^2} \\
& \& \ \lambda \textit{self}^{3DPoint}.\sqrt{\textit{self}.x^2 + \textit{self}.y^2 + \textit{self}.z^2} \\
)&
\end{aligned}$$

whose type is $\{2DPoint \to \text{Real}, 3DPoint \to \text{Real}\}$.

Indeed, this is how we implement methods, as branches of global overloaded functions. Let us now carry on with our example and add some more methods to have a look at what the restrictions in the formation of the types (see Section 2) become in this context.

The first condition, i.e. covariance inside overloaded types, expresses the fact that a version of a method which receives a more informative input returns a more informative output. Consider for example a method that updates the internal state of an object, such as the method *Erase* which sets the x component of a point to zero:

$$\begin{aligned}
\textit{Erase} \equiv (\ & \lambda \textit{self}^{2DPoint}.\langle x = 0; y = \textit{self}.y\rangle^{2DPoint} \\
& \& \ \lambda \textit{self}^{3DPoint}.\langle x = 0; y = \textit{self}.y; z = \textit{self}.z\rangle^{3DPoint} \\
)&
\end{aligned}$$

whose type is $\{\text{2DPoint} \to 2DPoint, \text{3DPoint} \to 3DPoint\}$. Here covariance arises quite naturally.[9] In object-oriented jargon, covariance says that an overriding method must return a type smaller than the one returned by the overriden one.

As for the second restriction it simply says that in case of multiple inheritance the methods which appear in different ancestors not related by $\leq$, must be explicitly redefined. For example suppose we also have these definitions:

$\textit{Color} \doteq \langle\!\langle c : \text{String} \rangle\!\rangle$
$\textit{2DColPoint} \doteq \langle\!\langle x : \text{Int}; y : \text{Int}; c : \text{String} \rangle\!\rangle$

and that we extend the ordering on the newly defined atomic types in the following (feasible) way: $\textit{2DColPoint} \leq \textit{Color}$ and $\textit{2DColPoint} \leq \textit{2DPoint}$. Then the following function is not legal, as formation rule 3.c in Section 3.2 is violated:

$$\begin{aligned}
\textit{Erase} \equiv (\ & \lambda \textit{self}^{2DPoint}.\langle x = 0; y = \textit{self}.y\rangle^{2DPoint} \\
& \& \ \lambda \textit{self}^{3DPoint}.\langle x = 0; y = \textit{self}.y; z = \textit{self}.z\rangle^{3DPoint} \\
& \& \ \lambda \textit{self}^{Color}.\langle c = \text{"white"}\rangle^{Color} \\
)&
\end{aligned}$$

In object-oriented terms, this happens since *2DColPoint*, which is a subtype of both *2DPoint* and *Color*, inherits the *Erase* method from both classes. Since there is no reason to choose one of the two methods and no general way of defining a notion of "merging" for inherited methods, we ask that this multiply inherited method is explicitly redefined for *2DColPoint*. Note that some object-oriented languages do

[9] In the example the notation we used is quite cumbersome since we did not use field update operations on records like those of [6] or [36]. Such operations may be derived in our system, by exploiting the & operator and by a clever use of explicit coercions: see [9].

not force this redefinition, but use some different criterion to choose from inherited methods, usually related to the order in which class definitions appear in the source code. As discussed in [19], our rule 3.c in Section 3.2 can be easily substituted to model these different approaches to the problem of choosing between inherited methods, allowing a formalization and a comparison of these approaches in a unique framework. The approach we have chosen in this foundational study is just the simplest one in a context where the set of atomic types is fixed.

In our approach, a correct redefinition of the *Erase* method would be:

$$
\begin{aligned}
\mathit{Erase} \equiv (\ & \lambda \mathit{self}^{2DPoint}.\langle x = 0; y = \mathit{self}.y\rangle^{2DPoint} \\
& \&\ \lambda \mathit{self}^{3DPoint}.\langle x = 0; y = \mathit{self}.y; z = \mathit{self}.z\rangle^{3DPoint} \\
& \&\ \lambda \mathit{self}^{Color}.\langle c = \text{"white"}\rangle^{Color} \\
& \&\ \lambda \mathit{self}^{2DColPoint}.\langle x = 0; y = \mathit{self}.y; c = \text{"white"}\rangle^{2DColPoint} \\
)\ &
\end{aligned}
$$

which has type:

$$
\begin{aligned}
\{\ & \mathit{2DPoint} \to \mathit{2DPoint}, \\
& \mathit{3DPoint} \to \mathit{3DPoint}, \\
& \mathit{Color} \to \mathit{Color}, \\
& \mathit{2DColPoint} \to \mathit{2DColPoint}\ \}
\end{aligned}
$$

The way we have written these methods may seem complicated with respect to the simplicity and modularity of object-oriented languages. Indeed the terms above can be regarded as the result of a compilation (or translation) of a higher-level object-oriented program like:

```
class 2DPoint
  state       x:Int;
              y:Int
  methods     Norm = sqrt(self.x^2 + self.y^2);;
              Erase = x <- 0;;
  interface   Norm: Real;
              Erase: Likeself
endclass

class 3DPoint is 2DPoint and
  state       z:Int
  methods     Norm = sqrt(self.x^2+self.y^2+self.z^2);;
  interface   Norm: Real
endclass

class Color
  state       c:String
  methods     Erase = c <- "white";;
  interface   Erase: Likeself
endclass
```

```
class 2DColPoint is Color, 2DPoint and
  methods    Erase = x <- 0; c <- "white";;
endclass
```

8.1 Inheritance

Inheritance is the ability to define the state, interface and methods of a class "by difference" with respect to another class; inheritance on methods is the most important one. In the record based model, inheritance is realized using the record concatenation operation to add to the record of the methods of a superclass the new methods defined in the subclass. However, the recursive nature of the hidden *self* parameter forces one to distinguish between the "generator" associated with a class definition, which is essentially a version of the methods where *self* is a visible parameter, from the finished method set, obtained by a fix point operation which transforms *self* into a recursive pointer to the object which the methods belong to. This operation is called "generator wrapping". Inheritance may be defined by record concatenation over generators.[10]

To be able to reuse a generator, the type of *self* parameter must not be fixed: it must be a type variable that will assume as value the type for which the generator is reused. A first approach is to consider the type of self as a parameter itself; let us call it *Likeself*. In this case, if this "recursive type" appears in the result type of some method, then, when a generator is wrapped, the same operation must be performed on the type, to bind *Likeself* to the type of the class under definition, hence we need a fix point operator at the type level too. If, furthermore, there is some binary method, then *Likeself* must be linked to the type of the class under definition on the left hand side of arrows too. But, if a generator G has such a binary method, and a generator G' is obtained by extending G, then the type obtained by wrapping G' is not a subtype of the one obtained by wrapping G, as explained in more detail below. Hence, subtyping cannot be used to write functions operating on objects corresponding to both G and G', but F-bounded polymorphism must be introduced. F-bounded polymorphism is essentially a way of quantifying over all types obtained by wrapping an extension of a generator F. For an account of this approach see for example [5,12,27,4].

The feeling is that in the approach outlined above, recursion is too heavily used. An approach close to the previous one but that avoids the use of recursive types has been recently proposed in [30]. The idea is to separate the state of an object from its methods and then encapsulate the whole object by existentially quantifying over the type of the state. The type of a method that works on the internal state does not need to refer to the type of the whole object (as in the previous approach) but only to its state part; therefore recursive types are no longer needed. The type of the state is referred by a type variable since it is the abstract type of the existential

[10] To be fair, we must note that the generator based approach may account for the special identifier *super* used in object-oriented languages to refer to a method as it is implemented in a superclass, while we do not have this possibility in our system.

quantification. The whole existential type is passed to the generator as in the previous case but without any use of recursive types. Finally, the behavior of F-bounded polymorphism is obtained by a clever use of higher order quantification.

Our approach to method inheritance is even simpler since we also separate the state from the methods. In our system, every subtype of a type inherits all the methods of its supertypes, since every overloaded function may be applied to every subtype of the types which the function has been explicitly written for. Moreover, the behavior of an inherited method M appearing as a branch of an overloaded function (i.e. a message) N can be overridden, i.e. defined in a way which is specific for a subtype T, by defining a branch for T inside the overloaded function N. Finally, new methods may be defined for a subtype by defining new overloaded functions. By this, we may say that, in our system, inheritance is given by subtyping plus the branch selection rule. This can be better seen by an example: suppose to have a message for which a method has been defined in the classes $U_1 \ldots U_n$; thus this message denotes an overloaded function of type $\{U_i \rightarrow T_i\}_{i=1..n}$ for some T_i's. When this overloaded function is applied to an argument, the *branch selected* is the one defined for the class $\min_{i=1..n}\{U_i | U \leq U_i\}$, where U is the class (type) of the argument. If this minimum is exactly U, this means that the receiver uses the method that has been defined in its class; otherwise, i.e. if this minimum is strictly greater, then the receiver uses the method that its class, U, has *inherited* from this minimum (a superclass); in other terms, the code written for the class which resulted to be the minimum, is *reused* by the objects of the class U.

The reader should note that, although our system has a static nature (the set of atomic types is fixed), it is possible to extend it to a dynamic one, along the lines drawn in [19].

8.2 Binary methods and multiple dispatch

Let us now see the problem with binary methods in greater detail. Let us see what happens in the "objects as records" analogy: if we add a method *Equal* to *2DPoint* and *3DPoint* then, in the notation typical of formalisms built around this analogy, we obtain the following recursive record types (we forget the other methods):

$$2DEPoint \equiv \langle\langle x : \mathrm{Int}; y : \mathrm{Int}; Equal : 2DEPoint \rightarrow \mathrm{Bool}\rangle\rangle$$

$$3DEPoint \equiv \langle\langle x : \mathrm{Int}; y : \mathrm{Int}; z : \mathrm{Int}; Equal : 3DEPoint \rightarrow \mathrm{Bool}\rangle\rangle.$$

The two types are not comparable because of the contravariance of the arrow type in *Equal*: since one would expect $2DEPoint$ to be larger, as a record, than $3DEPoint$, the type at the left of the outer arrow in $2DEPoint$ should be larger, which is impossible by contravariance.[11] Note that this should not be considered a flaw in the system but a desirable property, since a subtyping relation between the two types,

[11] Recursive types should be considered as denotations for their infinite expansion, and an infinite type is a subtype of another one when all the finite approximations of the first one are subtypes of the corresponding finite approximation of the second one; see [2].

in the record based approach, could cause a run-time type error (see [11] for an example). Hence, there is an apparent incompatibility between the covariant nature of most binary operations and the contravariant subtyping rule of arrow types.

Our system is essentially more flexible, in this case. Indeed if we set

$$\mathit{3DPoint} \leq \mathit{2DPoint}$$

then an equality function, with type:

$$\mathit{Equal}\colon \{\mathit{2DPoint} \to (\mathit{2DPoint} \to \text{Bool}),\ \mathit{3DPoint} \to (\mathit{3DPoint} \to \text{Bool})\}$$

would not be well-typed in our system either, since $\mathit{3DPoint} \leq \mathit{2DPoint}$ while $\mathit{2DPoint} \to \mathit{Bool} \leq \mathit{3DPoint} \to \mathit{Bool}$. This expresses the fact that a comparison function cannot be chosen only on the basis of the type of the first argument. In our system, on the other hand, we can write an equality function where the code is chosen on the basis of both arguments

$$\begin{aligned}\mathit{Equal} \equiv (\ & \lambda(p,q)^{2DPoint \times 2DPoint}.(p.x = q.x) \text{ AND } (p.y = q.y) \\ \&\ & \lambda(p,q)^{3DPoint \times 3DPoint}.(p.x = q.x) \text{ AND } (p.y = q.y) \\ & \qquad\qquad\qquad\qquad\qquad\qquad \text{AND } (p.z = q.z) \\ )\ & \end{aligned}$$

the function above has type:

$$\{(\mathit{2DPoint} \times \mathit{2DPoint}) \to \text{Bool}, (\ \mathit{3DPoint} \times \mathit{3DPoint}) \to \text{Bool}\}$$

which is well formed.[12]

In the presence of a subtyping relation, the covariance versus contravariance of the arrow type, w.r.t. the left argument (domain), is a delicate and classical debate. Semantically (categorically) oriented people have no doubt: the hom-functor is contravariant in the first argument. Moreover, this nicely fits with typed models constructed over type-free universes, where types are subsets or subrelations of the type-free structure, and type-free terms model runtime computations. Also the common sense of the type-checking forces contravariance: if we consider one type a subtype of another if and only if all expressions of the former type can be used in the place of expressions of the latter, then a function $g : T \to U$ may be substituted by a function f only if the domain of f is *greater* than T. However, practitioners often have a different attitude. In OOP, in particular, the "overriding" of a method by one, say, with a smaller domain (input type) leads to a smaller codomain (output type), in the spirit of a "preservation of information". Indeed, in our approach, we show that both viewpoints are correct, when adopted in the "right" context.

In fact, our general arrow types (the types of ordinary functions) are contravariant in the first argument, as required by common sense and mathematical meaning. However, the *families* of arrow types which are glued together in overloaded types form covariant collections, by our conditions on the formation of these types (see

[12] This is not surprising as, even if the types of the two versions of equal are componentwise isomorphic, in general isomorphisms of types do not preserve subtyping.

3.2). Besides the justification of this at the end of Section 2, consider the practice of overriding. The implementation of a method in a superclass is substituted by a more specific implementation in a subclass; or, more precisely, overriding methods must return smaller or equal types than the overridden one. For example, the "+" operation, on different types, may be given by two different implementations: one implementation of type $Int \times Int \rightarrow Int$, the other of type $Real \times Real \rightarrow Real$. In our approach, we can glue these implementations together into one global method, precisely because their types satisfy the required covariance condition.

We have already noted that part of the expressive power of our system derives from the ability to choose one implementation on the basis of the types of many arguments. This ability makes it even possible to decide explicitly how to implement "mixed binary operations". For example, besides implementing "pure" equality between *2DPoints* and between *3DPoints*, we can also decide how we should compare a *2DPoint* and a *3DPoint*, as below:

$$\begin{aligned} Equal \equiv (\ & \lambda(p,q)^{2DPoint \times 2DPoint}. \quad \dots \\ \& \ & \lambda(p,q)^{3DPoint \times 3DPoint}. \quad \dots \\ \& \ & \lambda(p,q)^{2DPoint \times 3DPoint}.(p.x = q.x) \text{ AND } (p.y = q.y) \\ \& \ & \lambda(p,q)^{3DPoint \times 2DPoint}.(p.x = q.x) \text{ AND } (p.y = q.y) \\ & \qquad \qquad \qquad \qquad \qquad \text{ AND } (p.z = 0) \\ ) & \end{aligned}$$

The ability to choose a method on the basis of several object parameters is called, in object-oriented jargon, *multiple dispatch*.

9 Conclusion: intersections, products and their semantics

This work is only the starting point of a new type discipline to be more extensively explored. We believe that we have proposed here a sound solution to the use of contravariant arrow types and of covariant ones in programming: the "purely functional" or external arrows are contravariant, in the first argument, while overloaded functions, as inspired by our understanding of message passing and methods in object-oriented programming, yield covariant families of arrow types. It should also be clear that our language essentially models message passing and inheritance, by the use of overloaded application and subtyping, as described in the previous sections, thus avoiding unnecessary use of recursion.

We have not dealt, though, with abstract data types nor with incremental class definitions: this may be a matter for future extensions. We have tried to present our perspective and motivations in the introduction, by stressing the need to found the so called "ad hoc" polymorphism onto decent mathematical grounds, in particular in view of its role in the understanding of the object-oriented features mentioned above. Reference has been given to the work we are aware of in this subject, all of which has, in fact, a quite different perspective.

As for the Type Theory proposed, one has first to stress that that "terms depending on types" is a concept entirely different from "types depending on terms", (as described in the —first order— types of Martin-Löf type theory or of the Calculus of Constructions). One should also quote possible connections with other type disciplines, in particular, the intersection types, originated in [13]. Indeed, an overloaded type, in our sense, is strictly related to an intersection of types: recent applications of intersection types in [29] and in the programming language Forsythe support this analogy [31]. However, the two notions are slightly different. An intersection type $T \cap U$ is a type whose elements can play both the role of an element of type T and of an element of type U, and this is the case for our overloaded types too. In the case of intersection, though, types, a coherence condition is imposed too, which means, essentially, that when a value can play different roles, we are free to choose any of these roles, without affecting the result of the computation [32]. In our context, this is not the case; a programmer may define an overloaded function "foo" of type $\{Int \times Int \rightarrow Int, Real \times Real \rightarrow Real\}$ which sums two integers but multiplies two real numbers, while in a coherent intersection type discipline an overloaded function with that type should behave in a consistent way on integers and reals.

Consider now higher order systems and observe that in Girard's system F (Reynolds' second order λ-calculus, [20]), second order terms may be fed with input types. These terms then may seem to express an explicit type dependency as the one we tried to formalize in this paper. We fully understand now that it is not so. On the model theoretical side, this is made clear by the interpretation of second order product types as intersections (in view of the semantic relation between intersection and dependent products given in [24], this is a delicate issue: see [22] for a discussion). From the point of view of proof theory, the low expressiveness of terms which may take types as inputs is explained by early intuitions of Reynolds on parametricity and the work in [25], [1] and [23]. Intuitively, Reynolds Abstraction Theorem says that a term, taking as inputs two "related" types, gives "related" terms as outputs and the Genericity Theorem in [23] shows that if two terms coincide on one input type then they coincide on all input types. The moral is that in system F, as a properly second order logical system, one cannot have terms whose output values truly depend on input types.

For all these reasons, we had to design a completely new language: no tools are available from (constructive) logic to express the simple fact of practice that the value of a term may depend on a type as input. We decided, consistently with the practice of object-oriented programming, to allow only a "finite dependency": overloaded terms are finitely branching terms and the essential richness of the discipline is largely due to the use of subtyping, which fulfills a quantification over an infinity of types. However, the way is open to further strengthening, once we set the safe grounds of a few, but crucial, consistency properties (Church-Rosser, Strong Normalization, Subject Reduction).

In particular, one may think to allow type variables and second order λ-abstraction, also in overloaded types and terms (e.g. allow $\lambda X.(\ldots \&^X \ldots)$) and study how the covariance constraints and the syntactic properties are transformed in this case. Explicit polymorphism would then be entirely revised as type dependency would be as uniform and as effective as ever. The border line, though, between safe systems and inconsistencies would then become narrow: the technical difficulties of the normalization theorem, at our propositional level, may suggest the major obstacles one may encounter in defining "sound" higher order systems.

We plan to explore this direction as well as three less ambitious projects. First the semantics of $\lambda\&$, a non trivial matter even in the propositional case (a preliminary proposal is in [10]). Second, the application of the ideas of this calculus to the implementation of a prototypical object-oriented language. Third, a more detailed investigation of "compile-time vs. run-time" types. In this paper we proposed a simple view of this "dualism", which fits our approach. More should be said, though, in particular regarding subtyping, coercions, etc., i.e. the various ways of dealing with "types evolving during computations".

As for the use of recursion, surely an essential tool for programming practice, we believe that the theoretic investigation of complex issues, like this, should be made into two steps, if possible. First, analyze type disciplines where some "unshakable grounds" can be set: following the analogy "types as propositions" in λ-calculus, this means consistency proofs, via normalization, say, and related facts. Then, if everything works fine, add recursion when really needed for computations, both for types and terms. This is another "methodological" point which distinguishes our approach from the current theoretical treatments of object-oriented features.

Acknowledgements. This work has been supported in part by grants from the C.E.C. under ESPRIT BRA No.6309 (FIDE2: Fully Integrated Data Environment) and 3020, by the Progetto finalizzato "Sistemi informatici e calcolo parallelo" of C.N.R. under grant No.93.001502.PF69, by the grant No.203.01.56 of the Consiglio Nazionale delle Ricerche – Comitato Nazionale delle Scienze Matematiche, and by "Ministero dell'Università e della Ricerca Scientifica e Tecnologica". G. Castagna would like to thank Maribel Fernández for her comments on an early draft and Roberto Di Cosmo for his help in the work and patience in sharing an office. Very special thanks to Franca and Nico, too.

References

1. M. Abadi, L. Cardelli, and P.-L. Curien. Formal parametric polymorphism. In Dezani, Ronchi, and Venturini, editors, *Böhm Festschrift*. 1993.
2. Roberto M. Amadio and Luca Cardelli. Subtyping recursive types. *ACM Transactions on Programming Languages and Systems*, 15(4):575–631, 1993. A preliminary version appeared in POPL '91 (pp. 104–118), and as DEC Systems Research Center Research Report number 62, August 1990.
3. H.P. Barendregt. *The Lambda Calculus Its Syntax and Semantics*. North-Holland, 1984. Revised edition.
4. Kim B. Bruce. The equivalence of two semantic definitions for inheritance in object-oriented languages. In *Proceedings of Mathematical Foundations of Programming Semantics*, Pittsburgh, PA, March 1991.
5. Peter Canning, William Cook, Walter Hill, Walter Olthoff, and John Mitchell. F-bounded quantification for object-oriented programming. In *Fourth International Conference*

on Functional Programming Languages and Computer Architecture, pages 273–280, September 1989.
6. L. Cardelli and J.C. Mitchell. Operations on records. *Mathematical Structures in Computer Science*, 1(1):3–48, 1991.
7. L. Cardelli and P. Wegner. On understanding types, data abstraction, and polymorphism. *Computing Surveys*, 17(4):471–522, December 1985.
8. Luca Cardelli. A semantics of multiple inheritance. *Information and Computation*, 76:138–164, 1988. A previous version can be found in Semantics of Data Types, volume 173 of *Lecture Notes in Computer Science*, pages 51–67. Springer-Verlag, 1984.
9. G. Castagna. Strong typing in object-oriented paradigms. Technical Report 92-11, Laboratoire d'Informatique, Ecole Normale Supérieure - Paris, June 1992.
10. G. Castagna, G. Ghelli, and G. Longo. A semantics for λ&-*early*: a calculus with overloading and early binding. In M. Bezen and J.F. Groote, editors, *Proc. of the International Conference on Typed Lambda Calculi and Applications (TLCA), Utrecht, The Netherlands*, volume 664 of *Lecture Notes in Computer Science*, pages 107–123, Berlin, March 1993. Springer-Verlag.
11. G. Castagna and G. Longo. From inheritance to Quest's type theory. In *Ecole Jeunes Chercheurs du GRECO de Programmation*, Sophia-Antipolis (Nice), April 1991. Talk given at the 5th Jumelage on Typed Lambda Calculus - Paris - January 1990.
12. W.R. Cook, W.L. Hill, and P.S. Canning. Inheritance is not subtyping. *17th Ann. ACM Symp. on Principles of Programming Languages*, January 1990.
13. M. Coppo, M. Denzani-Ciancaglini, and B. Venneri. Functional characters of solvable terms. *Zeit. Math. Logik*, 27:45–58, 1981.
14. P.-L. Curien and G. Ghelli. Coherence of subsumption, minimum typing and the type checking in $F_{\leq}$. *Mathematical Structures in Computer Science*, 2(1):55–91, 1992.
15. P.-L. Curien and G. Ghelli. Confluence and decidability of $\beta\eta\mathrm{top}_{\leq}$ reduction in $\mathrm{F}_{\leq}$. *Information and Computation*, 109(1, 2):57–114, 1994.
16. L.G. DeMichiel and R.P. Gabriel. Common lisp object system overview. In *Proc. of ECOOP '87 European Conference on Object Oriented Programming*, 1987.
17. G. Ghelli. *Proof Theoretic Studies about a Minimal Type System Integrating Inclusion and Parametric Polymorphism.* PhD thesis, Dipartimento di Informatica, Università di Pisa, March 1990. Tech. Rep. TD-6/90.
18. G. Ghelli Modelling features of object-oriented languages in second order functional languages with subtypes. In J.W. de Bakker, W.P. de Roever, and G. Rozenberg, editors, *Foundations of Object-Oriented Languages*, volume 489 of *Lecture Notes in Computer Science*, pages 311–340. Springer-Verlag, 1991.
19. G. Ghelli. A static type system for late binding overloading. In A. Paepcke, editor, *Proc. of the Sixth Intl. ACM Conference on Object-Oriented Programming Systems Languages and Applications (OOPSLA), Phoenix, Arizona*, number 26 (11) in ACM SIGPLAN Notices, pages 129–145, Reading, MA, 1991. Addison-Wesley.
20. Jean-Yves Girard, Yves Lafont, and Paul Taylor. *Proofs and Types*, volume 7 of *Cambridge Tracts in Theoretical Computer Science*. Cambridge University Press, Cambridge, 1989.
21. R. Hindley. The Church-Rosser property and a result of combinatory logic. Dissertation, 1964. University of Newcastle-upon-Tyne.
22. G. Longo. Parametric and type-dependent polymorphism. *Fundamenta Informaticae*, 1994. To appear.
23. G Longo, K. Milsted, and S. Soloviev. The genericity theorem and parametricity in functional languages. In *8th Annual IEEE Symposium on Logic in Computer Science*, Montreal, June 1993.

24. G. Longo and E. Moggi. Constructive natural deduction and its ω-set interpretation. *Mathematical Structures in Computer Science*, 1(2):215–253, 1991.
25. QingMing Ma and John C. Reynolds. Types, abstraction, and parametric polymorphism, part 2. In Stephen Brookes, Michael Main, Austin Melton, Michael Mislove, and David A. Schmidt, editors, *Mathematical Foundations of Programming Semantics*, volume 598 of *Lecture Notes in Computer Science*, pages 1–40. Springer-Verlag, 1992.
26. N. Martí-Oliet and J. Meseguer. Inclusions and subtypes. Technical report, SRI International, Computer Science Laboratory, December 1990.
27. J.C. Mitchell. Toward a typed foundation for method specialization and inheritance. *Proc. of 17th Ann. ACM Symp. on Principles of Programming Languages*, pages 109–124, January 1990.
28. John C. Mitchell. A type-inference approach to reduction properties and semantics of polymorphic expressions. In Gérard Huet, editor, *Logical Foundations of Functional Programming*, University of Texas at Austin Year of Programming Series, pages 195–212. Addison-Wesley, 1990.
29. B.C. Pierce. Intersection and union types. Technical report, Carnegie Mellon University, 1990.
30. Benjamin C. Pierce and David N. Turner. Simple type-theoretic foundations for object-oriented programming. *Journal of Functional Programming*, 4(2):207–247, April 1994. A preliminary version appeared in Principles of Programming Languages, 1993, and as University of Edinburgh technical report ECS-LFCS-92-225, under the title "Object-Oriented Programming Without Recursive Types".
31. J.C. Reynolds. Preliminary design of the programming language Forsythe. Technical Report CMU-CS-88-159, Carnegie Mellon University, June 1988.
32. J.C. Reynolds. The coherence of languages with intersection types. In T. Ito and A. R. Meyer, editors, *Theoretical Aspects of Computer Software (Sendai, Japan)*, volume 526 of *Lecture Notes in Computer Science*, pages 675–700. Springer-Verlag, September 1991.
33. B. K. Rosen. Tree manipulation systems and Church-Rosser theorems. *Journal of the ACM*, 20:160–187, 1973.
34. F. Rouaix. *ALCOOL-90, Typage de la surcharge dans un langage fonctionnel*. PhD thesis, Université PARIS VII, December 1990.
35. Philip Wadler and Stephen Blott. How to make "ad-hoc" polymorphism less "ad-hoc". In *16th Ann. ACM Symp. on Principles of Programming Languages*, pages 60–76, 1989.
36. Mitchell Wand. Type inference for record concatenation and multiple inheritance. *Information and Computation*, 93(1):1–15, 1991.

Chapter 1.3.2

Protection in Persistent Object Systems*

Ron Morrison[1], Fred Brown[1†], Richard Connor[1‡], Quintin Cutts[1§], Graham Kirby[1], Alan Dearle[2**], John Rosenberg[3††] and David Stemple[4]

[1] School of Mathematical and Computational Sciences, University of St Andrews, North Haugh, St Andrews KY16 9SS, Scotland
[2] Department of Computer Science, University of Adelaide, Adelaide 5005, Australia
[3] Department of Computer Science, University of Newcastle, New South Wales, Australia
[4] Department of Computer and Information Science, University of Massachusetts, Amherst, MA 01038, USA

Abstract. Persistent programming is concerned with the creation and manipulation of data with arbitrary lifetimes. This data is often valuable and therefore protected to ensure that it is free from misuse. The mechanisms used to protect the data vary with a tradeoff between static expression of the protection and the flexibility in modelling it. This paper explores the full range of protection mechanisms in persistent systems from static to dynamic checking and contrasts it with the corresponding balance between safety and flexibility in the system. Protection by capabilities, dynamic universal union types, encapsulation, subtype inheritance, existential quantification and predicate defined invariants are all explored with reference to manipulating long-lived data.

1 Introduction

Persistent object systems support large collections of data that have often been constructed incrementally by a community of users [1]. Such data is inherently valuable and requires protection from deliberate or accidental misuse. Protection is required to guard against system malfunction, such as hardware failure, to ensure that users do not misuse the common facilities such as the operating system and to protect users from other users and even themselves.

Protection mechanisms are concerned with conserving the integrity of data. There are two quite separate ways in which this integrity may be compromised. Firstly, some kinds of failure, which jeopardise this integrity, such as hardware malfunction, have little to do with protection and are best dealt with by other

---

* The original version of this paper appeared as [10].

† Present address: Department of Computer Science, University of Adelaide, Adelaide 5005, Australia
‡ Present address: Department of Computer Science, University of Glasgow, Glasgow G12 8QQ, Scotland
§ Present address: Department of Computer Science, University of Glasgow, Glasgow G12 8QQ, Scotland
** Present address: Department of Computing Science, University of Stirling, Stirling FK9 4LA, Scotland
†† Present address: Basser Department of Computer Science, University of Sydney, New South Wales 2006, Australia

techniques such as incremental dumping or stability strategies [2, 3]. That is, periodically the data is copied to a secure device from which it may be retrieved if a failure occurs. Failures may, of course, occur in all the multiple copies of the data simultaneously leading to the conclusion that there is no absolute notion of data integrity. Protection mechanisms are built on the assumption that the underlying system does not fail. In the case of hardware error this assumption is incorrect. Fortunately an acceptable level of stability can usually be obtained for an acceptable price but the notion of absolute integrity no longer exists.

Given an acceptable level of stability, the integrity of the data can still be compromised by users. A number of mechanisms, such as capability systems, encryption methods, type systems and database integrity constraints have been used to add protection against data misuse in persistent systems. All of these mechanisms add security but at some cost and furthermore there is also a limit to the level of security that can be achieved. For example, once a program gains access to data it may alter it in a legal but undesirable manner. This can happen because the constraints placed on the user by the capability system, type system or integrity constraint system provide rather coarse grain control over the data. This coarse grain control trades expressiveness for security. The principle of minimum necessary privilege often causes the protection mechanism to be too fine grained to be enforced efficiently or even expressed succinctly. For example, the granularity of most type systems allows the user to restrict the use of a variable to a particular type such as integer. A finer grained system may allow the specification of types that only allow a subrange of the values such as 3..4 on Tuesday and Wednesday and 2..5 on other days. This is fine grained but neither succinct nor easily efficiently enforced.

Thus the second problem with integrity is that the checking system may allow the integrity of the data to be preserved but still contain information that is no longer of real use or is even erroneous. That is, even when enforced, the protection mechanism will not guarantee that programs produce desirable transformations on the data. The challenge is to find an acceptable level of security that can be obtained for a reasonable price in terms of efficient checking and succinct expression.

In protection mechanisms there is always a tension between the time of checking and the flexibility of the system. Checks that can be performed by static analysis allow the programmer to state or even prove some properties of the program before it runs. This increases confidence that the program is correct and explains the desire of most programming language designers to employ static type checking as one of the mechanisms for protection. The same desire has also led to capability systems that can be statically checked [4] and to proposals for the static checking of database integrity constraints [5]. A second aspect of static checking is that programs so checked are usually more efficient. By performing the checking statically the need for dynamic checking is reduced making the program execute faster and in less space.

Taken to the extreme, statically checked languages are not very interesting since they have a very limited ability to accommodate change. Flexibility is introduced by dynamic checking. Constraints placed on the data that depend on the evaluation of the program may only be checked in this manner. For example, the integrity constraints checked just prior to a transaction commit usually employ dynamic checks of this kind.

Another dimension of static versus dynamic checking is the ability of the system to support its own evolution safely. This property is sometimes called reflection [6] and on other occasions type magic [7]. In capability systems, which are usually the most dynamic, the type magic is the ability to issue and check the validity of capabilities. Capabilities are only issued by a trusted kernel and may not be manufactured by a user program. Compilers may generate representations of programs which when given a capability by the kernel become programs within the system. Since the security checking is always performed by the kernel, programs may be generated by many different compilers. Thus mixed language facilities are available up to the constraints imposed by the capability system. An example of such a system is given in [8].

As the checking is made more static the ability to mix languages is lessened. The magic in the system now lies with the type checkers which can only check languages with related type systems. The reflection in the system is also restricted by the type systems since only languages that adhere to the type system can be checked by the type checker. This is usually less general than a capability system. Example of systems displaying high level reflection at the type system level are (Chapter 1.1.3), [9].

One final point is that the system security can be compromised if the type magic can be impersonated. This is often necessary for maintenance and repair of systems and again yields a weakness in the security system. It often depends on how difficult it is to break the password checking for initial access to the system.

The full version of the paper [10] presents a number of mechanisms that are used to preserve the integrity of data in persistent systems. In statically checked systems, these mechanisms range from the predicate defined invariants of the language ADATPBL, through the statically enforced existentially quantified types of Napier88, encapsulation by scoping, subtype inheritance and the software capabilities of Jones & Liskov. In dynamically checked systems, the universal union type **any** of Amber [11] and Napier88 may be used as software capabilities as may dynamically checked database integrity constraints. Hardware enforced capability systems form the most primitive but most efficiently implemented form of the techniques [12].

References

1. Atkinson MP, Bailey PJ, Chisholm KJ, Cockshott WP, Morrison R. An Approach to Persistent Programming. Computer Journal 1983; 26,4:360-365
2. Lorie RA. Physical Integrity in a Large Segmented Database. ACM Transactions on Database Systems 1977; 2,1:91-104
3. Rosenberg J, Henskens F, Brown AL, Morrison R, Munro D. Stability in a Persistent Store Based on a Large Virtual Memory. In: Rosenberg J, Keedy JL (ed) Security and Persistence, Proc. International Workshop on Security and Persistence, Bremen, 1990. Springer-Verlag, 1990, pp 229-245
4. Jones AK, Liskov B. A Language Extension for Expressing Constraints on Data Access. Communications of the ACM 1978; 21,5:358-367
5. Sheard T, Stemple D. Automatic Verification of Database Transaction Safety. ACM Transactions on Database Systems 1989; 12,3:322-368
6. Stemple D, Fegaras L, Sheard T, Socorro A. Exceeding the Limits of Polymorphism in Database Programming Languages. In: Bancilhon F, Thanos C, Tsichritzis D (ed) Lecture Notes in Computer Science 416 (EDBT '90). Springer-Verlag, 1990, pp 269-285
7. Atkinson MP, Morrison R. Polymorphic Names, Types, Constancy and Magic in a Type Secure Persistent Object Store. In: Proc. 2nd International Workshop on Persistent Object Systems, Appin, Scotland, 1987, pp 1-12

8. Rosenberg J, Abramson DA. A Capability-Based Workstation to Support Software Engineering. In: Proc. 18th International Conference on Systems Sciences, Hawaii, 1987, pp 222-230
9 PS-algol. PS-algol Reference Manual, 4th edition. Universities of Glasgow and St Andrews Report PPRR-12-88, 1988
10. Morrison R, Brown AL, Connor RCH et al. Protection in Persistent Object Systems. In: Rosenberg J, Keedy JL (ed) Security and Persistence, Proc. International Workshop on Security and Persistence, Bremen, 1990. Workshops in Computing, Springer-Verlag, 1990, pp 48-66
11. Cardelli L. Amber. In: Lecture Notes in Computer Science 242. Springer-Verlag, 1986, pp 21-47
12. Dennis JB, Van Horn EC. Programming Semantics for Multiprogrammed Computations. Communications of the ACM 1966; 9,3:143-145

Chapter 1.3.3

Subtyping and Assignment in Database Programming Languages*

Richard Connor†, David McNally and Ron Morrison

School of Mathematical and Computational Sciences, University of St Andrews, North Haugh, St Andrews KY16 9SS, Scotland

Our focus of interest is in the integration of programming languages and database management systems. In particular, the integration of type systems and data models is considered. One tension in this integration occurs when a type system with subtype inheritance is combined with a data model which contains mutable values, as described by Albano [2].

A description of some well-known problems in such systems is given. This is followed by a classification of possible trade-offs between the safety of static checking, normally required by type systems, and the flexibility of dynamic checking, normally found in data models. At each stage in the classification decreasing static safety is traded for an increasing class of correct programs.

For the examination of different classes of language we introduce the notion of type accuracy as the relevant common denominator of the concepts of coherence in data models and soundness in type systems. The concept of type accuracy is simply that any statically asserted meta-description correctly captures the run-time data associated with it.

In addition to an assumption that substitution preserves identity, three other assumptions are frequently made about database programming languages, and the combination of these is known to break the conditions of type accuracy. The assumptions are:

- the principle of substitutability itself: a value with more "functionality" may be always used in place of one with less,
- that the description of a value's functionality, i.e. its type, does not necessarily include information about whether its components are mutable or not, and
- that an assignment operation may always be statically determined to be safe.

Each assumption is derived from qualities that may reasonably be desired, the second and third from a language which features mutability and the first from one which features subtyping. It is shown that these desiderata are not mutually tenable. However any two of the three may be retained so long as a sufficient restriction is placed on the remaining one.

---

* The original version of this paper appeared as [1] and contains an in-depth analysis of the issues described here; this synopsis describes only the scope of the paper.

† Present address: Department of Computing Science, University of Glasgow, Glasgow G12 8QQ, Scotland

To maintain type accuracy a system with both subtyping and assignment must prevent any dangerous update from occurring. Restrictions sufficient to preserve the type safety of such a system may be made in any of the following categories:

- limit the contexts in which substitution using inclusion may occur,
- model mutability within the type system or data model, and restrict compatibility in some appropriate manner, or
- accept that there may be a dynamic failure at time of update.

A number of possible mechanisms are shown in each of these categories. The classification is intended to aid the designers of database programming languages in choosing a suitable mechanism to allow subtyping and mutability to coexist without compromising the overall safety of the system.

In strongly related and contemporaneous work, Zdonik and Maier [3] in a similar treatment of object-oriented languages list similar mutually untenable conditions. They describe one further condition, however, the presence of predicate subtyping, and state that a system with any three of their four conditions is safe. This difference is attributable to some subtle assumptions made about the object-oriented model, notably that assignment to fields within a value is performed only by an encapsulated procedure declared at the same scope level as the data.

References

1. Connor R.C.H., McNally D.J. and Morrison R. "Subtyping and Assignment in Database Programming Languages", in *Bulk Types and Persistent Data*, Morgan Kaufmann (1991), pp 363-382.
2. Albano, A. "Type Hierarchies and Semantic Data Models" ACM SIGPLAN 83: Symposium on Programming Language Issues in Software Systems (San Francisco, 1983) 178-186.
3. Zdonik, S.B. and Maier, D. *Readings in Object-Oriented Database Systems* Morgan-Kaufmann (1990).

Section 1.4

Bulk Types and Iterators: Introduction and State of the Art

Florian Matthes

Technical University Hamburg-Harburg, Harburger Schloßstraße 20, D-21071 Hamburg, Germany

A bulk type describes a homogeneous collection of values. These values are described by another type which is given as a parameter to the bulk type constructor. Many bulk types such as sets, lists and relations are already familiar and widely used in data-intensive applications. Additional bulk types, like bags and multisets, can be defined either by system providers or by expert users. Languages with multiple bulk types have a higher potential for problem-oriented data modelling. In particular, by using bulk types to describe data that resides in legacy databases one gains access to that data in a convenient, consistent and safe manner.

The regular structure of bulk type instances can be exploited to provide high-level iteration abstractions for declarative access to bulk data. An important topic in database language research is the development of strongly-typed language constructs like queries, views or iterators that generalize the successful iteration abstractions of relational algebra, relational calculus or SQL to other bulk types. Problem-oriented iteration abstractions not only increase programmer productivity but they can also be exploited to increase system performance by enabling query optimization and tailored storage allocation schemes. Furthermore, generic bulk types and iteration abstractions greatly simplify the construction of user-oriented tools like database browsers or ad-hoc query interfaces.

Several members of the FIDE consortium explored alternative strategies for the provision of bulk types. DBPL [14] (synopsis in Chapter 2.1.2), O_2 [5] and Fibonacci (presented in Chapter 1.1.2) are all equipped with type-complete bulk type constructors and a rich built-in query language over complex values of these bulk types. Another strategy to provide bulk types in a programming language setting is to reduce well-known complex-object query languages to a small set of primitive operations and iteration abstractions expressed as first-class abstract data types with polymorphic higher-order functions [2,17,7,15,6,10].

Motivated by the substantial progress in programming language genericity and expressiveness as well as recent advances in object store technology, members of the FIDE consortium also investigated an extensible approach to bulk data support [12] (synopsis in Chapter 1.2.2) and [4]. This approach aims at generalizing the expertise in language design and database system construction from a fixed set of bulk type constructors to larger families of collection types and to a broader range of services attached to collection types such as integrity checking, data visualization and viewing mechanisms. This *add-on* approach to bulk type and iterator support is based on the following architectural and conceptual separation of tasks:

- Data-model-independent object stores provide persistence, concurrency control and recovery abstractions over relatively simple, graph-structured data. The object store interface has to find a balance between the need for efficient bulk data access and the desire to support the implementation of a wide range of bulk data structures. These issues are discussed in more detail in Chapter 2.2.1 and 2.2.2.
- Abstract machine languages implemented on top of these object stores are used as well-defined, minimal interfaces for (bulk) data access and data manipulation. These canonical machine languages are generated by language-specific compilers and provide an ideal starting point for integrated program and query optimization as well as multi-platform language implementations (see also Chapter 2.1.3).
- Persistent higher-order programming languages provide a uniform, strongly-typed programming and interactive interface to volatile and persistent, small-scale and large-scale bulk data. As described in Chapters 1.1.1 to 1.1.3, all FIDE languages are based on a common set of design principles like uniform naming, strong typing, flexible R-value and L-value binding, static scoping, orthogonal persistence and type orthogonality that also apply to the design and implementation of bulk types and iteration abstractions.
- Type-safe, generic bulk type libraries implemented in the FIDE languages provide application programmers with prefabricated software components for bulk data storage, iteration abstraction, bulk data input, formatted data display, searching, sorting, integrity maintenance, etc. These bulk type libraries are typically pre-populated by the language designer or constructed by expert programmers. Significant effort has been devoted at both Hamburg and Glasgow Universities to the construction of extensible, but nevertheless easily understandable and efficient bulk type libraries [3,13].
- Extensible grammars, as developed in [8] allow library designers to provide tailored syntactic forms for library-defined bulk types without compromising the simplicity, optimizability and security of the core language. As described in more detail in Chapter 3.2.3, classical data description and data manipulation languages can then be captured directly via types, type constructors and polymorphic (higher-order) functions exported from bulk type libraries.

The first paper in this Section investigates typing issues of bulk types. The semantics of some bulk data models involves user-defined attributes like element equality, ordering or other domain predicates. In this paper, a statically-decidable typechecking scheme is presented where such attributes are part of the bulk type which makes it possible to reject semantically incorrect bulk operations already at compile-time.

The second paper raises the language and system design question whether there should be built-in bulk types in database programming languages at all. Instead, one could argue that bulk types should be realized exclusively as user-definable add-ons to unbiased core languages with appropriate primitives and abstraction facilities. The advantages and disadvantages of both approaches are presented by distinguishing between elementary and advanced bulk type support.

The last paper in this Section presents viewing mechanisms on type-complete database objects and compares their semantics with object extension and role manipulation operations. All of these operations are identity-preserving. The ability to provide multiple views on a database object and to modify the structure of an object without invalidating its identity is crucial to the management of bulk class extents and of class relationships [1]. This work is also related to the concept of viewers developed in the FIDE project and presented in [16].

Finally, several other papers in this collection should be referenced that also make contributions to the research topic of bulk types and iterators.

The paper [9] (summarized in Chapter 1.1.3) investigates which subtyping rules should apply to bulk type constructors. For example, under which circumstances is it safe to treat the type *List(Student)* as a subtype of *List(Person)*, assuming that *Student* is a subtype of *Person*?

Chapter 1.2.1 includes an explanation is given on how to implement type-dependent bulk operations like the relational natural join using type-directed reflective programming techniques.

Query optimization techniques for database programming languages where bulk expressions can be nested and mixed freely with application code are presented in Chapter 2.3.4 and Chapter 2.3.5 (synopsis of [11]), respectively.

Finally, the integration of legacy bulk data maintained outside the scope of integrated database languages (in files or commercial databases) as typed bulk data with iteration abstractions is described in Chapter 3.3.1 and 3.3.2.

References

1. A. Albano, G. Ghelli, and R. Orsini. A relationship mechanism for a strongly typed object-oriented database programming language. In *Proceedings of the Seventeenth International Conference on Very Large Databases*, pages 565–575, 1991.
2. M. Atkinson, P. Richard, and P. Trinder. Bulk types for large scale programming. In *Proceedings of the Kiev East/West Workshop on Next Generation Database Technology*, volume 504 of *Lecture Notes in Computer Science*. Springer-Verlag, April 1991.
3. M.P. Atkinson, P.J. Bailey, D. Christie, K. Cropper, and P.C. Philbrow. Towards bulk type libraries for Napier88. FIDE Technical Report Series FIDE/93/78, FIDE Project Coordinator, Department of Computing Sciences, University of Glasgow, Glasgow G128QQ, 1993.
4. M.P. Atkinson, P.W. Trinder, and D.A. Watt. Bulk type constructors. FIDE Technical Report Series FIDE/93/61, FIDE Project Coordinator, Department of Computing Sciences, University of Glasgow, Glasgow G128QQ, 1993.
5. F. Bancilhon, C. Delobel, and P. Kanellakis. *Building an Object-Oriented Database System: The Story of O_2*. Morgan Kaufmann Publishers, 1992.
6. C. Beeri and P. Ta-Shma. Bulk data types, a theoretical approach. In C. Beeri, A. Ohori, and D.E. Shasha, editors, *Proceedings of the Fourth International Workshop on Database*

Programming Languages, Manhattan, New York, Workshops in Computing. Springer-Verlag, February 1994.

7. V. Breazu-Tannen, P. Buneman, and S. Naqvi. Structural recursion as a query language. In *Database Programming Languages: Bulk Types and Persistent Data*. Morgan Kaufmann Publishers, September 1991.
8. L. Cardelli, F. Matthes, and M. Abadi. Extensible grammars for language specialization. In C. Beeri, A. Ohori, and D.E. Shasha, editors, *Proceedings of the Fourth International Workshop on Database Programming Languages, Manhattan, New York*, Workshops in Computing, pages 11–31. Springer-Verlag, February 1994.
9. R. Connor, D. McNally, and R. Morrison. Subtyping and assignment in database programming languages. In *Database Programming Languages: Bulk Types and Persistent Data*, pages 363–382. Morgan Kaufmann Publishers, 1991.
10. L. Fegaras. Efficient optimization of iterative queries. In C. Beeri, A. Ohori, and D.E. Shasha, editors, *Database Programming Languages, New York City, 1993*, Workshops in Computing, pages 200–225, Springer-Verlag, 1994.
11. A. Gawecki and F. Matthes. Exploiting persistent intermediate code representations in open database environments. In *Proceedings of the Fifth Conference on Extending Database Technology, EDBT'96*, volume 1057 of *Lecture Notes in Computer Science*, Avignon, France, March 1996. Springer-Verlag.
12. F. Matthes and J.W. Schmidt. Bulk types: Built-in or add-on? In *Database Programming Languages: Bulk Types and Persistent Data*. Morgan Kaufmann Publishers, September 1991.
13. F. Matthes and J.W. Schmidt. System construction in the Tycoon environment: Architectures, interfaces and gateways. In P.P. Spies, editor, *Proceedings of Euro-Arch'93 Congress*, pages 301–317. Springer-Verlag, October 1993.
14. J.W. Schmidt and F. Matthes. The DBPL project: Advances in modular database programming. *Information Systems*, 19(2):121–140, 1994.
15. D. Stemple and T. Sheard. A recursive base for database programming primitives. In *Proceedings of the Kiev East/West Workshop on Next Generation Database Technology*, volume 504 of *Lecture Notes in Computer Science*. Springer-Verlag, April 1991.
16. K. Subieta, F. Matthes, A. Rudloff, J.W. Schmidt, and I. Wetzel. Viewers: A data-world analogue of procedure calls. In *Proceedings of the Nineteenth International Conference on Very Large Databases, Dublin, Ireland*, August 1993.
17. P. Trinder. Comprehensions, a query notation for DBPLs. In *Database Programming Languages: Bulk Types and Persistent Data*. Morgan Kaufmann Publishers, September 1991.

Chapter 1.4.1

The Joy of Sets*

Richard Connor[1†], Malcolm P. Atkinson[2], Sonia Berman[3], Quintin Cutts[1†], Graham Kirby[1] and Ron Morrison[1]

[1] School of Mathematical and Computational Science, University of St Andrews, St Andrews, KY16 9SS, Scotland
[2] Department of Computing Science, University of Glasgow, Glasgow G12 8QQ, Scotland
[3] Department of Computer Science, University of Capetown, South Africa

Abstract. The semantics of many bulk data models depends on user-defined attributes such as definitions of element equality, ordering, and other domain predicates. While these attributes are an intrinsic part of the data model, they are not normally treated as part of the static type description. This leads to the occurrence of data modelling errors which are not statically detectable, such as a union operator accidentally being applied to two sets which have different equality semantics.

Here we introduce a model of bulk types which includes such attributes as part of the type definition, along with a typechecking scheme which is statically decidable. The model relies upon the value dependencies being manifest to the typechecker; one neat way of achieving this is through the new paradigm of hyper-programming.

1 Introduction

The semantics of many bulk data models depends on user-defined attributes such as definitions of element equality, ordering, and other domain predicates. While these attributes are an intrinsic part of the data model, they are not normally treated as part of the type description. This may lead to the occurrence of data modelling errors such as a union operator accidentally being applied to two sets which have different semantics for the equality of their elements.

Attributes such as the definition of element equality are typically held with instances of bulk data types, rather than with their type [2]. When a function such as union is applied, an arbitrary choice is made between the two possible equality functions. The chosen equality is used not only as an attribute of the newly constructed bulk value, but also to implement the application of the union function itself, as this depends upon the definition of element equality. Thus the semantics of union and similar set functions is compromised as, among other reasons, commutivity is lost.

By including these attributes as part of the type, however, it should be possible to define function types over bulk values such that the functions they describe are limited in application to bulk values where the element domain attributes are the

*The original version of this paper [1] includes a section on polymorphism which has been removed from this version for reasons of space.

†Present address: Department of Computing Science, University of Glasgow, Glasgow G12 8QQ, Scotland

same. Any attempt to apply these functions to bulk values with different attributes will be detected by the type system and the execution will be disallowed. A dynamically typed system will generate a type error or exception when the operator is erroneously applied, and a statically typed system will detect such errors before the program which contains them starts to execute.

A directory of Scottish names is used as an example of the inclusion of element attributes in the type. People may take a different view as to whether the names "MacFarlane", "Macfarlane", and "McFarlane" are really different names, but their owners are usually protective of their different forms. If they are used to retrieve data however it is likely that the retriever will not wish to distinguish between them. A telephone company's applications may require a number of directories, some of which distinguish between different spellings and some of which do not. For example a printed version of a telephone directory may distinguish between them whereas an electronic version used by an operator enquiry service may not. These directories are characterised in the system by bulk data dictionaries; whether different spellings are distinguished or not is characterised by different domain equality rules in these dictionaries.

Bulk operators such as union and intersection over directories whose elements have different equality rules are undefined and should be considered as an error. If such errors are not detected, and an arbitrary choice of equality is used, then no further mechanical error will result and the program will appear to execute correctly. The only way of detecting that an error has occurred is by analysing the directory which results. By including the equality definition in the type the error will be detected earlier in a strongly typed system, ideally during the program's typechecking.

Figure 1 shows a possible syntax for type definitions where domain equality attributes are described as a part of the type. The types *customerDirectory* and *operatorDirectory* are defined as specialisations of the type operator *Dictionary*, which has been previously defined. The structural attributes of the two dictionary types are the same, but different domain equality rules are associated with the types. These different rules for domain equality mean that the types *customerDirectory* and *operatorDirectory* are not equivalent types within this system.

```
type customerDirectory is Dictionary[ string, phoneNo ] with
        ! simple (system-defined) equality
        domainEq = proc( a,b : string -> bool ) ; a = b

type operatorDirectory is Dictionary[ string, phoneNo ] with
        ! some complex equality rules
        domainEq = proc( a,b : string -> bool ) ; ...
```

Fig. 1. Attributes associated with type

This restriction of bulk type equivalence must be carefully introduced to avoid losing flexibility within the programming system. The telephone company software may include a procedure *printDirectory*, which has a single operand of type *customerDirectory*. The application of *printDirectory* to a value of type *operatorDirectory* is an error, and the inequivalence of these types will lead to the reporting of a type error in such circumstances. However, there is also a large class of functions which may be correctly applied to bulk data values with any equality rule, such as a membership test. Figure 2 shows examples of such typings.

```
printDirectory( aCustomerDirectory )          ! typing is correct
printDirectory( anOperatorDirectory )         ! typing is incorrect

let x = member( "McPhee",aCustomerDirectory )    ! typing is correct
let y = member( "McPhee",anOperatorDirectory )   ! typing is also correct
```

Fig. 2. Correct typing of different functions

The importance of the examples is that they demonstrate not only the importance of treating domain equality as an attribute of type in some circumstances, but also the importance of an appropriate form of polymorphism to allow abstraction over domain equality where it is not required. In fact the type of the functions union and intersection also requires polymorphism over element equality: the correct restriction is that the operands must have the same definition of equality, but the functions are applicable to any such pair of bulk values.

Equality of elements is not the only value that might be associated with bulk types; for instance some bulk types require order, others may require a characteristic function that restricts the values in the domain. The rest of this paper considers in detail the example of a set with an associated element equality function only; the mechanisms outlined are sufficiently general to extend easily to other examples of bulk types that depend on function values.

2 Name and structural equivalence

In general, the equivalence of types may be defined either by name or by structure. In name equivalence regimes two types are considered to be the same if and only if they share the same instance of a definition. Thus in the above example *customerDirectory* and *operatorDirectory* are de facto different types irrespective of the particular equality semantics defined.

Name equivalence thus gives a trivial solution to the requirement that sets with different element equality rules should be regarded as different types. However there are a number of problems in the use of a strict name equivalence regime in the context of database programming languages; these may be solved, but only by the use of structural equivalence testing in some circumstances [3]. In particular, the ability to abstract over part of the type definition, as required in the typing of functions such as *member*, can not be achieved without the use of structural equivalence.

The structural type equivalence of bulk types whose specification includes attributes such as domain equality requires the following to be true:

- the two bulk constructors are the same,

- the element types are the same, and
- the two equality tests are the same.

Traditional type checking takes care of the first two but the final test is problematic, and is the subject of this paper. The first obvious problem is the definition of "sameness" over values which in this case are function types. The second problem is that to achieve static typechecking the particular instances of the values must be available to the typechecker during its analysis of the program text.

Thus to achieve the static structural checking of these types in the most general context it is necessary to solve two well known intractable problems: the equality of functions and the static checking of dependent types. However, the careful introduction of certain restrictions may be used to allow partial solutions to both problems. The good news is that these restrictions may be easily explained to a programmer and give a useful programming algebra which allows precisely the desired static typechecking over bulk types with value dependencies.

3 Decidable static checking

There are two major problems with the decidable static typechecking of types which depend upon function values. The first is that dependent types in general pose difficulties with decidable static checking; the second is that function values in general do not have a good decidable notion of equality.‡

An angle of attack is outlined here which provides partial solutions to both of these problems. The conjunction of these partial solutions gives a useful degree of static checking over dependent set types.

3.1 Dependent types

For dependent types to be structurally equivalent it is necessary for the values upon which they depend to be equal. For the equivalence of dependent types to be statically decidable it is therefore necessary for the values upon which the types depend to be statically available to the typechecker. For some simple examples this is not a problem. For example, array types in Pascal are dependent upon their bounds; as these values are constrained to being manifest constants, the values are available to the typechecker and their equality is statically decidable.

For types which are dependent on more complex values statically decidable typechecking causes more difficulties. There are however two circumstances in which static typechecking can be maintained: either when a manifest constant binding is set up between the types and the values upon which they depend , or else when the system can arrange for the values upon which the type depends to be available to the typechecker during static analysis. The first of these is of limited use in the context of database programming languages, as will be shown; the second is more useful, however, and may be provided by systems which support incremental compilation or hyper-programming.

‡To avoid confusion the term *equality* will be used to mean the usual equivalence relation as defined over values, and *equivalence* will be used to mean the usual equivalence relation as defined over types.

3.1.1 Value equality deduced by constant binding

Where the full equivalence of dependent types is not statically decidable, a syntactic rule may be introduced to constrain the use of dependent types to contexts where a more restrictive rule is statically enforceable. This mechanism relies upon the use of values being constrained to contexts where their equality is a consequence of that context. Such a mechanism is commonly used to constrain a value dependency which arises with existentially quantified types [4].

One way of enforcing this with bulk types is to allow type definitions only to use functions referred to by identifiers with constant bindings. This allows identity to be used to determine that the equality functions are the same. Figure 3 shows an example of equivalent set type definitions which have associated equality functions. Because the identifier *stringEq* is a constant binding, it is possible to deduce statically that any other set type which defines equality as the same binding will also share the same procedure. Notice that this is a different consideration from the procedure itself being manifest; *stringEq* may be bound to the result of an arbitrary computation.

```
let stringEq = proc( a,b : string -> bool ) ; ...
        !** = means constant binding **!

type dictType1 is set[ string ] with stringEq
type dictType2 is set[ string ] with stringEq
```

Fig. 3. Dependent set type definitions

That sound static typing can be achieved here is clear; however such a system is of limited use. The main problem is that only a subset of the desired equivalence semantics is achieved. Figure 4 shows a program where equivalent types cannot be determined statically.

```
let dictStringEq = if caseSensitive() then stringEq else ignoreCase

type dictType1 is set[ string ] with stringEq
type dictType2 is set[ string ] with dictStringEq
```

Fig. 4. Correct typechecking not statically decidable

This may be of limited consequence within a single program; a programmer would most likely use a single definition for all set types which share equality semantics, thus avoiding in any case the problems of structural type equivalence. The real limitation of this mechanism becomes apparent when separate compilation and the merging of independently prepared subsystems are considered; the ability to share a constant binding does not exist in these cases. To achieve correct type equivalence it is necessary to make the values available to the typechecker.

3.1.2 Values available to typechecker

Some programming language environments allow for the possibility of values of non-trivial types to be available in the typechecking domain. For example, the incremental compilation strategy of languages such as ML [5] and Galileo mean that structured values are potentially available to the compiler at typechecking time. The hyper-programming system of Napier88 (Chapter 1.1.3) allows arbitrary bindings to be performed at composition time, thus making the values potentially available to the typechecker. If all values upon which the types depend are available before the compilation of a program, and the typechecker has the ability to perform the required equality tests over them, then static typechecking may be achieved. An essential part of this mechanism is that, once references to dependent values are made, the system preserves these for the lifetime of the programs; that is, the system guarantees referential integrity.

The essential requirement is that any values upon which a type depends are evaluated before any equivalence testing is performed upon the type. This restriction of the general type description can be enforced in incremental compilation systems by restricting the stated dependencies to free identifiers which are resolved in the external environment, and in a hyper-programming system by restricting the dependencies to being hyper-links.

Figure 5 shows how the program shown in Figure 4 may be adapted for use in an incremental compilation system. Representing the same text as two compilation/evaluation sessions meets the requirement that the type dependencies appear as free identifiers with respect to the compilation unit. The point is that in this case, the function value *dictStringEq* has been evaluated, as has the value *stringEq*, before the compilation of the second program. The typechecker can therefore access these values during the static analysis of the program fragment and perform the necessary equality testing on them whenever a structural comparison of the two types is required.

let *dictStringEq* = **if** *caseSensitive*() **then** *stringEq* **else** *ignoreCase*

type *dictionary1* **is set**[**string**] **with** *stringEq*
type *dictionary2* **is set**[**string**] **with** *dictStringEq*

Fig. 5. Correct typechecking statically decidable by incremental compilation

The same technique may be used in a hyper-programming system where type dependencies are constrained to being represented as hyper-links; this guarantees in a subtly different manner that the required values have been evaluated before typechecking time. This will be explained in more detail later. There are two other situations discussed later where such values may be available at compilation time: these are where the value is a manifest literal, and where compile-time linguistic reflection (Chapter 1.2.1) is used.

There are two major advantages of this solution over that of constant binding. Firstly it allows a fully general type equivalence check, rather than a restricted subset of it. The second is a consequence of this particularly important in database programming languages: it is possible to merge independently constructed subsystems whilst preserving the type equivalence semantics.

The problem of how to determine whether two functions have the same behaviour as each other is now examined.

3.2 Functional equality

The most general notion of functional equality is that, for any two functions, they are equal if they produce an equal result for any equal operands. It is well known that there exists no decidable algorithm which tests this notion for any given pair of functions. As a consequence, many programming languages provide no notion of equality over values of function type.

There are however other less general equivalence relations which may be usefully defined over functions. In some languages for example the concept of identity may be defined for functions; the identity of a function is created when its closure is formed (Chapter 1.1.3). Another possibility is that the code, perhaps normalised according to some semantics preserving rule, is equal, and the bindings from that code are equal [6]. The point here is that there do exist a number of equivalence relations which may be tested by fully decidable algorithms and which are sub-partitions of the most general relation defined by functional equality. Thus although it is not possible in general to determine the equivalent behaviour of arbitrary functions, it is possible to determine the equivalent behaviour of particular subsets of functions. Figure 6 shows three pairs of equal functions, the detection of whose equality is of varying complexity.

Without further elaboration we define a notion of weak functional equality, which will detect that both the second and third pair of functions are equal. The important attribute of this equality over simple identity is that it does not preclude the equality of pairs of functions which are independently constructed in different environments. The usefulness of this weak notion of equality may be seen in two situations: the merging of sub-systems, and the copying of values between persistent environments.

```
let first = proc( a : int -> int ) ; if a = 0 then 1 else 37
let second = proc( x : int -> int )
begin
        let res := 37
        if x = 0 do res := 1
        res
end

let difficultToDecide = ( first = second )
```

```
let first = proc( a : int -> int ) ; if a = 0 then 1 else 37
let second = first

let easyToDecide = ( first = second )
```

```
let first = proc( a : int -> int ) ; if a = 0 then 1 else 37
let second = proc( x : int -> int ) ; if x = 0 then 1 else 37

let quiteEasyToDecide = ( first = second )
```

Fig. 6. Varying degrees of complexity for functional equality testing

The merging of sub-systems, including the merging of independently prepared program and data, may only be sensibly achieved in cases where the type of the data has been agreed beforehand. In the case of dependent set types, the type includes the description of the element equality function. The importance of weak equality in this context is that as long as the equality is agreed beforehand, different instances of the same equality function may be prepared in the sub-systems, and then mechanically detected as equal during the system merge.

Copying values between typed object stores is really a special case of merging. In a typed object store every object must have a strong association with a representation of its type, to allow the typechecking of programs which bind to it. When values are copied between stores their associated type representations must also be copied. The importance of weak equality over identity in this case is that the equality of functions is preserved over copying, thereby preserving type equivalence over values independently propagated from a common source.

4 Hyper-programming interface and examples

Hyper-programming (Chapter 1.1.3) is a new style of programming made possible when source code representations are stored inside a typed persistent store. A hyper-program is a source representation which contains, in addition to the normal linear text, embedded links to other values in the store. Since the linked values can be accessed by scanning the hyper-program, they are available to the compiler. If the language definition allows the values on which types depend to be denoted by links, those values will be accessible by the typechecker for static checking. This may only be allowed in cases where the links are known to refer to immutable values, so that a constant binding is maintained from type to value as above.

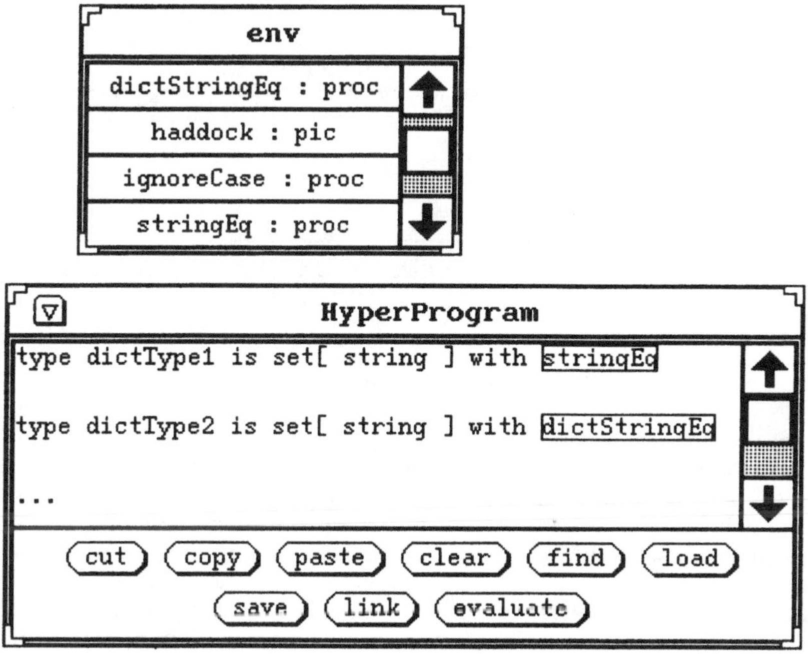

Fig. 7. An example hyper-program

Figure 7 shows the programmer's view of a simple hyper-program in which dependent set types may be checked statically. The values on which they depend are denoted by light-buttons which represent direct links to values already present in the persistent store. Although it is not possible to tell from the text of the program whether the types are the same, the typechecker is able to follow the links into the persistent store and perform arbitrary computation over the values in their closure.

Although the example above serves to illustrate the mechanism, it is unlikely to be used in practice since the programmer would not normally write separate equivalent type definitions within a single program. Figure 8 shows two separate compilation units using equivalent dependent types. They may be compiled in entirely separate environments, or in the same environment, so long as the function values are already present in the compilation environment.

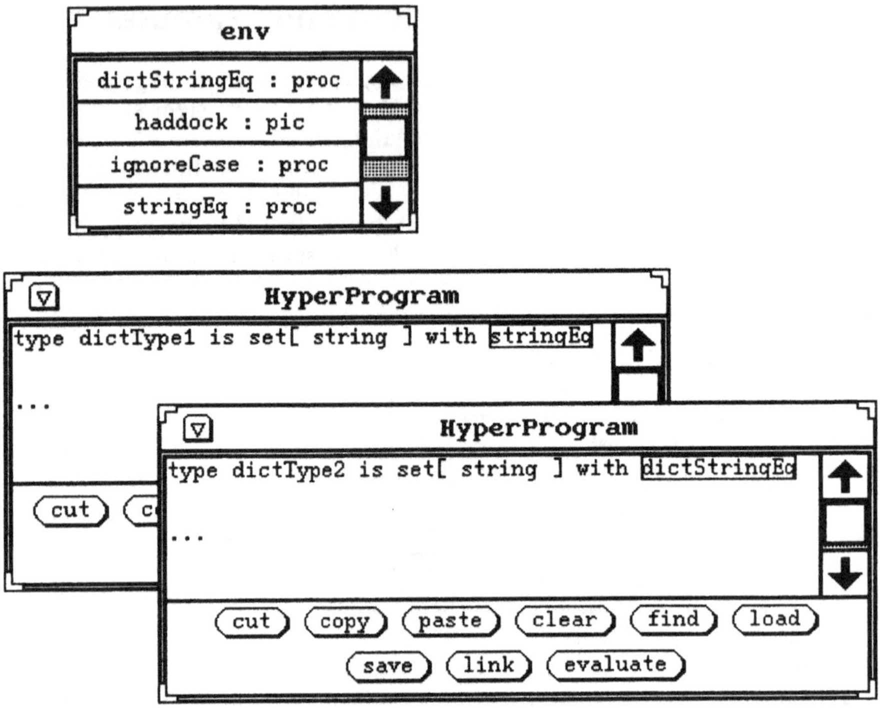

Fig. 8. Separate compilation units

If the types declared in the programs above are equivalent to each other, then data of these types which is created and placed in the persistent store will be seen to be typed equivalently in later use. Figure 9 shows an example of a hyper-program which applies the union operator to two values created by the programs in Figure 8. Note that these are typed set values whose type equivalence is checked at compilation time. It is not possible to see whether this program is typed correctly by a simple examination of the program text; however the typechecker is again able to access the closure of the embedded hyper-links, which contains the necessary information. It perhaps should be pointed out that in a hyper-programming system the programmer should also be given this ability!

One further point to make is that the light buttons named as *d1* and *d2* may refer to locations, rather than instances of the bulk types. After the program has been compiled it is possible for these locations to be updated with other values of the same type; however the program will work correctly with the new versions since their types, including dependencies, must be the same as the old versions. The significance of this in database terms is that the programs may be typechecked after the schema has been defined, rather than after it has been populated.

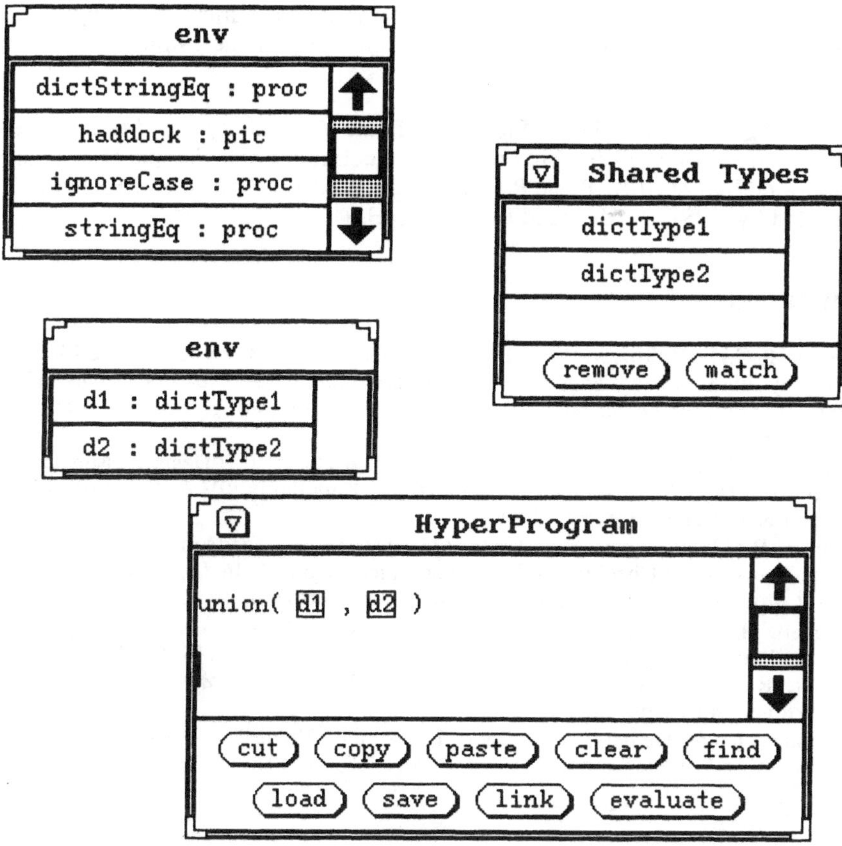

Fig. 9. Statically checkable union application

5 Polymorphism

The reader is referred to the original publication of this paper [1] for a discussion of polymorphism, which has been left out of this version due to space constraints.

6 Conclusions and further work

This paper has outlined how bulk data types that depend upon value based attributes may be statically type checked. The technique depends upon the equality relation over the value based attributes being decidable statically. One way of achieving this is by hyper-programming, a programming technique that allows links to persistent objects to be part of the source representation of a program. These links are available to the type checker and therefore can be used as part of the type equivalence relation for bulk types. To restore the flexibilty that has been lost by the introduction of static type checking, a polymorphic abstraction mechanism is introduced over these value dependent bulk types.

One expected result not discussed in this paper is that major efficiency gains may be made by using static knowledge of these functions in the implementation of the bulk values.

Acknowledgements. Dave Stemple of the University of Massachusetts at Amherst is to be thanked for his constructive comments on the paper. This work was supported by Esprit III Basic Research Action 6309 - $FIDE_2$, and Richard Connor is supported by EPSRC Advanced Fellowship B/94/AF/1921.

References

1. Connor R.C.H., Atkinson M.P, Berman S., Cutts Q.I., Kirby G.N.C. & Morrison R. "The Joy of Sets" In *Database Programming Languages*, New York City 1993, C. Beeri, A. Ohori & D. Shasha (ed), Workshops in Computing, Springer-Verlag 1994, pp 417-433.
2. Atkinson, M.P., Lécluse, C., Philbrow, P. & Richard, P. "Design Issues in a Map Language". In *Bulk Types & Persistent Data*, Kanellakis, P. & Schmidt, J.W. (ed), Morgan Kaufmann (1991) pp 20-32.
3. Connor, R.C.H., Brown, A.L., Cutts, Q.I., Dearle, A.,Morrison, R. & Rosenberg J. "Type Equivalence Checking in Persistent Object Stores". In *Implementing Persistent Object Bases - Principles and Practice*, Morgan Kaufmann, pp 154-170.
4. Mitchell, J.C. & Plotkin, G.D. "Abstract Types have Existential Type". ACM Transactions on Programming Languages and Systems 10, 3 (1988) pp 470-502.
5. Milner, R., Tofte, M. & Harper, R. *The Definition of Standard ML*. MIT Press, Cambridge, Massachusetts (1989).
6. Donahue, J. & Demers, A. "Data Types are Values". ACM Transactions on Programming Languages and Systems 7, 3 (1985) pp 421-445.

Chapter 1.4.2

Bulk Types: Built-In or Add-On?*

Florian Matthes and Joachim W. Schmidt

Technical University Hamburg-Harburg, Harburger Schloßstraße 20, D-21071 Hamburg, Germany

Bulk structures play a central rôle in data-intensive application programming. The issues of *bulk type* definition and implementation as well as their integration into database programming languages are, therefore, key topics in current DBPL research.

In this paper we raise a more general language design and implementation issue by asking whether there should be at all built-in bulk types in DBPLs. Instead, one could argue tat bulk types should be realized exclusively as user-definable add-s to unbiased core languages with appropriate primitives and abstraction facilities.

In searching for an answer we first distinguish two substantially different levels on which bulk types are supported. *Elementary Bulk* essentially copes with persistent storage of mass data, their identification and update. *Advanced Bulk* provides additional support required for data-intensive applications such as optimized associative queries and integrity support under concurrency and failure.

Our long-term experience with bulk types in the DBPL language and system clearly shows the limitation of the built-in approach: built-in *Advanced Bulk*, as elaborate as it may be, frequently does not cover the whole range of demands of a fully-fledged application and often does not provide a decent pay-off for its implementation effort. On the other hand, restriction to built-in *Elementary Bulk* gives too little user-support for most data-intensive applications.

Irrespective of the particular kind of bulk data structures present in a given database programming environment (e.g. lists, sets, relations in traditional DBPLs; class extents in object-oriented databases; base predicates in deductive databases or extensionally defined functions in functional databases), one can distinguish two fundamentally different approaches to bulk type support within a language framework:

Built-In Bulk Types are provided as first-class parameterized type constructors in several programming languages [13,6,12,11], their syntax, type rules, semantics and implementation being hard-wired into the language processor and the runtime system support.

Add-On Bulk Types are defined and implemented utilizing standard built-in language mechanisms (typing, naming, binding, scoping or recursion) of a sufficiently generic general-purpose base language like ML [10], Modula-3 [3], Napier88 (see Chapter 1.1.3) or Eiffel [9].

* This text is a summary of [8].

In this paper we analyze the motivations and basic assumptions behind both (extreme) approaches and explore their individual advantages and shortcomings. This investigation is based on the one hand on our substantial experience with the design and implementation of database programming languages incorporating powerful built-in bulk type support [13,5,7]. On the other hand it reports on the design rationale for Tycoon[1], a language and system environment with add- bulk types. The issue of built-in vs. add- bulk types has a longer tradition in the Persistent Programming Language community, in the DBPL camp, however, the main goal always consisted in building in advanced bulk types. By reporting on our own past experiences and future expectations we attempt to contribute to a more open and objective discussion on this important DBPL research issue.

We report on experience with built-in bulk types by referring essentially to DBPL, a set- and predicate-based procedural database programming language [14]. We illustrate issues in language design, system construction and application programming involving built-in bulk types.

The numerous requirements for bulk types (see, e.g. [1,2]) can be classified into *elementary* and *advanced* requirements which we will sumarize below. This discussion is valid for both, built-in as well as add- bulk types, and, therefore, also establishes a framework for an investigation of environments that enable their users to add-on bulk types meeting these elementary and advanced requirements.

As a first cut, the distinction between an elementary and an advanced requirement can be based on the kind of technology that is required to provide a particular bulk type support. Elementary requirements usually can be met by *local* modifications to language processors (compilers, abstract machines, run-time support libraries) essentially based on *programming language* technology. On the other hand, more advanced requirements, for example effective query optimization or stratification analysis of fixed-point queries, involve *global* analysis and modifications as provided by advanced *database* technology.

The built-in approach can be characterized by the following assumptions:

- All language implementation details are hidden from the application programmer (How is a bulk type implemented? How is a query represented, transformed and evaluated? How is serializability achieved?)
- The efficient implementation of the database language depends crucially on detailed language design time knowledge about permissible language constructs: Which (bulk) types exist? What is the syntax of the query (sub-)language? What are the algebraic properties of the built-in language primitives like equality predicates, comparison operations, aggregate functions?
- Significant optimizations are based on a careful case-analysis within the available language space. Examples are optimizations for special cases like flat relations, unordered collections, read-only transactions or one variable selection queries.

[1] Tycoon: Typed Communicating Objects in Open Environments

Some of these assumptions are in conflict with the programming language principles of orthogonality and free extensibility. Accordingly, much work in the database community aims at *extending database technology* to support, e.g.

- new aggregate functions in queries,
- new operations within queries (e.g. test for intersection of geometric objects),
- new bulk structures (e.g. ordered sequences),
- new operations in the target list of query expressions,
- new storage structures,
- new join algorithms, etc.

Despite progress made with extensible database systems [15], none of today's database programming language implementations provides adequate support for the above extensions.

The paper outlines the initial design of the Tycoon bulk type environment that aims at defining uniformly and implementing systematically declarative iteration abstractions applicable to a wide variety of bulk structures. Specifically, we explain how the concepts of data independence and query optimization can be generalized to liberally extensible systems. We also identify specific language mechanisms required for the efficient and robust construction of such open and extensible database application systems.

In our experience the main arguments against the traditional built-in approach to bulk types can be summarized as follows:

Reusability: It is difficult (often impossible) to safely re-use existing system components of the built-in system environment (buffer manager, polymorphic index structures, wait-for-graph management, clustering algorithms etc.).

Scalability: It is typically not possible to eliminate unnecessary functionality from the built-in system environment (concurrency control or recovery actions, components for recursive query evaluation).

Adaptability: Even if one has access to the implementations of the built-in bulk structures, modifications of these components (e.g. replacing B-Tree index structures by hashed structures or replacing a garbage collection algorithm) have to be performed in a "lower level" programming language with obvious negative consequences on the overall system correctness and long-term system evolution.

The apparent resistance of current DBPL *system implementations* against DBPL *language extensions* gives rise to the following important research question. Can one isolate "generic" language constructs that aid in the systematic construction of flexible DBPL processors and meet more than just a limited set of structures and algorithms foreseen at language design time? The second part of this paper addresses the relationship between DBPL language and system extensibility.

Recent advances towards expressive type systems as well as highly effective compilation schemes may allow the *elementary* requirements for bulk data storage (including persistence management) to be satisfied without resorting to the built-in approach. Given state-of-the-art language technology, a high investment in built-in bulk types (as exemplified by DBPL) can only be justified by the support it provides for *advanced* requirements like generalized associative queries or integrity constraint management in multi-user environments. We finally reported on our current work that aims to satisfy even these advanced requirements by user-definable add-ons to generic core languages focussing on linguistic and architectural aspects, since important component technology seems to be already available in extensible database systems.

Clearly there remain many open research issues for further theoretical and experimental work. What is a suitable formal framework for data models supporting generalized bulk types? Is it necessary to equip DBPLs with specific *syntactic* support for a concise notation of bulk data manipulations (e.g. list comprehensions)? Is there a taxonomy for general optimization strategies (algebraic vs. operational, static vs. dynamic, deterministic vs. probabilistic)? Where should the meta-information required for optimizations come from (static program analysis, program annotations via pragmas, access to program specifications, compile-time or run-time reflection)? Can standardized iteration abstractions be exploited for program verification tasks?

Acknowledgements. This work was supported by the European Commission under ESPRIT BRA contract # 3070 (FIDE).

References

1. M. Atkinson, F. Bancilhon, D. De Witt, K. Dittrich, D. Maier, and S. Zdonik. The object-oriented database system manifesto. In *Deductive and Object-oriented Databases*. Elsevier Science Publishers, Amsterdam, Netherlands, 1990.
2. M. Atkinson, P. Richard, and P. Trinder. Bulk types for large scale programming. In *Proceedings of the Kiev East/West Workshop on Next Generation Database Technology*, volume 504 of *Lecture Notes in Computer Science*. Springer-Verlag, April 1991.
3. L. Cardelli, J. Donahue, L. Glassman, M. Jordan, B. Kalsow, and G. Nelson. Modula-3 report. Technical Report ORC-1, Olivetti Research Center, 2882 Sand Hill Road, Menlo Park, California, 1988.
4. A. Dearle, R. Connor, F. Brown, and R. Morrison. Napier88 – a database programming language? In *Proceedings of the Second International Workshop on Database Programming Languages, Portland, Oregon*, June 1989.
5. J. Koch, M. Mall, P. Putfarken, M. Reimer, J.W. Schmidt, and C.A. Zehnder. Modula/R report, lilith version. Technical report, Department Informatik, ETH Zürich, Switzerland, February 1983.
6. C. Lécluse, P. Richard, and F. Velez. O_2, an object-oriented data model. In *Proceedings of the ACM-SIGMOD International Conference on Management of Data, Chicago, Illinois*, pages 424–433, 1988.
7. F. Matthes and J.W. Schmidt. The type system of DBPL. In *Proceedings of the Second International Workshop on Database Programming Languages, Portland, Oregon*, pages 255–260, June 1989.
8. F. Matthes and J.W. Schmidt. Bulk types: Built-in or add-on? In *Database Programming Languages: Bulk Types and Persistent Data*. Morgan Kaufmann Publishers, September 1991.

9. B. Meyer. *Object-oriented Software Construction.* International Series in Computer Science. Prentice Hall, Englewood Cliffs, New Jersey, 1988.
10. R. Milner, M. Tofte, and R. Harper. *The Definition of Standard ML.* MIT Press, Cambridge, Massachusetts, 1990.
11. S. Naqvi and S. Tsur. *A Logical Language for Data and Knowledge Bases.* Computer Science Press, 1989.
12. A. Ohori, P. Buneman, and V. Breazu-Tannen. Database programming in Machiavelli – a polymorphic language with static type inference. In *Proceedings of the ACM-SIGMOD International Conference on Management of Data, Portland, Oregon*, pages 46–57, 1989.
13. J.W. Schmidt. Some high level language constructs for data of type relation. In *Proceedings of the ACM-SIGMOD International Conference on Management of Data, Toronto, Canada*, August 1977.
14. J.W. Schmidt, H. Eckhardt, and F. Matthes. DBPL Report. DBPL-Memo 112-88, Fachbereich Informatik, Johann Wolfgang Goethe-Universität, Frankfurt, Germany, 1988.
15. M. Stonebraker. Special issue on database prototype systems. *IEEE Transactions on Knowledge and Data Engineering*, 2(1), March 1990.

Chapter 1.4.3

Extensible Objects for Database Evolution: Language Features and Implementation Issues

Antonio Albano, Milena Diotallevi, and Giorgio Ghelli

Dipartimento di Informatica, Università di Pisa, Corso Italia 40, 56125, Pisa, Italy

Abstract. One of the limitations of commercially available object-oriented DBMSs is their inability to deal with objects that may change their type during their life and which exhibit a plurality of behaviours. Several proposals have been made to overcome this limitation. An analysis of these proposals is made to show the impact of more general modelling functionalities on the object implementation technique.

1 Introduction

In the last decade many database programming languages and database systems have been defined which are based on the object paradigm. Some of these systems are based on designing from scratch an object data model, and a database programming language; for example, Gemstone, ObjectStore, Ontos, O_2, and Orion. Other systems are based on the extension of the relational data model with object-oriented features, as in the Illustra and UniSQL systems, and in the forthcoming new SQL standard, called SQL3. The success of the object data model is due to its high expressive power which is obtained by combining the notions of object identity, unlimited complexity of object state, class inclusion, inheritance of definitions, and attachment of methods to objects. However, this data model is not yet completely satisfactory when entities need to be modelled which change their class and their behaviour during their life, or entities which can play several roles and behave according to the role being played.

For example, consider a situation with persons classified either as generic persons, students or employees. This situation is modelled by three object types `Person`, `Student`, and `Employee`, in any object system. In this situation it is important to allow an object of type `Person` to become a `Student` or an `Employee`. However, this may lead to problems. Suppose that a `Code` field has been defined for both students and employees, with a different meaning and even a different type, integer and string respectively. Let a person John first become a student with code 100 and then an employee with code "ab200". At least four choices are possible:

1. The new `Code` overrides the old one, which makes no sense.
2. The situation is avoided, either statically, by preventing the declaration of a `Code` field in two subtypes of `Person`, or dynamically by forbidding any object which already has a `Code` field to acquire a new `Code` field. These two

approaches are unacceptable, since they create some form of dependency between two different object types, `Student` and `Employee`, which are "unrelated", i.e. such that they don't inherit from each other. In any object oriented methodology it is essential that a programmer defining a subtype only has to know about its supertypes, and must not fall into errors, either static or dynamic, which depend on the existence of another descendent of a common ancestor.
3. The situation can be prevented by stipulating that an object must always have a most specific type, i.e. that it can acquire a new object type only if this new type is a subtype of its previous most specific type. This solution is better than the previous one, since it does not link the possibility of extending an object to the rather irrelevant event of a common field name between two unrelated types, but it imposes too strong a constraint on the object extension mechanism.
4. A `Code` message to John gets a different answer depending on whether John is seen as a `Student` or as an `Employee`. This is the solution which best matches our intuitions.

The above problem is not just a consequence of using the same name `Code` for two different things. It is also an example of the fact that, when objects are allowed more than one most specific type, it is necessary to avoid interactions between these unrelated types. This can be achieved by allowing objects to have a "context dependent" behaviour, which can be supported in two different ways.

1. By static binding: the meaning of a message sent to an object is determined according to the type that the compiler assigns to the object, or in some other static way. This solution produces efficient executable code, since no method lookup is needed, but deleteriously affects extensibility and reusability which itself derives from combining inheritance with dynamic binding of methods to messages.
2. By dynamic binding (also called "late binding" or "dynamic lookup"): in this case an object may have several "entry points", which we call "roles". For example, when a `Student` is extended to become an `Employee`, it acquires a new role (or entry point) which will be used when it is seen as an `Employee`, without losing its old `Student` role. Messages are always addressed to a specific role of an object, and method lookup starts from the addressed role. An object which is always accessed through its most specific role behaves exactly like an object in a traditional object oriented language.

The languages proposed to deal with extensible objects may be classified as follows [2]:

- languages with *dynamic binding* and *uniform behaviour* (e.g. Galileo [3], [4]);
- languages with *static binding* and *context dependent behaviour* (e.g. Clovers [9], Views [8], IRIS [6] and Aspects [7]);
- languages with both *dynamic binding* and *context dependent behaviour* (e.g. Fibonacci — see Chapter 1.1.2).

In this paper we discuss some possible linguistic and implementation issues which arise when both dynamic binding and context dependent behaviour are supported. We draw on the experience gained in the design and implementation of the Galileo and Fibonacci object-oriented database programming languages.

The linguistic model we present is not essentially new, as it is based on the role mechanism of Fibonacci. The focus of the paper is not on the mechanism itself, but on its effect on object representation, a point which is not usually discussed in the literature. In particular, we show how the various parts of an object representation are related to the language features by showing how object representation changes when new features are introduced after each other.

The paper is organised as follows. Section 2 gives a basic linguistic and implementation model for an object-oriented language without extensible objects. Section 3 extends the linguistic model with extensible objects with uniform behaviour, and shows how extensibility affects the implementation model. Section 4 studies how the possibility of shrinking objects affects the implementation model. Section 5 further extends the language with a role mechanism, i.e. with context dependent behaviour with dynamic binding, showing the effects on the implementation model. Section 6 shows how the model must be further modified to deal with the possibility of giving different implementations for values of the same object type, as happens in Fibonacci. Section 7 draws some conclusions.

2 Non-extensible Objects

In this section we define a basic object-oriented language, without extensibility, with the associated object representation model. To fix a notation, throughout the paper we adapt the syntax and semantics of the Galileo95 language [1].

2.1 The language

2.1.1 Object Types

In Galileo95 objects are modelled using the so-called "object as record" analogy, adopted initially in Simula, formalised by Cardelli [5], and used in most object database systems: objects are essentially records that may have functional components to model methods; message passing is implemented as field selection. In this context, an object type specifies three pieces of information:

- the object type interface, i.e. (a) the set of messages which can be sent to the object, with the parameter and result types (signature) for every message, and (b) the public object instance variables, i.e. the components of the object state, which can be accessed from outside the object;
- the structure of the object state, i.e. the name, type, and mutability of the private instance variables;
- the method implementation, i.e. the code that an object of that type executes when it receives a message.

In other languages, such as Fibonacci, an object type only specifies the interface of objects of that type, while every object can have, in principle, its own implementation, i.e. its own state structure and method set. The consequences of this different approach are discussed in Section 6.

An object type is specified by a set of pairs of two kinds:

1. A label-type pair (A_i :T_i) represents one component of the object state (the identifiers A_i are called *attributes*); the value associated with an attribute A_i of an object O is extracted with the dot expression O.A_i and has type T_i.
2. A label-function pair (A_i := fun(...) ...) represents a method, i.e. a function shared by all instances of the object type. A method can access the attributes and methods of the object using the predefined identifier `self`. A message A_i with parameters p is sent to an object O employing the O.A_i(p) notation.

The following example shows the definition of the object type `Person`, with a method `Introduce`:

```
let type Person =
        object
          [Name :string;
           BirthYear :int;
           Phones :[House :string];
           Introduce:= fun () :string is
             implode({"My name is  ";
                      self.Name })
          ];
```

Where `[House :string]` is an example of a tuple type, `{"a";"b"}` is a sequence of strings, `implode` concatenates a sequence of strings, and the declaration `let type T = object [SoP]`, where `SoP` is a set of pairs as previously described, introduces into the current environment a new type `T` and the function `mkT` to construct values of type `T`. The input parameter of the `mkT` constructor is a record of type `[SoP']` with one field for each component in the object state, i.e. `SoP'` is the set of `SoP` label-type pairs. Each application of the `mkT` constructor returns an object of type `T` with a different identity.

An example of the construction of an object of type `Person`, and examples of state access and message passing are:

```
let John := mkPerson ([Name := "John Smith";
                       BirthYear := 1967;
                       Phones := [House := "06 222444"] ]);

john.BirthYear;
john.Introduce();
```

In general, object methods and attributes — called the *properties* of an object — may be either *public* or *private*. A private property is only accessible from within the type definition, while a public property may always be accessed. Hereafter, properties are assumed to be public, since this aspect is not relevant for the considerations we are interested in.

2.1.2 Subtyping and Inheritance

Subtyping and inheritance are two different mechanisms which are often related in object oriented languages. Subtyping is an order, or pre-order, relation among types such that, whenever T' is a subtype of T, written $T' \subseteq T$, any operation which can be applied to any object of type T' can also be applied to any object of type T. Inheritance is a generic name which describes any situation where an object type, object interface, or object implementation, is not defined from scratch but is defined on the basis of a previously defined entity of the same kind. For example, in our situation defining an object type T' by inheritance from T means defining T' by only saying how its state and method set differ from T's state and methods. For methodological and technical reasons, most object-oriented languages only allow strict inheritance, which means that T' can be defined from T only by:

- adding instance variables or methods to T;
- refining T's state and methods, where refining an instance variable means substituting its type with a subtype, and refining a method m means substituting it with a new method whose type is a subtype of the type of m.[1]

Whenever T' is defined by strict inheritance from T, T' is also a subtype of T, since T' supports the whole T interface.

Strict inheritance is also adopted in Galileo95, where this is the only way to define a subtype of an object type. To define an object type `T` by inheritance from another object type `T'`, we write:

```
type T := object is T' and H
```

`H` specifies the properties (attributes and methods) to add or redefine in `T`; below is an example.

```
let type Student := object is Person and
                        [Code :string;
                         Faculty :string;
                         Introduce := fun () :string is
                              implode({super.Introduce();
                                        "I am a student of ";
                                        self.Faculty}) ];
```

It is generally possible to define an object type by inheritance from several object types: `T := object is` T_1, ..., T_n `and` T_r (multiple inheritance).

[1] In any strongly and statically typed language the type $S' \to U'$ of m' is a subtype of the type $S \to U$ of m when $S \subseteq S'$ and $U' \subseteq U$; the inversion of the direction of the comparison between S and S' is explained in [5].

If the supertypes have a property with the same name and different types, the property is inherited from the last (w.r.t. the $T_1, \ldots, T_n$ order) supertype which defines it. In this case, strict inheritance means that every property which is either redefined *or* inherited from more than one type must have a type which is a subtype of the type of the same property in *all* the ancestor types $T_1, \ldots, T_n$. Not every object oriented language allows multiple inheritance; inheritance from a single supertype is the most common solution.

2.1.3 Method Lookup and Semantics of Self

When a message `m` is sent to an object `O`, two problems must be solved: (a) which method is used to answer the message, and (b) what is the semantics of the pseudo-variable `self` which may appear in the selected method.

In traditional object-oriented languages, with objects that cannot change their type dynamically, the run-time type `T` of an object `O` is fixed when the object is created. This run-time type is generally a subtype of the compile-time type of any expression whose evaluation returns `O`. When a message is sent to `O`, the method is first searched for in its run-time type `T`. If none is found, the method is searched for up the supertype chain of `T`. The search will stop, since static typechecking ensures that the method has been defined in one of the super-types. The fact that the method lookup starts from the run-time type `O`, rather than from the compile-time type of the expression which returns `O`, is called *dynamic binding*, while the specific algorithm used to look for the method (depth-first upward search, in this case) is called the *lookup algorithm*.

Consider now a `self.msg(...)` invocation found inside a method defined for the message *msg2* inside type T, and suppose that the method is executed by an object with a type T' inheriting from T. Two choices are possible, in principle, for the semantics of `self.msg(...)`:

- method lookup for *msg* may start from from T, the statically determined type of `O` (static binding of `self`)
- method lookup for *msg* may start from the dynamic type T' of the object which has received the message *msg2* (dynamic binding of `self`).

The second choice is the one adopted in all object-oriented languages, and is essential in many typical object-oriented applications. Hence, when the method where `self.msg(...)` is found is type-checked, the type checker can only assume that `self` will be bound to an object whose type inherits from T. This is not a problem in languages which only allow strict inheritance, such as the one we are describing, and this is the main justification for the strict inheritance constraint.

The pseudo-variable `super` can also be used in a method expression. `super` is statically bound, i.e. the method search for a message sent to `super` begins with the supertype of the type where the method is defined.

2.2 An Implementation Model

We now describe an implementation model for the basic language described so far. We only focus on the information that must be present in the run-time representation of an object to support the described functionalities. We give a simple, not unrealistic, way of representing this information, without discussing alternative representations and optimisations.

In our model, every object is represented by a reference to a representation of its run-time type (the object type descriptor) plus a representation of the object's own state. The object type descriptor and the object state representation are described in the following subsections.

2.2.1 The Object Type Descriptor

We need to make a distinction between the *compile-time object type descriptor*, which is used by the compiler to determine the correctness of message passing operations and of new object type definitions, and the *run-time object type descriptor*, which is used for method lookup. Both structures are persistent in an object oriented database system, but the first belongs to the schema while the second is managed by the run-time system.

A run-time object type descriptor thus only contains the method and state lookup table for that type. This is a table which associates every message accepted by an object of that type with the code of the corresponding method (even if inherited), and every component of the state of the object with its position inside the object state representation. The second piece of information is needed if the language supports multiple inheritance. When only single inheritance is supported, the offset of each state component can be directly computed by the compiler. It would also be possible, but more costly, to keep field names inside the object itself. We will also call this structure *extended* run-time object type descriptor, to emphasize that it contains both specific and inherited methods, while in most of the other implementation models we will present, the run-time object type descriptor will only contain information about specific (not inherited) properties.

2.2.2 The Representation of the Object State

The state of each object is simply represented as a tuple containing its non-method fields. The run-time representation of an object is depicted in Figure 1.

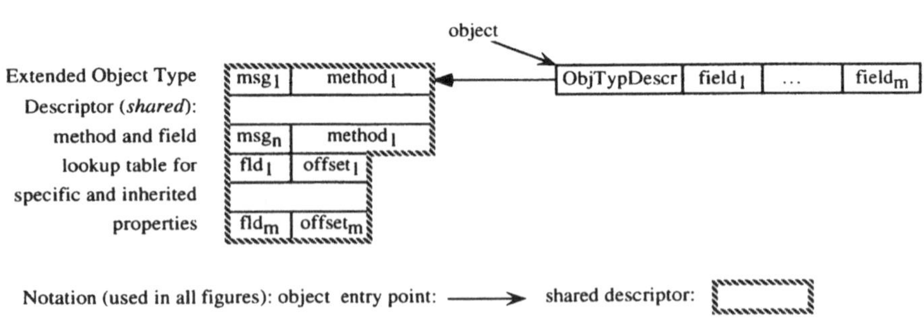

Fig. 1. The structure of an object which does not change type.

3 Extensible Objects with Uniform Behaviour

In this section we add to the basic model the possibility of extending objects, but without the possibility to revert the object to the original state, and without introducing the notion of a context dependent behaviour. We then show the linguistic and implementation effect of this first extension. This section is based on the linguistic and implementation model which underlies the first version of Galileo [3].

We first extend the basic language by stipulating that, when an object type `T'` is defined by inheritance from type `T`, two functions are automatically generated: `mkT'` to construct directly new instances of type `T'`, and the function `inT'` to extend an instance of type `T` with the new type `T'`, without affecting the object's identity.

The function `inT'` has two parameters: the value of the object `O` to be extended and a record which gives the values of the `T'` attributes which are not inherited from `T`.

To solve the problem created by the presence of two properties, in two independent subtypes, with the same name but a different type, the following *property type specialisation rule* is adopted: when an object `O` with a set of properties $\mathcal{A}$ is extended with a new type `T`, for every property `P` which is both in $\mathcal{A}$ and in `T`, the type of `P` in `T` (the new type of `P`) must be a subtype of the type of `P` in $\mathcal{A}$ (the old type of `P`).

For example, the object `john` may be extended with the type `Student` as follows:

```
let type Student = object is Person and
                   [Code :string;
                    Faculty :string;
                    Phones :[House :string; GuestHouse :string];
                    Introduce := fun () :string is
                                   implode({super.Introduce();
                                            "I am a student of ";
                                            self.Faculty})
                   ];
let johnAsStudent := inStudent(john,
                          [Code := "0123";
                           Faculty := "Science";
                           Phones := [House := "06 222444";
                                      GuestHouse := "552244"]]);
```

The extension operator does not change the object identity. Suppose now that the following types are also defined:

```
let type Athlete = object is Person and
                   [Code:int;
                    Sport: string;
                    Introduce:= fun () :string is
                       implode({super.Introduce();
```

```
                                  " I practice ";
                                  self.Sport}) ];

let type Employee = object is Person and
                    [Code:string;
                     Company: string;
                     Introduce:= fun () :string is
                        implode({super.Introduce();
                                 " I work at ";
                                 self.Company}) ];
```

An object of type `Person` which has never been extended to a `Student` can be extended to become an `Athlete`, but the property type specialisation rule (applied to `Code`) prevents the extension of a `Student` to an `Athlete`. However, a `Student` can be extended to an `Employee`.

Other operators defined on extensible objects in this language are:

- `Expr isalso T`, to test whether an object denoted by the expression `Expr` also has the type `T`; for example both `john isalso Student` and `johnAsStudent isalso Student` are true.
- `Expr As T`, to coerce an object denoted by the expression `Expr` to one of its possible types `T`; for example `john As Student` returns the object with type `Student`. This operation raises a run-time failure if the object never acquired type `T`, but has no other run-time effect in this language.

3.1 Method Determination

In Galileo, method lookup cannot only depend on the minimal type of an object, since, thanks to object extension, an object may have more than one minimal type. In Galileo, method lookup depends on the whole *object type history*, which is defined as the ordered set of types $\{T_1, \ldots, T_n\}$ such that T_1 is the type the object had when it was built, and every extension operation adds a new type at the end of the history.

When an object with a type history $\{T_1, \ldots, T_n\}$ receives a message `m`, the method to execute is searched for in two steps:

1. first, the method is looked for in methods that are specific to (i.e. are not inherited) the last type T_n acquired; if it is not found there, the search goes on in the type history, in the inverse temporal order $T_{n-1}, T_{n-2}, \ldots, T_1$;
2. then, if the method has not been found by the construction type T_1, the search goes up the supertype chain of T_1 as in the basic language. Static typechecking ensures that the search will eventually find an appropriate method.

For example, an object `john` created with type `Person`, and then extended with the subtypes `Student` and `Employee`, and finally with `Student` subtype `GraduateStudent`, will answer the message `Introduce` using the method defined in the type `GraduateStudent`.

3.2 Self-reference Semantics

When a method contains a `self.msg` invocation, the interpretation of the self-reference depends on how the method has been determined:

- if the method has been found in the type T_i by the search into the type history, the type of `self` is T_i, the type containing the selected method;
- if the method has been found by a search in the supertype chain of T_1, the type of `self` is T_1, the creation time type of the object that received the message `m`.

Hence, we can say that `self` is statically bound for methods found during the history search phase, while it is dynamically bound for methods found during the upward search phase. Performing a dynamic binding of `self` to T_1 for a method found in type T_i during the history search phase would not be sound since, when a message is compiled, `self` type it is assumed to be a subtype of the T_i type being defined, which is not true for T_1 (unless $i = 1$). On the other hand, this choice does not affect the language's expressive power because the method lookup mechanism is equivalent to the one adopted in the basic language for non extended objects. This means that this approach can represent every classical object-oriented construction based on the dynamic binding of `self` for non-extensible objects.

As an example of the `self` interpretation rule, let us consider the following definitions:

```
let type W1   := object [s := fun():int is 3;
                          r := fun():int is self.s()];
let type W11  := object is W1 and [s := fun():int is 4];
let type W12  := object is W1 and [s := fun():int is 5;
                                   r := fun():int is
                                           2*self.s()];
```

Let us construct a value `v1` of type `W11`, and send it the message `v1.r()`:

```
let v1 := mkW11([ ]);
v1.r();                    % returns 4
```

`v1.r()` returns 4 because the method for `r` is inherited from `W1`; here `self` is assigned type `W11` (dynamic binding), hence `self.s` returns 4. Let us extend `v1` with the type `W12`, and send it the message `v1.r()`:

```
let v2 := inW12(v1,[ ]);
v1.r();                    % returns 10
```

This time the method for `r` is found in `W12` by history search, hence `self` is statically bound to type `W12`, hence `self.s` returns 2*5. Note that there is no modification in the semantics of `super`.

3.3 The Implementation Model

The simplest run-time representation of objects in this language contains the object type history, represented as a modifiable sequence of references to type descriptors, and a modifiable sequence of label-value pairs to represent the state. In this case a type descriptor only contains the code for its own methods. Method search is executed through the two-phase algorithm described above, while field search is executed exploiting field labels. When an object is extended with a new subtype, the new type is added to its history and the new fields are added to its state; if an attribute of the supertype is redefined, its value is directly replaced by the new value.

More specifically, every method is represented as a function which receives, apart from the message parameter, a self parameter which is bound to the receiving object, as happens with objects that do not change type, plus a boolean parameter which says whether the method has been found during the history search phase or during the upward search phase. This boolean parameter is used to determine whether the history search must be used when a message is sent to `self`. This simple representation is shown in Figure 2. Note that the object is accessed indirectly to allow the object to be extended without modifying its identity, i.e. preserving any external reference to the object; any other technique to allow identity preserving extensibility (e.g. concatenating new fields to the object tail) would work.

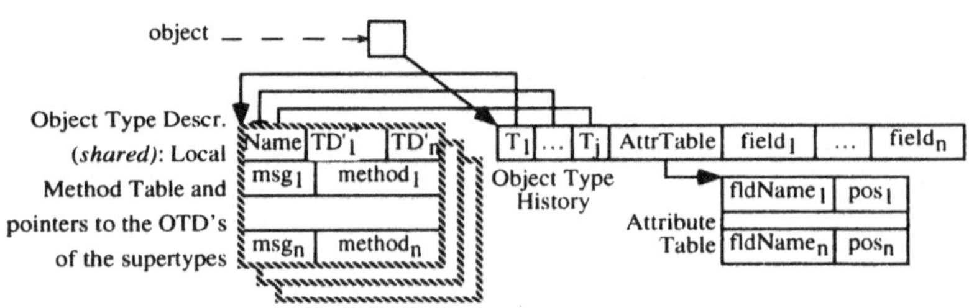

Fig. 2. The structure of an extensible object.

3.4 An Improved Implementation Model

To obtain a more efficient execution of message passing, an object representation can be used which closely resembles the one in Figure 1. In this case, each object only contains a reference to an *Object Type History Descriptor* (*OTHD*). An OTHD contains an object type history (i.e. a sequence of references to object type descriptors), a method lookup table and a field lookup table, which allow one to find the code of every method and the position of every field for any object with the story described by the OTHD. The system maintains a pool of OTHD's and creates a new one only when an object is created whose story is different from any story which is currently described in the OTHD. This optimised representation is shown in Figure 3.

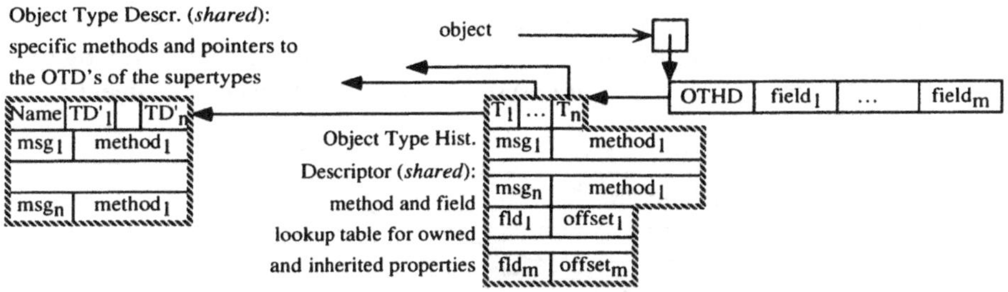

Fig. 3. A better structure for extensible objects.

4 Extensible and Shrinkable objects

As a further generalisation step, we now add an operator `dropT(Expr)` to the language, to cancel the type `T`, and all its subtypes, from the object denoted by the expression `Expr`. `dropT(Expr)` is a function which is declared automatically when a subtype is defined, as happens with `mkT` and `inT`.

In our linguistic model, object shrinkability adds a first kind of context-dependent behaviour. Let $\texttt{Ide}_1$ be an identifier bound to an object of type $\texttt{T}_1$ (e.g. $\texttt{Ide}_1$:= `mkPerson(...)`), and $\texttt{Ide}_2$ an identifier bound to the same object extended with the subtype $\texttt{T}_2$ (e.g. $\texttt{Ide}_2$:= `inStudent(`$\texttt{Ide}_1$`, ...)`). If type $\texttt{T}_2$ is removed from the object, by executing either $\texttt{dropT}_2(\texttt{Ide}_2)$ or $\texttt{dropT}_2(\texttt{Ide}_1)$, then:

- if the object is accessed through the identifier $\texttt{Ide}_2$, a run-time failure will arise when a message is sent it, either to execute a method or to extract the value of an attribute, irrespective of whether the property is defined in $\texttt{T}_2$ or is inherited from $\texttt{T}_1$;
- if the object is accessed through the identifier $\texttt{Ide}_1$, a message to execute a method or to extract the value of an attribute defined in $\texttt{T}_1$ is normally executed. Note that, in a well typed program, it is not possible to extract a property which is only defined in $\texttt{T}_2$ by going through $\texttt{Ide}_1$.
- the `isalso` and `As` operators can still be applied to $\texttt{Ide}_2$, to verify whether the object still belongs to some type and to send messages to the part of the object that is still valid.

Shrinkable objects thus have a behaviour which depends on the context they are accessed through, their *role* in our terminology. For this reason, the implementation model must be extended to take into account the fact that an object can be accessed through many different roles. Every role contains the following information: the type (e.g. $\texttt{Ide}_1$ is associated with the `Person` type while $\texttt{Ide}_2$ is associated with the `Student` type), the validity (e.g. $\texttt{Ide}_1$ is valid while, after the $\texttt{dropT}_2$ operation, $\texttt{Ide}_2$ is not valid any more), and a reference to the object. The object itself must contain a reference to all of its roles, both to implement `As` and `isalso` and to find every role associated with a subtype of `T` when `dropT` is executed.

This representation is shown in Figure 4, where an object with two valid roles and one removed role is represented. Note that the indirection level given by roles can also be exploited to allow identity preserving modifications of the object.

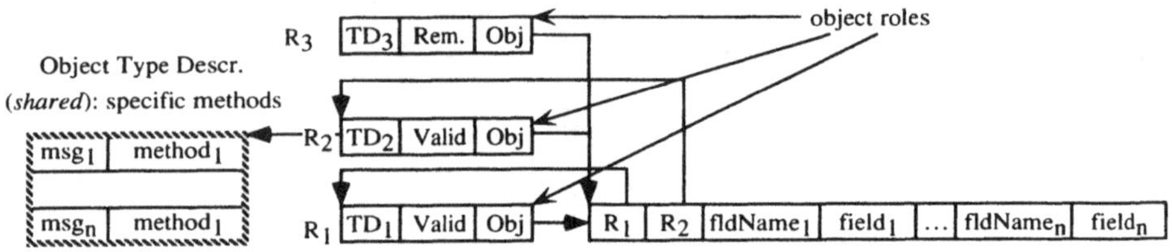

Fig. 4. The structure of a shrinkable object.

Every reference to an object is actually a reference to one of its roles. When an object is extended a new role is added, and when an object loses the type T_i, the following actions are executed:

- the status of the T_i role becomes `removed`;
- the type T_i is removed from the object type history;
- the first steps are repeated for every role of the object whose type is a subtype of T_i.

We do not discuss, in this case, any optimised implementation.

5 Extensible Objects with Context Dependent Behaviour

The most general solution to support objects which can dynamically acquire new types and exhibit a plurality of behaviours was first given in Fibonacci [2], and then adapted to Galileo95 [1]. The proposal has the following main features:

Objects with roles An object has an immutable identity and is organised as an acyclic graph of *roles*. Methods and fields are associated with the roles. Every message is addressed to a specific role of an object, and the answer may depend on the role addressed (*context dependent behaviours*);

Independence of extensions An object can be extended with unrelated subroles without interference;

Plurality of dynamic bindings A message can be sent to a role with two different notations to request a different lookup method:

- *upward lookup*: the message is sent with the exclamation mark notation, and the method is looked for in the receiving role and in its ancestors;
- *double lookup*: the message is sent with the dot notation, and the method is first looked for in all the descendants of the receiving role, visited in reverse temporal order, then in the receiving role, and finally in its ancestors.

Note that a traditional object oriented language can be seen as a role language where no object is ever extended and every message is always sent to the most specific role of the object. In this situation, upward lookup and double lookup coincide, and both coincide with the standard method lookup technique.

Role casting and role inspection Operators are provided to inspect the roles of an object and to dynamically change the role through which an object is accessed.

Multiple implementations An object type only describes the interface of the corresponding objects, while the implementation (i.e. method implementation and state structure) is defined, for every object, when the object is built.

We will first describe the Galileo95 model, which adopts the single implementation approach for objects. Let us consider again the definitions of the `Person` subtypes `Student` and `Athlete` given at beginning of Section 3.

In contrast to the previous model, in this model, an object with a role `john` of type `Person` may now be extended with the types `Student` and `Athlete` as follows:

```
let johnAsStudent := inStudent(john, [...]);
let johnAsAthlete := inAthlete(john, [...]);
```

The answer to the message `Code` sent to `johnAsStudent` is a string while the answer to the same message sent to `johnAsAthlete` is an integer. The answers to the message `Introduce` sent to `johnAsStudent` or to `johnAsAthlete` are also different. We say that `john`, `johnAsStudent` and `johnAsAthlete` are three roles of the same object, of type `Person`, `Student`, and `Athlete`, respectively.

Besides the functions `mkT` and `inT'`, the following operators, similar to those seen in the previous section, are also provided on objects and roles:

- `dropT(Expr)`, to drop the role with type `T` and all its sub-roles from the object reachable through the role `Expr` (hereafter "the object `Expr`"). A run-time failure will arise if a message is sent to a removed role.
- `Expr isalso T`, to test whether an object `Expr` also has the role type `T`; for example `johnAsStudent isalso Athlete` is true.
- `Expr As T`, to retrieve the role `T` of the object `Expr`. For example, `johnAsStudent As Athlete` returns the role with type `Athlete` of the object which is reached through the role `johnAsStudent`.
- `Expr isexactly T`, to test the run-time role type of the role denoted by the expression `Expr`; for example, `john isexactly Athlete` is false while `johnAsAthlete isexactly Athlete` is true.

5.1 Method Determination

When a valid role `r` with run-time type T_i receives a double lookup message `r.m`, the corresponding method is looked for in two steps:

1. first, the method is looked for in the object roles whose type is a subtype of T_i, in inverse time order;[2]
2. if the method is not found, the search proceeds in the role type T_i, and finally goes up the supertype chain of T_i until the root type is reached. Static type-checking ensures that the search will eventually find the appropriate method.

When a role `r` receives an upward lookup message `r!m`, only step 2 is performed. For example, the answer to the double lookup message `john.Introduce` changes once the object has been extended with the role type `Student`, and once again after its extension with the role type `Athlete`. To receive always the same answer from `john`, irrespective of any extensions, the message must be sent with the `john!-Introduce` notation.

The combination of double lookup with role casting allows *static binding*, and the `super` mechanism, to be simulated. For example, let us consider the following function:

```
let foo := fun(x:Person) :{string} is
          {x.Introduce;
           x!Introduce;
           (x As Person)!Introduce}
```

Let `johnAsStudent` be bound to a value of type `Student`, which has been later extended with a role of type `ForeignStudent`, subtype of `Student` which redefines the method `Introduce`. The value returned by `foo(johnAsStudent)` is a sequence of three answers produced by the methods defined in type `Foreign-Student` (*double lookup*), in type `Student` (*upward lookup*), and in type `Person` (*static binding*).

5.2 Self-reference Semantics

When the method selected by a role `r` to answer a message `m` contains a message whose receiver is `self`, the interpretation of the self-reference depends on how the method has been found:

- if the method has been found in the downward lookup phase, hence in a type `T` which is a subtype of the type of `r`, then `self` is bound to the `r As T` role;
- if the method was found by a search in the supertype chain, then `self` is bound to the `r` role.

The observations made in Section 3.2 apply in this case too.

[2] Note the difference with the corresponding rule given in the previous section: there the method was looked for in the whole object type history, here it is looked for in the subroles of the receiving role only.

5.3 The Implementation Model

In this language, methods and attributes are not associated with the object as a whole, but each property is associated with one specific role. For this reason, the simplest implementation model is obtained starting from the last model presented and moving methods and state fields from the object, whose only aim is now to collect the history of the roles it acquired, to the roles, as shown in Figure 5. A role now stores the following information:

- a reference to the role type descriptor;
- a status `valid` or `removed` to describe whether the object lost that type;
- a reference to the object;
- the values of the specific attributes of its role type.

A new role descriptor is created when the object is created in a root type (a type without supertypes), and when the object is extended with a new type. Creating an object in a non-root type is implemented in the same way as creating the object in the root type and then extending it. Object extension is only valid if the object has all the supertypes of the new type but does not have the type it is acquiring.

An object descriptor is a sequence of references to the roles of the object, kept in temporal order.

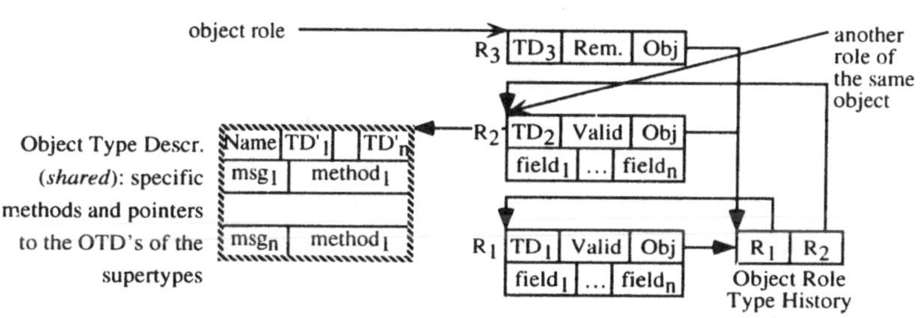

Fig. 5. The structure of an object with a plurality of behaviours.

This representation may easily be optimised, as will be shown in the next section.

6 Extensibility, Roles, and Multiple Implementations

The final feature of the language is separation between role type interfaces and implementations, as in Fibonacci, where:

- a role type only specifies the role interface but not the method implementation;
- a role implementation is only given when a role is constructed, or when an object is extended with new roles. Different role implementations can be given for the same role type;

- the state of a role is encapsulated and is accessible only through methods of the same role; this last point is not, however, essential for our discussion.

In this context, the definition of types `Person` and `Student` would only contain their interfaces as follows:

```
let type Person = object [Name :string;
                          BirthYear :int;
                          Phones :[House :string];
                          Introduce: string];

let type Student = object is Persona and
                 [Code :string;
                  Faculty :string;
                  Phones :[House :string; GuestHouse :string];
                  Introduce :string ];
```

The implementation of methods is given when a role is constructed:

```
let john = role Person with
             private
               MyName := "Antonio Rossi";
               MyBirthYear := 1950;
               MyPhone := [House :="565443"]
             method
               Name:= MyName;
               BirthYear := MyBirthYear;
               Phones := {MyPhone};
               Introduce:= implode({"My name is ";self.Name})
             end;
```

A student may be built either by extending a person, or from scratch, by defining the owned and inherited methods together; this second possibility affects the implementation model, as we will see.

Method determination and self-reference semantic rules are the same as in the previous section.

6.1 Implementation Model

The implementation model is shown in Figure 6. The main difference is that methods move from the role type descriptor to the role representation. Another difference arises because an object can acquire more than one role type in a single expression evaluation, both when it is created and when it is extended, hence it is not true that an object has as many roles as types. For example, suppose that four types $T_4 \subseteq T_3 \subseteq T_2 \subseteq T_1$ are defined. An object may be created in T_2 and then extended in type T_4. In this case the object would only have two roles, the first one returned by both `obj As` T_1 and `obj As` T_2, and the second one returned by both `obj As` T_3 and `obj As` T_4.[3]

[3] Note that this feature is orthogonal to multiple implementation; we might have introduced it in the previous section too.

The *role type descriptor* (*RTD*) now contains the following information:

- the type name (actually, its run-time representation);
- the list of all the supertypes of the type, in inheritance order. That is, if $T_1, \ldots,$ T_n is the list of immediate supertypes of T, then the list of all the supertypes of T contains first the list of all supertypes of T_n, then the list of all the supertypes of T_{n-1} which are not supertypes of T_n, and so on.
- the list of all the subtypes of the type.

We could have only kept immediate supertypes in the RTD, as in the previous sections. However, the increased complexity of the lookup method that would result, justifies the decision of making this small optimisation from the beginning.

The *role representation* contains the following information:

- a reference to the most specialised type associated with the role;
- a `valid` or `removed` status;
- the role local state, shared by all of the role's own methods;
- a table containing names and implementations for every owned method of the role;
- a reference to the object descriptor.

Finally, the object descriptor is a sequence, kept in temporal order, of pairs (types, role). Whenever an object acquires a new set *types* of types, thanks to an extension operation, a new pair *types,role* is added to the sequence, where *role* is the newly acquired role. Associating the set of types with each role in the object descriptor is a small optimisation, which helps us to implement message passing and the `As` operation.

Double lookup message passing is implemented as follows:

1. Downward lookup: if the object is accessed through a role R_i whose most specific type is T_i, the subtype list is obtained from the role type descriptor of type T_i, and the method is searched in every role R in the object role type history such that the most specific type of R is a subtype of T_i. The role type history is looked for in reverse temporal order.
2. Upward lookup: if downward lookup fails, then the supertype list is obtained from the role type descriptor of type T_i, and the method is searched in every role R in the object role type history such that at least one type of R is a supertype of T_i. Roles are examined in the inheritance order, i.e. according to the order of types in the supertype list.

Figure 6 below represents a situation where types T_2 and T_3 are two subtypes of type T_1, and the represented object has first been built from scratch in type T_2, and then has been extended to type T_3.

Note that no name is needed in the state representation, since it is only accessed by local methods, hence the position of each state component can be statically determined. On the other hand, the method lookup algorithm takes advantage of the fact that the method table associates names with method implementations.

The semantics of `self` is the same as in the previous section, and can be fully supported once the `As` operator is supported.

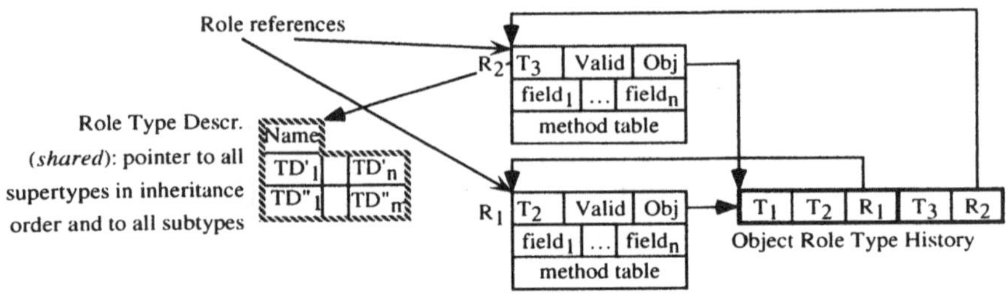

Fig. 6. The structure of an object with interface and implementation.

6.2 An Improved Implementation Model

The solution described so far is not realistic, since method lookup, which is the basic operation, requires an algorithm which is too slow. Hence, in the development of the Fibonacci system an optimisation similar to the one described in Section 3.4 was adopted.

In Fibonacci, every role is associated with a full method lookup table, i.e. a table which associates with each specific or inherited message, that the role can receive, the following information:

- a reference to the method code;
- a reference (`owner`) to the role *type* where the method implementation belongs;
- a field (`overriden`) to remember whether the method is defined in a subrole;

More precisely, each role contains a reference to two method lookup tables, one corresponding to double lookup and the second corresponding to upward lookup only; the "overridden" field is only present in the double lookup table.

The two lookup tables are built when a role is built, and in that moment they coincide. Later, whenever a new subrole `subr` defining a method `meth` for `msg` is added to the object, the `msg` field in the double lookup table of all superroles of `subr` is updated with the triple (meth, type of subr, true). The upward lookup table never changes. A method is a function which receives all the message parameters plus two roles, the "state role" which must be used to retrieve state variables and the "self role" which is bound to `self`.

To answer a message `msg` a role `r` just looks in the appropriate table to find the correct method `meth` and its owner type `owner`. Then, if overridden is `false` or is not applicable (upward lookup), it calls `meth` binding "state role" to `r As owner` and "self role" to `r`. If overridden is `true`, then `r As owner` must be bound to "self role" too.

Note that the lookup table contains the type of the role that owns the implementation, rather than the role itself, so that two different roles with the same message-method correspondence may share the table. Actually, the Fibonacci implementation contains a *lookup table pool* where every new lookup table is stored, associated with the object extension history. In this context an object extension history is not just a sequence of types since two objects may acquire the same type but with a different implementation. The history is a sequence of extension functions. This is because usually there are very few extension functions for every type, just one for most of them, and since almost every object construction or extension is made through a function, indexing the table pool with function histories is almost as effective as using type history in languages with one implementation per type.

The resulting situation is shown in Figure 7.

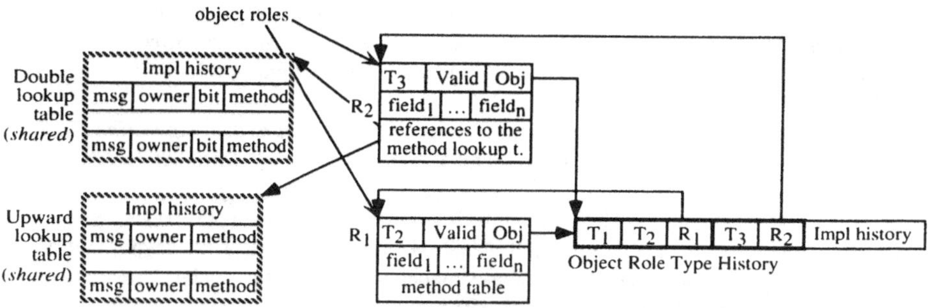

Fig. 7. The Fibonacci optimised implementation of roles.

7 Conclusion

We have described a sequence of object models of increasing complexity, starting with the standard model and ending with a model with the following features:

- extensible objects;
- context dependent behaviour (roles);
- shrinkable objects;
- multiple implementations for the same type.

Drawing on our experience in the implementation of Galileo, Galileo 95, and Fibonacci, we have presented a sequence of implementation models of increasing complexity, to show which implementation features are linked to every linguistic feature, and to help to distinguish the basic run-time information, which is strictly needed to implement every operation, from the structures that are added to obtain a faster implementation of message passing.

References

1. A. Albano, G. Antognoni, and G. Ghelli. View operations on objects with roles. ESPRIT BRA PROJECT 6309 ($FIDE_2$) Technical Report FIDE/95/129, Università di Pisa, Dipartimento di informatica, 1995.

2. A. Albano, R. Bergamini, G. Ghelli, and R. Orsini. An object data model with roles. In R. Agrawal, S. Baker, and D. Bell, editors, *Proc. of the Nineteenth Intl. Conf. on Very Large Data Bases (VLDB), Dublin, Ireland*, pages 39–51, San Mateo, California, 1993. Morgan Kaufmann Publishers.
3. A. Albano, L. Cardelli, and R. Orsini. Galileo: A strongly typed, interactive conceptual language. *ACM Transactions on Database Systems*, 10(2):230–260, 1985. Also in S. B. Zdonik and D. Maier, editors, *Readings in Object-Oriented Database Systems*, Morgan Kaufmann Publishers, Inc., San Mateo, California, 1990.
4. A. Albano, G. Ghelli, and R. Orsini. Objects for a database programming language. In P. C. Kanellakis and J. W. Schmidt, editors, *Proc. of the Third Intl. Workshop on Data Base Programming Languages (DBPL), Nafplion, Greece*, pages 236–253, San Mateo, California, 1991. Morgan Kaufmann Publishers.
5. L. Cardelli. A semantics of multiple inheritance. *Information and Computation*, 76:138–164, 1988. A previous version can be found also in *Semantics of Data Types*, LNCS 173, 51–67, Springer-Verlag, 1984.
6. D. H. Fishman, D. Beech, H. P. Cate, E. C. Chow, T. Connors, J. D. Davis, N. Derrett, C. G. Hoch, W. Kent, P. Lyngbaek, B. Mahbod, M. A. Neimat, T. A. Ryan, and M. C. Shan. IRIS: An object-oriented database management system. *ACM Transactions on Office Information Systems*, 5(1):48–69, 1987.
7. J. Richardson and P. Schwartz. Aspects: Extending objects to support multiple, indipendent roles. In *Proceedings of the ACM SIGMOD International Conference on Management of Data*, pages 298–307, Denver, CO, 1991.
8. J. J. Shilling and P. F. Sweeney. Three steps to view: Extending the object-oriented paradigm. In *Proceedings of the International Conference on Object-Oriented Programming Systems, Languages and Applications (OOPSLA)*, volume 10 of *ACM SIGPLAN Notices*, pages 353–361, 1989.
9. L. A. Stein and S. B. Zdonik. Clovers: The dynamic behavior of type and instances. Technical Report CS-89-42, Brown University Technical Report, 1989.

Section 1.5

Concurrency and Transactions: Introduction and State of the Art

Ron Morrison

School of Mathematical and Computational Sciences, University of St Andrews, North Haugh, St Andrews KY16 9SS, Scotland

Traditionally the database and programming language communities have taken different approaches to concurrency control. In programming languages, concurrency control is based upon the concept of the co-ordination of a set of co-operating processes by synchronisation. Language constructs such as semaphores [1], monitors [2], mutual exclusion [3], path expressions [4] and message passing [5] have been provided to support this concept. By contrast, in databases, concurrency is viewed as a system efficiency activity which allows parallel execution and parallel access to the data. However, each database process may have to suffer the indignity of abortion in order to sustain the illusion of non-interference. The key concept in databases is that of serialisability [6] which has led to the notion of atomic transactions [7] supported by locking or optimistic concurrency control methods [8].

In both cases the user must attempt to understand the computations in terms of some global cohesion. In programming languages the emphasis is on synchronisation and the overall cohesion is understood in terms of the conflation of all the synchronisations. A number of techniques, including CCS [9] and the π-calculus [10] have been developed to help with this. In database systems, global cohesion is understood in terms of the concept of serialisability but includes failure semantics such as abortion.

Figure 1, taken from [11], illustrates a spectrum of understandability from the points of view of programming language and database users. It represents the fact that databases tend to use atomic transactions to enforce isolation rather than co-ordinated sharing. Programming languages promote co-operation. Thus in integrating databases and programming languages, the designer must unify these established and provenly useful positions. The impetus does not altogether come from persistence however, since languages that support atomic transactions and databases that require non-serialisable and designer transactions [12, 13] have been identified as necessary by their respective communities.

Both camps agree that co-ordinating a set of computations that share data is a complex undertaking and that it is difficult to characterise the power and behaviour of the mechanisms and even more difficult to compare them with each other.

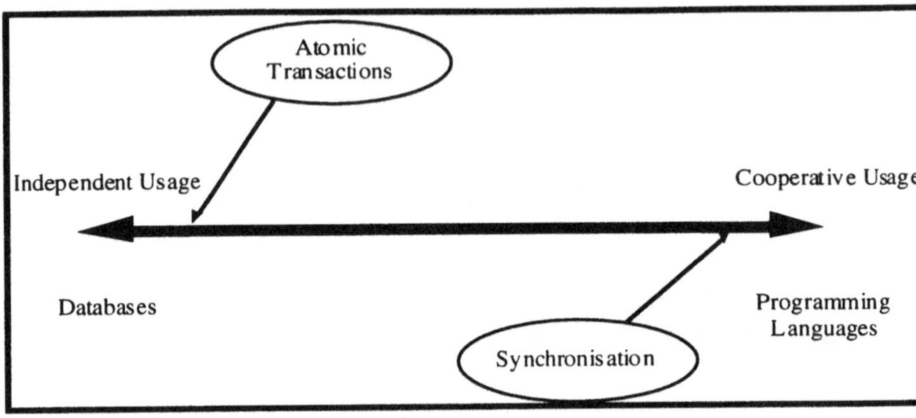

Fig. 1. A spectrum of understandability.

Previous attempts to provide concurrency in orthogonally persistent systems either have focused on a single model, provided a mechanism for extending synchronisation or provided basic persistent threads. The work of Krablin's CPS-algol [14, 15] is perhaps the most notable. CPS-algol added constructs to PS-algol to support processes and hence persistent threads. The concurrency model is co-operative based on synchronisation by conditional critical regions. Concurrency is provided by executing procedures as separate threads. Using these primitives and the higher-order functions of PS-algol, a range of concurrency abstractions can be constructed including atomic and nested transactions as well as more co-operative models. This work has been re-visited recently in [16] and [17].

Given that the overall goal is for the user to understand the computations in terms of some global cohesion the CACS system (Chapter 1.5.1), [18] proposes a mechanism for integrating concurrency control in programming languages and databases. It takes the point of view that the difficulty stems from both the low-level nature of the mechanisms and the inherent complexity of the problem.

The goal of the CACS approach is to control the coherence of sequences of operations on shared data in an understandable and flexible manner. The essence of the system is: understandability; the separation of concurrency control from data; formal capture; and a path to implementation. The global cohesion of an action in CACS is visualised as the movement of data among access sets. The visibility of the data to other users then becomes an issue of synchronisation. Where the visibility coincides with commit time, atomic transactions may be obtained, and where the visibility is immediate the synchronisation is present. By viewing the co-ordination of the use of data as the co-ordination of the movement of the data among access sets, then the same data may be used in a different manner at different times. Thus the data may take part in an atomic transaction one day, a saga the next and may be in a co-operative computation the next. A future goal of the work is to allow interaction of the concurrency control methods.

References

1. Dijkstra EW. The Structure of the T.H.E. Multiprogramming System. Communications of the ACM 1968; 11,5:341-346

2. Hoare CAR. Monitors: An Operating System Structuring Concept. Communications of the ACM 1974; 17,10:549-557
3. Dijkstra EW. Cooperating Sequential Processes. In: Genuys F (ed) Programming Languages. Academic Press, 1968, pp 43-112
4. Campbell RH, Haberman AN. The Specification of Process Synchronisation by Path Expressions. In: Lecture Notes in Computer Science 16. Springer-Verlag, 1974
5. Brookes SD, Hoare C, Roscoe A. A Theory of Communicating Sequential Processes. Carnegie-Mellon University Report CMU-CS-83-153, 1980
6. Eswaran KP, Gray JN, Lorie RA, Traiger IL. The Notions of Consistency and Predicate Locks in a Database System. Communications of the ACM 1976; 19,11:624-633
7. Gray JN. The Transaction Concept: Virtues and limitations. In: Proc. 7th International Conference on the Very Large Data Bases, 1978, pp 144-154
8. Kung HT, Robinson JT. On Optimistic Methods for Concurrency Control. ACM Transactions on Database Systems 1982; 6,2:213-226
9. Milner R. Lecture Notes in Computer Science Vol 92: A Calculus of Communicating Systems. Springer-Verlag, 1980
10. Milner R. The Polyadic π-Calculus: A Tutorial. University of Edinburgh Report ECS-LFCS-92-249, 1991
11. Munro DS, Connor RCH, Morrison R, Scheuerl S, Stemple D. Concurrent Shadow Paging in the Flask Architecture. In: Atkinson MP, Maier D, Benzaken V (ed) Persistent Object Systems, Tarascon 1994, Proc. 6th International Workshop on Persistent Object Systems, Tarascon, France. Workshops in Computing, Springer-Verlag, 1994, pp 16-42
12. Nodine MH, Zdonik SB. Co-operative Transaction Hierarchies: Transaction Support for Design Applications. VLDB Journal 1992; 1,1:41-80
13. Sutton S. A Flexible Consistency Model for Persistent Data in Software-Process Programming. In: Dearle A, Shaw GM, Zdonik SB (ed) Implementing Persistent Object Bases, Principles and Practice, Proc. 4th International Workshop on Persistent Object Systems, Martha's Vineyard, USA. Morgan Kaufmann, 1990, pp 305-319
14. Krablin GL. Transactions and Concurrency. Universities of Glasgow and St Andrews Report PPRR-46-87, 1987
15. Krablin GL. Building Flexible Multilevel Transactions in a Distributed Persistent Environment. In: Proc. 2nd International Workshop on Persistent Object Systems, Appin, Scotland, 1987, pp 86-117
16. Munro DS. On the Integration of Concurrency, Distribution and Persistence. Ph.D. thesis, University of St Andrews, 1993
17. Matthes F, Schmidt JW. Persistent Threads. In: Proc. 20th International Conference on Very Large Data Bases, Santiago, Chile, 1994, pp 403-414
18. Morrison R, Barter CJ, Connor RCH et al. Concurrency Control in Process Models. IOPENER 1993; 2,1:11-12

Chapter 1.5.1

Specifying Flexible Concurrency Control Schemes: an Abstract Operational Approach*

David Stemple[1] and Ron Morrison[2]

[1] Department of Computer and Information Science, University of Massachusetts, Amherst, MA 01038, USA

[2] School of Mathematical and Computational Sciences, University of St Andrews, North Haugh, St Andrews KY16 9SS, Scotland

Abstract. An abstract, operational model for specifying flexible concurrency control schemes within a persistent store is presented. The goal of the model is to allow concurrency control schemes to be specified in a manner that promotes understandability and supports their implementation. Schemes that support controlled sharing among autonomous computations are the primary targets of this work. An abstract machine programmed by a set of rules is employed to specify operational semantics for the concurrency control schemes.

1 Introduction

Co-ordinating a set of computations that share data is a complex undertaking. Mechanisms for such co-ordination have been designed for operating systems, programming languages and database systems. These include semaphores [1], monitors [2], mutual exclusion [3], path expressions [4], locks [5], and optimistic concurrency control systems [6]. Techniques for specifying transactions by means of an abstract machine have also been proposed in [7]. It has been difficult to understand the power and behaviour of these mechanisms and to compare them with each other. This difficulty stems from both the low level nature of the mechanisms and the inherent complexity of the problem. This paper addresses the task of building systems for controlling the co-ordination of computations on shared data in a persistent programming environment and attempts to alleviate the difficulties of understanding and comparing different control schemes.

The goal of this approach is to allow programs to control the coherence of sequences of their operations on shared data, called actions, in an understandable and flexible manner. The actions are programmed by specifying algorithms for manipulating the data and by annotating the algorithms with markers that specify how the data sharing is to be controlled. An extreme example of the coherence of a sequence of operations is the atomic transaction in which the operations are isolated from the effects of any other concurrent transaction and only allowed to have an effect on the database as a single unit. In systems supporting atomic transactions this strong coherence can be programmed simply by inserting `begin` and `end` transaction markers around a set of operations to delineate an atomic transaction. The effect of `begin` and `end` has to be specified separately at a lower level in the system. Examples of more complex coherence occur in design systems where parts of a

* This paper originally appeared as [11].

design are updated locally by multiple designers and the different changes are reconciled before their joint effect is made to the global design.

Many ways of achieving the isolation of atomic transactions have been devised and implemented and many mechanisms for co-ordinating co-operative computations have been proposed. This paper does not add another proposal to these efforts. Rather it presents an approach to specifying systems of concurrency control. The approach is based on the concepts of the ACTA framework [8-10] but is less general and more implementation oriented. It is flexible in that it allows more than one concurrency model to be specified, abstract in that it allows more than one implementation to realise a specification and operational in that specifications are written in terms of behaviour rather than invariants. The model is called the Communicating Actions Control System or CACS.

2 The Conceptual Framework

The conceptual framework of CACS may be explained in terms of the components used to specify concurrency control schemes. These are actions, objects, events, visibility control and dependencies.

The model of computation used in CACS is that of autonomous agents, called actions, making requests to access data in a globally shared database. The database consists of uniquely identified entities called objects. Objects are associated with types which define sets of operations, the details of which are not known to the control system. Access to objects in the database is made by actions requesting that operations be performed on database objects. When a request is granted by the control system, the effect of the operation appears in the requesting action's local access set but not in the database. Objects' identities remain the same in access sets and the database. Thus an object may have different states in different scopes of visibility. In order for the effect of an operation on an object to be made globally available the object must be committed to the database. Conceptually this is a separate operation which makes the database state of the object the same as its state in the local access set of the action performing the commit. Effects of operations may be shared among actions without their objects being committed to the database. This is accomplished by committing objects into shared access sets which are separate from the local access sets.

Actions interfere and co-operate with each other through the mediation of the control system via dependencies. Dependencies are formed as a by-product of actions making requests, and cause the control system to delay, disallow, require, or invoke by proxy operations by actions involved in the dependencies. The behaviour caused or prohibited by dependencies is defined as a part of a particular concurrency control scheme specified in CACS terms. The concept of a correct interleaving of actions is specified in CACS in terms of the behaviour induced by dependencies.

The interaction between actions and a control system specified in CACS is only partially modelled. The control system's reception of requests from actions is modelled as the control system taking events from an event stream. The way in which events are placed on the event stream is not specified. It is assumed that the activities of the control system are made known to the actions also through unspecified means. The creation of identifiers for actions, objects and shared access sets is independent of the control system.

3 Overview of CACS Mechanisms

A particular concurrency control scheme is defined by giving a set of rules for the behaviour of the CACS abstract machine. This yields the operational, abstract semantics of a particular scheme. The rules specify the behaviour of the control system when it takes an event from the event stream.

The abstract state of CACS has the following components:

- the event stream including its current position
- the rule base, which can change as a result of executing rules
- the action histories containing traces of actions in progress
- the visibility structure containing the database and the local and shared access sets along with their relationship to actions
- the dependency structure recording all current dependencies among actions.

The full paper [11] presents a method of specifying flexible concurrency control schemes using the concepts of actions, objects, events, visibility control and dependencies. The approach is to define a control environment in which protocols of data sharing can be defined operationally but are sufficiently abstract to allow significant freedom in implementing the protocols. The conceptual model of data sharing that is at the core of CACS is elaborated. Following this the details of CACS processing are presented. Finally two examples of specifications of concurrency control protocols are given: for atomic transactions and a co-operative sharing system.

References

1. Dijkstra E.W. The Structure of the T.H.E. Multiprogramming System. Communications of the ACM 1968; 11,5:341-346
2. Hoare CAR. Monitors: An Operating System Structuring Concept. Communications of the ACM 1974; 17,10:549-557
3. Dijkstra EW. Cooperating Sequential Processes. In: Genuys F (ed) Programming Languages. Academic Press, 1968, pp 43-112
4. Campbell RH, Haberman AN. The Specification of Process Synchronisation by Path Expressions. In: Lecture Notes in Computer Science 16. Springer-Verlag, 1974
5. Eswaran KP, Gray JN, Lorie RA, Traiger IL. The Notions of Consistency and Predicate Locks in a Database System. Communications of the ACM 1976; 19,11:624-633
6. Kung HT, Robinson JT. On Optimistic Methods for Concurrency Control. ACM Transactions on Database Systems 1982; 6,2:213-226
7. Nodine M, Skarra AH, Zdonik SB. Synchronisation and Recovery in Cooperative Transactions. In: Dearle A, Mitchell G, Zdonik SB (ed) Implementing Persistent Object Bases: Principles and Practice. Morgan Kaufmann, 1990, pp 329-344
8. Chrysanthis PK. A Framework for Modeling and Reasoning about Extended Transactions. Ph.D. thesis, University of Massachusetts, 1991
9. Chrysanthis PK, Ramamritham K. ACTA: A Framework for Specifying and Reasoning about Transactions. In: Proc. ACM SIGMOD, 1990, pp 194-203
10. Chrysanthis PK, Ramamritham K. A Formalism for Extended Transaction Models. In: Proc. 17th International Conference on Very Large Database Systems, Barcelona, Spain, 1990

11. Stemple D, Morrison R. Specifying Flexible Concurrency Control Schemes: An Abstract Operational Approach. In: Proc. 15th Australian Computer Science Conference, Hobart, Tasmania, 1992, pp 873-891

Chapter 1.5.2

Persistent Threads*

Florian Matthes and Joachim W. Schmidt

Technical University Hamburg-Harburg, Harburger Schloßstraße 20, D-21071 Hamburg, Germany

1 Introduction

A noticeable trend in database research and database system development is an increased interest in behavioural and procedural aspects of information systems. Data models that describe dynamic processes in addition to static data structures are capable of capturing more of the application semantics as exemplified by object-oriented models like Taxis, ADAPLEX, Galileo or Fibonacci. Similarly, database systems that support procedures, methods, rules or triggers in addition to persistent data values are capable of factoring-out procedural code from individual application programs into shared databases.

In this paper we focus on the intricate binding issues on the borderline between "active code" and "passive data" that arise in persistent object systems as soon as one gives up the classical separation between short-lived transactions expressed in a host language and long-lived data stored in a database. More specifically, we provide a classification scheme for bindings from code to persistent data and vice versa and we investigate bindings from persistent data and code to threads, which exhibit an interesting duality. On the one hand, threads can be viewed as activities that can be created, executed, synchronized, suspended, terminated, etc. Alternatively, they can be viewed as passive data that can be stored persistently, annotated with attributes, associated with other persistent data structures, moved between nodes in a network, and manipulated by computations.

This duality makes persistent threads a key technology for future persistent object systems and for applications that manage long-term, distributed or cooperative activities like computer-aided design, workgroup communication and workflow management. Unfortunately, this duality also invalidates many design assumptions on which today's volatile thread implementations are based. Therefore, we also discuss in some detail implementation aspects of persistent thread bindings.

The specific persistent thread model presented here has been developed within the context of the persistent programming environment Tycoon [5,3] (see Chapter 2.1.4) where it serves as an abstract model to shield programmers and application-oriented tools from details of the underlying system implementation (object store, database language evaluator, scheduler, recovery subsystem) while being sufficiently

* This text is a synopsis of [6].

low-level to support a variety of (possibly application-defined) scheduling and activity management strategies.

2 Bindings in persistent systems

A binding is an association between a name and a computational entity from a specific semantic domain. We also say that a name is bound to a computational entity. Different names can be bound to the same entity (sharing, aliasing). Entities can be flat (like records) or nested (like functions in Algol-like languages). As is shown in the full paper, the semantics of bindings from and to (dynamically) nested entities requires particular attention.

Entities can be transient (like local program variables) or persistent (like database tables). Virtually all database systems restrict persistent entities to contain only bindings to other persistent entities since bindings to volatile entities would lead to "dangling references". Such constraint violations are avoided in many systems by a transitive reachability rule: Every entity reachable from a persistent entity becomes persistent, too. In reachability-based systems, there is a so-called "persistent root". An entity is made persistent by making it reachable through chains of bindings (e.g. database definition, class extent) starting from this persistent root.

Conceptual Model	Language Model	Implementation Model
entity	variable	data
behaviour	function	code
activity	continuation	thread
relationship	name	binding

Fig. 1. Corresponding notions at different levels of conceptualization

The following three categories of structured entities are of particular interest in extended (higher-order) database modelling (see Fig. 1):

Persistent Data (D) describe the persistent state of an information system by a collection of computational entities related through bindings. The structure (types) of the persistent entities and their bindings are described by a database schema.

Code (C) is a description of operation sequences that query and update volatile or persistent entities and bindings. Code involves names to describe bindings to other code, bindings to persistent data, and bindings to volatile data.

A **Thread (T)** is a representation of code *in the process of being executed.* A thread describes a single sequential flow of control in a program. Having multiple threads in a program means that at any instant the program has multiple points of execution, one in each of its threads. Unlike operating system processes, multiple threads can execute within a single (persistent) address space, permitting multiple threads to access shared variables in addition to local variables.

A thread is created by submitting a parameterless code fragment and (persistent) data to an evaluator. The semantics of the evaluator can be defined inductively by rules that map thread states to thread states and that perform side-effects on data. A thread state subsumes bindings to the code fragments currently being executed and a dynamic environment that records the current bindings from names occurring in the code to local and global entities.

Since entities of each of the three categories above – data, code and threads – may contain bindings, there are nine possible binding patterns between computational entities in fully orthogonal object systems. In the full paper we list the binding patterns which we regard as "historic" milestones in the development of persistent system models.We review briefly the evolution of database languages in terms of their binding patterns. We argue that the expressiveness and usability of a database system model is related directly to the orthogonality of its binding patterns and that, in retrospect, many ad-hoc binding restrictions found in database systems are simply based on the choice of an improper implementation technology.

3 Programming with persistent threads

We propose a next step in the evolution of database languages by introducing the concept of first-class bindings to threads. The concept of threads (continuations, sessions, running transactions) is either non-existent or only implicitly available in today's database systems. We argue that an explicit and orthogonal handling of threads naturally leads to the concept of persistent threads, a systems abstraction suitable for novel high-level models for long-term activity management.

While threads managed by a DBMS scheduler are volatile (they are limited to the lifetime of their corresponding operating system processes), a limited form of persistent threads can be found in the (single-user) persistent higher-order systems Napier88 (see Chapter 1.1.3) and PQuest [4] that have an atomic *stabilize* operation. This operation can be called anywhere inside a program to define a consistent persistent system state. This state not only consists of the global database state variables but also includes the state of the program evaluator. If a system crash occurs during program execution, the execution can be resumed in the state valid at the last *stabilize* operation.

procedure *p(x:Int)* = **begin** *stabilize(), print("leave p, x=", x)* **end**
procedure *main()* = **begin** *print("call p"), p(3), print("; end")* **end**

For example, assuming that during the execution of *main* the system crashes after returning from *p*. On system restart, program execution would resume with the first statement after the *stabilize* operation, and the output would be *leave p, x=3; end.*

We illustrate how threads fit as first-class computational entities into the persistent object system Tycoon. In Tycoon, computational entities (data, code, threads) are either bound in the scope of individual programs or in the scope of persistent modules. The execution of a Tycoon program code *c* invoked from an operating-system shell leads to the creation and execution of a Tycoon thread bound to *c* in an initial environment that contains C→D bindings from all module names imported by *c* to corresponding linked persistent module values.

A thread is a first-class entity in Tycoon – it can be passed as a function argument, returned from a function, bound to a name in the scope of a persistent module, exported to a portable data file, or sent across a communication channel. Users or applications at the operating-system level can create independent Tycoon threads running against a shared set of persistent modules. Conceptually, the computational entities of all Tycoon threads and modules reside in a common persistent object store. This seamless integration of volatile and persistent store simplifies the access to databases represented as persistent modules. Furthermore, it facilitates the exchange of data, code and threads between threads via shared variables. These variables are bound in the scope of persistent modules and are typically protected by synchronization mechanisms like transactional locks, semaphores, monitors, or message queues.

The definition of persistence has to be revised because first-class threads are generalized from volatile to persistent. In addition to all persistent modules also all active threads act as "roots of persistence". Moreover, the transitive reachability rule introduced in section 2 has to be extended to also include T→C, T→D and T→T bindings.

Having threads as computational entities in a database language, programmers can benefit from the potential of multi-threaded programming [7]. By making a thread reachable from persistent data (persistent modules) and by checkpointing the state of the persistent store it becomes possible to protect long-running activities from system failures. After a crash, the thread can be restarted explicitly in the state that was valid at the last checkpoint.

More importantly, persistent threads support directly an activity-oriented style of information system modelling as promoted by scripts, by process-centered specifications, or by (visual) process languages of work flow management tools. The full paper shows a programming example using the Tycoon Language (see Chapter 1.1.1) that exploits persistent threads.

4 On thread implementation and formalization

Several important requirements on persistent thread implementations differ substantially from volatile thread implementations, for example:

- Thread state representations have to be made relocatable and portable in the sense that states need to be abstractly interpretable without reference to a specific machine architecture (e.g. SPARC register files).
- It is desirable to have automatic garbage collection that reclaims the storage of terminated or orphaned threads.
- It is necessary to formalize in sufficient detail the effects of thread execution on shared entities in the persistent store, in particular, if these entities have a complex structure. Only then reliable support can be provided for concurrency, recovery, or garbage collection.

- Store access in distributed persistent memory has different performance characteristics than store access in centralized shared-memory architectures.

In the full paper we first report on our implementation of persistent threads. We then sketch thread formalization with a clear emphasis on abstract representations of machine code (Tycoon Machine Language, TML, see Chapter 2.3.5), machine states and on explicit modelling of machine-store interactions (Tycoon Store Protocol, TSP, see Chapter 2.2.4). A complete definition of the Tycoon thread evaluation semantics is given in [3].

5 Concluding remarks

It should be noted that persistent threads are an expressive and efficient, but rather low-level concept for the management of cooperative activities. Therefore, we are currently investigating related database synchronization and communication models that have been proposed in the literature [2,8,1] and how such models can be realized as polymorphic libraries encapsulating Tycoon's persistent threads. This approach to a flexible reconciliation of system and user needs has proved to be highly successful in modern programming and operating environments which offer several higher-level models like monitors, ACID transactions, transactional RPCs and communicating processes on a common, standardized thread abstraction available on multiple system platforms.

Acknowledgements. This research is supported by ESPRIT Basic Research, Project FIDE, #6309 and by a grant from the German Israeli Foundation for Research and Development (*bulk data classification*, I-183 060).

References

1. Y. Breibart, A. Deacon, H.-J. Schek, A. Sheth, and G. Weikum. Merging application-centric and data-centric approaches to support transaction-oriented multi-system workflows. *ACM SIGMOD Record*, 12(3):23–30, September 1993.
2. H. Garcia-Molina and K. Salem. Sagas. In *Proceedings of the ACM-SIGMOD International Conference on Management of Data, San Francisco, California*, pages 249–259, May 1987.
3. F. Matthes. *Persistente Objektsysteme: Integrierte Datenbankentwicklung und Programmerstellung*. Springer-Verlag, 1993. (In German.).
4. F. Matthes, R. Müller, and J.W. Schmidt. Object stores as servers in persistent programming environments – the p-quest experience. FIDE Technical Report Series FIDE/92/48, FIDE Project Coordinator, Department of Computing Sciences, University of Glasgow, Glasgow G128QQ, July 1992.
5. F. Matthes and J.W. Schmidt. System construction in the Tycoon environment: Architectures, interfaces and gateways. In P.P. Spies, editor, *Proceedings of Euro-Arch'93 Congress*, pages 301–317. Springer-Verlag, October 1993.

6. F. Matthes and J.W. Schmidt. Persistent threads. In *Proceedings of the Twentieth International Conference on Very Large Data Bases, VLDB*, pages 403–414, Santiago, Chile, September 1994.
7. G. Nelson, editor. *Systems programming with Modula-3*. Series in innovative technology. Prentice Hall, Englewood Cliffs, New Jersey, 1991.
8. A. Reuter. ConTracts: A means for extending control beyond transaction boundaries. In *Third International Workshop on High Performance Transaction Systems*, 1989.

Part 2

Persistent Support Systems: Introduction and Overview

Florian Matthes

Technical University Hamburg-Harburg, Harburger Schloßstraße 20, D-21071 Hamburg, Germany

The goal of the persistent support systems developed in FIDE is to improve the construction, maintenance and operation of *persistent application systems* (PAS). A PAS is a software system that gives its users a flexible, problem-oriented and safe access to large sets of long-lived objects of application-specific types.

Due to technological and commercial developments there is an ever-increasing demand for persistent application systems that have to handle *non-standard* object types, such as texts (electronic mail, text retrieval, "intelligent" text manipulation), two- and three-dimensional graphics (CAD and geographic information systems), digitized raster images (picture and font databases, fax manager, character recognition software), voice data, or even image sequences (presentation software, scene analysis). Moreover, persistent application systems have to be implemented also in PC-based, interactive, networked, distributed, or semi-autonomous system environments. As a consequence of their longevity, PAS have to survive even under drastic changes of their underlying hardware and software platforms. As it is widely recognised today [4,8,12,1,11], classical database technology provides insufficient system support for these new object types and changing system environments.

In addition to the classical problems of large-scale application development, developers of a PAS are faced with three PAS-specific requirements:

Generic Programming and Data Modelling: PAS are typically characterised by highly repetitive algorithmic and structural patterns (set-oriented queries, integrity constraints, generic data structures, etc.). Therefore, many commercial tools utilise generator techniques to derive automatically stereotyped program fragments (form definitions, format conversions, sorting routines, iterators, etc.) from parameterised, high-level descriptions. But by no means all of their operations fit these regular patterns, and therefore, it is necessary to facilitate their use from general purpose languages, such as those presented in Part 1 of this book, as well.

Persistent Storage: The primary task in a persistent application system is the manipulation of the state of long-lived data objects shared by multiple, possibly concurrently executing applications. In advanced persistent application systems it is advantageous to be able to store, share and modify also program objects ("methods", "scripts") and programs in the process of being executed ("workflows", "activities", "processes") as first-class data objects.

External Server Integration: The buzzword "open architectures" is of particular relevance for persistent application systems since it is often necessary to interact with external devices (screens, printers, keyboards, pointing devices, scanners, CD-ROMs, modems, fax machines, etc.) and external servers (window libraries, RPC libraries, directory services, etc.) for data acquisition, data presentation, data transfer and data integration purposes.

In the following, we first sketch how these requirements are met partially in third- and fourth-generation languages, and we then outline FIDE's contributions to PAS construction in comparison with these more traditional approaches.

Low-Level Server Access from Third-Generation Languages

The majority of today's information systems are implemented in third-generation languages (COBOL, FORTRAN, C, Pascal). A severe limitation of these languages is their inability to capture correctly the genericity inherent even in simple persistent object models. For example, the relational data model supports the definition of unary, binary, ternary, ... relations over various domains and it includes generic operations over relation variables. These operations cannot be captured adequately by any of the commercial programming languages mentioned above [3].

As a consequence of this conceptual limitation, developers of database programming interfaces like Embedded SQL [7] restrict themselves to the least common denominator of all 3GLs and handle any information interchange via strings, addresses and untyped byte arrays that are transferred at the smallest possible granularity (attribute-wise) between application programs and the database systems. A similar situation can be observed at the interface between programming languages and (graphical) user interfaces.

The resulting POS scenario using 3GLs is depicted in Fig. 1: The overall functionality of a particular POS is provided by a coordinated manipulation of numerous heterogeneous objects on different media (D: database objects, P: program objects, S: screen objects, etc.). Objects on different servers are subject to server-specific naming, typing, lifetime, and binding rules (indicated by different line styles in Fig. 1) while inter-server communication takes place at a low level of abstraction using simple, machine-oriented protocols.

A crucial advantage of such a loose server coupling is the *openness* of the application development environment. If required, new servers can be integrated freely as libraries into existing persistent object systems. Furthermore, call interfaces provide a minimal common ground for data exchange between independently developed services and they also constitute a starting point for data abstraction and component exchangeability.

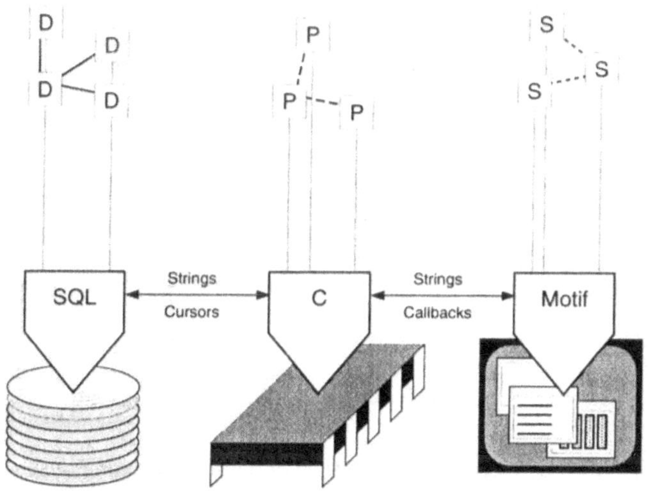

Fig. 1. Narrow and unsafe server interfaces in third-generation languages

Server Integration in Fourth-Generation Languages

Fourth-generation languages recognise the need for a uniform, safe and application-oriented development environment across a variety of servers and above the minimal interoperation level of strings and cursors. As depicted in Fig. 2, a well-designed 4GL provides high-level naming, typing and binding mechanisms for objects on different media (on disk, in memory, and on screen) and thereby eliminates a substantial amount of the low-level, repetitive data-conversion and data-transfer code found in 3GL applications. 4GLs are tailored to the specific requirements of traditional, commercial database applications:

Functional requirements: record- and set-oriented data modeling, data manipulation, data storage and data display; generic operations (search, iterate, insert, delete, update, format, display, validate, ...) applicable uniformly to record and set objects of different component structures.

Operational requirements: persistent storage of data, application code, integrity constraints and user-interface definitions; efficient manipulation of data on secondary storage; integration into transactional multi-user systems.

Modal requirements: interactive user-interfaces, access to pre-compiled queries and update transactions; support for incremental system evolution (e.g. schema changes); provision for *ad-hoc* queries.

Examples of relational 4GLs include Ingres-4GL [6], PL-SQL [10], Visual Basic for Microsoft Access and Informix-4GL [5]. Furthermore, several object-oriented database systems are shipped with 4GL languages to simplify application development (e.g. O_2SQL and CO_2 for O_2 [2]). Several client-server programming languages like Visual Basic or Power Builder can also be classified as 4GLs. Practical

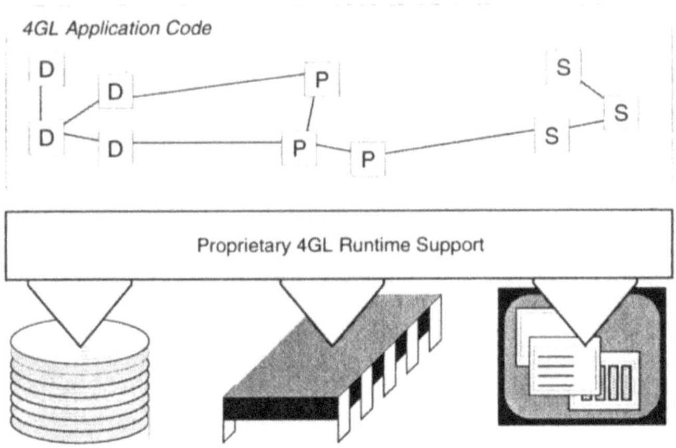

Fig. 2. Server integration in proprietary fourth-generation languages

experience shows that 4GL constitute a significant advance towards achieving faster software development, improved long-term software maintainability, better software portability, and even enhanced execution efficiency for specialised applications (e.g. queries) when compared with hand-coded third-generation language solutions such as written in C or COBOL [9].

There are, however, some severe limitations to current 4GL languages that hamper their success in today's open, continually evolving system environments: 4GLs are deeply integrated into proprietary DBMSs and it is therefore impossible to move 4GL applications from one DBMS to another. This situation is in sharp contrast to 3GL applications using standardised programming and database languages (e.g. C and OpenSQL). Moreover, applications developed in 4GLs do not scale well due to a lack of appropriate typing and modularisation support such as that found in Ada, C++, Modula-2 or Eiffel. On the system level, 4GL often incur an unnecessary system overhead since it is impossible to "downscale" the extensive 4GL runtime support (form management, event management, query support, report generation, transaction management, ...) to just the functionality needed by a particular application. When a problem does not match the patterns of computation captured by the 4GL models, the cost of coding the solution can rise very rapidly.

Support Systems for Persistent Higher-Order Languages

Most of the above 4GL limitations reflect the deficiencies of the commercially available persistent system technology. This technology simply does not support the abstractions required for a more flexible, systematic 4GL service integration.

To overcome these limitations and to achieve 4GL openness and extensibility, FIDE undertook the integrated effort of not only developing higher-order languages with appropriate abstraction capabilities (see Part 1), but also of designing persistent

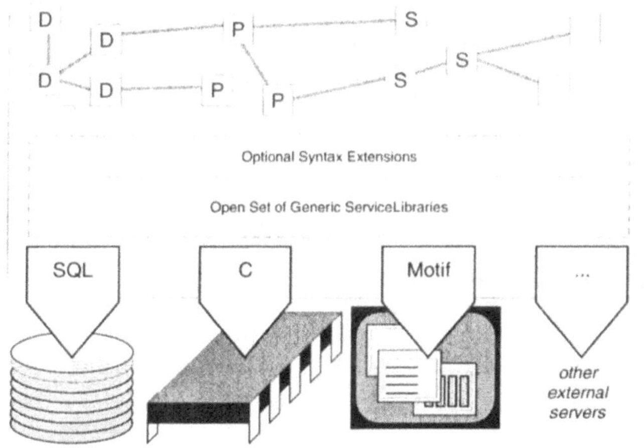

Fig. 3. Scalable application frameworks in persistent higher-order languages

system architectures (Chapter 2.1), realising object store managers (Chapter 2.2) and experimenting with novel implementation techniques (Chapter 2.3).

The FIDE system support architectures and their implementation techniques are influenced heavily by *language concepts* which are described in more detail in Part 1. For example, orthogonal persistence requires a uniform and highly efficient management of volatile and persistent data, higher-orderness requires a uniform persistent storage of data, code and threads, genericity calls for polymorphic value representations, and reflection leads to a tight integration of the PAS development and execution environment.

Fig. 3 sketches the architecture of a PAS implemented in a persistent higher-order language. Similar to a 4GL, the relevant application objects (persistent database objects, volatile program objects, virtual screen objects, etc.) are subject to uniform naming, typing and binding rules, indicated by uniform line styles connecting the corresponding symbols in Fig. 3. In contrast to a 4GL, most of these object types are not built into the base language but are provided by an open set of libraries that are an integral part of the programming environment. Some of the libraries are simply interfaces to external services (database systems, language compilers, GUI toolkits), other libraries provide functionality that is implemented in the persistent higher-order language itself (see Chapter 3.1.4). Furthermore, Fig. 3 indicates that access to some of the libraries may be supported by tailored syntactic forms provided by the persistent languages or by application-specific syntax extensions.

References

1. M. Atkinson, F. Bancilhon, D. De Witt, K. Dittrich, D. Maier, and S. Zdonik. The object-oriented database system manifesto. In *Deductive and Object-oriented Databases*. Elsevier Science Publishers, Amsterdam, Netherlands, 1990.

2. F. Bancilhon, C. Delobel, and P. Kanellakis. *Building an Object-Oriented Database System: The Story of O_2*. Morgan Kaufmann Publishers, 1992.
3. P. Bunemann, J. Hirschberg, and D. Root. A Codasyl interface to Pascal and Ada. In *Proceedings of the Second British National Conference on Databases*. Cambridge University Press, 1982.
4. R.G.G. Cattell. Next-generation database systems. *Communications of the ACM*, 34(10), October 1991.
5. Informix Software Corp. Informix-4GL reference manual. Technical report, Informix Software Corp., 1986.
6. Ingres Corporation. INGRES ABF/4GL reference manual for the UNIX and VMS operating systems. Technical Report INGRES Release 6.3, Ingres Corporation, 1080 Marina Village Parkway, Almeda, California, November 1989.
7. Ingres Corporation. INGRES embedded SQL companion guide for C. Technical Report INGRES UNIX Release 6.3, Ingres Corporation, 1080 Marina Village Parkway, Almeda, CA 94501, December 1990.
8. F. Manola, S. Heiler, D. Georgakopoulos, M. Hornick, and M. Brodie. Distributed object management. *International Journal of Intelligent and Cooperative Information Systems*, 1(1), March 1992.
9. V.M. Matos and P.J. Jalics. An experimental analysis of the performance of 4GL tools on PCs. *Communications of the ACM*, 32(11):1340–1352, 1989.
10. Oracle Corporation. PL/SQL user's guide and reference, version 1.0. Technical Report Part No. 800-V1.0, Oracle Corporation, June 1991.
11. M. Stonebraker, L.A. Rowe, B. Lindsay, J. Gray, M. Carey, M. Brodie, and P. Bernstein. Third-generation data base system manifesto. *ACM SIGMOD Record*, 19, September 1990.
12. S.B. Zdonik and D. Maier. *Readings in Object Oriented Database Management Systems*. Morgan Kaufmann Publishers, 1989.

Section 2.1

Architecture and Abstract Machines: Introduction and State of the Art

Malcolm P. Atkinson

Department of Computing Science, University of Glasgow, Glasgow G12 8QQ, Scotland

Abstract. The search for an appropriate architecture for Persistent Systems is still in its infancy and can be compared with the original exploration of operating system architectures. Indeed it is not clear whether a favoured architecture will emerge or whether there will remain a variety of architectures.

In a recent paper [6] the following classes of architecture were discussed:

Combined Existing Systems Here an existing storage technology and an existing programming language are combined re-using varying amounts of existing knowledge, designs and implementations.

Extended Existing Systems In these architectures an existing technology is chosen to provide one of these two major components and then extended to encompass more of the functionality of the other.

Systems Based on an Integrated Design Combined requirements are identified and a system is then designed and built "from scratch" to fulfill those requirements. However, this construction utilises conventional operating systems and potentially other pre-existing technology.

Persistent Worlds The constructors of these systems start with a few primitives to provide persistence and build from these. In this category we find work on novel persistent operating systems [24,15].

It may be useful to use this classification to study the current $FIDE_2$ work and its relationship with other work. By definition, the work of $FIDE_2$ Fully Integrated Data Environment, is directed towards the final two classes. In practice, all the $FIDE_2$ implementations end up in the third category.

1 Architectures in $FIDE_2$ systems

The original work on DBPL (Chapter 2.1.2) had aspects of the first two classes: it derived from an attempt to synthesise from existing relational systems [32] and it was implemented by successive extensions and changes to Modula-2. The recent systems developed by that group (Chapters 1.1.1, 1.4.2, 2.1.4, 2.2.4 and 2.3.5) are an evolution of Quest [11] but are essentially a design and implementation according to the model of Integrated Design. Even here, work to link these systems with existing technology, relational databases for example [25] or to provide open technology [26] can be viewed both as a route to incorporate legacy systems and as an implementation strategy combining technologies. This example, taken from just one

$FIDE_2$ partner's work serves to show that the architectures of actual systems are not simply classified.

The work at Pisa developing Fibonacci (Chapters 1.1.2, 1.3.1 and 1.4.3) is clearly in the third category of architectures. Nevertheless, it takes a predominantly language approach with the provision of orthogonal persistence being considered a normal language requirement. This provision is made by utilising the FLASK store from St Andrews [28] (Chapter 2.3.1). That store was designed as a general purpose platform for supporting persistent languages (Chapter 2.2.1).

The development of Napier88 has consistently been within the third class of these architectures (Chapter 1.1.3). The integrated design has led to pressures to explore various implementation strategies and a variety of stores [9] with FLASK being the current platform (Chapter 2.3.1).

The PIOS architecture demonstrates a different emphasis within the overall style of $FIDE_2$ systems (Chapters 2.2.2 and 2.3.3). In the three systems introduced so far it is considered reasonable to develop a simple object store that accommodates all data structures. Access methods and optimisations are then performed in the higher-level language parts of the system. A good example is the query management technology developed in Tycoon (Chapter 2.3.5). PIOS takes a different architectural view and builds some of the access structures into the lower-level object store (Chapter 2.3.3) but uses the FLASK store as its lowest-level substrate. The INRIA group have also explored similar strategies (Chapter 2.3.4) utilising the commercial object store O_2 [16]. The trade-off that is being explored in these experiments is whether intimate knowledge of the physical storage structure is more exploitable than information about the application load.

The nested transactional stores developed at INRIA and Glasgow [21,12] is perhaps nearest to the fourth class of architectures (Chapters 2.2.3 and 2.3.2). Here is an attempt to build a new lowest substrate on which a variety of persistent object stores and orthogonally persistent languages can be supported. However, it still depends on a component, Mach, that was conceived with conventional loads in mind. More recently, the techniques developed for this store have been re-engineered to work with more conventional operating systems (as illustrated by [13,1]) and can now be applied to the third class of architecture as well.

2 Persistent Foundations

The $FIDE_2$ research has not attempted to build from the foundations, not because we think that unimportant but because limited resources would not permit us to explore in this direction at the same time as exploring high-level integration issues. We have, nevertheless, sketched the architectures which we would envisage if such a strategy was followed [7] (Chapter 2.1.1). Others are exploring this route, for example, Rosenberg's group in Sydney [14] and Dearle's group in Stirling [15] with both operating system and hardware research. One of their planned test loads is Napier88.

3 Commercially Available Architectures

It is interesting to contrast these architectures with those in use in commercial object stores. The majority of commercial object stores have started with a language, often C++ or SmallTalk, and have augmented it with facilities to provide persistence. Many cases are of the form of an additional library based on a persistent object class. This has the advantage of leaving the language and existing code unperturbed, but has drawbacks regarding safety, application programming complexity and performance.

Others have taken similar languages and revised their implementation to give persistent versions, this are again examples of the second class of architectures. This can eliminate all but the first problem with the library variant of the extension architecture. That problem remains because languages like C++ lack type safety and so programs have the capability to damage long-lived data unconnected with them.

A solution to this is emerging as type-safe variants of C++ such as Java are developed [22] and persistent platforms for it are implemented [27]. There is something of a rush to deliver ODMG compliant bindings for Java [18] which is an example which falls between the two architectures *Combined Existing Systems* and *Systems Based on an Integrated Design*. For here, there is an attempt to re-use existing object stores and Java itself is fixed. This dissonance shows through in the *current* treatment of static variables which are treated as transient, and in arrangements for locking, concurrency, etc. On the other hand, the binding has been carefully rethought, so that modelling and operations can be expressed entirely in Java without recourse to ODL and OQL.

The first architecture in its pure form is also represented in Java. There is the standard JDBC that allows Java programs to interact via SQL with relational databases. Various aids to forming this combination have been built. Bridges simplify the connection to databases and hide variations between different RDBMS's facilities. Automated mapping technology then helps Java programmers avoid having to be too knowledgeable about the RDB world. One form of this automatically generates Java classes that are surrogates for the conceptual entities percieved to underly the relations. The Java programmer uses these without having to pay much attention to the hidden relational system. This is clearly a productivity enhancer for those that need to utilise legacy systems.

There are also systems that provide persistence for Java by automatically mapping the Java classes to relations and then using JDBC [17]. Again the goal is to minimise the attention that programmers need to pay to the fact that an RDB is being used to hold their data. It is a strategy to provide orthogonal persistence for Java entirely on top of the standard Java VM [33] and hence to retain applet mobility.

Starting from relational systems both of the first classes are represented. For example, the use of BLOBs to hold collections of C++ objects is a straightforward example of combining two existing systems [31]. In other cases the relational system continues to be extended with programming facilities, so, for example, the latest versions of ORACLE have an interactive language that permits more programming operations than earlier ones.

O_2 is an interesting case, as it is built as an independent data model along the lines of category three architectures. It utilises detailed physical knowledge to build efficient object and list type access mechanisms and uses a procedural interface to translate between the O_2 data model and any programming language's data types. This allows multi-lingual applications to be built around an O_2 database service.

Readers interested in a further survey are referred to [6] and to [34].

4 Specialised Architectures

It is clear that in extreme cases, particular architectures are required for object stores. For example, service commitments with multi-media require special caching arrangements, but have particular knowledge about the VCR-simulation operations [8,29]. Similarly, when large volumes of data are collected but not updated, special architectures are appropriate [20]. The strategy of integration taken by $FIDE_2$ militates against such special architectures since, once a general purpose language or open system is offered the application builders may impose a wide variety of loads. It still remains a challenge to develop adequate engineering, and perhaps adaptive strategies [23].

4.1 Store Interfaces

Among the various issues in persistent object system design is how to partition the total task. That is, what interfaces are appropriate and what should the functionality of the partitions be. There is general agreement within $FIDE_2$ that there should be an abstract store interface. However, the level of that interface and the information that may flow across it is varied. It can in principle vary from the store administration data structures being known to the compiler writers to every store operation including field access and update being via a procedural interface, as in the case of O_2 above.

The first extreme locks together compiler and store development, but may provided the highest performance as many store interface calls can be optimised away. The Haskell and standard ML compiler writers have explored this strategy though not with persistent stores which normally contain data of higher value [30,2,19]. This approach also leaves the long-term data vulnerable to compiler errors and makes the store language specific.

The second extreme normally has high cpu costs due to the path length across the interface and repeated traversals of that interface. Methods of ameliorating this cost result in some intermediate form of interface. In the FLASK/Napier88 store some aspects of the store are revealed via privileged procedures available to the Napier88 system builders. Care has been taken to avoid making the store language specific. In the Tycoon store, there is a general interface intended to encapsulate the provisions of independently developed stores. If the operations across these interfaces are on high-volume bulk objects the interface overhead becomes unimportant.

5 Abstract Machine Interfaces

The three $FIDE_2$ languages all depend on an abstract machine to separate implementation details from the language analysis system and to achieve machine independence through a precise definition. All three have to accommodate persistent higher-order procedures and both Napier88 and Tycoon have to accommodate reflection (Chapter 1.2.1), persistent processes and inter-process communication. This combination leads to considerable complexity in the abstract machine design which led us to conclude that a common abstract machine was not feasible for the time being as it would have inhibited experimentation. However, this was partly due to the limited resources available in a research context. The large number of languages that are being mapped to the Java virtual machine [33] indicates that given the resources a mapping can be constructed.

The Tycoon abstract machine (Chapter 2.1.4) is based on the continuation passing style [3]. The Napier88 compiler utilises a different strategy to minimise the unnecessary costs of frame formation (Chapter 2.1.3).

The generation of acceptable quality machine code from these abstract machines faces several difficulties due to the combination of reflection, persistence and higher-order procedures [10].

6 Summary

The architectures and intermediate interfaces of particular research groups have reached sufficient maturity that systems of good quality can be built and used for extensive application programming. But in each case this is achieved via the exploration of a particular locality in the space of possible architectures and interfaces. It is now necessary to carry out a synthesis of these experiments and to explore other regions in order to provide a useful map for future excursions in this space.

References

1. L. Amsaleg, M. Franklin, and O. Gruber. Efficient incremental garbage collection for workstation/server database systems. Technical Report FIDE/94/110, ESPRIT Basic Research Action, Project Number 6309—$FIDE_2$, 1994.
2. Andrew W. Appel. Simple generational garbage collection and stack allocation. *Software Practice & Experience*, 19(2):171–183, March 88.
3. A.W. Appel. *Compiling with Continuations*. Cambridge University Press, 1992.
4. M.P. Atkinson, editor. *Fully Integrated Data Environments*. Springer-Verlag, 1995.
5. M.P. Atkinson, V. Benzaken, and D. Maier, editors. *Persistent Object Systems*. Workshops in Computing. Springer-Verlag in collaboration with the British Computer Society, 1994. Proceedings of the Sixth International Workshop on Persistent Object Systems (Tarascon, Provence, France, 5th–9th September 1994).
6. M.P. Atkinson and R. Morrison. Orthogonal persistent object systems. *VLDB Journal*, 4(3), 1995.

7. M.P. Atkinson, D.I.K. Sjøberg, and R. Morrison. Managing change in persistent object systems. In *JSSST International Symposium on Object Technologies for Advanced Software (Kanazawa, Japan, 4th–6th November 1993)*, 1993. Invited paper.
8. S. Blott, H. Kaufmann, L. Relly, and H.-J. Schek. Buffering long externally-defined objects. In Atkinson et al. [5], pages 45–59. Proceedings of the Sixth International Workshop on Persistent Object Systems (Tarascon, Provence, France, 5th–9th September 1994).
9. A.L. Brown, G. Mainetto, F. Matthes, R. Mueller, and D.J. McNally. An open system architecture for a persistent object store. In R. Morrison and M.P. Atkinson (minitrack coordinators), editors, *Proceedings of the Twenty-Fifth Hawaii International Conference on System Sciences, Volume II, Software Technology, Persistent Object Systems*, pages 766–776, 1992.
10. S.J. Bushell, A. Dearle, A.L. Brown, and F.A. Vaughan. Using C as a compiler target language for native code generation in persistent systems. In Atkinson et al. [5], pages 164–183. Proceedings of the Sixth International Workshop on Persistent Object Systems (Tarascon, Provence, France, 5th–9th September 1994).
11. L. Cardelli. Typeful programming. Digital Systems Research Center Report 45, Digital Eqipment Corp., Systems Research Centre, 130 Lytton Avenue, Palo Alto, Calif., USA, May 1989.
12. L. Daynès and O. Gruber. Nested actions in Eos. In A. Albano and R. Morrison, editors, *Persistent Object Systems: Implementation and Use*, Workshops in Computing, pages 144–163. Springer-Verlag in collaboration with the British Computer Society, 1992. Proceedings of the Fifth International Workshop on Persistent Object Systems (San Miniato, Italy, 1st–4th September 1992).
13. L. Daynès, O. Gruber, and P. Valduriez. Locking in OODBMS client supporting nested transactions. In Atkinson [4], chapter 2.3.2.
14. A. Dearle, R. di Bona, J. Farrow, F. Henskens, D. Hulse, A. Lindström, S. Norris, J. Rosenberg, and F. Vaughan. Protection in Grasshopper: A persistent operating system. In Atkinson et al. [5], pages 60–78. Proceedings of the Sixth International Workshop on Persistent Object Systems (Tarascon, Provence, France, 5th–9th September 1994).
15. A. Dearle, R. di Bona, J. Farrow, F. Henskens, A. Lindstrom, J. Rosenberg, and F. Vaughan. Grasshopper: An orthogonally persistent operating system. *Computer Systems*, 7(3):289–312, 1994.
16. O. Deux et al. The O_2 system. *Communications of the ACM*, 34(10):34–49, 1991.
17. Souza dos Santos C. and Theroude E. Persistent java. In *Proceedings of the First International Workshop on Persistence and Java, Drymen, Scotland, Sept. 1996*, M/S 29-112, 2550 Garcia Avenue, Mountain View, CA 94043, USA, 1997. Sun Microsystems Laboratories.
18. Cattel R. (ed). *The Object Database Standard — ODMG-97.* Morgan Kaufmann, 1997.
19. Marcelo J. R. Goncalves and Andrew W. Appel. Cache performance of fast-allocating programs. Technical Report CS-TR-482-94, Princeton University, December 1994.
20. R.L. Grossman, N. Araujo, X. Qin, and W. Xu. Managing physical folios of objects between nodes. In Atkinson et al. [5], pages 217–234. Proceedings of the Sixth International Workshop on Persistent Object Systems (Tarascon, Provence, France, 5th–9th September 1994).
21. O. Gruber. *Eos, an Environment for Persistent and Distributed Applications over a Shared Object Space.* PhD thesis, Université Pierre et Marie Curie, Paris VI, France, December 1992.
22. Gosling J., Joy B., and Steele G. *The Java Language Specification.* The Java Series. Addison-Wesley, 1996.

23. A. Kemper and D. Kossmann. Adaptable pointer swizzling stategies in object bases: Design, realization, and quantitative analysis. *VLDB Journal*, 4(3), 1995.
24. J. Liedtke. Improving IPC by kernel design. In *Proceedings of the Fourteenth ACM Symposium on Operating System Principles (5th–8th December 1993, Asheville, NC)*, pages 175–187. Association for Computing Machinery, 1993.
25. F. Matthes, A. Rudloff, J.W. Schmidt, and K. Subieta. A gateway from DBPL to Ingres. In T. Risch W. Litwin, editor, *Applications of Databases, First International Conference, ADB-94*, volume 819 of *Lecture Notes in Computer Science*, pages 365–380, Vadstena, Sweden, June 1994. Springer-Verlag.
26. F. Matthes, G. Schroeder, and J.W. Schmidt. Tycoon: A scalable and interoperable persistent system environment. In Atkinson [4], chapter 2.1.4.
27. Atkinson M.P., Daynès L., Jordan M.J., Printezis T., and Spence S. An orthogonally persistent java. *ACM SIGMOD Record*, 25(4), December 1996.
28. D.S. Munro, R.C.H. Connor, R. Morrison, S. Scheuerl, and D.W. Stemple. Concurrent shadow paging in the Flask architecture. In Atkinson et al. [5], pages 16–42. Proceedings of the Sixth International Workshop on Persistent Object Systems (Tarascon, Provence, France, 5th–9th September 1994).
29. B. Özden, A. Biliris, R. Rastogi, and A. Silberschatz. A low-cost storage server for movie on demand databases. In *Proceedings of the Twentieth International Conference on Very Large Data Bases (Santiago, Chile, September 1994)*, pages 594–605, 1994.
30. S.L. Peyton-Jones. Implementing lazy functional languages on stock hardware: the spineless tagless G-machine. *Journal of Functional Programming*, 2(2):127–202, April 1992.
31. B. Reinwald, S. Dessloch, M. Carey, T. Lehman, H. Pirahesh, and V. Srinivasan. Making real data persistent: Initial experiences with SMRC. In Atkinson et al. [5], pages 202–216. Proceedings of the Sixth International Workshop on Persistent Object Systems (Tarascon, Provence, France, 5th–9th September 1994).
32. J.W. Schmidt. Some high level language constructs for data of type relation. *ACM Transactions on Database Systems*, 2(3):247–261, September 1977.
33. Linholm T. and Yellin F. *The Java Virtual Machine*. The Java Series. Addison-Wesley, 1996.
34. F. Vaughan. *Implementation of Distributed Orthogonal Persistence Using Virtual Memory*. PhD thesis, University of Adelaide, Faculty of Mathematical and Computer Sciences, 1994.

Chapter 2.1.1

Persistent Foundations for Scalable Multi-Paradigmal Systems

Malcolm P. Atkinson

Department of Computing Science, University of Glasgow, Glasgow G12 8QQ, Scotland

Abstract. Problems with the inconsistent behaviour of system construction components for building large and long-lived application systems are identified. They make the programmer's task harder and the user's world more confusing in the same way that the disharmonies between programming languages and databases did. Persistent programming languages overcame those disharmonies.

This paper challenges researchers to design and build a common substrate to the construction components. The construction components would be re-built using the substrate to achieve consistent behaviour. Application systems would then use this new family of construction components. The substrate, called the Scalable Persistent Foundation promises several advantages: consistent application system behaviour even when under stress, accelerated application system building and maintenance, genuine longevity of application systems and improved operational efficiency.

The search for a design and implementation of this foundation will provoke debate about what behaviour, in the context of distribution, overload, failure, change, concurrency, transactions, safety, security, etc. is wanted.

Experiments using short-lived computations and small-scale systems are rarely useful in predicting large-scale and long-term behaviour. Therefore large-scale apparatus and long-term experimental procedures are required.

1 Introduction

The concept of persistence was introduced [3] as a means of simplifying the task of programming. In essence the task of programming had not been simplified by the introduction of database systems as intended[1], instead *application programmers* had an increasingly difficult conceptual task managing the eternal triangle (see Figure 1). They had to match a mapping between the modelled system and the programs with a pair of mappings: the mapping from modelled system to database and thence from database to program. If users are to be convinced that the system is operating correctly then the operations on a database conducted directly and those conducted via the program have to appear consistent.

Achieving this consistency for a few simple programs operating against a *simple* (relational?) database was moderately easy provided the mappings were simple. As

[1] Other benefits had been achieved, such as a basis for physical independence and a methodology for large system construction by incrementally binding programs to the central repository of data, which we revisit later in this paper.

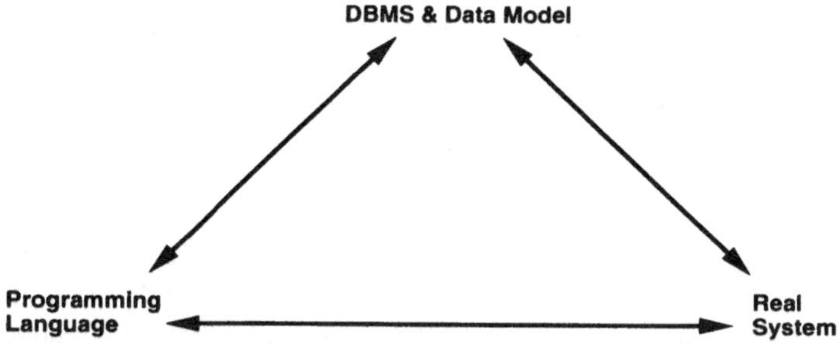

Fig. 1. A programmer has to keep three mappings consistent

soon as there were many programs or the models, programs and mappings became complex, this illusion of consistency became almost unachievable.

In the previous case there are two *constructional components* used to build the application: the programming language and the DBMS. If only one constructional component, a *persistent programming language* is used only one mapping is maintained — a considerable simplification of the conceptual context. This is illustrated in Figure 2 and further described in Section 2. Persistent systems were proposed that used automated data management techniques to maintain the one model across all the time scales encountered. Medium-scale demonstrations showed that programming was simplified and that application systems using them were easier to understand. A summary of relevant work is given in Section 4.

Fig. 2. Persistence requires a single mapping

Fundamental to the implementation of all persistent systems is the management of identity (references) and a consistent treatment of program and data. In order to have simple semantics and the potential for large system construction, programs must have the same semantics however long they have been stored in the system and whatever the lifetime of the data on which they operate. An illustration of the engineering issues these requirements raise is given in Section 5. The challenges encountered are typical of any database management system.

It can be argued that any persistent programming language provides an object-oriented database, though some definitions of object-orientation would restrict the set of persistent programming languages (PPLs) that provide OODBs to those with inclusion polymorphism), i.e. subtyping or bounded parametric polymorphism [31]. Certainly the experiences of trying to implement persistent programming languages has relevance to object-oriented systems and vice versa. On the other hand some object-oriented database systems are not true persistent systems as they require different treatment of long-lived and short-lived data. The code to manipulate a long-lived object's data is different in some respects from code applied to transient data or the types available in the two contexts differ. This re-introduces the dual model problems; essentially there are now lots of little triangles to manage rather than one big one.

A major concern in large-scale and long-lived system construction is safety. This requires protection which in most persistent programming languages is provided via a strong type system (that is a type system that cannot be evaded, not necessarily an entirely static one). The strength of this protection depends on a closed world. Any chink might let in a malevolent or erroneous piece of code. Realisation of the full potential of persistent systems requires a transformation in application system building habits that cannot be incremental. These issues are further described in Section 6.

The author has recently been involved in the construction of a large system (HMS), distributed over several hospitals and designed to support health care management [6]. It is probably typical of many large application systems in that it was built using a variety of construction components. One of these was a tailored scripting and control language with persistent tables [61]. But other construction components, for example, a relational system, filing systems, an operating system and a distributed window manager, were also in use. The intention is that for all application programmers (domain experts) and all end-users the illusion of a seamless consistent single system operating on a single HMS model would be maintained. Significant effort was invested by the HMS team who constructed the HMS system software to automate data movement, update propagation, conflicting change notification, distributed databases and queries. This is successful for *most* of the time. The problem is that the illusion is not permanently maintained. The moment a system failure occurs, for example the windowing system mysteriously loses a font on one machine or all the machines in a room stop when a fan fails, the illusion of a consistent system fails catastrophically. It requires a guru with a black belt[2] in systems software to organise a restart quickly i.e. with only a moderate amount of file copying, keyboard activity, etc. The distributed and duplicated databases recover themselves and the scripts still run but other parts of the system don't recover.

It is informative to consider why this is so. An attempt is made to identify the cause of the problem in Section 7. It can be seen as a consequence of attempting to use in combination construction components with different semantics for their preservation and management of data. It is argued that such construction components inevitably have different semantics for their persistence and hence that problems will arise whenever they are stressed. This problem will be manifest in any application system built from heterogeneous construction components, particularly those that are distributed.

An examination of the task of building a complete DBMS for whatever model, a well-engineered PPL or an operating system reveals a certain commonality. It is proposed that by identifying that common substrate and by implementing that once

[2] Matters are usually made *much* worse when a would-be-guru with a green belt attempts to intervene!

as a low-level persistent language with well defined semantics the problem of inconsistent behaviour from construction components will be overcome. A simple solution is not feasible whereby total applications are re-implemented in this persistent language for two reasons:

- existing investment is lost, particularly: the training of programmers, the existing data and the existing software; and
- different construction components and paradigms may be best for different parts of an application.

A two-level architecture, Scalable Persistent Foundations (SPF), is therefore proposed (see Section 8) whereby the traditional construction components are *all re-implemented* in a common persistent programming language, call it LLPL. These components then exhibit their familiar behaviour except with respect to persistence where they all exhibit a common semantics. The applications are then built out of these re-implemented construction components, LLPL and any other components that are made possible by the new architecture such as a variety of programming languages, all of which will have become PPLs, new software engineering tools and extensive libraries relevant to persistent application programming.

This architecture is proposed because:

1. it is more likely to yield understandable contexts for application programming and predictable application system behaviour for users and programmers than alternative architectures;
2. it is necessary if the data currently being committed to Object-Oriented Databases and Persistent System stores is to remain useable over typical application system life-times;
3. it is expected to provide a basis for building construction components more economically, in research initially and when proven, in industry;
4. the attempt to identify its properties will focus the discussion on what common behaviour is required irrespective of whether it is achieved by this or some other architecture;
5. it will draw research in operating systems, database systems, persistent languages and distributed systems into a collaborative effort towards achieving a common goal; and
6. a clearly identified substrate would result in sharply defined demands on hardware architectures, network protocols and operating system micro-kernels.

It is a complete inversion of the approach to disharmony being advocated elsewhere [66]. In those approaches a layer is placed *above* the construction components to try to hide their intrinsic behaviour and expose a consistent composite behaviour. This is a natural short-term approach and is valuable as a mechanism for developing collaborative working in the software industry [59] but the extent to which consistent behaviour and long-term persistence can be achieved in this way is limited, while it does little if anything to simplify the application programmer's task.

The claims of an alternative architecture cannot be trivially evaluated. In the case of a putative architecture for large-scale, long-lived and distributed-application systems this is particularly true. A radically different architecture requires an investigation on the scale of large science to validate its claims. Such an experiment is proposed here (see Section 14). It is an example of a new requirement for experimental facilities and large-scale coordinated research in computing science.

The remainder of this paper is presented in two parts:

1. a brief survey (Sections 2 to 7) of current work in persistent languages aimed at providing the reader with entry points to that work and at filling in the background that motivates the SPF proposal; and
2. a development of the SPF idea, identifying some of the major questions and requirements, leading to a sketch of the proposed experiment and the way in which it might be conducted (see Sections 8 to 14).

This attempt to bring together all the issues concerned with a complete persistent architecture inevitably treats each individual issue cursorily. But it is the juxtaposition of all these issues that is the real challenge for the large and long-term persistent architecture. Individually they may be difficult challenges but not intractable. Consistent and feasible solutions to carefully chosen subsets can also be envisaged but where is the research that tackles the whole problem, by this or any other architecture?

2 Persistence Defined

This section and the following five are an introduction to the issues explored by persistent programming research over the last twelve years. Readers familiar with these issues may wish to skip to Section 8.

Persistent systems make *uniform* provision for the storage and use of data irrespective of those data's lifetimes.

For example, if particular data, say relations, can be created and stored for very long periods then it should be possible to have similar data that is short-lived, as a local variable in a procedure perhaps. Similarly, if a datum such as a list or tree can be created and used within a program's execution it should also be given the potential for a longer useful lifetime.

Two principles guide the provision of persistence:

1. **Persistence Independence**: The semantics of all or part of a program is not changed by changes in the longevity of the data to which it is applied; and
2. **Persistence Orthogonality**: The same facilities for persistence are accorded to data irrespective of the type of that data.

These principles arise from the original motive for providing persistence. Persistence is intended to make it much easier to build application software that works with combinations of short-term and long-lived data. Initially the need was recognised in the context of building CAD systems. In that context, sophisticated programs manipulate complex data which models some aspects of an artefact (electrical circuit, diesel engine, digital chip, aircraft, etc.) on behalf of designers. During a calculation or a design session there is much transitory data, but the design is of enduring interest, in the examples given measured in years or decades. Usually there is the added complication of many programs, each modelling different aspects of the common design.

Programmers are already challenged to build adequate models of the real artefact. Consider for a moment the design of a diesel engine. The shape of the cylinder and piston has to be modelled. The structure, stresses and heat flow in the cylinder head has to be modelled. The injection, mixing of the fuel and the chemistry and physics of its explosion has to be modelled. Interfaces have to be provided that enable designers to visualise this total system and adjust its parameters, e.g. the shape of the piston, and assess aspects of its manufacture and performance.

Building tools to make and manipulate such models just once is enough effort for any application programming team. They should be able to build them with data structures appropriate for the task in hand, i.e. manipulating the model and making it simulate the real system. Lumbering those programmers with the additional intellectual task of moving that data in and out of some long-term repository, organising its reliable storage and worst still requiring them to map it to a different stored form based on a different data model is clearly an impediment to their work.

The principles follow in consequence. If persistence were provided non-orthogonally then the "natural" model would sooner or later use some data structure whose type had limited persistence. If it only existed transiently within executions the programmers would need to remember to always translate it to something else whenever they stored a designer's work. If it had only long-term storage rights they would find themselves having to build some equivalent to hold the related data that was generated during calculations.

If program had different semantics depending on the longevity of the data on which it worked programmers would continually have to write two versions of their code, one that worked correctly when the data came from earlier design sessions and one for the data recently created. Then they have to contrive to use the correct mixtures of code according to the sources of data in any given calculation.

It is boring to re-iterate the case for these principles, however, it is necessary. Systems appear today, which as a short cut to the market place or in the pursuit of local rather than global economies, fail to comply with the principles and generate the programming problems caricatured in the preceding two paragraphs: object-oriented systems where the data types available in objects aren't identical with those used in the language(s) in which program (methods, procedures, programs) are written; object-oriented systems in which the data has to be explicitly fetched from the database; object-oriented systems which have different name spaces in their long-term repositories from those in programs; and object-oriented systems which present a different semantics when viewed via their query language from the semantics they present to programmers. The motivation for these object-oriented systems is to facilitate the construction of large and sophisticated applications such as the ones illustrated above. If the market place is rational, those where these fundamental flaws are obvious will be a short-lived novelty as they will soon be found out. We should be concerned about those where the flaws are less obvious and the cases where the market is irrational through ignorance. There the investments made in application building on shaky foundations may be very substantial and totally wasted.

There are many consequences of the two principles of persistence. For example the principle of persistence independence ultimately requires that type checking should not be any different if data is generated by one program, stored for an arbitrary period and then used in another program. Persistence independence also forbids constructs which expect programmers to explicitly organise data movement and requires that constructs used to organise concurrency, transactions and recovery are equally available for short-term and long-lived data.

The main consequence of persistence orthogonality is that all types have to be supported over the full range of lifetimes. This includes the recursive types [40] which have references in their implementations. In consequence providing long-lived and reliable identity was one of the principle challenges facing PPL implementors from the beginning.

3 Persistent Application Systems

Persistent Application Systems (PAS) are a class of applications in which the provision of good quality persistence is a prerequisite for their success. The health care and diesel engine design examples already given are indicative of their general form. Other examples are: support for the work of a city engineer's office, support for the operational management of a power distribution network, computer integrated manufacturing, scientific databases built and maintained by an extensive group of scientists and geographic information systems. PAS are systems where computers (together with communications and other technology) are deployed to support *co-operative* human activity. The people involved are attempting to construct and/or operate some complex system (the target) and use a shared computer model to help them do it.

The shared model is important as:

1. it represents the state of the target and it is easier to get useful information from the model than the target;
2. it allows people to communicate with others as they input details into the model and others extract them, not necessarily in the same combinations or in the same form;
3. it supports analysis, experiment and consistency checking; and
4. in the operational management, control and manufacturing contexts at least may be the intermediary, implementing in the target system operations that humans have performed on the model.

Communication is often the most significant of these when assessing the impact of a PAS on an organisation. That communication takes place in both space (to someone in some other place) and in time (to someone trying to find out what was done hours or even decades later). Builders of PAS have a responsibility to recognise and honour both these forms of communication requirement.

The trend in PAS is towards much more sophisticated models requiring very large amounts of program. At the same time the scope of a typical PAS is broadening, larger and more disparate groups are to be supported in a wider range of cooperative work. Finally, the groups of people do not operate in isolation, but interact with other groups, hence PAS must interact with other PAS on their behalf. The requirements of a group change, groups split and merge, and consequently a PAS must also have the ability to evolve, adapt, merge and split.

Our long-term goal must therefore be to make it easier to build and maintain such PAS. To cope with the volumes of program and data, the very long time scales and the ability to evolve that they require.

4 Survey of Persistent Programming Systems

The requirements for persistent programming languages were first published in 1978 [13]. An initial implementation of a data type complete PPL was achieved by 1981 [3,5,4]. A fuller story of the development of a variety of persistent languages can be obtained by reading the references of "Figure 1 History of Persistent Programming" in [14].

Important landmarks in the development of these languages were:

1. development and exploitation of persistent procedures [9] which have provided the basis for encapsulation and protection, active and object-oriented models and incremental system construction;
2. a recognition of the rôle played by dynamic and incremental binding [2];
3. the provision of a construct to hold an extensible set of bindings and to localise dynamic binding, so that incremental system development is safely achievable [33]; and
4. the development of type-safe linguistic reflection [72].

A general issue in these languages, partly driven by research into programming languages and partly by the special needs of persistence, is the development of type systems which are further discussed in Section 6. The relationship of PPLs with database programming languages has been surveyed [1].

There are a number of workshops and conferences where current work on persistent languages may be found, these are summarised in Table 1.

5 Engineering Persistent Systems

Several challenges have been encountered while trying to produce well engineered PPLs and associated programming environments. Mechanisms had to be developed

Table 1. Sources of papers on persistence

Event	Proceedings
POS1	Data Types and Persistence, Atkinson, Morrison & Buneman (eds), Springer-Verlag, 1988
POS3	Persistent Object Systems, Rosenberg & Koch (eds), Springer-Verlag, 1989
POS4	Implementing Persistent Object Bases, Dearle, Shaw & Zdonik (eds), Morgan Kaufmann, 1990
POS5	Proceedings of the Fifth Int. Workshop on Persistent Object Systems, Albano & Morrison (eds), Springer-Verlag, 1992
POS6	Proceedings of the Sixth Int. Workshop on Persistent Object Systems, Atkinson, Maier & Benzaken (eds), Springer-Verlag, 1994
POS7	Proceedings of the Seventh Int. Workshop on Persistent Object Systems, Connor & Nettles (eds), Morgan Kaufmann, 1996
POS8/PJW3	Proceedings of the Eighth Int. Workshop on Persistent Object Systems and the Third Int. Workshop on Persistence and Java, Morrison, Jordan & Atkinson (eds), Tiburon, California, 1998
DBPL1	Advances in Database Programming Languages, Bancilhon & Buneman (eds), ACM Press with Addison-Wesley, 1990
DBPL2	Database Programming Languages, Hull, Morrison & Stemple (eds), Morgan Kaufmann, 1989
DBPL3	Proceedings of the Third Int. Workshop on DBPLs, Kanellakis & Schmidt (eds), Morgan Kaufmann, 1991
DBPL4	Proceedings of the Fourth Int. Workshop on DBPLs, Beeri, Ohori & Shasha (eds), Morgan Kaufmann, 1993
DBPL5	Proceedings of the Fifth Int. Workshop on DBPLs, Atzeni & Tannen (eds), Springer-Verlag, 1995
DBPL6	Proceedings of the Sixth Int. Workshop on DBPLs, Cluet & Hull (eds), Springer-Verlag, 1997
Bremen	Security and Persistence, Rosenberg & Keedy (eds), Springer-Verlag, 1990
HICSS22	Persistent Programming Systems Sections in Proceedings of the Twenty Second Hawaii International Conference on Systems Sciences, Shriver, IEEE Press, 1989
HICSS25	Architectural and Operating Systems for Persistent Object Systems & Persistent Object Systems Sections in Proceedings of the Twenty Fifth Hawaii International Conference on Systems Sciences, Shriver, IEEE Press, 1992
IWOOOS2	Proceedings of the Int. Workshop on Object-Orientation in Operating Systems, Cabrera, Russo & Shapiro (eds), Palo Alto, IEEE Computer Society Press, 1991
IWOOOS3	Proceedings of the Int. Workshop on Object-Orientation in Operating Systems, Lea & Jul (eds), Dourdan, France, IEEE Press, 1992
PJW1	Proceedings of the First Int. Workshop on Persistence and Java, Atkinson & Jordan (eds), Drymen, Scotland, Sun Microsystems Laboratories, Tech Report, SMLI TR-96-58, 1996
PJW2	Proceedings of the Second Int. Workshop on Persistence and Java, Atkinson & Jordan (eds), Half Moon Bay, California, Sun Microsystems Laboratories, Tech Report, SMLI TR-97-63, 1997

for incremental binding between existing data[3] and new programs. To prevent this invalidating the type system, incremental checking of the structural equivalence of types had to be implemented with sufficient efficiency to accommodate relatively rare dynamic binding events during execution [21]. Representing and storing all the types that may occur is an interesting problem; polymorphic procedures, ADTs and the data they produce are examples [53].

Perhaps the most challenging problem is to implement a store that meets the following combination of requirements:

- manage the various memories and storage devices, allocating and recovering space, giving the illusion of an indefinitely large store;
- provide stable references (needed to implement all recursive types [40] and to provide persistent block retention semantics for procedures [41]);
- provide a reliable store that offers recovery after various kinds of failure [19];
- provide mechanisms for concurrent use of data; and
- provide a transactional mechanism to allow programs to voluntarily withdraw updates that they have grouped together and to control their release of revised information.

Many solutions to parts of the problem exist. For exampling swizzling can be combined with various disc block copying strategies to provide the references and the recovery over large stores [54]. In this case reasonably explicable recovery is provided but the transaction and concurrency mechanisms are likely to exhibit phantom recovery and locking. An extreme example is the simple provision of recovery and transactions by manipulating the paging mechanism [70]. Remember that when paging or block copying is used the copies and recovery and therefore probably the locking are of whole pages. Consequently items co-resident with objects in use will be locked and recovered. This generates locking and recovery effects that are nothing to do with the logic of programs or data, but are coincidences generated by the placement and usage patterns. Such phenomena subvert the intended goal of freeing the programming task from distracting anomalies.

These anomalies can be entirely unpredictable in the higher-order languages. For example, a procedure collected from a library may have been the result of some earlier procedure application and contain encapsulated data, probably stored in a remnant of the generating procedure's activation record. The user of the procedure from the library doesn't wish to know about its life history. Even if that is known there is nothing the programmer can do to predict a lock on or recovery of the activation record, let alone program around such events. Furthermore, several procedures could have been generated in the original activation and these will interact on their common hidden data even if they are used in different transactions. Lock interference here may be intentional or one of the coincidences just described. How can the application programmer be informed as to which kind of event has really occurred?

[3] Henceforth in this paper it is assumed that procedures, abstract data types and other values which contain code are **all** included as first class values in the type system. Hence "data" will normally mean all data including the data that is program such as procedures.

It may be tempting to ignore the problem, arguing that the application program is only delayed until the lock clears. But if the system is stressed these problems may occur often leading to deadlocks or performance degradation which will become the concern of the hapless programmer.

Pursuing the details of these challenges is not appropriate in this paper. For recent work the reader is referred to [18,17,76,74,70,75].

6 Persistent Type Systems

In persistent programming languages the type system has three rôles:

1. to describe data so that its use and interpretation may be better understood by programmers;
2. to limit the programs that may be written in order to make programming safer; and
3. to describe data so that its properties are communicated from the programmer to the compiler and onward to the run-time support and storage machinery so that they may store and manipulate it more efficiently.

Type systems are languages for describing types and the mechanisms whereby sentences in those languages are interpreted. *Types* are denoted by expressions in the type algebra provided by the type system. *Variables* have types which denote the subset of values they may hold. Each *value* has a type. It is useful to note how this vocabulary relates to that used in databases [57]; see Table 2.

Table 2. Vocabulary equivalences

Programming Languages	Databases
Type System	Data Model
Type	Schema
Variable	Database
Value	Instantaneous DB Extent

There are many conflicting forces influencing the designer of a type system, as shown in Figure 3.

Research into type systems has attempted to make program parts more re-usable through the use of various kinds of polymorphism [31]. In the context of persistent languages this has been developed as universal parametric polymorphism [52], and various forms of inclusion polymorphism providing subtyping and inheritance [25,26,7]. Recently Connor has analysed the options for resolving some of the difficulties that occur when sharing, update and inclusion polymorphism are combined [29] and developed a model of bounded parametric polymorphism [28] which solves the type information loss problem encountered in subtyping. Quest [20], Modula-3

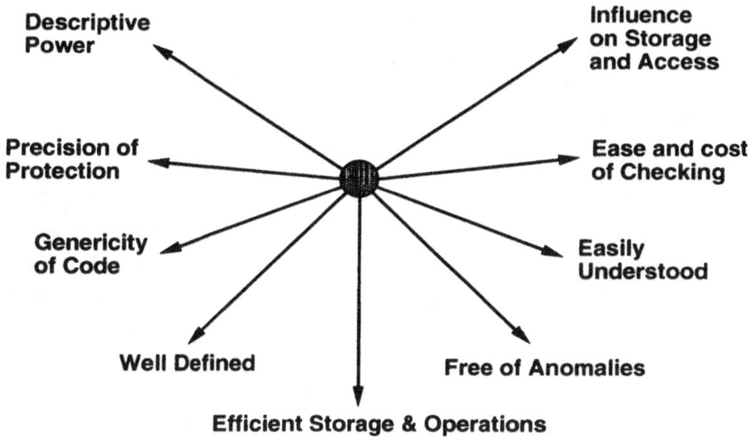

Fig. 3. Forces influencing type system design

[22] and Tycoon [51,56] (see also Chapter 1.1.1) are also developing practical and sophisticated typing systems.

The advantage of these more sophisticated type systems is that they allow more programs to be written by being more precise about the exact restrictions placed on the combination of operations and data. This not only allows for more re-usable code but it also enables better type description from the programmer's point of view. The expressions in the type algebra may now describe a set of possible values and their usage very precisely and may also be given a suggestive name and used by name in other type expressions. Furthermore these expressions may be parametric and so describe a way of combining types with which they are parameterised. This allows application specific or general purpose structures to be named. For example:

type Set [ElementType] **is** . . .
. . .
type Students **is** Set[Student]
type Staff **is** Set[Employee]
. . .

In the above example the structure *Set* was named and later it was used to name two set types *Students* and *Staff*.

Abstract data types are used to completely encapsulate data, making the operations on it precisely limited to those provided. In Napier88 the type **any** is used to denote an infinite discriminated union type so that limits may be placed on type checking. This allows incremental matching of types; essential when they reach the scale encountered in schemata.[4] Any operation that projects a value out of **any** will invoke further typechecking. Other significant uses of **any** are:

[4] A particular program is usually concerned only with data described by some small subgraph of the schema against which it runs.

1. to allow code to be written which will handle data not yet specified;
2. to provide an interface for type enquiry when generating type-safe code that provides type dependent behaviour via reflection [32,44,72];
3. to act as place holders for parts of schemata that are yet to be specified while code operates against the parts already defined.

The type **env** in Napier88 denotes an updateable set of bindings [33]. Each binding holds an identifier, a locality in which a value may reside, the type constraining that value and constancy information. Thus the **env** values in the language act as the locus of incremental construction as additional bindings are added to them. To permit safe incrementality the type requirements of any identifier being introduced into scope are verified dynamically. If the data made accessible in this way are large and/or the introduction occurs in the outer scopes of programs then the cost of dynamic checks is relatively small. As the constructional tools now run in a persistent environment it is also possible to perform the introduction and verification earlier, e.g. this leads to early feedback to programmers, to further reduction in text input and checking costs, and to novel program structures [42,37].

A recurring interest in the type system research for persistent languages is the appropriate treatment of bulk types [1]. These types describe regular structures such as: sets, relations, finite maps, sequences and trees. The description is advantageous to programmers as it identifies the regularity and this may then be exploited via an algebra of bulk operations. The description is also advantageous to implementors as the scale and regularity make optimisation both possible and worthwhile. Questions arise about the form of these types, the extent to which they should be built-in and their prerequisites such as equality and order [8,55]. Consistent notations may be provided over such types with the power and convenience of query languages but with a natural and consistent relationship with the rest of the programming language [73].

The repertoire of constructs available in type systems would appear to offer similar descriptive power to that in the data models. The ability to declare new parametric constructs should allow all semantic description to be captured. These claims are difficult to verify since equivalent care in developing and presenting definitions has to be taken and assessment of the efficacy of descriptions in communication with humans is difficult. Valid comparisons also require supporting tools and real applications.

For recent work the reader is referred to [23,24,60,21,8,29,30,28].

7 Using Multiple System Components

The target of the research considered here is to better support the construction, maintenance and operation of PAS (see Section 3). It is informative to consider their present support. This comprises a number of construction components: operating system, user interface management system (UIMS), various DBMS, various programming languages, a communications system, etc. Consequently, for the programmer or user the PAS looks more complex than the eternal triangle (see Figure 1). A more realistic current structure is shown in Figure 4.

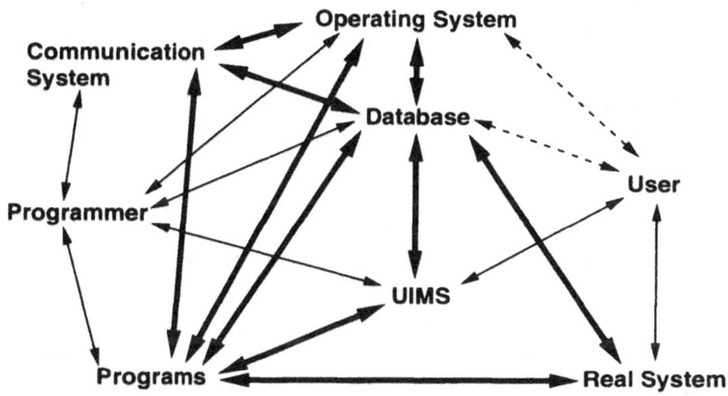

Fig. 4. Structure of a typical PAS

The heavy arrows denote mapping or relationships that have to be understood and maintained by programmers, the light arrows denote the components each class of person has to understand and the interrupted arrows are undesirable awareness by users of construction components. As explained above these intrude into the user's awareness due to the failure modes of the PAS. An alternative view depicting the method of constructing a PAS is shown in Figure 5. This shows part of the cause of the problem. The various constructional components that support the PAS are designed and built independently, guided by different research and industrial cultures. During their construction little consideration was given to consistency which would aid interworking with other construction components. Large and complex PAS need a multiplicity of construction components. Therefore a strategy saying that only one generalised component can be used is doomed from the start.[5]

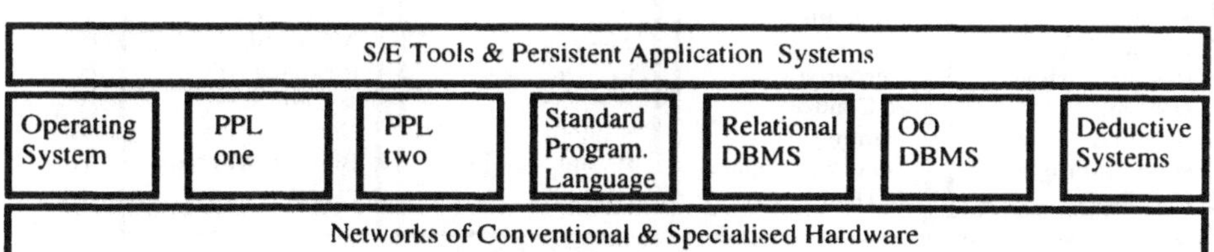

Fig. 5. Complex PAS support

The multiplicity of construction components serve three purposes:

[5] It is about as sensible as saying all buildings will be built using only concrete, albeit very good concrete, denying the use of windows, doors, lifts, etc.

1. they identify and provide services and subsystems that are useful, capturing particular ways of handling *different* parts of the computational and constructional processes;
2. as such they each embody the accumulated understanding of how to perform *their* part of the PAS task and hence it is a significant economy to re-use them; and
3. they provide a means of dividing the labour of building PAS so that subsidiary industries may make the construction components and recover their cost over many PAS.

Figure 6 exposes a property of the implementation of the construction components themselves. Many of them, despite the fact that they service very different needs, have a substantial number of sub-components serving common functional requirements. These repeated sub-components are just those that deal with the provision of generalised persistence, such as recovery, concurrency, distribution, accounting, etc. They typically account for a large part of the construction component (95% in the case of System R [43]). It is marginal differences in the behaviour of sub-components that purport to provide the same service that cause the problems when systems are under stress, whereas differences in the special part of each construction component are precisely those that are useful. The replicated common functionality can also be seen as unnecessary repetition of work that would be better amortised over many construction components.

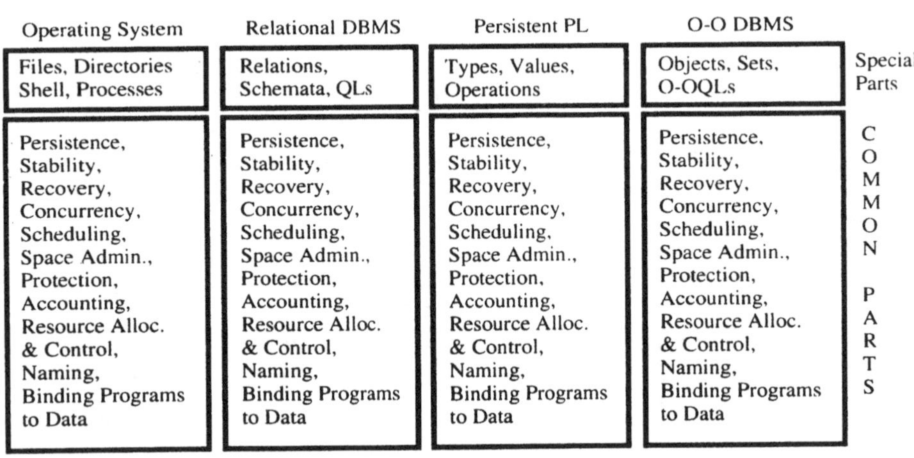

Fig. 6. Undesirable replication of effort

The model of PAS so far presented is a simplification. It omits to distinguish several types of programmer[6] and system builder and ignores the fact that many additional

[6] Those that provide generic packages and those that work with high levels of domain specific knowledge are examples.

construction components are built within the PAS or for a family of PAS[7] using the original construction components. Similarly the construction components themselves may often be built out of other families of construction components, so the decomposition may be recursive. The construction and the relationships are indeed more complex but the simplified picture will suffice for most of the arguments in this paper.

8 A Scalable Persistent Architecture

Figure 7 depicts the illusion of a single coherent PAS that it is desirable to present to the user.

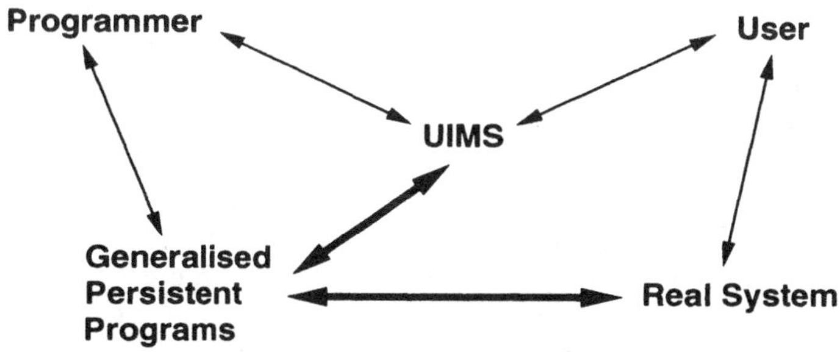

Fig. 7. The goal of simpler PAS

The UIMS has remained distinct as it may play a major rôle in allowing users to work with many PAS and will certainly develop independently. It will however be changed by and will exploit good quality mechanisms for persistence. For example it will store its fonts and user profiles in the reliable store provided. The application programmer, particularly those that work in the domain specific end of the work should now be given a simple[8] environment in which to program.

A challenge for computing science research is to establish the best architecture for the construction of PAS, call it a Scalable Persistent Architecture. Four lines of response are possible:

Laissez faire Ignore the problem either hoping it will go away or be resolved by market forces;

Obtain Standard Behaviour Coerce *all* the construction component providers to adopt a precise common standard for *all* the issues in the common parts;

Arrange a Cover Up Provide a "veneer" that hides *all* the inconsistencies; or

[7] For example, a shape modelling solid geometry package and a fluid dynamics package, in the diesel engine design PAS.

[8] In the sense of free of distractions, as it will probably be rich in available construction components — only some of which are relevant to any given programmer.

Simplify Components Provide a common substrate that provides most of the critical functionality of construction components but leaves them able to exhibit their essential differences when they have been re-written using this substrate.

The OMG [66] initiative is adopting the second policy. Their call for common service specifications is however a step in the direction of the fourth policy. Clearly any research programme that makes significant progress on the fourth policy will, *inter alia*, benefit the second policy. The cover up policy is a caricature of many of the efforts in interoperability and heterogeneous system technology [49]. It has the advantage that some of the uniformity of behaviour can be obtained with relatively little effort compared with the second and fourth policies. However, to get truely uniform behaviour may take a very thick "veneer" or may even be unachievable given the behaviour of underlying systems. It does however offer the best promise for short- and medium-term results, as it avoids re-implementation of large constructional components, and will remain important technology for managing PAS transitions and for interworking between PAS where strongly coupled behaviour is not required and inconsistency will be expected and tolerated.

This paper espouses the fourth policy for reasons given above (see Section 1) and because it is believed that in the long term it will give best PAS behaviour and performance and will significantly encourage the provision of more useful construction components. The proposed architecture is shown in Figure 8 modulo the caveat about simplification that was given above and with the reminder that the particular construction components actually shown are illustrative examples.

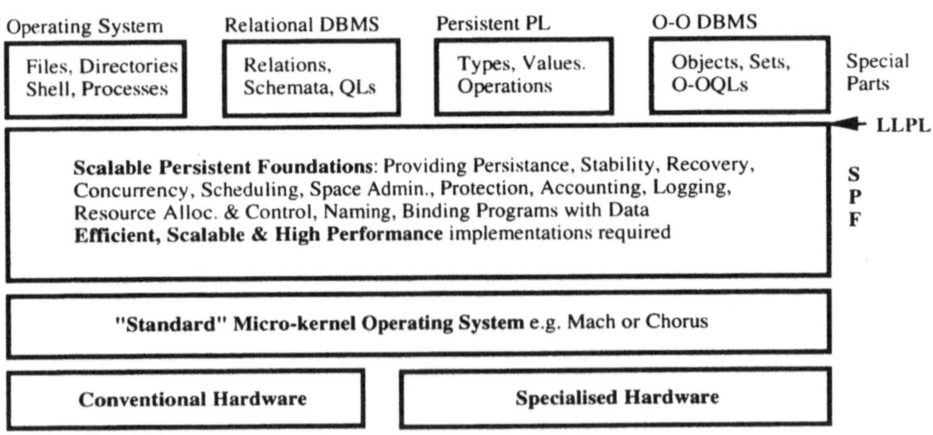

Fig. 8. Common PAS support

The important new system component proposed by this architecture is the Scalable Persistent Foundation (SPF). This provides all the common services needed by programmers building construction components but is not normally used directly by application programmers. Its facilities are exercised via one interface called

LLPL (Low-Level Persistent Language). Once the actual facilities to be provided by SPF through LLPL have been precisely identified it would be constructed to very high engineering standards, possibly on top of a micro-kernel platform. In order to achieve the goal of longevity for PAS the commitments made by the SPF definition must be sufficiently independent of particular technology that they can be kept for many decades.

The remaining sections of this paper begin the discussion of the form that SPF and LLPL should take. The only strong statement this paper makes about the architecture is that this common substrate should be identified and built. It does not claim to have a definitive list of its required functions. Nor does it claim to specify any one of those functions, these are matters for research and debate. What is clear is that:

- the maximum gain from the SPF is achieved if it offers significant functionality to the construction component builders;
- there is a minimum functionality necessary to ensure reasonably consistent construction component behaviour, which would be enforced, i.e. there would be no direct access to the micro-kernel from construction components; and
- there is a maximum enforced functionality tolerable before it starts impeding the construction components from meeting their validly different goals.

A possible outcome of this research is that it will discover that there are no realistic SPF because the minimum functionality exceeds the maximum functionality as defined above. If this is a problem is encountered it may be relieved by building SPF for useful subsets of constructional components.

9 Achieving Reasonable Longevity

An example of a PAS given in Section 3 was a system supporting the work of city engineers. The main sewers of Paris were built by Napolean's engineers about 180 years ago. In contrast files I have constructed with various applications on my computer in the last three years are no longer useable as the technology moved on and the application packages didn't. Today we mostly store data indirectly, via some applications package and its direct use and interpretation is extremely difficult. Imagine the consternation in a city engineer's office if the data about the sewers (or any other service) became inaccessible after only twenty years.

Yet more and more of the data within PAS are being stored in forms that are only known to programs and are virtually meaningless without the corresponding code. The trend towards object-oriented systems (persistent programming for that matter) exacerbates this problem. Now the code and data are intimately bound together and with proper encapsulation the data are not even accessible without the code. So in the future, in order to achieve reasonable longevity, not only the data values but also all the code will need to migrate across the successive technologies that support the SPF and hence the PAS.

The old solutions will no longer work. Old databases and files were moved forward by effective data translation technology, for example EXPRESS [67]. This will no longer be possible because humans are no longer aware of the precise formats in use (they are the results of decisions by applications programmers compounded with those of construction component builders, for example compiler writers) and it is no longer straightforward to locate all the data. In any case, if that data were translated the programs (e.g. methods in objects) would no longer function correctly. They too would need translation to the equivalent code. But these translations have to be done in tandem while preserving the bindings between program and data.

No technology is available at present that can perform this, but, unless we postulate that contrary to previous experience computer technology will stop developing, this technology is an essential prerequisite of persistence over moderate timescales. SPF has to guarantee such longevity.

How might this be achieved? If the LLPL ensured that all data (including program) was stored with a sufficient description this would suffice. The interface that it provided could require this whenever types and code were deposited. The additional information could normally be provided by compilers and other constructional components and would not be a further burden on applications programmers. The volume of data involved is small since it could be factored out of individual items and be reachable by reference or context.

The challenge is to identify precisely what extra data is needed and to find ways of expressing it that are independent of the current computer architectures so that there is confidence that equivalent code and representations can always be found. A similar architectural independence was required for ANDF/TDF [34,35]. In the case of code, reverse translation is not possible, so it will be necessary to store some intermediary form of code from which the executable code can be regenerated.

10 Safety Requirements

Another prerequisite is that the data be adequately protected against accident and malevolence. The relative merits of various forms of protection have been discussed elsewhere [15]. At the very least the fundamental properties of the data managed by the SPF and on which the SPF depends for its correct functioning must be inviolable.

For example, the SPF will need to distinguish between persistent references[9] and the scalar (bit pattern data) so that the integrity of references and of space allocation can be maintained under changing circumstances. The LLPL interface must not allow a program to present an arbitrary bit pattern as a reference or to overwrite a location constrained to hold references without ensuring the replacement is a valid reference and that any protocols needed for space and reference management have been completed.

Similarly code must be distinguished from the scalar data and references. It is clear that fundamental damage could be done if an LLPL implementation were ever to let a sequence of references or scalars be executed as code. Furthermore any code cannot be let into the SPF domain; it must have been checked that it complies with any rules that are not checked dynamically.

[9] At least the subset that can traverse space management boundaries.

Consequently, at the very least, for safety the SPF/LLPL must ensure that scalar data, references and code are immiscible. That is, there must be no operations available in the LLPL interface that could violate their separation.

But this leaves a problem; a major class of construction components, the compilers or linkers, need to generate code.[10] Conventional compilers overcome this problem by creating files as some kind of scalar data that happens to have the same bit pattern as the required code. The file is then re-opened as an executable program. This is not a safe operation — the file appears to have changed type and the operation could have been applied to a file not produced by a compiler.

In order to perform this operation in a persistent store or any other context that relies on type checking to preserve safety and integrity it is necessary to supply the compiler with "magic" which is a small amount of trustworthy code that takes the data in a form that the compiler was able to produce, e.g. a vector of integers into which the compiler was able to write, and turns it into a form which is no longer available for read and write operations but is now succeptable to execute operations [10]. This provides a minimum foundation for reflection [72] which then allows the system to become populated with code. All the constructional tools will then use this reflection as they enable people to build constructional components and PAS.

One way in which this reflective magic could be provided is for LLPL to include operations which take code, in the form output by compilers, and transform it to the form required in the store. It could, at the same time, verify that the necessary information for longevity had been provided as the ANDF [34] installers do.

The minimal protection considered above could be extended towards a more complete and modern type system (see Section 6). The problem here is to be certain that this did not unduely restrict the efficiency with which the construction components could store data. For example, if a language that uses LLPL as its target traditionally packs records and vectors, or an image handling package wishes to compress the data they should be able to do this. The choice of the appropriate level of types in LLPL and the extent, above the minimum given above that they are mandatory is a major design issue. However, the type information can provide the framework for providing the information needed for data longevity.

If a more sophisticated type system is used then the magic needs to be extended to include a mechanism for introducing new types, or more precisely new identification via type algebraic expressions of types, into the SPF. Again this can be part of the reflection mechanisms accessible through LLPL.

11 Distribution and its Visibility

Consider the traditional requirements of a distributed system as categorised under various forms of transparency [12]:

- *Access transparency* enables local and remote data to be used with exactly the same operations;

[10] This is just a special, but obvious case; there is a problem creating any new value and placing it in the store — it has to be denoted in some way before it can be put in the store.

- *Location transparency* enables objects to be used without knowledge of their location;
- *Concurrency transparency* enables several processes to operate concurrently on shared data without interference between them;
- *Replication transparency* enables multiple instances of data to be used to increase reliability and performance without knowledge of the replicas by users or application programs;
- *Failure transparency* enables the concealment of faults, allowing users and application programs to complete tasks despite the failure of hardware or software components;
- *Migration transparency* allows the movement of data within a system without affecting the operation of users or application programs;
- *Performance transparency* allows the system to be reconfigured to improve performance as loads vary; and
- *Scaling transparency* allows the system and applications to expand in scale without change to the system structure or the application algorithms.

However few if any of these transparencies are wanted *all the time* by the implementors of construction components. A few examples are offered. Remember that in all these examples we are considering the needs of computer science experts writing highly tuned construction components, other programmers may always need the transparencies and even the experts may accept them as a useful simplification much of the time.

- *Access transparency* may be undesirable when a program wishes to evaluate *a priori* whether the cost or delay of an operation may be unacceptable;
- *Location transparency* is undesirable when optimisers wish to arrange operations and code to be co-located, and programs organising reliability will want to arrange for replicas to be stored in widely separated locations;
- *Concurrency transparency* will be inappropriate since the construction components will need to mediate their own concurrency regimes and process interaction is essential for prompt communication;
- *Replication transparency* is often provided in particular ways by construction components which will therefore need access to the replicas and will use this access for optimisation;
- *Failure transparency* is undesirable when the construction component is required to inform its users of the cause when it is unable to perform a service on schedule; and
- *Migration transparency* is also contraindicated when construction components are themselves attempting to optimise operations.

Whenever a transparency is usually appropriate the normal operations provided by LLPL should provide it. However, *enquiry operations* are necessary which allow the construction component to see behind the transparency mechanism. Design of these enquiry operations and identification of the information they should reveal is a research issue. It may also be desirable to provide operations that allow the construction component to give advice or even specify object attributes like locality. Both classes of operation would obviously need to be handled with care and may not be available to all programmers. They need to use information and interfaces that are sufficiently independent of current hardware and the particular implementation of SPF so that the programs still operate as the technology changes.

12 Accommodating Change

A particular feature of any PAS is that it is continuously subject to change. There are external pressures for change on the PAS such as new organisational requirements, repairs and new domain specific techniques. A set of measurements on the HMS system showed very high rates of change [69].

There are also changes in the supporting technology. In some ways the SPF must protect the construction components and the PAS from untoward effects of change but nevertheless allow them to exploit significant progress.

The challenge is to:

- ensure that all the necessary consequences of any change are propagated; and
- avoid all unnecessary propagation of the consequences of change.

It is necessary that the SPF will be well designed to support change. For example the incremental binding described with the type **env** (see Section 6), reflection and inclusion polymorphism all allow certain kinds of system evolution without the changes impacting program and data that are not directly using the changed parts. Reflection and type **any** can be combined to automate some consequential changes. Tools can be built that assist the programmer in keeping track of the consequences of changes [68].

These mechanisms are necessary but not sufficient to meet the changes that PAS will encounter. For example, it is likely that new base types will be supported by underlying (specialist) hardware, e.g. to represent and process images. To utilise such facilities LLPL will need to be extensible with new base types and operations without these perturbing existing code. The need to accommodate changes of support architecture, value representations and instruction sets below the SPF has already been introduced.

13 Standard Programming Language Issues

Several issues have been addressed specifically in the preceding sections, this section identifies a few of the general issues that must also be considered.

One obvious requirement is a requirement for high performance. This should be addressed in two ways. The measures of performance established for SPF should take account of its ability to perform all its operations including stability operations, etc. and accommodation of change. Indeed any short-term performance measures may be misleading. Another set of enquiry operations and perhaps advisory operations should be provided in LLPL so that construction components can enquire about the expected performance and indicate preferences about the treatment of code or objects. Of course, the final implementation of SPF should be particularly well-engineered with high quality optimised code generation available through LLPL.

It is necessary to decide whether the language provided via LLPL is higher order. A higher-order language would probably assist significantly with the coding of construction components and the SPF already has to accommodate code as data. If it is a higher-order language then components requiring fast execution and compilers using LLPL[11] as their route to code generation should be able to avoid any overheads of the provisions for higher-order code if they do not use it.

The exact primitives for transactions and concurrency need to be chosen so that common regimes, such as serialisability, are easily obtained but other mechanisms may also be efficiently supported. A promising set of primitives has been suggested for ACTA [62] and its use is being investigated as CACS [71]. Other languages, such as Concurrent CLU [47,38,27] and Argus [48], have explored different concurrency provision.

The primitives for distribution have also to be chosen. Candidates may be found in Emerald [16], Argus, Hermes [65] and Guide [63].

A major choice is the level of type system that should be provided. Some aspects of this choice have already been considered (see Section 10). Additionally we may consider their effectiveness in aiding construction component implementation. If a high-level type system were provided, then a dialect of the language that inhibited the transgression of transparencies might also be useful for direct use by application programmers. This may be expecting too much of one language. At the very least it would be necessary to guarantee that any overheads introduced by the advanced type system could be avoided by compilers and other construction components that only used simple types.

This is an incomplete[12] list of the design aspects of SPF/LLPL that have yet to be addressed. The challenge is to meet all the requirements reasonably well rather than some of them exceptionally well at the expense of ignoring others. It is also necessary to restrict the language features so that the language is easily understood and can be precisely defined.

14 Summary of Issues

The achievements of persistence have been surveyed. These suggest that it might be possible to continue the process of integration and provide a much simpler and more reliable basis for application programming. The present construction components all exhibit different behaviour with respect to persistence particularly when stressed. This leads to difficulties building PAS and the resulting PAS have unsatisfactory behaviours that force users to become aware of some of the construction components.

[11] In an efficient binary form.

[12] For example, accounting and resource usage control have been omitted.

A new architecture, SPF, which arranges that all the construction components rest on a common substrate and which ensures certain consistencies is proposed. This is an inversion of the approach currently used to obtain interoperability where a layer of software is placed over the construction components that attempts to translate their existing behaviour into consistent behaviour.

It is argued that the SPF approach is the only approach that will obtain completely consistent behaviour and that it also has the advantage of reducing the cost of building construction components. Its advantages however, can only be realised in the longer term.

Research into the design of SPF is proposed as a means of identifying the common goals of the persistence, distributed object management and distributed operating systems communities. This identification of the required common behaviour is of value whether it is realised via the OMG's common services, the interoperability surface layers or SPF's common substrate.

An experiment is necessary to evaluate the efficacy of the SPF architecture; specifically that the SPF architecture gives a better environment in which to build, maintain and operate PAS than the interoperability inversion or the attempts to strait-jacket all the construction components into a common behaviour without the benefit of the substrate. This research cannot be conducted entirely on a small scale and by minor perturbations of the existing research and commercial systems. Perturbations will not accomplish the change in structure. Small scale experiments will not exercise the architecture in relevant ways and will not yield measurements of behaviour over lifetimes that approximate the target longevity.

An experimental plan is therefore proposed.

1. Develop an agreed design of SPF and LLPL, during this phase prototypical experiments would be necessary to test specific constructs, their use and implementation.
2. Build a well-engineered version of SPF and LLPL ensuring they are adequately equipped with instrumentation.
3. Re-build a selection of major construction components to a high standard on top of SPF.
4. Run experiments building and operating realistic PAS using these revised components. Measure and analyse their behaviour when they operate over significant volumes of data under typical loads for a sufficiently long period that independent and typical application programmers take the PAS through several evolutionary steps.

The first phase requires a collaborative effort from the distributed object management community, the operating systems community and the persistent programming researchers as rival designs are proposed and reviewed. It would conclude with one design[13] being chosen which had probably already been taken to a prototype stage.

[13] If resources permit, continuing the experiment with two rival designs would test the architecture's sensitivity to design details, explore a larger application space and add the spice of rivalry.

Phase 2 would commence with the construction of the foundation which can be considered as an experimental apparatus. Much of the quality software production and its subsequent maintenance should be subcontracted to the industry's leading experts in each technology. Similarly the long term maintenance should be contracted to such companies.[14]

During phase 3 the standard construction components and tools would be re-implemented using the SPF. Again this should be mostly subcontracted — for example a relational system should be set up by a company already expert in building relational systems.[15] At the same time researchers would begin to use SPF to build new construction components and extend libraries giving new variations of persistent behaviour.

During phase 4 groups of computer scientists would "book time" on the SPF and construction components to run experiments. These would vary between those that operated some artificial PAS that characterised some perceived property of PASs and the operation of actual PAS with independent application programmers and users.[16] In both cases the instrumentation would be used to obtain measurements of relevant properties from any level of the system and on any scale from the measurement of changes in PAS structure and code to the measurement of data movements across various interfaces. The experimenters would be expected to establish in advance the possible outcomes and the way in which the experiment would test some relevant hypothesis or provide data to guide the improved design of the SPF, construction components or PASs. This phase is illustrated in Figure 9.

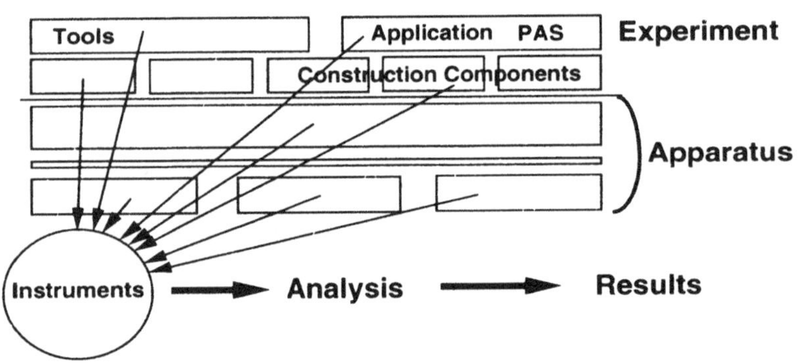

Fig. 9. The form of a typical experiment in Phase 4

[14] This is analogous to specialist companies building and maintaining a particle accelerator — physicist do not have to dig their own tunnels, build their own vacuum pumps and make their own superconducting magnets — though they are rightly involved in their design and in verifying that performance goals are met.

[15] This would develop and propagate ideas about SPF and provide expert criticism as well as producing necessary experimental apparatus.

[16] For example the astronomical data processing suggested by Kersten [45].

To obtain relevant measurements the PAS may need to be operated for many years, with a large and geographically extensive network. The whole experimental plan needs to be executed as a large, long-term and well-funded programme. This is, however, worthwhile as it will answer questions that cannot be answered with small-scale experiments. These may be important answers as architectures may otherwise be limited to evolve by a succession of minor perturbations. In computing science we are not limited by the constraints of Darwinian evolution, we can intervene and try a new architecture.

Acknowledgements. The European Community supported parts of this work via two ESPRIT projects: FIDE, Basic Research Action 3070 and $FIDE_2$, Basic Research Action 6309. The author is grateful to the programme committee of IW-DOM92 for the invitation to prepare and present this paper, particularly to Tamer Özsu who showed both forbearance and kind hospitality. He also readily acknowledges the considerable help given in preparing the paper by João Lopes and Paul Philbrow.

References

1. M.P. Atkinson and O.P. Buneman. Types and persistence in database programming languages. *ACM Computing Surveys*, 19(2):105–190, June 1987.
2. M.P. Atkinson, O.P. Buneman, and R. Morrison. Binding and type checking in database programming languages. *The Computer Journal*, 31(2):99–109, April 1988.
3. M.P. Atkinson, K.J. Chisholm, and W.P. Cockshott. PS-algol: An algol with a persistent heap. *ACM SIGPLAN Notices*, 17(7):24–31, July 1982.
4. M.P. Atkinson, K.J. Chisholm, and W.P. Cockshott. CMS—a chunk management system. *Software Practice and Experience*, 13(3):273–285, March 1983.
5. M.P. Atkinson, K.J. Chisholm, W.P. Cockshott, and R.M. Marshall. Algorithms for a persistent heap. *Software Practice and Experience*, 13(3):259–272, March 1983.
6. M.P. Atkinson and A. England. Towards new architectures for distributed autonomous database applications. In Rosenberg and Keedy [64], pages 356–377.
7. A. Albano, G. Ghelli, and R. Orsini. A relationship mechanism for a strongly typed object-oriented database programming language. In *Proceedings of the Seventeenth International Conference on Very Large Data Bases (Barcelona, Catalonia, Spain, 3rd–6th September 1991)*, 1991.
8. M.P. Atkinson, C. Lécluse, P.C. Philbrow, and P. Richard. Design issues in a map language. In Kanellakis and Schmidt [46]. Proceedings of the Third International Workshop on Database Programming Languages (Nafplion, Greece, 27th–30th August 1991).
9. M.P. Atkinson and R. Morrison. Procedures as persistent data objects. *ACM Transactions on Programming Languages and Systems*, 4(7):539–559, October 1985.
10. M.P. Atkinson and R. Morrison. Polymorphic names, types, constancy and magic in a type secure persistent object store. In R. Carrick and R.L. Cooper, editors, *Persistent Object Systems: Their Design, Implementation and Use*, pages 1–12. Universities of Glasgow and St Andrews Technical Report PPRR-44-87, 1987. Proceedings of the Second International Workshop on Persistent Object Systems (Appin, Scotland, 25th–28th August 1987).

11. A. Albano and R. Morrison, editors. *Persistent Object Systems: Implementation and Use*. Workshops in Computing. Springer-Verlag in collaboration with the British Computer Society, 1992. Proceedings of the Fifth International Workshop on Persistent Object Systems (San Miniato, Italy, 1st–4th September 1992).
12. ANSA, Poseidon House, Castle Park, Cambridge, UK CB3 0RD. *ANSA Reference Manual Volume A*, 1989.
13. M.P. Atkinson. Programming languages and databases. In S.B. Yao, editor, *The Fourth International Conference on Very Large Data Bases (Berlin, West Germany, September 1978)*, pages 408–419, September 1978.
14. M.P. Atkinson. Questioning persistent types. In Hull et al. [39], pages 2–24. Proceedings of the Second International Workshop on Database Programming Languages (Salishan Lodge, Gleneden Beach, Oregon, June 1989).
15. A.L. Brown, A. Dearle, R. Morrison, D.S. Munro, and J. Rosenberg. A layered persistent architecture for Napier88. In Rosenberg and Keedy [64], pages 155–172.
16. A. Black, N. Hutchinson, E. Jul, H. Levy, and L. Carter. Distribution and abstract types in Emerald. *IEEE Transactions on Software Engineering*, SE-13(1), January 1987.
17. A.L. Brown, G. Mainetto, F. Matthes, R. Mueller, and D.J. McNally. An open system architecture for a persistent object store. In Morrison and Atkinson (minitrack coordinators) [50], pages 766–776.
18. A.L. Brown and J. Rosenberg. Persistent object stores: An implementation technique. In Dearle et al. [36], pages 199–214. Proceedings of the Fourth International Workshop on Persistent Object Systems, Their Design, Implementation and Use (Martha's Vineyard, USA, September 1990).
19. A.L. Brown. *Persistent Object Stores*. PhD thesis, University of St Andrews, 1988.
20. L. Cardelli. The Quest language and system (tracking draft). Technical report, Digital Equipment Corporation, Systems Research Center, 130 Lytton Avenue, Palo Alto, CA 94301, June 1990.
21. R.C.H. Connor, A.L. Brown, Q.I. Cutts, A. Dearle, R. Morrison, and J. Rosenberg. Type equivalence checking in persistent object systems. In Dearle et al. [36], pages 154–167. Proceedings of the Fourth International Workshop on Persistent Object Systems, Their Design, Implementation and Use (Martha's Vineyard, USA, September 1990).
22. L. Cardelli, J.E. Donahue, L. Glassman, M. Jordan, Kalsow. W., and G. Nelson. Modula-3 report (revised). Technical Report 52, DEC Systems Research Centre, 130 Lytton Avenue, Palo Alto, Ca, USA, October 1989.
23. R.C.H. Connor, A. Dearle, R. Morrison, and A.L. Brown. An object addressing mechanism for statically typed languages with multiple inheritance. In *Proceedings of the Conference on Object-Oriented Programming Systems, Languages and Applications (New Orleans, Louisiana, October 1989)*, pages 279–285, 1989.
24. R.C.H. Connor, A. Dearle, R. Morrison, and A.L. Brown. Existentially quantified types as a database viewing mechanism. In F. Bancilhon, C. Thanos, and D. Tsichritzis, editors, *Proceedings of the Second International Conference on Extending Database Technology (Venice, Italy, March 1990)*, number 416 in Lecture Notes in Computer Science, pages 301–315. Springer-Verlag, 1990.
25. P.L. Curien and G. Ghelli. Coherence of subsumption. *Mathematical Structures in Computer Science*, 2(1):55–91, 1992.
26. G. Castagna, G. Ghelli, and G. Longo. A calculus for overloaded functions with subtyping. In *ACM Conference on LISP and Functional Programming—LFP (San Francisco, Ca, June 1992)*, 1992.
27. R.C.B. Cooper and K.G. Hamilton. Preserving abstraction in concurrent programming. Technical Report 76, University of Cambridge Computer Laboratory, 1985.

28. R.C.H. Connor and R. Morrison. Subtyping without tears. In *Proceedings of the 15th Australian Computing Science Conference—ACSC-13 (Tasmania, January 1992)*, pages 209–225, 1992.
29. R.C.H. Connor, D. McNally, and R. Morrison. Subtyping and assignment in database programming languages. In Kanellakis and Schmidt [46], pages 305–324. Proceedings of the Third International Workshop on Database Programming Languages (Nafplion, Greece, 27th–30th August 1991).
30. R.C.H. Connor. *Types and Polymorphism in Persistent Programming Systems*. PhD thesis, University of St Andrews, 1991.
31. L. Cardelli and P. Wegner. On understanding types, data abstraction and polymorphism. *ACM Computing Surveys*, 17(4):471–523, December 1985.
32. A. Dearle and A.L. Brown. Safe browsing in a strongly typed persistent environment. *The Computer Journal*, 31(3), 1988.
33. A. Dearle. Environments: A flexible binding mechanism to support system evolution. In B.H. Shriver, editor, *Proceedings of the Twenty-Second Annual Hawaii International Conference on System Sciences, Volume II Software Track (January 1989)*, pages 46–45, 1989.
34. Defence Research Agency. TDF specification part I. Technical report, United Kingdom's Defence Research Agency, RSRE, Malvern, 1991.
35. Defence Research Agency. TDF facts & figures. Technical report, United Kingdom's Defence Research Agency, RSRE, Malvern, 1992.
36. A. Dearle, G.M. Shaw, and S.B. Zdonik, editors. *Implementing Persistent Object Bases, Principles and Practice*. San Mateo, CA: Morgan Kaufmann Publishers, 1990. Proceedings of the Fourth International Workshop on Persistent Object Systems, Their Design, Implementation and Use (Martha's Vineyard, USA, September 1990).
37. A.M. Farkas, A. Dearle, G.N.C. Kirby, Q.I. Cutts, R. Morrison, and R.C.H. Connor. Persistent program construction through browsing and user gesture with some typing. In Albano and Morrison [11], pages 376–393. Proceedings of the Fifth International Workshop on Persistent Object Systems (San Miniato, Italy, 1st–4th September 1992).
38. K.G. Hamilton. *A Remote Procedure Call System*. PhD thesis, University of Cambridge Computer Laboratory, 1984.
39. R. Hull, R. Morrison, and D. Stemple, editors. *Database Programming Languages*. San Mateo, CA: Morgan Kaufmann Publishers, 1989. Proceedings of the Second International Workshop on Database Programming Languages (Salishan Lodge, Gleneden Beach, Oregon, June 1989).
40. C.A.R. Hoare. Recursive Data Structures. *International Journal of Computer and Information Science*, 4(2):105–132, 1975.
41. J.B. Johnston. The contour model of block structure processes. *ACM SIGPLAN Notices*, 6(2):56–82, 1971.
42. G.N.C. Kirby, R.C.H. Connor, Q.I. Cutts, R. Morrison, A. Dearle, and A.M. Farkas. Persistent hyper-programs. In Albano and Morrison [11], pages 86–106. Proceedings of the Fifth International Workshop on Persistent Object Systems (San Miniato, Italy, 1st–4th September 1992).
43. W.F. King. Future directions in data base management systems. In B. Shaw, editor, *Data Base Systems. Proceedings of the Joint IBM/University of Newcastle upon Tyne Seminar (4th–7th September 1979)*, page 129. University of Newcastle upon Tyne Computing Laboratory, 1980.
44. G.N.C. Kirby. Persistent programming with type-safe linguistic reflection. In Morrison and Atkinson (minitrack coordinators) [50], pages 820–831.

45. M.L. Kersten, S. Plomp, and C.A. van der Berg. Object management in Goblin. In Özsu et al. [58]. The final proceedings will be published as: M.T. Özsu, U. Dayal and P. Valduriez (eds.), *Distributed Object Management*, Morgan Kaufmann, 1992.
46. P. Kanellakis and J.W. Schmidt, editors. *Database Programming Languages: Bulk Types and Persistent Data.* San Mateo, CA: Morgan Kaufmann Publishers, 1991. Proceedings of the Third International Workshop on Database Programming Languages (Nafplion, Greece, 27th–30th August 1991).
47. B. Liskov, R. Atkinson, T. Bloom, E. Moss, J.C. Schaffert, R. Scheifler, and A. Snyder. *CLU Reference Manual*, volume 114 of *Lecture Notes in Computer Science*. Springer-Verlag, Berlin, 1981.
48. B. Liskov. Overview of the ARGUS language and system. MIT Programming Methodology Group Memo 40, MIT, February 1984.
49. T. Landers and R.L. Rosenberg. An overview of Multibase. In H.-J. Schneider, editor, *Distributed Databases*, pages 153–184. North-Holland Publishing Company, 1982.
50. R. Morrison and M.P. Atkinson (minitrack coordinators), editors. *Proceedings of the Twenty-Fifth Hawaii International Conference on System Sciences, Volume II, Software Technology, Persistent Object Systems*, 1992.
51. F. Matthes. *Generic Database Programming: A Linguistic and Architectural Framework.* PhD thesis, Fachbereich Informatik, Universität Hamburg, Germany, September 1992. (In German).
52. R. Morrison, A.L. Brown, R. Carrick, R.C.H. Connor, A. Dearle, and M.P. Atkinson. The Napier type system. In J. Rosenberg and D. Koch, editors, *Persistent Object Stores*, Workshops in Computing, pages 3–18. Springer-Verlag in collaboration with the British Computer Society, 1989. Proceedings of the Third International Workshop on Persistent Object Systems (10th–13th January 1989, Newcastle, New South Wales, Australia).
53. R. Morrison, A. Dearle, R.C.H. Connor, and A.L. Brown. An ad hoc approach to the implementation of polymorphism. *ACM Transactions on Programming Languages and Systems*, 13(3):342–371, July 1991.
54. J.E.B. Moss. Addressing large distributed collections of persistent objects: The Mneme project's approach. In Hull et al. [39], pages 358–374. Proceedings of the Second International Workshop on Database Programming Languages (Salishan Lodge, Gleneden Beach, Oregon, June 1989).
55. F. Matthes and J.W. Schmidt. Bulk data types; built-in or added-on? In Kanellakis and Schmidt [46]. Proceedings of the Third International Workshop on Database Programming Languages (Nafplion, Greece, 27th–30th August 1991).
56. F. Matthes and J.W. Schmidt. Preliminary definition of the Tycoon language TL. DBIS Tycoon Report 062-92, Fachbereich Informatik, Universität Hamburg, Germany, June 1992.
57. R.S. Nikhil. Functional databases, functional languages. In M.P. Atkinson, O.P. Buneman, and R. Morrison, editors, *Data Types and Persistence*, Topics in Information Systems, series editors M.L. Brodie, J. Mylopoulos and Schmidt, J.W., chapter 5, pages 51–67. Springer-Verlag, 1988. Edited Papers from the Proceedings of the First Workshop on Persistent Object Systems (Appin, Scotland, August 1985).
58. M.T. Özsu, U. Dayal, and P. Valduriez, editors. *Pre-Proceedings of the International Workshop on Distributed Object Management (Edmonton, Canada, 18th–21st August 1992)*, 1992. The final proceedings will be published as: M.T. Özsu, U. Dayal and P. Valduriez (eds.), *Distributed Object Management*, Morgan Kaufmann, 1992.
59. The common object request broker: Architecture and specification. Published jointly by Object Management Group and X/Open, 1991.

60. A. Ohori, I. Tabkha, R.C.H. Connor, and P.C. Philbrow. Persistence and type abstraction revisited. In Dearle et al. [36], pages 141–153. Proceedings of the Fourth International Workshop on Persistent Object Systems, Their Design, Implementation and Use (Martha's Vineyard, USA, September 1990).
61. Perihelion Technology Ltd, The Maltings, Charleton Road, Shepton Mallet, Somerset, England BA4 5QE. *Polyhedra Application Generation Environment, Version 2.0*, 1992.
62. K. Ramamritham and P.K. Chrysanthis. In search of acceptability criteria: Database consistency requirements and transaction correctness properties. In Özsu et al. [58]. The final proceedings will be published as: M.T. Özsu, U. Dayal and P. Valduriez (eds.), *Distributed Object Management*, Morgan Kaufmann, 1992.
63. M. Riveill. An overview of the Guide language. In *Second Workshop on Objects in Large Distributed Applications (18th October 1992, Vancouver, Canada)*, 1992.
64. J. Rosenberg and J.L. Keedy, editors. *Security and Persistence. Proceedings of the International Workshop on Computer Architectures to Support Security and Persistence of Information (Bremen, West Germany, 8–11 May 1990)*, Workshops in Computing. Springer-Verlag in collaboration with the British Computer Society, 1990.
65. Strom, Bacon, Goldberg, Lowry, Yellin, and Yemini. *Hermes: A Language for Distributed Computing*. Prentice-Hall, 1991.
66. C. Schaffert. CORBA: OMG's object request broker. In Özsu et al. [58]. The final proceedings will be published as: M.T. Özsu, U. Dayal and P. Valduriez (eds.), *Distributed Object Management*, Morgan Kaufmann, 1992.
67. N.C. Shu, B.C. Housel, R.W. Taylor, S.P. Ghosh, and V.Y. Lum. EXPRESS: A data EXtraction, Processing, and REStructuring System. *ACM Transactions on Database Systems*, 2(2):134–174, June 1977.
68. D.I.K. Sjøberg. Measuring name and identifier usage in Napier88 applications. Technical Report FIDE/92/37, ESPRIT Basic Research Action, Project Number 3070—FIDE, 1992.
69. D.I.K. Sjøberg. Measuring schema evolution. Technical Report FIDE/92/36, ESPRIT Basic Research Action, Project Number 3070—FIDE, 1992.
70. V. Singhal, S.V. Kakkad, and P.R. Wilson. Texas: An efficient, portable persistent store. In Albano and Morrison [11], pages 11–33. Proceedings of the Fifth International Workshop on Persistent Object Systems (San Miniato, Italy, 1st–4th September 1992).
71. D. Stemple and R. Morrison. Specifying flexible concurrency control schemes: An abstract operational approach. Technical Report FIDE/92/35, ESPRIT Basic Research Action, Project Number 3070—FIDE, 1992. 17pp.
72. D. Stemple, R.B. Stanton, T. Sheard, P.C. Philbrow, R. Morrison, G.N.C. Kirby, L. Fegaras, R.L. Cooper, R.C.H. Connor, M.P. Atkinson, and S. Alagic. Type-safe linguistic reflection: A generator technology. Technical Report FIDE/92/49, ESPRIT Basic Research Action, Project Number 3070—FIDE, 1992. 29pp.
73. P.W. Trinder. Comprehensions, a query notation for DBPLs. In Kanellakis and Schmidt [46]. Proceedings of the Third International Workshop on Database Programming Languages (Nafplion, Greece, 27th–30th August 1991).
74. F. Vaughan and A. Dearle. Supporting large persistent stores using conventional hardware. In Albano and Morrison [11], pages 34–53. Proceedings of the Fifth International Workshop on Persistent Object Systems (San Miniato, Italy, 1st–4th September 1992).
75. M. Wolczko and I. Williams. Multi-level garbage collection in a high-performance persistent object system. In Albano and Morrison [11], pages 396–418. Proceedings of the Fifth International Workshop on Persistent Object Systems (San Miniato, Italy, 1st–4th September 1992).

76. P. Zezula and F. Rabitti. An efficient store for object bases. In Morrison and Atkinson (minitrack coordinators) [50], pages 756–765.

Chapter 2.1.2

The DBPL Project: Advances in Modular Database Programming*

Joachim W. Schmidt and Florian Matthes

Technical University Hamburg-Harburg, Harburger Schloßstraße 20, D-21071 Hamburg, Germany

1 Introduction

In the DBPL project we tackled the problem of supporting data-intensive applications in a single framework, clean and simple in its conceptual foundation and free of technical mismatches. Our development of specific language extensions required by data-intensive applications was guided by a strict adherence to the language design principles of simplicity, orthogonality and abstraction. The project started in the mid 70ies with Pascal/R [16–18,6] and Modula/R [10,12] where we first suggested some high-level language constructs for data of type relation. This research culminated in the delivery of a mature implementation of the DBPL system [23,22,15,14,19], a database programming language based on Modula-2.

2 DBPL Language Concepts

In the full paper [23] we describe the rationale, the conceptual basis for the language design [21] and the specific language elements in detail. Conceptually, we based the DBPL language on Modula-2 with built-in extensions for data-intensive applications:

- a parametric bulk type constructor for "keyed sets" or relations;
- a module concept which supports sharing across programs and implies persistence;
- a procedure concept with transactional semantics, i.e. serializability and recovery;
- abstraction from bulk iteration through associative access expressions.

In particular, we eliminated the competence and impedance mismatch between programming languages and database management systems by providing

orthogonal persistence, a uniform treatment of volatile and persistent data,
type completeness, a uniform treatment of large quantities of objects with a simple structure and small quantities of objects with a complex structure, as well as
strong static typing, a uniform (static) compatibility check between the declaration and the utilization of each name.

* This text is a synopsis of [23].

In implementing the DBPL system we adopted a rather strict approach by aiming for

- full orthogonality in our relationally extended type space, leading especially to nested relations;
- type-complete persistence, i.e. longevity of data from Booleans to relations;
- functional abstraction for relational expressions including recursion.

Without going into details it should be noted that naming (of statements, expressions etc.) naturally leads to the concept of recursion (see Fig. 1). The semantics of a recursive query expression in DBPL is not defined operationally (as is common practice for procedures) but as a least fixed point of recursive set equation [2,5].

```
TYPE NumPairType = RELATION OF RECORD
                               Super, Sub : PartNumType END;

CONSTRUCTOR TransitiveMadeFrom: NumPairType;
BEGIN
  {p.Name, mf.Num} OF
     EACH p IN PartRel, EACH mf IN p.MadeFrom:
       p.State = comp,
  {mf1.Super, mf2.Sub} OF
    EACH mf1 IN {TransitiveMadeFrom},
    EACH mf2 IN {TransitiveMadeFrom}:
      mf1.Sub = mf2.Super
END TransitiveMadeFrom;
```

Fig. 1. Recursive query (access expression) in DBPL

3 DBPL System Architecture

In the full paper we report on experience gained during DBPL system implementation and refinement in

- removing conventional compiler implementation restrictions [20],
- extending the expressiveness of the bulk query language,
- generalizing the storage model, and
- reducing system performance bottlenecks resulting from mismatches between independently developed contributing technologies [4].

A repeating pattern in the development of the DBPL system was the need to generalize existing database solutions to meet the requirements imposed by the orthogonal DBPL language model.

DBPL was not the end of our efforts in supporting database programming. We embedded it into a network of DBPL-based spin-off projects ranging from distributed DBPL [8,11] to DBPL-oriented programming environments (DAIDA) [3,7,24]. The Open DBPL/SQL gateway [13] and the bidirectional call interfaces between DBPL and other languages demonstrated that it requires a surprisingly small effort to embed a "closed" database programming language with a well-designed internal architecture into "open" system environments.

4 On Project Termination

Over the years, we encountered several data modeling concepts (inheritance, object identifiers, ordered bulk data structures, triggers, etc.) and database system requirements (communication between concurrent processes, exception handling, etc.) that did not fit nicely into the original DBPL language framework (see, for example, [1,9]). We regard the monomorphic type system of Modula-2, the lack of first-class procedures, and the strict separation between built-in and user-defined system functionality in the DBPL system architecture as hard, built-in limitations which prevent, without violating our design principles, DBPL extensions beyond the realms of set- and predicate-based data models and first-order programming languages.

The DBPL project results in a mature product for modular database application programming and a follow-up project Tycoon (see Chapters 1.1.1 and 2.1.4) based on polymorphic types and other higher-order concepts. Thus the Tycoon project carries forward in a more general linguistic and architectural framework the experience gained with bulk data typing, iteration abstraction, and modularization in DBPL.

Acknowledgements. The research presented here was supported by ESPRIT Basic Research, #892 (DAIDA), #3070 (FIDE), #6309 ($FIDE_2$).

References

1. S. Böttcher, M. Jarke, and J.W. Schmidt. Adaptive predicate managers in database systems. In *Proceedings of the Twelfth International Conference on Very Large Databases, Kyoto, Japan*, 1986.
2. J. Eder, A. Rudloff, F. Matthes, and J.W. Schmidt. Data construction with recursive set expressions in DBPL. In *Proceedings of the Kiev East/West Workshop on Next Generation Database Technology*, volume 504 of *Lecture Notes in Computer Science*, April 1991.
3. M. Jarke. *Database Application Engineering with DAIDA*. Springer-Verlag, 1993.
4. M. Jarke and J. Koch. Range nesting: A fast method to evaluate quantified queries. In *Proceedings of the ACM-SIGMOD International Conference on Management of Data*, pages 196–206, May 1983.
5. M. Jarke, V. Linnemann, and J.W. Schmidt. Data constructors: On the integration of rules and relations. In *Proceedings of the Eleventh International Conference on Very Large Databases, Stockholm*, August 1985.
6. M. Jarke and J.W. Schmidt. Query processing strategies in the Pascal/R relational database management system. In *Proceedings of the ACM-SIGMOD International Conference on Management of Data, Orlando, Florida*, 1982.

7. M. Jeusfeld, M. Mertikas, I. Wetzel, Jarke. M., and J.W. Schmidt. Database application development as an object modelling activity. In *Proceedings of the Sixteenth International Conference on Very Large Databases, Brisbane, Australia*, August 1990.
8. W. Johannsen, L. Ge, W. Lamersdorf, K. Reinhard, and J.W. Schmidt. Database application support in open systems: Language support and implementation. In *Proceedings of the IEEE Fourth International Conference on Data Engineering, Los Angeles, California*, February 1988.
9. W. Johannsen, W. Lamersdorf, K. Reinhard, and J.W. Schmidt. The DURESS project: Extending databases into an open systems architecture. In *Proceedings of the First Conference on Extending Database Technology, EDBT'88*, volume 303 of *Lecture Notes in Computer Science*, pages 616–620. Springer-Verlag, 1988.
10. J. Koch, M. Mall, P. Putfarken, M. Reimer, J.W. Schmidt, and C.A. Zehnder. Modula/R report, lilith version. Technical report, Department Informatik, ETH Zürich, Switzerland, February 1983.
11. W. Lamersdorf, H. Eckhardt, W. Effelsberg, K. Reinhard, and J.W. Schmidt. Database programming for distributed office systems. In *Proc. Int. Conf. on Office Automation*, Washington, 1987.
12. M. Mall, M. Reimer, and J.W. Schmidt. Data selection, sharing and access control in a relational scenario. In M.L. Brodie, J.L. Myopoulos, and J.W. Schmidt, editors, *On Conceptual Modelling*. Springer-Verlag, 1984.
13. F. Matthes, A. Rudloff, J.W. Schmidt, and K. Subieta. A gateway from DBPL to Ingres. In T. Risch W. Litwin, editor, *Applications of Databases, First International Conference, ADB-94*, volume 819 of *Lecture Notes in Computer Science*, pages 365–380, Vadstena, Sweden, June 1994. Springer-Verlag.
14. F. Matthes and J.W. Schmidt. The type system of DBPL. In *Proceedings of the Second International Workshop on Database Programming Languages, Portland, Oregon*, pages 255–260, June 1989.
15. F. Matthes and J.W. Schmidt. DBPL: The system and its environment. In M. Jarke, editor, *Database Application Engineering with DAIDA*, pages 319–348. Springer-Verlag, 1993.
16. J.W. Schmidt. Some high level language constructs for data of type relation. In *Proceedings of the ACM-SIGMOD International Conference on Management of Data, Toronto, Canada*, August 1977. (Also appeared in ACM TODS, 2(3), September, 1977 and A. Wasserman (editor), IEEE Tutorial on Programming Language Design, and M. Stonebreaker (editor), Readings in Database Systems, Morgan Kaufmann Publishers, 1988 and 1993).
17. J.W. Schmidt. Type concepts for database definition. In B. Shneiderman, editor, *Databases: Improving Usability and Responsiveness*. Academic Press, New York and London, 1978.
18. J.W. Schmidt and M. Mall. Pascal/R report. Bericht 66, Fachbereich Informatik, Universität Hamburg, Germany, January 1980.
19. J.W. Schmidt and M. Mall. Abstraction mechanisms for database programming. In *Proc. SIGPLAN Symp. on Programming Language Issues in Software Systems*, San Francisco, June 1983.
20. J.W. Schmidt and F. Matthes. Naming schemes and name space management in the DBPL persistent storage system. In *Proceedings of the Fourth International Workshop on Persistent Object Systems, Martha's Vineyard, Massachusetts*. Morgan Kaufmann Publishers, January 1991.
21. J.W. Schmidt and F. Matthes. The rationale behind DBPL. In *3rd Symposium on Mathematical Fundamentals of Database and Knowledge Base Systems*, volume 495 of *Lecture Notes in Computer Science*. Springer-Verlag, May 1991.

22. J.W. Schmidt and F. Matthes. Modular and rule-based database programming in DBPL. In M. Jarke, editor, *Database Application Engineering with DAIDA*, pages 85–124. Springer-Verlag, 1993.
23. J.W. Schmidt and F. Matthes. The DBPL project: Advances in modular database programming. *Information Systems*, 19(2):121–140, 1994.
24. J.W. Schmidt, I. Wetzel, A. Borgida, and J. Mylopoulos. Database programming by formal refinement of conceptual designs. *IEEE – Data Engineering*, September 1989.

Chapter 2.1.3

The PamCase Machine

Quintin Cutts*, Richard Connor* and Ron Morrison

School of Mathematical and Computational Sciences, University of St Andrews, North Haugh, St Andrews KY16 9SS, Scotland

Abstract. The application of orthogonal persistence to a number of traditional programming language mechanisms has produced significant results for the modelling power of persistent languages. Many of the implementation techniques for these mechanisms have been copied or adapted from non-persistent systems for use in early persistent language implementations. As the appearance of integrated persistent programming environments becomes more widespread, an examination of these implementation techniques shows that they may not be well-suited to a persistent environment. The premise of this paper is that the techniques do not take into account the increased object management costs involved in a persistent system. Aspects of the PamCase abstract machine architecture are presented that efficiently implement a number of common language mechanisms as well as some novel ones enabled within the persistent environment. The machine has been implemented and measurements support the initial premise.

1 Introduction

The application of orthogonal persistence to a number of traditional programming language mechanisms has produced significant results for the modelling power of persistent languages. However, the implementations of these mechanisms have not been significantly evolved to meet the changed execution environment of an orthogonally persistent system. The run-time environment of a non-persistent language may manipulate highly structured representations of program and data, all of which are discarded at the end of the program execution. Any data required to persist long-term is copied and translated into a flat format suitable for storage in a file system. By comparison, in an orthogonally persistent system, where all data types have the full range of persistence, it is the structured representations used in the run-time environment that are passed directly to the long-term store by the underlying persistence mechanism. It is the premise of this paper that traditional language implementation mechanisms are profligate in their use of objects, possibly to gain fast execution speeds, and that it is the consequent high and unnecessary object management costs that significantly reduce the performance of persistent systems. This paper describes aspects of the PamCase abstract machine architecture, designed to support efficient execution in a persistent-object based system. The aspects under discussion support efficient implementation of three important persistent programming language mechanisms. By way of motivation, these mechanisms are now described.

---

* Present address: Department of Computing Science, University of Glasgow, Glasgow G12 8QQ, Scotland.

1.1 Persistent First-class Procedures

A first-class procedure has the same rights as any other value, e.g. it may be declared, assigned, passed as parameter, returned as result, or be a component of a record or array. In an othogonally persistent system, it is further entitled to the full range of persistence. Persistent first-class procedures [2] are used heavily in new paradigms for program construction and modelling. Two examples follow:

- **Application Construction**: First-class procedure values are the primary components used to construct an executable application within the persistent store. Using the application construction methodology described in [16], executable code is treated as a structured and extensible data type where each node within the structure is a first-class procedure. A blend of static and dynamic binding and type checking is used to construct applications that are statically type checked whilst permitting type safe incremental linking of new or updated components. The entire Napier88 programming environment (Chapter 1.1.3), over 100,000 lines of code, is constructed using this methodology.

- **Protection Mechanisms**: First-class procedures are used in persistent systems to implement protection mechanisms, for example, password protection techniques and first order information hiding [22]. Descriptions of these may be found in Chapter 1.1.3 of this book.

In implementation terms, a first-class procedure is a segmented executable code unit, usually containing encapsulated state, that may be retained long-term within the persistent environment. This is in contrast to traditional systems where first-class procedures only exist for the duration of the program's execution and executable code stored long-term is held in non-segmented, non-updateable code files containing no encapsulated state beyond simple manifest values. An efficient representation for a persistent first-class procedure is required to ensure low storage costs and fast automatic transfer between long and short-term storage devices. The representation must also support efficient execution.

1.2 Manipulation of Store Locations

Traditional store semantics languages have the concept of a store of locations into which values may be assigned. In a non-persistent language, the store exists for the duration of a program's execution; if required, a separate mechanism copies the values contained in the locations to long-term storage. In a persistent language, first-class store locations with the full range of persistence may be created and manipulated within the persistent store. Additionally new programming paradigms enabled by an integrated persistent programming environment allow the locations associated with the free identifiers of a procedure to be manipulated in novel ways. The benefits of persistent first-class store locations are described using the following three sections.

1.2.1 Hyper-programming

In an integrated persistent programming system, source code construction takes place in an environment that may contain persistent values created during earlier program executions. By analogy with hyper-text, where a structured textual document may contain direct links to other documents, a *hyper-program* is a structured source code representation that may include links to other code and data values present in the environment. Many of the benefits of hyper-programming are described in detail in [18], and in Chapters 1.1.3 and 3.1.3. These include the ability to bind to the values and locations of free identifiers within a procedure closure.

Using the hyper-program representation, a unique source code representation of a first-class executable value may be given where the free identifiers of the procedure value are replaced by hyper-program links to the corresponding identifiers' locations and values. For example, consider the code in Figure 1 written in the persistent programming language Napier88 (Chapter 1.1.3) in which a procedure is created within the outermost, procedure-valued, *begin..end* block and then assigned to the identifier *counter*. The value of the identifier *val* and its associated location are bound into the procedure value created in the block, and must be retained with it to ensure correct execution of the procedure. Depending on the persistence of the procedure value, the location and value of *val* may also be required to persist.

```
let counter = begin
                    let val := 1

                    proc( → int ) ! fn header - takes no params
                    begin         ! and returns an integer
                         val := val + 1
                         val
                    end
              end

let one = counter()   ! '()' is procedure application
```

Fig. 1. Procedure with free identifier

The hyper-program representation of the *counter* procedure is shown on the left side of Figure 2 below. Note that this is a representation of the *value* associated with the identifier *counter* once it has been instantiated and called once. The free identifiers of the procedure value are represented using boxes; these are direct links to a location object associated with the identifier *val*.

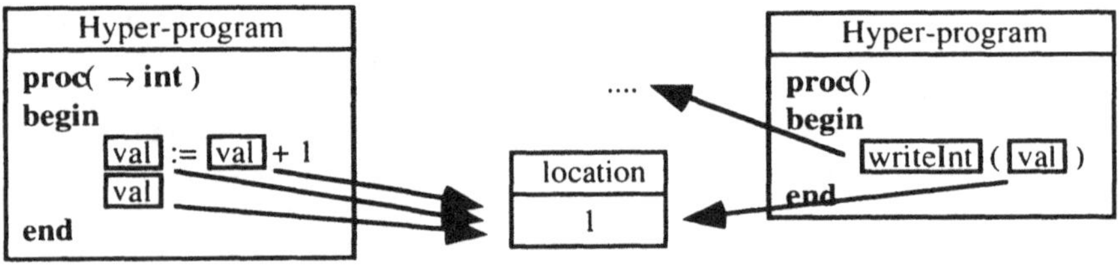

Fig. 2. Hyper-programs for *counter* value and for the new display procedure

An additional procedure may subsequently be required to write out the current value of the counter without updating it. This is achieved by writing a new hyper-program containing a copy of the link to *val* found in the hyper-program for *counter*. The new hyper-program is shown on the right hand side of Figure 2 and also contains a direct link to a procedure that writes out integer values. Both *counter* and the display procedures operate on the same integer location. Note that the construction of the new program violates the protection described in Section 1.1 of this chapter and in Chapter 1.1.3.

1.2.2 Partial Representations

Programming languages and programming environments typically support many binding processes between code and data, where the data may itself be other code values. For example, manifest data values may be included in source code; code and data may be bound during compilation in interactive programming environments; the static and dynamic linking processes common in imperative languages binds code segments together; and within run-time systems the mechanisms of closure formation and parameter passing are used to bind code to data, including locations.

Within an integrated persistent system, all these binding activities may be performed within a single environment, as shown in Chapter 1.1.3. The goal here is to find a uniform low-level mechanism that may be used to implement the range of binding times and processes described above.

Each binding process consists of the following components:

- A body of code that cannot be executed because some bindings, to values or locations, are incomplete
- A description of how the bindings should be formed
- A binding process taking the code, the binding description and an environment of values and locations and producing an executable code value or at least a version of the body of code with some of its incomplete bindings resolved

The first two components form a *partial representation*. Ongoing research is attempting to show how each of the binding processes mentioned above can be mapped onto this partial representation model.

1.2.3 Application construction

The application construction methodology introduced in Section 1.1 is based on the use of persistent locations. Each component of the application is held in a separate location. When a new version of a component is constructed, it is bound to the *locations* of the components to which it refers before being assigned into its own location. Since the locations are typed, type-safety is assured. During execution of an application, each component performs a dereference of the locations to which it is bound in order to access the latest version of the other components. Relinking a new version of a component involves overwriting the location with the new version (although if the type of the component has changed, a little more work is required).

The efficient implementation of these three programming paradigms depends on the provision of mechanisms to create, access, update and manipulate first-class persistent store locations. Additionally, the implementation of first-class procedures should ideally enable easy access to and manipulation of the locations containing values of free identifiers.

1.3 Dynamic Structural Type Checking

Static and dynamic type checking may be used heavily in the context of long-lived, data-intensive application environments to support increased reliability and productivity, evolution, data modelling and protection [21, 11, 22, 25, 10]. Additionally, type equivalence by *structure* rather than by *name* is necessary for some operations in persistent systems [7].

Structural type equivalence requires the construction of complex representations of the type's structure over which the checking algorithms are performed. Type system operations performed during execution are typically restricted or avoided partly because of the inherent cost of transferring complex type information (type representations) between compile-time (static) and run-time (dynamic) environments.

In an integrated persistent system, compilation takes place within the execution environment and so the separate concepts of static and dynamic checking are merged. This offers both advantages and disadvantages to the type checking exercise:

- Type representations constructed during compilation are readily available during execution. No complex transfer operation is required.
- The efficiency of the execution environment may be adversely affected by the presence of complex type representations which are frequently required to persist long-term.
- The same type system operations are used for both static and dynamic type checking. Although type equality is usually the only operation available during execution, other type operations are also useful then [12].

The goals in implementing a type system of this nature involve: minimising the size of type representations whilst maximising performance of the type system operations; allowing the same type checking operations to be accessed both from high-level programs (such as the compiler) and from the machine implementation (for type system operations required by the language semantics) – using the same type checking module aids implementation, reliability and portability.

1.4 Minimising Object Management Costs

The preceding sections have highlighted some of the goals required for the efficient implementation of particular persistent programming mechanisms. Inherent in each of the goals is a more general requirement to minimise object management costs. In a persistent system where provision must be made to move the objects used for store locations, type representations and the implementation of first-class procedures between long and short-term storage, it is essential that the size and number of objects is held to a minimum. Particular sub-goals for persistent object management are:

- minimising object creation
- minimising object retention long-term within the persistent store
- simplifying location access

It is expected that the achievement of these goals will have the overall result of improved space and time efficiency for persistent systems. This paper describes the aspects of the design of the PamCase abstract machine that enable the goals to be met. The following sections describe: the use of an independent object manager as part of the machine's design; value formats and the machine's execution model; the first-class procedure implementation; and the mechanism by which the machine accesses the high-level type system module. Finally, a measurements section indicates the success of the machine design in achieving the stated goals.

2 Object Management

The PamCase machine uses storage facilities provided by an object manager. Apart from the machine's registers, the object manager supplies all storage required by the machine through a well-defined interface. Low-level object store operations such as garbage collection and stabilisation are performed by the object manager. The separation of object management functions from the abstract machine simplifies the machine design, aids the provision of orthogonal persistence [3] and improves the potential for portability and experimentation.

A consequence of relying on the object manager for low-level object management operations is the machine's dependence on the particular object format specified by the interface to the manager. All abstract machine objects must be mapped onto this format, for example, first-class procedure implementation objects, type representations and store locations.

The format allows the object manager to support operations such as garbage collection and stabilisation without any knowledge of an object's semantic interpretation. The object format used within this architecture, specified for the object managers designed by Brown [4] (Chapter 2.2.1), is illustrated in Figure 3. An object consists of a number of contiguous words in memory. The first word of the object is known as the *header* and contains the number of pointer components in the object, held in the low-order 24 bits of the word; the remaining bits may be used for implementation experiments. The next word contains the size of the object in words. Each pointer component takes up one word and these come directly after the size word. Pointers address the first word of an object. The remaining space in the object after the pointers contains non-pointer components: the formatting of these components is of no interest to the object manager. This format has been successfully implemented on differing hardware architectures.

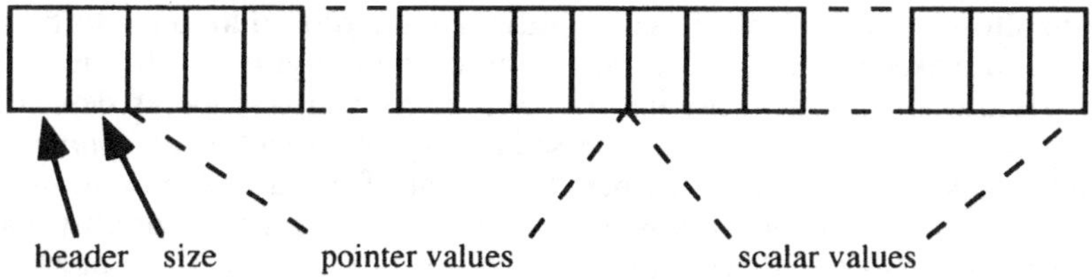

Fig. 3. Uniform object format

3 Value Formats and the Execution Model

For reasons of efficiency, the abstract machine provides separate instructions to operate over data in a small number of different value formats. Language data types are mapped onto these formats. This allows values to be stored in formats which coincide with their respective hardware operations and this minimises any translation costs. For example, integers and booleans are represented using a single non-pointer (scalar) word; reals are represented using two scalar words; objects such as arrays and records are referenced using a single pointer; and procedure values are represented using two pointers as will be seen in Section 4. Mixed pointer and scalar formats are also available. All the formats are described in detail in [8].

The execution model, developed from one of the machine's predecessors, the S-machine [20], is based on the use of two stacks. One stack holds pointer values, the other, scalars. The two stacks were originally used to aid the pointer-following required for garbage collection in a machine architecture supporting multiple value formats, essentially the same reason that the uniform object format requires the segregation of pointers from non-pointers. The machine instructions may operate on either or both stacks. The stacks are represented within the definition of objects provided by the object manager: their format is described in Section 4.

A consequence of the execution model's support for multiple value formats is the method of implementation of **polymorphic** code. Polymorphism allows code to be written which abstracts over the type of the data upon which it operates [5].

The PamCase machine uses an implementation technique described fully in [23] in which values are converted to a uniform format in polymorphic contexts and tag information, to be be used for type-sensitive operations, is associated with the values. Examples of such operations are equality and the conversions between the monomorphic and polymorphic formats. Of relevance to this paper is the fact that neither the uniform format nor the tagging impose significant object management costs, instead a slight penalty in execution speed is suffered. The implementation supports polymorphism without compromising the efficiency of monomorphic code.

4 First-class Procedure Implementation

Many techniques have been developed for the implementation of first-class procedures, from Landin's classical SECD-machine [19] to the Continuation Passing Style popularised in the Standard ML of New Jersey systems [1]. The mechanism described here is derived from the CASE machine [15], itself derived from the machine used to implement the language IDEA [14].

The primary issue involved in first-class procedure implementations is the mechanism allowing the values of free identifiers in the procedure body to be accessed during procedure execution. Consider again the code in Figure 1. In the figure, the extent or lifetime of the identifier *val* has escaped its static scope as defined by the outer *begin-end* block since it can be accessed during the execution of *counter*. Using a traditional stack execution model, where the extent of an identifier is limited by its static scope, the location for *val* would have been reclaimed and possibly reused by the time *counter* was called, resulting in incorrect evaluation. A mechanism is required therefore to retain the values of the free identifiers of a procedure. The combination of the free identifier values and the procedure code is known as the procedure *closure* and the point during execution at which the two are associated together is known as *closure formation*.

4.1 Procedure closure representation and formation

In PamCase, a procedure closure consists of the code of the procedure held in a code vector object and an *environment* object containing the values of the procedure's free identifiers.

During execution, values for identifiers declared locally within a procedure are created and accessed on the stack, whilst the values of free identifiers are accessed via the environment. Executing code can access only values in the local stack frame and in the associated environment object.

On closure formation, a new environment object is created and the appropriate values are copied into it from the enclosing procedure's local stack and environment. The form closure operation uses an *environment template* object constructed, along with the code vector, during compilation of the procedure. The template describes the layout of the new environment and the locations in the local stack or enclosing environment of the values required to populate it.

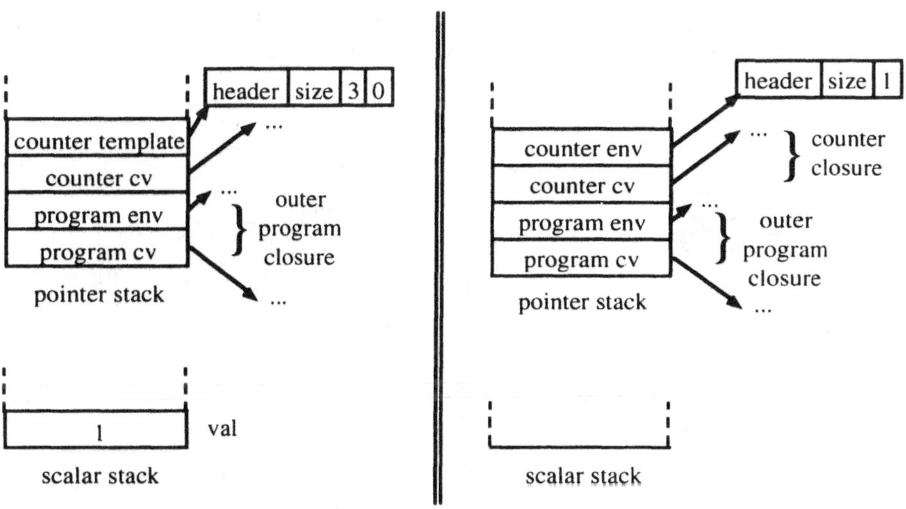

Fig. 4. The form closure operation

Consider the formation of the closure for the *counter* procedure of Figure 1. Just before the form closure operation takes place, pointers to the code vector and the environment template are placed onto the pointer stack. The template, illustrated in part A of Figure 4, is a persistent object and so has the header and size in the first two words, followed by an integer describing where to find the value for *val*. Finally, the object contains another integer indicating how many pointers the new environment object should contain. During closure formation, the size of the template less one (that is the word in the template indicating the number of pointers) gives the size of the new environment. The information for *val* in the template is interpreted as an offset from the stack frame base, the choice of stack determined by the position of the offset in the template. In this case, the environment contains no pointer values and so the *val* offset *3* refers to position 3 on the scalar stack (indexing from zero). Were the offset negative, the offset would be interpreted as relative to the start of the enclosing environment object. Using this information, the new environment is constructed and the appropriate values copied in, shown in part B of Figure 4. The new environment object replaces the template on the stack.

4.2 Procedure call and return

Setting up a procedure call consists of loading the procedure closure, that is a pointer to the code vector and a pointer to the environment object, onto the stack, followed by the procedure argument values if any. On application, the closure and arguments form the base of the new activation frame. Information required for correct procedure return is stored on the stack above the arguments. The return information consists of the return-address (in fact an offset within the calling procedure's code vector) within the calling procedure's code vector and the offset from the new frame base to the calling procedure's frame base. This offset is the dynamic link. Two frame base offsets are required as there are two stacks. Note that the frame-base return information is required to find and reinstate the code pointer and environment registers†. Stack base and code pointer registers may then be reset before execution continues in the new context. The call of *counter* in Figure 1 is shown in Figure 5.

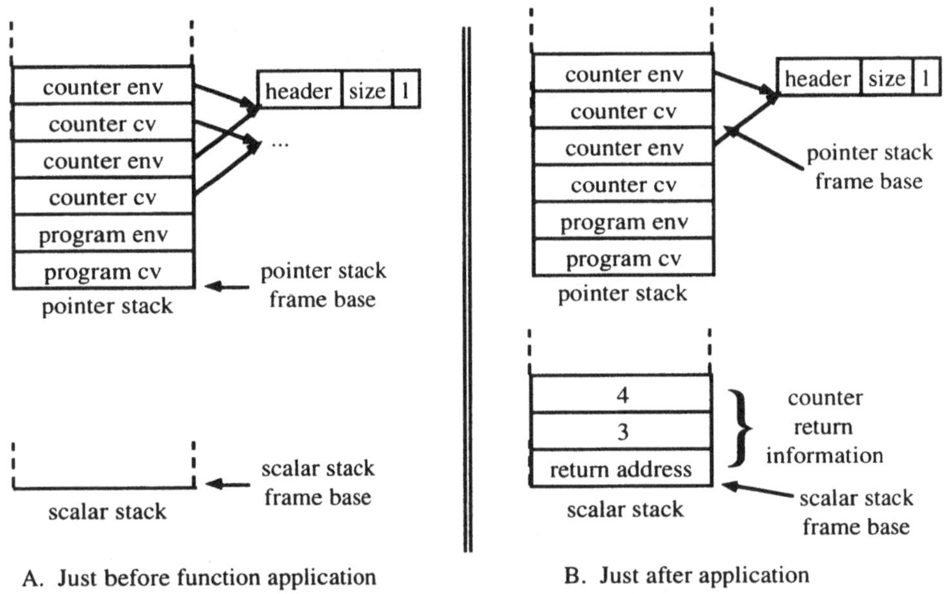

Fig. 5. Procedure call

The return instruction takes an offset parameter indicating the position relative to the top of the scalar stack of the return information which is used to reinstate the calling procedure's context.

† and also because the machine's instruction set currently uses a mix of frame base and stack top addressing.

4.3 Maintaining referential integrity of variable locations

The above mechanism works correctly for the example of Figure 1. However, if two procedures are created both operating over the identifier *val*, as in Figure 2, then the two closure formation operations would each take a copy of *val* into the respective environment objects, resulting in the loss of referential integrity over *val*'s location.

The environment mechanism for retaining free identifier values is developed from the CASE machine, designed to support lazy functional languages. Such languages have the property of referential transparency. It is the referential transparency property that allows the potential loss of referential integrity to be ignored in functional languages since without update it has no semantic impact. The store semantics of the languages for which PamCase is designed to support mean that each shared free variable location must be held within an object accessible both from the local stack and from the environment objects of the associated procedure closures.

A choice here is whether to marshall free variable locations into a single object where possible or to hold each location in a separate object. The former method reduces the number of objects required thereby lowering object management overheads, whilst the latter simplifies the addressing mechanism for free variables and supports the desirable property that ultimately only live values will be retained by the underlying object management system. The latter method is used in PamCase.

The cost of encapsulating every variable value in an independent object is suspected to be prohibitive and to negate the low object overhead of the CASE model. Note additionally that procedure parameters are subject to the same requirements as locally declared variables. The following analysis however allows the number of location objects to be restricted. The value for an identifier must only be encapsulated within a independent location object, or *boxed*, when

- it is a stack value, i.e. a procedure parameter or local variable
- it is accessible simultaneously from more than one procedure scope
- it is variable

The program of Figure 1 works correctly only because *val* is only ever accessible from a single procedure. Constant values may be freely copied between the stack and environments.

The use of this analysis allows the number of boxed values to be significantly reduced. Measurement of the reduction in boxing in given in Section 6.

4.4 Stack implementation

As described in Section 2, the machine uses two stacks. The two stacks are held within a single persistent object: the pointer stack grows up from the base of the object, the scalar stack back from the end. When the stack object becomes full, a new larger object is created and the stacks are copied over from the old stack object. The following reasons make this choice of a non-segmented, single-object representation the simplest and usually the most efficient:

- Only one test for stack overflow is required. The test is made on each procedure call and compares the statically-calculated size of the new activation frame against the remaining space between the two stack top pointers.

- No underflow test is required when the stacks are retracted – as would be required with a segmented stack where each segment contains a number of activation frames. A *halt* instruction signals the end of a thread's execution, removing the need to test for when the bottom of the stack is reached.
- Empty space in a stack object, remaining after a long series of recursive procedure calls for example, is not expected to be significant compared to the total amount of space used in the persistent system. It is accepted that pathological cases can be constructed.

4.5 The machine architecture

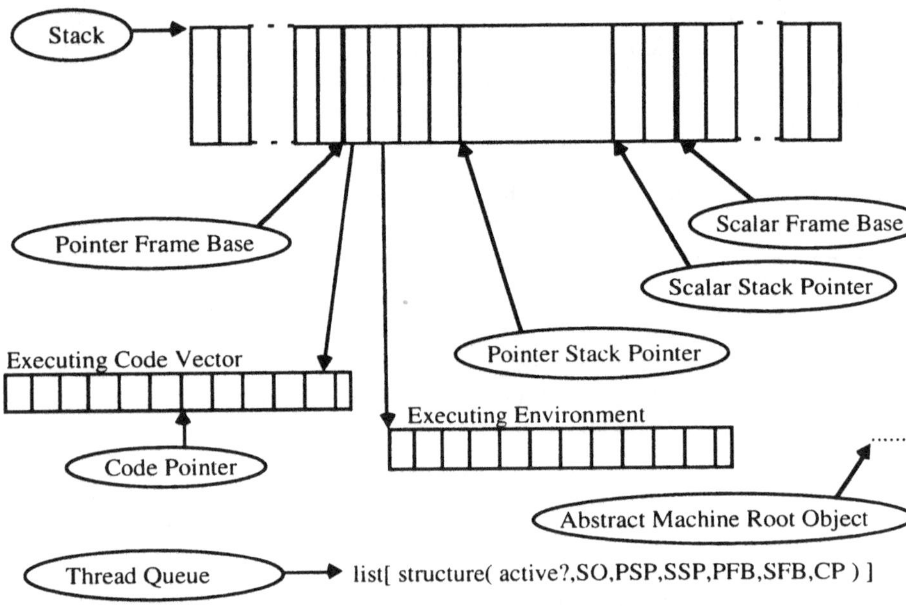

Fig. 6. The machine architecture

Figure 6 depicts the machine architecture. The ovals are machine registers. The machine supports multiple threads as described in [24]. Each thread is represented using a thread object which is a tuple of the various stack registers and an indication of whether the thread is currently active. The thread queue register points to a list of these objects and the abstract machine ensures fair execution between the threads.

The abstract machine root–object register points to an object that is used to record the entire state of the machine prior to a garbage collection or checkpoint, which are based on reachability from this object. The root object also contains pointers to functions and system-wide constant values required by the machine during execution and also to the root of all programmer-specified persistent data.

Whilst many of the machine registers point directly to positions within heap objects, in particular the stack and the code vector, such pointers may not be stored within persistent objects, in line with the uniform object format used throughout the system. Instead, offsets from object bases are stored within the thread objects.

5 High-level Parameterisable Type System

In Section 1.3, one of the stated goals towards implementing a suitable type system is the provision of a single type–checking module that can be used across the entire environment. That is, the module is accessible both to the high-level language code implementing for example a compiler and also to the abstract machine instructions that perform type–checking operations. Note that this module contains functionality to construct, examine and test the equivalence of type representations.

It is desirable to write the type–checking module in the host language for two reasons: it is easier to manipulate the structured, recursive type representations required to implement a complex type system using the data structures provided by a high-level language; secondly, once constructed, the type–checking module may be simply incorporated into the compiler, written in the host language and forming part of the integrated persistent environment.

Having written the type checking module in the host language (more on this in a moment) the module is assigned to a known location in the abstract machine root object. Abstract machine instructions involving type checking can access it from the root object and apply the appropriate operations as required. If the compiler writer needs to generate type system operations to be called dynamically, they can be accessed by root object accessing instructions and applied using the standard calling conventions. Finally the module may be made accessible in the persistent store to users for inclusion in their own programs (although since the integrity of the entire environment depends on the safe application of the type operations when constructing representations, this privilege may be seriously restricted!)

In Napier88, the persistent environment is bootstrapped using a compiler for the Napier88 constructed on an external system. The type checker is written in Napier88 using this compiler and assigned into the root object during execution of the program in which the type checking module is generated. Dynamic type checking may now be performed within the environment, which can now be populated with persistent values. Once the bootstrapping compiler has been used to construct a compiler for Napier88 written in Napier88 within the persistent environment, it may be discarded. The persistent environment subsequently may support its own evolution.

The second goal stated in Section 1.2 relates to the efficiency of object representations and operations. This depends primarily on two factors:

- The efficient implementation of the high-level language used to implement the type module. Of particular interest here is the first-class procedure implementation since the type module is implemented using procedures. This is covered in Section 4.
- A choice of efficient type checking algorithms and type representations for implementation in the high-level language. There are many trade–offs here associated with fast type equivalence checking, fast type representation construction and analysis (decomposition) functions and compact type representations. Detailed discussion of these matters may be found in [6,12].

6 Measuring up to the Goals

The PamCase machine was designed to support a class of polymorphic persistent languages efficiently. PamCase is derived from the Persistent Abstract Machine

(PAM) [9] an it is therefore sensible to compare the two in terms of execution speed and space requirements for both code and data. To reiterate, the primary goals of PamCase towards achieving improved space and speed efficiency are the minimising of object creation and retention and the simplification of access to locations. More specific goals are efficient procedure execution and type system operations.

The analysis is backed up by measurements of the machine's execution. An interpreter for the PamCase machine has been implemented in C and runs on Sun Sparcstations and DEC Alphas. The measurements provided here, taken using a Sun Sparcstation ELC with 40Mb memory and a local disk, running SunOS 4.1.3, are relative to the performance of the PAM while running Napier88 programs. The PAM interpreter is also implemented in C and uses identical mechanisms for components such as the decode loop.

6.1 First-class Procedures

The following points are made about the first-class procedure implementation before giving measurements of its performance.

- The only data retained by a closure, in its environment object, is that required for the correct execution of the procedure. This is in comparison with for example the PAM model, which uses a segmented stack and retains free variables in stack frame objects. The stack frame objects must be retained along with any contained pointers to objects that do not form part of the procedure's environment though they are conceptually garbage.
- Procedure call is efficient, by comparison to PAM which uses a segmented stack, requiring an object creation on every call to hold the activation record. As non-segmented stacks may be used in PamCase, no object creation is required on procedure call. Closure formation by comparison is expensive, requiring an object creation, but it is expected that its cost is usually amortised over many calls to the resulting value.
- Free identifier access is efficient, requiring only a dereference of the environment object. Traditional displays or static-chaining are not required.

Boxing free variables. A static analysis of the entire body of code for the Napier88 hyper-programming environment, more than 100,000 lines of code, has determined that only 3% of all identifiers need be boxed. In conjunction with the measurements given below for the execution of a large application, the overhead of boxing does not appear to be significant. It is planned to carry out a dynamic analysis to determine more accurately the exact boxing overhead.

The compiler and the analysis above use a slightly weaker rule to check where boxes are required than that given in Section 4.3, in that the value for an identifier is boxed whenever it is accessed from an inner–procedure's scope, irrespective of whether that scope is the only one to access it. As such, Figure 4 and Figure 5 should be adjusted to show that *val* is boxed on creation and it is a pointer to the box that is copied into the environment object for *counter*.

Closure formation times. Figure 7 gives a measure of the closure–formation time, varying the number of free variables required to make up the environment. In this case these were all integer values. In PAM, the closure–formation time is constant, whereas in PamCase it is proportional to the number of free variables in the procedure.

Procedure call times. Figure 8 shows procedure call and return times, varying the number of (integer) parameters. The *PamCase* data represents calls where the parameters did not require boxing: in the *PamCase (boxing)* they all did. When boxing is performed it causes a significant overhead. The PAM requires the creation of a new object on every call to be used for the new stack frame. It can be seen that the object allocation is the major cost in PAM's procedure call by comparing it to the PamCase (boxing) call with one boxed parameter - the costs for each are the same. Note also that by extrapolating the graph of Figure 7, a closure formation with around 12 environment values in PamCase takes the same time as a single procedure call in PAM.

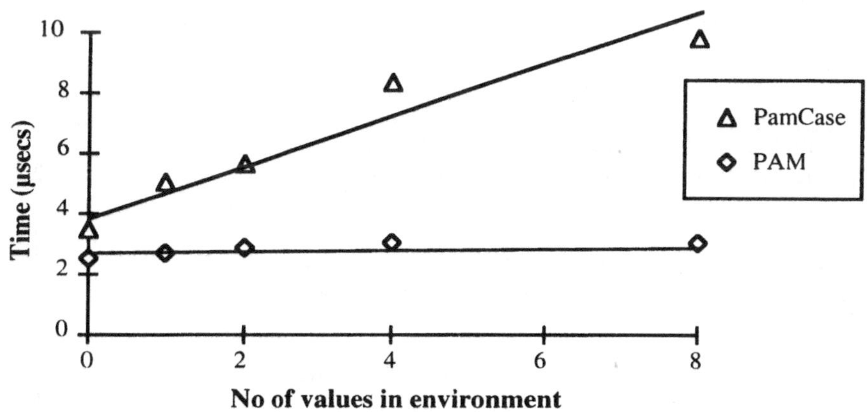

Fig. 7. Closure-formation times

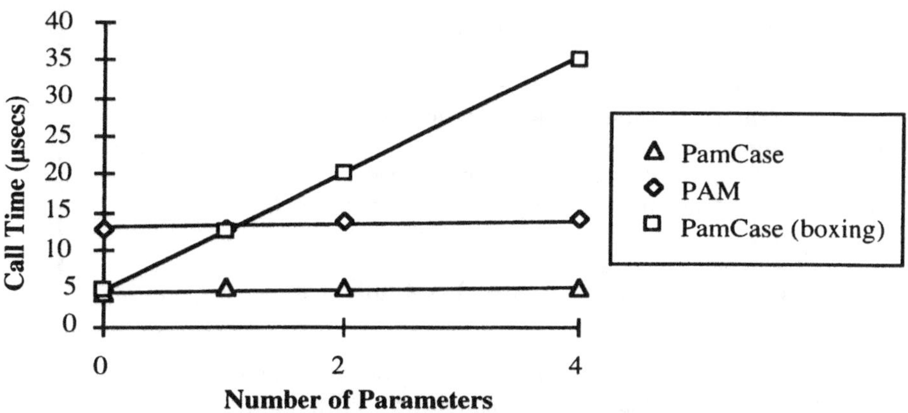

Fig. 8. Procedure call and return times

Object retention. Figure 9 gives the code for a very simple database application written in Napier88, taken from [17], designed to show object retention characteristics. The code generates two procedures, *addPerson* and *findPerson*, places them into a structure type *DB* and then stores the structure into the persistent store.

Figure 10 displays the result of measuring the number of objects reachable from the structure object, *exampleDatabase*, when it is removed from the store. The measurement compares the efficiency of the first-class procedure representations since the database at this stage contains almost no data. Both the number and size of individual objects and the total size of all objects are given. The PamCase machine retains only a quarter of the data retained by the PAM. This saving consists of two components: firstly, the PAM implementation retains the code vector for the outermost program; secondly, it retains type representations used to place the database structure into the store. Neither of these can ever be accessed by the database subsequently and are therefore not retained by the PamCase implementation. Note that in this example, the only free variable requiring boxing is *current*.

```
type Person is structure( name : string ; age : int )
type DB is structure( add : proc( string,int ) ;
                      find : proc( string → Person ) )

let nilPerson = Person( "",-1 ) ; let dbSize = 10
let database = vector 1 to dbSize of nilPerson
let current := 1

let addPerson = proc( name : string ; age : int )
begin
        database( current ) := Person( name,age )
        current := current + 1
end

let findPerson = proc( name : string → Person )
begin
        let tmp := 1 ; let found := false
        while tmp <= current and ~found do
        begin
                if database( tmp )( name ) = name
                then found := true else tmp := tmp + 1
        end

        if found then database( tmp ) else nilPerson
end

! Construct the database and place it in the persistent store
in PS() let exampleDatabase = DB( addPerson,findPerson )
```

Fig. 9. Placing procedures into the persistent store

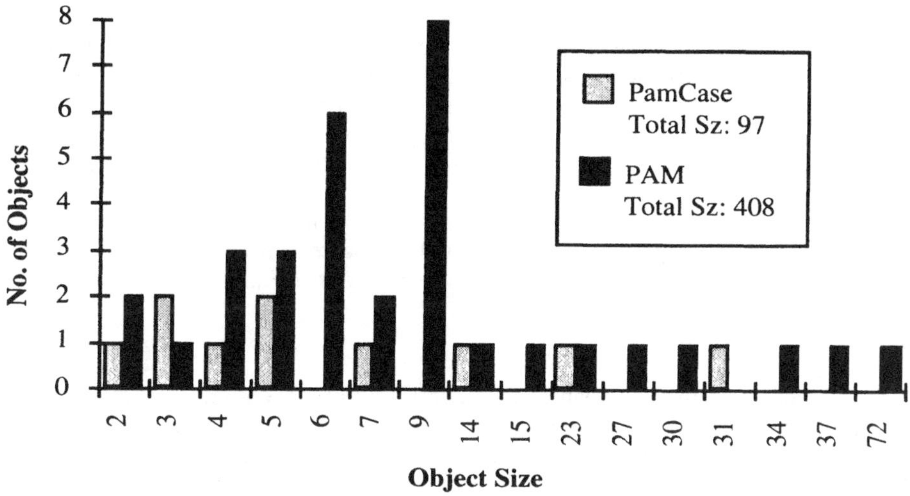

Fig. 10. Object retention measurements

Effect on a populated store. Measurements were taken using two persistent stores, each populated with an identical compiler written in the persistent language Napier88 for Napier88, compiling to PamCase abstract machine code. The compiler consists of about 20,000 lines of code. One store was implemented using the PAM, the other used PamCase.

Examining the size of the stores, the PAM store retained 287,047 objects, using up 12.113Mb of storage; the PamCase store retained only 29,775 objects, using up 1.362Mb of storage. Both stores were slightly larger than this though, caused by the addition of management space overheads. Since the two abstract machines use essentially the same instruction set, the code size between the two systems is about the same.

To measure the execution speed, the compiler was run against a wide variety of programs. On average, the PAM version took 2.3 times longer to execute than the PamCase version. The speed-up has two potential causes: the non-segmented stack, allowing faster procedure call; and the smaller store size, giving improved object faulting and clustering performance.

6.2 The type system implementation

The type representation described in [12] is the result of work to determine a representation suitable for persistent systems, good both for fast equivalence checking and for efficient construction and information-gathering (decomposition) operations. In stores using the PAM to implement the Napier88 type system, this representation offers at least an order of magnitude improvement in space characteristics over the first type system implementation. The latter's design was based on a traditional static/dynamic checking divide where different type representations were used for static and dynamic type checking, instead of the holistic approach taken in the new system.

As described in Section 5, the type checking module is implemented in the host high-level language as a package of procedures. The reduced object retention of the

PamCase procedure implementation has had a significant effect since a very large proportion of type information is no longer retained within the store. About 70% of the reduction in store size reported above for the compiler store is due to the reduced object retention of the new procedure implementation. However a simple type merging program was run against both stores which coalesced all equivalent but not identical representations. The merged type representations were those attached to store objects subject to dynamic type checking. These are the only type representations retained in the PamCase store, whereas the PAM version retains many conceptually garbage type representations within procedure closures. The merging program gives the remaining 30% space improvement for PamCase.

6.3 Location access

The individual boxing of variable free identifier values chosen for the first-class procedure implementation was considered when first discussed in Section 4 to be a hazard to efficiency. However, the separation of these program components into individually-addressable components may be viewed as a benefit as it simplifies the use of such values in the new programming paradigms enabled within an integrated persistent environment.

The ability to insert free variable locations of first-class procedures into hyper-programs increases the requirement for efficient access to such locations. The procedure–closure representation of PamCase is well suited here. The code vector includes a source code representation that contains descriptions of the free identifiers' name, type, constancy and location in the closure's environment object. The information is used by programming environment tools to access and manipulate free identifier values.

The three components of the *partial representation* model outlined in the Introduction map closely to the code vector, environment template and closure formation operation used in PamCase's first-class procedure implementation. On-going research is showing that the same technique may be extended to support the other binding processes as well. The environment template is extended to include descriptions of all identifiers within the code that may be unbound. The form closure operation is adjusted to perform binding in an incremental manner in which both the input and output of the operation may be a partial representation. When all bindings are complete, the partial representation becomes an executable code segment. The freeing up of individual locations made possible by the environment model will simplify the process of choosing appropriate components with which to specialise a partial representation.

7 Related and Ongoing Work

Another derivative of the PAM has been constructed in parallel by Dearle and Farkas to support the Octopus model. The primary goal of their research is to provide low-level mechanisms to support the manipulation of locations and values bound into persistent values, in line with the goals described here in Section 1.3. Their machine uses the environment model for procedure closures but retains the segmented stack of the PAM. Details of their implementation can be found in [17] .

Both the PAM and PamCase machines were designed primarily for the implementation of the persistent programming language Napier88. The goal of engineering an integrated orthogonally-persistent programming environment has thus far overriden the requirement high performance. Ongoing work is now examining performance issues within the PamCase implementation, and in particular is assessing how the performance of the interpreter can be tuned through analysis of the object graphs retained within the persistent store. Such work can benefit both object–management and machine–execution costs [13].

8 Conclusions

It is stated in the Introduction that object management costs constitute a significant proportion of the execution cost, in terms of space and time, in an orthogonally persistent system. Further, traditional language implementations are not tuned to this object cost and when used in the implementation of a persistent language can seriously degrade performance.

Aspects of the PamCase machine architecture have been presented that reduce the object management overhead involved in implementing some common and novel language mechanisms. The reduction in object costs supported by the first-class procedure implementation combined with the type system implementation, both designed to reduce object overheads, is shown by the measurements of a Napier88 system to give significant improvements in performance: a factor of nearly 10 in space usage and of of around 2.3 in execution speed by comparison with an earlier machine, the PAM. It has also been shown that the implementation's support for manipulation of first-class persistent locations may be advantageously used to support novel programming language mechanisms enabled within a persistent system.

References

1. Appel, A. W. and MacQueen, D. B. (1991) Standard ML of New Jersey. In Proceedings of the Third International Symposium on Programming Language Implementation and Logic Programming, New York.
2. Atkinson, M. P. and Morrison, R. (1984) Persistent First Class Procedures are Enough. In M. Joseph and R. Shyamasundar (eds), *Lecture Notes in Computer Science 181*, pp. 223-240, Springer-Verlag,
3. Brown, A. L. (1989) Persistent Object Stores. *Ph.D. Thesis,* University of St Andrews.
4. Brown, A. L., Mainetto, G., Matthes, F., Müller, R. and McNally, D. J. (1992) An Open System Architecture for a Persistent Object Store. In *Proceedings of the 25th International Conference on Systems Sciences*, pp. 766-776, Hawaii.
5. Cardelli, L. and Wegner, P. (1985) On Understanding Types, Data Abstraction and Polymorphism. *ACM Computing Surveys*, **17** (4), 471-523.
6. Connor, R. C. H. (1990) Types and Polymorphism in Persistent Programming Systems. *Ph.D. Thesis,* University of St Andrews.
7. Connor, R. C. H., Brown, A. B., Cutts, Q. I., Dearle, A., Morrison, R. and Rosenberg, J. (1990) Type Equivalence Checking in Persistent Object Systems. In A. Dearle, G. M. Shaw and S. B. Zdonik (eds), *Implementing Persistent Object Bases, Principles and Practice*, pp. 151-164, Morgan Kaufmann,
8. Connor, R. C. H., Brown, A. L., Carrick, R., Dearle, A. and Morrison, R. (1989) Design Issues in The Persistent Abstract Machine. Universities of Glasgow and St Andrews.

9. Connor, R. C. H., Brown, A. L., Carrick, R., Dearle, A. and Morrison, R. (1990) The Persistent Abstract Machine. In J. Rosenberg and D. M. Koch (eds), *Persistent Object Systems*, pp. 353-366, Springer-Verlag,
10. Connor, R. C. H., Cutts, Q. I., Kirby, G. N. C. and Morrison, R. (1994) Using Persistence Technology to Control Schema Evolution. In *Proceedings of the 9th ACM Symposium on Applied Computing*, pp. 441-446, Phoenix, Arizona.
11. Connor, R. C. H., Dearle, A., Morrison, R. and Brown, A. L. (1990) Existentially Quantified Types as a Database Viewing Mechanism. In F. Bancilhon, C. Thanos and D. Tsichritzis (eds), *Lecture Notes in Computer Science 416* (EDBT '90), pp. 301-315, Springer-Verlag,
12. Cutts, Q. I. (1992) Delivering the Benefits of Persistence to System Construction and Execution. *Ph.D. Thesis*, University of St Andrews.
13. Cutts, Q. I., Hosking, A. L. (1997) Analysing, Profiling and Optimising Orthogonal Persistence for Java. In Proceedings of the Second International Workshop on Persistence and Java, Sun Microsystems Laboratories, Mountain View, California. (Available from: http://www.dcs.gla.ac.uk/rapids/publications.html)
14. Davie, A. J. T. (1979) Variable Access in Languages with Higher Order Procedures. University of St Andrews Department of Computational Science Technical Report CS/79/2.
15. Davie, A. J. T. and McNally, D. J. (1989) CASE - A Lazy Version of an SECD Machine in a Flat Environment. In Proc. 4th IEEE TENCON International Conference on Information Technologies for the 90's, IEEE, Bombay, pp 864-872.
16. Dearle, A., Cutts, Q. I. and Connor, R. C. H. (1993) Using Persistence to Support Incremental System Construction. *Journal of Microprocessors and Microprogramming*, **17** (3), 161-171.
17. Farkas, A. M. and Dearle, A. (1994) The Octopus Model and its Implementation. In *Proceedings of the 17th Australasian Computer Science Conference*, pp. 581-590, Christchurch, New Zealand.
18. Kirby, G. N. C., Connor, R. C. H., Cutts, Q. I., Dearle, A., Farkas, A. M. and Morrison, R. (1992) Persistent Hyper-Programs. In A. Albano and R. Morrison (eds), *Persistent Object Systems*, pp. 86-106, Workshops in Computing, Springer-Verlag.
19. Landin, P. J. (1964) The Mechanical Evaluation of Expressions. *Computer Journal*, **6** (4), 308-320.
20. Morrison, R. (1979) On the Development of Algol. *Ph.D. Thesis*, University of St Andrews.
21. Morrison, R., Brown, A. L., Carrick, R., Connor, R. C. H., Dearle, A. and Atkinson, M. P. (1987) Polymorphism, Persistence and Software Reuse in a Strongly Typed Object Oriented Environment. *Software Engineering Journal*, (December), 199-204.
22. Morrison, R., Brown, A. L., Connor, R. C. H. *et al.* (1990) Protection in Persistent Object Systems. In J. Rosenberg and J. L. Keedy (eds), *Security and Persistence*, pp. 48-66, Springer-Verlag.
23. Morrison, R., Dearle, A., Connor, R. C. H. and Brown, A. L. (1991) An Ad-Hoc Approach to the Implementation of Polymorphism. *ACM Transactions on Programming Languages and Systems*, **13** (3), 342-371.
24. Munro, D. S. (1993) On the Integration of Concurrency, Distribution and Persistence. *Ph.D. Thesis*, University of St Andrews.
25. Stemple, D., Morrison, R., Kirby, G. N. C. and Connor, R. C. H. (1993) Integrating Reflection, Strong Typing and Static Checking. In *Proceedings of the 16th Australian Computer Science Conference*, pp. 83-92, Brisbane, Australia.

Chapter 2.1.4

Tycoon: A Scalable and Interoperable Persistent System Environment

Florian Matthes, Gerald Schröder, and Joachim W. Schmidt

Technical University Hamburg-Harburg, Harburger Schloßstraße 20, D-21071 Hamburg, Germany

Abstract. We describe the Tycoon persistent system architecture that achieves a high degree of scalability and interoperability through a full integration of persistent data, programs and threads while maintaining a strict separation of storage, manipulation, modelling and representation tasks into well-defined system layers. For several of these layers alternative implementations with distinct operational support are provided that can be configured dynamically to match best the requirements of a given application. Moreover, we present Tycoon's architectural contributions to enable interoperability with existing generic services like databases, user-interface toolkits and C++ program libraries.

1 Introduction and Motivation

Modern information systems provide their users with a flexible and problem-oriented access to large repositories of complex persistent objects. The efficient and cost-effective implementation of such information systems has to be based on *generic services* provided by commercially available systems like relational or object-oriented databases, graphical user-interface toolkits, program libraries or standardized communication services.

The goal of the Tycoon[1] project carried out by our group since 1992 in the context of the ESPRIT Basic Research Project FIDE is to improve substantially the programmer productivity and modelling flexibility in such an *open* heterogeneous system environment through contributions at two levels. First, Tycoon provides a persistent polymorphic programming language with an elaborate higher-order type system to uniformly describe existing generic services and to enable the consistent integration of these services via high-level application code. This language aspect of the Tycoon project is described in more detail in Chapter 1.1.1, [12,17] (synopses in Chapters 1.4.2 and 3.3.3) and [18,14].

In this paper we focus on the second contribution of the Tycoon project, the development of a *persistent system architecture* to support the Tycoon language and a seamless generic server integration. Several innovative components of the Tycoon system have been described already in [15,11,5] (synopses in Chapters 1.5.2, 2.2.4 and 2.3.5) and [8,9]. Here we present and explain Tycoon's overall system architecture which excels through its scalability and interoperability.

Tycoon's system *scalability* makes it possible to cover in a single linguistic and architectural framework system implementations that range from a stand-alone main memory Tycoon implementation on a personal computer to a large, networked, multi-user, optimizing persistent Tycoon implementation. Contrary to monolithic information system architectures such

[1] Tycoon: Typed communicating objects in open environments

as SAP/R3 or Oracle, Tycoon applications that require only a limited system functionality can work with an efficient and lean system version that nevertheless can be scaled easily to cope with increasing operational demands over the lifetime of the application.

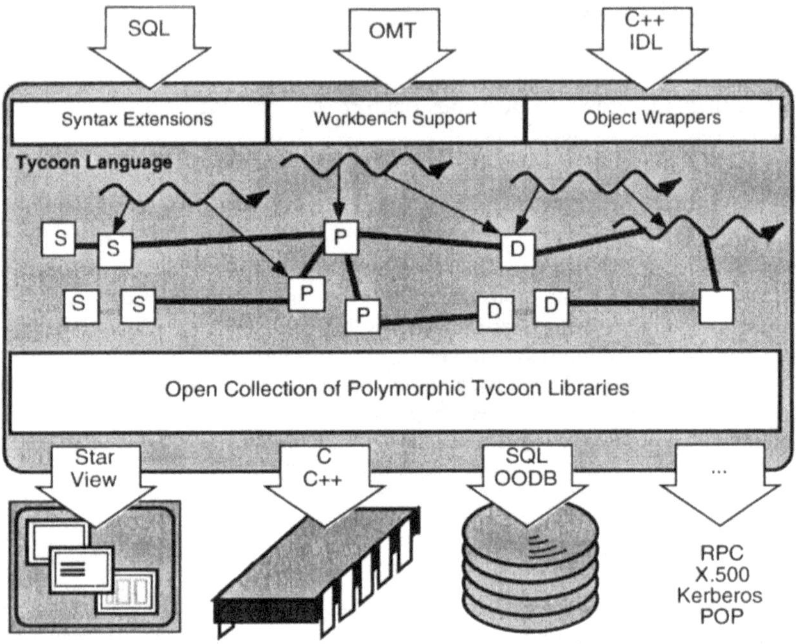

Fig. 1. Interoperability in the Tycoon environment

Figure 1 describes Tycoon's contributions to *interoperability*:

- Existing and evolving generic services are integrated in a *uniform manner* as polymorphic Tycoon libraries that provide type-safe access to external data and code. Using this approach, several generic services such as window systems (OpenWindows/NeWS), user-interface management systems (StarView), database systems (Ingres, Oracle), remote procedure call libraries (SunRPC), authentication services (Kerberos) and information retrieval engines (Inquery) have been integrated successfully in an add-on fashion into the Tycoon system.
  Within the Tycoon language, uniform naming, typing, binding and lifetime rules apply to screen, program and data objects (S, P, D in figure 1). In contrast to closed systems like fourth generation languages, Tycoon enables programmers to integrate also new generic services into their applications, that is, interoperability is not limited to a fixed set of object types like tables or forms. This extensibility is indicated by ellipses in the server icon list of figure 1.
- Integrated services are indistinguishable from services implemented in Tycoon itself. In particular, *type safety* and *persistence abstraction* can be obtained systematically also for

external services in the context of the Tycoon system. As a result, many programming errors can be found by static type checking at compile-time. This should be seen in contrast, for example, to untyped or string-oriented bindings as found in user-interface toolkits or SQL databases. Furthermore, Tycoon programmers are relieved from storage management issues like garbage collection, data transfer from and to disk, and recovery of persistent data.

- It is not only possible to integrate existing services into the Tycoon programming environment, but Tycoon is designed to be itself easily ***integrated as a subsystem*** into larger systems. For example, parts of the Tycoon compile-time and run-time environment can be reused as servers for persistent data storage, for portable code representation and evaluation, or for dynamic type checking. Similarly, Tycoon application code can be called from main programs written in C, C++, FORTRAN, COBOL etc. This interoperability aspect is indicated by the arrows at the top of figure 1.

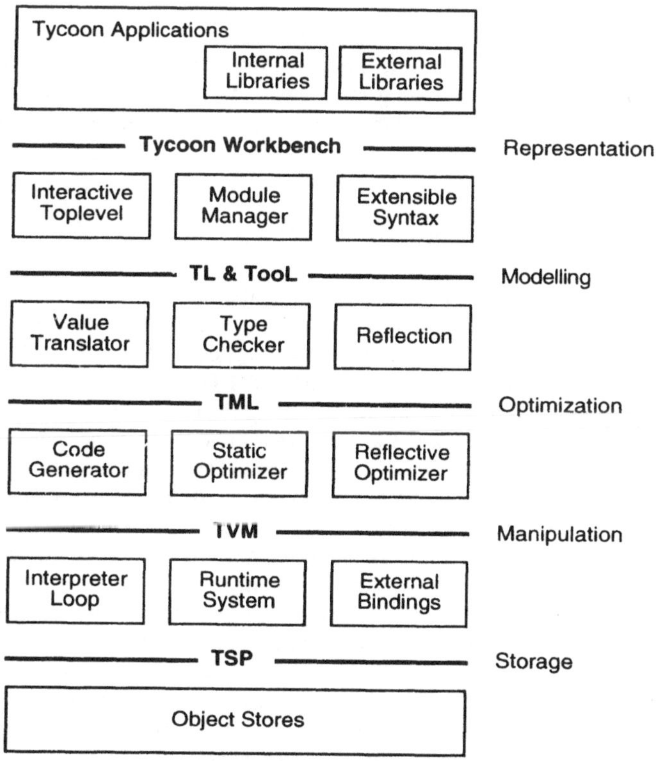

Fig. 2. Overview of the Tycoon persistent system layers

Figure 2 provides an overview of Tycoon's persistent system architecture that strictly separates storage, manipulation, modelling and representation tasks into well-defined system layers. For several of these layers, alternative implementations with distinct operational support are provided that can be configured dynamically to match best the requirements of a given application.

In this paper we discuss these layers of the Tycoon system environment in a bottom-up fashion: As described in section 2, full persistence abstraction for data and code is achieved already at the lowest layer of the Tycoon system defined by the Tycoon Store Protocol (TSP). The Tycoon Virtual Machine (TVM) presented in section 3 provides a platform-independent higher-order execution model that also supports calls, callbacks and exception handling involving external code written in other languages. In addition to executable TVM code, our persistent system architecture relies heavily on a persistent intermediate code representation (Tycoon Machine Language, TML) presented in section 4 which is used for static and reflective run-time code analysis and optimization. Since TML is an untyped language it is possible to implement multiple (polymorphically-typed) languages using a common TML intermediate representation. In Section 5 we highlight how modern language features like dynamic typing and reflection are supported by Tycoon's persistent system architecture. The wide range of services to be integrated into the Tycoon languages calls for a syntactic flexibility supported by the concept of extensible grammars as described in section 6. In section 7 we sketch how the Tycoon system components are integrated into a self-contained persistent programming environment including mechanisms for separate compilation and global optimization. The paper ends with a short summary of our experience using the Tycoon environment.

2 The Tycoon Store Protocol (TSP)

The Tycoon Store Protocol defines a *uniform* data-model-independent call-level interface to multiple (commercially distributed) persistent object stores. TSP is defined as an ANSI C header file which fully abstracts from implementation details of the underlying persistent stores. TSP is discussed in detail in [11] (see Chapter 2.2.4).

A TSP client can switch freely from one store implementation to another and work with more than one persistent store at once, but references between stores are not supported. Furthermore, TSP defines a portable linear data representation (TXR) to achieve store-level interoperability between all TSP server implementations. TSP concentrates on that subset of store functions that is provided by existing, widely used commercial and public-domain persistent object stores. TSP has a slight bias towards the needs of clients that have to implement persistent and possibly distributed programming languages.

A typical TSP server is implemented by writing a store adaptor that maps TSP data structures and functions to data structures and operations of an existing object store. As of today, this has been carried out for the commercial multi-user store ObjectStore (ObjectDesign) and the research prototype FLASK (Chapter 2.3.1). Moreover, our group has implemented two additional stand-alone TSP servers particularly well-suited for personal computers.

TSP contributes significantly to Tycoon's system scalability since TSP clients can choose between

- different garbage collection strategies;
- different object faulting mechanisms;
- optional error recovery, logging and persistent savepoint mechanisms;
- single-user or multi-user access;
- alternative commit protocols (for distributed systems);

- optional security and authentication support.

At present we are investigating the orthogonal combination of these features through a layering of (partial) TSP implementations.

As an experiment in store-level interoperability, an NFS (Network File System) server was written that exports selected TSP store objects as files and directories. In this way, all file-level commands are available on TSP stores, for example, *cd* and *ls* for browsing through an object graph.

A primary design goal behind TSP has been to provide efficient data storage as independently as possible from the data and language model supported by TSP store clients. In particular, TSP should be capable of supporting polymorphically typed models where the components of store objects contain values of multiple types that cannot be fixed in a separate schema definition phase. TSP therefore uses an *untyped* low-level store model, i.e. there is no separate dictionary of type or schema information maintained by the store. Instead of this, store values are made self-descriptive by imposing a regular object layout and a uniform tagging scheme. As a result, TSP achieves data model independence without sacrificing the advantages of self-descriptive statically-typed databases.

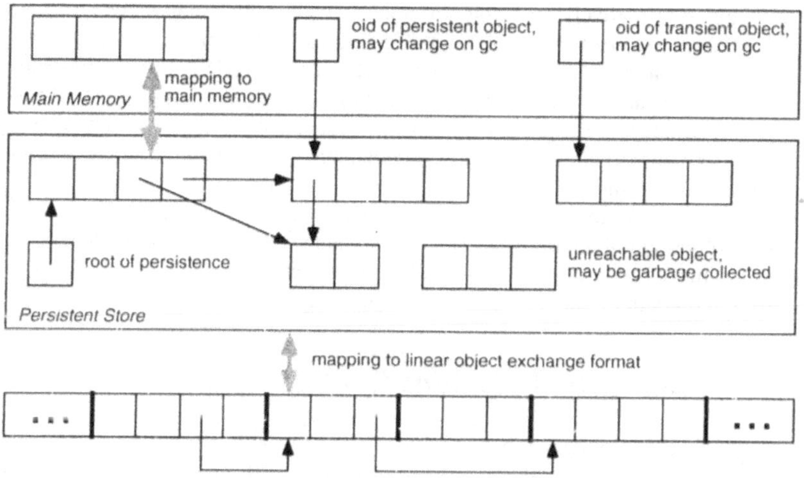

Fig. 3. Accessing a persistent store via the Tycoon Store Protocol (TSP)

The access to persistent store objects via the TSP is depicted in figure 3. Store objects are identified by unique persistent object identifiers (OIDs) that are also used to establish bindings between persistent objects. Each store has a single root of persistence (a location that holds the OID of a distinguished root object). Every object reachable from the root of persistence is stored persistently. Store objects can be created through TSP operations but are never explicitly destroyed by clients. The space of store objects that are not reachable from the persistent root object or from a (transient) OID held outside the persistent store during a session is reclaimed by a garbage collector. In general, all object access is performed using TSP function calls. TSP also supports the mapping of store objects into main memory to reduce the overhead incurred by repeated TSP calls.

Concurrency control and recovery on TSP stores is based on a flat transaction model. The TSP operations issued between two consecutive calls of the TSP *commit* operation are regarded as a single atomic transaction. Transactions of concurrently executing TSP clients are serialized. Furthermore, a TSP client can trigger an explicit TSP *rollback* operation to undo all side-effects on a TSP store since the last *commit* operation.

TSP provides customization facilities to support a tight integration of TSP servers into client systems. A TSP client can install callback functions that are called whenever certain state transitions occur in the backend.

- If a failure occurs, a failure handler is called with an error code. Depending on this code, the client can try to recover from the failure. This is especially useful in handling deadlocks or commit failures.
- If garbage collection is to be performed, a garbage collection handler is called. The client can decide to perform some additional operations (e.g. in an interactive user mode) before the internal garbage collection is triggered.
- The garbage collector of a TSP backend calls a client-provided enumerator function that has to enumerate all store object identifiers (OIDs) which are held outside the object store. Objects transitively reachable through these OIDs are not garbage collected. Since some persistent stores change OIDs during garbage collection, the client-provided enumerator function is also used to propagate OID changes to TSP client data structures.
- To transfer arbitrarily complex object store subgraphs between multiple TSP servers via sequential streams, a handler is needed that encapsulates the byte stream access. In this way, the TSP implementation remains independent of file systems, network protocols or other input/output facilities.
- TSP provides hooks to enable a portable transfer of client-specific data types like unique symbols, floating point numbers, matrices, etc. not supported by the predefined TSP data formats. This is accomplished by so-called *extern/intern* handlers that are called on data export and on data import via sequential byte streams.

3 The Tycoon Virtual Machine (TVM)

The Tycoon Store Protocol defines a passive data repository that is independent of a particular evaluation model. Executable code is stored as persistent data by the store manager. The store manager is thus independent of code representations that can be tailored to specific application purposes.

The Tycoon Virtual Machine (TVM) is an abstract call interface above the TSP layer that defines a bytecoded instruction set based on a higher-order, functional execution model. TVM bytecode is either interpreted by a virtual machine or is compiled on the fly into target machine code. The TVM interpreter and its associated run-time system are written in ANSI-C and have been ported to SunOS 4.1.x, Solaris 2.x, Linux, Windows-NT and MacOS.

The platform-independence of the TVM model makes it possible to dynamically transfer portable bytecode between heterogeneous nodes in a distributed programming environment without recompilation. Utilizing TSP's linear external data representation (TXR), it is also possible to migrate a persistent thread (code in the process of being executed) across system boundaries [8,9,15]. A thread is represented as an object graph describing bindings between code and data objects.

In addition to the interpreter vs. compiler alternative, scalability at the TVM level is achieved by switching between single-threaded and multi-threaded TVM implementations or between TVM implementations that support first-class persistent threads or transient evaluation contexts only. The set of TVM instructions can also be extended with new instructions to meet the needs of specific application domains like floating-point-intensive simulation software.

Individual TVM instructions are guaranteed execution atomically w.r.t. their effects on TSP stores. This property can be implemented rather efficiently at the TVM level and simplifies the implementation of higher system layers in a multi-threaded and multi-user persistent system scenario.

To enable interoperability with existing and future libraries written in other programming languages, TVM includes a portable and efficient mechanism to access functions stored in statically or dynamically bound object libraries. This mechanism is also exploited heavily in the Tycoon architecture to support an open set of "base" types like fixed point and floating point numbers of different precisions, date and time values, etc.

In the TVM bytecode there is no distinction between calls to static and dynamic libraries so the TVM code remains independent of the binding mechanism employed by a particular TVM implementation. The name of the external library and the symbol name (the name of the function to be called) are specified as run-time values along with a description of the function argument values and types. The interpreter maintains a list of statically bound libraries and symbols that is searched first. If no matching static library is found, a dynamic binding via the dynamic linker of the underlying operating system is attempted. On platforms that do not support dynamic linking, all required external servers (like window libraries or databases) have to be bound statically to the TVM. This requires only the insertion of the library name and the exported symbol names into a table in the source code of a distinguished TVM module. Then the TVM has to be rebuilt, compiling this module and relinking the executable. Again, these binding mechanisms are motivated by the desire to support a scalable system architecture.

Much care has been devoted in addition to support callbacks from external code to TVM byte code through a binding mechanism that exports an arbitrary TVM function object (closure) as an external function pointer. This is achieved by a generic wrapper function that takes a TVM argument type descriptor list and a function closure and dynamically generates a wrapper function that maps external function arguments to TVM function arguments.

The parameters that can be transferred between the TVM and external languages are limited to unstructured values, i.e. numbers, strings, words (including pointers and OIDs). Structured values have to be handled by wrapper functions written in C or in TVM code that construct and decompose these values.

To ensure a seamless interoperability at higher system layers, the external call and callback interface has to ensure that TVM exceptions are propagated correctly across language boundaries even in multi-threaded TVM applications.

A non-trivial problem arises if persistent TVM programs and threads work with pointers to data structures outside TSP stores. The lifetime of such data structures is limited to the lifetime of a single operating system process. Therefore, TVM offers mechanisms to log the construction and destructtion of these *volatile* values so that these values can be reconstructed automatically if a persistent thread is resumed. The log is essentially a list of TVM constructor and destructor functions stored persistently. As a result, it is possible, for example, to open and close windows in a windowing system, commit a state of the store, and to have the the windows that existed in the committed state automatically recreated on startup of the store.

Note that this feature does not assume that the window system or other external libraries have been prepared specifically for usage in a persistent system architecture but that this persistence support is added independently by the TVM layer. This is discussed in more detail in [7].

4 The Tycoon Machine Language (TML)

While TVM code is designed for efficient executability on multiple platforms, our persistent system architecture relies heavily on an additional persistent *intermediate* code representation (Tycoon Machine Language, TML) to unify static compile-time and reflective run-time code analysis and optimization. TML is an untyped language that is used for the implementation of multiple (polymorphically-typed) languages using a common TML intermediate representation. A detailed description of the syntax and semantics of TML and of the TML optimization algorithms can be found in [5] (a synopsis appears in Chapter 2.3.5).

A TVM bytecode sequence is generated for a given TML term by a compiler backend written in TL, the Tycoon Language. TML is a Continuation Passing Style (CPS) program representation that is well-suited for standard code optimizations and for algebraic query optimizations.

TML is a powerful yet simple program representation technique. The advantage of TML lies in the dramatic reduction of the number of program constructs that have to be handled by an optimizer, namely variable access, function abstraction, function application and primitive function application only. TML is particularly well-suited for control and data flow analysis by making the flow of control explicit through the uniform use of one language construct: the function application. Since TML does not have implicit function returns this language construct can be viewed as a generalized *goto* with parameter passing.

TML has a simple and clean semantics based on the λ-calculus. It is effectively a call-by-value λ-calculus with store semantics. By representing programs in TML, many well-known optimization techniques become special cases of a few simple and general λ-calculus transformations. Due to certain syntactical restrictions on TML trees, these transformations can be applied freely even in the presence of side-effecting calls to primitive functions.

Primitive functions (such as: conditional operations, integer arithmetic, object store access) encapsulate most of the semantics of a specific application programming language and operate on an implicit, hidden store. This separation between generic CPS functionality and specific application language functionality is also reflected by the implementation of the TML optimizers where all information about primitive procedures (meta evaluation function, cost attributes, target code generation function, etc.) is factored-out from the generic TML analysis and rewrite algorithms.

The TML optimizers and the TML to TVM translator do not perform checks on TML trees to test their well-formedness, e.g. whether a function receives more or different parameters than expected. This is the responsibility of the clients of these tools, i.e. of a frontend for a specific application programming language.

5 The Tycoon High-Level Languages

As depicted in figure 2, the task of the Tycoon high-level languages (like TL and TooL) is to support flexible high-level modelling of data, programs and threads independent of execution and storage details.

Again, scalability is achieved by supporting multiple high-level languages within the Tycoon architecture. The implementation of a particular high-level language is encapsulated by a tailored compiler function that takes typed data structures (an abstract syntax tree of the program to be compiled and a compile-time environment) as its input and returns typed data structures (a TML tree and a possibly extended compile-time environment) as its result. Target code generation and code optimization are performed in a second phase based on the returned TML tree. The TML tree may contain bindings to arbitrary store values like string literals or function closures that are preserved by all rewriting and code generation steps of the backend. The possibility of passing typed persistent bindings from the source code through to the executable code is exploited, for example, in persistent hyper-programming systems like the one described in [6].

Based on the backend functionality provided by TML, TVM and TSP, and by utilizing the generic frontend functionality provided by extensible grammars (see section 6), a special-purpose database language *L* can be implemented rather rapidly in the Tycoon persistent system architecture. A tailored compilation function for *L* can check the static semantics of *L* (scoping and typing rules) by a recursive traversal of the abstract syntax tree and can realize the dynamic semantics of *L* by a structure-directed mapping of language terms into TML terms. If necessary, language-specific TML primitives (e.g. *method-lookup*) and run-time support libraries (e.g. implementing operations on bulk data structures like relations) can be utilized to extend the higher-order TML core execution model by semantic primitives required by *L*.

Our group in Hamburg has implemented two high-level languages based on expressive *polymorphic* type systems. As discussed, for example, in [1] and [12,17] (synopses in Chapters 1.4.2 and 3.3.3) such languages can serve as meta models to describe and integrate existing relational, functional and object-oriented database models.

- The Tycoon Language (TL, [13,10]) excels by its very expressive type system based on existential and universal type quantification, recursive types and structural subtyping similar to the type system of the experimental polymorphic programming language Quest [2]. Contrary to Quest which is based on the notion of values, types and kinds (types of types), TL has a full ***higher-order*** type system where type quantification and subtyping applies uniformly to types, type operators and higher-order type operators, eliminating the need for a separate kind level.
  In addition to very few built-in types like *Int*, *String* or *Bool*, TL defines a small set of data type constructors: Tuples aggregate a fixed number of value and type bindings, arrays aggregate a flexible number of value bindings with homogeneous signatures, variant records define types that consist of a finite union of tuple types distinguished by a discriminator. The orthogonal combination of these type constructors along with recursive type definitions and (recursive) type operators covers virtually all data structures that appear in persistent programming.
  The TL execution model is mainly imperative and includes updatable locations. Since functions and types are first-class language objects, powerful generic higher-order functions can be written. To cope with run-time errors, exceptions and exception handlers are supported. Furthermore, TL includes mechanisms for reflective programming, dynamic typing and external language bindings as described in the remainder of this section.
- The Tycoon object-oriented language (TooL) is organized around (parameterized) classes and message passing. The type system of TooL captures much of the flavor of Smalltalk within a safe static typing discipline. Following the spirit of Smalltalk that provides a highly flexible and extensible programming environment based on a small set of ex-

pressive language primitives, TooL provides only a few built-in type concepts with rich semantics that achieve power through systematic use and orthogonality. TooL integrates type concepts that are well understood in isolation like object types, subtyping, type matching and type quantification into a practical database programming language.

In the following subsections we point out some innovative language implementation techniques that are utilized in our Tycoon language processors and that are also relevant for other high-level persistent language implementations.

5.1 Dynamic Types

In long-lived and distributed applications there are situations where type checking cannot be performed completely at compile-time. For example, if values are transmitted (via files or communication channels) between independently developed applications, there is no common scope in which a static type check could be performed to guarantee compatibility between data and programs.

For such situations, the Tycoon languages provide dynamically-typed values. A dynamic value is a pair of value *v* and run-time type representation *t* that describes the type of *v*. A type representation is created automatically by the compiler whenever a dynamic value is created. If a value component *v* is extracted at run-time from a dynamic value, its associated type representation *t* can be inspected. Most languages that support dynamic types limit this inspection to a simple boolean subtype test: is *t* subtype of a given supertype *T* defined at compile-time? Tycoon provides a much richer set of strongly-typed functions for the algorithmic inspection of dynamic values, for example, to iterate over the attribute values and attribute types of a tuple or to construct a tuple from a list of typed bindings.

Another application area for dynamic types is the implementation of generic functions with type-dependent behavior. These functions take a type representation, usually along with a value of this type, analyze the type and exhibit different behavior depending on the type. An example is a generic persistent store browser that is capable of displaying and manipulating values of any type.

In the Tycoon scenario where the compile-time and run-time environment reside in the same persistent store, it is advantageous to use the same type representation at compile-time and at run-time. A dynamic type representation is a compile-time value (a run-time value of the compiler) that is stored persistently until the run-time of the application. More generally, the Tycoon compilers provide a binding mechanism for making arbitrary compile-time values accessible to the generated code. Furthermore, the functions to inspect, check and create type representations are shared (as persistent store objects) between the compile-time type checker and the run-time environment.

The higher-order Tycoon language TL provides a limited form of *dependent* types, i.e. TL type expressions may depend on value identifiers. For example, an abstract data type depends on a specific implementation represented as a tuple value with functional components. Dynamic type representations for such dependent types involve bindings to run-time values. Therefore, the concept of compile-time name equivalence has to be mapped to the concept of run-time value equivalence (e.g. based on OIDs) and type representations may need to be constructed dynamically, depending on the result of value computations.

5.2 Compile-Time and Run-Time Reflection

The Tycoon languages TL and TooL are implemented using a compiler bootstrapped in the Tycoon language TL. In many Tycoon applications the compiler is used as a *black box* to develop a self-contained stand-alone application program. Advanced Tycoon applications like object-oriented database systems, programmable simulators or compilers for high-level languages can also access the functionality offered by the Tycoon compiler in a structured way. This is called compile-time or run-time reflection depending on the point in time the compiler functionality is used [19] (see Chapter 1.2.1).

Compile-time reflection is achieved by executing user-definable code during the compilation process if so-called *reflective* expressions appear in the source code of a program being compiled. This makes it possible to write code that depends on information that is known statically at compile-time, maybe inferred by the compiler. For example, generic code to traverse recursively defined data structures that depend on statically inferred type information can be written using compile-time reflection.

Run-time reflection is achieved by making typed bindings to compiler subcomponents (parser, type checker, code generator, evaluator, module manager, ...) available to applications at run-time. In this case, code is evaluated or even generated depending on run-time (computed) values that are not known statically at compile-time. Note that this kind of reflection, although very flexible, may lead to unexpected run-time type checking errors during reflective compiler calls.

Full type safety even in the presence of run-time and compile-time reflection is guaranteed by the consistent use of dynamic types in the Tycoon compile-time and run-time environment.

5.3 Typing of External Bindings

The flexible but untyped TVM mechanisms described in section 3 to establish bindings from TVM code to external, dynamically-bound library functions is the basis for high-level data and code interoperability of the Tycoon languages with an open set of external servers.

External functions are inherently type unsafe since neither object files nor linked libraries contain type information. This type information is available in the sources of the generating languages but is lost after compilation. This means that Tycoon cannot automatically check the parameters of function calls to external libraries. However, the correctness of calls to these functions can be enforced by the Tycoon programmer who binds the external libraries into the Tycoon system by assigning appropriate Tycoon signatures to these external functions.

The following example shows the binding of a function *int_add* that takes two integers and returns an integer stored in an external library *math* to the Tycoon identifier *intAdd* with the function type **Fun**(*:Int :Int):Int.*

let *intAdd* = *bind(:***Fun***(:Int :Int):Int "math" "int_add" "iii")*
let *sum* = *intAdd(12 23)*

The string value *"iii"* specifies the low-level parameter-passing conventions to be used at the TVM level (here: call-by-value with two integers and return by value of an integer). All subsequent applications of *intAdd*, like *intAdd(12 23)*, can be checked for type correctness assuming that the binding has been typed correctly. Note that an external function like *intAdd* has true first-class status in Tycoon, for example, it can be passed as a parameter or can be stored persistently without restrictions.

As a more elaborate example of strongly-typed access to external functions, the following excerpt of the TL interface *SQL* exports polymorphic functions to perform dynamic SQL database access from Tycoon applications:

```
interface SQL import ... export
  error :Exception with sqlError:String end
  Table(E <:Tuple end) <:Ok
  ...
  openTable(Dyn E <:Ok  tableName :String) :Table(E)
  ...
  insertTuple(E <:Ok table :Table(E)  tup:E) :Ok
  ...
end
```

In the Tycoon libraries there exist two distinct modules *ingresSQL* and *oracleSQL* that implement this interface with bindings to the dynamic SQL call interfaces of these relational database systems. The unary type operator *Table(E)* exported from the interface describes the type of SQL tables with element type *E*. For example, a value of type *oracleSQL.Table(Person)* is an Oracle table with rows that have attributes as defined by the Tycoon tuple type *Person*.

The polymorphic function *openTable* opens an existing named table for further processing and takes a dynamic type variable *E* as its first argument to ensure that the database table structure matches the Tycoon type information. If a schema mismatch is detected, the Tycoon exception *error* is raised at run-time. All other operations of the SQL interface (queries, table updates) can be checked statically by the Tycoon compiler based on the polymorphic signatures assigned to the SQL functions. For example, the signature of the function *insertTuple* expresses the type constraint that into a table of type *Table(E)* only tuples of a matching type *E* can be inserted.

6 Extensible Grammars

The high-level Tycoon languages described in the previous section aim at minimality and orthogonality of concepts. The definition and implementation of these languages is based on a restricted *abstract syntax* represented by typed data structures in a Tycoon store. The mapping of a concrete syntax (a linear source text or a two-dimensional graphical notation) to an abstract syntax is not part of the language definition proper.

Most programming languages provide a fixed mapping from concrete syntax to abstract syntax. For convenience, several syntactic variants are often provided for the same construct of the abstract syntax. For example, the TL abstract syntax provides only one iteration construct (**loop** ... **exit** ... **end**). Other common loop constructs (**while**, **repeat**, **for**) can be expressed using **loop** in combination with **if**.

For languages like TL and TooL that have to support a wide spectrum of data and execution models, it is desirable to keep the concrete syntax adaptable to the needs of a particular application domain (see also Chapter 3.2.3). For example, declarative bulk data access can be supported by a tailored query language syntax (relational calculus, SQL, comprehensions notation) and parallel programming can be supported by tailored control structures (**par**, **alt**, etc.).

The Tycoon technology of *extensible grammars* [3,4] makes it possible to provide syntactic support for such add-on data and control abstractions.

Extensible grammars are implemented as a library of compiler tools written in TL. They were used to define the core syntax of TL and TooL thereby supporting the syntactic extension of both languages in a uniform way. Extensible grammars are parameterized by the abstract syntax tree constructors of the respective high-level Tycoon language.

The extensible grammar library also defines an abstract syntax for the dynamic definition and extension of grammars. Grammars describe the concrete syntax (EBNF notation) and the translation into abstract syntax trees using typed term constructors. Checks at grammar-definition time ensure that only well-formed abstract syntax trees are generated and that no syntactic ambiguities arise during grammar extension.

In a first step, the TL extensible grammar library is applied reflectively to define an initial concrete syntax for the definition of grammars using term constructors of the grammar library itself. In a second step, this grammar is used for the definition of a core programming language (e.g. TL or TooL abstract syntax). Although this initial syntax would be sufficient to express any well-typed program, it is not user-friendly. Thus, the initial version of the programming language syntax is used in further redefinitions, for example, to provide **while**, **repeat** and **for** loops and higher-level abstractions like **select from where** queries implemented on top of a bulk type library.

7 Integrated Persistent Programming Environment

In this section we sketch how the building blocks of the Tycoon persistent system architecture described in the previous sections are fully integrated into a persistent programming workbench to support the development of large data-intensive applications by teams of cooperating programmers. Since computer-aided software engineering itself is a data-intensive task, it is natural to implement a Tycoon workbench in one of the Tycoon languages exploiting orthogonal persistence, reflection, and dynamic typing (see also figure 2).

The interactive top level of the current TL workbench gives access to all tools in the environment via a command-line interpreter. A graphical workbench based on the concept of direct manipulation of persistent data and code is under construction. Separate compilation and incremental linking is currently built into the workbench, but we are implementing a generic separate compilation manager that exploits dynamic types, first-class environments, generic dependency checking and version management.

The development of large applications requires separate compilation. This facilitates teamwork by dividing the problem into manageable parts and eases the re-use of software components. Furthermore, type correctness of software components can be verified based on explicit assumptions about the interfaces of other software components.

TL supports separate compilation through three language constructs, namely, interface, module and library. A library defines a scope for nested module, interface and library declarations. An interface is syntactic sugar for a type- and value-parameterized tuple type definition. A module is syntactic sugar for a type- and value-parameterized link function that computes a tuple value as defined by the type of the module interface. The TL module manager tracks the dependencies between modules, interfaces and libraries and controls automatic recompilation and incremental linking based on these dependencies.

The TL programming environment has to inter-operate with commercial tools for project management and source-code version management. For example, our group is using SunSoft's TeamWare to coordinate the parallel Tycoon development by five full-time employees and approximately 35 students. Therefore, the TL workbench has to maintain the source code of library definitions, modules and interfaces as well as compiled modules and interfaces in the file system. The object store holds linked modules and persistent data only. This makes it necessary to assign version keys, check-sums and time stamps to source code and to compiled modules and interfaces to inform the module manager of changes performed by external tools on individual source or object files.

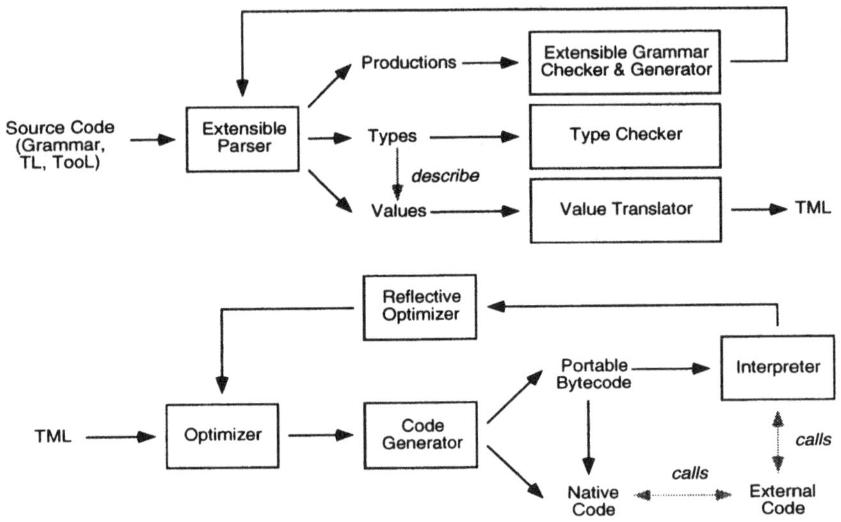

Fig. 4. Data flow between the language processors of the Tycoon workbench

The data flow between the components of the various Tycoon system layers described in this paper is shown in figure 4. Source files or interactive user input is parsed by the extensible parser (based on the TL or TooL syntax definition). Input phrases that contain grammar definitions are checked for consistency by the grammar checker and then transformed into parse rules for the extensible parser. Type expressions represented as abstract syntax trees are checked by the type checker for well-formedness according to static semantic rules of the respective Tycoon high-level language. Values are translated into (untyped) TML terms. TML terms may be optimized locally before they are submitted to the target code generator for the TVM. The TVM handles transparently the switching between the interpretation of portable bytecode and the direct execution of native machine code (external library code or compiled TVM code).

An interesting detail in figure 4 is the run-time reflective code optimizer. On request, the Tycoon target code generator augments the executable TVM code of each function by a (persistent) binding to its abstract intermediate code representation (a TML tree). This makes it possible to inspect function implementations at run-time. This is exploited in Tycoon to perform link-time and run-time optimizations across abstraction barriers.

To explain this form of optimization, consider the compilation of the *stack.empty(s)* expression in a module *m*. At compile-time, the only information available about the identifier *stack.empty* is the signature of the function. As soon as module *m* is linked, a binding to the module *stack* and its function *empty* is established. Tycoon's reflective optimizer exploits the binding information available after linking or more generally during program execution to compose the TML trees of separate functions into aggregated TML trees (dynamic inlining) that can then again be submitted to a (global) optimizer and code generator. The expansion and optimization of TVM functions in the persistent store are controlled by a tagging scheme and a cost model that avoid repeated optimizations of shared subfunctions and limit the increase in code size resulting from inlining.

8 Concluding Remarks

We have described the layers of the Tycoon persistent system architecture that emphasizes system scalability and interoperability with external servers. Currently, the following set of server gateways is available as TL source code:

- NeWS window system based on display PostScript: 48 modules; 6300 lines of code;
- StarView cross-platform user-interface toolkit: 131 modules; 6700 lines of code generated automatically from C++ header files;
- Oracle RDBMS: 3 modules; 1300 lines of code;
- Ingres RDBMS: 3 modules; 1300 lines of code;
- Kerberos authorization and authentication server [16]: 6 modules; 1055 lines of code;
- Inquery text retrieval engine: 3 modules; 1000 lines of code;
- RPC and socket communication: 13 modules; 1700 line of code.

An additional set of approximately 80 Tycoon modules with 29000 lines of TL code exports reusable library code like standard data types (date, time, string), bulk data types with uniform iteration abstractions, strongly-typed graphical data browsers and generic compiler toolkits (scanner, parser).

Through the bootstrap of the Tycoon language processors (TML, TL and TooL) and the implementation of an integrated object-oriented data modelling workbench (STYLE, see Chapter 3.2.2) we already have some experience with the development of complex Tycoon applications by cooperating teams of programmers.

system component	number of modules	total lines of code
TML	13	7600
TL	36	18200
TooL	22	9200
STYLE	250	41000

Since 1994, a WWW-driven information system implemented in TL has been operational at Hamburg University. This server was developed in the context of the ESPRIT Network of Excellence IDOMENEUS and utilizes Tycoon as a persistent store for data that is supplied by WWW forms and displayed on dynamically-generated WWW pages. Persistent TL threads are used to read, check and transform the data and to emulate persistent sessions between WWW clients and the WWW server. In particular, it is not necessary to install the Tycoon system as a demon, but Tycoon is started dynamically on request since persistent threads lead to very fast system startup sequences.

Acknowledgements. This research was supported by ESPRIT Basic Research, Project FIDE$_2$, #6309.

References

1. M.P. Atkinson and P. Bunemann. Types and persistence in database programming languages. *ACM Computing Surveys*, 19(2), June 1987.
2. L. Cardelli. Typeful programming. Technical Report 45, Digital Equipment Corporation, Systems Research Center, Palo Alto, California, May 1989.
3. L. Cardelli, F. Matthes, and M. Abadi. Extensible grammars for language specialization. In C. Beeri, A. Ohori, and D.E. Shasha, editors, *Proceedings of the Fourth International Workshop on Database Programming Languages, Manhatten, New York*, Workshops in Computing, pages 11–31. Springer-Verlag, February 1994.
4. L. Cardelli, F. Matthes, and M. Abadi. Extensible syntax with lexical scoping. Technical Report 121, Digital Equipment Corporation, Systems Research Center, Palo Alto, California, February 1994.
5. A. Gawecki and F. Matthes. Exploiting persistent intermediate code representations in open database environments. In *Proceedings of the Fifth Conference on Extending Database Technology, EDBT'96*, volume 1057 of *Lecture Notes in Computer Science*, Avignon, France, March 1996. Springer-Verlag.
6. G.N.C. Kirby, R.C.H. Connor, Q.I. Cutts, R. Morrison, A. Dearle, and A.M. Farkas. Persistent hyper-programs. FIDE Technical Report Series FIDE/92/53, FIDE Project Coordinator, Department of Computing Sciences, University of Glasgow, Glasgow G128QQ, 1992.
7. M. Kornacker. Persistente Sicherungspunkte für langlebige Aktivitäten in offenen Umgebungen. Diplomarbeit, Fachbereich Informatik, Universität Hamburg, Germany, August 1995. (In German.).
8. B. Mathiske, F. Matthes, and J.W. Schmidt. On migrating threads. In *Proceedings of the Second International Workshop on Next Generation Information Technologies and Systems, Naharia, Israel*, June 1995. (Also appeared as TR FIDE/95/136).
9. B. Mathiske, F. Matthes, and J.W. Schmidt. Scaling database languages to higher-order distributed programming. In *Proceedings of the Fifth International Workshop on Database Programming Languages, Gubbio, Italy*. Springer-Verlag, September 1995. (Also appeared as TR FIDE/95/137).
10. F. Matthes. *Persistente Objektsysteme: Integrierte Datenbankentwicklung und Programmerstellung*. Springer-Verlag, 1993. (In German).
11. F. Matthes, R. Müller, and J.W. Schmidt. Towards a unified model of untyped object stores: Experience with the Tycoon store protocol. In *Advances in Databases and Information Systems (ADBIS'96), Proceedings of the Third International Workshop of the Moscow ACM SIGMOD Chapter*, 1996.
12. F. Matthes and J.W. Schmidt. Bulk types: Built-in or add-on? In *Database Programming Languages: Bulk Types and Persistent Data*. Morgan Kaufmann Publishers, September 1991.
13. F. Matthes and J.W. Schmidt. Definition of the Tycoon language TL – a preliminary report. Informatik Fachbericht FBI-HH-B-160/92, Fachbereich Informatik, Universität Hamburg, Germany, November 1992.
14. F. Matthes and J.W. Schmidt. System construction in the Tycoon environment: Architectures, interfaces and gateways. In P.P. Spies, editor, *Proceedings of Euro-Arch'93 Congress*, pages 301–317. Springer-Verlag, October 1993.
15. F. Matthes and J.W. Schmidt. Persistent threads. In *Proceedings of the Twentieth International Conference on Very Large Data Bases, VLDB*, pages 403–414, Santiago, Chile, September 1994.

16. A. Rudloff, F. Matthes, and J.W. Schmidt. Security as an add-on quality in persistent object systems. In *Second International East/West Database Workshop, Klagenfurt, Austria*, Workshops in Computing, pages 90–108. Springer-Verlag, 1995. (Also appeared as TR FIDE/95/138).
17. J.W. Schmidt and F. Matthes. Lean languages and models: Towards an interoperable kernel for persistent object systems. In *Proceedings of the IEEE International Workshop on Research Issues in Data Engineering*, pages 2–16, April 1993.
18. J.W. Schmidt, F. Matthes, and P. Valduriez. Building persistent application systems in fully integrated data environments: Modularization, abstraction and interoperability. In *Proceedings of Euro-Arch'93 Congress*, pages 270–287. Springer-Verlag, October 1993.
19. D. Stemple, R. Morrison, and Atkinson M. Type-safe linguistic reflection. In *Database Programming Languages: Bulk Types and Persistent Data*, pages 357–362. Morgan Kaufmann Publishers, 1991.

Section 2.2

Object Store Design
Introduction and State of the Art

Fausto Rabitti

CNUCE-CNR, Via S.Maria 36, Pisa, Italy

1 Introduction

The development of persistent store technology is a fundamental research issue in the FIDE/FIDE$_2$ framework. In FIDE's envisaged architectures, data and programs are held in the persistent store. As such, the reliability, integrity, capacity, performance, and functionality of persistent stores are crucial to the achievement of FIDE's goals.

There is a growing interest in store architectures motivated by the need to support new object oriented database systems, database programming languages and persistent programming languages. Furthermore, there is a strong commercial interest in adding persistence to popular programming languages such as Common LISP, C++ and Java.

A persistent object store should have a number of intrinsic properties such as type security, unbounded capacity, infinite speed and total reliability. In implementation terms, none of these is realistically achievable and hence store design is concerned with technological approximations.

In the context of the FIDE/FIDE$_2$ project, we explored different research directions, trying different techniques for a better understanding of their characteristics. The Napier store (Chapters 1.1.3 & 2.2.1) was developed at the University of St. Andrews and from it the new FLASK store (Chapter 2.3.1) has been developed during FIDE$_2$; EOS is a project at INRIA (Chapters 2.2.3 & 2.3.2), that has been completed within FIDE$_2$; PIOS (Chapters 2.2.2 & 2.3.3) and Tycoon (Chapters 1.1.1, 2.1.4, 2.2.4 & 2.3.5) were new projects developed in the framework of FIDE$_2$: PIOS at IEI-CNR and Tycoon at the University of Hamburg.

The Napier persistent object store is founded on an open layered architecture that has been designed with the aim of supporting cost effective experimentation with the implementation of persistence. Each layer supports a distinct architectural mechanism and has a well-defined interface. The architecture is generic whereby different implementations of a layer may be interchanged without the need to alter the layers above or below. The Napier persistent object store architecture is discussed in Chapter 2.2.1.

PIOS is designed as the server of a database management system organised accordingly with the well–known *client-server* architecture. The role of the server is to provide integrated storage management of persistent data for a number of clients. An overview of PIOS is given in Chapter 2.2.2.

The most important feature of PIOS is the support of *physical object independence*. In PIOS, two levels of data model are recognised: the *canonical level*, in which the logical schema of object database is defined, and the *storage level*, in which the *storage schema* of physical object database is defined. Thus the database designer can choose among different storage organisations in order to fulfil application performance requirements. In general, *clustering* and *partitioning* of canonical objects are supported by PIOS while designing the physical (storage) objects. The current version of PIOS does not support schema evolution.

EOS is a project at INRIA that aims at defining and prototyping a minimal object-oriented foundation for persistent and concurrent computing environment over a distributed hardware platform. A minimalist approach is advocated for maximum extensibility. Furthermore, extensibility is really interesting if transparency with respect to programming hindering issues is provided. In this context, such issues are persistence, concurrency control as well as fault tolerance and distribution.

The object space is persistent, unique and logically flat. Flat refers to a complete absence of structure of the object space from the point of view of programmers, and not to the fact that objects cannot be aggregated. In other words, object identity is system-wide, and supports both method invocation and arbitrarily complex aggregation of objects. There are no visible physical containers such as segments or nodes, where objects could be allocated, and that would scope the identity of objects. Objects persist as long as they are reachable from a root of persistence, which is a built-in catalogue object associating an external name with an object. One part of this work, on efficient incremental garbage collection in client-server object database systems, is described in Chapter 2.2.3.

The Tycoon system is divided into three conceptual layers with three *public* interfaces. The layers are: the Tycoon Language (used by Tycoon programmers); the Tycoon Machine Language; the Tycoon Store Protocol.

The aim of the Tycoon Store Protocol is to provide a minimal set of abstractions. Examples are functions for creating and accessing objects and object stores. The idea of a generic and relatively simple object store interface is not new (Napier Store, Mneme, etc.). However, these interfaces are typically targeted to specific implementations. The Tycoon Store Protocol tries to unify the different approaches by defining a generic store interface, thus enabling Tycoon Store Protocol clients to use as much existing store technology as possible. Experience with using the Tycoon Store Protocol is described in Chapter 2.2.4.

These architectural approaches intend to explore different research directions, covering different assumptions in terms of functions of the object stores and trying sometimes different techniques to solve the same problem, for a better understanding of their characteristics. An example of these different and complementary assumptions underlying the various object stores is the level of query support built in the store level. Object stores for general purpose persistent languages, such as in Napier, do not provide any specific mechanism for physical store organisation, object indexing and query optimisation, leaving all these functions to the above levels (namely, language compiler and/or application programmer). EOS gives a limited support of this kind, in terms of physical object clustering. This is justified by its database programming language orientation. Finally, PIOS has as its main design goal the broadest support to set-oriented object access and query optimisation (namely, physical object independence, with object clustering and declustering, support of indexing mechanisms, cost-based query optimisation), at the expenses of severe limitations in the query language.

At the same time, we have tried to exploit as much as possible the synergy among the partners of the project in building these architectures. An example is the use of the Stable Heap layer of the Napier store inside PIOS the First, and the use of the FLASK store inside PIOS the Second. Comparison of these approaches depends upon the development of a measurement and analysis technology. Early work in this area is presented in Chapter 2.2.5.

2 State of the art

Many different object stores have been proposed and constructed, for example: [1-9]. Because the models that these stores are attempting to support are motivated from different sources, they vary considerably in their functionality and architectural design. However, one factor that is common to all these designs is that they must address the fundamental properties of persistent object stores.

Each store designer has his own starting point and his own goals and motives. The product will be the outcome of a unique set of compromises. For the store to be understood the requirements and the compromises need to be understood; it is therefore difficult to meaningfully summarise how one store compares with another. A more severe difficulty is that a programming system will typically be a combination of several different stores: for example there's the store abstraction provided by a programming language (perhaps locations with type, mutability, persistence properties) and which itself will typically be implemented from other stores (machine registers and caches, main memory, virtual memory, stable storage). A store design may be targeted for any one of a number of levels. Typically the higher the level the more specialised the store. This makes it difficult to compare stores with a single set of criteria. It is necessary to look at stores and store management in relation to the architecture of the complete system.

As a general observation, we can say that the common ground in the development of object stores, from object database stores to persistent stores, is the concept of a unified view of data and program.

In the context of FIDE and $FIDE_2$, the research on object store design contributed in a significant manner to increase the insight in many technical issues, to improve the understanding of the inter-relationships of many internal architectural factors, to clarify the interfaces with other architectural modules. However, one of the main contributions is not related to specific technical results but has been to extend the interest of the scientific and industrial community into this research area, that still needs to channel new research efforts into new directions such as distribution, extended transaction management, handling of new data types (e.g., multimedia), etc.

References

1. Atkinson, M.P., Chisholm, K.J., & Cockshott, W.P. CMS - A chunk management, Software - Practice and Experience, 13, 3, 273-285, March 1983
2. Brown A.L. (Ph.D. Thesis) Persistent Object Stores. Universities of Glasgow and St.Andrews PPRR-71, Scotland, 1989.
3. Brown A.L. & Rosenberg J. Persistent Object Stores: An Implementation Technique. in Dearle, Shaw, Zdonik (eds.), Implementing Persistent Object Bases, Principles and Practice, Morgan Kaufmann, 1991, pp199-212.
4. Cockshott W.P., Atkinson M.P., Chisholm K.J., Bailey P.J., & Morrison R. POMS: A Persistent Object Management System. Software Practice and Experience, vol. 14, no. 1, 1984, pp49-71.

5. Liskov B.H. Refinement - From Specification to Implementation, The Argus Language and System. Lecture Notes for the Advanced Course on Distributed Systems - Methods and Tools for Specification, Institute for Informatics, Technical University of Munich, 1984.
6. Moss, J.E.B. & Sinofsky, S. Managing persistent data with Mneme: Designing a reliable shared object interface, in In Advances in Object-Oriented Database Systems, Lecture Notes in Computer Science, Springer-Verlag, vol. 334, 1988, pp298-316.
7. Ross G.D.M. (Ph.D. Thesis) Virtual Files: A Framework for Experimental Design. University of Edinburgh, 1983.
8. Skarra A., Zdonik S.B. & Reiss S.P. An Object Server For An Object-Oriented Database System. Proc. International Workshop on Object-Oriented Database Systems, Pacific Grove, California, 1987, pp196-204.
9. Thatte S.M. Persistent Memory: A Storage Architecture for Object Oriented Database Systems. Proc. ACM/IEEE 1986 International Workshop on Object Oriented Database Systems, Pacific Grove, CA, September 1986, pp148-159.

Chapter 2.2.1

An Open System Architecture for a Persistent Object Store

Fred Brown[1], Giovanni Mainetto[2], Florian Matthes[3], Rainer Müller[3], and David McNally[4]

[1] Department of Computer Science, University of Adelaide, Adelaide 5005, Australia
[2] CNUCE, Institute of CNR, Via S. Maria 36, Pisa, Italy
[3] Technical University Hamburg-Harburg, Harburger Schloßstraße 20, D-21071 Hamburg, Germany
[4] School of Mathematical and Computational Sciences, University of St Andrews, North Haugh, St Andrews, KY16 9SS, Scotland

1 Introduction

An essential feature of a persistent programming system is a store capable of supporting complex objects. A number of proposals and implementations of persistent object stores have been made [1-8]. Each store has its own set of design goals since each has been used with a particular view of the persistence abstraction.

The aim of this work is to provide a suitable platform upon which programming language implementors may build a persistent version of their particular system. The hypothesis is that persistence is orthogonal to the programming paradigm and should be available as an abstraction for all systems [9]. Towards this view a platform is provided in a manner that can be tailored to the particular system. This is achieved by providing a set of reusable components within an open architecture for persistence. The major goal in designing the open architecture is to achieve high levels of performance whilst supporting cost effective experimentation and system maintenance.

To date, the open architecture has been employed to provide persistence in a variety of programming paradigms including imperative programming with first class procedures, Napier88 (Chapter 1.1.3); object-oriented database programming, Galileo [10]; typeful programming, Quest [11]; and lazy functional programming, STAPLE [12]. Each of these programming languages defines a different model of persistence and in the case of STAPLE a different model of computation. The interface to the persistent object store is sufficiently flexible to support any one of these programming languages. However, any particular instance of the open architecture would only be configured to support a single programming language. To date no mixed language systems have been attempted.

2 The open architecture

The open architecture has been designed with the aim of supporting cost effective experimentation with the implementation of persistence. The key to achieving this aim is the separation of the distinct architectural mechanisms into well defined layers. For example, a persistent object store requires a large, stable, heap of persistent objects [4]. Within the open architecture this is realised by a layer which provides non volatile storage, a layer which provides a large stable virtual memory and a layer which organises that virtual memory into a stable heap of persistent objects. The architectural layering is illustrated in Figure 1.

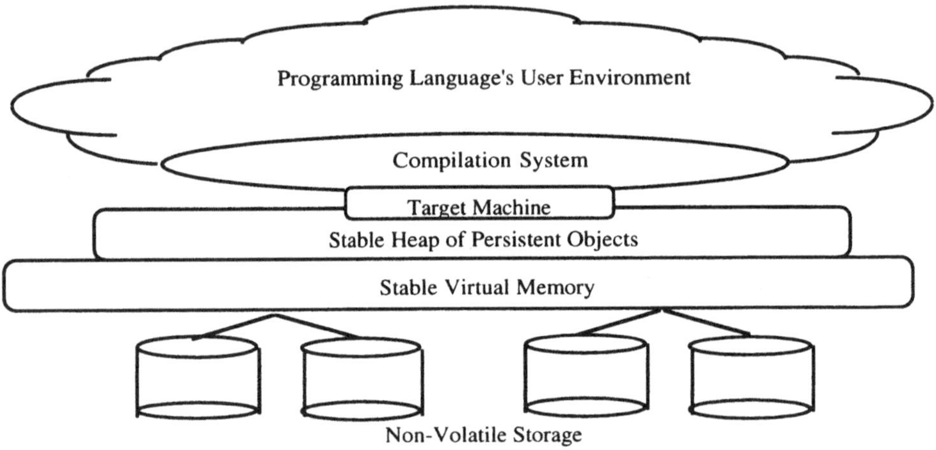

Fig. 1. The generic architecture.

The architectural layering reflects the persistence abstraction by ensuring that the programming language levels of the architecture are not able to discover details of how objects are stored. This divides the architecture between those architectural layers that provide the persistent object store and those architectural layers that manipulate objects. A complete description of each layer interface and a possible implementation is given elsewhere [13].

Each of the layers in the persistent object store has an interface which provides the functionality of the layer to the next higher layer. These interfaces can be adhered to strictly and will yield a functioning system. However, the potential inefficiency of strict interfaces may prove unsatisfactory for production systems which demand as much performance as possible. In many cases these systems are prepared to discard interfaces and make dangerous assumptions about implementations in order to gain speed.

The open architecture recognises the need to enhance efficiency by by-passing the interfaces and getting at the implementation directly, but it is also concerned with preserving safety and preventing chaos from breaking loose. The interface to each architectural layer may be opened up using quality of service information provided by the layer's implementation. This information may be used to optimise access to a layer by higher layers or to extend the functionality of a layer. However, a dependency on particular quality of service information effectively redefines a layer interface which may restrict the potential for system maintenance and experimentation. Subject to the use made of quality of service information, individual layers may be independently reimplemented without reference to the implementation of the other layers. This scheme may be provided at every level of the open architecture.

3 Conclusions

The open architecture design is aimed at providing a suitable platform upon which programming language implementors may build a persistent version of their system. Towards this end, the architecture provides a set of reusable components that can be tailored to an individual system. In particular the design of the open architecture addresses the issues of cost-effective experimentation, system maintenance and high performance.

Cost-effective experimentation is supported by the highly modular structure of the open architecture. Provided that a module's interface is maintained it may be reimplemented without requiring the reimplementation of other modules. This also simplifies the task of system maintenance.

The issue of high performance is addressed in the provision of a quality of service interface that reports selected details of a module's implementation. This may permit efficient access to data without the overhead of function calls via an interface. However, the choice of quality of service information must be made with regard to the trade off between performance and flexibility.

The open architecture may be employed with any programming system that may be mapped onto the single object format provided. To date, implementations of the open architecture exist for the persistent programming language Napier88, the object-oriented database programming language Galileo, the typeful programming language Quest and the functional programming language STAPLE. Each of these systems uses the same implementation of the persistent object store and demonstrates the cost-effectiveness of using the open architecture to integrate persistence with a particular programming paradigm.

Acknowledgements. The work was supported by SERC Grants GR/F 28571, GR/G 17578 and GR/G 33011, SERC Post-doctoral Fellowship B/ITF/199, ESPRIT II Basic Research Action 3070 - FIDE and a grant from the DTI Awareness Initiative in Object Oriented Programming. Gianni Mainetto worked in St.Andrews supported by Italian NRC Fellowship 203.07.17 "Progetto Finalizzato: Sistemi Informatica @ Calcolo Parallelo."

References

1. Atkinson MP, Chisholm KJ, Cockshott WP. CMS - A Chunk Management System. Software Practice and Experience, vol. 13, no. 3, 1983, pp259-272.
2. Cockshott WP, Atkinson MP, Chisholm KJ, Bailey PJ, Morrison R. POMS: A Persistent Object Management System. Software Practice and Experience, vol. 14, no. 1, 1984, pp49-71.
3. Brown AL, Cockshott WP. The CPOMS Persistent Object Management System. Universities of Glasgow and St.Andrews PPRR-13, Scotland, 1985.
4. Brown AL (Ph.D. Thesis) Persistent Object Stores. Universities of Glasgow and St.Andrews PPRR-71, Scotland, 1989.
5. Moss JEB, Sinofsky S. Managing Persistent Data with Mneme: Designing a Reliable Shared Object Interface. In Advances in Object-Oriented Database Systems, Lecture Notes in Computer Science, Springer-Verlag, vol. 334, 1988, pp298-316.
6. Skarra A, Zdonik SB, Reiss SP. An Object Server For An Object-Oriented Database System. Proc. International Workshop on Object-Oriented Database Systems, Pacific Grove, California, 1987, pp196-204.

7. Ross GDM. (Ph.D. Thesis) Virtual Files: A Framework for Experimental Design. University of Edinburgh, 1983.
8. Thatte SM. Persistent Memory: A Storage Architecture for Object Oriented Database Systems. Proc. ACM/IEEE 1986 International Workshop on Object Oriented Database Systems, Pacific Grove, CA, September 1986, pp148-159.
9. Atkinson MP, Bailey PJ, Chisholm KJ, Cockshott WP, Morrison R. An Approach to Persistent Programming. The Computer Journal, vol. 26, no. 4, 1983, pp360-365.
10. Albano A, Cardelli L, Orsini R. Galilieo: A Strongly Typed, Interactive Conceptual Language. ACM Transactions on Database Systems, vol. 10, no. 2, 1985, pp230-260.
11. Cardelli L. Typeful Programming. DEC SRC Report, No. 45, May 1989.
12. Davie AJT, McNally DJ. Statically Typed Applicative Persistent Language Environments (STAPLE) User's Manual. Computational Science Research Report, CS/90/14, University of St.Andrews, Scotland, 1990.
13. Brown, A.L. & Rosenberg J. Persistent Object Stores: An Implementation Technique. in Dearle, Shaw, Zdonik (eds.), Implementing Persistent Object Bases, Principles and Practice, Morgan Kaufmann, 1991, pp199-212.

Chapter 2.2.2

Overview of *PIOS*: a Physically Independent Object Server

Giuseppe Amato[1], Salvatore Biscari[2], Giovanni Mainetto[2] and Fausto Rabitti[2]

[1] IEI, Institute of CNR, Via S.Maria 46, Pisa, Italy
[2] CNUCE, Institute of CNR, Via S.Maria 36, Pisa, Italy

Abstract. *PIOS* (Physically Independent Object Server) is a prototype implementation of an object store intended to test some new ideas and techniques in the framework of the $FIDE_2$ project.

The main idea in PIOS is the support of physical objects' independence in an object store. Physical Independence allows the change of strategies in storing physical objects in the database without affecting the applications since they always see the same logical database schema. Physical Independence opens up opportunities to enhance performance in areas such query optimisation and high performance concurrency control.

In this paper, an overview of the PIOS architecture is presented, stressing the new techniques implemented in the system to exploit physical independence in improving system performance.

1 Introduction

Few years ago, a comprehensive survey of the next–generation database systems was largely dedicated to Object–Oriented Database Management Systems (ODMSs) [1]. Since then, enhancements have been added to ODMSs that are now reaching the technological maturity. Several ODMSs, such as: O2, GemStone, ObjectStore and others not mentioned in that survey, are beginning to appear on the market as complete products.

Even if ODMSs are not having the great commercial success that database experts foresaw, they are occupying relevant positions in the new DMS[1] market areas, such as communication network management, geographical information management, computer aided design, etc. However, ODMSs have not been able to penetrate the enormous traditional DMS market, firmly held by relational systems.

The ODMSs' inability to compete with relational systems in the traditional market of DMSs probably depends on the fact that this market requires applications that just need efficiency in the associative accesses to simply structured data, that is here the efficiency of set–oriented queries on trivial data is of paramount importance. On the contrary, the first generation's ODMSs are better suited for complex applications that require an efficient program guided navigation within a graph of complex persistent data.

Research is currently trying to overcome the limits of the first generation ODMSs. One research challenge is the exploitation of new techniques for a better engineering of ODMS specific mechanisms.

---

[1] We use the acronym DMS instead of the more traditional DBMS.

PIOS (*Physically Independent Object Server*) is a research prototype intended to explore new development directions in ODMSs. The most important feature of *PIOS* is the support of *physical independence*. The introduction of physical independence has lead to a revision of some of the most important functionalities provided by an ODMS and to a redesign of its supporting architecture. *PIOS* is interested in the experimentation of concurrency control techniques that guarantee an efficient and correct management of the same kind of transactions as those used in traditional applications. Thus *PIOS* grants *strict* and *serialisable* executions of *short–duration* transactions. *PIOS* is the server component of a client–server architecture, where a centralised server manages the shared persistent object database on behalf of several clients. At run time, *PIOS* is made of a set of processes that communicate through messages with client processes. Typical *PIOS* clients are: the compiler of an external language and its run–time support, a query language processor, a tool that supports database administration and design, a browser, etc.

This paper concentrates its attention on the introduction of the physical independence support in an ODMS, on the underlying client–server database architecture, and on the technical solution of the concurrency control problem.

The paper is organised as follows. Section 2 introduces the most important ideas that have driven the development of *PIOS* prototype, outlines *PIOS* main features and the supporting architecture; Section 3 describes in detail how *PIOS* deals with physical data independence; Section 4 deals with the concurrency control problem in *PIOS*, it describes the new protocols that we propose and the new techniques that have been developed to increase efficiency; Section 5 gives a complete description of *PIOS* architecture, focusing on the concurrency control techniques.

2 *PIOS* rationale

The main research directions pursued in the development of *PIOS* can be summarised as follows:

1. Effectiveness of physical independence in ODMSs;
2. Investigation of object–oriented query processing in presence of physical independence support, with particular emphasis on the optimisation phase;
3. Effectiveness of *navigation accelerators* in ODMSs;
4. Investigation of *concurrency control techniques* that use serialisability as correctness criterion in an ODMS supporting physical independence;
5. Design and realisation of an easy–to–maintain architecture that implements an ODMS supporting physical independence.

In the rest of this Section, these issues will be sketched to provide the reader a complete survey of *PIOS* features. In the next sections, issues 2) and 3) will not be further described since they are already covered from other papers that can be found in the literature and in this book (see Chapter 2.3.3).

2.1 Physical independence in *PIOS*

A DMS supports physical data independence if the application programs do not need to be rewritten when the physical organisation of data is changed. The possibility of adapting the physical database organisation to changes in the performance requirements of application programs is an important and well–known feature of traditional DMSs: twenty years ago, the ANSI/X3/SPARC committee proposed a three–level architecture to guarantee physical and logical independence properties in DMSs [2]. Vice versa, in the ODMS area this issue has not received any particular attention probably because most ODMSs are strictly bound to a specific object–oriented database programming language and the initial development efforts were concentrated in designing an architecture able to ensure an adequate performance, tailoring it on the specific language.

Successively, developers and researchers have dedicated attention to the definition of the ODMS storage–level subsystem to use it as the kernel to support a large number of different object–oriented data models (see for example DASDBS [3] and O2 [4]). A different higher layer may be built on top of the common kernel to directly support a specific object–oriented data model. The storage–level subsystem is often called *object store*. The presence of the object store component facilitates the introduction of the physical independence notion in an ODMS because of the need to organise the supporting architecture with at least two levels of abstraction. *PIOS* follows this stream of research and development.

In *PIOS* two object data models are provided: a *logical data model* and a *physical data model*. The logical data model is a classical object–oriented data model in which a single logical object can simultaneously belong to several logical classes that are in an *ISA* relationship. The physical data model is an object–oriented data model too, in which every physical object belongs to exactly one physical class. Physical classes are flat: there is no *ISA* relationship among them.

PIOS logical data model is supposed to support several high level languages (i.e. object-oriented database programming languages, like Orion [5] and O2 [6], and conceptual database programming languages, like Galileo [7] – see Chapter 1.1.2).

The traditional physical data models are used to describe complex data structure at the lowest level (see for example the *unifying model* [8] and the *frame memory* [9]). In contrast to these traditional physical data models, *PIOS* physical data model allows the description of data at a higher level of abstraction. In fact, the abstraction mechanisms provided from *PIOS* physical data model are much closer to those of a relational data model than to those defined in one of the previously mentioned traditional physical data models.

Inside *PIOS*, two database schemata correspond to the two data models: the *logical schema* and the *physical schema*. The former schema, which allows the definition of types of logical objects in the database, is exported to every client. In principle, the logical schema of a client should provide its users with a special view of shared persistent objects (e.g. an *external schema* or a *user view* of the logical schema). The latter schema, which is not visible to *PIOS*'s clients, allows the definition of types of physical objects, that is the types of those objects that are used to represent logical objects (Figure 1).

For a given logical schema, *PIOS* enables the database designer to choose among different physical organisations. This choice should be guided by performance requirements of applications that run in *PIOS* clients. At the physical level the *PIOS* database designer can also operate to set-up *value and navigation indexes*. Value and navigation indexes are defined in *PIOS* physical schema. Section 3 describes the range of physical mappings from the logical schema provided by *PIOS* to the database designers.

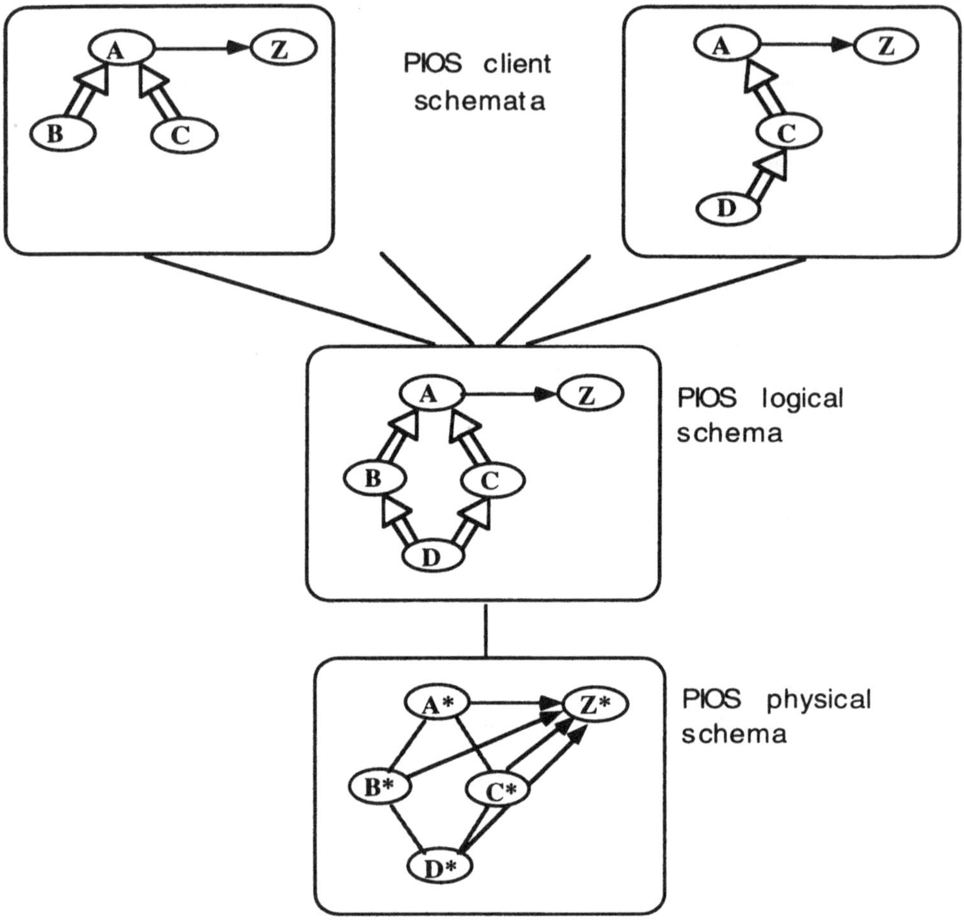

Fig. 1. PIOS schemata

2.2 Navigation accelerators in *PIOS*

A *Navigation Index* is used to efficiently support the navigation along references between related objects in the store of *PIOS* [10]. The basic strategy of this index is to avoid disk accesses to intermediate objects by determining (whenever possible) identities of target objects by calculation and by use of a simple auxiliary storage structure in all other cases. In fact, a navigation index appends codes to objects, which not only uniquely identify the objects, but also reflect relationships with other objects in the store. The important feature of the coding technique – applying the theory of *simple continued fractions* [11] – is that, once an object code is given, codes of all the objects referencing the given object can also be provided. This approach to coding structures was previously suggested by [12] as a method for hierarchy processing in relational systems. Obviously, the application to the object store is more general, because it must manage navigation in directed graphs.

2.3 Query processing in *PIOS*

The *PIOS* system provides the database designer with a powerful set of construction rules to design a specific physical database schema. This schema can be quite different from the logical schema and obviously implies a more complex translation of a logical query (i.e., a query on the logical schema) into a physical query (i.e., a query on the physical schema), compared to analogous procedures followed by most of the other ODMSs. Query optimisation in *PIOS* is a two–phase process: (i) algebraic optimisation is performed through application of rewriting rules and (ii) physical optimisation is performed based on a cost model and a local search procedure. Algebraic optimisation also consists of two steps: (i) algebraic optimisation of logical queries, applied at the very beginning of the query optimisation and (ii) algebraic optimisation of physical queries (pruning), which completes the translation of physical queries. A detailed description of the *PIOS* Query Optimiser can be found in [13] and in Chapter 2.3.3 of this book.

2.4 Concurrency control in *PIOS*

ODMSs provide their transaction programmers with two alternatives for controlling concurrent accesses to shared persistent objects. The first possibility is the direct interaction with simple system–provided synchronisation primitives and data structures. In the second possibility, the transaction programmer transparently uses system–provided access primitives that automatically guarantee the correctness of the access. This second approach is safer but it is also usually less efficient than the first one because the ODMS must implement a general policy for concurrency control that cannot be tailored to specific application requirements and that cannot take advantage of any semantic knowledge of the transaction behaviour.

The concurrency control mechanisms provided from *PIOS* are of the second type. The programs, running on the external client machines, interact with *PIOS* server by sending messages containing information that identify the beginning and the ending of each transaction as well as object access primitives. These messages can be automatically generated by the compiler of the external language and thus a programmer can write a transaction program that transparently accesses the data stored in a *PIOS* database. The *PIOS* system will automatically ensure the serialisability and strictness of the overall transaction execution.

This design decision provides advantages in terms of the reliability of the overall system, the simplification of external clients and the centralisation of concurrency control activity inside *PIOS*. If the accesses to database objects had not been transparently granted, then the problem of the correct use of some concurrency control protocol from an external client would have to be faced. It is not realistic to expect an external client, that can be a complex piece of software such as the run–time support of a language, to include a detailed knowledge of the concurrency control protocol implemented by its object server.

Despite the choice of transparency, *PIOS* provides a satisfactory solution to the concurrency control problem mainly because *PIOS*'s concurrency control mechanisms can take advantage of several sources of semantic knowledge about a transaction's behaviour.

In *PIOS* the presence of two data models directly reflects on the concurrency control activity. *PIOS* distinguishes two kinds of concurrency control: *logical level concurrency control* and *physical level concurrency control*.

Two different and integrated techniques have been developed to control concurrent accesses to shared persistent data. The technique used at the logical level is an optimistic one that bases its safety on the pessimistic technique provided at the physical level. Two original protocols have been developed for the two levels of concurrency control.

The protocol used at the logical level is called *Two–Level Access Validation.* It relies on the semantic knowledge that comes from a transaction model richer than the usual read–write model of transactions. This transaction model contains several items of information related to the temporal ordering of access operations, the existence of physical objects and the presence of a pessimistic technique at the underlying physical level.

The protocol used at the physical level is a version of the *Multigranularity Locking* protocol called *Expandable*. Being a version of the *Multigranularity Locking* protocol, this protocol allows us to strike a balance between the locking overhead and the amount of transaction parallelism. To this purpose, it takes advantage of semantic information about an active transaction provided from several components of the *PIOS* system. One source of knowledge is *PIOS* query processor that performs a simple analysis of the dynamic semantics of a complete query transaction. Another source of semantic knowledge regards the organisation of important *PIOS* data structures such as the value indices.

2.5 Process structure of *PIOS*

PIOS as a whole represents the server component of a client-server ODMS. When the unit of transfer between the server and one client is a single object, the server component is called *object server* [14]. *PIOS* is an object server that supports *prefetching*, i.e. every client can send a single object at a time to *PIOS*, while *PIOS* can send back a set of objects in a single unit of transfer.

Internally, *PIOS* is in turn structured according to a client-server architecture in which several *User Supervisors* (*USs*) are the clients of a single *Physical Object Server* (*PHOS*). Every *US* is a process that acts on behalf of an external *Client* process. Peer *US–Client* processes can run on different machines connected through an interconnection structure that is usually a LAN. The *USs* interact with *PHOS* through a *Message Queue*. The process structure of *PIOS*, the data structures used for interprocess communication, the most important persistent information and the information about *PIOS* schemata are all shown in Figure 2.

2.5.1 User Supervisor

The main purposes of each *US* are the translation of logical access operations (to logical objects) into physical access operations (to physical objects) and the recomposition of the logical results from the results of physical operations. The translation and optimisation of logical queries are of paramount importance for the overall *PIOS* performance.

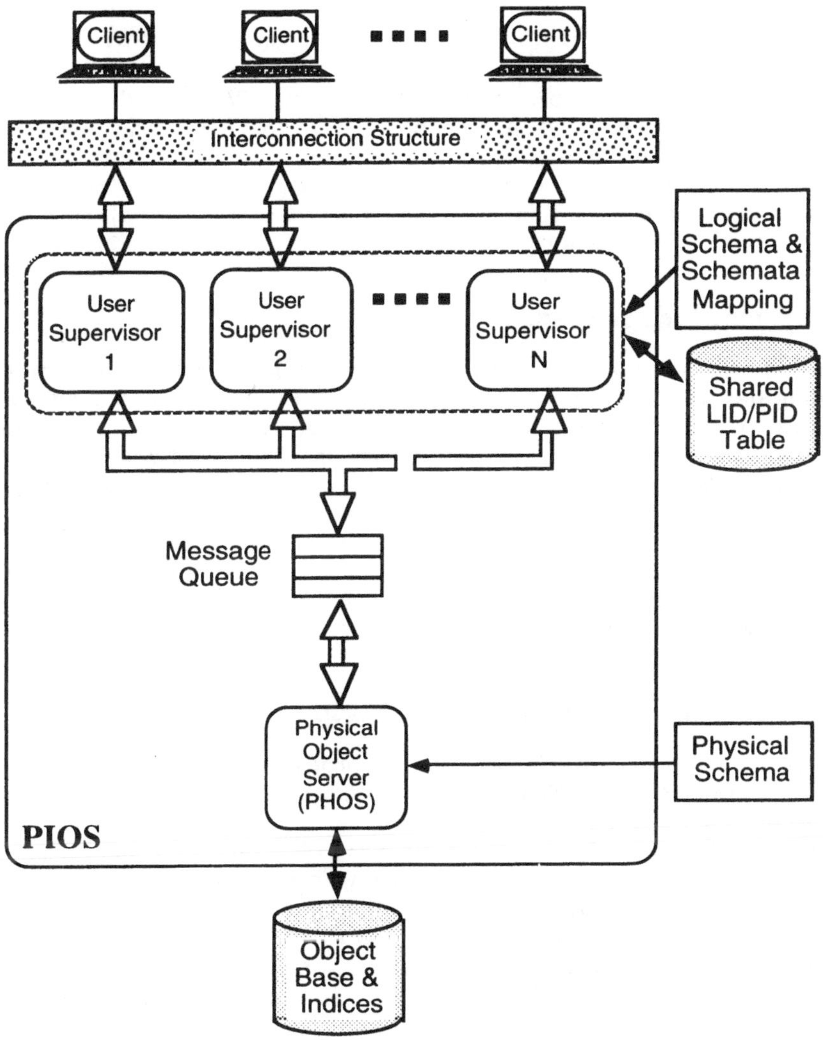

Fig. 2. *PIOS* process structure

The information recording the correspondence between logical classes and their physical counterparts is stored in a file that is accessed from every *US* when it starts. This information is *statically* defined. The file is created off-line as the result of the logical and physical design of a *PIOS* database. A *US* mainly uses this information during the translation of logical set–oriented access operations.

The translation of a navigational access to a single logical object requires that *US* interacts with a shared data structure called *LID/PID table*. This table maintains all the *dynamic* information about the correspondence between logical object identifiers (*LIDs*) and the corresponding physical object identifiers (*PIDs*) (see Figure 2).

2.5.2 Physical Object Server

The main task of *PHOS* is to provide *USs* with the operations of *PIOS* physical data model that include the operations for accessing navigation and value indices. All these operations must be serialisable and recoverable. Thus *PHOS* is the subsystem of *PIOS* that implements the functions usually provided from both a scheduler and a data manager.

Before initialising the physical database, *PHOS* gets all the information about physical classes and indices from a read-only file (*Physical Schema*), that has been created off-line as outcome of the logical and physical design (Figure 2).

3 Physical independence

The goal of supporting physical independence in an ODMS becomes the problem of translating the access operations provided by the *PIOS* logical data model into the operations provided by the *PIOS* physical data model. A data model is made of three ingredients: data structures, explicit and implicit integrity constraints, and operators to manipulate the data structures without violating the integrity constraints. It will thus be necessary to give rules for translating data structures, integrity constraints and operators of the logical data model into the corresponding data structures, integrity constraints and operations of the physical data model, while preserving their semantics. In the following, we will concentrate on the data structures and we will sketch the operators. A complete and detailed description of this process can be found in [15].

3.1 Data structures of the two data models

PIOS logical data model is a classical object–oriented data model [16]. Classes with multiple inheritance (*ISA* relation) and objects are the two distinguishing data structures of the data model.

Objects are instances of record types and every object has a *unique logical object identifier* (*LID*). A *LID* is univocally associated with a logical object when the object itself is created. A *LID* remains unchanged during all the object's life. The same object can simultaneously belong to several classes, those that are in an *ISA* relation. Every logical object has a logical (immaterial) *state*, consisting of the set of the actual values of its *attributes*. An object state can change during the object's life. There are two kinds of attribute: *descriptive attributes* and *references*. Descriptive attributes take on values of a primitive type (e.g. integers, reals, strings and images). References take on *LID*s as values and they are used for modelling the association among objects. Both a descriptive attribute and a reference can evaluate to a single value or to a set of values of the same type.

A *class* data structure has an extensional meaning. A class is a "bulk" type constructor, like *set_of* or *list*, characterised by two facts: an *instance_of* relation exists between a class and the set of actual objects belonging to it that at a certain moment exist in the logical (immaterial) database state. This set of objects is the *extension* of the class. A subset relation exists between the extensions of two classes that are in an *ISA* relation.

The logical data model also provides an abstraction mechanism for modelling *dependent* objects. For every class, the database designer specifies whether its objects are *dependent* or *independent* and *shared* or *not shared*. An object is *independent* if its existence does not depend on the existence of any other object. An object is *dependent* if it can exist in the logical database only when referenced, possibly indirectly, by an *independent* object. The *dependent/independent* specification can be useful in translating *composite* objects, as in [5]. An object is defined as *not shared* if it can be referenced by no more than one object, otherwise it is *shared*. If an object belongs to a *shared* class, then, for each reference to it, a specification is required as to whether that reference is *shared* or *not shared*, i.e. whether more than one object of the same class may be associated with it. The last specification is not important for the translation mechanisms discussed in this paper, and therefore it will not be considered in the examples.

PIOS does not store any logical object in the database; it only stores *physical objects*. Physical objects are similar to logical ones. In the general case, there is no one–to–one correspondence between a logical object and its physical counterpart.

A physical object has an *identifier* and a *state*. Every *physical object identifier* (*PID*) is unique in the database: *PIOS* automatically generates a new *PID* when it creates a new physical object and such *PID* will never change. The *state* of a physical object consists of the set of the actual values of its *physical attributes* and these can change during the object's life. Similarly to the logical level, an attribute can be descriptive or reference (in the latter case it takes on *PID*s as values), and it can take a single value or a set of values. In particular circumstances, *PIOS* automatically generates special physical references called *system references* that do not correspond to any reference defined at logical level. *PIOS* uses system references to reconstruct logical objects starting from physical ones.

The physical-level counterpart of a logical class is the *collection*, a set–like type constructor used to group physical objects. Several collections at physical level can correspond to a single logical class. Collections differ from classes because their organisation is flat, i.e. there is no implicit subset relation defined on them.

PIOS's physical data model also captures the notions of value index, defined on a (physical) descriptive attribute of the (physical) objects of a collection, and navigation index, defined on a path constituted from a sequence of (physical) reference attributes.

3.2 Mapping of data structures

In this section, we describe how the *PIOS* database designer defines the mapping of the logical data structures to a physical one. We will also make clear how the *PIOS* system can reconstruct logical data starting from physical ones.

The mapping definition involves the application, in a given order, of a sequence of mapping operations to *PIOS* logical schema. The database designer interactively submits these operations to the *Mapping Definition Manager*, a specific tool of the *PIOS* system that operates off–line producing as outcome: the logical schema, the physical schema and the schemata mapping information.

A *PIOS* database designer has firstly to decide the representation of the generalisation hierarchies, i.e. the way in which a logical object, that can simultaneously belong to several classes of a generalisation hierarchy, is represented from physical objects, each of them belonging to exactly one collection. Then, he can decide *partitioning* and *grouping* physical objects. Before these operations, the *Mapping Definition Manager* automatically performs an initial *one-to-one* transformation of the logical schema.

3.2.1 One-to-one transformation

The first step of the mapping definition consists of the automatic application to the logical schema of the following transformations:

- every class of the logical schema becomes a collection of the physical schema;
- every descriptive attribute of an instance of a logical class becomes a descriptive attribute of a physical object in the corresponding physical collection;
- every reference from an instance of a logical class to another instance becomes a reference between the two corresponding physical objects of the corresponding physical collections.

3.2.2 Generalisation hierarchy mapping

PIOS supports two alternative techniques for the resolution of the generalisation hierarchies: the *Schema Division Solution* (SDS) and the *Objects Distribution Solution* (ODS). Similar techniques have been proposed in the literature and in several systems.

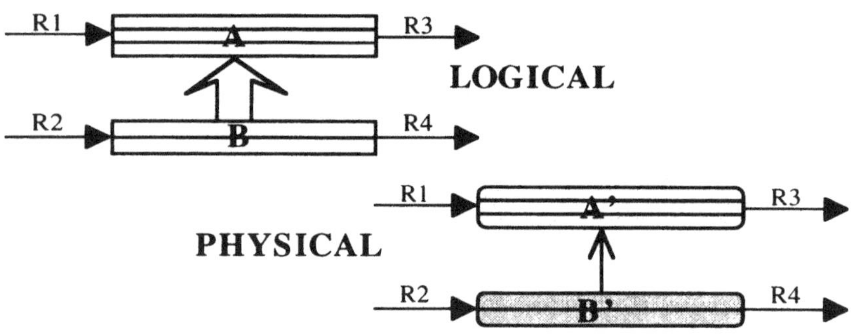

Fig. 3. Schema Division Solution

SDS breaks a logical object into several physical objects. Given two classes in an *ISA* relationship, SDS produces two collections: the first that will contain physical objects with values only for the logical attributes defined in the more general class, and the former that will contain physical objects with values only for those logical attributes defined in the more specific class. This means that the physical objects of the second collection contain values representing only the part of a logical object corresponding to the specialised attributes and that these values have a meaning only if they are related to that subset of the physical objects of the first collection representing those logical objects that are in both classes. Thus a generalisation reference is system generated for each physical object of the second collection. The generalisation reference will connect the physical objects representing one logical object. References entering and exiting the two classes will respectively enter and exit the two corresponding collections.

In Figure 3, a graphical representation of this solution is shown. The rectangles A and B represent classes of the logical schema with the specific parts of their logical objects (internal thin rectangles), the ovals A' and B' represent the corresponding collections and physical objects. Arrows represent references and the double arrow the *ISA* relationship. All the objects have the same structure, thus we have simplified the graphics by drawing one single arrow for the entire class (collection). Notice that the *ISA* relationship has been replaced by a system generated reference in the physical counterpart (a system reference has a distinguishing head of the arrow). This reference will connect every physical object of B' with a physical object of A'.

ODS breaks the extension of classes in an *ISA* relationship, while it maintains the entirety of the representation of a logical object. Given two classes in an *ISA* relationship, ODS also produces two collections: in the first there will be physical objects with values for all the attributes (both inherited and not) of the logical objects of the subclass, where as in the second the physical objects that represent those logical objects belonging to just the superclass will be placed. Each reference entering the superclass will correspond to two references entering both of the generated collections. A reference to or from the subclass will enter or exit the corresponding collection. A reference exiting the superclass corresponds to two references exiting both the collections. No system reference between the two collections will be generated. ODS is graphically described in Figure 4.

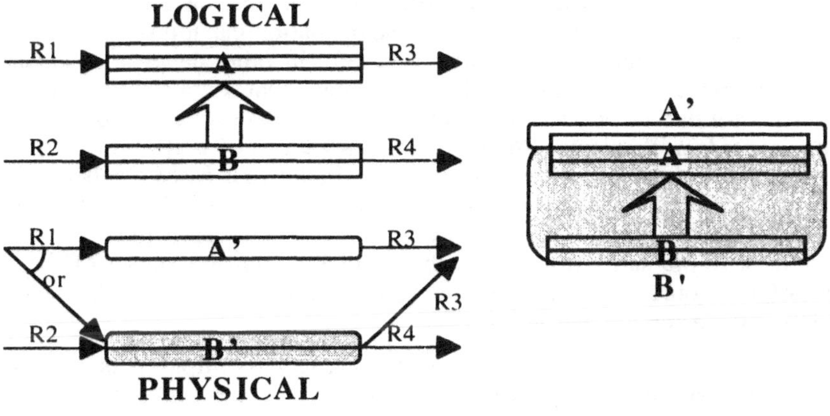

Fig. 4. Object Distribution Solution

After the initial transformation previously described, the *Mapping Definition Manager* automatically resolves all logical generalisation hierarchies according to SDS. If desired, the database designer can change this default solution and he can apply ODS. The syntax of the ODS operation is the following:

ODS <$\texttt{coll}_0$>

where <$\texttt{coll}_0$> is the name of a physical collection corresponding to the logical class which is the root of a generalisation hierarchy.

The result of the ODS operation will be that the definitions of the collections corresponding to the subclasses of the hierarchy will be modified to contain all inherited descriptive attributes and references, and to remove generalisation references. Moreover, all collection definitions will be searched and each time a collection

<coll$_0$> of an ODS hierarchy is encountered as a referent, it will be decomposed into an expression of the form:

<coll$_0$><pred$_1$> **OR** <coll$_1$> <pred$_2$> **OR** ... **OR** <coll$_n$><pred$_{n+1}$>

where <coll$_1$> ... <coll$_n$> are all the subclasses of <coll$_0$> and where <pred$_i$> are the following predicates:

<pred$_i$> ::= **IS_NOT_OF** <coll$_i$> ... <coll$_n$>

Remember that every logical object belongs to exactly one most specific class (among those that are in an *ISA* realationship) and thus the previous expression represents an exclusive or. This allows a simple representation of the logical expression analogous to the representation of an element of a (small) set. In general, it is not possible to evaluate statically the logical expression. In this case, a tag associated with every referent reference must be inspected.

3.2.3 Collection partitioning

PIOS allows the classes at the logical level to be fragmented into two or more collections of the physical level. Fragmentation problems have been investigated in depth in distributed database research. The fragmentation capability is not necessarily restricted to data distribution, it can also be useful in other database architectures for efficiency purposes and to supply the capabilities that implement specific access mechanisms for particular portions of data (e.g. image data stored on optical disks) or security devoted mechanisms. *PIOS* supports two kinds of collection fragmentation: *vertical partitioning* and *horizontal partitioning.* In the first case, a collection is split into two or more collections, each of which contains a subset of the attributes of the starting collection. In the second case, a collection is split into two or more collections with the same structure, each of which contains a subset of the physical objects of the source collection according to a fragmentation predicate. The two operations can be applied repeatedly.

Vertical partitioning. When an operation for vertical partitioning is applied, some parts (i.e. some subsets of the descriptive attributes or references) of the objects of the initial collection are stored as objects of the newly generated collections and a reference is created from the rest of the object to each of its parts, i.e. to each new object. All newly generated collections are *dependent* on the starting collection and are *not shared.* All references entering the starting collection remain unchanged. An existing reference will come from the initial collection or from one of its parts, depending on whether it remains in the initial collection. Figure 5 shows a graphical example of vertical partitioning. The syntax of the vertical partitioning operation is:

VERTICAL_PART <coll-name>:
<coll-name$_1$> (<list-of-descr-attributes$_1$>,<list-of-references$_1$>),
<coll-name$_2$> (<list-of-descr-attributes$_2$>,<list-of-references$_2$>),
...
<coll-name$_n$> (<list-of-descr-attributes$_n$>,<list-of-references$_n$>)

The result of this operation is the creation of *n* new *dependent* and *not shared* collections that contain the descriptive attributes and references indicated.

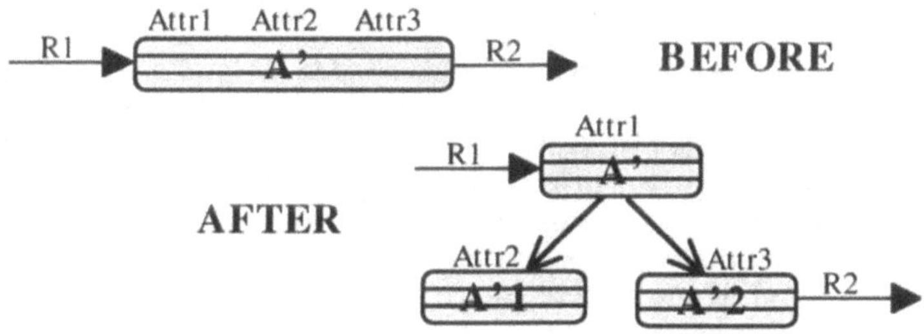

Fig. 5. Vertical partitioning

The source collection will also be changed. The descriptive attributes and references cited in the operation are discarded, and a set of system generated references called *vertical references* will connect the source collection to the new collections.

Horizontal partitioning. When an operation for horizontal partitioning is applied, the collection is divided into a set of new collections with the same structure, such that the physical objects belonging to each collection satisfy certain conditions, given by predicates. The syntax of this operation is the following:

```
HORIZONTAL_PART <coll-name>:
        <coll-name1> IF <predicate1>
        <coll-name2> IF <predicate2>
        ...
        <coll-namen> IF <predicaten>
```

The result of this operation is the creation of n new collections with the same structure as the source collection <coll-name> (see Figure 6). The semantics of this operation consists of replacing every reference to <coll-name> in the physical schema with a complex expression such as:

```
<coll-name1> <predicate1> OR ... OR
        <coll-namen> <predicaten> OR <coll-name><predicate>
```

where `<predicate>::= NOT<predicate1> AND ... AND NOT<predicaten>`.

Finally, every complex expression is simplified.

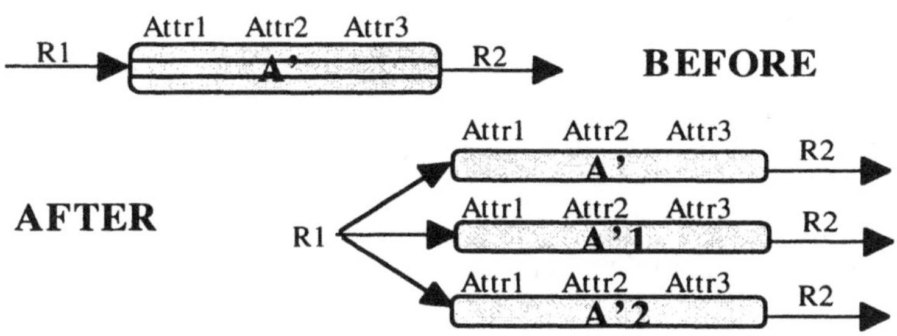

Fig. 6. Horizontal partitioning

3.2.4 Collection grouping

The *clustering* mechanism has been investigated in traditional DMSs for a long time. This mechanism consists in storing, in close proximity, data items that are supposed to be frequently accessed together. This mechanism has also been proposed for ODMSs. What we call *grouping* is a kind of static clustering (that is determined at schema definition time). Conceptually, the collection obtained by grouping two or more different collections will contain physical objects that have values for all the attributes of all the grouped collections. A collection generated by a grouping operation can have physical objects with different structures. For instance, let us consider the following definition:

$$C = A \oplus B$$

in which C, A and B are collections and $\oplus$ is the grouping operation. Let A and B correspond to the classes A_C and B_C of the logical data model. A physical object of collection C may correspond to one or two different objects, each belonging to one of the logical classes A_C and B_C. A problem arises here concerning how to understand whether a given physical object of C represents one or two logical objects at a given moment. The problem has already been solved in the clustering techniques of CODASYL DMS [17] and consists in assigning to each physical object of the resulting collection a binary code of n bits, where n is the number of the source collection. The i-th bit indicates whether the object contains the values of an object of the i-th collection or not.

To make the grouping operation feasible, we stipulate some restriction rules:

Rule 1. Two collections can be grouped if and only if there is a reference from one to the other.

Rule 2. When defining a group, all collections except the root collection must be dependent and not shared.

The first rule avoids groups that have no sense from semantic point of view, while the second avoids replications of values and the problem of managing dynamic re-grouping.

After the grouping operation, all references originally entering the root collection will enter the grouped collection and all references exiting the collections will exit from the grouped collection (see Figure 7). Grouping can be performed in two different ways depending on the type of reference that relates the two collections. If it

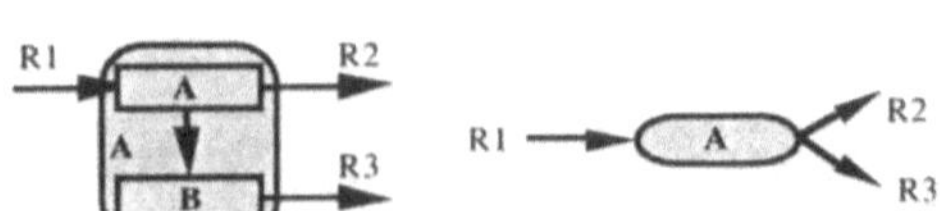

Fig. 7. Grouping

is a reference, we have to deal with *grouping by reference*. The syntax of the operation in this case is the following:

GROUP <coll-name$_1$>,<ref-name>,<coll-name$_2$>

The reference <ref-name> must be present in the references of the first collection. It may be a simple reference or a reference with a tag (e.g. an OR-list as described in 3.2.2). The result of the grouping operation is that for each of its objects the first collection will also contain the descriptive attributes and the references of the referred objects of the second collection. All attributes and references of the second collection will be added to the definition of the first collection, each of them followed by the predicates specified in the definition of <coll-name$_2$>, and then a simplification takes place.

The case when the reference is vertical is called *grouping by vertical reference.* The syntax of the grouping operation in this case is the following:

GROUP <coll-name$_1$>,<coll-name$_2$>

As in the first case, all attributes and all references of the second collection are added to the first one. The vertical reference between <coll-name$_1$> and <coll-name$_2$> is then removed from the list of vertical references of <coll-name$_1$> in the way described in the previous case. Besides this, in both cases, if the second collection is not referred to by other collections, its definition is cancelled, that is it does not exist any more.

3.3 Operators of the two data models

At the *logical level*, we have defined three groups of operations. The first group consists of operations for creating and modifying logical objects. There are operations for:

- creating a new object in a given class;
- updating the object with a given *LID* or the set of objects which satisfy a given clause;
- deleting the object with a given *LID* or the set of objects which satisfy a given clause.

The *creation* operation will generate the state of a logical object and it will insert the *LID* in the extensions of all its classes. The *deletion* operation will remove an object from all the classes to which it belongs. The deletion of a logical object may cause a cascade of deletions of referenced objects in *dependent* classes.

The second group of operations are intended to support the migration of objects from a class to its specialisation classes (using the *specialise* operation) or generalisation classes (using the *generalise* operation). In the case of *specialise* operations, the values for the new attributes must be supplied. The *generalise* operation, like the *delete* operation, may cause the recursive deletion of some referenced *dependent* objects.

The last group consists of operations for object access and retrieval. It is possible either to directly indicate the *LID*s of the objects to access, or to specify a query clause, which determines the set of objects needed. The first operation is called *retrieve*, while the second is the query operation *find* (see Chapter 2.3.3 of this book).

The operations at the *physical* level are similar to the operations of the logical data model but they operate on physical objects belonging to just one collection. There are operations for:

- creating, deleting and modifying physical objects;
- adding and deleting references between physical objects;
- retrieval of physical objects;
- access to the extension of a collection;
- access to value and navigation indexes.

The first and second groups include operations for the management of physical objects. Each logical operation for creation, deletion and modification of logical objects is translated in a sequence of physical operations. Thus, each logical operation consists of one or more physical operations. For example, because of the fragmentation of a logical class, a logical *creation* operation may be translated into a sequence of operations for creating physical objects and references.

The third group consists of two operations. The first is the *get* operation that returns the state of a given *PID*. The logical operation *retrieve* can give raise to a sequence of *get* operations. The second operation (*search*) is set-oriented. This operation returns the set of physical object identifiers in the specified collection that satisfies a given specification. The specification is analogous to the condition that can be expressed by the select operator of the relational algebra.

The operation that given a collection identifier returns the set of *PID*s belonging to the collection is useful in the mapping of logical set–oriented operations. The last group consists of operations that deal with the management of the index structures.

3.4 Mapping of operators and system composite objects

The mapping of a logical *creation* operation consists of three steps:

- construction, in a temporary buffer of the logical level, of the sets of basic values of the physical objects corresponding to the logical object to be created;
- determination of the physical collections of these objects;
- creation of the physical objects and transfer of their values from the temporary buffer into the collections.

Updating a logical object may cause changes in its structure, that is after performing the logical *update* operation we may obtain a set of physical objects that belong to collections which are completely different from the initial ones. For example, if a horizontal fragmentation has been declared, changing a simple value of an attribute that is involved in the fragmentation predicate may cause a migration of a physical object from one collection to another. This means creation of a new physical object and deletion of the old object.

The algorithm used for the mapping of the *update* operator is also useful for the mapping of the *generalise* and *specialise* operations. The mapping of the *delete* operation consists of removing those physical objects that correspond to the given logical object and all their references. In turn, the deletion of each physical object may cause a cascade deletion of all *dependent* objects referenced by it that are not referenced by other *independent* objects.

The mapping of the *retrieve* operation is trivial: for each of the given *LID*s the corresponding physical objects that contain the values for the attributes specified in a <target-list> are read. If there is no <target-list> given in the logical operation, all the physical objects corresponding to the entire logical object will be read. If the

<target-list> is present, a considerable amount of data transfer can be avoided when there is a vertical fragmentation.

Operations like creation, deletion, migration and update (of certain attributes) of a logical object, can lead to changes in the corresponding set of physical objects that represents the logical entity. This set is organised as a hierarchy. One hierarchy of physical objects corresponds to every logical object, i.e. to every *LID*, and vice versa. In *PIOS* this hierarchy is called *system composite object* (*SCO*). One *SCO* is represented by a *rooted direct acyclic graph* (*RDAG*) in which the nodes are physical objects and the edges are system references. Being one *RDAG*, every *SCO* is univocally identified from the *PID* of its root object, called its *initial object*. Correspondingly, the *PID* of an initial object univocally identifies one *SCO*: that represented from those objects belonging to the transitive closure of objects reachable through system references from the given physical object.

4 Concurrency control

PIOS clients transparently interact with the database of physical objects through the operations provided from the logical data model. These operations deal with classes and logical objects, where as a *PIOS* database is made of physical objects belonging to collections derived from classes according to the schemata mapping. Therefore a translation has to be dynamically performed between logical-level operations and physical-level ones. This translation uses the information stored in the shared and persistent *LID/PID* table.

The persistent shared data of *PIOS* are the object database and the *LID/PID* table. Two different and integrated techniques have been developed to control concurrent accesses to the shared persistent data. The first technique, that can be seen as operating at the logical level, is an optimistic technique that bases its safety on the pessimistic technique provided from the physical level. The second is a pessimistic technique that takes advantage of semantic knowledge about transaction behaviour to increase parallelism and to reduce the system overhead due to concurrency control. Two original protocols have been developed for the two levels.

4.1 Logical level concurrency control

At logical level, the data shared among *UserSupervisors* (*US*s) are those contained in the *LID/PID* table, that maintains the correspondence between logical objects and *SCO*s. This table is shared and concurrently accessed from the instances of *US*s, both for reading and updating, during the translation of an operation from the logical level to the physical level. The table has a functional interface that guarantees the atomicity of the single access operation. Notice that the granularity of the accessible data item is a single table entry.

Since the *LID/PID* table is shared among the instances of *US*, a concurrency control protocol that guarantees table consistency is necessary. The table is the only persistent data structure shared at logical level for which such a policy is necessary because it is the only one that is dynamically updated during transaction executions.

4.1.1 Possible solutions

There are three possible approaches to the solution of the concurrency control problem in the *LID/PID* table accesses:

1. A first approach could be to adopt a pessimistic technique such as *Strict Two–Phase Locking* (*S2PL*) to control accesses to the database and indices, and also to the table. In this hypothesis, a suitable lock should be acquired on every table entry before accessing it. This solution is correct, but severely inefficient. The whole translation process performed by every *US* passes through the table: therefore, setting a lock on one entry means, as side effect, setting a sort of implicit lock on the whole *SCO* referenced by that entry. The result is, on the one hand, an overhead due to the 'redundancy' of replicating the locks at both levels and, on the other hand, a reduction of parallelism between concurrent transactions.
2. A second approach could be to adopt a pessimistic protocol such as *S2PL* only to control accesses to table entries, and not to physical objects in the database. Thus the control of the concurrent accesses to the database, at physical level, would be implicitly enforced through the control of the table accesses at the logical level. Unfortunately, this approach is not suitable to *PIOS*: setting locks only at logical level could make sense only if all accesses were performed to logical objects (that is *SCO*s) considered as a whole. This is exactly what we want to avoid with the physical independence. The purpose of physical independence is to decouple a database's physical organisation from the logical structure, in order to take advantage of the differences between logical and physical schemata for the sake of performance enhancement. In *PIOS* the way to enhance performance is to allow parallelism in the accesses to different parts of the same logical object. This would be impossible if a transaction must set a lock on the logical object as a whole. This approach is therefore not correct for *PIOS* and should be discarded.
3. The third approach, the one we adopted, consists of the integration of a classical pessimistic technique with an original technique of optimistic type. The former is *S2PL* and it is used for controlling concurrent accesses to the physical database, the latter is used for controlling accesses to the *LID/PID* table entries. While a transaction must set a lock on all physical objects before accessing them, the accesses to the table entries can go on without locking, thus leading to less overhead compared with the previous two previous proposals.

4.1.2 The 2LAV protocol

The optimistic technique adopted for controlling concurrent accesses to the *LID/PID* table relies on the following rules of the *Two-Levels Access Validation* (*2LAV*) protocol:

1. Before or after reading a table entry, a transaction must either read or write the physical object referenced by that entry.
2. Before creating a table entry, a transaction must write the new physical object to be referenced by that entry.
3. Before updating a table entry related to a given *LID*, the transaction must delete the physical object referenced by that entry.

The *2LAV certifier* aborts the transaction whenever a failure is generated from the physical level during the access to a physical object. The failure is the consequence of the non existence of a physical object. Of course all the accesses to physical objects must obey *S2PL* protocol rules: before performing an access a transaction must successfully set a suitable lock.

Table 1. Correspondence between logical and physical level operations

Logical Objects	Physical Objects	*LID/PID* table entries
Creation	Creation of the corresponding *SCO*	Creation of an entry for every initial object in the *SCO*
Deletion	Deletion of the corresponding *SCO*	Deletion of an entry for every initial object in the *SCO*
Specialisation	*ODS* Deletion from the collection corresponding to the superclass Creation in the collection corresponding to the subclass	*ODS* Update of the entries related to the superclasses Creation of the entry related to the subclass
	SDS Creation in the collection corresponding to the subclass	*SDS* Creation of the entry related to the subclass
Generalisation	*ODS* Deletion from the collection corresponding to the subclass Creation in the collection corresponding to the superclass	*ODS* Deletion of the entry related to the subclass Update of the entries related to the superclasses
	SDS Deletion from the collection corresponding to the subclass	*SDS* Deletion of the entry related to the subclass
Update	*Horizontal Partitioning* Deletion from the collection corresponding to the old value of the attribute Creation in the collection corresponding to the new value of the attribute	*Horizontal Partitioning* *ODS*: Update of the entries related to the class and the superclasses *SDS*: Update of the entry related to the class

A formal proof that the *2LAV* protocol allows serialisable histories can be found in [18]. Here we are interested to show, informally, how the correctness of the protocol is based on three logical presuppositions:

- the semantics of the utilisation of the table implies that every access to one entry is always preceded or followed by an access to the physical object referenced in that entry;
- the information maintained in the table pertains only to physical objects' existence, and not to their state;
- the serialisability of the accesses to each physical object is guaranteed by *S2PL*.

The first point follows from the analysis of the table access patterns. As shown in Table 1, every access to a table entry is always followed (when the entry is read) or preceded (when the entry is written) by an access to the physical object referenced (or to be referenced) by that entry. This peculiarity is fundamental for the correctness of the protocol: it allows us to 'hook' concurrency control on table entries to concurrency control on physical objects.

The second point follows from the observation that no table update is performed when only the state of a physical object is modified. For this reason, a failure when accessing a physical object can take place only as a consequence of incorrect information about the existence of that object, which, in turn, can only occur as a consequence of a nonserialisability in table accesses.

Notice also that, for a typical application, the number of object creations or deletions is much lower than the number of object state retrievals or updates. It is therefore reasonable to expect a lower number of conflicts in table accesses compared with the number of conflicts in object accesses: this could justify, in more general terms, the utilisation of an optimistic technique for concurrency control, which is known to be inefficient when the number of conflicts is high.

About the third point, we will only say that, upon examination of the proof in [18], it is easy to be convinced that the underlying *S2PL* protocol is fundamental for the correctness of the *2LAV* protocol. Most of the possible conflicts in table entry accesses are in fact avoided thanks to the locking of physical objects.

The correctness and the efficiency of this protocol are possible because the protocol uses a rich transaction model that contains more information: on the temporal ordering of accesses, on the existence of physical objects, and on the *S2PL* protocol.

4.2 Physical level concurrency control

In the previous section, it has been shown that the concurrency control protocol used for *PIOS* at the logical level relies on an underlying pessimistic protocol. The pessimistic protocol adopted in *PIOS* is the classical *strict two phase locking* (*S2PL*). If we compare *S2PL* with basic two phase locking, we can verify that, beside serializability, this protocol has the advantage of guaranteeing the strictness of interleaved executions of concurrent transactions [19].

The *multigranularity locking* (*MGL*) protocol has also been adopted at the physical level. In this protocol, persistent values are hierarchically organised in data items of different sizes and the transaction can choose the size of the data items to lock. Determining the size of data items to lock makes it possible to strike a balance between locking overhead and amount of transaction parallelism [20].

In *PIOS* these two protocols are co-operatively used. In short, *S2PL* tells *when* to set or release a lock, *MGL* tells *how* to do it, i.e. which data items of what size to lock, with which lock type and in which order.

Accurate answers to several important questions must be given when the design of a system that uses *MGL* protocol has to be faced. Some of the important questions are the following:

1 For a given data model, what is the best hierarchical organisation of data items?
2 For a given transaction, which are the most appropriate data items to lock and in which mode?
3 For a given layered system, which is the system component that has the suitable semantic knowledge to decide the most appropriate data item to lock?

The attempt to give answers to these questions has led to the proposal of a version of *MGL* called *Expandable MGL*. The description of this topic is preceded by a short survey of *MGL* protocol and its use in ODMSs.

4.2.1 Multiple Granularity Locking protocol and ODMS

MGL protocol was first proposed in the context of relational DMSs [21]. In this context, the use of *MGL* aims at minimising the number of locks to set while a transaction accesses a set of tuples of a relation. The *MGL* protocol organises data items in a tree where small items as tuples are nested within larger ones like relations. Each non–leaf node represents the data associated with all its descendants; thus the root of the tree represents the whole database. Nodes of the tree are called *granules*. Transactions can lock nodes *explicitly*, which in turn result in setting *implicit* locks on descendants. Nodes can be locked in five different modes. An *exclusive* (X) lock excludes any other transaction from accessing (i.e. reading or writing) the node; a *shared* (S) lock permits other transactions to concurrently read the same node but prevents any concurrent updating of the same node. A non–leaf node is locked in *intention–shared* (IS) mode to specify that descendant nodes will be explicitly locked in S mode. Similarly, an *intention–exclusive* (IX) lock implies that explicit locking is being performed in some descendant nodes in X mode. A *shared and intention–exclusive* (SIX) lock on a non–leaf node implies that the whole subtree rooted at the node is being locked in S mode and that explicit exclusive locking will be performed for some descendant nodes.

Table 2. Compatibility matrix for Multigranularity Locking protocol

	NL	IS	IX	S	SIX	X
NL	√	√	√	√	√	√
IS	√	√	√	√	√	No
IX	√	√	√	No	No	No
S	√	√	No	√	No	No
SIX	√	√	No	No	No	No
X	√	No	No	No	No	No

A compatibility matrix for the five kinds of locks is shown in Table 2, where NL mode represents the absence of a request. The matrix is used to determine when to grant or deny lock requests on a data item.

Data items are organised in hierarchies. A *Lock Type Graph* (LTG) represents the hierarchy among the types of the data items, as shown in Figure 8. The *Lock Instance Graph* (LIG) represents the same hierarchy instantiated on the actual data items stored in the database.

Given a LIG G and the previous compatibility matrix, [20] defines the following *MGL* protocol:

1 A transaction T can lock a non–root node *n* of G in S or IS mode only if T holds an IX or IS lock on *some* parent of *n*.
2 A transaction T can lock a non–root node *n* of G in X, SIX or IX mode only if T holds an SIX or IX lock on *all* of *n*'s parents.
3 To read the contents of a node, a transaction T must own an S or X lock on some ancestor of the node (including the node itself). To write the contents of a node, a transaction T must own, for *every* path from

the root to the node, an X lock on some ancestor of the node along that path (including the node itself).

An *MGL* protocol for ODMS has been proposed and realised in ORION, an ODMS with multiple inheritance [22]. The motivation for using this protocol in the context of ODMSs is that the object-oriented data model provides a natural hierarchical organisation of data items in granules of different size: every object is a member of the set representing the extension of a class; a class can be a subclass of one or several superclasses, which implies that there is a subset relationship among the extension of a subclass and the extensions of its superclasses. In this context, when most of the objects belonging to the extension of a class are to be accessed, it makes sense to set one lock for the class, rather then one lock for each object.

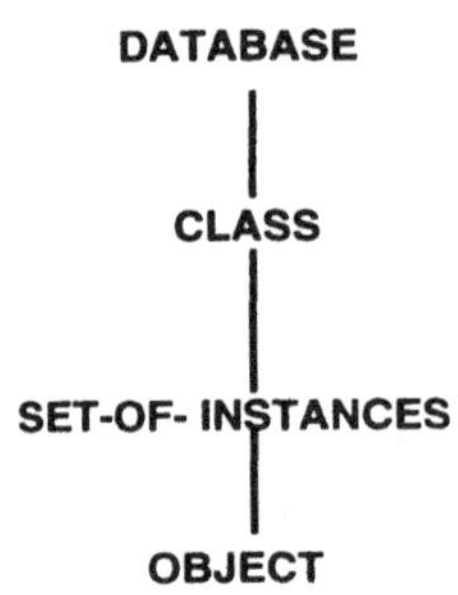

Fig. 8. ORION Lock Type Graph

In [22] the hierarchies representing the *ISA* relationship and the *instance_of* relationship are inserted into the traditional LTG (Figure 8). Given an ORION database schema, a LIG will be a rooted DAG that directly connects the database root node to base class nodes (roots in the *ISA* hierarchy). Subclasses of base classes are represented as subnodes of base class nodes, and so on to represent all of the *ISA* hierarchy. Class nodes are connected to their extensions and extensions to objects thus representing the *instance_of* relationship. The LIG is a rooted DAG because in ORION there is multiple inheritance.

We notice that the LTG in Figure 8 distinguishes common properties of classes such as class variables and class definition from class extensions (set of instances). Unfortunately, these two different aspects of the notion of class are related in the hierarchy: if a class is locked because a transaction is changing a class variable, then the set of instances of the class is also implicitly locked. This seems to be a weak point of the ORION LTG.

4.2.2 Design of PIOS Lock Type Graph

Let us reformulate the first two questions in a more technical manner:

1 What is the best LTG for *PIOS* physical data model?
2 Which are the most appropriate granules of *PIOS* LIG to lock and in which mode for a *PIOS* transaction?

A trivial choice of the LTG for *PIOS* can lead to modest performance and it can render of no use the decision to adopt a complex protocol such as the *MGL*. To understand the origins of these possible shortcomings, we will first attempt to adapt the LTG proposed in [20] to *PIOS*, as shown in Figure 9.

In this hypothesis, a *PIOS* physical database will be the topmost granule of a containment relationship that has collections and indices in intermediate positions, and physical objects as the smallest granules. Physical objects have as parents both collections and indices because a physical object is contained in the extension of a collection and it can also be accessible through an index if for example a value index has been defined for the collection that contains such a physical object (for simplicity we will limit our attention to value indices).

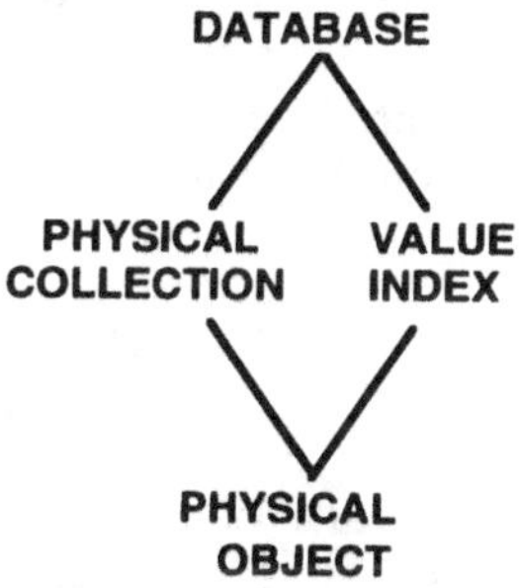

Fig. 9. A trivial *PIOS* Lock Type Graph

This LTG is simple and easy to understand, but a deeper analysis reveals its inadequacy. Let us suppose that at a certain moment in *PIOS* there are two running transactions T1 and T2. T1 counts the number of objects in a collection. T2 updates the state of a physical object that belongs to the same collection accessed from T1.

T1 does not need to access any object state: it just has to access the data structure that represents the collection, where as T2 does not access any collection since it accesses directly the physical object state by means of the *PID*.

These considerations lead us to conclude that T1 and T2 should be able to execute in parallel because there is no logical conflict between them. However, the trivial LTG generates a conflicting situation. According to the *MGL* protocol previously described, T1 should set one single shared lock S on the collection it wants to count, and T2 should lock the same collection in intention-exclusive IX mode, since it has to lock in X mode a physical object that belongs to the same collection. S and IX lock modes on the same granule are not compatible and so the two transactions cannot execute in parallel. Similar examples could be provided for indices.

The origin of this shortcoming comes from the meaning of the collection granule. A collection in this putative LTG has a double meaning because it is used for representing a set of individuals (the extension of the collection intended as a set of *PID*s of physical objects) and the set of values that the individuals take (the extension of the collection intended as a set of *states* of physical objects). A LTG with two types of granules for the two concepts should increase parallelism. If a system is able to separate the two concepts, then it could allow to execute in parallel: two operations that change the values of single different individuals without modifying the set of individuals, an operation that increments or decrements the set of individuals with another operation that just accesses the value of a different individual, an operation that queries the cardinality of the set of individuals from an operation that modifies the value associated with an individual, and so on. In terms of LTG this separation means that both of the data structures representing the set of individuals and the data structure representing the set of values of individuals should be leaf granules.

From a pragmatic point of view, we notice that a DMS can arrange for a greater parallelism if it organises granules according to criteria that strictly depend on the operations that it provides. Here are the general criteria we believe should be followed:

- all the data structures representing persistent values that can individually be accessed from a single operation should be leaf granules;
- non-leaf granules should be introduced in the hierarchy when the system provides at least one operation that manipulates a set of granules as a whole.

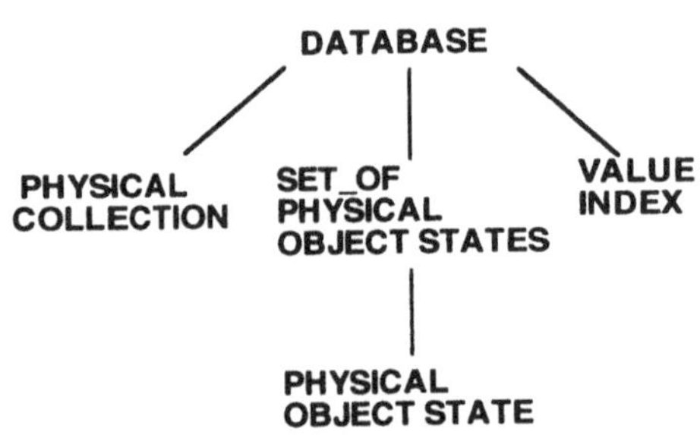

Fig. 10. *PIOS* Lock Type Graph

Following these two criteria, *PIOS* LTG becomes that shown in Figure 10. The previous granule has been split into two granules. The first one, still called Physical Collection, represents the collection data structure that realises the extension of a collection and it is not a parent of the Physical Object State granule. The second granule is called Set_of Physical Object State and it is the unique parent node of all physical object states of the collection. This last granule allows us to reduce the lock overhead, since *PHOS* provides a simple query primitive based on the values stored in the states of physical objects (belonging to one collection). There are also more complex situations in which, with the help of statistical information, the *PIOS* query manager can foresee whether a large percentage of the physical objects of a collection will be accessed during the execution of a query, and thus it can order a single shared lock instead of a set of shared locks, one for each physical object.

The index granule has been positioned in a different place with respect to the trivial LTG. A *PIOS* value index plays the same role as a collection in the LTG. The reason is that a value index is defined on some descriptive attributes of a collection and thus it can be considered a sort of associative collection that maps a value to a set of *PID*s. Similarly to collections, a value index will contain all the *PID*s of the physical objects of the collection over which it has been defined.

With this solution, the transactions T1 and T2 can run in parallel without any interference. T1, the transaction that counts, only asks for a shared lock on a Physical Collection granule and an intention–share lock on the Database. T2, the transaction that updates, asks for an exclusive lock on a Physical Object State granule, an intention–exclusive lock on Set_of Physical Object State and Database granules. In this case, there is only one shared entity, the Database, between the two transactions, and its IS and IX lock modes are not conflicting.

4.2.3 MGL and abstraction layers: the Expandable MGL protocol

We are now going to answer the third question, which is:

> For a complex layered system such as *PIOS*, which is the system component that has the semantic knowledge to decide the most appropriate data item to lock?

Firstly we must have an idea of the semantic knowledge in which we are interested. There are two kinds of semantic knowledge that can be useful in the exploitation of parallelism among transactions.

The first one is related to an analysis of the semantics of a transaction in its entirety. It would be useful if *PIOS* could infer properties of the submitted transactions that allow it to choose the most appropriate granule to lock. An example of this is the previously mentioned analysis performed by *PIOS* query processor when it foresees, using statistical information, the percentage of the physical objects accessed during the navigation of collections. To obtain this knowledge it is usually necessary to perform a complex analysis using components of the system that are close to the end user as suggested in [23]. These components of a layered system such as *PIOS* are placed in the highest layers of abstraction and they can infer information to reduce the locking overhead in the *MGL* protocol, i.e. they can reason about properties that concern coarse granules of LTG.

The second kind of semantic knowledge concerns the organisation of the data structures used in the implementation of a complex system. In a complex system organised in layers of different abstractions, only the system component that realises an abstract data type knows the details about the data structures used in the implementation. For example, in *PIOS* only the index manager holds the semantic information to decide the strategy that guarantees the greater parallelism when a transaction uses an index, because it alone knows the organisation of the data structures used in the implementation of the index. Similar examples in *PIOS* could be provided concerning the implementation of collections or physical objects. The components of a layered system such as *PIOS* that hold this knowledge are those placed at the lowest layers of abstraction. They can provide information for increasing parallelism of the *MGL* protocol, that is they can use properties that regard fine granules of LTG.

The previous considerations suggest that the following properties should characterise the layers of a complex system (see Figure 11):

- The higher layers of abstraction know how to choose coarse granules to reduce overhead
- The lower layers of abstraction know how to choose fine granules to increase parallelism

It is worth noting that if a system only shows the first property, then there can be a low overhead in the management of concurrency control and little parallelism among transactions since coarse granules can potentially raise several conflicts. However, if a system only presents the second property, then it could achieve a greater parallelism at the price of a greater overhead.

The *PIOS* approach aims at providing a unifying framework that takes advantage of both types of semantic knowledge. The idea is to allow each *PIOS* layer to claim locks on granules corresponding to its level of semantic knowledge. If a higher layer infers from its own semantic knowledge that it cannot take a final decision on a coarse granule, then it can delegate to lower layers of the system the task of exploiting their semantic knowledge of finer granules. Conversely, if a higher layer holds all the knowledge necessary to take a definite decision on a coarse granule, then it can inhibit lower layer claiming any lock on finer granules.

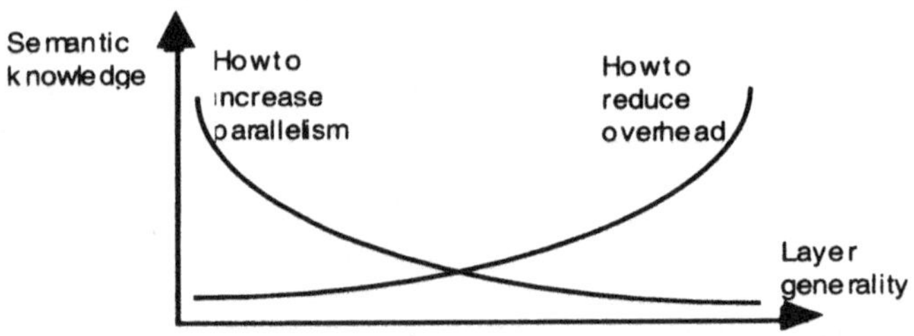

Fig. 11. Different kinds of semantic knowledge in a layered system

In *PIOS* this is obtained by modifying the LTG and extending the *MGL* protocol. As far as *PIOS* LTG is concerned, we introduce the idea of *a node's expandability*: a granule, that is viewed as a leaf from a higher layer, can be expanded from a lower layer with a subtree of finer granules (Figure 12). The *MGL* protocol has been extended in such a way that an intermediate layer can also lock what it sees as a leaf granule in IS or IX mode. These apparently unnatural lock modes are used to communicate among layers. When a higher layer wants to allow a lower layer to expand a granule, it will set an intention lock on the interested granule. We call this version of the *MGL* protocol *Expandable.*

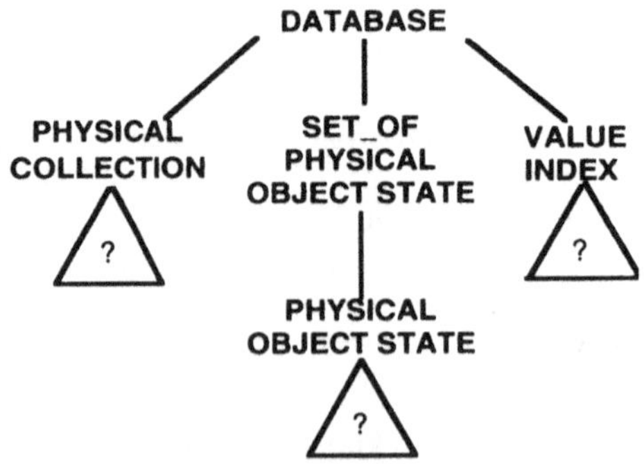

Fig. 12. Nodes' expandability

Let us consider a *PIOS* example that illustrates this protocol. There are two concurrent transactions T3 and T4. T3 is going to insert a new physical object in an indexed collection. T4 is willing to update the state of a physical object belonging to the same indexed collection.

Let us first analyse the case in which Expandable *MGL* protocol is not used. T3 during its execution has to lock in X mode a Physical Collection granule representing the extension of the collection and a Value Index granule representing the index defined over the collection. T4 must lock in X mode a Physical Object State granule and the Value Index granule. T3 and T4 cannot run in parallel since they ask for an incompatible lock on the same Value Index granule. This happens because some higher layer of *PIOS* did not have a detailed semantic knowledge of the index data structure and it decided to lock the whole index.

The use of Expandable *MGL* protocol and leaves' expandability can permit parallel executions. Both T3 and T4 ask for a IX lock on the same Value Index granule, and the index manager adopts its own ad-hoc policy for expanding this granule. If for instance T3 and T4 work on different pages of the B-Tree data structure, then they can run in parallel without interference.

It is important to point out that the lower layers of the system can use different concurrency control protocols during the expansion of granules. For example, in *PIOS* the protocol used for access control to physical object states is the strict two-phase locking and the protocol used for indices is a customised version of B-Tree locking. The two protocols are quite different because the second is not a two-phase protocol and it makes use of instant duration locks.

5 Overall *PIOS* Architecture

The client–server architecture of *PIOS* was outlined in Figure 1. We remind readers that the clients communicate by means of their peer processes *US*s with *PHOS*, which is responsible for the management of the physical database and its indices. *PHOS* and *US*s communicate through a message queue.

The distinction between logical level and physical level is reflected in the architecture in the following way. External clients manage entities at the logical level and issue commands to *USs* that, hopefully after some optimisations, translate these commands into *PHOS* statements. *PHOS* represents the physical level.

In the following, we give a complete description of *US* and *PHOS* functionalities.

6.1 *User-Supervisor* architecture

The *US* architecture is shown in Figure 13. A *US* consists of three main modules: *Logical Level Interface*, *Query Manager*, and *Translation Manager*.

Each *US* receives commands originated from the corresponding peer client process through it's Logical Level Interface. This provides two different kinds of external interfaces: a programming interface and an interactive interface. The programming interface is a library that contains a function for every logical level operation of *PIOS*. Interactive sessions made of sequences of *PIOS* commands use the interactive interface of *US*. Independently from the interface, the sequences of operations are organised as transactions, so they start with Begin Transaction operation and they terminate with Commit Transaction or Abort Transaction operation. The Logical Level Interface submits query operations to the *Query Processor*, while all the other operations directly go to the *Translation Manager*.

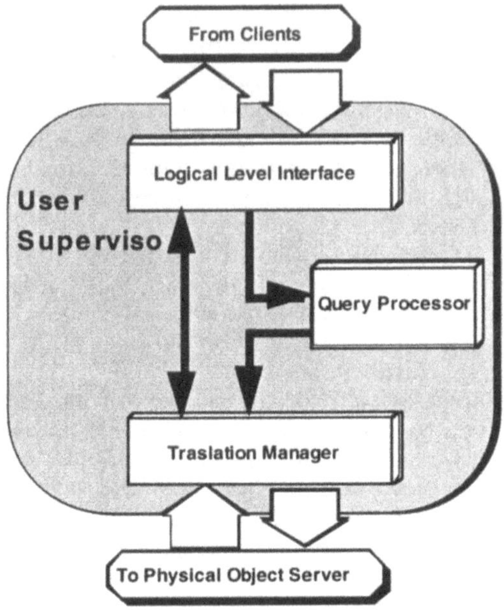

Fig. 13. *User Supervisor* architecture.

The *Query Processor* translates logical queries into physical queries and it prepares an optimal execution plan [13]. The query optimisation starts with an *algebraic optimisation* of the logical query. After the algebraic optimisation, the logical query is translated into a physical one and the algebraic optimisation is repeated — it eliminates redundancies which can appear during the translation — before the *physical optimisation* starts. The algebraic optimisation is performed by means of a set of rewrite rules applying heuristics for ameliorating the expression and using schema information for pruning. On the other hand, physical optimisation is based on a randomised cost model which uses as input data distribution statistics and applies heuristics for reducing the search space. The optimised physical query is sent to the *Translation Manager.*

The *Translation Manager* translates logical operations into physical operations — at this stage queries have already been translated by the *Query Processor* — and then it submits them to *PHOS*. *PHOS* returns a physical-level result that is then retranslated into a logical-level result and given back to the client.

To translate logical objects into physical ones, the *LID/PID* table is maintained to keep the correspondences between the logical and physical object identifiers. That table is shared among *USs* and is dynamically updated (see Section 4.1).

The high expressiveness of logical operations and semantic information obtained by the *Query Processor* are used by the *Translation Manager* to generate the most appropriate physical lock requests corresponding to the portion of LTG that is seen by the *US* (see Section 4.2).

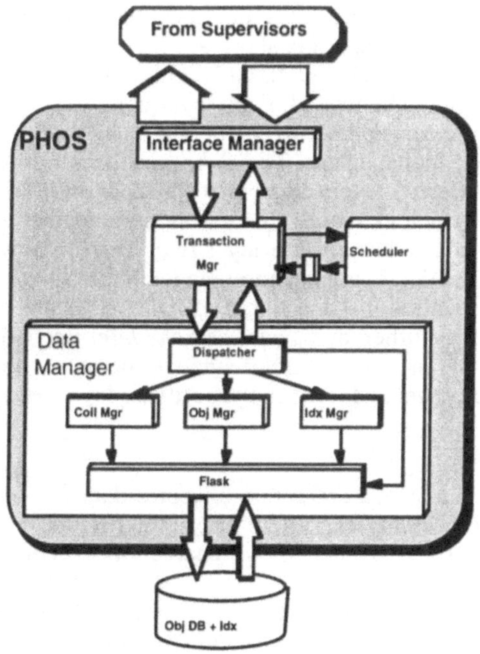

Fig. 14. *PHOS* architecture.

6.2 *PHOS* architecture

PHOS, whose architecture is shown in Figure 14, is the *PIOS* component that mainly implements the following functions:

- Direct access to the state of physical objects or to fragments of the state (access by identity);
- Associative and navigational accesses to physical objects (value and navigation indices);
- Concurrency control;
- Recovery from failures;

The *Interface Manager* receives the operations of the physical data model through a message queue and passes them to the *Transaction Manager* (TM). After some consistency controls, TM passes operations to the *Scheduler*. The *Scheduler* decides whether an operation can be immediately executed, or whether it must be delayed or rejected due to conflicts with operations requested by other transactions. The only type of operations that can be delayed or rejected by the *Scheduler* is a lock request. All the other operations are immediately executed.

Lock requests are submitted to the *Scheduler* (through TM) from the *US*s or the *Data Manager* (DM) - see the observation concerning *Expandable MGL* in Section 4.2. In both the cases, if the *Scheduler* decides to delay an operation, the transaction containing it is stopped until the scheduler allows the operation to start. The *Scheduler* also detects deadlock situations and it can decide to abort some of the transactions involved in the deadlock. In this case, the lock request is rejected and the transaction that generated the request is aborted.

The *Scheduler* does not work on a fixed LTG but it supports a variable number of *anonymous granule types* to be locked. Each layer can use anonymous granules of its own, provided that name conflicts are avoided, and it can adopt ad-hoc hierarchies and ad-hoc policies for lock management. The *Scheduler* does not know what hierarchies are adopted by the different layers and what interpretation is given to a granule because it only checks if a lock request for a granule conflicts with other requests for the same granule. In fact, it is only the layer requiring locks which knows the LTG portion it is using and which guarantees to manage locks correctly, that is as expected by *MGL*. This feature allows the portion of LTG used by a specific layer to be changed without affecting other layers and the *Scheduler* itself. This type of *Scheduler* can be seen as a general purpose *Scheduler* since it operates without any knowledge of concurrency control protocols adopted in the software layers of the system.

6.2.1 Data Manager

The DM is the component of *PHOS* that executes database operations requested by the TM. Firstly, the DM analyses an operation, then it delivers the access operation to the subcomponent of DM that is in charge of executing a specific type of operations.

To realise *Expandable MGL*, the DM has been implemented using co-operative threads communicating by message passing. In this way, the execution of an operation can be suspended in a subcomponent and resumed after some time when specific conditions occur.

The main component of DM is the *Dispatcher* (DISP). It starts threads, kills threads, and decides which thread operations have to be dispatched. A thread is created whenever a new transaction starts (that is when the operation Begin Transaction occurs). The purpose of a thread is to execute operations belonging to the transaction foe which it has been created.

PHOS threads are co-operative: there is only one active thread at a time. A thread can be suspended because it might be waiting for a new operation (submitted by TM) or because it needs data locked by other threads. When the operation that caused the suspension is completed, the corresponding thread will be resumed.

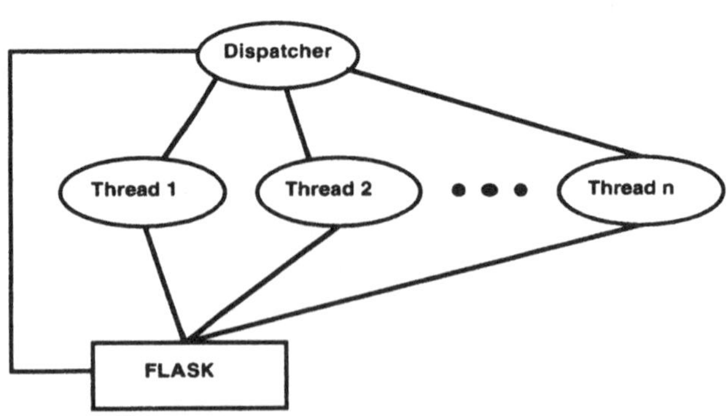

Fig. 15. Threads interaction

It is worth noting that when a thread is waiting for the authorisation to continue the processing of an operation, it cannot begin the execution of a new operation. Any authorisation different from that expected will lead to a *System Failure*.

The physical object store used is FLASK ([24] and Chapter 2.3.1 of this book) and its functionalities are shared among threads and DISP. FLASK offers basic functionalities to put, get and modify physical objects on database. All update operations are recoverable because FLASK provides a *Concurrent Shadow Page* mechanism.

Interaction with FLASK is made by procedure calls. FLASK procedures are called by threads, to accomplish basic actions on the database, and by DISP to begin, abort and commit a physical level transaction.

DM's subcomponents are the *Storage Level Object Manager* (SLOM) and the *Index Manager* (IDXM). The first manipulates physical objects and collections. The second executes the operations involving the indices.

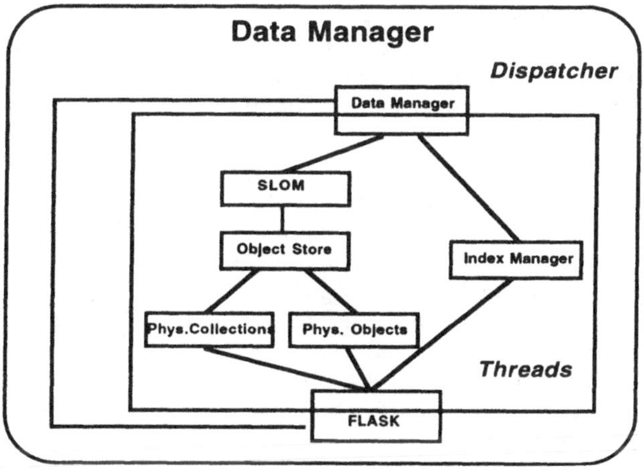

Fig. 16. *Data Manager* architecture

SLOM initially performs a translation between data formats and then it gives the control to the *Object Store* (OS). The OS decides whether an operation on the database involves objects, collections, or both and it transfers the flow of control to the *Physical Object Manager* (POM) or the *Physical Collection Manager* (PCM), respectively. From POM, PCM and from IDXM, execution at last passes to FLASK.

Figure 16 shows that the DM is distributed among threads and the DISP; the DISP decides which thread has to execute an operation, threads have to decide which subcomponent has to execute the operation. Some FLASK functionalities are requested directly by DISP when a Begin Transaction, Commit Transaction, or Abort Transaction occurs, or by threads for basic operations on database.

6.2.2 Index Manager and the realisation of Expandable MGL protocol

Indices have been implemented using B^Ltrees [25], a variant of B^+trees. In a B^+tree, each internal node has the structure $<p_1, k_1,..., k_{n-1}, p_n>$, where p_i is a pointer to an other node (either internal or leaf) and k_i is a key such that all keys in the node pointed by p_i are smaller (or equal if the pointed node is a leaf) than k_i. All keys in the node pointed by p_{i+1} are greater than k_i. Each leaf of a B^+tree in an ODMS has the structure $<o_1, k_1, ..., o_n, k_n>$, where o_i is a pointer to a persistent data structure that contains the set of the object identifiers with key equal to k_i. A B^ltree differs from a B^+tree only for the meaning of the last pointer of a node. The internal nodes which have the structure $<p_1, k_1, ..., p_{n-1}, k_{n-1}, link>$, where *link* is a pointer linking a node with the next son of the same parent. The last son and the root of the tree have a null *link*. The leaves have the structure $<o_1, k_1, ..., o_n, k_n, link>$. Because of the concurrency control policy, it can happen that when a transaction is looking for a key in a node, it does not find the key because another transaction has split the node. In this case, the key can be found by following the *link* pointer.

The concurrency control policy used in *PIOS* on indices is a version of that defined in [26] which allows to use Concurrent Shadow Paging. In the following the pseudo code defining a simplified version of the concurrency control policy is reported. Problems coming from the B^Ltree management, such as checking if a node is valid or splitting and propagating split of nodes, will not be reported. The interested reader can find a complete description of the technique in [27].

The aims of the proposed solution are both to use as few locks as possible and to avoid deadlocks. The algorithm that we propose just requires instant duration locks on intermediate node during the descent phase. When a transaction finds an inconsistent node, because some other transaction has partially modified the index structure, the consistent situation is recovered since the actions that lead to inconsistency could be foreseen. A special treatment is provided for the management of locks on the leaf node. This prevents the phantom problem and avoids to ask for key locks instead of node locks accessing keys of the leaf nodes.

The supported operations are *Insert, Search,* and *Delete*. Deletion of keys is logical. When a new key is inserted, if in the node there is a logically deleted key, the new key will overwrite it.

The pseudo code for leaf nodes of a tree is in Figure 17. When we search for a key or when we insert a new key, the next key is locked to avoid the phantom problem; if a searched key is not found, a commit-duration lock on the next key prevents the key from being inserted before the read transaction commits. When a new key is inserted, the lock on the next key prevents the new key from being read before the write transaction commits.

```
function Search(leaf,key):Objects;
begin
  lock(NextKey(key),S);          {to be checked after the
                                  lock has been granted}
  lock(key,S);
  if(exists(key))                {the key could have been
                                  locked during a deletion}
  then begin
         unlock(NextKey(key),S);
         Search:=get(leaf,key);
  end
  else begin
         unlock(key,S);
         Search:=NULL_OBJ;
  end;
end;

procedure Insert(Leaf,key);
begin
  lock(leaf,X);
  lock(NextKey(key),X);          {to be checked after
                                  the lock has been granted}
         put(leaf,key);
end;

procedure Delete(Leaf,key);
begin
  lock(leaf,X);
  lock(key,X);
         logically_delete_key(leaf,key);
end;
```

Fig. 17. Concurrency control and leaves of the B^Ltree.

When the searched key is found, it is locked both to prevent the key from being deleted before the read transaction commits and to prevent the key deleted by a uncommitted transaction from being used.

When we insert or delete a key, we lock the updated node to prevent two transactions from modifying the same node since this could lead to inconsistencies in the concurrent shadow paging mechanism.

When we delete a key, we lock the key to prevent a read transaction from using the key before the delete transaction commits.

As far as internal nodes are concerned, the rules are the following:

1 if an internal node is updated (e.g. when a new key is inserted) a commit duration lock is requested on the node;
2 if an internal node is only read, an instant duration lock is requested on the node.

Two transactions cannot update the same node simultaneously, but a transaction updating a node does not stop a transaction from reading the same node.

This is correct under our assumptions, because if the update transaction has to commit, the read transaction, because of the shadow paging, sees the page before the modification.

6 Conclusions

In this paper we have provided a survey of the *PIOS* system. *PIOS* is an attempt to use new technology for supporting ODMS. The main feature of *PIOS* is the support of physical independence in the context of object databases. The introduction of physical independence in an ODMS has lead us to revisit several important functionalities such as query management and optimisation, concurrency control and navigation accelerators. The general architecture of an ODMS has been revisited too.

The *PIOS* system has been fully implemented on Sun Sparc hardware with Unix Sun Operating System. The performance of the concurrency control subsystem has been tested via benchmarks. These experiments have shown results that are similar to those of other research prototypes of object stores (details can be found in [27] and [28]). The main advantages with respect to performance improvements concern query processing (see Chapter 2.3.3 for details). These advantages are made possible by several architectural choices (e.g., low-level support of value indices and navigation indices, possibility to define specific data structures at physical level thanks to the physical independence support, etc.), at the price of making more cumbersome, and possibly less efficient, other system functions.

In our opinion, the current *PIOS* prototype shows quite appealing functionalities but some other research efforts should be invested in order to validate the efficiency of the technical solutions proposed. One controversial point to be furtherly investigated is our choice in favour of an *object* server architecture. We remind readers that usually ODMSs choose in favour of *page* server, that is the architecture where the shared server exchanges pages of the database with external clients. In practice, the object server architecture is determined by our approach to physical independence. Our approach allows to exploit some semantic information related to the logical level during object accesses. Such knowledge could be furtherly extended with information about global behaviours of transactions expressed in the external language that could improve the *PIOS* performance via a clever prefetching of persistent objects. This implies the integration of *PIOS* with an external persistent programming language, which is one of the issue we are currently working on. Only when all the types of semantic information provided by our approach could be exploited, we could be able to exhaustively compare the efficiency of our technical solutions.

Another important development direction of *PIOS* is towards multimedia object repositories. In this case the advantage of an object server architecture, supporting physical independence, surely overcomes any eventual performance limitations. Applying our approach in supporting multimedia database systems, we can exploit the advantage of specifying the dabase schema at our logical level, without making any distinction between different multimedia data types, and then accomodating the specific storage requirements of the multimedia objects (e.g., data contiguity for continuous media, synchronization requirements, very large data sizes) at our physical level. Our present implementation of *PIOS* is limited by the fact that the physical level is based on a single-level memory mapped object store. Such architecture can be extended if we base the physical level on a more suitable object store, designed for supporting hierarchical memory levels, including tertiary storages, horizontal and vertical migration policies, parallel data accesses, etc. We are currently exploring the requirements for extending our physical specification language with the information necessary by these new multimedia hierarchical stores (e.g., Kydonia [29]).

Acknowledgements. We would like to thank Prof. Malcolm Atkinson for his careful reading of the draft version of the paper and for his suggestions that greatly contributed in improving the quality of this paper. We also acknowledge the efforts of Emma Criscuoli, Filomena Giannasio, Andrea Bioli, Ugo Pasquali and several other obscure students that contributed to the implementation of *PIOS*.

References

1. "Next–Generation Database Systems", *Comm. of the ACM, Vol. 34, N. 10,* 1991.
2. ANSI/X3/SPARC, "Interim report ANSI/X3/SPARC study group on data base management systems", *FDT Bulletin of ACM SIGMOD, Vol. 7, No. 2,* 1975.
3. Paul H., et al., "Architecture and implementation of Darmstadt Database kernel system", *Proc. ACM SIGMOD Int. Conf. Management Data,* San Francisco, CA, 1987.
4. Velez F., G. Bernard and V. Darnis, "The O2 object manager: an overview", *Proc. 15th Int. Conf. on Very Large Data Bases,* Amsterdam, The Netherlands, 1989.
5. Kim W., Ballou N., Chou H. T., Garza J. F., Woelk and D. "Features of the ORION Object-Oriented Database", In *Object-Oriented Concepts, Databases, and Applications,* W. Kim and F. H. Lochovsky (eds.), ACM Press Frontier Series, 1989, pp. 251-282.
6. Deux O. et al. "The Story of O2". IEEE Transactions on Knowledge and Data Engineering, Vol. 2, No. 1, March 1990.
7. Albano A., Cardelli R. and Orsini R. "Galileo: a Strongly Typed, Interactive Conceptual Language", *ACM Trans. on Database Systems,* Vol.10, No.2, 1985, pp. 230-260.
8. Batory D. S. and C. C. Gotlieb, "A Unifying Model of Physical Databases", *ACM Transactions on Database Systems, Vol. 8 N. 2,* pp. 509–539.
9. March S. T., D. G. Severance and M. Wilens, "Frame Memory: A Storage Architecture to Support Rapid Design and Implementation of Efficient Databases", *ACM Transactions on Database Systems, Vol. 3, N. 3,* pp. 441–463.
10. Zezula P. and Rabitti F. "Object Store with Navigation Accelerator". Information Systems, 18(7):429-460, 1993.
11. Olds D. C. "Continued Fractions." *New Mathematical Library.* Random House, New York, 1963.
12. Ciaccia P., Maio D., and Tiberio P. "A Method for Hierarchy Processing in Relational Systems." *Information Systems,* Vol. 14, No. 2, pp. 93-105, 1989.
13. Rabitti F., Benedetti L. and Demi F., "Query Processing in *PIOS*", *Proc. of Sixth International Workshop on Persistent Object Systems,* Tarascon, France, September 6-9, 1994. Workshops in Computing, Springer Verlag, pp. 415-440, 1995.
14. Joseph J. V., Thatte S.M, Thompson C.W. and Wells D.L., "Object-Oriented Databases: Design and Implementation", *Proc. of IEEE,* Vol. 79, No.1, pp. 42-63,1991.
15. Aloia N., S. Barneva and F. Rabitti, "Supporting physical independence in object databases", *Database Technology,* Vol. 4, No. 4, pp. 265–286.
16. Atkinson M.P., Bancilhon F., DeWitt D., Dittrich K., Maier D. and Zdonik S., "The Object–Oriented Database System Manifesto", *Proc. Int. Conf. DOOD,* Kyoto, Japan, pp. 40–57, 1989.
17. Teorey T. and Fry J. P. "Design of Database Structures" Prentice-Hall Inc., Englewood Cliffs, New Jersey, 1982
18. Biscari S., Mainetto G., and Rabitti F., "Logical Concurrency Control in *PIOS*". *FIDE Report* FIDE/95/119 1995.
19. Bernstein P., V. Hadzilacos and N. Goodman, *Concurrency Control and Recovery in Database System,* Addison–Wesley, Reading, MA, 1987.
20. Gray J., "Notes on Database Operating Systems", *IBM Res. Rep. RJ2188,* IBM Research Laboratory, San Jose, CA also in *Operating Systems – An Advanced Course,* R. Boyer, R. M. Graham and G. Siegmüller (eds.), Springer Verlag, LNCS 60, 1978.

21. Gray J., R. Lorie and G. Putzolu, "Granularity of locks and degrees of consistency in a shared database", *IBM Res. Rep. RJ1654,* IBM Res. Lab., San Jose, CA also in *Modeling in Database Management Systems*, Nijssen (ed.), North Holland, 1976.
22. Garza J. F. and W. Kim, "Transaction Management in an Object–Oriented Database System", *Proc. ACM SIGMOD Intl. Conf. on Management of Data*, Chicago, Illinois, pp. 37–45, 1988.
23. Amato G., Giannotti F., Mainetto G.,"Data sharing analysis for a database programming language via Abstract Interpretation", *19th International Conference on Very Large Data Base,* Dublin (Ireland) 24-27 August 1993, pp. 405-415.
24. Munro D.S., Connor R. C. H., Morrison R., Scheuerl S. and Stemple D.W. "Concurrent Shadow Paging in the Flask Archiecture", *Proc. 6th Intl. Workshop on Persistent Object Systems*,Tarascon (FR), September 6-9, 1994. Workshops in Computing, Springer Verlag, pp. 16-42, 1995.
25. Lehman P. and Yao S., "Efficient Locking for Concurrent Operations on B–Tree", *ACM Transactions on Database Systems*, Vol. 6, No. 4, 1981, pp. 650-670.
26. Mohan C. and Levine F., "ARIES/IM:An Efficient and High Concurrency Index Management Method Using Write-Ahead Logging", *Proceedings of the ACM SIGMOD Conference*, SanDiego California, 1992.
27. Amato G. and Mainetto G., "Concurrent Index Management Using Shadow-Paging", *Proc. of the 4th SEBD Conference*, San Miniato (PI), Italy, pp. 237-250, 1996.
28. Amato G., Biscari S., Mainetto G. and Rabitti F., "Multigranularity Locking with the Use of Semantic Knowledge in a Layered Object Server", *Proc. 7th Intl. Workshop on Persistent Object Systems*, Cape May, New Jersey (USA), May 29-31, 1996.
29. Christodoulakis S., Anestopoulos D., Argypopoulos S., "Data Organization and Storage Hierarchies in a Multimedia Server", *Proc. IEEE Compcon*, 1993.

Chapter 2.2.3

Efficient Incremental Garbage Collection for Client-Server Object Database Systems*

Laurent Amsaleg[1], Michael Franklin[2†], Olivier Gruber[3‡]

[1] Projet RODIN, INRIA Rocquencourt, BP. 105, 78153 Le Chesnay Cedex, France
[2] Department of Computer Science, University of Maryland, A. V. Williams Building, College Park, MD 20742, USA
[3] IBM Research Division, Almaden Research Center, 650 Harry Road, San Jose, CA 95120-6099, USA

Abstract. We briefly outline the main characteristics of an efficient server-based algorithm for garbage collecting object-oriented databases in a client-server environment. The algorithm is incremental and runs concurrently with client transactions. Unlike previous algorithms, it does not hold any locks on data and does not require callbacks to clients. It is fault tolerant, but performs very little logging. The algorithm has been designed to be integrated into existing OODB systems, and therefore it works with standard implementation techniques such as two-phase locking and write-ahead-logging. In addition, it supports client-server performance optimizations such as client caching and flexible management of client buffers. The algorithm has been implemented in the EXODUS storage manager before being evaluated.

1 Introduction

A primary strength of Object Oriented Database Management Systems (OODBMS) lies in their ability to model complex objects and the inter-relationships among them. This modelling power, while allowing for a more natural representation of many real-world application domains, also raises new problems in the design of fundamental lower-level functions such as storage management and reclamation. It has long been recognized that explicit storage management (e.g. *malloc()* and *free()*) places a heavy burden on the developers of large programs. Manual detection and reclamation of garbage increases code complexity and is highly error-prone, raising the risk of memory leaks and dangling pointers. For these reasons *automated* garbage collection for programming languages has long been an active area of investigation (see [8] for a survey).

The shared and persistent nature of databases provides further motivation for automated garbage collection. Because a database is shared, the knowledge of data

* The full version of this paper has been published in the Proceedings of the 21st VLDB Conference, Zürich, Switzerland, 1995.

† This author's work was partially performed as a Visiting Researcher at INRIA Rocquencourt, and was supported by NSF RIA IRI-94-09575 and a grant from the University of Maryland General Research Board.

‡ This author's work was performed while he was with INRIA Rocquencourt.

interconnection may be distributed among many programs and/or users, making it difficult for programmers to determine when to explicitly reclaim storage. Furthermore, sharing and persistence increase the potential damage caused by storage management errors, as mistakes made by one program can inadvertently affect others. These considerations argue for a very cautious approach to storage reclamation, however, neglecting to reclaim wasted space can degrade performance due to increased I/O.

In an OODBMS, the notion of persistence (and hence, garbage) can be tied to *reachability*. Reachability is a simple, implicit way to express persistence that is orthogonal to object type [4,10]. The database is an object graph in which some objects are designated as persistent roots. Objects that can be reached by traversing a path from a root will persist beyond the execution of the transaction that created them. Objects that are not reachable from a root or from the transient program state of an on-going transaction are garbage; such objects are inaccessible and thus, they can be safely reclaimed. Reachability-based persistence is used in the GemStone and O2 systems, and garbage collection is required in the Smalltalk binding for the ODMG object database standard. In general, however, most existing systems still rely on explicit object deallocation and/or off-line storage management utilities. The lack of acceptance of reachability-based persistence is due in part to the absence of efficient implementation techniques that can be integrated with existing systems. The work described here is aimed at addressing this need.

2 OODBMS Garbage Collection Issues

In recent years, there has been increasing research activity in OODBMS garbage collection [7,6,9,3,1,2]. OODBMS have several features that can impact the correctness and/or performance of traditional garbage collection approaches:

Concurrency: A garbage collector must co-exist with concurrent transactions and must not adversely impact their ability to execute.

Client Caching: OODBMS typically cache and update data at clients. The dynamic, replicated, and distributed nature of these updates makes client-based garbage collection problematic. Server-based collection is difficult because a server may have an inconsistent snapshot of the database.

Atomic Transactions: The rollback of partially completed transactions violates the fundamental assumption that unreachable objects always remain unreachable.

Persistence: Modern garbage collection algorithms assume that the volume of live (i.e, non-garbage) objects is small. Persistence invalidates this assumption.

Fault Tolerance: OODBMS provide resilience to system failures. Garbage collection must also operate in a fault tolerant manner.

Disk-Resident Data: Much of the data in an OODBMS is on disk — the collector cannot ignore I/O.

3 Garbage Collecting Client-Server OODBMS

In [3], we describe a server-based GC designed to work in the specific context of client-server OODBMS. We consider page servers that provide efficient and flexible features like inter-transaction caching, write-ahead-logging (WAL) based recovery, "steal-based" management of clients' buffers and 2-phase page-level locking. These flexibilities, while providing opportunities for improved performance, also raise potential problems for garbage collection algorithms. To validate our ideas, we integrated (and measured) our scheme in the EXODUS storage manager [5].

Our garbage collector has the following main characteristics:

- It is based on a Mark and Sweep approach. This approach can be more efficient and easier to integrate into an existing OODBMS. For example, the clustering produced by a copying-based GC may be in conflict with database requirements or user-specified hints.
- It is server-based, but requires no callbacks to clients. Our solution enforces its safety by being conservative with respect to the effect of transactions.
- It is incremental and non-disruptive. It holds no locks on data and performs only minimal synchronization with client transactions. It has been designed to be efficient with respect to I/O.
- We use a partitioned approach in order to avoid having to scan the entire database before reclaiming any space.
- It works in the context of ACID transactions with standard implementation techniques such as two-phase locking and write-ahead-logging.
- It is fault-tolerant but requires minimal logging — crashes of clients or servers during garbage collection will not corrupt the database.
- It can co-exist with performance enhancements such as inter-transaction caching at clients and "steal" buffer management between clients and servers.

[3] presents in detail several problem that must be addressed when designing a garbage collector for a client-server OODBMS. It then describes our partitioned Mark and Sweep collection algorithm. Finally, it details its implementation in the EXODUS system and presents our performance studies of the implemented system.

References

1. L. Amsaleg. *Conception et réalisation d'un glaneur de cellules adapté aux SGBDO client-serveur.* PhD thesis, Université Paris 6 Pierre et Marie Curie, Paris, France, June 1995.
2. L. Amsaleg, P. Ferreira, M. Franklin, and M. Shapiro. Evaluating Garbage Collectors for Large Persistent Stores. In *The 1995 OOPSLA Workshop on Object Database Behavior, Benchmarks, and Performance, Addendum to the Proceedings*, Austin, Texas, October 1995.
3. L. Amsaleg, M. Franklin, and O. Gruber. Efficient Incremental Garbage Collection for Client-Server Object Database Systems. In *Proc. of the 21th VLDB Int. Conf.*, Zürich, Switzerland, September 1995.

4. M. Atkinson, P. Bailey, K. Chisholm, P. Cockshott, and R. Morrison. An Approach to Persistent Programming. *Computer Journal*, 26(4):360–365, 1983.
5. M. Carey, D. DeWitt, J. Richarson, and E. Shekita. Object and File Management in the EXODUS Extensible Database System. In *Proc. of the 12th VLDB Int. Conf.*, pages 1–27, Kyoto, Japan, 1986.
6. E. Kolodner and W. Weihl. Atomic Incremental Garbage Collection and Recovery for Large Stable Heap. In *Proc. of the ACM SIGMOD Int. Conf.*, pages 177–185, Washington D.C., June 1993.
7. J. O'Toole, S. Nettles, and D. Gifford. Concurrent Compacting Garbage Collection of a Persistent Heap. In *Proc. of the 14th SOSP Int. Conf.*, pages 161–174, Asheville, North Carolina, December 1993. ACM Press.
8. P. Wilson. Uniprocessor Garbage Collection Techniques. In *Int. Workshop on Memory Management*, volume 637 of *Lecture Notes in Computer Science*, pages 1–43, St. Malo, France, September 1992. Springer-Verlag.
9. V. Yong, J. Naughton, and J. Yu. Storage Reclamation and Reorganization in Client-Server Persistent Object Stores. In *Proc. of the Data Engineering Int. Conf.*, pages 120–133, Houston, Texas, February 1994.
10. S. Zdonik and D. Maier. *Readings in Object-Oriented Database Systems*. Morgan-Kaufmann, San Mateo, California, 1990.

Chapter 2.2.4

Towards a Unified Model of Untyped Object Stores: Experience with the Tycoon Store Protocol*

Florian Matthes, Rainer Müller, and Joachim W. Schmidt

Technical University Hamburg-Harburg, Harburger Schloßstraße 20, D-21071 Hamburg, Germany

1 Introduction

Systems that have to work with large-scale persistent data have a system architecture where there is a clean separation between a *frontend* performing data manipulation and visualization and a *back end* responsible for reliable persistent bulk data storage. Since actions in the frontend trigger data access operations performed by the backend, this separation leads to a client-server architecture, where a *store protocol* defines possible interactions between a client program and a database server.

The Tycoon Store Protocol (TSP) specifies a clean interface between the frontend and the backend of fully integrated persistent environments. TSP is designed to match the flexibility requirements of persistent languages (see [1,3] for a more detailed discussion):

- Full persistence abstraction requires uniform, efficient element-oriented access to persistent and non-persistent data, code and threads.
- Orthogonal persistence for polymorphic data structures, higher-order (polymorphic) functions and user-defined abstract data types require an untyped persistent heap.
- Incremental program construction and reflective programming techniques require schema modifications at runtime and dynamic binding techniques.

Despite the fact that TSP has been implemented and evaluated in the context of the Tycoon project (see Chapter 2.1.4), TSP is fully independent of the Tycoon system.

2 On the Construction of Scalable Persistent Systems

TSP has been designed to support the construction of *scalable* persistent systems, i.e. configurable systems where the complexity and size of the entire system is proportional to the operational support required by a particular client.

Figure 1 explains the role of TSP in such a persistent system scenario. The data access operations defined in TSP are issued by client programs and executed by

* This text is a synopsis of [2].

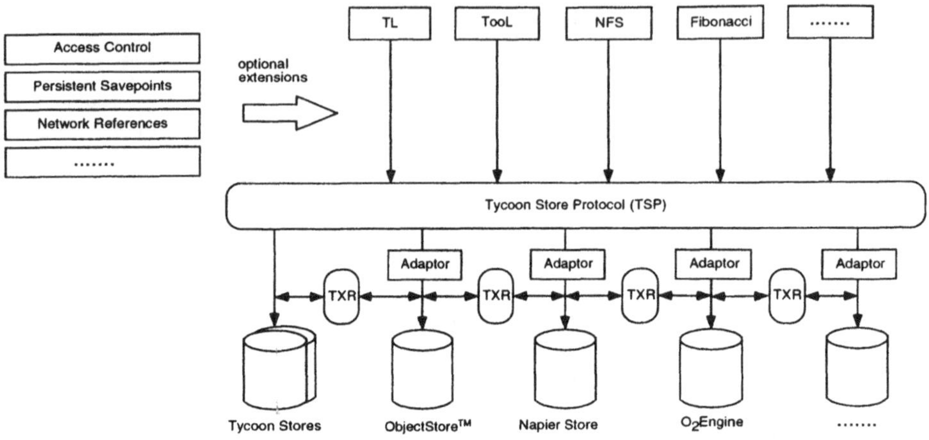

Fig. 1. The role of the Tycoon Store Protocol in scalable persistent systems

database servers. In the full paper we report on our experience in implementing TSP backends including adaptors to existing object stores, e.g. ObjectStore.
TSP defines a stable application programming interface for client programs (expressed by a standard C header file). TSP is intended to be a stackable protocol. These optional system layers utilize TSP as their lower and upper interfaces and extend the semantics of individual TSP operations (e.g. store object update) and provide additional TSP operations (e.g. rollback to savepoint). In the full paper we report on extending the TSP functionality systematically by TSP-compliant layers for persistent savepoints and access control.

TSP is complemented by a platform-independent external data representation (TXR) that can be generated and parsed by all TSP backends. The TXR makes it possible to transfer arbitrary complex, graph-structured persistent store objects via a linear data representation from one backend to another without exposing private implementation details of individual persistent stores.

A TSP client can choose dynamically between different backends and can access multiple stores (possibly of multiple architectures) concurrently. A multi-user database server like ObjectStore supports multiple TSP clients at a time which may run on different client nodes in a local area network accessing a shared persistent store.

3 An Untyped Store Model

A primary design goal behind TSP has been to provide efficient data storage as independent as possible from the data and language model supported by TSP store clients. In particular, TSP should be capable of supporting polymorphically typed models where the components of store objects can contain values of multiple types that cannot be fixed in a separate schema definition phase. TSP therefore uses an *untyped* low-level store model, i.e. there is no separate dictionary of type or schema information maintained by the backend. Instead of this, store values are made self-descriptive by imposing a regular object layout and a uniform tagging scheme. As a result, TSP achieves data model independence without sacrificing the advantages of self-descriptive statically-typed databases. In the full paper the store model is described in detail.

4 Overview of the Tycoon Store Protocol

Due to the simplicity of TSP's data model, it is possible to define concisely all its operations. The following clusters of operations are described in the full paper:

- operations on persistent stores,
- failure handling and recovery,
- operations on store objects,
- main memory mapping of store objects,
- management of object identifiers, and
- lineraziation of store subgraphs.

5 Concluding Remarks

The main contribution of this paper is the in-depth description of an object store protocol that we regard as an excellent starting point for a *standardized* interface between the frontend and the backend of fully integrated persistent environments. In developing the TSP specification, its implementations and its adaptors to commercial object stores available to other research groups, we hope to establish TSP as a widely accepted protocol within persistent language implementations. This would not only simplify the development of new persistent languages but also facilitate system measurements, comparative performance studies and interoperability experiments between multiple persistent languages.

References

1. F. Matthes, R. Müller, and J.W. Schmidt. Object stores as servers in persistent programming environments – the P-Quest experience. FIDE Technical Report Series FIDE/92/48, FIDE Project Coordinator, Department of Computing Sciences, University of Glasgow, Glasgow G128QQ, July 1992.
2. F. Matthes, R. Müller, and J.W. Schmidt. Towards a unified model of untyped object stores: Experience with the Tycoon store protocol. In *Advances in Databases and Information Systems (ADBIS'96), Proceedings of the Third International Workshop of the Moscow ACM SIGMOD Chapter*, 1996.
3. R. Müller. Language processors and object stores: Interface design and implementation. Master's thesis, Fachbereich Informatik, Johann Wolfgang Goethe-Universität, Frankfurt, Germany, November 1991. (In German).

Chapter 2.2.5

Measuring Persistent Object Systems*

Malcolm P. Atkinson, Anthony Birnie, Niall Jackson, and Paul C. Philbrow

Department of Computing Science, University of Glasgow, Glasgow G12 8QQ, Scotland

Abstract. Measurements of persistent systems are reported. A discussion of issues and criteria that should guide measurements and their interpretation is initiated. Measurements which may inform the engineering of persistent object stores are discussed and in particular a proposal is made for the formulation of laws governing the behaviour of persistent object stores. Some initial laws are presented. Experiments examining adherence to these laws are briefly reported.

1 Introduction

This paper is intended to fulfil two goals: to report on recent measurements of persistent systems conducted by the authors and to initiate a discussion of the issues and criteria that should guide measurements and their interpretation. There have been repeated calls for measurement of persistent object stores [1]. The intuition behind these calls and our measurement work is that measurement is a necessary component of developing well engineered persistent object stores. The measurements are required for two purposes: to validate or refute our theories about the behaviour of persistent object stores and their work loads and to allow better comparison of the effectiveness of various technologies.

There appear to be two quite distinct reasons for measuring the properties of a persistent object store: to establish the gross behaviour of a store implementation for the benefit of consumers; and to better understand mechanisms and hence to conduct more precise engineering.

The criteria for these two classes of measurement are quite different. For the gross behaviour the principal concern is marketing. Here the measurements have to be understandable, have to bear a reasonable relationship to the way the consumer will use the product and have to be trustworthy in the sense that they are consistently measured.

The criteria for engineering measurements are far more complex. Primarily they should serve the rôle of enabling better engineering. This means that they need to be related to precise and validated models of the system that they are intended to improve. The measurements are used both to establish the validity of the models and

---

* Synopsis of M. P. Atkinson, A. Birnie, N. Jackson, and P. C. Philbrow, Measuring Persistent Object Systems. In A. Albano and R. Morrison, editors, *Persistent Object Systems: Implementation and Use*, Workshops in Computing, pages 63–85. Springer-Verlag in collaboration with the British Computer Society, 1992.

to determine parameters. Comparisons are of interest to engineers in their capacity as consumers and generators of designs. In persistent object systems both the models and measures have yet to be established.

The paper consists of two almost independent parts. In the first our initial efforts in establishing gross behavioural measurement techniques are presented. Two benchmarks are described and the results with Napier88 (see Chapter 1.1.3) are reported. The second part discusses the kind of measurements and models which may inform the engineering of persistent object stores. In particular there is an initial proposal about formulating laws governing the behaviour of persistent object stores and some of the experiments examining that behaviour are briefly reported.

2 Measurements of external behaviour

Measurements produced in this category should meet four criteria: relevance, reliability, feasibility and independence. To be *relevant* the measurement must be one which measures aspects of performance which concern the wider audience of consumers and which is determined under conditions of typical load. For example, the typical metric is elapsed time or response time and the typical load is a complex mixture of operations on large, complex data structures that are intended to be characteristic of real loads. The complexity of any remotely representative load makes these measurements difficult to interpret for engineering purposes and we have therefore concluded that those measurements should be designed and conducted separately.

To be *reliable* the measurement must be such that if it were repeated by an independent body the result would be the same. This requires that the measurement be well specified so that there is no ambiguity in its parameters that could be interpreted differently on different occasions. For example the precise structure and size of the test data, the sequence of operations, the concurrency, recovery and stabilisation, and the performance characteristics of the supporting machine will all need to be specified.

To be *feasible* the measurement must not require excessive resources to set up. For example, it is unlikely that teams will write very large amounts of application code or arrange complex transformations of large volumes of data. To gain confidence in measurements they usually require repetition. The total testing time must therefore be reasonable, both in the labour costs of setting up and running the tests and in the computational costs.

To be *independent* the measurement must be re-usable in all the other persistent object stores activated by all conceivable persistent and database languages. This requirement indicates that the measurement will be specified in a language independent form. There are conflicts here between the precision required for reliability and the necessary freedom to allow many different approaches to handling the data and operations. These four criteria are in mutual conflict, for example the complexity and size of relevant workloads are in conflict with the feasibility requirement.

The paper reports on use of two external behaviour measures. One of these is Cattell and Skeen's Object Operations benchmark (OO1) [3,4], recently used to measure a number of OODBMS [2], and the other is a new MAPS benchmark. The experiments are presented and then an analysis of their performance against the four criteria leads to suggestions about future external behaviour measures.

The external measurement results were found to be reproducible within limits. Beyond these limits overload conditions set in. We argue that an important measure is the point at which overload sets in; this measure isn't often published. We refer to this point as a phase change.

We propose that the measurement strategy of applying a controlled mixture of reproducible and re-usable batches of operations, developed in the MAPS benchmark are a good foundation both for achieving better reliability while retaining feasibility and for allowing greater relevance to be achieved while allowing controlled erosion of independence. The operations can more or less be specified independently of one another and as a result the OO1 case would be a special case where the appropriate operations were run. The framework allows the research and development community to argue separately about the characteristic operations that might run in a persistent object store and consequently develop their specification.

3 Engineering measurements: Internal behaviour

In contrast to the previous group of measurements these measurements are not concerned with being realistic, instead the measurement should select some particular property of the store's behaviour and enable it to be better understood. For this purpose two new criteria come into play: the measurement should have a *theoretical* foundation and it should be reasonably *isolatable*.

By being *theoretically* founded we mean that there should be some postulated *law* that is likely to describe the persistent object store's behaviour which the measurement may confirm or refute. More often the measurement shows that the law only holds under certain circumstances and the measurements are valuable in determining the limits of validity. This requirement is necessary for the measurement to be useful in predicting behaviour, more importantly the proposition of these laws and their verification by measurement drives and verifies the process of trying to understand the resultant behaviour of the store mechanisms that are built. Frequently the measurements also serve to determine parameters that are significant in these laws.

By requiring the properties be *isolatable* we seek to separate one set of measurements from another so that the results are more easily interpreted and combined. This requirement is often difficult to meet as the present store implementations are complex and there are interactions between many of the mechanisms.

The original four criteria remain important though their interpretation changes in this context. They will only be *relevant* if the store properties that are described by the measurement are useful in developing better engineered persistent stores. They can only be trusted if they attain *reliability* but some measures may well be context specific so that it is only the work-load parameters that need be precise in the first instance. *Feasibility* in this class of measurements is more concerned with

Heisenberg-effects and with data volumes. *Independence* here should be sufficient for different groups to test the same laws, measure the same parameters and usefully compare their values. These requirements suggest that the laws should satisfy gauge theory.

At present, because of the complexity of store implementations, internal behaviour measurements are likely to be the best path to better understanding of store processes and improved engineering of persistent object stores. Laws are proposed that correspond to the behaviour under specific circumstances that is expected of a well engineered store. Specific and reproducible measurement experiments are then devised to test the laws and to determine the associated parameters. The laws proposed so far are:

1. Any given operation takes the same time to execute however many times it has executed previously
2. The point at which a phase change occurs should be predictable in terms of the store's and operation's parameters
3. Phase changes should not occur when benign operations are repeated
4. At most one phase change should occur when space churning operations are repeated
5. The onset of a phase change occurs after a number of operations proportional to the size of the medium that becomes exhausted and inversely proportional to the average space required per operation
6. The rate at which benign operations are executed may depend on the size of data read or written but it should be independent of the contextual volume of data

The behaviour for a given store is investigated for a given operation over a space explored via four parameters: *size*, *load*, *locality* and *repetitions*. To facilitate measurement a standard approach to organising the collection of data has been prototyped.

A strategy of investigating laws has been adopted where the simplest possible laws are tested first. These are refined only if necessary, otherwise other independent laws are developed. We illustrate this by considering three categories of store operation: benign (leaving the store unchanged), churning and expanding. It is desirable to develop laws that provide properties that may be relatively straightforwardly combined to predict composite behaviour.

Some ingenuity is needed to conduct the measurements. Problems include: isolation of one activity; modification of behaviour by the measurement apparatus itself; and the difficulty of obtaining accurate and meaningful timing information or other measures such as disc traffic or page faults.

There are challenges in the formulation of laws. Laws should: encapsulate relevant behaviour that is understandable and useful to engineers; be intuitively sensible and sufficiently independent; and be formulated so that they may be tested by experiment and if validated the relevant parameters may be determined. It is not easy to formulate laws that meet these requirements. A particular difficulty is that there does not appear to be a comprehensive and consistent view of the way a store should behave.

4 The future of laws and measurement

One motive of this paper is to provoke discussion on the laws and on the validity and implications of the measurements. It is hoped that the initial laws will be challenged and tested, in particular it is intended that rival and additional laws will be proposed. The discussion about their desirability as a description of persistent object stores will sharpen the community's understanding of the behavioural goals for persistent object stores.

Phase changes are viewed as a crucial issue. They are probably inevitable. The important requirement is that store designers and store users should know about them. Ideally, the properties of stores should be sufficiently well-understood that phase changes can be predicted.

Only when the laws concerning the simple behaviour of actual stores have been established and their parameters and limits of applicability determined will it be possible to return to benchmarks and interpret them as anything more than an indication of how the benchmark itself runs under certain measurement conditions. But if the laws are that well understood benchmarks will not be needed.

References

1. M.P. Atkinson and D. Maier. Perspectives on persistent object systems (concluding remarks on workshop). In A. Dearle, G.M. Shaw, and S.B. Zdonik, editors, *Implementing Persistent Object Bases, Principles and Practice*, pages 425–426. San Mateo, CA: Morgan Kaufmann Publishers, 1990.
2. R.G.G. Cattell, editor. *Next Generation Database Systems*. October 1991. Special Issue of Communications of the ACM, 34, 10.
3. R.G.G. Cattell and J. Skeen. Engineering database benchmark. Database Engineering Group, Sun Microsystems, March 1990.
4. R.G.G. Cattell and J. Skeen. Object operations benchmark. *ACM Transactions on Database Systems*, 17(1):1–31, March 1992.

Chapter 2.3

Implementation Techniques: Introduction and State of the Art

Ron Morrison

School of Mathematical and Computational Sciences, University of St Andrews, North Haugh, St Andrews KY16 9SS, Scotland

Persistent system environments are expected to provide the data management facilities required by languages, such as those presented in Chapters 1.1.1 to 1.1.3, and with at least the performance of traditional database systems. In FIDE the major research issue was the choice of architectures for complete, extensible and tailorable systems. This includes work on:

- canonical store mechanisms relating to transactions, concurrency, distribution, global optimisation and inter-operability,
- efficient programming language implementation, and
- query processing and optimisation.

The state of the art relevant to the persistent system environments can be summarised as follows. Digital's Trellis/Owl project has developed a statically type checked object oriented language [1]. This persistent system relies heavily on an object server designed and built by Zdonik at Brown University [2]. Similar object-oriented database server systems have been developed by Servio Logic [3], Ontologic and O_2 [4].

Texas Instruments have developed a layered architecture known as the Persistent Memory System. This persistent system is designed for use on the TI Explorer Computer and is currently being extended to operate as a distributed system within a network of Explorers. Texas Instruments are also heading a DARPA/ISTP project, DAAB07-90-B920, to design "A modular and open object-oriented database system". Efficient implementation of persistent object stores is being investigated by Rosenberg at the University of Sydney, Australia. The system is based on a uniform virtual memory with very large addresses [5]. Object store technology is also being investigated by Moss at the University of Massachusetts, Amherst [6]. Distributed stores are the subject of research in Adelaide in the CASPER project [7] and operating systems support for persistence in the Grasshopper project [8] in a joint investigation with the University of Sydney. The main thrust of the FIDE research in finding efficient implementation centred around the following questions:

- What store primitives are appropriate for the required concurrency, transactions and distribution?

- How can accelerators and optimisations be incorporated into the stores and used by the languages?
- What information should flow between the store and the language processors about store and query organisation?
- What is a good architecture for the persistent system environment?
- How may persistent polymorphic languages be implemented efficiently?
- What performance is achievable from a fully integrated system?

In FIDE, stable object stores capable of supporting the languages were developed, tested and measured (see Chapters 2.2.1 to 2.2.5). The research linked into the development work and in that context optimisation and clustering were investigated (see Chapters 2.3.3 to 2.3.5). Sophisticated store designs to handle object-oriented indexing were developed and evaluated by simulation (see Chapter 2.2.3) [9]. A number of persistent abstract machines were designed, built and used. An example of one, PAM/CASE is described in one of the papers in this section.

The investigation of alternative construction architectures was a major theme and was enhanced by the link to the EOS project [10] at INRIA where the relationship with operating systems was investigated (see Chapters 2.3.2 & 2.3.3). The stable stores were extended to support distribution and then to provide finer grained concurrency and transaction support (see Chapter 2.3.1) [11]. Research into the efficient implementation of polymorphic persistent languages was also undertaken (see Chapter 2.3.6) [12]. The synopsis of the results of all of these are contained in the papers in this section.

References

1. O'Brien PD, Halbert DC, Kilian MF. The Trellis Programming Environment. In: Proc. International Conference on Object-Oriented Programming Systems, Languages and Applications (OOPSLA'87), Orlando, Florida, 1987, pp 91-102
2. Skarra A, Zdonik SB. An Object Server For An Object Oriented Database System. In: Proc. International Workshop on Object-Oriented Database Systems, Pacific Grove, California, 1986, pp 196-204
3. Bretl B, Maier D, Otis A et al. The GemStone Data Management System. In: Kim W, Lochovsky F (ed) Object-Oriented Concepts, Databases and Applications. ACM Press and Addison Wesley, 1989, pp 283-308
4. Deux Oea. The O_2 System. Communications of the ACM 1991; 34,10:34-48
5. Rosenberg J, Koch DM, Keedy JL. A Massive Memory Supercomputer. In: Proc. 22nd International Conference on System Sciences, Hawaii, 1989, pp 338-345
6. Moss E, Sinofsky A. Managing Persistent Data with Mneme: Designing a Reliable, Shared Object Interface. In: Advances in Object-Oriented Database Systems, Proc. 2nd International Workshop on Object-Oriented Database Systems, Bad Münster am Stein-Ebernburg, Germany. Springer-Verlag, 1988, pp 298-316
7. Vaughan F, Schunke T, Koch B, Dearle A, Marlin C, Barter C. A Persistent Distributed Architecture Supported by the Mach Operating System. In: Proc. Proceedings of the 1st USENIX Conference on the Mach Operating System, 1990, pp 123-140
8. Dearle A, di Bona R, Farrow J et al. Grasshopper: An Orthogonally Persistent Operating System. Computer Systems 1994; 7,3:289-312

9. Zezula P, Rabitti F. Navigation Index for an Object Store. In: Proc. 25th International Conference on System Sciences, Hawaii, 1992, pp 756-765
10. Gruber O. Eos, an Environment for Persistent and Distributed Applications over a Shared Object Space. PhD thesis, Université Pierre et Marie Curie, Paris VI, 1992
11. Munro DS, Connor RCH, Morrison R, Scheuerl S, Stemple D. Concurrent Shadow Paging in the Flask Architecture. In: Atkinson MP, Maier D, Benzaken V (ed) Persistent Object Systems, Tarascon 1994, Proc. 6th International Workshop on Persistent Object Systems, Tarascon, France. Workshops in Computing, Springer-Verlag, 1994, pp 16-42
12. Morrison R, Dearle A, Connor RCH, Brown AL. An Ad-Hoc Approach to the Implementation of Polymorphism. ACM Transactions on Programming Languages and Systems 1991; 13,3:342-371

Chapter 2.3.1

Concurrent Shadow Paging in the Flask Architecture*

David Munro[1], Richard Connor[1†], Ron Morrison[1], Stephan Scheuerl[1] and David Stemple[2]

[1] School of Mathematical and Computational Sciences, University of St Andrews, North Haugh, St Andrews, Fife, KY16 9SS, Scotland
[2] Department of Computer Science, University of Massachusetts, Amherst, Massachusetts, MA 01003, U.S.A.

Abstract. The differing requirements for concurrency models in programming languages and databases are widely diverse and often seemingly incompatible. The rigid provision of a particular concurrency control scheme in a persistent object system limits its usefulness to a particular class of applications, in contrast to the generality intended by the provision of persistence. One solution is to provide a flexible system in which concurrency control schemes may be specified according to the particular task in hand, allowing the same data to be used in conjunction with different concurrency control schemes according to the needs of the application.

A major difficulty in the engineering of such a system lies in the building of generic mechanisms to provide the facilities of data visibility restriction, stability, and atomicity, *independently* of the combination of these employed by a particular concurrency control scheme. Flask is a architecture which is designed to achieve this goal by defining a layering whereby the memory management is not tied to any one concurrency control scheme operating above. This paper outlines the Flask architecture and focuses on an implementation based on concurrent shadow paging.

1 Introduction

With an increase in the number and diversity of models of concurrency, there is a growing need within database and persistent programming systems to support different styles of concurrency control scheme operating in conjunction over the same data. Flask is a layered architecture which has the flexibility to support different models of concurrency over the same data. The architecture eschews any fixed notion of concurrency control. Instead it provides a framework in which models can be defined and supported. One of the major difficulties in engineering such a system lies in the building of generic mechanisms to provide the facilities of data visibility restriction, stability, and atomicity, independently of the combination of these employed by a particular concurrency control scheme.

---

* The full version of this paper appeared in: Atkinson MP, Maier D, Benzaken V (eds) Persistent Object Systems, Tarascon 1994, Proc. 6th International Workshop on Persistent Object Systems, Tarascon, France. Springer-Verlag, 1994, pp 16-42

† Present address: Department of Computing Science, University of Glasgow, Glasgow, G12 8QQ.

One of the key features of the Flask architecture is that as little as possible is built-in to the lower layers providing increased functionality moving up the levels of abstraction. This provides the necessary flexibility but may also permit efficiency gains since many optimisations are achievable at a higher-level.

The Flask architecture challenges the orthodoxy whereby most database systems, such as System/R [1], Ingres [2], O2 [3] and Oracle build in specific models of concurrency, usually at the store level. This design decision is taken for reasons of simplicity of implementation and arguably trades efficiency for flexibility. A drawback with the approach is that the specification of a particular concurrency control model is often described in terms of its implementation.

2 Overview of Flask

The framework of the Flask architecture is shown in Figure 1 as a "V-shaped" layered architecture to signify the minimal functionality built-in at the lower layers. At the top layer the specifications of the model are independent of the algorithms used to enforce them and can take advantage of the semantics of these algorithms to exploit potential concurrency [4]. For example a particular specification may translate into an optimistic algorithm or alternatively a pessimistic one while the information they operate over remains the same. More importantly such an approach can accommodate different models of concurrency control.

Fig. 1. V-shaped layered architecture

In Flask, the significant events defined by a particular concurrency control scheme are generated from and reported to the higher layers enabling these schemes to undertake conflict detection. This assumption frees the lower layers from the onus of interference management. The theme here is concerned with low-level memory management implementations in the Flask architecture under the assumptions given above. The focus of interest then centres on the visibility of data from different actions. In Flask, the visibility is expressed in terms of the control of movement between a globally visible database and conceptual stores called access sets. Each action is associated with a local access set and may use other shared access sets. At the lowest level the atomicity layer ensures consistent update to the access sets and the global database. The failure resilience layer utilises this atomicity to effect an action *meld*.

The approach taken marries the notion of data visibility as expressed by access sets to a concurrent shadow paging mechanism. It is argued that in moving the programming algebra and the concurrency control to higher layers many of the perceived difficulties concerning concurrent shadow paging have been abstracted out. Shadow paging is then seen as a mechanism worthy of consideration for such an architecture in essence because it can stabilise over arbitrary address ranges without requiring knowledge of objects and program behaviour.

3 The Flask Concurrent Shadow Paged Store

The main problem of concurrency and shadow paging is that transactions may make conflicting requests to modify the same page. When one of the transactions melds the modified page is written to its shadow page on non-volatile store. This of course will include the changes made by any unmelded transaction that modified objects on the same page. One common solution is to use page-level locking whereby an atomic transaction obtains an exclusive lock on a page before shadowing the page [5, 6]. Each transaction maintains its own page table of shadows and the locking guarantees that a page is never in more than one page table. The main drawbacks of this solution are firstly that it introduces phantom locking where two atomic actions are prevented from modifying different parts of the same page. Secondly it employs a built-in concurrency control mechanism at a low level.

The Flask solution involves not only keeping a disk page table of shadows for each process but to also maintain per-process shadow pages, i.e., an access set. Flask also maintains a global disk page table of pages which constitute the last meld point. When a process first modifies a page a shadow copy is made and its address is added to the process's shadow page table. To resolve a disk address on a page fault the process shadow page table is searched first and, if still unresolved, then the global disk page table. This mechanism ensures that the changes made by one process are completely isolated from other processes and the global state. Action abort is thus a trivial matter of discarding a process's shadow pages. When an action melds its changes must become globally visible to all other actions. There is therefore a requirement in the Flask architecture to ensure that the changes made to a page by the melding action are propagated to any other action holding a shadow copy of the same page.

Because the meld resolution is at a page-level then the changes made by the melding action must be propagated to other actions' per-process shadows. Suppose that two actions A and B share a page but modify different objects on that page. Because of the isolation of the concurrent shadow paging mechanism A can meld without affecting B. For B to subsequently meld it must retain the changes that A made. And so a mechanism is required for B to ingest the changes made by A. The algorithm that meld uses to propagate changes is dependent on the particular concurrency model in operation. Under the assumption that the higher-layer concurrency control can detect object-level conflicts there a number of methods of achieving this.

In concurrency models that require isolation, where the concurrency control ensures that two transactions do not modify the same object, it is possible to use logical operations to propagate the changes. For example, in an atomic transaction model, suppose two actions A and B have changed different objects on the same page P and action A melds. The changes made by A to page P can be calculated by an xor of P onto the original page, i.e., as it was at the last meld. This derives a page of changes made by A to page P. These changes can now be xor'd onto action B's copy of page P. So the meld propagation formula can be written as (P_A **xor** P_O) **xor** P_B where P_A is the action A's shadow page P, P_O is the page P as it was at the last meld and P_B is action B's shadow page P. Thus B's version of page P now includes the changes made by A. This approach is not restricted to atomic transactions. In co-operative models where the actions agree to change an object to the same value using majority rules logical operations can also be used.

3.1 The Flask Implementation

The concurrent shadow paging scheme in the implementation of Flask works much the same as single-user shadow paging whereby the virtual address space is mapped to non-volatile storage through a disk page table. Modified pages are shadowed and the transient disk page table reflects the current global state of the address space. In addition a separate disk page table is created for each access set used. Entries to the disk page tables are added for each page modified by the action. When an action first modifies a page a shadow copy is made and the action works on the copy. The concurrency control specification dictates whether the update is local or shared.

References

1. Chamberlin, D.D., Astrahan, M.M., Blasgen, M.W., Gray, J.N., King, W.F., Lindsay, B.G., Lorie, R.A., Mehl, J.W., Price, T.G., Selinger, P.G., Schkolnick, M., Slutz, D.R., Traiger, I.L., Wade, B.W. & Yost, R.A. "A History and Evaluation of System R". CACM 24,10 (1981) pp 632-646.
2. Stonebraker, M. (Editor) "The Ingres Papers". Addison-Wesley, Reading, MA (1986).
3. Deux, O. "The Story of O2". IEEE Transactions on Data and Knowledge Engineering. March 1990.
4. Garcia-Molina, H. "Using Semantic Knowledge for Transaction Processing in a Distributed Database". ACM Transactions on Database Systems, 8,2 (1983) pp 186-213.
5. Lorie, A.L. Physical Integrity in a Large Segmented Database, ACM Transactions on Database Systems, 2,1 (1977) pp 91-104.
6. Agrawal, R. & DeWitt, D. "Integrated Concurrency Control and Recovery Mechanisms: Design and Performance Evaluation". ACM Transactions on Database Systems, 10,4 (1985) pp 529-564.

Chapter 2.3.2

Locking in OODBMS Clients Supporting Nested Transactions*

Laurent Daynès[1†], Olivier Gruber[3‡], and Patrick Valduriez[3]

[1] Sun Microsystems Laboratories, 901 San Antonio Road, MS-MTV29-111, Palo Alto, CA 94303, USA
[2] IBM Research Division, Almaden Research Center, 650 Harry Road, San Jose, CA 95120-6099, USA
[3] Projet RODIN, INRIA Rocquencourt, BP. 105, 78153 Le Chesnay Cedex, France

Abstract. Nested transactions facilitate the control of complex persistent applications by enabling both fine-tuning of the scope of rollback and safe intra-transaction parallelism. In this paper, we are concerned with supporting concurrent nested transactions on client workstations of an OODBMS. Use of the traditional design and implementation of a lock manager results in a high CPU overhead: in-cache traversals of the OO7 benchmark perform, at best, 4.5 times slower than the same traversal achieved in virtual memory by a non-persistent programming language. We propose a new design and implementation of a lock manager which cuts that factor down to 1.8. This lock manager supports nested transactions with both sibling and parent/child parallelisms, and provides object locking at a cost comparable to page locking. Object locking is therefore a better alternative due to its higher functionality.

1 Introduction

Object-Oriented Database Management Systems (OODBMS) are advocated for complex applications such as CAD/CAM and CASE environments. Most of today's OODBMSs have adopted a client-server architecture. The server sends data to clients on demand, and clients keep these data in their cache for as long as possible. A cache coherency protocol deals with consistency between the caches of the different clients. Each client usually runs on a workstation dedicated to a single user. Ideally, the user should be able to work on a client's cached data using powerful mechanisms to control the structure of their applications. Typically, rich and flexible transaction models, such as design transactions or cooperative transactions, are advocated for this purpose. The common basis of most of these transaction models is the nested transaction model of Moss [10].

In this paper, we investigate solutions allowing users to run several hierarchies of nested transactions working concurrently on their client cache. To achieve this

* A shorter version of this paper has been published in the Proceedings of the 11th International Conference on Data Engineering, Taipei, Taiwan, 1995.

† This author's work was performed while he was seconded to the University of Glasgow by INRIA Rocquencourt.

‡ This author's work was performed while he was with INRIA Rocquencourt.

goal, we introduce a local concurrency control built on top of the cache consistency protocol, which controls locally the access to data already covered with stronger or equal cache consistency locks. Given this architecture, the main design issue is the granularity of locking used at the client.

An OODBMS context is less favourable to a coarse grain locking. Because arbitrary composition of objects is allowed, because users can write arbitrary code to operate on objects and because multiple transactions may be running concurrently, each time a transaction executes a method on an object O, it has to request a lock for protecting that object O. As a result, *page locking will issue the same number of lock requests as object locking*. Thus, the difference in cost between page and object locking comes from all operations whose cost is proportional to the number of acquired locks. This includes (1) the cost of acquiring locks, (2) the cost of space management to store and retrieve locks, (3) the cost of releasing locks when a hierarchy of transactions commits, and (4) the cost of *lock inheritance*. Lock inheritance is that mechanism which ensures isolation between each level of a hierarchy of nested transactions, allowing intra-transaction parallelism [8].

In this paper, we study three lock manager implementations which support nested transactions. One corresponds to the traditional implementation of a lock manager [6,7,4]. A second derives from the first one but uses a solution similar to that proposed in [5] for optimising lock access. The third lock manager implements our original proposal. These three implementations cover all the published lock manager implementations of which we are aware of.

We used the OO7 benchmark to compare the performance of these three lock managers, using page and object locking alternatively on the client's cached data. Our results confirm that using a local concurrency control within clients introduces a significant overhead that must not be underestimated. They further show that our lock manager used with object locking adds an overhead in the range of the best page locking scheme studied, under the same nested or flat transaction workloads, and performs at least 27% better than the two other object locking alternatives.

The rest of this paper is organised as follow. Section 2 discusses the nested transaction locking rules as defined by Moss, and describes the traditional implementation of a lock manager supporting these rules. Section 3 presents our new design of lock inheritance and section 4 introduces our implementation of a lock manager. Section 5 reports the comparative measurements we achieved.

2 Traditional Implementation of Lock Inheritance

A nested transaction is a tree of transactions with a *top-level transaction* as root and *sub-transactions* as leaves or intermediate nodes. A sub-transaction can either commit or abort, but commitment will take effect only when the top-level transaction commits. Thus, the top-level transaction has the ACID (Atomicity, Consistency, Isolation, Durability) property while the sub-transactions are only ACI.

Each transaction of a transaction tree is uniquely identified in the system, and within its transaction tree by the set of its superior transactions, which uniquely defines its position in the tree. The ancestors of a transaction T, hereafter denoted $Ancestor(T)$, includes T and its superiors.

This section assumes a nested transactions model with sibling parallelism only. In this context, each transaction is provided with the visibility of its ancestors' working set, that is, a transaction is able to read or modify objects already used by its ancestors. When a transaction commits, its working set is merged with those of its parent transaction, making the results of the committing transaction also visible to the inferiors of the parent transaction. In the now ubiquitous locking protocol formulated by Moss [10], these visibility rules are supported through two distinct mechanisms: conflict detection and delegation of locks.

Each transaction keeps track of the identities of its ancestors, and uses them to check if their lock requests conflict with the current state of locks. We formally represent the set of transactions owning a lock l in a mode M by $Owners(l, M)$, and the set of transactions owning l in a mode incompatible with a mode M by $I_{owners}(l, M)$. Using these notations, conflict detection can be expressed by the following rule:

$$I_{owners}(l, M) \subseteq Ancestors(T)$$

That is, a transaction T requesting a lock l in mode M does not conflict with the urrent lock settings if **all incompatible owners** of the lock are ancestors of T.

Transactions record all the locks they own in a book-keeping structure which we call a *lockset*. Each time a transaction T acquires a lock l, it adds it to its lockset.

At commit time, a sub-transaction delegates its locks to its parent transaction, which means the sub-transaction's locks become the parent transaction's. Delegation is implemented by exchanging, within locks, the identities of the committing child and its parent transaction. Applying the aforementioned conflict detection rule, these delegated locks can then be granted to the descendants of the parent transaction. The combination of the conflict detection rule and the delegation of locks forms the so-called lock inheritance mechanism.

Figure 1 illustrates the implementation of a lock manager as commonly described in the literature [6,7,4,5]. (Each flag represents a latch.) A lock is implemented by a Lock Control Block (LCB) which contains information such as its name, its current mode (read or write), a latch, and links. A fixed-size hash table is used to store and retrieve LCBs using their name. The LCB is also the head of two doubly-linked lists of Lock Request Blocks (LRBs). One list implements the granted requests (i.e. $\forall M : Owners(l, M)$). The other list holds pending requests, and corresponds to blocked transactions. Each LRB relates to one transaction, and contains information such as its transaction's identity, the requested locking mode, and links to its lockset.

The lock manager also maintains a pre-allocated free pool of LCB's per hash table slot and a pre-allocated free-pool of LRB's per transaction. This strategy allows to reduce the number of latch operations to one per lock operation.

To set a lock on a resource (e.g. a page or an object), the lock manager first selects a hash chain using the resource's name as the hashing key. If there is no LCB for the resource, it initialises a new one and appends it to the hash chain. Otherwise,

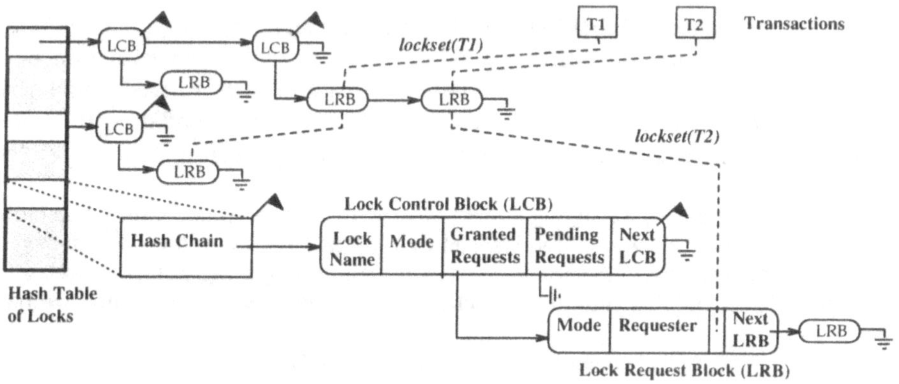

Fig. 1. Lock Manager Implementation

it scans the LCB's LRB chain to see if the requester already has one LRB. If there is no LRB for the requester, it allocates a new LRB, chains it to the requester's lockset, and chains it to the right LCB chain according to the conflict detection result. Conflict detection is performed when the LRB chain is scanned to look up the LRB of the requester.

This implementation of lock managers does not give good supports to nested transactions locking at the client for several reasons. First, hash-table lookups severely hurt performance when locks are often re-checked, which is the case for workloads involving a lot of pointer-chasing. OODBMSs are particularly optimised for these workloads using either single-level store or pointer swizzling techniques to efficiently implement object identity [11–13]. Hash table lookup would spoil the benefits of these optimisations.

Second, the locksets of committing transactions have to be entirely scanned either for delegating (sub-transaction case) or for releasing (top-level case) locks, as well as for re-scheduling pending transactions. The processing of a lockset involves, per lock, several latches, updates to linked list, and de-allocation of either an LCB or LRBs. These scans have a noticeable impact on performance when they are repeatedly performed because of transactions are nested, and when they involve large locksets (which is typical of object locking).

Third, nested transactions whose working sets overlap augment the length of LRB chains. Where a single LRB was sufficient in a flat transaction model, several LRBs are needed when several transactions within the same hierarchy all request the same lock. This yields both a space overhead and a time overhead: more LRBs have to be allocated and deallocated, increasing memory management and latching costs.

3 Lock Inheritance Revisited

Two observations allow us to dramatically optimise lock inheritance. First, one can see that the effect of Moss's conflict detection rule is to filter out any ancestor transactions from the requested lock's owner set, prior to checking for conflicts. In other words, all superiors of a transaction are "*non-conflicting*" with that transaction. Second, when a transaction T_c commits, only the descendants of T_c's parent can inherit T_c's locks. Since in Moss's formulation $parent(T_c)$ does not conflict with its descendants, the inheritance of locks is simply achieved by changing T_c's locks to be $parent(T_c)$'s locks.

However, instead of changing locks, we could change the conflict detection rule of every one of $parent(T_c)$'s descendants, by adding T_c to their set of "*non-conflicting*" transactions. The price to pay is a walk through the transaction tree to update these descendants' conflict detection rules. However, one can observe that generally:

$$| \, Descendant(Parent(T_c)) \, | \ll | \, lockset(T_c) \, |$$

where $lockset(T_c)$ denotes the set of locks T_c owns at commit-time. Therefore lock inheritance should be dramatically improved if the operation of making a transaction non-conflicting with another is as expensive as changing a lock's ownership.

Table 2 summarizes both Moss's approach and ours, using a simple hierarchy made of a transaction T_1 and its two child transactions T_2 and T_3. In Moss's approach, when T_2 commits, it delegates its locks by changing their ownership. Thereafter, using Moss's conflict detection rule, T_1 and T_3 are allowed to see T_2's effects. In our approach, when T_2 commits, T_2's locks are left unchanged. Instead T_2 is declared non-conflicting with both T_1 and T_3. This is done by updating the conflict detection rule of T_1 and T_3. Using their updated conflict detection rule, both T_1 and T_3 will be able to see T_2's effects.

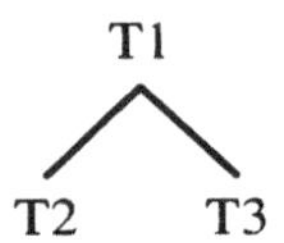

	Moss's approach		New approach	
T2 is	running	committed	running	committed
T1 is non-conflicting with	{}	{}	{}	{T2}
T3 is non-conflicting with	{T1}	{T1}	{T1}	{T1,T2}
T2's Lock Ownership	{T2}	{T1}	{T2}	{T2}

Fig. 2. Two approaches to implement lock inheritance

More formally, each transaction manages two transaction identity sets: an Upward Inherited Identity Set (denoted UIIS), and a Downward Inherited Identity Set (denoted DIIS). These sets are defined as follows for a transaction T:

$$UIIS(T) = \bigcup_{\forall T_i \in Committed(T)} (\{T_i\} \cup UIIS(T_i))$$

$$DIIS(T) = UIIS(Parent(T)) \cup DIIS(Parent(T))$$

where $Committed(T)$ denotes T's committed sub-transactions.

New transactions are initialised with empty identity sets. Then, each time a transaction T_c commits, its identity is inserted in $Committed(parent(T_c))$, which triggers updates to some $DIIS$ and $UIIS$ of the transaction hierarchy, according to these set definitions. Figure 3 illustrates these updates.

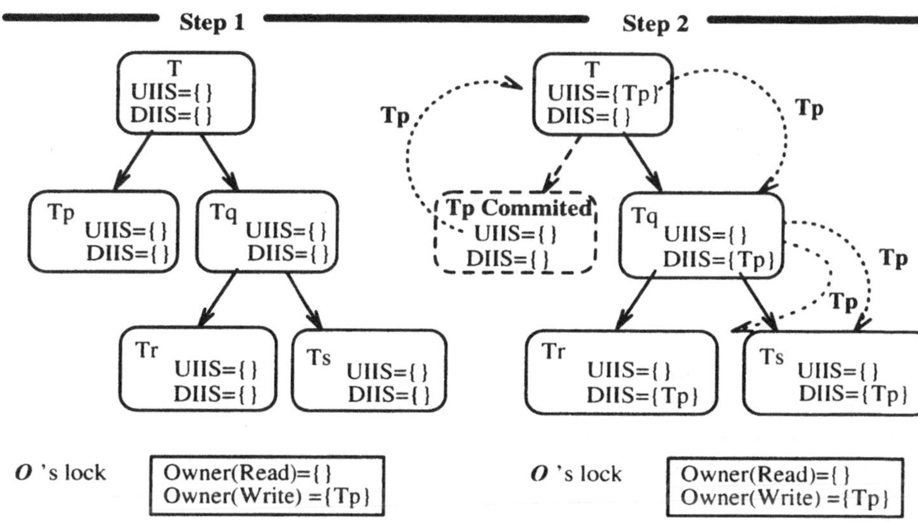

Fig. 3. Updates upon Delegation

The first step depicts a transaction T which started two parallel sub-transactions T_p and T_q. T_p took an exclusive lock on an object O. T_q started two sub-transactions T_r and T_s. All $UIIS$s and $DIIS$s are empty since no transactions have committed yet. The second step shows the updates that the commit of T_p triggers (dotted arrows). First, notice that O's lock is left unchanged, and that it is still owned in a exclusive mode by T_p, now in a committed state. Second, notice how the $UIIS$s' and $DIIS$s' updates follow the definitions given above.

Using Moss's terminology, $UIIS(T)$ represents the committed sub-transactions of T whose locks should be retained by T. $DIIS(T)$ represents T's committed sub-transactions whose locks should be retained by T's superiors. This distinction is needed because if T aborts, it must delete from its locks only its own identity and those of its committed sub-transactions, i.e. only $\forall T_i \in (\{T\} \cup UIIS(T))$.

Both the $UIIS$ and $DIIS$ of a transaction T represent the part of T's conflict detection rule that must be updated to enforce the nested transaction semantics with respect to visibility each time a sub-transaction of any T's ancestors is committed. This new technique simply extends Moss's conflict detection rule by adding these variable parts. Thus, when sibling only parallelism is assumed, the conflict detection rule for a transaction T requesting a lock l in a mode M is:

$$I_{owners}(l, M) \subseteq Ancestors(T) \cup DIIS(T) \cup UIIS(T)$$

When supporting parent/child parallelism, all superiors of the requester T must conflict with T if they hold incompatible lock requests. The rationale for this is that a parent transaction cannot allow its parallel sub-transactions to access its own resources without endangering the correctness of its computation. However, a parent can allow its running child transactions to access the resources of its already committed child transactions. Therefore, the conflict detection rule for parent/child parallelism is:

$$I_{owners}(l, M) \subseteq \{T\} \cup DIIS(T) \cup UIIS(T)$$

Indeed, one can see that each transaction may have its own conflict detection rule, parameterized by various sets of non-conflicting transactions. The conflict detection rule can be refined to provide finer control on lock inheritance. Refinements are achieved by adding sets of transaction identities that filter, out of the requested lock's owner sets, all transactions which allow visibility to their working sets [3].

4 Implementation

In this section, we propose a new implementation of a lock manager. Our goal is twofold. First, to come up with an implementation that supports our lock inheritance technique efficiently. Second, to avoid the shortcomings of traditional lock manager design when used in an OODBMS context.

In section 2, we identified hash lookups for finding locks as a major overhead for an OODBMS using pointer swizzling. Swizzling works as follows. When an object is brought into the client cache, a *handle* describing that object is created. Basically, the handle points to the object's location in the cache. The cache maintains a hash table which maps OIDs to handles. We call this table the *object table*. Initially, cached objects reference each other using their OIDs, and de-referencing requires looking up the object's handle in the object table. Swizzling an object pointer is overwriting the OID within that pointer with the address of the corresponding object in the cache. Thus, subsequent de-referencings avoid looking up the object table. Pointers within an object are un-swizzled when that object leaves the cache [12].

The object table can be used to avoid hashed accesses to locks when object locking is used. The idea is to pre-allocate a LCB in the handle of each shared object. The pointer to this LCB is appended to the beginning of the cache's region where the shared object was copied at fault-time. That way, (1) the lock table is merged with the object table, (2) the same latch prevents both concurrent swizzling and locking, reducing latching cost, (3) LCB's memory management is eliminated from the processing of lock requests and factorised with those of handles, and (4), accessing the LCB costs a pointer de-reference.

If page locking is used, a LCB is pre-allocated when the page is loaded from the server, and a pointer to that LCB is set in a page header. This is done once and transactions follow this pointer without any existence check to get the lock. The LCB is indeed pre-allocated in the page hash table which is used to keep track of the pages loaded in the client cache.

Using LRB chains to implement granted lock requests leaves a high overhead during the processing of lock requests: it involves space management, and scanning for detecting conflicts. On the other hand, we believe that the client activity would not exceed one hundred simultaneous transactions. On this assumption, we found fixed-size bitmaps an ideal structure for representing lock owner sets: they incur very low space overhead compared to LRB chains, and efficiently support the set-oriented operations we are interested in.

In this new approach, each client manages a bitmap structure. Each client's transaction is allocated a bit number within that bitmap, which uniquely identifies that transaction within the client. Each LCB is composed of one status word and one bitmap per locking mode (i.e. for each $Owner(M), \forall M$). Bitmaps are also used to implement the ancestor set, $DIIS$, and $UIIS$ of each transaction. All bitmaps use the same mapping of transactions to bit numbers, i.e. the ith bit always identifies the same transaction. Bits that are set to 1 indicate the transactions that currently own the lock in the mode corresponding to the bitmap. Finally, the lockset of a transaction is implemented as a stack of LCB's references.

Figure 4 depicts, in the case of object locking, a global overview of the data structures at the client. It includes the cache, the object table, object locks and the transaction to bit number mappings.

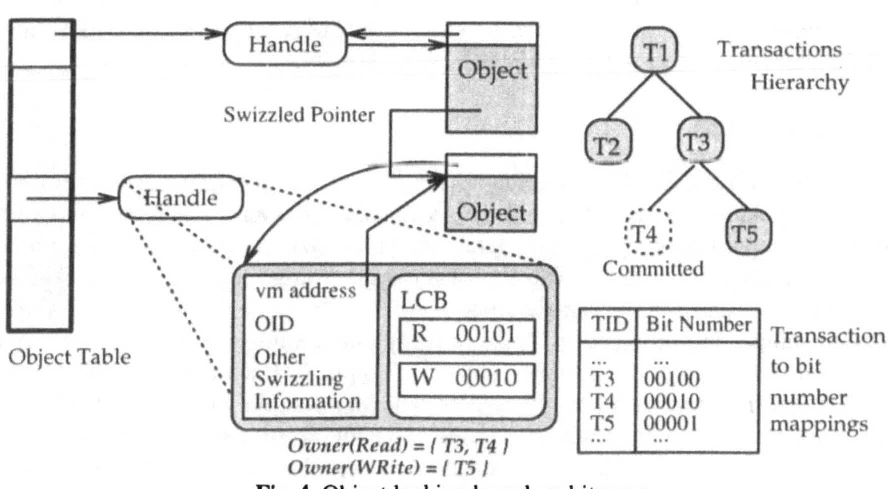

Fig. 4. Object locking based on bitmaps

Bitmaps name transactions on a per client basis and we expect that bitmaps of between 64 and 128 bits will be sufficient for most clients. However, our design increases the probability of bitmap overflow since the identities of all committed sub-transactions accumulate within owner sets until their top-level transaction's commitment.

Our solution to this problem is to free the bits of committed sub-transactions before bitmaps overflow. Indeed, all the bits of the committed inferiors of a transaction T can be exchanged, within locks, by the unique bit of T. These bits correspond exactly to $UIIS(T)$. Doing this exchange respects the isolation property of T, and frees bit numbers which can be re-used earlier than the commitment of T's top-level, thus limiting the probability of bitmap overflows. A more detailled description of this mechanism is given in [2].

5 Performance Measurements

We described three designs of lock manager supporting nested transaction semantics. The first one (denoted HASH) uses the state of the art implementation techniques advocated in [6,7]. The second (denoted PTR) keeps the representation of locks used by HASH, but pre-allocates LCBs when swizzling pointers and uses a direct pointer to access LCBs. The third (denoted BITMAP) derives from PTR by changing its chain of granted LRBs to two fixed-size bitmaps stored in the pre-allocated LCBs.

This section shows how the use of these lock managers to implement client-local concurrency control can degrade the client's performances. Our measurements are based on the OO7 benchmark [1]. We measured the three aforementioned lock managers using alternatively page and object locking, which gives us 6 different options. Each option is named hereafter with the name of its lock manager, prefixed with the locking granule used: "P-" for page locking (P-BITMAP, P-PTR, P-HASH), and "O-" for object locking (O-BITMAP, O-PTR, O-HASH).

5.1 Overview of OO7

The OO7 benchmark emulates applications managing complex data structures such as CASE or CAD/CAM systems. It defines a canonical database's schema, and a set of canonical operations against this database. Three sizes of database are defined, and three levels of complexity can be set by augmenting/reducing the number of inter-connections between database objects.

The database is organised in modules (only one actually). Each module has a manual and a hierarchy of assembly objects of depth 7. Each assembly object recursively references other assembly objects. The leaf assembly objects, called Base assemblies, differ from the other assemblies of the hierarchy, called complex assemblies. A base assembly has three bi-directional links to three shared composite parts. There are 500 composite parts shared among the 729 base assembly objects.

A composite part has a bi-directional link with a document object and a bi-directional link to the root of a graph of 20 atomic parts. Each atomic part is inter-connected to the other atomic parts of its composite part. Three degrees of interconnection are defined (3,6,9). Connections hold some data and are therefore implemented as objects in the database.

Our measurements rely essentially on the read-only and read-write traversals of the OO7 benchmark, namely T1 and T2b. These traversals corresponds to pointer-chasing workloads. Each traversal navigates through the assembly hierarchy and visits each composite part of each base assembly. For each visited composite part, a depth first search on its graph of atomic parts is performed. Fields of atomic parts are read or updated according to the nature of the traversal. For a detailed review of OO7, please refer to [1].

5.2 Testbed Configuration

We obtained the Exodus version of the code from the Wisconsin University ftp site, turned the E[1] code back to pure C++ code, and added lock requests to each object method's invocations. Basically, all instances of a shared object's class are protected with a lock (their own lock, or those of the page they belong to): this includes the module, all the assembly, the composite and atomic parts as well as connection objects.

The three lock managers and the client's cache have been implemented in C++ on a 486 DX PC at 33 MHz (with 16 Megabytes of main memory), running the OSF/MK operating system. We used the Gnu C++ compiler, version 2.2.2. We set the size of bitmaps to 64 bits for the BITMAP lock manager. All measurements were made using only the small database, which fits entirely in main memory so as to avoid paging. This corresponds to the "hot traversals" experiments of the OO7 benchmark, where the client's cache is warmed by running the measured operation once. As specified in OO7, our results are the average times of three executions.

5.3 Traversals as Flat Transactions

We first instrument the OO7 benchmark running each traversal as a flat transaction. Figure 5 reports the results T1 yields with object and page locking for the three different degrees of interconnections between atomic parts (reported in horizontal axis). For comparison, we also report the performance of T1 without locking, i.e. in native C++.

We first observe that page locking produces a high locking overhead: At best (P-BITMAP and P-PTR, fanout 3), it is 1.6 times slower than the equivalent C++ traversal, and up to 4 times slower at worse (P-HASH, fanout 9).

The explanation lies in the following numbers. The small OO7 database, set with a fanout 3, contains 41,594 shared objects which require protection. These objects fit in 314 pages of 4kB. Therefore, T1 traversal acquires *at most* 314 locks. But T1 does 353,201 lock requests. Locks have to be requested so many times because there is no way to factorise the lock requests of several accesses to the same object, or to objects belonging to the same page.

[1] E is the persistent programming language derived from C++ which interfaces Exodus.

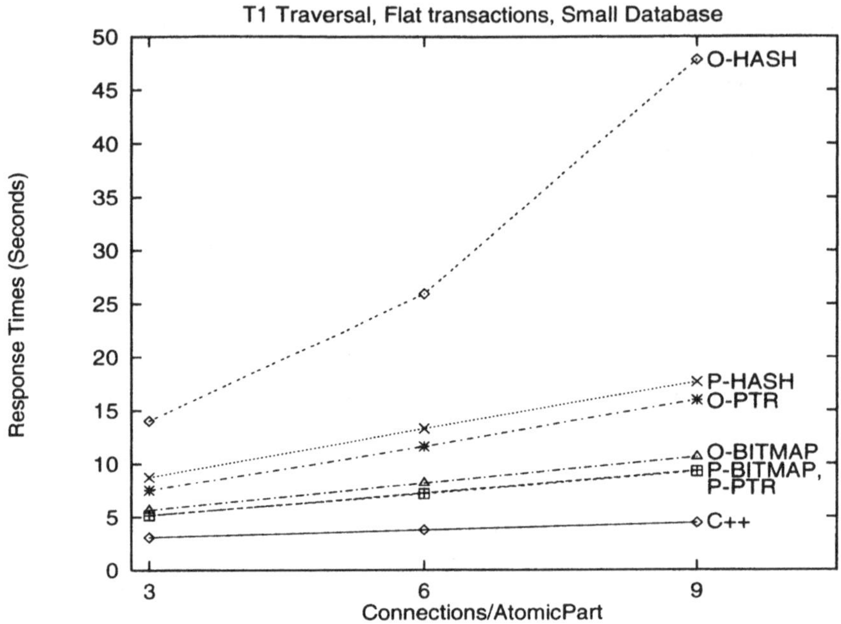

Fig. 5. Locking overhead with flat transactions

P-BITMAP and P-PTR exhibit the same performances, that is between 1.6 and 2 times slower than C++. This occurs because re-checking a lock costs almost the same in both implementations. In contrast, P-HASH adds a hash look-up to P-PTR's re-check cost, which nearly doubles the locking overhead with respect to P-PTR, and makes P-HASH even slower than O-PTR and O-BITMAP.

When moving from page to object granule, the number of lock requests stays the same, but the locking overhead increases because more locks are acquired and released. O-PTR is up to 1.7 times slower than P-PTR (i.e. 3.6 slower than C++), and O-HASH is up to 2.7 times slower than P-HASH (i.e. 10.8 slower than C++). The added overhead is the cost of allocating and de-allocating space for more LRBs, since more locks are manipulated. In addition, O-HASH suffers from the cost of dynamically allocating/de-allocating LCBs, and from the high rate of collision in the hash table of locks, increasing lookup times. Collisions are responsible for the non-linear behaviour of O-HASH.

In comparison, O-BITMAP is only 14% slower than the best page locking scheme (P-PTR). This results from bitmaps being pre-allocated in handles, making a lock acquisition as expensive as a lock re-check. Thus, most of the degradation that O-BITMAP introduces with respect to P-PTR comes from that 130 times more locks are released at commit time. Globally, O-BITMAP performs between 1.83 and 2.4 times slower than C++.

5.4 Traversals as Nested Transactions

Typical OODBMS's applications are complex tasks such as CAD/CAM's design process and programming in CASE environments. In these applications, users' transactions are complex and may involve several database operations such as traversals. Nested transactions provide the opportunity to control finely the structure of the transaction, either its degree of multi-programming by launching parallel sub-transactions, or its grain of rollback by nesting or chaining sub-transactions sequentially. Thus, at run-time, users can either run a set of traversals in a single transaction, or map these traversals to as many sub-transactions as necessary to obtain the desired transaction's structure. This section evaluates how each of the studied options degrades the client performance to support these structuring features. For simplicity, we only study non-parallel nested transactions in this paper.

The benchmarks we used are derived from the traversal *CU* of OO7. The original specification, quoted from [1], is: *"Perform Traversal T1, followed by T2a, in a single transaction"*. We slightly change this specification to produce a new traversal that takes nesting of transactions into account. The resulting traversal, we call *Nested CU*, is defined as: *Perform Traversal T1, followed by a sub-transaction performing T2b*[2]. We further refine Nested CU to a *D-Nested CU*, which nests update traversals down to a depth D. That is, the top-level transaction performs a traversal T1, and starts a sub-transaction which performs a traversal T2b, which in turn starts a sub-transaction to perform T2b again, and so on down to a depth D.

Figure 6 reports our measurements of D-Nested CU with object locking. For the sake of comparisons, we add the best times we got after running the same number of traversals in a single flat transaction using alternatively page and object locking Our best shots come from O-BITMAP for object locking (denoted Best-O-Flat), and P-PTR for page locking (denoted Best-P-Flat). As observed earlier, the degradation of performances between the best page and object locking option is very low.
When moving from flat to nested transaction, the costs of lock inheritance become crucial for performance. First of all, both O-HASH and O-PTR do not reach depth 4 because they exhausted the available swap space. At depth 4, the nested transaction creates 4 times more LRB than for the same traversal with a flat transaction. This is because the isolation property is required at each level of the nested transaction hierarchy. This illustrates how bitmaps dramatically reduce the space overhead of locking: An LCB including bitmaps is no larger than a single pair of one LCB and one LRB.

Second, the management of large locksets goes against options which implement delegation by updates on locks. At depth 4, both O-PTR and O-HASH update $4 \times 40,895$ locks, whereas O-BITMAP does an update 4 times to a bitmap implementing a transaction's $DIIS$.

The overhead O-BITMAP introduces with respect to Best-O-Flat has two origins. First, for a depth of D, O-BITMAPS performs $D \times 40,895$ more lock acquisitions than Best-O-Flat, since each sub-transaction has to acquire locks for its

[2] We use T2b instead of T2a as T2b performs the highest ratio of updates, thus making the cost of lock inheritance higher.

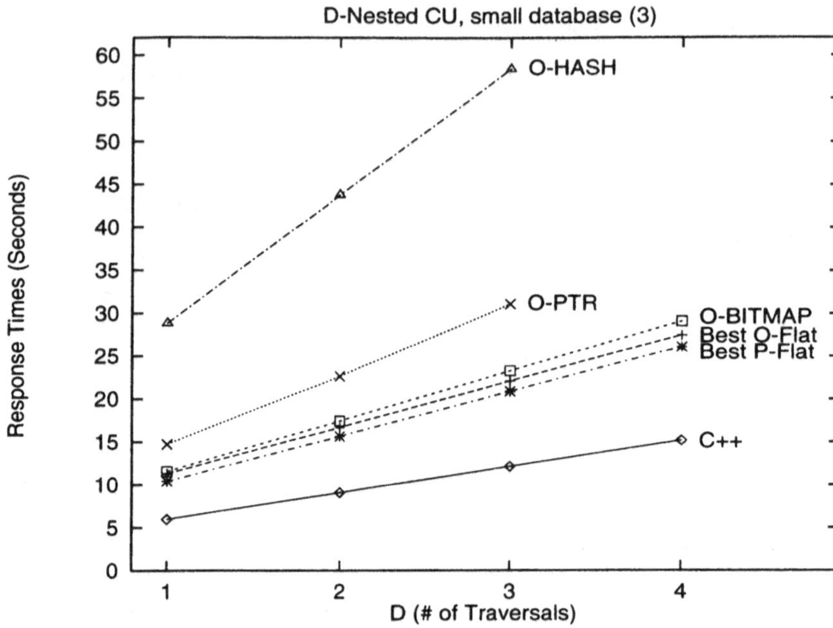

Fig. 6. D-Nested T2b, varying *D* from 1 to 4

own isolation. Second, since all transactions of the hierarchy take a lock in a mode incompatible with those owned by their ancestors, each lock acquisition by a sub-transaction checks for hierarchical relationships. This is more costly than checking locks in a flat transaction. Despite these two additional overheads, O-BITMAP is at most 6% slower than Best-O-Flat, and 11.5% slower than Best-P-Flat.

5.5 Transactional Encapsulation

Nested transactions are also advocated as a natural extension to the modularity principle of Abstract Data Type (ADT) [6]. Such an extension consists of coupling ADT's encapsulation with automated invocation of a sub-transaction. Thus, modularity and re-use properties are augmented with failure atomicity. This usage of nested transactions, we refer to hereafter as *Transactional Encapsulation*, has been intensively studied in the Argus project [9].

Applying this principle to all objects populating a database would obviously result in a very high overhead. In practice, transaction properties are not needed at the finest grain of encapsulation. In the following, we report the measurement of a traversal T2b when transactional encapsulation is applied to a grain smaller than an OO7 module (denoted TE-T2b). We map transaction invocations to the OO7's hierarchy of complex assembly objects, and measure the locking overhead for different depth of the transaction hierarchy, that is for various grains of transactional encapsulation. The deeper the hierarchy is, the smaller the grain.

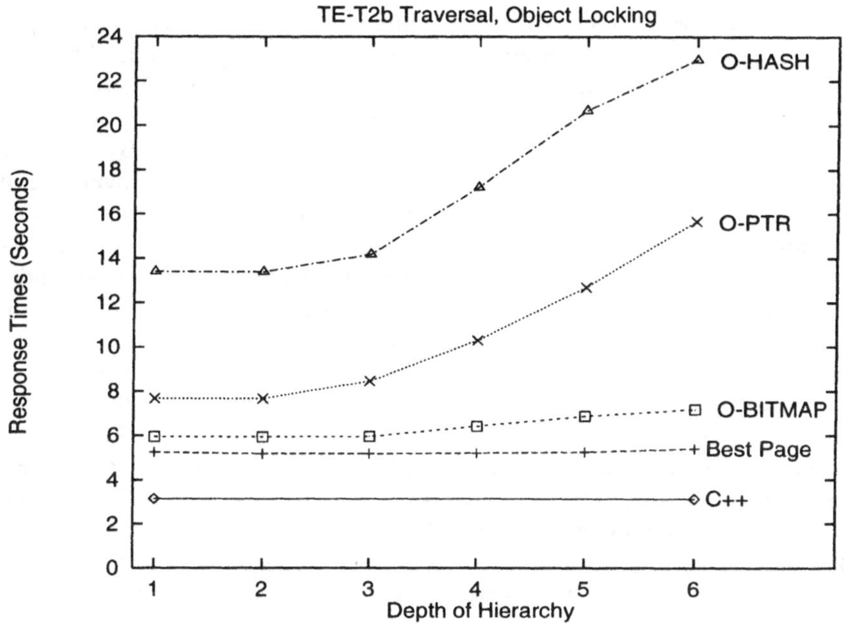

Fig. 7. Transactional Encapsulation Performance

Figure 7 reports the measurements that TE-T2b yields for each of the object locking option, when it is run against the small database with a fanout of 3. The bottom line represents the time a pure C++ TE-T2b yields. We also add the best time of TE-T2b when it is run with page locking.

All executions, whatever their depth, produce the same number of lock requests, and use the same number of locks. Thus, the performance loss between two grains of transactional encapsulation is only due to lock inheritance. The fanout of complex assembly hierarchy being 3, applying transactional encapsulation to a depth 6 creates $(3^6 - 1)/2 = 364$ transactions for traversing the module. While O-BITMAP supports this well, both O-HASH and O-PTR suffer from the hindering effect of scanning locksets at sub-transaction's commit. The shift starting at depth 5 for O-BITMAP is due to bit number collections which were done synchronously for the measurements. That is, when there are no more free bits, a collection is started on behalf of the transaction that raises it. Five collections are raised at depth 6. Even with these synchronous collections, O-BITMAPS outperforms the best times of the two other object locking options, and is between 14% and 32% slower than the best page locking scheme.

6 Conclusions

In this paper, we have studied several options for synchronising access to an OODBMS's client cache by multiple parallel nested transactions. OODBMS's data structures and programs are so complex that it is almost impossible to cover an object with a single lock request. As a result, the number of lock requests issued by programs is the same whatever the locking granule used. However, the fraction of requests acquiring a lock counts for 11% of the total number of requests when object locking is used, and for less than 0.1 % when page locking is used. By reducing the cost of acquiring a lock to the cost of re-checking it, we made the overhead of processing lock requests independent of the locking grain used. Techniques used include a low-overhead lock representation using bitmaps, fast detection of conflicts involving hierarchical relationships between transactions, and allocation/deallocation of lock structures at swizzling/unswizzling times. Furthermore, our implementation of delegation is independent of the number of locks. Therefore, the only cost impacted by granularity is that of releasing locks at commit time.

This explains the good performances of our solution compared to those of the techniques advocated in [6,5]. Using our lock manager with object locking on the OO7's small database set with 3 interconnections per object, (1) traversals performed by flat transactions are 9% times slower than the best page locking option when state-of-the-art solutions are at least 45% slower, (2) set of traversals structured in nested transactions are less than 6% slower than the same traversal done in a single flat transaction, when state-of-the-art solutions are at least 30% slower.

References

1. M. Carey, D. DeWitt, and J. Naughton. The OO7 Benchmark. Technical report, Computer Sciences Department, University of Wisconsin-Madison, April 1993.
2. L. Daynès. *Conception et réalisation de mécanismes flexibles de verrouillage adaptés aux SGBDO client-serveur.* PhD thesis, Université Pierre et Marie Curie (Paris VI – Jussieu), 1995.
3. L. Daynès and O. Gruber. Efficient Customizable Concurrency Control using Graph of Locking Capabilities. In *Persistent Object Systems (Proc. of the Sixth Int. Workshop on Persistent Object Systems)*, Workshops in Computing, pages 147–161, Tarascon, Provence, France, September 1994. Springer-Verlag in collaboration with the British Computer Society.
4. J.L. Eppinger, L.B. Mummert, and A.Z. Spector. *Camelot and Avalon : A Distributed Transaction Facility*. Morgan Kaufmann, San Mateo, CA, 1991.
5. V. Gottemukkala and T.J. Lehman. Locking and Latching in a Memory-Resident Database System. In *Proc. of the 18th Proc. of Int. Conf. on Very Large Data Bases*, pages 533–544, 1992.
6. J. Gray and A. Reuter. *Transaction Processing : Concept and Techniques*. Morgan-Kaufman, 1993.
7. T. Härder, M. Profit, and H. Schöning. Supporting Parallelism in Engineering Databases by Nested Transactions. Technical Report 34/92, Kaiserslautern University, December 1992.
8. T. Härder and K. Rothermel. Concurrency Control Issues in Nested Transactions. *VLDB Journal*, 2(1):39–74, 1993.
9. B. Liskov. Distributed Programming in Argus. *Communications of the ACM*, 31(3):300–312, March 1988.

10. J.E.B. Moss. *Nested Transactions : An Approach to Reliable Distributed Computing.* PhD thesis, Massachussets Institute of Technology, April 1981.
11. J.E.B. Moss. Working With Objects: To Swizzle or Not to Swizzle? *IEEE Transactions on Software Engineering*, 18(8):657–673, August 1992.
12. S. White and D. DeWitt. A Performance Study of Alternative Object Faulting in Pointer Swizzling Strategies. In *Proc. of the 18th Proc. of Int. Conf. on Very Large Data Bases*, pages 419–431, Vancouver, British Columbia, Canada, 1992.
13. P.R. Wilson and S.V. Kakkad. Pointer Swizzling at Page Fault Time: Efficiently and Compatibly Supporting Huge Addresses on Standard Hardware. In *Proc. of the 1992 Workshop on Object Orientation in Operating Systems (24th-25th September 1992, Dourdan, France)*, pages 364–377. IEEE Computer Society Press, 1992.

Chapter 2.3.3

Query Processing in *PIOS*

Fausto Rabitti, Leonardo Benedetti and Federico Demi

CNUCE, Institute of CNR, Via S.Maria 36, Pisa, Italy

Abstract. An approach to query processing in object-oriented stores supporting physical data independence is proposed in this Chapter.

In particular, the problem of query optimisation (i.e. finding efficient execution plans for declarative queries) is investigated. A set of rewrite rules has been defined in order to allow an algebraic optimisation phase. A local search procedure, based on a cost model of the store, has been tailored to the task of physical optimisation. To support the physical data independence in the store, a translation algorithm, dealing with the actual storage organisation of the database, has been studied. A comprehensive example illustrates these mechanisms. Finally, performance results are presented.

1 Introduction

Object-oriented database management systems (OODBMSs) are the result of new technologies which aim at tackling the data management problem of engineering applications like CASE and CAD systems. In the last few years, a number of prototypes (e.g. IRIS, Gemstone, Object Store, ORION, and O) have been developed.

If we consider the performance of such systems, a key problem to solve is the optimisation of queries formulated with the declarative query languages supported. Several techniques that have been designed for other environments (e.g. query optimisers for relational DBMSs, code optimisation strategies for object-oriented programming languages) may turn out to be useful in this context.

This chapter presents the study, description, and evaluation of query processing and query optimisation strategies implemented in PIOS (*Physically Independent Object Server*) [1], an object server which supports an object–oriented data model as defined in [3] and physical data independence: it allows the definition of a *logical schema*, that describes logical aspects of the database and against which operations are requested, and a *storage schema* which defines how objects are actually stored. A complete description of PIOS can be found in Chapter 2.2.2 of this book.

As explained in that chapter, PIOS supports two different strategies for storing class hierarchies (*ODS* and *SDS*), *grouping* and *partitioning* of logical objects. Grouping allows several logical objects to be stored by means of a single physical object. Partitioning is the fragmentation of logical objects into several physical objects (*vertical partitioning*) and the choice of their storage bucket according to a predicate (*horizontal partitioning*). Moreover, in order to speed-up retrieval operations, PIOS allows the definition of value and navigation indices [5]. All these designing choices are submitted to the system using a specific language: the *Object Store Definition Language* [4]. The physical independence in PIOS implies that queries have to be translated by the system in order that they operate against the storage schema.

An example logical schema that will be used for formulating queries and the definition of a physical schema with value and navigation indices are presented in Appendix A.

Query processing is essentially the mapping of a declarative query expression into a procedural sequence of access plan primitives (i.e. an execution plan). Query optimisation is the selection of an efficient execution plan belonging to the set of all the equivalent plans for a given query (i.e. search space). For non-trivial queries, this selection process can become quite expensive, therefore the search strategy has to be carefully tuned, possibly taking into account results gathered over a sequence of queries being optimised. Moreover, as new query evaluation techniques prove to be useful, the optimiser has to be sufficiently extensible to allow their integration.

All the above aspects have been studied during the design of the PIOS query processor (a more comprehensive description can be found in [2]). A set-oriented, non-procedural query language has been defined that is easily manageable and efficiently optimisable. Its expressions are checked for type consistency and submitted to a two-step optimisation process: (*i*) *algebraic optimisation*, performed by means of a set of rewrite rules using heuristics for ameliorating the expression and schema information for pruning it, (*ii*) *physical optimisation*, a randomised search based on a cost model exploiting data distribution statistics, in addition to heuristics for reducing the search space.

The search space is modelled by annotating with *roles* the operators of the physical expression resulting from the algebraic optimisation phase. It includes the choice of traversal order for path navigations starting everywhere in the path expression (i.e. join reordering) and the selection of existing indices. Adaptable rules for annotating the expressions should guarantee the optimiser's extensibility and improvability.

The cost-driven physical optimisation is not usually implemented in existing OODBMSs (e.g. O, Object Store), or it is oversimplified (e.g. ORION). Without a cost model, it is not obvious which query transformation rules have to be applied in order to reach an optimised plan. Therefore, the PIOS query processor performs a rather simple algebraic optimisation, using rewrite rules that in the vast majority of cases are able to improve the expression. However, the PIOS query processor emphasises the cost-driven physical optimisation, which is the main focus of this paper. An important contribution of is that, within the PIOS context, we are able to compare, in orders of magnitude, the relative improvement of algebraic optimisation and cost-driven physical optimisation.

The rest of the chapter is organised as follows. In Section 2, an overview of related research on query processing and query optimisation is presented: this serves as introduction for our specific work which covers Section 3 and Section 4. In particular, in Section 3 the algebraic optimisation phase and the translation algorithm between logical and physical level are described, while the physical optimisation phase is presented in Section 4. Conclusions are in Section 5.

2 Related Work

Almost all existing query optimisers for OODBMSs can be partitioned into two different classes: those based on a system of rewrite rules (e.g. [6, 7, 8]) and those exploiting the concept of class extent (e.g. [9, 10, 11]).

An optimiser belonging to the first class is the one designed for the O_2 system [8]. Its main features are the algebraic optimisation of the queries, exploiting the semantic properties of the language, and the factorisation of constant and/or duplicated subexpressions. To complete the approach, a set of heuristics for reducing the rewriting phase and for the selection of suitable indices is defined. The important thing to note here is that the entire process is carried out without the support of a comprehensive cost model.

The other approach has been explored in the design of the query optimiser for the ORION system [9]. Several techniques for the query optimisers of relational DBMSs have turned out to be useful and easily employable in this project. In particular: the enumeration of all valid permutations of the classes involved in a query, the choice of the best join algorithm and the exploitation of a cost model based on data distribution statistics. A graphical representation of queries and tree traversal algorithms are proposed. There are three methods for evaluating a (sub)query (i.e. for traversing its tree representation). The *forward traversal* starts at the root node and consists of: (*i*) a projection on the children attributes, (*ii*) an evaluation of the qualified children that allows the qualification of their parents. The *backward traversal* starts at the leaves: the qualified attributes are evaluated through a selection, then a semi-join returns the qualified parents. The *mixed traversal* combines the two previous methods.

As stated in the introduction, complex queries give rise to many alternative execution plans that have to be examined in order to produce an *optimised plan*. Query optimisers deal with non-trivial queries, possibly executed only once: therefore, they have to take into account the combinatorial nature of the search space. For common queries of OODBMSs, the latter is usually even wider than the analogous queries of relational DBMSs. This is due to the fact that path expressions can be viewed as *implicit joins*. Hence, the search strategy may result in a quite time consuming search process (i.e. there is a trade-off between optimisation cost and quality of the solution obtained), therefore it needs to be carefully designed and tuned. Two approaches have been proposed [12]: *enumerative* (or *deterministic*) search and *randomised* search.

Enumerative search inspects for optimality several solutions by *depth-first* order (e.g. greedy strategy with augmentation heuristic [13]) or *breadth-first* order (e.g. branch-and-bound algorithm [14] with heuristics for early pruning of inefficient plans). The latter algorithm, combined with restrictions on the search space, has been chosen for the design of the optimiser of the relational DBMS System R [15].

Randomised search aims at improving start solutions until a *local* optimum is obtained. Two algorithms have been proposed: *iterative improvement* (or *local search*) [13] and *simulated annealing* [16]. Comparisons between enumerative and randomised strategies can be found in [17] where, in the context of parallel execution, access plans are modelled as processing trees.

3 Query Processing in PIOS: Algebraic Optimisation and Translation

Queries are submitted to PIOS using a specifically defined non-procedural query language: a brief overview of it and of the three-step algebraic optimisation phase (see Figure 1) is presented in this section (see [2] for details). As far as the latter is concerned, the input is a type-consistent expression of the query language (*initial logical expression*) to which a set of schema-independent rewrite rules is applied. The resulting expression (*simplified logical expression*) is then translated into an equivalent one formulated against the storage schema (*initial physical expression*). This expression is finally pruned by means of schema-dependent rewrite rules in order to obtain a *simplified physical expression*.

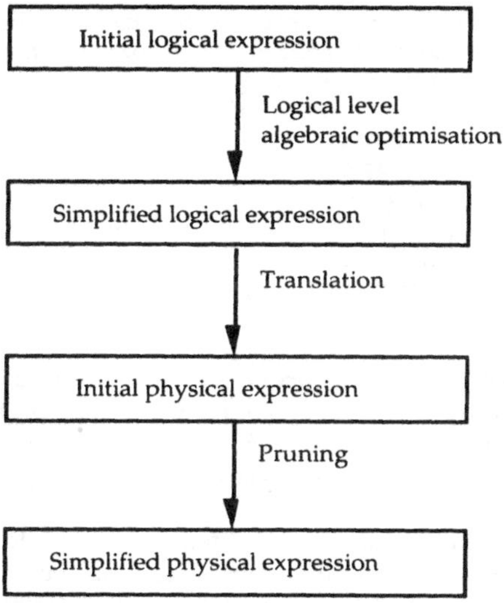

Fig. 1. Algebraic optimisation phase

3.1 Query Language

Queries are expressed in PIOS through a *formal*, *object-preserving*, efficiently optimisable query language. Formal languages provide a sound foundation for equivalence-preserving transformation rules. Object-preserving languages return as query results objects that already exist in the database (they cannot create new objects as side-effects of query executions).

In the following the query language operators are presented. Operands and results are sets of LIDs (*unique logical object identifiers*), thus the language maintains the *closure property*. A query expressed against the logical schema (i.e. *logical query*) is an expression *e* compliant with the following grammatical rules:

```
e ::= UN(e, elist) Union
      | IN(e, elist)                 Intersection
      | DF(e, elist)                 Difference
      | F(class, expression)         Selection (Filter)
      | MB(quantifier, attribute, class, e) Map Backward
      | MF(quantifier, attribute, class, e) Map Forward
elist ::= e | e, elist
expression ::= simplePredicate
             | simplePredicate  and expression
             | simplePredicate  or expression
             | (expression)
simplePredicate ::= attribute relOp const
                  | TRUE
                  | FALSE
attribute ::= class_field
relOp ::= < | <= | = | <> | >= | > | has
quantifier ::= A   Universal Quantifier
             | E   Existential Quantifier
```

The semantics of the query language operators is straightforward. Only map operators need an explanation: **MB(E**, *A_ref*, *A'*, *S*) is the subset of LIDs of class *A'* that reference, via *A_ref*, at least one object in *S*; meanwhile **MB(A**, *A_ref*, *A'*, *S*) is the subset of LIDs of class *A'* that reference, via *A_ref*, objects in *S* only. Semantics of Map Forward operators is defined similarly.

The query language presented above is rather simple. It must have a simple structure in order to be highly optimisable. The main restriction is that method invocation is not allowed, since it is not possible to predict the result during the optimisation phase. Other restrictions (arithmetic is not present, *attribute relOp attribute* is not defined, etc.) are due to the fact that we have preferred to leave out some standard features, that can be handled in well known ways, in order to keep more understandable the basic principles of the optimisation process. This query language can also be used for defining *envelopes* (i.e. portions of database which are sufficient for executing a transaction) as a result of queries executed at the server level, and which can be then transmitted to the client for further processing.

In subsequent examples, simple queries formulated using the query language are presented. Of course, they are expressed against the logical schema defined in Appendix A.

Examples

1. Find all Italian libraries

```
MB(E, Library_Addr, Library,
        F(Address, Address_Country = 'Italy'))
```

2. Find all Italian university libraries

```
MB(E, Library_Addr, UnivLibrary,
        F(Address, Address_Country = 'Italy'))
```

3. Find all technical books written in English by John Smith, having at least a topic different from Object Store.

```
IN(   IN(F(TechBook, Book_Language='English'),
         F(TechBook, Book_Author='John Smith')),
      MB(E, TechBook_Topics, TechBook,
         F(Topic, Topic_Description<>'Object Store')))
```

This query will be used throughout this paper in order to describe the various phases of query processing.

3.2 Logical Level Algebraic Optimisation

After that the logical query is checked for type consistency, a set of rewrite rules is applied. These query transformation rules are based on pattern matching and textual substitution and create equivalent expressions (see [2] for details). The overall logical-level algebraic optimisation process aims at:

1. eliminating the redundancy possibly contained in the expression;
2. easily checking for contradiction the conditions specified in each selection operator, in order to simplify the entire expression;
3. standardising the expression structure, in order to make it easier its translation into an equivalent query formulated against the storage schema.

This phase is particularly useful when queries are the result of an automatic process of translation. Next, a very simple transformation (i.e. filter aggregation) performed on the example query is presented.

Example

Initial logical expression:

```
IN(IN(F(TechBook, Book_Language='English'),
      F(TechBook, Book_Author='John Smith')),
   MB(E, TechBook_Topics, TechBook,
      F(Topic, Topic_Description<>'Object Store')))
```

Simplified logical expression (after logical level algebraic optimisation):

```
IN(F(TechBook, Book_Language='English' ∧
               Book_Author='John Smith'),
   MB(E, TechBook_Topics, TechBook,
      F(Topic, Topic_Description<>'Object Store')))
```

3.3 Translation

Since PIOS supports physical data independence, the simplified logical expression has to be translated into an equivalent query formulated against the storage schema (*initial physical expression*). The target language for this translation (*physical query language*) is similar to the logical query language presented in Section 3.1 and is still declarative enough to enable the subsequent phase of physical optimisation. Its operands and intermediate results are sets of *physical object identifiers* (PIDs). In general, the final result of a physical query is a multi-set of PIDs, which eventually is transformed back by the system into a set of LIDs.

In order to allow an easy factorisation of common subexpressions, the working structure for the representation of physical queries is a DAG (*Directed Acyclic Graph*) instead of a tree. Due to space constraints, translation algorithms are not presented here, instead the resulting physical expression for the example query is shown.

Example

Initial physical expression (after translation against storage schema):

```
IN(F(TechBook*, TechBook*_Book.Language='English'
                 ∧ TechBook*_Book.Author='John Smith'),
   MB(E, TechBook*_TechBook.Topics,
         ──► F(Topic*, Topic*_Topic.Description <> 'Object Store')))
   IN(F(ItalTechBook, ItalTechBook_Book.Language='English'
                 ∧ ItalTechBook_Book.Author='John Smith'),
   MB(E, ItalTechBook_TechBook.Topics, • ))
```

This expression reflects the fact that *TechBook* class has been horizontally partitioned into two collections: *ItalTechBook* that contains technical books written in Italian and *TechBook** that contains technical books not written in Italian. The arrow is the result of the common subexpression detection mechanism performed at translation time (i.e. *Topic** collection can be accessed only once).

3.4 Pruning

This phase is performed by means of a set of schema-dependent rewrite rules. In particular, every predicate contained in a selection operator of the initial physical query is checked for contradiction against the condition verified by the collection on which it is defined (these conditions stem from partitioning). Contradictory selection operators are replaced with the expression **F**(*collection*, **FALSE**). The effects of such replacements are then propagated through the entire expression. This process avoids accessing a collection when its objects have primitive values not compliant with those requested by the query.

Example

Simplified physical expression (after pruning phase):

```
IN(F(TechBook*, TechBook*_Book.Language='English'
          ∧ TechBook*_Book.Author='John Smith'),
  MB(E, TechBook*_TechBook.Topics,
      F(Topic*, Topic*_Topic.Description<>'Object Store')))
```

It is obtained after that selection operator on *ItalTechBook* collection has been replaced with **F**(ItalTechBook, **FALSE**) and the intersection operator has been subsequently pruned. The result of all the entire algebraic optimisation is a *simplified physical expression* that becomes the feasible starting point for the subsequent physical optimisation phase.

4 Query Processing in PIOS: Physical Optimisation

Physical optimisation is the kernel of the entire query optimisation process in PIOS. In fact the *simplified physical expression*, obtained from the previous algebraic optimisation phase, can be mapped into several (typically many) equivalent access plans, each exploiting different strategies for accessing data. In order to speed up the evaluation of queries, the physical optimisation phase must take into account the low-level features of PIOS storage system. In particular: the direct access to physical objects via PIDs, navigations among objects performed through forward and backward references stored in the object's states and the exploitation of value and navigation indices.

The task of choosing an efficient plan is a computationally intractable problem as discussed in Section 2. In PIOS, it has been attacked using a local search procedure [14] in addition to a cost model. The latter is able to estimate the cardinalities of each temporary set involved in an access plan and the number of accesses to secondary storage needed for the plan's execution. In order to reduce the search space, a set of heuristics and a set of tuning parameters have been defined.

4.1 Physical Level Access Primitives

A PIOS access plan is a sequence of physical level access primitives (*primitives* for short). Each of them takes either one or two sets of PIDs as parameters and produces one set of PIDs as a result. There are *set primitives*, *navigation primitives* (possibly performed through a navigation index) and *selection primitives* (possibly performed using a value index). In the following, a survey of all primitives is presented. Meta identifiers such as *T*, *T1*, *T2* etc. stand for temporary sets of PIDs.

These are the *set primitives* supported:

```
T = T1 UN T2            Union
T = T1 + T2             Disjoint union
T = T1 INT T2           Intersection
T = T1 \ T2             Difference
T = sort T1
T = pids collectionName
```

It stores in T all the PIDs of the objects belonging to *collectionName* collection. These are the navigation primitives:

```
T = MF [attributeName] T1 by link
T = MF [attributeName1... attributeNamen] T1 by navIndexId
T = MB [attributeName ] T1 by link
T = MB [attributeName1... attributeNamen] T1 by navIdxId
```

Each navigation primitive specifies the reference(s) to be navigated and the physical access method to be used. The latter can be: (*i*) **by link** if physical pointers are to be used; (*ii*) **by** *navigationIndexId* if a navigation index is to be accessed without materializing the physical objects stored in the collections. Finally, these are the *selection primitives*:

```
T = F [ conjunct ] T1
```

The objects of T1 are accessed and the PIDs of those verifying *conjunct* are stored in T.

```
T = F [ conjunct ] collectionName by valueIndexId
```

The value index *valueIndexId* is accessed to select the subset of the objects stored in *collectionName* which satisfy *conjunct.*

4.2 Cost Model

For assuring high quality results, the task of choosing an efficient plan must be guided by the minimisation of the expected time needed for its execution. For that purpose the definition of a *cost model* is needed. In particular, it has to exploit a mathematical model able to estimate the cardinalities of each temporary set of PIDs involved in an access plan. In PIOS, such a model is based on statistics of (*i*) *primitive attributes*: uniform distribution and independence among values of distinct attributes is supposed; (*ii*) *references*: statistics on referenced and referencing objects are collected; (*iii*) *collections*: the number of objects belonging to each collection is maintained; (*iv*) *indices*: the number of levels and leaves of the B-trees implementing the indices is maintained as well. In order to avoid an unjustified overhead, the above statistics are only periodically updated (e.g. when the system is shut down).

The approximation adopted for the execution time of an access plan is the estimated *number of pages* accessed by the underlying persistent object store, thus ignoring the delay caused by the CPU for internal processing. As in most cost models for database systems, we neglect specific cost modifications due the history of read and write and the physical properties of disks and controllers, since these factors do not change the order of magnitude of the results and would make much more complex the cost model. This also reflects the characteristics of the persistent object store used in PIOS (see Chapter 2.2.2). Moreover, the interleaving of transactions and the presence of a cache memory are not taken into account by the cost model.

In PIOS, all physical objects belonging to a certain collection are stored in a set of pages that they use exclusively (i.e. it cannot exist a page containing objects belonging to two different collections). A PID contains information about the physical placement on the storage device of the object it refers to. This enables the direct access to an object via its PID. As far as the cost model is concerned, a physical object is always considered to be accessed as a whole (this is rather sensible in a system supporting physical data independence, where very large objects could be stored in contiguous physical pages, and simplifies the overall estimation process).

4.3 Search Space

In this section the technique implemented in the PIOS query processor for obtaining different, but equivalent, plans for a given physical expression is described. Plans differ in their exploitation of existing indices (value and navigation indices) and in the ordering of navigation executions.

The general idea is to annotate every operator of the simplified physical expression with a *role* and to provide an algorithm for translating an annotated physical expression into an access plan. Not all the annotations can be mapped into a correct access plan. Section 4.4 will describe how the local search procedure is constrained to generate only legal annotations (i.e. annotations that give rise to correct access plans).

Definitions

Given a physical expression:

- the *result set* attached to an operator *O* is the temporary set of PIDs representing the result of the subquery rooted in *O*.
- the *advance set* attached to an operator *O* is a temporary set of PIDs that is a superset of the result set of *O*.

Every physical operator is annotated with one of the following *roles*: *generator* (gen), *propagator* (pro), and *bottom-up* (bup).

An operator annotated with *generator* role creates an advance set for its operands. Operators eligible to be generators are intersections and navigation operators.

An operator annotated with *propagator* role has an advance set attached to itself, and uses it for speeding up its execution and/or for providing an advance set for its operands. Any operator is eligible to be propagator.

An operator that is neither generator nor propagator is said to be annotated with *bottom-up* role.

Subsequent examples are intended to show how different annotations of the same simplified physical expression yield different but equivalent plans.

Example

```
<bup> IN(
<bup>  F(TechBook*, TechBook*_Book.Language='English'
                    ∧ TechBook*_Book.Author='John Smith'),
<bup>  MB(E, TechBook*_TechBook.Topics,
<bup>        F(Topic*, Topic*_Topic.Description<>
              'Object Store')))
```

Annotating every operator with *bottom-up* role, the resulting plan is obtained translating the physical expression in a bottom-up way.

```
10000#     314$    T0   = pids Topic*
 9999#   20314$    T1   = F[Topic*_Topic.Description<>Object Store] T0
10000#   25569$    T2   = MB[TechBook*_TechBook.Topics] T1 by link
10000#    1303$   *T3   = sort T2
10000#     314$    T4   = pids TechBook*
    1#   20158$    T5   = F[TechBook*_Book.Author=John Smith ^
                             TechBook*_Book.Language=English] T4
    1#       1$   *T6   = sort T5
    1#     159$ !*T7    = T3 INT T6
Execution cost:   68132$.
```

Each primitive has two numbers preceding it: the first one (i.e. it is followed by *#*) represents the estimated cardinality of the resulting temporary set of PIDs, while the second one (i.e. it is followed by *$*) is the estimated number of accesses to the secondary storage needed for its computation. Moreover, the * character means that the temporary set is sorted, while the *!* character marks the final result set. In this case, the plan entails the scan of two collections: *Topic** and *TechBook** (the result set is *T7*). In our sample database, objects are usually supposed to span over two physical pages, and a single-page buffer of the same dimension of a physical page is assumed (i.e. reading data of two different pages always implies two accesses to the secondary storage).

Performing a naive selection of indices on the above plan, the following one is obtained (navigation indices are not exploitable for this query):

```
10000#     314$    T0   = pids Topic*
 9999#   20314$    T1   = F[Topic*_Topic.Description<>Object Store] T0
10000#   25569$    T2   = MB[TechBook*_TechBook.Topics] T1 by link
10000#    1303$   *T3   = sort T2
    4#     161$    T4   = F[TechBook*_Book.Author=John Smith] TechBook*
                              by Vix# 2
    1#      10$    T5   = F[TechBook*_Book.Language=English] T4
    1#       1$   *T6   = sort T5
    1#     159$  !*T7   = T3 INT T6
Execution cost:   47831$.
```

The *Vix# 2* value index is used for solving the condition on author attribute, therefore *TechBook** collection is not scanned (only a few objects of its extent are accessed). In contrast, the *Vix# 1* value index (defined on *Topic*_Topic.Description*) is ignored because the condition on topic is not selective enough (i.e. all topics but one are different from Object Store). Changing the physical expression annotation as follows, yields a plan that entails accessing only those technical books having at least a topic different from Object Store:

```
<gen>   IN(
<pro>     F(TechBook*, TechBook*_Book.Language='English'
                          ∧ TechBook*_Book.Author='John Smith'),
<bup>     MB(E, TechBook*_TechBook.Topics,
<bup>      F(Topic*, Topic*_Topic.Description<>'Object Store')))
```

```
10000#     314$    T0   = pids Topic*
 9999#   20314$    T1   = F[Topic*_Topic.Description<>Object Store] T0
10000#   25569$    T2   = MB[TechBook*_TechBook.Topics] T1 by link
    1#   20158$  ! T7   = F[TechBook*_Book.Author=John Smith ^
                             TechBook*_Book.Language=English] T2
Execution cost:   66355$.
```

Advance set *T2* is generated by the intersection operator (through its navigation operand) and then propagated to the selection operator on *TechBook** collection.

If the annotation is the following, a plan that avoids the scan of collections is obtained. Only those topics referenced by at least a technical book stored in *TechBook** collection (i.e. technical books not written in Italian) are accessed:

```
<bup>   IN(
<bup>     F(TechBook*, TechBook*_Book.Language='English'
                          ∧ TechBook*_Book.Author='John Smith'),
<gen>     MB(E, TechBook*_TechBook.Topics,
<pro>      F(Topic*, Topic*_Topic.Description<>'Object Store')))
```

```
10000#     314$    T0   = pids TechBook*
 9504#   25563$    T1   = MF[TechBook*_TechBook.Topics] T0 by link
 9504#   19306$    T6   = F[Topic*_Topic.Description<>Object Store] T1
10000#   24281$    T7   = MB[TechBook*_TechBook.Topics] T6 by link
10000#    1303$   *T8   = sort T7
    4#     161$    T9   = F[TechBook*_Book.Author=John Smith] TechBook*
                               by Vix# 2
    1#      10$    T10  = F[TechBook*_Book.Language=English] T9
    1#       1$   *T11  = sort T10
    1#     159$  !*T12  = T8 INT T11
Execution cost:   71098$.
```

In this case, advance set *T1* is created by the map operator and propagated to the selection operator on *Topic** collection. Next, the annotation that gives rise to the optimised plan is presented: it performs a join reordering, only those topics referenced by technical books written in English by John Smith are accessed.

```
<gen>   IN(
<bup>     F(TechBook*, TechBook*_Book.Language='English'
                     ∧ TechBook*_Book.Author='John Smith'),
<pro>     MB(E, TechBook*_TechBook.Topics,
<pro>       F(Topic*, Topic*Topic.Description<>'Object Store')))
    4#     161$    T0   = F[TechBook*_Book.Author=John Smith] TechBook*
                               by Vix# 2
    1#      10$    T1   = F[TechBook*_Book.Language=English] T0
    4#       7$    T2   = MF[TechBook*_TechBook.Topics] T1 by link
    4#      10$    T7   = F[Topic*_Topic.Description<>Object Store] T2
   12#      13$    T8   = MB[TechBook*_TechBook.Topics] T7 by link
   12#       1$   *T9   = sort T8
    1#       1$   *T10  = sort T1
    1#       3$  !*T11  = T9 INT T10
Execution cost:     206$.
```

The next section will present an effective method for changing the physical expression annotation, so that various plans exploiting different access strategies can be evaluated and compared.

4.4 Local Search

The physical optimisation problem (i.e. the selection of the optimum access plan for a given physical query) is a hard combinatorial problem. Various general techniques have been developed for tackling this kind of problem. In particular, randomised search strategies do not enumerate the entire search space (in our case the set of equivalent plans associated with the simplified physical expression), but attain a *local optimum* possibly different from the global optimum: *local search* [14] is the one chosen for the design of the physical optimisation phase in PIOS.

Two concepts are very important for the local search technique:

- *Move*: a perturbation applied to a state belonging to the search space to get another state;
- *Neighbourhood of a state P*: the set of states reachable from *P* with a single move.

The procedure (see Figure 2) begins with an *initial state*; a move is accepted if the adjacent state being moved to is of lower cost than the current state. This is done repeatedly until the algorithm attains a state whose cost is lower than that of all neighbouring states (i.e. *local optimum*). After that, a *new starting state* is obtained by making a fixed number of moves from the local optimum; this time each move is accepted irrespective of whether it increases or decreases the cost. When a certain stopping condition is satisfied the entire process is halted and the best local optimum encountered is returned.

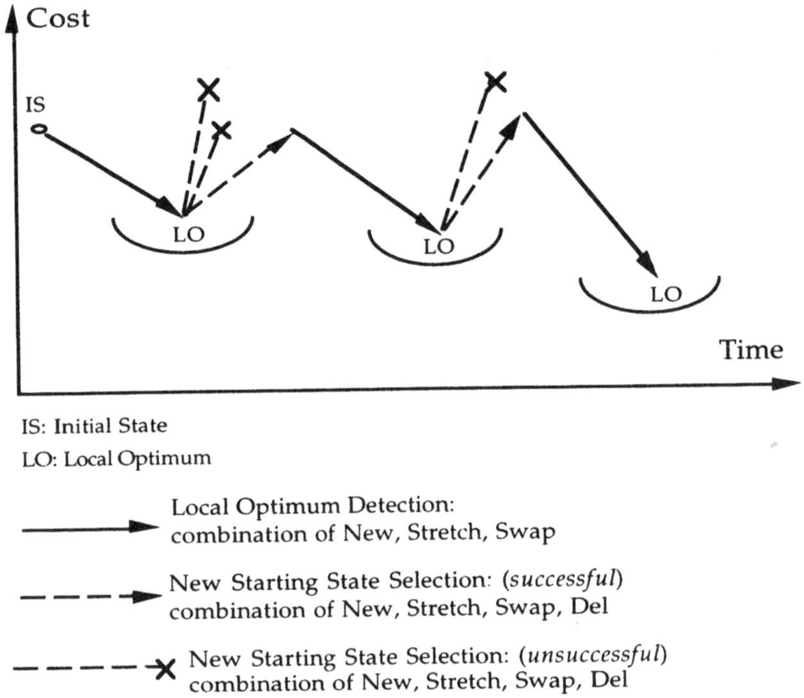

Fig. 2. Local Search algorithm

This general technique has been tailored to the specific problem of query optimisation by defining the following aspects:

1. *Selection of the initial state*: all operators of the physical expression are tagged with the *bottom-up* role. Navigation indices to be used are selected through heuristics based on the length of the navigation [5]. The problem of choosing the best value index for the execution of a certain selection condition has already been widely studied, therefore standard criteria are used. For each new plan inspected by the search, the choice of value indices is repeated.

2. *Move set*: moves are functions that take as input the annotated physical expression and a particular operator belonging to it and change the annotation according to a certain rule. Three moves have been defined for the local optimum search phase:

New: a filter operator, annotated with *bottom-up* role and deemed particularly slow to perform, is selected, and an attempt to provide an advance set for it is made. For that purpose an operator with advance set propagation capabilities (i.e. an operator with an already attached advance set or an operator that can generate such a set) is selected from the filter's ancestor operators.

Stretch: an operator annotated with *generator* role is selected and, in a fashion similar to that devised for the *New* move, an attempt to provide an advance set for it is made.

Swap: an intersection operator with either *generator* or *propagator* role is selected, and the order of propagation of the advance sets towards two of its operand expressions is reversed.

3. *Local optimum detection*: it would be impractical to exhaustively enumerate all the neighbours of the current state to verify its local optimality. Instead, an approximation based on random sampling is used.

4. *New starting state selection*: it is obtained by making a fixed number of moves from the local optimum without evaluating the cost of the associated plans. Another type of move is added to the move set for this phase only:

   Del: an operator annotated with *generator* role is selected and the advance set it creates is deleted. Of course, the annotation of the entire subexpression may be affected.

5. *Stopping criterion*: the process is stopped either by a timeout or when the cost of the current plan is less than a previously estimated lower bound on the cost of global minimum.

6. *Move selection criterion*: moves are chosen from the move set at random. The probability associated with selecting any particular move is specified along with the move set. Every time an infeasible move is attempted its selection probability is diminished, and those of the other moves are increased accordingly.

The latter mechanism leads to a twofold adaptability aspect in the random selection of a move: (*i*) *topological adaptability*: probabilities tend to adjust in a way that reflects the shape of the physical query DAG (e.g. a shallow DAGs will force the Stretch move probability to a low value); (*ii*) *temporal adaptability*: certain moves are more useful at an early stage of the local search, others at a later stage. As the former start failing, the latter start being selected more and more often (e.g. *New* move is generally needed at the beginning of the search, in order to create several advance sets, while *Stretch* move and *Swap* move start being useful later for circulating the previously created advance sets).

Local optimum detection, new starting state selection, stopping criterion, and move selection probabilities allow the definition of several parameters that can be used for the fine tuning of the local search procedure. Moreover, modifying the moves guarantees the optimiser adaptability and extensibility.

Example

Let's examine how the local search procedure can change the bottom-up annotation in order to obtain the one that gives rise to the optimised plan. Bottom-up annotation is a local optimum: changing the annotation of whatever selection operator increases the estimated execution cost. Therefore a new starting state must be reached. Let's suppose that *New* move is performed on selection operator on *Topic** collection: the latter is annotated with the *propagator* role, while a map operator is tagged with the *generator* role.

Our goal is eventually attained if the *Stretch* move is then performed on a map operator: the latter is annotated with the *propagator* role, while intersection operator is annotated with the *generator* role. This is feasible because the intersection operator creates an advance set using the result computed by the filter operator on *TechBook** collection.

4.5 Performance Results

In this section we present some meaningful examples of performance gains resulting from algebraic and physical optimisation, considering four sample queries. Remember that the numbers reported are the results (also intermediate results) of the processing of these queries on the PIOS system. The database used contains synthetic data, artificially generated with uniform distribution of attribute values. Uniform distribution is considered a worst case assumption for database query optimisation, since non-uniform distributions, allowing a more efficient clustering of data on disk, can give better performance. Therefore, we have used a uniform distribution to show an upper-bound of costs. Selected queries are the following:

Query a: Find all technical books written in English by John Smith, having at least a topic different from Object Store. It is the example query used throughout this paper.

Query b: Find all technical books written in English by an author different from John Smith, having Object Store as topic. It similar to the preceding, except that conditions on author and topic are inverted.

Query c: Find all technical books written in English by John Smith that do not have History as topic. It is formulated using a universally quantified map operator (i.e. **MB**(**A**, TechBook_Topics, ...)).

Query d: Find all Italian libraries in a "baroque style" building. It involves a collection (i.e., *Building*) which contains very large objects (the BuildingPicture attribute contains a bit-map image), therefore the optimiser has to try to avoid its scan.

For each of the above queries, the following four plans are estimated (results are presented in Figure 3):

1. *Plan without optimisation*: the initial logical expression is directly translated into a physical expression. Therefore both algebraic and physical optimisation are ignored.

2. *Initial plan*: it is obtained by performing algebraic optimisation only (i.e. logical level algebraic optimisation and pruning).

3. *Initial plan with naive indices*: it is obtained by performing a naive selection of value and navigation indices on the preceding plan. Selection of existing indices is based on heuristics.

4. *Optimised plan*: it is the standard result of the process of query optimisation as described in Sections 3 and 4.

Comparing the values of *Plan without optimisation* with those of *Initial plan with naive indices*, we can observe how algebraic optimisation, combined with an index selection guided by heuristics, is generally able to reduce by an order of magnitude the expected execution time. This gain is particularly notable for queries that can be pruned according to the actual storage organisation and when predicates involving primitive attributes on which value indices are maintained are rather selective.

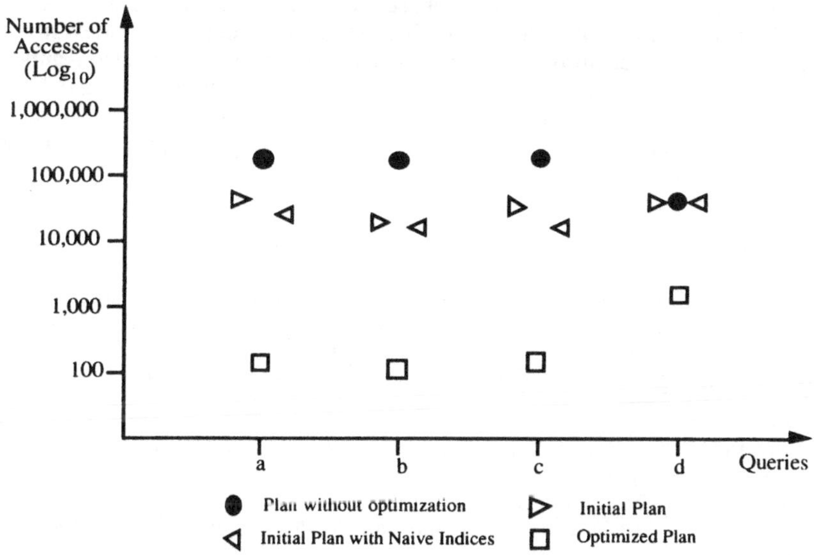

Fig. 3. Performance results (accesses to secondary storage)

However, the cost-driven process of physical optimisation (i.e. notice the values of *Optimised plan*) can further reduce by two orders of magnitude the expected execution time. Considering that the local search procedure has to make only a few attempts to obtain the annotation giving rise to the optimised plan of the above queries, the physical optimisation process proves its effectiveness.

5 Conclusion

In this paper, we have presented the entire process of query processing in PIOS, an object server which supports physical data independence. In particular, the declarative, set-oriented query language and the various phases which allow a sound and complete algebraic optimisation have been described. The result of this phase is a physical expression that becomes the feasible starting point for the critical process of physical optimisation: a local search procedure, which exploits a specific cost model based on statistics of stored data, has been designed in order to obtain an optimised access plan within a reasonable amount of resource (i.e. CPU time and central memory).

The search space is modelled by annotating with *roles* the physical expression operators. It includes the selection of the best ordering for path navigations (starting everywhere in the path expression) and the choice of available value and navigation indices: experimental results on artificial data, assuming uniform distribution, show that these techniques, combined in a system supporting fragmentation of objects, are capable of speeding up the execution of queries by orders of magnitude. In particular, the cost-driven physical optimisation phase, usually ignored by existing query optimisers of OODBMSs, has proved its effectiveness. In fact, it is able to generate and estimate plans that would be discarded by systems based on rewrite rules and heuristics.

The overall physical optimisation phase has been designed in order to be easily extensible to new advanced query processing techniques and/or new index structures: adding new local search moves able to change the physical expression annotation should be sufficient to extend the search space. Moreover, various parameters have been defined for the local search procedure, so that its progressive fine tuning can tackle the traditional trade-off between the resources used for optimisation and the quality of the results produced.

References

1. F. Rabitti, G. Mainetto, P. Zezula, S. Barneva, N. Aloia, L. Benedetti, S. Biscari, P. Carcaci, E. Criscuoli, F. Demi, F. Giannasio, and U. Pasquali. Design and Implementation of PIOS: a Physically Independent Object Server. In Technical Report FIDE/93/70, ESPRIT BRA Project No. 6309, FIDE-2 (Formally Integrated Data Environment), 1993
2. F. Rabitti, L. Benedetti, and F. Demi. Query Processing in PIOS. In Technical Report FIDE/94/83, ESPRIT BRA Project No. 6309, FIDE-2 (Formally Integrated Data Environment), 1994
3. M. Atkinson, F. Bancilhon, D. DeWitt, K. Dittrich, D. Maier, and S. Zdonik. The Object-Oriented Database System Manifesto. In Proceedings of DOOD-89, Kyoto, Japan, 1989
4. N. Aloia, S. Barneva, and F. Rabitti. Supporting Physical Independence in an Object Database Server. In Proceedings of ECOOP-92, 1992
5. P. Zezula and F. Rabitti. Object Store with Navigation Accelerator. In Information Systems Vol. 18, No. 7, Springer-Verlag, 1993
6. G. Shaw and S. Zdonik. An Object-Oriented Query Algebra. In Proceedings of DBPL-89, Salishan Lodge, Oregon, 1989
7. D. D. Straube and M. T. Özsu. Queries and Query Processing in Object-Oriented Database Systems. In ACM Transactions on Information Systems Vol. 8, No. 4, 1990
8. S. Cluet. Langages et Optimisation de Requêtes pour Systèmes de Gestion de Base de Données Orientés-Objet. Thèse de doctorat présentée à l'Université de Paris-Sud - Centre d'Orsay, 1991
9. P. Jenq, D. Woelk, W. Kim, and W. Lee. Query Processing in Distributed ORION. In Proceedings of EDBT, Venice, Italy, 1990

10. A. Kemper and G. Moerkotte. Advanced Query Processing in Object Bases Using Access Support Relations. In Proceeedings of VLDB-90, Brisbane, Australia, 1990
11. R. Lanzelotte, P. Valduriez, M. Ziane, and J. Cheiney. Optimization of Nonrecursive Queries in OODBs. In Proceedings of DOOD-91, 1991
12. R. Lanzelotte and P. Valduriez. Extending the Search Strategy in a Query Optimizer. In Proceedings of VLDB-91, Barcelona, Spain, 1991
13. A. Swami. Optimization of Large Join Queries: Combining Heuristics and Combinatorial Techniques. In Proceedings of ACM-SIGMOD-89, 1989
14. C. H. Papadimitriou and K. Steiglitz. Combinatorial Optimization: Algorithms and Complexity. Prentice Hall, 1982
15. P. Selinger, M. Astrahan, D. Chamberlin, R. Lorie, and T. Price. Access Path Selection in a Relational Database Management System. In Proceedings of ACM-SIGMOD-79, 1979
16. Y. Ioannidis and Y. Cha Kang. Left-Deep vs. Bushy Trees: an Analysis of Strategy Spaces and its Implications for Query Optimization. In Proceedings of ACM-SIGMOD-91, 1991
17. R. Lanzelotte, P. Valduriez, and M. Ziane. On the Effectiveness of Optimization Search Strategies for Parallel Execution Spaces. In Proceedings of VLDB-93, Dublin, Ireland, 1993

Appendix A. Example Database

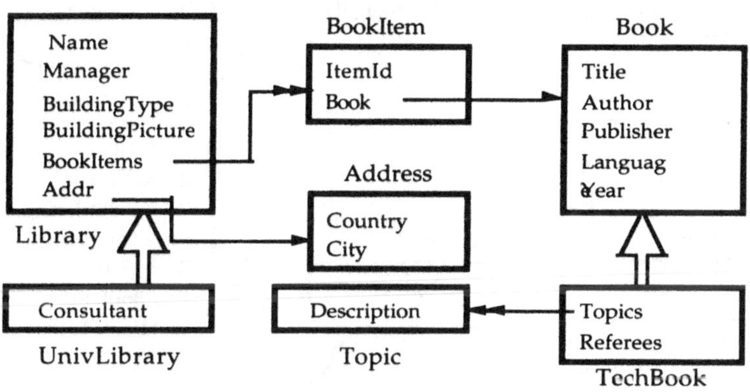

Fig. A.1 Logical schema

An example of a *logical schema* is presented in Figure A.1. The main entities represented in it are libraries and books. Libraries contain book items referring to books. Moreover, there exist university libraries characterised by a consultant and technical books characterised by a set of topics. In Figure A.2 is depicted an example of a *storage schema* obtained as result of a process of storage level design. In particular,

- the class hierarchy involving *Library* and *UnivLibrary* classes is stored with the SDS strategy, while the other class hierarchy, involving *Book* and *TechBook*, is stored with the ODS strategy;

- the *BuildingPicture* attribute (a long binary data field) is stored separately from its library object (together with the associated *BuildingType*);
- technical books written in Italian are stored in a different collection (*ItalTechBook*);
- libraries are stored together with their address;
- three value indices (the associated attributes are underlined in Figure A.2) are defined: *Library.Name*, *Book.Author* and *Topic.Description*;
- a navigation index id defined: the references involved have a circle in Figure A.2.

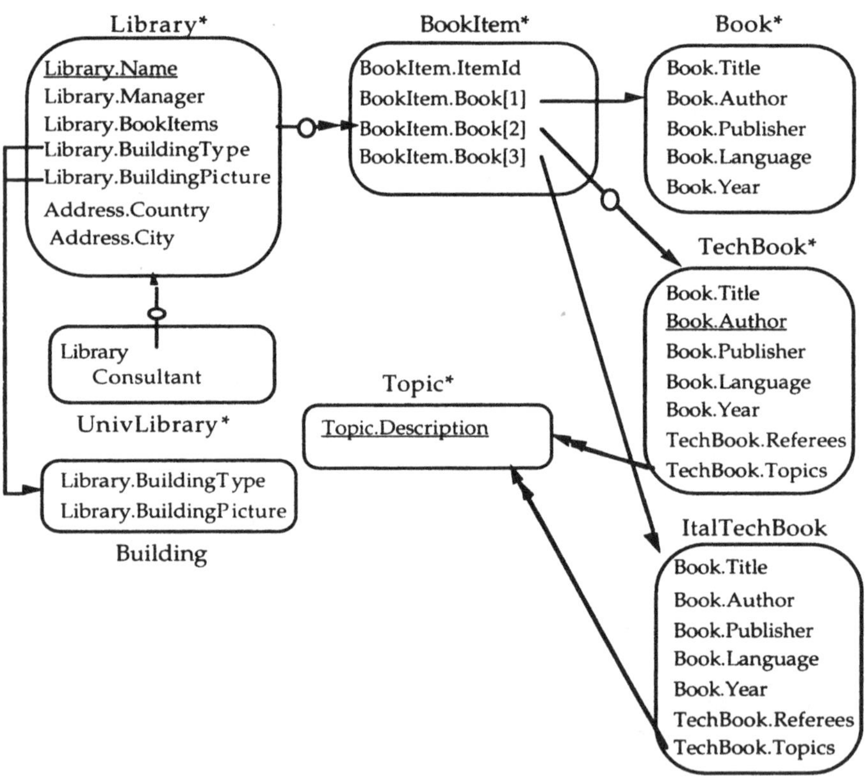

Fig. A.2 Storage schema

Chapter 2.3.4

Optimization of Nested Queries in Object Bases

Sophie Cluet[1] and Guido Moerkotte[2]

[1] INRIA, BP 105, 78153 Le Chesnay Cedex, France
[2] Lehrstuhl für Informatik III, RWTH-Aachen, 52074 Aachen, Germany

1 Introduction

A fundamental characteristic of declarative query languages is the nesting of queries (embedding of a query within another query). In the object-oriented (oo) context, nested queries are used to (i) express complex conditions, (ii) access nested structures and (iii) produce nested results. We propose novel techniques for efficiently evaluating nested queries in oo languages.

Until recently, optimization of oo nested queries has remained largely unexplored. Although most oo algebras [1,2,5,12,20,22,23] support nested algebraic expressions (e.g. a join may occur within the predicate of a selection), no rewrite rules have been proposed to deal with these nested parts. Thus, they remain nested throughout the rewriting process and are finally evaluated by potentially inefficient nested loops.

In [6], we presented some original optimization techniques for simple nested queries. In [21], more optimization was supported using the ADL algebra. Compared to these previous works, our present contribution is threefold: (i) we cover the whole spectrum of nested queries, (ii) for most queries, we propose several rewriting alternatives whose efficiency depends on the context and (iii) we present the exact equations on which the rewriting relies. These equations may seem intricate but are essential to the design of an optimizer.

Naturally, our research has been influenced by the work on the optimization of relational nested queries [15,14,9,8,10,17,18]. The classification introduced in [15] proved to be useful for relational unnesting. Based on this observation, we extended this classification to the oo context. This extension is necessary due to the orthogonality of oo SQL-like query languages compared to the relational SQL.

Also, the relational idea of using different join operators for unnesting nested queries will be carried over to the oo context [15,8,10,17]. However, as opposed to the relational context, where unnesting is performed at the SQL level, we use algebraic equivalences. Thus, our work can be applied to different query languages, if a translation procedure into the algebra is given. Further, we show that, due to the nesting in the oo data structures ($\neg$1NF), there exist more elegant and efficient alternatives for unnesting queries. First, we can avoid null values. They are needed in the relational context to represent mis-fits in the joins (outer-joins) introduced by the unnesting process. This is more naturally captured by empty sets in the oo context. Secondly, the **group-by** of SQL is captured in the relational context in a distorted manner using operations that couple grouping with aggregation. In the oo context, explicit grouping operations are a necessity but they also yield more flexibility for expressing and rewriting queries. This results in alternative unnesting techniques not known in the relational context.

Due to space limitation, this paper concentrates on one-level nested queries without quantification. Queries with quantification as well as more complex unnesting strategies including the treatment of several levels of nesting, non-neighbour predicates and outer restrictions can be found in [7]. The paper is organised as follows. The next section introduces some preliminaries, namely the algebra and the translation of SQL-like queries into the algebra. The core of the paper is contained in Section 3. It represents the classification of oo nested queries together with the algebraic equivalences used for unnesting. We review some results of [6] and introduce new unnesting techniques for those cases which could not be unnested so far. Section 4 concludes the paper.

2 Preliminaries

2.1 Algebra

We assume standard knowledge on oo data models. Our underlying data model conforms to the Object Database Standard [3]. It features objects that have an identity, that are manipulated through user-defined methods, whose structures are complex and that belong to classes that may be refined into subclasses. Each class has an extension which is a set containing the object identifiers of all its instances. The model also features complex values (or literals) with no identity, that are manipulated by standard operators and do not belong to classes. Hence, there are no extensions for them.

The algebra is an extension of the GOM algebra [13]. Its main characteristic is that — with the exception of the map operator — it is defined on sets of tuples. This guaranties some nice properties among which is the associativity of the join operator.

We now restate the algebraic operators that will be used in the sequel. Union, intersection and difference operators, that are part of the algebra, are not reviewed.

Map Operations (and Projection): These operators are fundamental to the algebra. Since the other operators are defined on sets of tuples, sets of non-tuples (mostly sets of objects) must be transformed into sets of tuples. This is one purpose of the map operator. Other purposes are dereferencing, method and function application. Also, our translation process pushes all nesting into map operators.

The first definition corresponds to the standard map [13] or materialize [2] operator. The second and third definition are just shorthands: the second is a map with tuple concatenation and the third a map with tuple construction.

$$\chi_{e_2}(e_1) = \{e_2(x) | x \in e_1\}$$
$$\chi_{a:e_2}(e_1) = \{y \circ [a : e_2(y)] | y \in e_1\}$$
$$e[a] = \{[a : x] | x \in e\}$$

In the definitions, the e_i's denote both expressions (in the left hand side) and their evaluation (in the right hand side). Note that the oo map operator obviates the need for relational projection. Sometimes the map operator is equivalent to a simple projection or renaming. In these cases, we will use π instead of χ.

Selection: Note that in the following definition there is no restriction on the selection predicate. It may contain path expressions, method calls, nested algebraic operators, etc.

$$\sigma_p(e) = \{x|x \in e, p(x)\}$$

Join Operations: On top of the standard join operator ($\bowtie$), the algebra features the semi-join ($\ltimes$), anti-join ($\triangleright$) and left outer-join ($⟕$) operators that, as in the relational context, are needed for unnesting purposes. They are defined similarly to their relational counterparts. One difference is that the left outer-join accepts a default value to be given, instead of null, to one attribute of its right argument.

$$\begin{aligned}
e_1 \bowtie_p e_2 &= \{y \circ x | y \in e_1, x \in e_2, p(y,x)\} \\
e_1 \ltimes_p e_2 &= \{y | y \in e_1, \exists x \in e_2, (p(y,x))\} \\
e_1 \triangleright_p e_2 &= \{y | y \in e_1, \neg\exists x \in e_2\ p(y,x)\} \\
e_1 ⟕_p^{g=c} e_2 &= \{y \circ x | y \in e_1, x \in e_2, p(y,x)\} \cup \\
&\quad \{y \circ z | y \in e_1, \neg\exists x \in e_2\ p(y,x), \mathcal{A}(z) = \mathcal{A}(e_2), g \in \mathcal{A}(e_2), \\
&\quad z.g = c, \forall a \in \mathcal{A}(e_2)(a \neq g \Rightarrow z.a = NULL)\}
\end{aligned}$$

The function $\mathcal{A}$ used in the last definition returns the set of attributes of a relation.

Another join operator is called *d-join* ($< \cdot >$). It is a join between two sets, where the evaluation of the second set may depend on the first set. It is needed to translate **from** clauses into the algebra (see below). Whenever possible, d-joins are rewritten into standard joins.

$$e_1 < e_2 > = \{y \circ x | y \in e_1, x \in e_2(y)\}$$

As an example, let us consider a set whose name is *Emps* ant that contains two objects. The objects represent employees and their identifiers are e_1 and e_2. Let us consider another set whose name is *Sales* and that contains three objects s_1, s_2 and s_3 representing sales. Let us further suppose that employees have an attribute whose name is *sales* and that $e_1.sales = \{s_1, s_2\}$, $e_2.sales = \{s_3\}$. Then,

$$\begin{aligned}
Emps[e] &= = \{[e : e_1], [e : e_2]\} \\
Emps[e] < e.sales[s] > &= \{[e : e_1, s : s_1], [e : e_1, s : s_2], [e : e_2, s : s_3]\} \\
&= Emps[e] \bowtie_{s \in e.sales} Sales[s]
\end{aligned}$$

Grouping Operations: Two grouping operators will be used for unnesting purposes. The first one — called *unary grouping* — is defined on a set and its subscript indicates (i) the attribute receiving the grouped elements (ii) the grouping criterion, and (iii) a function that will be applied to each group.

$$\begin{aligned}
\Gamma_{g;A\theta;f}(e) = \{&y.A \circ [g : G] | y \in e, \\
&G = f(\{x | x \in e, x.A\theta y.A\})\}
\end{aligned}$$

Note that the traditional nest operator [19] is a special case of unary grouping. It is equivalent to $\Gamma_{g;A=;id}$. Note also that the grouping criterion may be defined on several attributes. Then, A and θ represent sequences of attributes and comparators.

As an example, let us consider again the set $Emps$ of employee and let us suppose that e_1 and e_2 have an attribute whose name is *age* and whose value is respectively 32 and 33. Then,

$$\begin{aligned} Map_{a:e.age}(Emps[e]) &= \{[a:32, e:e_1], [a:33, e:e_2]\} \\ \Gamma_{g;a\leq;id}(Map_{a:e.age}(Emps[e])) &= \{[a:32, g:\{[a:32, e:e_1]\}], \\ &\quad [a:33, g:\{[a:32, e:e_1], \\ &\quad [a:33, e:e_2]\}\} \\ \Gamma_{c;age\leq;count}(Map_{a:e.age}(Emps[e])) &= \{[age:32, c:1], [age:33, c:2\} \end{aligned}$$

The second grouping operator — called *binary grouping* — is defined on two sets. The elements of the second set are grouped according to a criterion that depends on the elements of the first argument.

$$e_1 \Gamma_{g;A_1\theta A_2;f} e_2 = \{y \circ [g:G] | y \in e_1, G = f(\{x | x \in e_2, y.A_1 \theta x.A_2\})\}$$

Below is an example of binary grouping.

$$\begin{aligned} R1 &= Map_{bsa:e.bestsale.amount}(Emps[e]) \\ &= \{[e:e_1, bsa:10000], [e:e_2, bsa:15000]\} \\ R2 &= Map_{a:s.amount}(Sales[s]) \\ &= \{[s:s_1, a:10000], [s:s_2, a:9000], [s:s_3, a:15000]\} \\ R1\ \Gamma_{c;bsa<a;count} R2 &= \{[e:e_1, bsa:10000, c:1], [e:e_2, bsa:15000, c:0]\}\} \end{aligned}$$

In the sequel, the following abbreviations will be used: $\Gamma_{g;A;f}$ for $\Gamma_{g;A=;f}$ and $\Gamma_{g;A}$ for $\Gamma_{g;A;id}$.

New implementation techniques have to be developed for these grouping operators. Obviously, those used for nest operator can be used for simple grouping when θ stands for equality. For the other cases, implementations based on sorting seem promising. We also consider adapting algorithms for non-equi joins.

Max Operation: The Max operator has a very specific use that will be explained in the sequel. Note that an analogous Min operator can be defined.

$$Max_{g;m;a\theta;f}(e) = [m : max(\{x.a | x \in e\}), g : f(\{x | x \in e, x.a\theta m\})]$$

The algebra is defined on sets whereas most OODBMS also manipulate lists and bags. We believe that our approach can be easily extended by considering lists as set of tuples with an added positional attribute and bags as sets of tuples with an added occurrence counter attribute.

2.2 Translating SQL-like Queries into the Algebra

We use the ODMG standard query language OQL [3] for the examples. However, since we unnest at the algebraic level, the techniques that we present are not restricted to OQL but can be applied to any other reasonnable oo query language. The schema on which the queries are defined represents a company. It can be easily inferred from the queries and, hence, we will not detail it.

In [6], we showed the importance of factoring out constant or locally constant subqueries as well as common subexpressions. For this purpose, we introduced a phase preceding the optimization process. This phase — called *dependency-based optimization* — transforms the SQL-like query by introducing one variable per subquery. Thereby, common subexpressions are factorized; two occurrences of the same subquery are represented by only one variable. Further, expressions not dependent on the current block are pushed into higher-level blocks.

Below is an OQL query before (left hand-side) and after (right hand-side) the dependency-based transformation. With each employee's age, the query associates the number of sales made by younger employees.

```
select [age:x2.age,
        nb:count(select s
                 from  x in Emp
                       s in x.sales
                 where x.age < x2.age)]
from  x2 in Emp
```

```
select [age:x2a, nb:cs]
from   x2 in Emp
define x2a = x2.age,
       cs = count(select s
                  from  x in Emp
                        s in x.sales
                  where xa < x2a
                  define xa = x.age
```

The transformed query features a new **define** clause in every block. Here, variables are introduced that represent expressions dependent on its owner block only. Thus, the operation $x.age$ is now part of the outer block.

The following algebraic expression corresponds to the outer block of the query:

$$q \equiv \chi_{[age:x2a,nb:cs]}(\chi_{cs:e_{inner}}(\chi_{x2a:x2.age}(Emp[x2])))$$

The **from** clause contains only one variable whose definition is translated by $Emp[x2]$. This allows us to view the set of object identifiers, i.e. the extension of *Emp*, as a unary relation with attribute $x2$. Note that this attribute allows us to avoid λ-expressions found in other oo algebras. The next two map operators correspond to the **define** clause. Their effect is to augment the initial relation with two more attributes representing the *age* and the result of the nested block (e_{inner}). The last map operator corresponds to the **select** clause.

Let us now take a look at the inner block's algebraic expression.

$$e_{inner} \equiv count(\chi_s(\sigma_{xa<x2a}(\chi_{xa:x.age}(Emp[x] < x.sales[s] >))))$$

The **from** clause of the inner block contains two variable definitions: this is translated by a d-join ($Emp[x] < x.sales[s] >$). Note that a standard join could not be used since the evaluation of *x.sales* obviously depends on the value of *x*. The inner block features a **where** clause. This is represented — as might be expected — by a selection. Note that in this example, the last map operator (χ_s) is used to transform a relation into a set of objects.

In the sequel, for readability, we will sometimes combine map operations with other operators.

3 Classification and Algebraic Optimization

In this section we present a classification of oo nested queries along with appropriate algebraic optimization techniques. The classification extends the relational classification of [15] which introduced five types of nested queries. One of them is not used here (Type D). The reason is that unnesting of Type D queries is subsumed by our generalized treatment of Type N and J queries. The four remaining types from [15] are:

- **Type A** nested queries have a constant inner block that returns a single element.
- **Type N** nested queries have a constant inner block that returns a set.
- **Type J** nested queries have an inner block that is dependent on the outer block and returns a set.
- **Type JA** nested queries have an inner block that is dependent on the outer block and returns a single element.

Obviously, the need for extending the original classification arises from the richness of the oo model compared with the relational one and its impact on the query language. The classification we propose has three dimensions: the original one plus two that are required by the following oo characteristics. In the oo context, as opposed to the relational, (i) nested blocks may be located in any clause of a **select-from-where** block and (ii) a dependency (i.e. reference to a variable defined in an outer block) may occur in any clause. The organisation of this section follows the three dimensions. We start by presenting nested queries of Type A/N/J/JA with nesting and dependency in the **where** clause. This will allow us to show the differences and similarities between relational and oo unnesting techniques. We continue by explaining the treatment required by other locations of nesting (i.e. **select** and **from** clauses). We end with the optimization of Type J/JA queries with range (**from** clause) or projection (**select** clause) dependencies.

3.1 Different Types of Nesting

3.1.1 Queries of Type A

Below is an example of a type A query. It returns the employees with the maximum sales. The inner block is constant and returns a single numerical value.

```
select x2
from   x2 in Emp
where  x2.TotSales =
         max (select x.TotSales
              from   x in Emp)
```

```
define m = max(select xs
               from   x in Emp)
               define xs = x.TotSales
select x2
from   x2 in Emp
where  x2s = m
define x2s = x2.TotSales
```

Note that the first **define** clause is written before the outer block because its entry does not depend on any variable. The algebraic translation of the query is:

$$q \equiv \chi_{x2}(\sigma_{x2s=m}(\chi_{x2s:x2.TotSales}(Emp[x2])))$$
$$m \equiv max(\chi_{xs}(\chi_{xs:x.TotSales}(Emp[x])))$$
$$\equiv max(\chi_{x.TotSales}(Emp[x]))$$

For most queries of this kind, we rely on a technique similar to that of [15]. The constant inner block (m in the example) is evaluated first and its result is used for the evaluation of the outer block (q in the example).

However, for this query, as well as all min/max queries where inner and outer blocks have a common domain (Emp in the example), it is possible to do better than just pushing out the constant block [6]. The requirement of having a common domain seems rather restrictive but retrieving the elements exhibiting the min/max value implies just this. The idea is to use the scan needed for the evaluation of the inner block to also evaluate the outer block. This is exactly what the *Max* operator does. It is introduced by the following algebraic equivalence which is a slightly generalized version of the one found in [6]:

$$f(\sigma_{a\theta max(e_2)}(e_1)) \equiv Max_{g;m;a\theta;f}(e_1).g \qquad (1)$$
$$\text{if } e_2 = \pi_a(e_1)$$

Remember that the $Max_{g;m;a\theta;f}(e)$ operation returns a tuple containing (i) an attribute m representing the maximum value for the attribute a in the set e and (ii) an attribute g representing the result of f applied to the set of elements of e satisfying $a\theta m$.

Applying Eqn. 1 to the above query yields

$$q \equiv Max_{g;m;x2s;\chi_{x2}}(\chi_{x2s:x2.TotSales}(Emp[x2])).g$$

Note that the *Max* operator can be computed within a single pass (linear time) for $Max_{g;m\theta;f}$, if f is linear. Also note that an equivalent treatment for min can be applied. Furthermore, although the equivalence we used can easily be adapted to the relational context, we are not aware of any such optimization.

3.1.2 Queries of Type N

Below is an example of a Type N query. It returns the employees who have sold all the expensive products. As can be seen, the inner block is constant and, as opposed to type A queries, returns a collection that has to be scanned for every element of the outer block. This inner scan is the reason for considering techniques different from that of type A queries.

```
select x
from   x in Emp
where  x.SoldItems ⊇
         (select i
          from   i in Item
          where  i.price > 20000)
```

```
define ExpItems = select i
                  from   i in Item
                  where  p > 20000
                  define p = i.price
select x
from   x in Emp
where  xsi ⊇ ExpItems
define xsi = x.SoldItems
```

Its algebraic translation is the following:

$$q \equiv \chi_x(\sigma_{xsi \supseteq ExpItems}(\chi_{xsi:x.SoldItems}(Emp[x])))$$
$$ExpItems \equiv \chi_i(\sigma_{p>20000}(\chi_{p:i.price}(Item[i])))$$

In the above example, the predicate that connects outer and inner blocks is based on a set comparison. Set comparators are not supported by standard SQL. However, they are in the non-standard SQL of [15], where this query would be considered as **Type D** — resolved by division. Relational division implements very specific queries: i.e. there is a non strict inclusion relationship between outer and inner blocks (as in the above query). However, other set comparators are as likely as non-strict set inclusion and, should we choose the division solution, we would then have to introduce one division-like operation per set comparator. Furthermore, the division operation does not have particularly nice algebraic properties that we would like to exploit. This is why we rejected the Type D treatment of applying division.

We chose to leave type N queries with set comparisons as they are. We will explain our choice using the above query. First, note that the nesting itself has been solved by constant factorization. The nested query $ExpItems$ can be evaluated first, independently of expression q. Secondly, remember that, in the oo context, attributes may be sets. Thus, comparing set attributes in algebraic operations will arise commonly. Accordingly, it seems natural to support good algorithms for their evaluation.

Other possible predicates connecting inner and outer blocks are based on membership. For these, we could also rely on good implementations of the selection operator. We prefer to adapt techniques from the relational context [4,8,15] and use semi-join and anti-join for unnesting the **in** and **not in** cases. The interest for unnesting using join operations, apart from existing efficient algorithms, is that they have algebraic properties that can be used for further rewriting. Since these equivalences are not totally new, we refer the reader to [7].

3.1.3 Queries of Type J

In Type J, as opposed to Type N, the inner query is dependent on a variable of the outer block. Thus, it cannot be factored out. An example is given below. As for type N queries, the predicate connecting inner and outer blocks is based either on membership or on a set comparator. Again, queries with **in** (**not in**) can be transformed using semi-joins (anti-joins). The corresponding equivalences can be found in [7].

Now let us consider the following query with set comparison.

```
select x
from   x in Emp
where x.sales⊇
         (select s
          from   s in Sale
          where s.dept=x.dept and
                  s.amount>20000
```

```
select x
from   x in Emp
where xs⊇BestSales
define xs=x.sales
          xd=x.department
          BestSales = select s
                            from   s in Sale
                            where sd=xd and
                                     sa > 20000
                            define sd=s.dept
                                     sa=s.amount
```

The query returns the employees who have done all the expensive sales of their department. Note that it also corresponds to a relational Type D query. The algebraic translation of the query is split for clarity:

$$q \equiv \chi_x(\sigma_{xs \supseteq BestSales}(q_1))$$
$$q_1 \equiv \chi_{BestSales:\chi_s(\sigma_{sd=xd}(q_3))}(q_2)$$
$$q_2 \equiv \chi_{xd:x.dept,xs:x.sales}(Emp[x])$$
$$q_3 \equiv \sigma_{sa>2000}(\chi_{sd:s.dept,sa:s.amount}(Sale[s]))$$

The problem here is that the nested query q_1 evaluating $BestSales$ is not constant. In order to unnest the query and avoid several costly scans over the *Sale*s extension, we associate with each employee, the set of expensive sales of his/her department. For this, we rely on the following equivalence. It uses binary grouping.

$$\chi_{g:f(\sigma_{A_1\theta A_2}(e_2))}(e_1) \equiv e_1 \Gamma_{g;A_1\theta A_2;f} e_2 \quad (2)$$
$$\text{if } A_i \subseteq \mathcal{A}(e_i),\ \mathcal{F}(e_2) \cap \mathcal{A}(e_1) = \emptyset,\ g \notin A_1 \cup A_2$$

The conditions state that the A_i's are attributes of the e_i's, e_1 and e_2 must be independent, and g must not be an attribute of e_1 or e_2. Applying Eqn. 2 to q_1 yields:

$$q_1 \equiv q_2 \Gamma_{BestSales;xd=sd;\chi_s} q_3$$

If employees and sales are both sorted on their department, this binary group operation can be evaluated very efficiently in a single scan over the two sets. This simple evaluation is not possible when the grouping criterion is based on an operation different from equality. The selection in q_3 can be evaluated independently, e.g. using an index, or can be combined with the χ_s operator in the group. Note that the selection with set comparator $\supseteq$ is now evaluated between two attributes. As for type N queries, we rely on good algorithms for such selections.

The above equation is the most general and can be applied in all Type J queries (as well as to Type JA cases as will be shown in the sequel). There exist two other equations which may deal more efficiently, using simple grouping, with two special cases. The equation

$$\chi_{g:f(\sigma_{A_1=A_2}(e_2))}(e_1) \equiv \pi_{\overline{A_2}}(e_1 ⟕_{A_1=A_2}^{g=f(\emptyset)} (\Gamma_{g;A_2;f}(e_2))) \quad (3)$$
$$\text{if } A_i \subseteq \mathcal{A}(e_i),\ \mathcal{F}(e_2) \cap \mathcal{A}(e_1) = \emptyset,\ A_1 \cap A_2 = \emptyset,\ g \notin \mathcal{A}(e_1) \cup \mathcal{A}(e_2)$$

relies on the fact that the comparison of the correlation predicate is equality, as in the above example. The expression $\pi_{\overline{A_2}}$ eliminates the attribute(s) A_2 from the relation it is applied to. If we apply this equation on the original q_1 expression, it yields a new alternative:

$$q_1 \equiv \pi_{\overline{sd}}(q_2 ⟕_{sd=xd}^{BestSales=\emptyset} (\Gamma_{BestSales;sd;\chi_s}(q_3)))$$

Note that the binary grouping operation in the previous expression of q_1 now corresponds to a simple grouping followed by an outer-join (see below, also). The outer-join does not introduce null values for those employees whose department do not have expensive sales. The $\emptyset$ default value corresponds to the application of the operation χ_s on the empty set. The $\pi_{\overline{sd}}$ expression can be dropped due to the χ_x operation in q.

The next equation relies on the fact that there exists a common range for the variables of the correlation predicate (third condition). Its application will be illustrated in Subsection 3.2.1.

$$\begin{aligned} \chi_{g:f(\sigma_{A_1 \theta A_2}(e_2))}(e_1) &\equiv \pi_{A_1:A_2}(\Gamma_{g;A_2\theta;f}(e_2)) \\ \text{if } A_i \subseteq \mathcal{A}(e_i), \mathcal{F}(e_2) \cap \mathcal{A}(e_1) &= \emptyset, g \notin \mathcal{A}(e_1) \cup \mathcal{A}(e_2), \\ e_1 = \pi_{A_1:A_2}(e_2) &\text{ (this implies that } A_1 = \mathcal{A}(e_1)) \end{aligned} \tag{4}$$

It is important to note that the applicability of the above equivalences does not depend on the set comparison of the predicate in the outer **where** clause but, instead, on the correlation predicate within the inner block. This is opposed to the relational unnesting techniques which solely depend on the predicate restricting the outer block. This has one important consequence: a uniform treatment, independent of the predicate in the outer block, is possible. Hence, they enable the derivation of alternative unnested expressions for the **in** and **not in** cases. To see this, consider $\sigma_{A \in e_2}(e_1) \equiv \sigma_{A \in B}(\chi_{B:e_2}(e_1))$. Further, as illustrated in the next subsection, the equations can be used (unchanged!) for unnesting Type JA nested queries. That is why they should be considered *the core* of unnesting nested queries in the oo context. Also, since these equations also hold for set comparators as the predicate in the outer block, they obviate a special treatment of Type D queries as needed in the relational case.

Let us finally clarify the correspondence between the binary grouping and the unary grouping in conjunction with an outer-join:

$$\begin{aligned} \chi_{g:f(\sigma_{A'_1 \theta A'_2}(e_2))}(e_1) &\equiv \Gamma_{g;A_1;f \circ \pi_{\overline{A_1}} \circ \sigma_{A_2 \neq \perp_{A_2}}}(e_1 ⟕_{A'_1 \theta A'_2} e_2) \\ \text{if } A_i = \mathcal{A}(e_i), A'_i &\subseteq A_i, g \notin A_1 \cup A_2, \mathcal{F}(e_2) \cap A_1 = \emptyset \end{aligned} \tag{5}$$

Here, $\circ$ represents function composition and $\perp_A$ is a tuple with attributes A and null values only. This alternative first produces an intermediate flat result which is subsequently grouped. The range of applicability of this equation is the same as for Eqn. 2 which introduces a binary grouping. Concatenating Eqns. 2 and 5 gives the correspondence between binary and unary grouping in conjunction with an outer-join. If several of the Eqns. 2–5 apply, chosing the most appropriate is a matter of costs.

3.1.4 Queries of Type JA

The difference between Type J and Type JA queries is that, for the latter, an aggregate function (e.g, count, max) is applied to the inner block.

However, this difference between Type J and Type JA queries does not necessitate new unnesting techniques. Indeed, the grouping operators, that we used for unnesting type J queries, have been defined to allow the application of an arbitrary function to each formed group. For Type J queries, this function usually is a map operator. For Type JA queries this is an (additional) aggregate function. Thus, by applying Equations 2–5, aggregated Type JA queries are treated in exactly the same manner as Type J queries. The following subsection will give an example.

It is interesting to note that Eqn. 3, when used on Type JA queries (i.e. with an aggregate function), captures the technique introduced by [8] for relational type JA queries. His technique relies on an operator called *generalized aggregation* combining a grouping with an aggregate.

3.2 Different Locations of Nesting

So far, we studied queries where the nesting was used to express complex conditions (nesting in the **where** clause). Nesting has other purposes in the oo context, too. It can be used to produce nested results (**select** clause) or access nested structures (**from** clause). This is what we study now.

3.2.1 Nesting in the *select* Clause

Although nothing forbids it, Type A or N nesting rarely occurs in **select** clauses. Indeed, there is not much sense in associating a constant (set or element) with each element of a set. Should that happen, we rely on the first phase of the optimization process to factor out the constant block. Thus, it will only be evaluated once. We do not believe in or consider further optimization.

For Type J/JA queries, nesting in the **select** clause is equivalent to nesting in the **where** clause. Remember that the application of Eqns. 2–5 did not depend on the predicate in the outer **where** block but on the correlation predicate within the inner block. I.e. it did not depend on the location of the nesting, but on the fact that a dependency between inner and outer block existed in the form of a selection. Hence, Eqns. 2–4 can be used whenever nesting occurs in the **select** clause. To illustrate this, let us consider the following Type JA query that associates to each employee's age, the number of sales made by younger employees.

```
select [age:x2.age,
        nb:count(select s
                 from   x in Emp
                        s in x.sales
                 where  x.age < x2.age)]
from  x2 in Emp
```

```
select  [age:x2a, nb:cs]
from    x2 in Emp
define  x2a = x2.age,
        cs =  count(select s
                    from   x in Emp
                           s in x.sales
                    where  xa < x2a
                    define xa = x.age
```

The algebraic expression is the following:

$$q \equiv \chi_{[age:x2a,nb:cs]}(\chi_{cs:e_{inner}}(\chi_{x2a:x2.age}(Emp[x2])))$$
$$e_{inner} \equiv count(\chi_s(\sigma_{xa<x2a}(\chi_{xa:x.age}(Emp[x] < x.sales[s] >))))$$

Assume that every employee has at least one sale. Then, we may use advantageously the fact that one variable (x) of the inner block ranges over the same set (all of the employees) as the variable of the outer block (x2) to apply equivalence 4.

$$q \equiv \chi_{[age:x2a,nb:cs]}(\pi_{x2a:xa}\Gamma_{cs;xa\leq;count\circ\chi_s}(e'_{inner}))$$
$$e'_{inner} \equiv (\chi_{xa:x.age}Emp[x]) < x.sales[s] >$$

Note that we pushed the map operation before the d-join in expression e'_{inner}. The Γ operation can be efficiently implemented by first sorting the argument on its *age* values. If the argument is already sorted, e.g. due to an index scan, the Γ operation can be evaluated in linear time during a single scan of e_{inner}, if f is linear.

There exists one Type J case where another more powerful technique can be applied: a *flatten* operation is performed on the outer block, and there is no tuple constructor within the outer block's **select** clause. As shown in [6], these queries can be optimized by pushing the *flatten* operation inside until it is applied on stored attributes, thus eliminating the nesting.

3.2.2 Nesting in the *from* Clause

For the moment, we consider that inner blocks are constant or that their dependency on outer blocks are expressed through a selection. Other dependencies are studied in the sequel. In the current context, nesting in the **from** clause is easily optimized. Due to space limitations, we do not illustrate this with an example but the following two equivalences should clarify the matter.

$$\begin{aligned} e_1 < \sigma_p(e_2) > &\equiv \sigma_p(e_1 < e_2 >) \\ \sigma_p(e_1 < e_2 >) &\equiv e_1 \bowtie_p e_2 \\ &\qquad \text{if } \mathcal{F}(e_2) \cap \mathcal{A}(e_1) = \emptyset \end{aligned}$$

Let us consider that $e_1$and e_2 are, respectively, the outer and inner block of an O_2SQL query. Since the nesting is located in the **from** clause, this results in a d-join between e_1 and e_2. If there is a predicate dependency between inner and outer block, it can be pushed out of the d-join (first equivalence). When no dependency exists between inner and outer blocks, the d-join can be transformed into a standard join (second equivalence).

3.3 Different Kinds of Dependency

Remember that we distinguish three kinds of dependencies: projection dependency (a reference to an outer variables occurs in the **select** clause), range dependency (...in the **from** clause) and predicate dependency (...in the **where** clause). Above, we studied queries with predicate dependency. In the sequel, we concentrate on optimization techniques required for range and projection dependencies.

3.3.1 Range Dependency

Consider the following query exhibiting a range dependency. It associates with each employee, the names of their customers living in Roma. The inner block's variable s depends on the outer block.

```
select [ ( e: x.name,
           c: select s.cust.name
              from   s in x.sales
              where s.cust.city = "Roma"]
from     x in Emp
```

```
select [(e: xn, c: SCN]
from   x in Emp,
define xn = x.name
       xs = x.sales
       SCN = select scn
             from   s in xs
             where scc = "Roma"
             define sc = s.cust
                    scn = sc.name
                    scc = sc.city
```

Translation into the algebra yields:

$$q \equiv \chi_{[e:xn,c:SCN]}(\chi_{SCN:nq}(\chi_{xn:x.name,xs:x.sales}(Emp[x])))$$
$$nq \equiv \chi_{scn}(\sigma_{scc=\text{"Roma"}}(\chi_{scc:sc.city}(\chi_{scn:sc.name}(\chi_{sc:s.cust}(xs[s])))))$$
$$\equiv \chi_{sc.name}(\sigma_{scc=\text{"Roma"}}(\chi_{sc:s.cust,scc:sc.city}(xs[s])))$$

The only unnesting technique that can be applied to this query, and those of same kind, consists of reducing the range dependency to a predicate dependency. Once this has been done, we can apply the above equations. The reduction, from range to predicate dependency, is based on *type-based rewriting* as found in [5,11,16]. This technique relies on the existence of type extents for rewriting queries. Since type based rewriting itself has already been described, we just comment on its application to unnesting using the above example.

Relying on the fact that the elements of the attribute *sales* of an employee belong to the extent of the class *Sale*, the inner block of the query can be rewritten as

$$nq \equiv \chi_{sc.name}(\sigma_{scc=\text{"Roma"}}(\chi_{sc:s.cust,scc:sc.city}(\sigma_{s\in xs}(Sale[s]))))$$

Type-based rewriting can be performed again using the extent of class *Customer*. This allows us, for instance, to use indexes on *Customer.city* and *Sale.cust* to evaluate the query. However, since our goal is unnesting and not general optimization, we do not detail this. Concerning unnesting, it is important to note that the dependency no longer specifies the range ($xs[s]$) but now represents a predicate ($\sigma_{s\in xs}$). Herewith, the algebraic expression is of the same form as one resulting from a predicate dependency. Hence, the above mentioned unnesting techniques apply.

However, in our model, the domain of an attribute is not always covered by an extent. Thus, we cannot always apply type-based rewriting. In these cases, we do not unnest and rely on existing optimization techniques for path expressions crossing sets (e.g. *x.sales.cust.city*).

3.3.2 Projection Dependency

In the algebra, the inner block of a query with a projection dependency ends with a map operation that has a function argument depending on both, the inner and the outer blocks. This kind of query should be rare which is fortunate because they cannot be unnested. Nested loops or cross products have to be used for their evaluation. The only optimization that can be done is to push those parts of the expression that depend only on the outer block out of the inner block and to memoize (e.g. using an hash table) the results of the complex expressions depending solely on the inner block to avoid evaluating them more than once.

Remarks Nothing restricts variables of the outer block to occur at only one place within the inner block. If there exist several dependencies, all the corresponding unnesting techniques can be applied selectively. Hence, if, for example, a range and a predicate dependency occur, the latter should be used for unnesting if the range dependency cannot be resolved by type-based rewriting.

Queries containing several nested blocks at the same level are unnested by successive rewritings as in the relational context. Note that if the nesting occurs in a disjunctive **where** clause, the query has to be transformed first into a union.

Finally, note that queries containing several levels of nesting cannot always be treated with the above techniques. In [7] we extend our techniques to the more complex cases.

4 Conclusion

As opposed to the relational context where unnesting is performed at the SQL-level, we have introduced a technique which allows unnesting at the algebraic level. This frees us from query language dependencies. We introduced an algebra and showed how nested SQL-like queries are translated into nested algebraic expressions. Then, we reported several unnesting strategies in the form of algebraic equations. While some of them merely recast known relational strategies, most of them make use of and are concerned with features specific to object-oriented queries. Our presentation was concerned with one-level nested queries without quantifiers. More complex unnesting strategies can be found in [7].

References

1. C. Beeri and Y. Kornatzky. Algebraic optimization of object-oriented query languages. In *Int. Conf. on Database Theory (ICDT)*, pages 72–88, 1990.
2. J. A. Blakeley, W. J. McKenna, and G. Graefe. Experiences building the oodb query optimizer. In *ACM SIGMOD Conf. on Management of Data*, pages 287–296, 1993.
3. R. Cattell, editor. *The Object Database Standard: ODMG 93*. Morgan Kaufmann, to appear.
4. S. Ceri and G. Gottlob. Translating SQL into relational algebra: Optimization, semantics and equivalence of SQL queries. *IEEE Trans. on Software Eng*, pages 324–345, 1985.
5. S. Cluet and C. Delobel. A general framework for the optimization of object-oriented queries. In *ACM SIGMOD Conf. on Management of Data*, pages 383–392, 1992.
6. S. Cluet and G. Moerkotte. Nested queries in object bases. In *Int. Workshop on Database Programming Languages*, pages 226–242, 1993.
7. S. Cluet and G. Moerkotte. Classification and optimization of nested queries in object bases. Technical report, University of Karlsruhe, 1994.
8. U. Dayal. Of nests and trees: A unified approach to processing queries that contain nested subqueries, aggregates, and quantifiers. In *Proc. Int. Conf. on Very Large Data Bases (VLDB)*, pages 197–208, 1987.
9. G. Lohman et al. Optimization of nested queries in a distributed relational database. In *Int. Conf. on Very Large Data Bases (VLDB)*, 1984.

10. R. Ganski and H. Wong. Optimization of nested SQL queries revisited. In *ACM SIGMOD Conf. on Management of Data*, pages 23–33, 1987.
11. P. Jenq, D. Woelk, W. Kim, and W. Lee. Query processing in distributed ORION. In *Proc. Int. Conf. on Extended Database Technology (EDBT)*, Venice, 1990.
12. A. Kemper and G. Moerkotte. Advanced query processing in object bases using access support relations. In *Proc. Int. Conf. on Very Large Data Bases*, pages 294–305, 1990.
13. A. Kemper and G. Moerkotte. Query optimization in object bases: Exploiting relational techniques. In *Proc. Dagstuhl Workshop on Query Optimization (J.-C. Freytag, D. M aier und G. Vossen (eds.))*. Morgan-Kaufman, to appear 1993.
14. W. Kiessling. SQL-like and Quel-like correlation queries with aggregates revisited. ERL/UCB Memo 84/75, University of Berkeley, 1984.
15. W. Kim. On optimizing an SQL-like nested query. *ACM Trans. on Database Systems*, 7(3):443–469, Sep 82.
16. G. Mitchell, S. Zdonik, and U. Dayal. *Object-Oriented Database Systems (A. Dogac, M. T. Özsu, A. Biliris, and T. Sellis (eds.)-*, chapter Optimization of Object-Oriented Queries: Problems and Applicatios. NATO ASI. Springer, 1993.
17. M. Muralikrishna. Optimization and dataflow algorithms for nested tree queries. In *Int. Conf. on Very Large Data Bases (VLDB)*, 1989.
18. M. Muralikrishna. Improved unnesting algorithms for join aggregate SQL queries. In *Int. Conf. on Very Large Data Bases (VLDB)*, pages 91–102, 1992.
19. H.-J. Schek and M. H. Scholl. The relational model with relation-valued attributes. *Information Systems*, 11(2):137–147, 1986.
20. G.M. Shaw and S.B. Zdonik. A query algebra for object-oriented databases. In *IEEE Conference on Data Engineering*, pages 154–162, 1990.
21. H. Steenhaben, P. Apers, H. Blanken, and R. de By. From nested-loop to join queries in oodb. In *Int. Conf. on Very Large Data Bases (VLDB)*, pages 618–629, 1994.
22. D. Straube and T. Özsu. Queries and query processing in object-oriented database systems. *ACM Trans. on Information Systems*, 8(4):387–430, 1990.
23. S. L. Vandenberg and D. DeWitt. Algebraic support for complex objects with arrays, identity, and inheritance. In *ACM SIGMOD Conf. on Management of Data*, pages 158–167, 1991.

Chapter 2.3.5

Integrating Query and Program Optimization Using Persistent CPS Representations*

Andreas Gawecki and Florian Matthes

Technical University Hamburg-Harburg, Harburger Schloßstraße 20, D-21071 Hamburg, Germany

1 Introduction and Motivation

The traditional focus of database language research has been on high-level languages for data access and manipulation (query languages, trigger definition languages, 4th generation languages, script languages) or on implementation-oriented languages which capture the characteristic operations of a specific target system at hand (relational algebra, object algebra, structural recursion, ...).

A closer look at tools working on such code representations like query and program optimizers reveals a large number of common tasks which at present are addressed with often icompatible technologies:

Binding analysis: Which entity (table, index, view, function, method, variable, etc.) is denoted by an identifier? Are there multiple references to the same entity?

Identifier substitution by a bound value or expression: View expansion, method or procedure inlining, constant folding, substitution of host programming language parameters, etc.

Free variable analysis: Does a variable appear in a query predicate? Does a procedure depend on global variables? Does a query contain programming language variables? Are there independent subexpressions? Which base relations do appear inside an integrity constraint?

After a decade of experience in our group with building integrated database programming languages [15,13,16] (see also synopsis in Chapter 2.1.2) and optimizers for their query languages [9,8,7,2,3], we made the radical decision to replace special-purpose representations for queries, programs and scripts with a single, expressive *intermediate* language. We thereby avoid incompatibilities and redundancies arising from the repeated implementation of the above functionality.

This intermediate language of the Tycoon System (see Chapter 2.1.4), the Tycoon Machine Language (TML), is presented in more detail in [6,5,11]. Here, we only demonstrate its use for integrated program and query optimization in a persistent programming environment.

* This is a synopsis of [6].

2 Continuation Passing Style

Continuation Passing Style (CPS) [1,12,10,17,4] is a powerful yet simple program representation technique. The main advantage of CPS over other intermediate representations lies in the drastic reduction of the number of program constructs which have to be handled by the compile-time and run-time optimizer while preserving much of the structural information of the source language input. CPS has simple and clean semantics based on the λ-calculus. TML is a CPS representation based on a call-by-value λ-calculus with store semantics. A number of predefined *primitive procedures* operate on an implicit, hidden store.

TML supports higher-order languages, i.e. languages where functions may take other functions as arguments (see Chapter 1.1.1 which describes the Tycoon Language). For example, the selection operation $\sigma_p(R)$ in relational algebra takes two arguments, a range relation R and a selection predicate p where p can be understood as a boolean function on the element type of R.

Like terms in the λ-calculus, CPS terms provide an integrated representation of code fragments and their associated data bindings. To meet the specific requirements of persistent languages and database languages, TML terms may contain simple literal values and object identifiers that denote arbitrarily complex objects (tables, indices, ADT values) in the persistent Tycoon object store (see Chapter 2.2.4).

By representing programs in CPS, many well-known program and algebraic query optimization techniques become special cases of a few simple and general λ-calculus transformations. These transformations can be applied freely even in the presence of nonterminatating computations and/or side-effecting calls to primitive procedures. This is due to the syntactical restrictions on TML terms which require actual parameters to function calls to be be constants, variables or abstractions. The complete abstract syntax of TML is defined by only four productions (literals, identifiers, abstractions and applications). Although the semantics of TML is based on the general λ-calculus, well-formed TML programs must satisfy a number of additional constraints which are preserved by the TML rewrite rules. These constraints and rewrite rules are given in the full paper.

In TML, most of the "real work" needed to implement source language semantics (e.g. integer arithmetic, query evaluation) is factored out into primitive procedures which are not considered part of the intermediate language itself. By definition, each primitive calls exactly one of its continuation arguments tail-recursively, passing the result of its computation, if any. For example, some arithmetic primitives take two continuations: the *normal* continuation which receives the calculated result, and an *exception* continuation which is invoked if the primitive fails due to overflow or division by zero. The set of primitive procedures used for the compilation of TL (see Chapter 1.1.1) and the information needed by the generic TML rewriting tools for additional (possibly language -specific) primitive procedures is described in the full paper).

3 Analysis and Rewriting

The TML optimizer is organized into two separate passes, namely a *reduction* pass and an expansion pass. During the reduction pass, a number of generic rewrite rules are applied to the TML tree until no more rules are applicable. Termination is guaranteed because each of the rewrite rules reduces the size of the TML tree if it is applied.

The subsequent *expansion* pass tries to substitute bound λ-abstractions (procedures or continuations) at the positions where they are applied. Effectively, this CPS transformation performs *procedure inlining* in terms of traditional compiler optimization or view expansion in database terminology. The decision whether a given use of a bound abstraction is to be substituted is based on a heuristic cost model similar to the one described by [1].

When one or more abstractions are substituted during the expansion pass, there usually is the opportunity to perform more reductions on the TML tree. Likewise, the reduction pass may reveal new opportunities to perform expansions, so the two passes are applied repeatedly until no more changes are made to the TML tree. To guarantee the termination of this process even in obscure cases, a penalty is accumulated at each round of the reduction/expansion phases.

The optimization rules are described in [6] in detail using the notation

$$\begin{array}{l}(precondition):\\ A \xrightarrow{\underline{rule\ name}} B\end{array}$$

This indicates that the TML expression A may be rewritten to the TML expression B if $precondition$ evaluates to true.

3.1 Optimization across Abstraction Barriers

Effective optimization of highly modular languages and of database languages requires the analysis and rewriting of CPS terms that have been declared and compiled in separate scopes (logical schema, physical schema, query modules, embedded query, application program), at different times and most often by different users.

The Tycoon approach to overcome these abstraction barriers is (1) to wait until link or execution time, when all the bindings between the contributing parts of a persistent application are established, and (2) to keep sufficiently abstract code and binding information until that point in time. Based on this approach it is rather straightforward to collect (via transitive reachability) all declarations that contribute to a given TML term (for example an embedded query) into a single scope (represented again as a TML term) and to invoke the TML optimizer to generate a globally optimized TML term.

For each exported source code function *f* in a compilation unit, the compiler back end augments the generated code for *f* with a reference to a compact persistent representation of the TML tree (Persistent TML, PTML) for *f*. At run-time, it is possible to map PTML back into TML, re-invoke the optimizer and code-generator, link the newly-generated code into the running program, and execute it (Fig. 1).

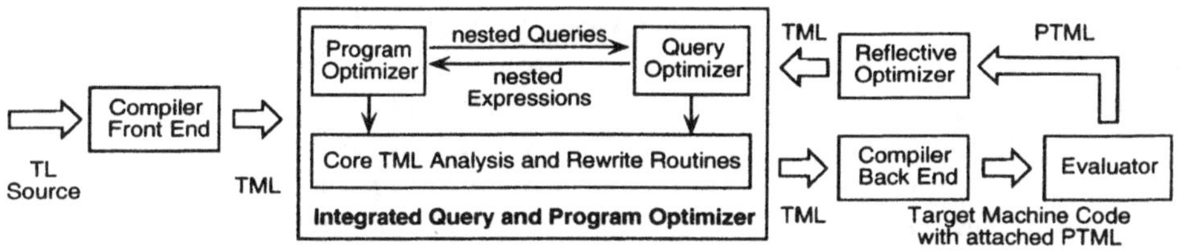

Fig. 1. Compilation, optimization and evaluation in the Tycoon system

The mapping from PTML back to TML also returns the set of R-value bindings ([identifier, OID] pairs) established at runtime. These bindings correspond to free variables (module names, database names, table names, function names, constant names, etc.) in the source text and they naturally give rise to context-dependent, inter-procedure and inter-module optimizations. The full paper describes this process in more detail.

4 Towards Integrated Program and Query Optimization

The syntax of many modern query languages allows programming language variables, function and method calls to appear in the **select** and **where** clauses of SQL statements. Furthermore, the body of element-at-a-time iterators (**for each** statements) and of database triggers may refer to programming language statements. User-defined data types lead to further interaction between query expressions and programming language expressions.

Since traditional query optimizers do not have access to an abstract representation of these program fragments, they have to work under worst-case assumptions (dependencies between subexpressions, side-effects), or they have to rely on programmer-supplied information (commutativity, idempotence, side-effects) which is difficult to keep consistent in large, long-lived systems. In particular, current query representations do not cover any form of control flow (conditionals, case analysis, loops, exceptions) which is "inherited" through embedded programming language expressions.

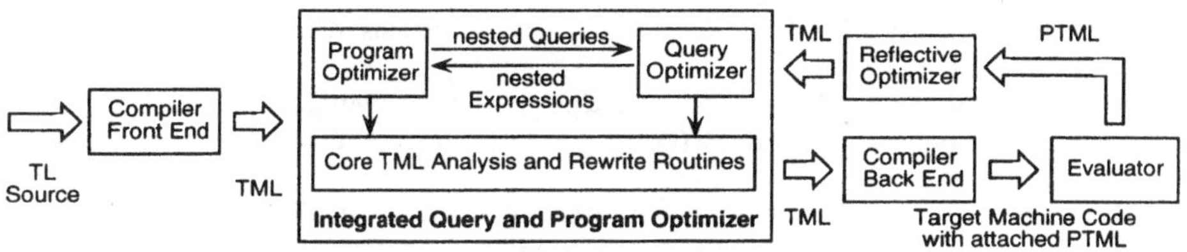

Fig. 2. Embedded Query Optimization

Given an integrated database language where user-defined code and query expressions are fully integrated [14], query and program optimization have to interact closely (see Fig. 2): Whenever the program optimizer encounters an embedded query construct like a set-at-a-time (bulk) query or update, an element-at-a-time iterator, or a view definition, it invokes the query optimizer on the respective TML subtree with a TML environment which describes the global bindings (free variables) for that expression. Similarly, the query optimizer invokes the program optimizer to analyze and optimize nested programming language expressions which appear in query constructs (target list, selection predicate, iterator body). Again, binding information for free variables (e.g. range variables in queries or loop control variables in **for each** iterators) is passed along with the respective TML subtree. Recursive declarations of functions, values, or queries are represented uniformly through applications of the fixpoint combinator Y and do *not* lead to repeated traversals of TML terms.

Acknowledgements. This research was supported by ESPRIT Basic Research, Project FIDE, #6309.

References

1. A. Appel. *Compiling with Continuations*. Cambridge University Press, 1992.
2. S. Böttcher, M. Jarke, and J.W. Schmidt. Adaptive predicate managers in database systems. In *Proceedings of the Twelfth International Conference on Very Large Databases, Kyoto, Japan*, 1986.
3. J. Eder, A. Rudloff, F. Matthes, and J.W. Schmidt. Data construction with recursive set expressions in DBPL. In *Proceedings of the Kiev East/West Workshop on Next Generation Database Technology*, volume 504 of *Lecture Notes in Computer Science*, April 1991.
4. A. Gawecki. An optimizing compiler for Smalltalk. Bericht FBI-HH-B-152/92, Fachbereich Informatik, Universität Hamburg, Germany, September 1992. (In German).
5. A. Gawecki and F. Matthes. The Tycoon machine language TML: An optimizable persistent program representation. FIDE Technical Report FIDE/94/100, Fachbereich Informatik, Universität Hamburg, Germany, August 1994.
6. A. Gawecki and F. Matthes. Exploiting persistent intermediate code representations in open database environments. In *Proceedings of the Fifth Conference on Extending Database Technology, EDBT'96*, volume 1057 of *Lecture Notes in Computer Science*, Avignon, France, March 1996. Springer-Verlag.
7. M. Jarke and J. Koch. Query optimization in database systems. *ACM Computing Surveys*, 16(2):111–152, 1984.
8. M. Jarke, J. Koch, M. Mall, and J.W. Schmidt. Query optimization research in the database programming languages (DBPL) project. *IEEE – Data Engineering*, pages 11–14, September 1982.
9. M. Jarke and J.W. Schmidt. Query processing strategies in the Pascal/R relational database management system. In *Proceedings of the ACM-SIGMOD International Conference on Management of Data, Orlando, Florida*, 1982.
10. R.A. Kelsey. Compilation by program transformation. Technical report, Yale University, Department of Computer Science, May 1989.

11. P. Kiradjiev. Dynamic optimization in CPS-based intermediate languages. Master's thesis, Fachbereich Informatik, Universität Hamburg, Germany, December 1994. (In German).
12. D. Kranz, R. Kelsey, J. Rees, P. Hudak, J. Philbin, and N. Adams. ORBIT: An optimizing compiler for Scheme. *ACM SIGPLAN Notices*, 21(7):219–233, July 1986.
13. M. Mall, M. Reimer, and J.W. Schmidt. Data selection, sharing and access control in a relational scenario. In M.L. Brodie, J.L. Myopoulos, and J.W. Schmidt, editors, *On Conceptual Modelling*. Springer-Verlag, 1984.
14. F. Matthes and J.W. Schmidt. Bulk types: Built-in or add-on? In *Database Programming Languages: Bulk Types and Persistent Data*. Morgan Kaufmann Publishers, September 1991.
15. J.W. Schmidt. Some high level language constructs for data of type relation. In *Proceedings of the ACM-SIGMOD International Conference on Management of Data, Toronto, Canada*, August 1977.
16. J.W. Schmidt and F. Matthes. The DBPL project: Advances in modular database programming. *Information Systems*, 19(2):121–140, 1994.
17. D. Teodosiu. HARE: An optimizing portable compiler for Scheme. *ACM SIGPLAN Notices*, 26(1):109–120, January 1991.

Chapter 2.3.6

An ad hoc Approach to the Implementation of Polymorphism*

Ron Morrison, Alan Dearle†, Richard Connor‡ and Fred Brown§

School of Mathematical and Computational Sciences, University of St Andrews, North Haugh, St Andrews KY16 9SS, Scotland

Abstract. Polymorphic abstraction provides the ability to write programs that are independent of the form of the data over which they operate. It has proved difficult to provide efficient implementations of polymorphism. This paper addresses this problem and describes a new technique which can implement all forms of polymorphism, use a conventional machine architecture and support non-uniform data representations. Furthermore, the method ensures that any extra cost of implementation applies to polymorphic forms only and allows such polymorphic forms to persist over program invocations.

1 Introduction

Polymorphism in a programming language is the ability to write programs that are independent of the form of the data objects that they manipulate. Thus it provides an abstraction over the form of the data which is often categorised by type.

This paper [1] concentrates on machine architectures and code generation techniques required to support polymorphism. First of all it reviews some known techniques and then suggests a new method which has been used to implement the language Napier88. This utilises the block retention architecture of the Persistent Abstract Machine [2, 3] and allows polymorphic expressions to manipulate values of non-uniform sizes. Other features of the method are that only polymorphic expressions, and not others, pay the extra cost of genericity and that the technique is suitable for implementation on traditional architectures. Finally, the system also supports the persistence of polymorphic values.

2 Implementations of Polymorphism

In polymorphic expressions, a computation is described independently of the type of the data being manipulated. This polymorphic description can be at several levels of abstraction - the computation can be expressed at the level of source code, machine

* This is a synopsis of [1].

† Present address: Department of Computing Science, University of Stirling, Stirling FK9 4LA, Scotland

‡ Present address: Department of Computer Science, University of Glasgow, Glasgow G12 8QQ, Scotland

§ Present address: Department of Computer Science, University of Adelaide, Adelaide 5005, Australia

code, μ-code or any combination of these. Therefore the meaning of polymorphism in any system is interpreted with respect to a level of abstraction.

There are three extremities in implementation techniques for polymorphism that depend upon the level of abstraction at which the polymorphism is expressed. For any polymorphism to exist, the source code of a program must exhibit expressions that are independent of the type of the data. If this is the limit of the polymorphic expression then we use the term *textual polymorphism* to categorise it. For example, in Ada generics [4], only the source code displays polymorphism since different machine code may be generated for each different instantiation type. Similarly, languages which exhibit ad hoc polymorphism may execute the same code for different types at the source level but may in fact execute different code at the machine level.

A second perhaps more pure form of polymorphism is found in systems where both the source and machine code for polymorphic expressions are independent of the data types manipulated. This we term *uniform polymorphism.* In ML [5], which uses uniform polymorphism, all data has a uniform representation and the same code is executed at both the source and machine level for polymorphic expressions regardless of the type of the data being manipulated. This has implications for the efficient representation of data, including non-polymorphic objects.

Finally, other systems have source and machine code uniformity but non-uniform store representations. This means that machine instructions must take account of the differing store formats. Thus, the machine code for a polymorphic expression takes account of type information when it is executed. Many of the object-oriented languages are implemented in this manner and all systems that depend on a tagged architecture also fall into this last category which we term *tagged polymorphism.*

In the paper each of the above implementation categories is explored in turn since each yields different tradeoffs for the efficient implementation of polymorphism. Textual, uniform and tagged polymorphism represent extremities in the range of implementation techniques. Most languages will be implemented by a mixture of techniques within this range. The reason for exploring the extremities is to expose the limits of each technique and therefore the tradeoffs available to the implementor.

3 Conclusions

The paper presents a technique for implementing polymorphism which has been used to support the language Napier88. It is a variant of tagged polymorphism and can be used to implement parametric and built in ad hoc polymorphism. Combined with the work of Wadler & Blott [6] it can be used to implement user defined ad hoc polymorphism, although, as yet, this has not been done. The technique has been used to implement the existentially quantified types of Mitchell & Plotkin [7]. It has been demonstrated elsewhere that since the method can implement ad hoc polymorphism in a non-uniform store, it can also implement bounded universal quantification, bounded existential quantification and inclusion polymorphism [8].

The technique may also be used to implement all data types that exhibit universal quantification. This is a direct consequence of the fact that all values in the λ-calculus are functions and it is sufficient to provide a technique that will implement polymorphic functions such as the one described in this paper.

The technique is unique in achieving the following properties:

- implementation of all forms of polymorphism,
- the use of a conventional architecture,
- support for non-uniform data objects,
- support for first class polymorphic forms,
- support for the persistence of polymorphic forms,
- only requiring extra space and execution of additional code in polymorphic contexts, and
- the generation of compact and fast code.

References

1. Morrison R, Dearle A, Connor RCH, Brown AL. An Ad-Hoc Approach to the Implementation of Polymorphism. ACM Transactions on Programming Languages and Systems 1991; 13,3:342-371
2. Brown AL, Carrick R, Connor RCH, Dearle A, Morrison R. The Persistent Abstract Machine. Universities of Glasgow and St Andrews Report PPRR-59-88, 1988
3. Connor RCH, Brown AL, Carrick R, Dearle A, Morrison R. The Persistent Abstract Machine. In: Rosenberg J, Koch DM (ed) Persistent Object Systems, Proc. 3rd International Workshop on Persistent Object Systems, Newcastle, Australia. Springer-Verlag, 1990, pp 353-366
4. Ichbiah et al. The Programming Language Ada Reference Manual. In: Lecture Notes in Computer Science 155. Springer-Verlag, 1983
5. Milner R. A Proposal for Standard ML. University of Edinburgh Report CSR-157-83, 1983
6. Wadler P, Blott S. How to Make ad-hoc Polymorphism Less ad-hoc. In: Proc. 16th ACM Symposium on Principles of Programming Languages, Austin, Texas, 1989
7. Mitchell JC, Plotkin GD. Abstract Types have Existential Type. ACM Transactions on Programming Languages and Systems 1988; 10,3:470-502
8. Connor RCH, Dearle A, Morrison R, Brown AL. An Object Addressing Mechanism for Statically Typed Languages with Multiple Inheritance. In: Proc. OOPSLA'89, New Orleans, Louisiana, 1989

Part 3

Using Persistent Languages: Introduction and Overview

Ray Welland

Department of Computing Science, University of Glasgow, Glasgow, G12 8QQ, Scotland

This Part focuses on making use of the persistence technology, described in Parts 1 and 2 of this book, to build Persistent Application Systems (PASs). In order to fully exploit the $FIDE_2$ technology we need to provide the application builder with techniques, tools and environments to support system building. We also want to demonstrate that the main features of the $FIDE_2$ languages such as orthogonal persistence, strong typing and referential integrity can be exploited to construct better application building environments. The characteristics of a PAS are that it is a large-scale, long-lived, data-intensive application system. Therefore, we need to identify and prototype techniques and tools which address these aspects of application systems.

The data-intensive aspects of PASs are the focus of the $FIDE_2$ work as our technology is aimed at bridging the gap between programming languages and databases, providing both computational power and long-term data storage and retrieval facilities. Therefore, our development environments for PASs will combine features which one would expect to find in both a software engineering environment and those commonly provided to build and support database applications. The long-lived nature of a PAS means that we have to support the evolution of systems as long-lived systems will inevitably change over time. We have to support the evolution of both large-scale software and complex data. Again this means that we need to consider both maintenance techniques which traditionally come from the software engineering field and schema evolution aspects from the database field. Investigating the building of large-scale systems is something which is difficult within a research environment although we have at least one experiment which is now beginning to reach a realistic size for a PAS.

Much of our work on programming environments has centred around providing tools for a single $FIDE_2$ language, the so called 'closed world' model. However, at some stage we will need to be able to import external services into our environment without compromising the integrity of the environment. Therefore, the problem of interoperability of systems was a major research issue in $FIDE_2$.

The original workplan for $FIDE_2$ proposed three lines of research within the PAS Workbench theme:

- building prototype Persistent Programming Environments (PPEs) to provide homogeneous development environments for PASs;
- providing prototype visualisations of PASs and a human factors evaluation of their effectiveness and usability;

- investigating the problems of interoperability in order to fully exploit the $FIDE_2$ functionality.

The work on visualisation has become closely inter-dependent on the PPE work and therefore these two lines of research are described together in Section 3.1. On the other hand, it became obvious that, as the project progressed, there was a need to investigate and prototype data modelling tools. The description of this work fits more naturally into this third section rather than being discussed with the work related to types and language elements in Part 1.

Section 3.1 describes two major experiments in building prototype PPEs. St Andrews have investigated a new paradigm, *hyper-programming*, in the Napier88 language (described in chapter 1.1.3) and investigated how this can be used to support application building. The Glasgow Persistent Workshop is built on the Napier88 platform exploiting the language without hyper-programming. Both of these experiments contain elements of visualisation which are described in this section.

Section 3.2 describes work on data modelling tools. Again there are two parallel experiments, one exploiting Napier88 at Glasgow and the other built on top of Tycoon (described in chapter 1.1.1) at Hamburg. In both cases these could be seen as part of the work on PPEs. It is envisaged that the Glasgow work on data modelling tools will be integrated with the Workshop in order to provide a complete application development environment. The STYLE Workbench is already effectively a PPE but is described in section 3.2 because of its strong connection with the data modelling work.

Section 3.3 is concerned with work on interoperability. One strand of this work investigates interoperability between structured files and databases; it shows how database languages can be used to query and update files at a high level of abstraction. The other strand concerns investigating how to achieve type-safe inter-operation between persistent objects supported by independently generated generic servers. This work utilises the Tycoon programming language, TL, and the Tycoon programming environment.

Section 3.1

Persistent Programming Environments: Introduction and State of the Art

Ray Welland

Department of Computing Science, University of Glasgow, Glasgow, G12 8QQ, Scotland

1. Introduction

A Persistent Programming Environment (PPE) is the environment within which all the enabling tools for persistent software engineering will operate. Our objectives in this work were to identify the minimal set of elements which are essential in a PPE and to prototype some of the tools which would be required for the development of Persistent Application Systems (PASs).

This Section concentrates on the tools which are mainly concerned with supporting programming activities, as the data modelling aspects of PAS development are dealt with in Section 3.2. This is an artificial distinction because ultimately we see all these tools operating within the same common framework. For example, one might start building a PAS by defining the data model and generating the framework of an application as described in Section 3.2. To fully define the functionality of the application will require the use of the programming tools described in this Section.

The chapters in this Section describe two different approaches to the development of a PPE. The work on *hyper-programming* defines a new paradigm for program construction and the first part of this Section outlines how this can be exploited to develop a PPE. We then describe the construction of a prototype PPE, built on top of Napier88, which supports the construction of PASs and exploits the features provided in the language. The STYLE Workbench, described in Chapter 3.2.2, could also be considered as a third example of a prototype PPE built within $FIDE_2$.

2. The Hyper-programming approach

The team at St Andrews have developed a prototype Persistent Programming Environment (PPE) for Napier88 which is an integrated environment which supports composition, compilation and execution of programs, and browsing of the persistent store. It is self-contained in that the entire environment, including the user interface, is implemented as objects in a persistent store. The PPE supports hyper-programming which allows programs composed within the environment to contain embedded direct links to other values, locations and types extant in the store. This provides programmers with a new binding mechanism, *composition-time binding*, in addition to the run-time binding mechanism previously used in Napier88. Composition-time binding gives greater safety and run-time efficiency than run-time binding, but less flexibility. A third mechanism, compile-time binding, which represents an intermediate point on the efficiency/flexibility spectrum, is also supported. With compile-time binding free identifiers are resolved at the time that a program is compiled. The provision of the three binding mechanisms allows the programmer to choose a particular trade-off as appropriate for each particular case. Hyper-program editors are integrated with a browsing tool which is used both to identify values, locations or types (bindings) for linking into hyper-programs under construction, and to display representations of the bindings linked into existing hyper-programs. The PPE automatically records, as hyper-program fragments, the source code from which procedures and type declarations are derived. This means that the original source code for an application component can always be displayed.

Chapter 3.1.1 provides an overview of the principles of persistent linkage and how these can be exploited to build a PPE. It describes how the combination of persistent linkage, strong typing and referential integrity could be exploited to build tools for program construction, version and configuration management, and documentation management. An integrated PPE must support the manipulation of program, data and meta-data within a single framework and Chapter 3.1.2 focuses on how the hyper-programming paradigm may be used to support schema evolution. Chapter 3.1.3 discusses visualisation in the hyper-programming paradigm; it describes a new integrated browser and editor for Napier88. This tool provides a uniform treatment of executable and source forms of programs, and thus provides a single interfacing tool to perform queries of any complexity against the database or introduce new data or program into the persistent store.

3. The Persistent Workshop

The team at Glasgow has undertaken the design of a new PPE supported solely by the Napier88 platform. It is intended that persistent software engineering will be fully supported by this PPE, but that it will also demonstrate that other computer-based design and development activities could be equally well supported using the same architecture and technology. Only a representative sample of parts of a PPE could be implemented within the constraints of $FIDE_2$. Critical parts are: the supporting software organising information sharing among tools; consistent user interfaces to operate the PPE; a suite of tools intended to aid in the development of moderate scale PAS; a collection of tools that support the construction and maintenance of well organised libraries of components in the persistent object store; and a collection of library components . These components of the PPE all make extensive use of the orthogonal persistence, strong typing, higher-order procedures, incremental binding mechanisms and reflection provided by Napier88.

Chapter 3.1.4 briefly describes the 'Glasgow Persistent Workshop' concentrating on the Workshop framework and tools, and its evaluation. The Workshop framework provides paradigms for application development and mechanisms for tool interaction and to verify the utility of this framework the Workshop is populated with a number of prototype tools. Chapter 3.1.5 describes the Libraries which provide a collection of re-usable software components which have a regular structure, to which rigorous quality assurance techniques have been applied and which can be retrieved using appropriate tools. In addition to providing software components which are useful to Napier88 programmers, the Libraries experiment also aims to demonstrate that the effort of writing and documenting re-usable components of high quality is worthwhile. There is a close relationship between the work on the Libraries and that on the Workshop. The tools supporting the use of the Library run within the

Workshop, while the construction of the Workshop itself relies heavily on the use of Library components. The Libraries and Workshop together now form a substantial PAS which can be used for experimental purposes. One such set of experiments concern visualisation. Prototype visualisation tools have been built, installed in the Workshop and evaluated; this has led to improved visualisation tools. Results of the first cycle of these evaluations are discussed in Chapter 3.1.6.

4. The State of the Art

The $FIDE_2$ work on PPEs is focused on a *closed-world* environment, i.e. an environment which is language-dependent, allowing tight integration of tools and exploitation of specific language features. Early examples of language-oriented environments were Interlisp [10] and the Smalltalk environment [5]. More recently there have been a number of commercial language environments available on PC or Macintosh from companies such as Borland [3], Metrowerks [7] and Symantec [9].

Another approach to integration is to let tools operate on common data structures that contain information about programs and other system components, and that are stored in a database. The tools access these data structures through the database system being used, which help ensure consistency and integrity of the processes. In Ada programming support environments, e.g. Rational's Apex Ada [4, 8], the internal program database consists of DIANA structures [6]. These are attributed, abstract syntax representations of programs that combine source code and executable code of Ada objects into one unit and record additional semantic information.

The Glasgow Persistent Workshop also provides a common database with program and system information. The ease of storing data structures of any type, enabled by Napier88, was of considerable significance when the Workshop was implemented. This contrasts markedly with the context of most programming environments whose developers have to map all their data structures to files or some relatively rigid data model, particularly if a relational DBMS is used. However, development of programming environments for process modelling supported by the OODBMS O_2 [1] may also have benefited from persistent data structures [2].

References

1 F. Bancilhon, C. Delobel, and P. Kanellakis. *Building an Object-Oriented Database System: The Story of O2*, Morgan Kaufmann Publishers, San Mateo, CA, 1992.

2 S. Bandinelli, M. Braga, A. Fuggetta, and L. Lavazza. The architecture of the SPADE-1 process-centered SEE. Technical Report No. 18, ESPRIT-III Project GOODSTEP (6115), May 1994. Appeared in: B. Warboys (ed.): *3rd European Workshop on Software Process Technology*, Grenoble, France, LNCS 772, Springer, 1994.

3 Borland C++, User's Guide, Version 4.5, Borland International Inc., 1994.

4 P.H. Feiler, S.A. Dart and G. Downey. Evaluation of the Rational Environment. *Technical Report CMU/SEI-88-TR-15*, Software Engineering Institute, Carnegie Mellon University, Pittsburgh, Pa, 1988.

5 A. Goldberg. *Smalltalk-80: The Interactive Programming Environment*. Addison-Wesley, 1984.

6 G. Goos, W.A. Wulf, A.J. Evans and K.J. Butler. *DIANA – An Intermediate Language for Ada*. Lecture Notes in Computer Science 161, Springer-Verlag, Berlin, 1983.

7 CodeWarrior® User's Guide, Metrowerks, Inc., Austin, TX, USA, December 1995.
8 Rational Apex Ada, User's guide, Release 2.0, Rational Software Corporation, 1995.
9 Symantec Café for Windows 95/NT, 1.0, Symantec Corporation, 1996.
10 W. Teitelman and L. Masinter. The Interlisp Programming Environment. *IEEE Computer*, 14(4):25–33, April 1981.

Chapter 3.1.1

Exploiting Persistent Linkage in Software Engineering Environments*

Ron Morrison, Richard Connor†, Quintin Cutts†, Vivienne Dunstan and Graham Kirby.

School of Mathematical and Computational Sciences, University of St Andrews, North Haugh, St Andrews KY16 9SS, Scotland

Abstract. This paper examines some of the advantages of providing software engineering environments within a persistent object system with strong typing and referential integrity. Persistent linkage allows persistent objects to be included in the binding process. Strong typing guarantees that objects are only manipulated in a manner consistent with their type system descriptions. Referential integrity ensures that once a link (reference) to an object is established, its identity is unique and it persists over time. As a consequence no object can be deleted while another refers to it. It is shown how the integration of system specifications, programs, configuration management tools and documentation all within a single persistent environment leads to powerful new techniques. This new power is achieved by sharing structured persistent data across the hitherto enclosing boundaries of system components.

1 Introduction

The benefits of orthogonal persistence can be summarised as:

- improving programming productivity as a consequence of simpler semantics;
- avoiding *ad hoc* arrangements for data translation and long term data storage; and
- providing protection mechanisms over the whole computational environment.

Some persistent programming systems allow software engineering environments to be completely supported within the persistent system [1, 2, Chapter 1.1.3]. Thus each software environment component or activity, including process modelling, can take advantage of the persistent system. The full paper [3] focuses on the combination of three particular advantages, those of persistent linkage, strong typing and referential integrity. Although other integrated programming environments have been developed [4-13], the authors do not know of any that use persistent linkage, strong typing and referential integrity to gain the benefits described here.

The hypothesis presented in this paper is that persistent linkage (which allows persistent objects to be included in the binding process, thereby increasing the range of binding times), strong typing (which ensures type security), and referential integrity (which preserves identity) may be used in combination to improve both the construction and use of software engineering environments.

---

* Synopsis of paper originally published in Computer Journal 1995; 38,1, 1-16.

† Present address: Department of Computer Science, University of Glasgow, Glasgow G12 8QQ, Scotland

To illustrate the power of the combination of persistent linkage, strong typing and referential integrity in a persistent environment the following examples are used:

- the construction, editing, compilation, linking and execution of programs;
- the versioning of application components;
- the configuration of applications from component programs and data; and
- the documentation of application components.

Orthogonally persistent environments are by definition strongly typed, highly structured, and enforce referential integrity. File systems are traditionally composed of weakly typed, weakly structured components, and do not generally enforce referential integrity. The advantages to software environments described here all rely upon these differences in the objects manipulated by the program editors, compilers, linkers, version controllers and configuration managers. Thus hyper-programs [14] are possible only because the typed links in the programs are guaranteed to be maintained during and after manipulation by an editor. Hyper-code is possible only because the compiler can cause source and executable versions of the same code to be reliably linked to each other, thus enabling them to be presented as a unified view of the program. The version control and configuration management strategy outlined in the paper is possible only because links placed in versions of code and data by the version controllers can be reliably interpreted to discover the dynamically changing configuration of a component. The documentation control strategy outlined is possible only because reliable links and reverse links can be inserted between documents and the objects which they describe.

The combination of these concepts yields a programming environment in which a programmer need understand only the programming task. Hyper-programming removes any complexity introduced by an explicit linking mechanism; hyper-code removes the unnecessary conceptual gap between source and executable code, and the version control mechanism avoids the description of complex configuration information by allowing configuration details to be discovered as well as imposed.

The paper deliberately does not touch on a number of aspects that are essential to a complete software environment, such as scale, support for requirements and design, and support for programmer teams. Rather the message is illustrative of what can be achieved by using persistent linkage. The concept of having actual and target configurations can be extended to requirements and design. For example a requirements document may refer to other existing objects and other requirements documents and as such may become hyper-text mixed with hyper-code. The same is obviously true for design documents. However the utility of the persistent linkage can only be evaluated after experimentation.

Support for programmer teams and collaborative working requires concurrency control mechanisms that may be non-serialisable in nature. Much preliminary work is being undertaken in this area but at present solutions tend to be one-off rather than general. The Communicating Actions Control System (CACS) [Chapter 1.5.1] addresses this problem within the context of persistent systems. The essence of the system is: understandability; the separation of concurrency control from data; formal capture; and a path to implementation. Global cohesion of an action in CACS is visualised as the movement of data among access sets. The visibility of the data to other users then becomes an issue of synchronisation. Where the visibility coincides with commit time, atomic transactions may be obtained, and where the visibility is immediate then synchronisation is being used. By viewing the co-ordination of the use of data as the co-ordination of the movement of the data among access sets, then the same data may be used in a different manner at different times. Thus the data may take part in an atomic transaction [15] one day, a saga [16] the next and may be in a co-operative computation [17] the next. This work is at an early stage but would utilise hyper-links to ensure that specifications and implementations of the concurrency control are kept in lock step.

Scaling the notion of hyper-links is difficult in engineering terms and not always desirable in conceptual terms. Supporting hyper-links over a distributed system means that the user may be unaware of the topology of that system and that failure semantics differ from that of a local system. An obvious application of this is the use of hyper-links to support the World Wide Web. The WWW links are written in HTML and are unreliable whereas the persistent links require reliability. Mixing the descriptive technology of HTML with the reliability of persistent links provides an interesting research area. The work on structured access to files by Abiteboul, Cluet & Milo [18, 19] provides a possible avenue for solving this problem.

The present use of persistence for constructing programming environments and software engineering tools is in its infancy but some notable experiments are being undertaken. The Glasgow Workshop [Chapter 3.1.4] controls the use of a set of software engineering tools in order to guide the programmer through the construction of persistent application systems. Present tools include application construction via design in a conventional data model [20], a methodology tool, SPASM [21], which tracks the dependencies between software components accurately and a thesaurus tool [22] which aids the programmer by recording the use of names within the software system. All of these tools would benefit from the use of hyper-links to increase their safe use.

At present the hyper-programming system has been constructed, released to other users and is in regular use. The version control, configuration management and documentation systems have been prototyped. It should, however, be emphasised that the techniques described in this paper are not meant to be definitional on how to construct version control, configuration management and documentation systems. Rather the paper illustrates how strongly typed persistent linkage with referential integrity may be used to provide new techniques for their construction and use.

References

1. Currie IF. Filestore and Modes in Flex. In: Proc. 1st International Workshop on Persistent Object Systems, Appin, Scotland, 1985, pp 325-334
2. Bretl B, Maier D, Otis A et al. The GemStone Data Management System. In: Kim W, Lochovsky F (ed) Object-Oriented Concepts, Databases and Applications. ACM Press and Addison Wesley, 1989, pp 283-308
3. Morrison R, Connor RCH, Cutts QI, Dunstan VS, Kirby GNC. Exploiting Persistent Linkage in Software Engineering Environments. Computer Journal 1995; 38,1:1-16
4. O'Brien PD, Halbert DC, Kilian MF. The Trellis Programming Environment. In: Proc. International Conference on Object-Oriented Programming Systems, Languages and Applications (OOPSLA'87), Orlando, Florida, 1987, pp 91-102
5. Reiss SP. Graphical Program Development with PECAN Program Development Systems. ACM SIGPLAN Notices 1984; 19,5:30-41
6. Sweet RE. The Mesa Programming Environment. In: Proc. ACM SIGPLAN Symposium on Programming Languages and Programming Environments, 1985, pp 216-229

7. Teitelbaum T, Reps T. The Cornell Program Synthesizer: A Syntax-Directed Programming Environment. Communications of the ACM 1981; 24,9:563-573
8. Teitelman W, Masinter L. The Interlisp Programming Environment. In: Barstow DR, Shrobe HE, Sandewall E (ed) Interactive Programming Environments. McGraw-Hill, 1984
9. Habermann AN, Notkin D. Gandalf: Software Development Environments. IEEE Transactions on Software Engineering 1986; 12,12:1117-1127
10. Thomas I. Tool Integration in the Pact Environment. In: Proc. 11th International Conference on Software Engineering, 1989, pp 13-22
11. Dowson M. Integrated Project Support with Istar. IEEE Software 1987; 4,6:6-15
12. Akima N, Ooi F. Industrializing Software Development: A Japanese Approach. IEEE Software 1989; 6,2:13-21
13. Bott MF. ECLIPSE: An Integrated Project Support Environment. Peter Peregrinus, 1989
14. Kirby GNC, Connor RCH, Cutts QI, Dearle A, Farkas AM, Morrison R. Persistent Hyper-Programs. In: Albano A, Morrison R (ed) Persistent Object Systems, Proc. 5th International Workshop on Persistent Object Systems, San Miniato, Italy. Springer-Verlag, 1992, pp 86-106
15. Moss JEB. Nested Transaction: An Approach to Distributed Computing. MIT Press, Cambridge, Massachusetts, 1985
16. Garcia-Molina H, Salem K. Sagas. In: Proc. ACM SIGMOD International Conference on Management of Data, 1987, pp 249-259
17. Nodine MH, Zdonik SB. Co-operative Transaction Hierarchies: Transaction Support for Design Applications. VLDB Journal 1992; 1,1:41-80
18. Abiteboul S, Cluet S, Milo T. Querying and Updating the File. In: Proc. 19th International Conference on Very Large Data Bases, Dublin, Ireland, 1993, pp 73-84
19. Abiteboul S, Cluet S, Milo T. A Database Interface for File Updates. ACM SIGMOD Record 1995; 24,2:386-397
20. Cooper RL, Qin Z. A Graphical Data Modelling Program With Constraint Specification and Management. In: Proc. 10th British National Conference on Databases, Aberdeen, 1992, pp 192-208
21. Sjøberg DIK, Cutts QI, Welland R, Atkinson MP. Analysing Persistent Language Applications. In: Atkinson MP, Maier D, Benzaken V (ed) Persistent Object Systems, Tarascon 1994, Proc. 6th International Workshop on Persistent Object Systems, Tarascon, France. Springer-Verlag, 1994, pp 235-255
22. Sjøberg DIK. Thesaurus-Based Methodologies and Tools for Maintaining Persistent Application Systems. Ph.D. thesis, University of Glasgow, 1993

Chapter 3.1.2

Using Persistence Technology to Control Schema Evolution*

Richard Connor†, Quintin Cutts†, Graham Kirby and Ron Morrison

School of Mathematical and Computational Sciences, University of St Andrews, North Haugh, St Andrews KY16 9SS, Scotland

Preface to Chapters 3.1.2 and 3.1.3

The content of these chapters derives from two papers which explore further the possibilities of the hyperprogramming and hypercode concept. Neither paper describes engineered systems, but rather both are workshop papers which explore long-range possibilities of systems built around the hyperprogramming model. Although most FIDE research is based upon engineering practice as well as ideas, these papers are purely conjectural; the hyperprogramming and hypercode systems are built and in use, but a second generation of such systems is a prerequisite before the engineering aspects of systems such as those outlined here can be investigated, and so at the time of writing these remain descriptions of potential research projects.

This chapter shows how given the a single semantic context within which the data, the schema and the queries all reside, hyperlinks may be used to track between parts of the schema and the data and queries which depend on it. The tracking of such dependencies would allow more leverage than is possible within traditional systems, and should be of significant use during the process of schema evolution. The paper describes a set of schema evolution tools, which should be feasible to construct on top of a database where both hypercode and linguistic reflection are available in the support system.

The following chapter, 3.1.3 "Unifying Interaction with Persistent Data and Program", shows how a unified user interface can be presented to programmers of a database system in which the code of the system is represented as manifest closures, rather than pre-linked text. User-level interactions, such as browsing and editing, can thus be unified over data of all types, including program fragments.

---

* The original form of this paper describes how the hyper-programming paradigm may be used as a base technology to control schema evolution within database programming language systems. It contains a full description of one such interface; interested readers are encouraged to access the full form of the paper [1].

† Present address: Department of Computing Science, University of Glasgow, Glasgow G12 8QQ, Scotland

1 Introduction

Databases become obsolete when they can no longer meet the changing needs of the applications that they support. Evolution is inevitable in a long running system as the people who use the data, the data and the uses to which the data is put all change. This is reflected within the database system by changes to the data, the programs which use the data and the meta-data. Changes to program and data with the invariant of fixed meta-data are normally handled by updates to program libraries and the database respectively. The outstanding problem is to change the meta-data while keeping all the existing programs and data consistent with the semantics of the change.

It is shown here how traditional database technology may be extended by taking advantage of the facilities of an integrated persistent programming environment. The persistent environment can provide an underlying technology which allows the schema editor to locate and change, either manually or automatically, all affected program and data. The advantages of the mechanism are that it provides understandable semantics for evolution by controlling when the changes are made and by ensuring that changes to schema, program and data are consistent and made in lock step. Furthermore, these changes may be grouped together as a transaction within a live system; the accommodation of lazy data changes allows minimum loss of availability.

An integrated persistent environment is self supporting in that it allows all the activities of manipulating program, data and meta-data to be provided by the same mechanisms. The advantages of integrated persistent environments are described elsewhere in this book. For the purposes of controlling schema evolution, the persistent environment must:

- allow programs to be manipulated as data;
- provide an incremental loader; and
- guarantee referential integrity: once a link to an object in the persistent environment has been established, the object will remain accessible for as long as the link exists.

The incremental loader and the guarantee of referential integrity provide the basic facilities that allow hyper-programming [2]. The importance of hyper-programming in the context of this paper is that it provides a mechanism for representing all executable programs, since free variables in closures may be represented as links within hyper-programs. This means that the system may enforce associations between all executable programs in the environment and their corresponding hyper-program source representations [3].

2 Controlling Schema Evolution

To be able to control schema evolution, there is a requirement to locate and translate affected queries and data; the essential elements are at hand in the hyper-code system. The schema may keep a record of which programs (queries) and data are associated with particular parts of the schema via secure links. The programs always have hyper-code source and therefore source code and data translation is possible.

The schema evolution mechanism transforms the programs and data affected by a schema edit. This is achieved as follows:

1. Locate, from the schema, all affected programs and data.
2. For each program which may be affected, obtain its hyper-code.
3. Locate the points in the hyper-code which access the changed part of the schema and edit the hyper-code to reflect the new logical schema structure. This will involve establishing new links both to and from the changed part of the schema.
4. Update the old program with the new one.
5. Update the affected data with new versions.

The extent to which this process can be automated depends upon the complexity of the schema change incurred. The essential point is that all interrogation and manipulation of schema, program and data occurs within a single integrated environment, and may therefore be represented as a meta-level program within that environment.

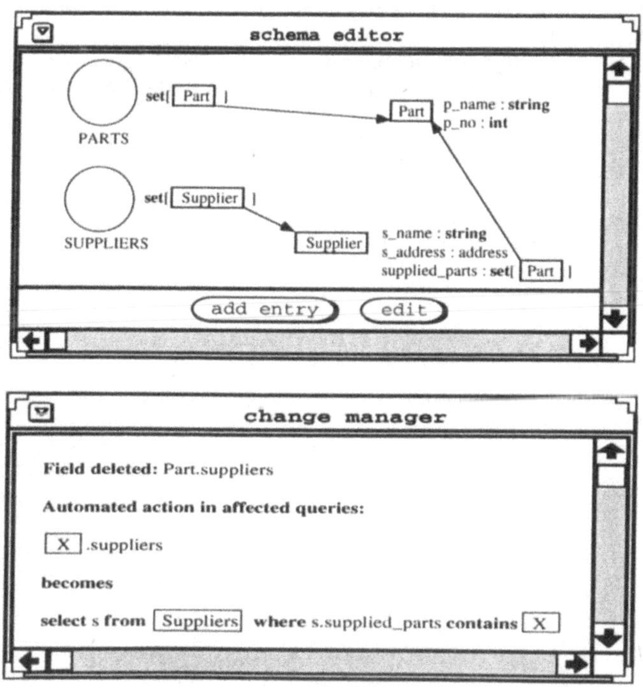

Fig. 1. Schema evolution and change management tool interface.

Figure 1 shows an example of the interface presented by the schema editing and change management tool. It is important to note that the research described here is not a matter of user interface design; the essential properties of the feasible implementation of this system rely upon the hyper-programming technology, which is in turn dependent upon the integrated environment.

The mechanism relies heavily upon the self-contained nature of the persistent environment. As all the data and code is held in the same environment as the schema, it is possible to keep not only links from the schema to the data it describes but also reverse links from the schema to programs which bind to particular points of it. The hyper-code concept makes it possible to map between executable and source representations. The fact that these representations are themselves values within the persistent environment, along with the provision of a compiler in the same environment, makes the strategy possible.

References

1. Connor RCH, Cutts QI, Kirby GNC, Morrison R. Using Persistence Technology to Control Schema Evolution. In: Proc. 9th ACM Symposium on Applied Computing, Phoenix, Arizona, 1994, pp 441-446
2. Kirby GNC, Connor RCH, Cutts QI, Dearle A, Farkas AM, Morrison R. Persistent Hyper-Programs. In: Albano A, Morrison R (ed) Persistent Object Systems, Proc. 5th International Workshop on Persistent Object Systems, San Miniato, Italy. Springer-Verlag, 1992, pp 86-106
3. Morrison R, Connor RCH, Cutts QI, Dunstan VS, Kirby GNC. Exploiting Persistent Linkage in Software Engineering Environments. Computer Journal 1995; 38,1:1-16.

Chapter 3.1.3

Unifying Interaction with Persistent Data and Program*

Richard Connor†, Quintin Cutts†, Graham Kirby, Vivienne Dunstan and Ron Morrison

School of Mathematical and Computational Sciences, University of St Andrews, North Haugh, St Andrews KY16 9SS, Scotland

1 Introduction

Some general comments relevant to the contents of this chapter are given in the **Preface to Chapters 3.1.2 and 3.1.3** at the beginning of Chapter 3.1.2.

Visual interaction with object-oriented databases, such as that provided by generic object browsing systems, has proved to be a convenient and natural way for database users to address informal queries over a database. The users of such tools can browse freely around the data structures and values of a database, avoiding the necessity to write down algebraic expressions to perform the equivalent accesses. Where appropriate it is also possible to perform updates or invoke more complex methods over the objects depicted on the screen. Such tools are greatly preferred to a traditional algebra-based approach for simple queries and updates to object-oriented databases.

The advantages of this style of access are comparable to the advantages of a modern iconic operating system interface over a traditional command-line based approach. In addition, however, a more general programming algebra is required so that more complex and longer-running queries may be handled. This frustratingly gives rise to two quite separate mechanisms for manipulating the same values within a system, with the choice of mechanism being somewhat arbitrary for tasks in the middle ground between trivial and complex.

This paper describes a new browser/editor that is being developed for the Napier88 system. The significance of this new browser is that it includes three very strong unifying concepts, the combination of which makes the browser the only mechanism which is required for interaction with the database system. The three important unifying concepts are:

---

* The original form of this paper describes how the hyper-programming paradigm may be used as a base technology to present a unified high-level database interface to the programmer. It contains a full description of one such interface; this synopsis addresses only the issue of how a hyper-programming system allows the unification to occur. Interested readers are encouraged to access the full form of the paper [1].

† Present address: Department of Computing Science, University of Glasgow, Glasgow G12 8QQ, Scotland

1. Data of any type supported by the system may be browsed and edited in a uniform manner. This includes a uniform treatment of procedure closures; a drawback of previous browsers is that they could not adequately handle procedures.

2. Source code is treated not as a fundamental building block within the programming system, but instead as a transient text-based view of any value. The source does not have a conceptual permanent existence within the system, but is apparently generated from any value that may be browsed. Compilation and linking still occur within the system, but are presented to the programmer simply as a reification of the transient source.

3. As a further consequence of the generic treatment of procedure values and source code, the artificial distinction between source and executable values within a running system is completely removed. If a run-time error occurs, for example, the actual value of the procedure in which it occurred may be displayed by the browser. The source will still be available for necessary purposes such as correction and adaptation; however the source will not exist as a separate entity accessible in isolation from the executable value.

The major difference between this and other browsers is therefore in the uniform treatment of the executable and source code forms of procedures, and hence programs. Furthermore, the manipulation of code made possible by the unification strategy is sufficiently general to subsume the usual process of program editing, compilation and linking which is normally associated with the manipulation of code bodies within a system. This means that the browser/editor is the only interfacing tool required to perform queries of any complexity against the database, or to introduce new data and program to it.

2 Unifying Source and Executable Forms

The essential problem with the uniform visualisation of persistent source and executable code representations is that many different executable forms may share the same source representation. The paradigm of hyper-programming [2], however, may be used to create a one-to-one mapping between source and executable, with the direct consequence that the concepts may be merged in the programmers' view of the system [3].

There is normally a clear distinction in systems which support first-class procedures between the concept of procedure code, and the concept of closure; it is this distinction which traditionally makes the unification of source and executable values impossible. The concept of closure represents the executable version of code; it is formed by a pair consisting of the procedure code and the environment in which this code is to be evaluated. Thus the difference between code and closure can be summed up as the meaning of any free variables in the code at the time the procedure value is instantiated.

For a procedure without free variables, the environment is not significant and there is no conceptual difference between code and closure. The system's compiler performs a mapping from source to executable; it is quite possible to construct a reverse mapping from executable to source. This is true in any system, and indeed many systems do keep such reverse mappings for debugging purposes. If all procedures within a system have the property of containing no free variables, then this mapping is one-to-one; that is, no two semantically different executables map to the same source. This is a direct consequence of the executable semantics being wholly captured by the procedure code. If all the code in the system may be defined in terms of such source-executable pairs, then the conceptual unification of source and executable may be achieved with an appropriate user interface design.

However, many procedures in database systems do contain free variables. Thus in general the conceptual division of the code and closures into pairs cannot take place as many different executable procedures, each with its own different semantics, may derive from the same source description. It is therefore not possible at the interface level to unify the concepts of code and closure.

By a simple extension of the hyper-programming paradigm it is possible to describe a hyper-source representation for any executable procedure. The concept of composition time binding is slightly widened to one of binding all free variables at closure formation time; these variables may be represented by hyper-links in exactly the same way. An example of a procedure with a free variable is shown in Figure 1.

```
let counterGen = proc( → proc( → int ) )
        begin
                let a := 0

                proc( → int )
                begin
                        a := a + 1
                        a
                end
        end

let myCounter = counterGen()
let val1 = myCounter()
let val2 = myCounter()

let anotherCounter = counterGen()
let val3 = anotherCounter()
```

Fig. 1. Free variable binding.

Each time the outer procedure *counterGen* is called, it creates a new integer variable *a* and returns a new procedure operating on *a*. The action of the procedure returned is to increment the variable and return its new value. All the procedures generated by *counterGen* share the same code. Their closures differ, however, since the name *a* is bound to a different location in their respective environments.

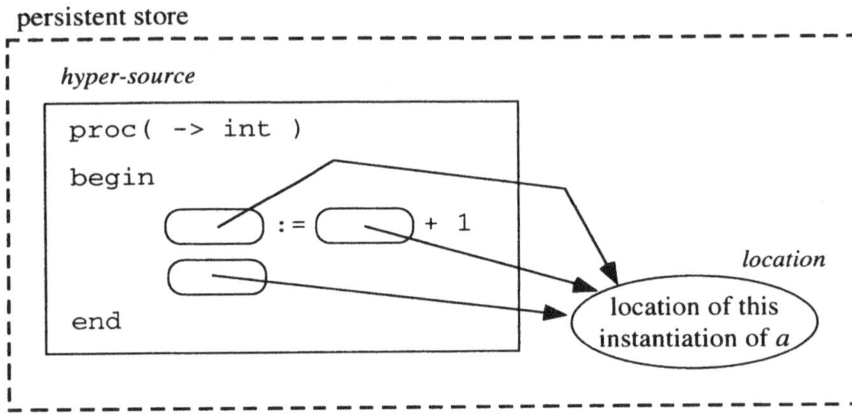

Fig. 2. Corresponding hyper-source.

The procedure *myCounter* in Figure 1, whose meaning depends critically upon its evaluation context, may be represented by the hyper-source shown in Figure 2. Thus hyper-source may be used to give a source representation for any arbitrary procedure, with the property that its semantics is independent of its evaluation environment. This is quite simply achieved by representing the necessary parts of the traditional evaluation environment within the source itself, by means of hyper-links. Notice for example that successive evaluations of the procedure *counterGen* will result in different hyper-source representations, as although the textual code is the same the hyper-links are different, reflecting the different semantics. The use of hyper-source is thus able to achieve the desired one-to-one mapping between procedure source and executable forms This clears the way to the presentation of a unified visualisation of the two representations to the programmer, leaving concepts such as compilation and linking to be matters of system efficiency rather than system building essentials.

References

1. Connor RCH, Cutts QI, Kirby GNC, Moore VS, Morrison R. Unifying Interaction with Persistent Data and Program. In: Sawyer P (ed) Interfaces to Database Systems, Proc. 2nd International Workshop on Interfaces to Databases, Lancaster, 1994. Workshops in Computing, Springer-Verlag, 1994, pp 197-212
2. Kirby GNC, Connor RCH, Cutts QI, Dearle A, Farkas AM, Morrison R. Persistent Hyper-Programs. In: Albano A, Morrison R (ed) Persistent Object Systems, Proc. 5th International Workshop on Persistent Object Systems, San Miniato, Italy. Springer-Verlag, 1992, pp 86-106
3. Morrison R, Connor RCH, Cutts QI, Dunstan VS, Kirby GNC. Exploiting Persistent Linkage in Software Engineering Environments. Computer Journal 1995; 38,1:1-16.

Chapter 3.1.4

The Persistent Workshop – a Programming Environment for Napier88*

Dag Sjøberg[1], Ray Welland[2], Malcolm P. Atkinson[2], Paul Philbrow[2], Cathy Waite[2] and Stewart Macneill[2].

1 Department of Informatics, University of Oslo, PO Box 1080 Blindern, N-0316 OSLO, Norway
2 Department of Computing Science, University of Glasgow, Glasgow, G12 8QQ, Scotland

Abstract. The Persistent Workshop is a programming environment to support the construction of application systems in Napier88, a persistent programming language. In addition to supporting programming activities, the Workshop provides a demonstration of the persistence technology together with an environment in which various experiments can be conducted. The basic structure of the Workshop is outlined, together with a short summary of the tools provided within the programming environment. Finally, the evaluation of the Workshop is briefly described.

1 Introduction

The Glasgow Persistent Workshop (the 'Workshop') was built to facilitate the construction of medium-scale persistent applications in the persistent programming language Napier88 (see Chapter 1.1.3) and to allow a number of experiments to be performed. Individual tools for program construction, library management and use, visualisation, methodology support and data modelling are provided. The strongly-typed, persistent context in which these tools work is exploited to provide them with guarantees about the items on which they work, to furnish them with information about those items and to support communication between tools.
The reasons for engaging in this line of research are fourfold:

- to demonstrably exploit the opportunities provided by orthogonal persistence;
- to validate a model for building persistent application systems (PASs) and to better support programmers using persistence;
- to provide a context in which to carry out various research projects such as visualisation experiments and prototyping of build-management tools;
- to gain experience with a live persistent application, providing a real test load with genuine users.

Present persistent systems provide an excellent context in which to write software engineering components. Particular data structures to model software and

* The full version of this paper was published in the Nordic Journal of Computing 4(1997), pp123-149.

maintenance processes need only be formulated once and then both persist and may be manipulated directly. The powerful and orthogonally persistent type systems are well suited to representing these data structures and the persistent stores can accommodate all of the data and program involved.

Persistent researchers need access to the experience of building PASs and need to be able to observe the operational use and maintenance of PASs. The construction of the persistent Workshop provided us with the experience of using orthogonally persistent technology on a larger scale than we had previously experienced. The Workshop is in intensive use and continues to undergo evolution and maintenance. This should lead to the verification of the reliability, scalability and flexibility of persistent technology and also provides data to characterise loads on persistent stores and the evolution of PASs.

The utility of the persistent Workshop as an observable test-bed in an academic computing science department, is extremely valuable. To make the observations we wish to make, it is necessary that the current version of the system is actively used by a reasonably sized sample of people and that it is under development. Of course, we cannot build on these observations alone as this environment may exhibit idiosyncratic behaviour. But it is a convenient first source of operational information.

2 Structure of the Workshop

The initial design of the Workshop was intended only as a foundation for a persistent programmers' programming environment. However, as one of the main motives was to demonstrate that an orthogonally persistent system makes an excellent platform for such applications we also wished to demonstrate its wider utility, e.g. for design systems and other tool sets where professionals gain support for long-lived tasks from a sophisticated body of application software and data. It was soon apparent that the architecture we had chosen for this demonstration did indeed have wider applicability as for all PASs the application software must continue to evolve while the user community continues to use the existing data.

The architecture chosen for the Workshop is expected to have relevance to a variety of systems. An instance of the Workshop will have the following elements:

- WorkItems which are units on which the Workshop users are working;
- Tools which are subsystems that enable Workshop users to perform operations on WorkItems; and
- Workbenches which define the context in which an individual carries out a particular kind of work within a Workshop and contain instances of Tools, a collection of WorkItems and data concerning the work in progress and user's preferences.

Some user interface, window-based or textual, is required to allow manipulation of a Workshop instance. We are interested in the user interface design of some Tools and in the design of the software-interface between this user interface and the other Workshop components. We are less interested in the design of the Workshop's user interface, accepting a utilitarian model until the content and usage of the Workshop are well developed.

The construction of the Workshop has benefited from and is closely related to the work on the Glasgow Libraries (see Chapter 3.1.5). The Libraries contain many facilities used by the Workshop and tools; some of these were stimulated by the requirements of the Workshop. The Workshop also provides a set of tools and an environment for constructing and maintaining the Libraries. A goal of the Libraries research is to make it so convenient to use the library mechanisms that application programmers choose them to administer and document the parts of their own programs. This depends on the integration with, and quality of, the Workshop itself.

The principal Tools available at present are outlined below; more detailed descriptions of the Tools and User manuals for the majority can be found in [5]. In addition to general tools , such as those for administering WorkItems, the following groups of tools are available:

- programming tools for constructing, editing and compiling Software WorkItems;
- library management tools, for constructing, validating, viewing, searching and using Library WorkItems (see Chapter 3.1.5);
- visualisation tools that allow programmers to inspect and understand the contents of the persistent store (see Chapter 3.1.6);
- software engineering tools that manipulate PAS WorkItems [4];
- data modelling tools that provide generic data modelling and rapid prototyping facilities (see Chapter 3.2.1).

3 Evaluation of the Workshop

One of the primary purposes of building the Workshop was to use it as the subject of experiments and as a test bed for other experiments. The Workshop was built over a period of 18 months by nine developers (who all had other work and most worked on the project for only a few months). It comprises about 36000 lines of Napier88 code, excluding the Libraries and Napier88 technology, and had more than 50 users. It provided an opportunity to observe:

- user behaviour and responses;
- the sequence of changes a body of software, types and data undergoes during development; and
- actual loads imposed on the software and stores.

We conducted talk-alouds, interviews and other observations to identify user reactions to some of the tools in the early versions of the Workshop [1, 2]. These evaluation techniques were augmented with automatically recorded logs of Workshop usage. We recorded the activities of several groups of programmers who were given a series of four maintenance tasks to carry out on a large application program. In this experiment each programming team started with a pre-populated persistent store of approximately 200 Mbytes, containing the software to be maintained and the operational data. We have detailed records of each team's use of the Workshop over a period of eight working weeks. We analysed the log entries recorded for 11 users in a period of about 6 weeks (totalling about 9400 entries). Examples of analysis include use frequency of tools and operations (cf. our earlier analysis of use of Napier88 language constructs [3]). Popular tools and operations may be the subject of optimisation. Moreover, we may ask questions about why a particular tool is heavily used or, alternatively, why it is not used as much as we would expect. More details of this work can be found in [6].

References

1. D.O. Lavery. A Napier88 programmer study. Technical Report FIDE/95/140, ESPRIT Basic Research Action, Project Number 6309—FIDE2, 1995.
2. D.O. Lavery and G. Cockton. Iterative development of early usability evaluation methods for software visualisations. In *Proceedings of the Sixth Workshop of Empirical Studies of Programmers*. Ablex Publishing, 1996.
3. D.I.K. Sjøberg, Q. Cutts, M.P. Atkinson, and R.C. Welland. Analysing persistent language applications. In M.P. Atkinson, V. Benzaken and D. Maier (eds.), *Sixth International Workshop on Persistent Object Systems (Tarascon, Provence, France, 5–9 September, 1994)* pp. 235–255, Springer-Verlag and British Computer Society, 1994.
4. D.I.K. Sjøberg, R.C. Welland, M.P. Atkinson, P.C. Philbrow, and C.A. Waite. Exploiting persistence in build management. *Software Practice and Experience*, **27(4)**, 447-480 (April 1997).
5. C.A. Waite, P.C Philbrow, M.P. Atkinson, R.C. Welland, D.O. Lavery, S.D. Macneill, T. Printezis, and R.L. Cooper. Programmer's persistent workshop—principles and user guide. Technical Report FIDE/95/125, ESPRIT Basic Research Action, Project Number 6309—FIDE$_2$, 1995.
6. R. Welland, D. Sjøberg and M.P. Atkinson Empirical Analysis based on Automatic Tool Logging. *EASE-97 (Empirical Assessment and Evaluation in Software Engineering Workshop)*, Keele University, 24-25 March 1997.

Chapter 3.1.5

The Glasgow Persistent Libraries

Malcolm P. Atkinson, Ray Welland, Paul Philbrow, Cathy Waite, Richard Cooper, Darryn Lavery, Alan Froggatt, Claudia Herzig, Stewart Macneill, Miguel Mira da Silva, Greig Montgomery, Alex Pirmohamed and Tony Printezis.

Department of Computing Science, University of Glasgow, Glasgow, G12 8QQ, Scotland

Abstract. This chapter describes the development of the Glasgow Persistent Libraries for Napier88. Our overall goals are to increase software re-use and accelerate software construction and maintenance. The objectives of this work were to investigate the creation of high-quality library components and the provision of accurate retrieval mechanisms enabling users to find relevant library components. We discuss the basic principles which guided our research and describe the tools which were built to support the construction and use of the Libraries. To conclude, we outline possible future work in the area of large component libraries.

1 Introduction

This chapter describes part of the work undertaken at Glasgow University to develop a Persistent Programming Environment (PPE) for Napier88 (Chapter 1.1.3). This work on programming environments brings together three major areas of work: the Glasgow Persistent Libraries (the 'Libraries'), the Persistent Programming Workshop (the 'Workshop'), see Chapter 3.1.4, and visualisation, see Chapter 3.1.6.

The aim of the Libraries work is to produce libraries of re-usable software components which will overcome what we perceive as the major hurdles to successful re-use discussed below.

- *The difficulty of discovering what is available and understanding how to use it.* These problems have been tackled by ensuring that all libraries have a regular structure, providing a tool for finding components based on Information Retrieval techniques, and using a uniform documentation style throughout the libraries.

- *Uncertainty about the quality of library components.* To address this issue a rigorous quality assurance (QA) process has been defined, together with a tool to assist with this work.

- *The extra effort required to write and document code of sufficient quality that it can be re-used.* This is essentially a trade-off between the amount of effort required and how much the Libraries are used in practice. As part of the Libraries experiment the level of usage of the Libraries needs to be monitored.

The construction of the Workshop has benefited from and is closely related to the work on the Libraries. The Libraries contain many facilities used by the Workshop and tools; some of these were stimulated by the requirements of the Workshop. The Workshop also provides a set of tools and an environment for constructing and maintaining the Libraries. A goal of the Libraries research is to make it so convenient to use the library mechanisms that application programmers choose them to administer and document the parts of their own programs. This will depend on the integration with, and quality of, the Workshop itself.

In the remainder of this chapter we describe the common context for this work before discussing the work on the Libraries in more detail.

2 The Context of the work

The work described in this chapter has been carried out using the Napier88 system developed at St Andrews and utilises a wide range of the facilities in release 2.2 (Chapter 1.1.3). The majority of these facilities are common to all the $FIDE_2$ languages, as described below. However, the environment values and the reflective facilities which are exploited extensively in our work are particular to Napier88.

2.1 Orthogonal Persistent Systems

All the languages of the $FIDE_2$ project support *orthogonal persistence.* The definition, utility and provision of orthogonal persistence are discussed elsewhere [4]. Essentially, orthogonal persistence means that data structures of any type may have arbitrarily long lifetimes, potentially exceeding the lifetimes of individual program executions or even the period for which some programs or parts of the whole PAS remain in use.

Orthogonal persistence has two implications for the library research:

- values (objects) of any type, e.g. procedures, abstract data types, images, lists, tables, etc., may be library items; and
- all the data structures required to implement libraries are automatically preserved by persistence.

The first of these has not been explored significantly in the work at Glasgow to date, though it is exploited in the St Andrews standard library for Napier88 [11]. Orthogonal persistence was of considerable significance. It allowed the library developers to focus on the information and structure of the data for indexes, retrieval, etc. without distracting concern for preservation mechanisms.

2.2 Higher-order, Reflective Persistent Languages

All of the $FIDE_2$ languages: Tycoon, Fibonacci and Napier88 are polymorphic and higher-order (see Chapters 1.1.1 to 1.1.3). By *polymorphism* we mean that code can be written that operates on data of a number of different types. Polymorphism increases the potential re-usability of libraries of procedures, abstract data types and objects.

By *higher-order* we mean that procedures (or other values that include code, such as abstract data types and objects) are first-class values that can be used in the same way as any other values in the language [3]. In particular, they can be values in data structures, can be parameters, and can be produced by other procedures. These properties are exploited in two ways in the construction of the Libraries:

- libraries of procedures and other code objects can be readily stored by making procedures be values in persistent data structures, and
- these procedures can be managed using other procedures that manipulate them.

For example, the `Library Inspector`, our Quality Assurance tool, manipulates procedures in the store and is itself built from procedures in the store.

As section 3.4 describes, the polymorphism and higher-order properties are particularly important in providing libraries with bulk-type properties.

All three $FIDE_2$ languages are *strongly typed*: no operation is permitted unless a check has been made to verify that it will not break the type rules. This ensures that library components are correctly used. Its combination with persistence provides a type-checked linking mechanism that ensures that the combined components are compatible (at least with respect to their types). We have the impression that this type checking has accelerated development by rapidly detecting coding blunders, particularly when interfaces are being changed, without constraining our ability to code system functions.

Programmers using the Libraries must describe the types of the components they wish to use. This minor impediment to re-use is overcome by editing tools that utilise information from the library management system to automatically generate the type information and other details.

Two of the $FIDE_2$ languages support *reflection* (Chapter 1.2.1) which allows a program to generate new pieces of code while it is executing and then incorporate that code in the execution. This facility is important in the libraries work because it allows type dependent code to be generated, at the moment when it is first needed. Thus library management facilities can be generated for each type of value held in the library. Consequently, the library has the potential to provide values of any of the infinite set of types available in the language and yet it can tailor its operations to the finite set of types that actually occur.

2.3 Napier88

The language Napier88 (Chapter 1.1.3) is a well developed example of an orthogonally persistent language with the facilities described in the previous two sections. It is released with its own extensive standard library [11] which includes basic facilities, user-interface facilities (WIN), reflective facilities and basic inter-process communication. This has proved an adequate foundation for building the Libraries without stepping outside the language and its type-checking regime.

The Libraries research makes particular use of the following additional facilities:

- *environments*, which manage sets of bindings between names and values;
- the *callable compiler*, which allows programs to be dynamically constructed; and
- *incremental binding*, which allows programs to be incrementally linked during execution still under the regime of the type checker.

Values which are environments are first class, and may be components of other data structures, including values in other environments. Operations allow bindings to be added (and removed) from an environment, and allow names from an environment to be introduced into scope in program sources after a run-time check to verify that the entry still exists and that its type matches the expected type. We use these environment values to collect together related values as a library and to organise related libraries. The reader should note that the cost of the type check is only incurred when the programmer introduces the identifiers from an environment. These identifiers are subsequently used in a statically checked regime since the run-time system can be trusted not to permit that code to be executed if the check fails.

The callable-compiler (part of the reflective facilities, see Chapter 1.2.2) is called by tools that automatically complete programs with information from the library and then compile and save or execute them. This enables the library system to be well-integrated with the compilation and execution system without tying the library development to the compiler's implementation. That is, no special system interfaces or type-checking evasions are needed anywhere in the implementation of the whole of this library system.

Incremental binding is used to compose constructed programs with library components. This permits incremental resolution of library procedure references. The use of persistent references to library components from library components avoids a cascade of linking operations when a library component is used and avoids multiple inclusion of indirectly used sub-components.

3 The Glasgow Persistent Libraries

The increased re-use of code and other data structures is a major goal in software engineering. It is clear that there are many economic advantages to re-use, for example, the reduction of software production and maintenance costs. The provision of components also guides the solving of a problem by providing basic building blocks (c.f. windowing systems).

Perhaps the most important reason for encouraging re-use is intellectual synergy. Different programmers in a community can become expert in subdomains of their common application domain. In consequence they can prepare better quality code for tasks within that particular subdomain. This code can then be re-used by the other programmers in that community to produce better quality application systems.

There are, however, several impediments to achieving higher levels of re-use:

- the difficulty programmers have discovering what is already available and understanding how to use it;
- the uncertainty programmers have about the quality of library components; and
- the extra effort required to write and document code of sufficient quality that it can be re-used and to validate that it is of re-usable quality for all the circumstances under which it will be used.

It is frequently the case that the ad hoc solution to a particular task is expedient even though it increases the overall costs or reduces application program quality. In particular, a programmer under pressure to deliver an application will not take risks with unvalidated library components; you stick to what you know works, including a quickly developed particular solution, even though it increases the total volume of code to be maintained.

In $FIDE_2$ we have sought to overcome these difficulties and to achieve higher volumes of re-use via our work on libraries. Libraries are an appropriate metaphor for tackling this problem as they capture the idea of organising the information so that it can be found (classification) and the idea of a repository where people seek useful information. Additionally, in a library, information retrieval mechanisms and indexes are tools that people expect to use. Finally, a librarian is expected to maintain a level of quality in the collected material.

It is probable that for many programming systems the greatest re-use is achieved through the initial (standard) libraries. It is common to find that much investment goes into re-designing and re-implementing these initial libraries and the work reported here can be viewed both as an initial design of such a library for a persistent polymorphic higher-order language [4] and as the development of a set of tools and techniques that is pertinent to a wide range of such libraries. For example, these tools and techniques might be used with the collections of libraries that are obtainable in conjunction with Java [9] or with the initial library of objects in a system such as O_2 [6].

In the Java case, the standard libraries are called the core classes. In JDK 1.1.1 (March 1997) there were 1,400 classes in this core set. By JDK 1.2 (January 1998) there were 2.500. This investment in core classes indicates their commercial importance. Their volume indicates the need for tools to assist programmers in finding and using components they need.

An aim of this work is to extend the habit of preparing and supplying useful libraries from the ambit of the language and system providers to the programmers of sophisticated applications. The tools and processes that have been designed to facilitate the former group are intended to be sufficiently simple and lightweight that many application programmers will also use them to develop validated, documented and indexed components for their own use as well as for their colleagues to use.

3.1 Library Management Principles

Four principles have guided our library research.

Quality Control To overcome programmer reluctance to use existing library components it is essential that quality is assured. That is, reasonable measures are taken to verify that a library entry performs as specified and that that specification is clear. We include in the Quality Assurance (QA) requirement, that the supplier of an item provides a set of test programs that fit in a harness so that they can be used for regression testing. We also require that a separate person perform the QA, which involves inspecting the library entry, verifying that the tests are thorough, that the regression tests are passed and that the documentation is complete and consistent with the tests.

Regular Classification An attempt is made to impose a regular structure on the contents of the library. It is not necessarily the case that a programmer will know which leaf of this structure holds the item they want. Other mechanisms deal with this. However, once an item is located those in its proximity should perform related functions and therefore also be of interest. Within this classification, regular naming schemes help programmers remember and guess names.

Free Text Retrieval It is inevitable that many programmers will not perceive a collection of facilities in the same way as the facility providers. No matter how carefully the classification is refined, many programmers will not find it intuitive. To avoid this being a serious impediment to re-use, search tools based on information retrieval techniques and indexes, and browsing tools are provided. Once the collection of facilities is usefully large, browsing tools alone are ineffective. The search tools need to be based on natural language descriptions of the library items. We use the documentation of the facilities and their names as sources for this information, and the QA process includes validation that this is present, has the correct form and is of reasonable quality. This same information is used to produce paper documentation and WWW pages [27, 28].

Automation Building and maintaining a library is an onerous task. We wish to encourage many programmers, some of them remote, to contribute to the collected library. Therefore, the production of skeletons, the organisation of library entries and the processes involved in installation, QA and release must be sufficiently automated. We are able to use the protection afforded by strong typing to reduce the possibility of steps in this process being circumvented. There is some labour in making use of a library item after it has been found. This is also minimised by integration of editors, search tools and compilers, so that once an item has been located, any relevant information may be easily captured and used.

The four principles identified above lead to many detailed design issues. For example, when a higher-order procedure is documented, often the items of primary interest to programmers are the procedures that it generates. How can the structure of the library lead sensibly to that information when those procedures never reside in the library? Space does not permit a full discussion of all such issues in this chapter.

3.2 Library Management Tools

To support library work according to the principles identified above a set of related tools are required. These have been developed in Napier88 and are fully described in [26]. Outlines of the principal tools are included below.

The Explorer This tool includes information-retrieval facilities and mechanisms to present the documentation of selected entries via those facilities. Selected library entries may then be copied to a program under construction. The Explorer builds a weighted index of keywords extracted from the documentation of all the library components using well-established techniques from Information Retrieval [25]. Keywords are identified by removing noise words (such as `a` and `the`) and stemming words [21] to remove grammatical variations (e.g. `sort`, `sorted` and `sorting` will map to the common stem `sort`). The weighting of a key word is *inversely* proportional to its frequency of occurrence in the library documentation so that infrequently occurring words get the highest weighting as they are the best discriminators [24]. The keyword `list` will get a very low weighting as it occurs in more than one hundred library entries! The user types a free text query and the keywords are extracted from it using the same process as indexing. The Explorer then returns a list of matches between the query and the library entries, all possible matches are identified in a scrollable menu in descending order of total weighting. The user can retrieve the detailed documentation from any library entry simply by clicking on the name of the entry in the menu of possible matches. Documentation for a library entry consists of a definition of the procedure, a description of its purpose, an example of use, the current status and where the procedure is located (defined by the path to that procedure). The performance depends on the quality of the documentation provided for each library entry.

The Inspector This tool is the basis for all QA and documentation operations. It carries out a variety of standard consistency checks on all or part of a library and identifies those parts which are incomplete or unsatisfactory. All documentation, which is stored with the library items, is updated via the Inspector. Inspector facilities can then be used to format the documentation as hard copy manuals, or to construct WWW pages. This has the advantage of maintaining *one* primary source for the documentation and information retrieval, with all other material being derived from it to reduce the incidence of out-of-date documentation sapping programmers' confidence. Book-keeping, such as recording when a QA operation was done, and by whom, is also performed by this tool. When programmers wish to prepare new library entries (the item and its description) the Inspector can be invoked to create the skeleton of this entry and to guide the insertion of relevant information.

The Search Path Editor Programmers may wish to work with several versions of their own libraries or of standard libraries. In any case, it is unrealistic to attempt to keep all item names unique. To manage this, the Search Path Editor is provided which combines the visualisation of the libraries with facilities for organising how they are searched. Each program part under construction has its own search path, so that different parts of the system may be built using different libraries. The Search Path Editor defines the current search path which is used by the Completer in resolving ambiguities (see Chapter 3.1.6).

The Completer The use of a procedure (or other library item) requires the insertion of a call at its point of use and of a reference to its source and type earlier in the program. If a programmer simply inserts the call into their program, the Completer processes the code which includes the new procedure call and obtains the reference to its source and type information from the rest of the relevant library entry. The programmer may be asked to resolve ambiguities and problems encountered while locating the information.

Viper is a visualisation tool (Chapter 3.1.6, 15) which gives a view of the contents of the store and hence of the libraries as they are organised via environment objects in the store. The libraries are presented as a tree, emphasising their classification. The content of a node can be examined in more detail by selecting it, and search facilities enable programmers to look for things when they do not know in which node they are located. A separate program is available to produce (via PostScript) printed tree diagrams as an aide-mèmoire for programmers, Figure 1 shows an example of such a diagram.

3.3 Library Component Classification

The libraries are structured according to major subdivisions based on current application programming activities using Napier88. Currently the majority of applications are concerned with the support of persistent programming (including the library system itself and the Persistent Programmers' Workbench (Chapter 3.1.4), with Data Modelling (Section 3.2), with user interfaces [20] and with GIS [12, 13].

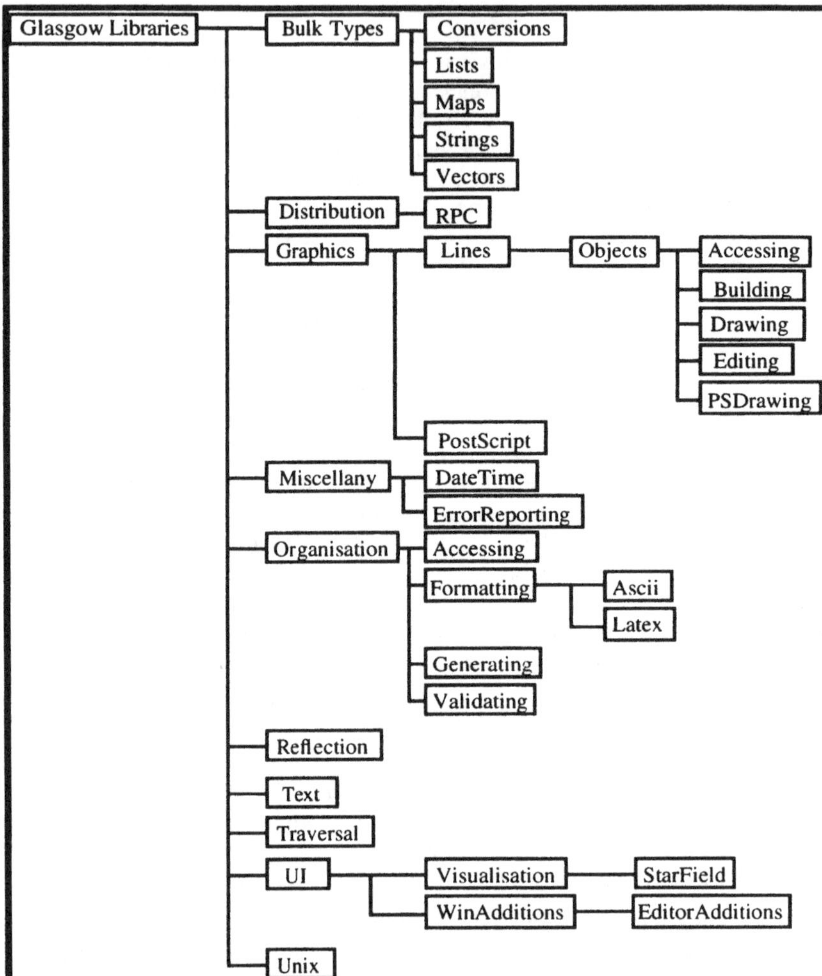

Fig. 1. The Structure of the Glasgow Libraries

The library's major components are presented in Figure 1. The library includes a major section, `BulkTypes` [1], to provide and manipulate Lists, Vectors, Strings and Maps [2].

Also included is a major section, `UI` within which is `WinAdditions`, which consists of extensions to the WIN user interface manager. There are also components for the `Visualisation` work. For example components exist to automatically generate menus from maps and to use star fields [5] to allow the values of bulk types to be understood via queries with sufficient feedback that users understand them.

Two sections, `Reflection` and `Traversal`, provide support for the reflective programming style in use (Chapter 1.2.2), for scanning structures in the store and for manipulating representations of types. The `Distribution` section provides programmer access to a data-type complete, type-safe RPC [18].

The `Organisation` section provides the procedures required for building the Library tools. Components for formatting the library documentation are stored under `Formatting`, while the Library Inspector is built from components in the `Generating` and `Validating` sub-sections.

Other major sections exist as is shown in Figure 1. Each may be further divided into collections of more closely related items, for example, all the list processing procedures in section `Lists`. The reader is reminded that we provide the search facilities in Explorer and Viper to remove the need for programmers to have an accurate intuitive grasp of the classification. One reason for this, is that we want to encourage remote users to contribute collections of library items. It is impracticable to expect to sustain a simple classification when there are multiple contributors.

3.4 Library Experiments

Several groups of students (a total of approximately 40) and about 10 staff have used these libraries at Glasgow. They have also been in use in Oslo and Cape Town. A study has been made of the user's reactions to the language, library and tools in combination [14, 16, 17, Chapter 3.1.6].

It was apparent that most programmers could make good use of the library components, but more analysis was needed to discover whether they make appropriate use (choose the most appropriate existing item) and whether the new tools were leading to more extensive use of the libraries. The former requires manual analysis of programs. The latter may be accomplished by comparing the use of libraries by successive cohorts of students undertaking similar tasks. For this analysis, we expected to use the existing thesaurus tools [23, 22] to count the number of different items used. We also considered analysing code to see if it was replicated in the library, indicating that programmers were 're-inventing the wheel' rather than using library components.

Events overtook this line of research. In 1995 we were invited by SUN Microsystems Laboratories to investigate orthogonal persistence for Java™. At the same time the enthusiasm with which Java was greeted has meant that many student projects are now conducted in Java. Consequently, we neither had the maintained test platform nor the test loads provided by cohorts of students to continue this work in Napier88. We are about to reach the stage where we have re-tooled for Java and can make equivalent measurements.

The Napier88 libraries were built by students and staff. The initial work required much supervision and care to ensure library conventions were adopted, and many programmers complained of bureaucratic tedium. In 1995, two students undertook projects to generate collections of library components. Claudia Herzig produced a star field viewer library [10] and Alan Froggatt a line drawing interactive graphics library [7, 8]. As the library tools were still under development, the students suffered from tedious book keeping tasks. However, the influence of the tools was apparent in that their work was conformant with library requirements and passed quickly through QA and into use. Staff and research students contributing to the library after the tools became available reported a considerable reduction in labour. It was immediately apparent that they were much more likely to prepare components, *ab initio*, as library components. We hoped to measure these effects and show that they were significant and we intend to do this when we have re-tooled for Java. An ultimate goal is to have persuaded programmers to use the library technology for all their program parts (even if they do not intend to release them) because the testing, documentation and support arrangements are sufficiently worthwhile and low cost.

We were keen to enfranchise others to contribute to a common library, but were concerned with maintaining the standards necessary for programmers to remain confident. A group at the University of Cape Town and individuals in northern Norway and Santiago, Chile produced code that might have been incorporated into the library. If we can make the supporting technology sufficiently strong we would hope such co-operation can be continued with little extra effort at the central repository of library items. As we remark below, Java has opened up this model of co-operation so that it operates on a grand and global scale.

If the total library grows large, then there is good reason to keep a well identified central repository and to allow local stores to have locally useful subsets of this. This will minimise storage and version release costs. As a first step a distributed version of the Explorer was developed, that allowed other stores to be searched for useful library items [19]. These could then be acquired locally. Both the remote searching and the transfer of library items were built on the RPC mechanisms described above.

4. Conclusions and Evaluation

We have developed a library of several hundred persistent components for Napier88 and demonstrated that it can be successfully used. Tools to support the construction of high-quality components and the retrieval of components from the Persistent Libraries have been prototyped and evaluated. However, the focus of our research work has now shifted from Napier88 to Java. We need to carry over the lessons learned from the work in the Napier88 environment to our new research platform.

The work reported here, mainly conducted in the period 1993 to 1995, developed library technology to facilitate and encourage re-use. A similar interest in extensive libraries can be found in object-oriented languages such as Modula-3, SmallTalk and C++. However, there are significant differences.

In the case of these other languages, the tools to support the production and organisation of libraries have not been discussed. On the other hand, recent interactive program development environments (IDEs) such as Visual Basic, Visual C++, Symantec, Code Warrior and Visual Age, have provided even closer integration between the component library system and the source code production editors. Sophisticated insertion, expanded from the current context is achieved with wizards.

These IDE tools are different from those described here. In particular, they typically do not include the information retrieval technology to search for appropriate items. Nor do they include tools to assist with the construction, organisation and QA of the libraries of components. It is possible that the IDE and component library vendors may have such tools but there is no general attempt to enfranchise the wider community to build application-specific libraries.

Since our original experiments using Napier88, two major developments presage trends that make our research more applicable:

- the blossoming of strongly-typed, object-oriented programming based on Java means that the proportion of the software industry that would benefit from the tools we have prototyped is growing very rapidly;

- the increasing use of the Internet to support globally distributed programming teams and software component "commerce" is extending the need to support programmers in finding components in ever larger search spaces.

Each of these trends is now examined.

4.1 Java Applicability

As remarked above, the current JDK (exemplar of the Java standards) contains approximately 2,500 classes. Even an experienced Java programmer has difficulty keeping track of this volume of components, particularly as each class has many methods. The problem is further extended by the many other collections of Java classes available across the WWW. Java beans are an attempt to both encourage the growth of such component libraries and to encourage systematic structures and naming to facilitate re-use.

4.2 Distributed Software Development

Partly to exploit cost differentials and partly to exploit the effective extension of the working day, it is becoming common to develop and maintain software with a distributed programming team. Say a group in California, a group in Scotland, a team in Moscow and a team in Japan, all working on the same example. Such an extended team has added difficulty keeping track of the components team members produce because there is little opportunity for the casual dialogue that propagates such information in a localised group. Even within the local group this propagation is unreliable.

4.3 The Java Opportunity

The integration of documentation with the source code and its automatic conversion to HTML using `javadoc` presents several advantages. The common source for the program and documentation encourages programmers to keep them in step. The structure imposed within the source file and between source files increases the contextual information.

This means that there is a potential for good (rapid and with high relevance) retrieval of useful components utilising the sources or the derived HTML. A specialised tool, in contrast with the general web indexers, would exploit this structure, restrict itself to the component sources and be integrated with program construction tools.

The two properties: multiple large libraries and distributed software development, mean that there is a particular need for an extended Explorer tool integrated with an IDE.

It is not yet apparent to what extent JavaSoft and other library producers can maintain quality and structure in their libraries. However, we suspect that at present they do this without tools similar to the Inspector. Were they to have such tools they might directly save labour while enhancing the consistency of the libraries and components produced.

4.4 The Way Ahead

The next step is to develop a more advanced version of the Explorer for Java, with controlled network searching capabilities exploiting Java's software organisational packages, which could be integrated with IDEs with immediate advantage.

A more difficult challenge is to develop further the QA and consistency verification essayed in the Inspector and to persuade the "standards bodies" to take due notice of the issues of quality and structure of a language's associated libraries.

Both of these steps are likely to generate significant cost reduction and improved product quality for all software projects using languages with extensive libraries. If they are adequately supported with tools the same benefits will be available for company and project specific component libraries. Finally, we can envisage redeploying these same techniques to other domains of re-use, such as system components on VLSI chips.

References

1. M.P. Atkinson, P.J. Bailey, D. Christie, K. Cropper, and P.C. Philbrow. Towards bulk type libraries for Napier88. Technical Report FIDE/93/78, ESPRIT Basic Research Action, Project Number 6309—FIDE2, 1993. 36pp, including index.
2. M.P. Atkinson, C. Lécluse, P.C. Philbrow, and P. Richard. Design issues in a map language. In P. Kanellakis and J.W. Schmidt, editors. *Database Programming Languages: Bulk Types and Persistent Data.* San Mateo, CA: Morgan Kaufmann Publishers, 1991.. Proceedings of the Third International Workshop on Database Programming Languages (Nafplion, Greece, 27th–30th August 1991).
3. M.P. Atkinson and R. Morrison. Procedures as persistent data objects. *ACM Transactions on Programming Languages and Systems*, 4(7), pp 539–559, October 1985.
4. M.P. Atkinson and R. Morrison. Orthogonal persistent object systems. *VLDB Journal*, 4(3), 1995.
5. C. Ahlberg and B. Shneiderman. Visual information seeking: tight coupling of dynamic query filters with starfield displays. In *Proceedings of ACM CHI'94 (Boston, MA, April 24th–28th 1994)*, pages 313–317, 1994.
6. F. Bancilhon, C. Delobel, and P. Kanellakis, editors. *Building an Object-Oriented Database System: The Story of* O_2 Morgan Kaufmann Publishers, 1992.
7. A. Froggatt. A line drawing library for Napier88. Senior Honours 1993–5, Solo Project, Department of Computing Science, University of Glasgow, April 1995.
8. A. Froggatt. Line drawing library: User manual. Programming Notes for Glasgow Napier88 Libraries, Department of Computing Science, University of Glasgow, April 1995.
9. J. Gosling, B. Joy and G. Steele. The Java™ Language Specification, Addison-Wesley 1996.
10. C. Herzig. A parametric generator for starfield displays. Senior Honours 1993–5, Solo Project, Department of Computing Science, University of Glasgow, April 1995.
11. G.N.C. Kirby, A.L. Brown, R.C.H. Connor, Q.I. Cutts, A. Dearle, V.S. Moore, R. Morrison, and D.S. Munro. The Napier88 standard library reference manual (version 2.2). Research Report CS/94/7, Department of Computational Science, University of St Andrews, 1994.
12. Y.J. Kuo. The development of an integrated GIS based on a persistent programming language. In *Proceedings of the Fifth EGIS Conference (Paris, France, 29th March–1st April 1994)*, 1994.

13. Y.J. Kuo. *The Design and Implementation of a Truly Integrated GIS Using the Persistent Programming Language Napier88.* PhD thesis, University of Glasgow, June 1995.
14. Lavery D. A Napier88 programmer study. FIDE Technical Report FIDE/95/140, Department of Computing Science, University of Glasgow, 1995.
15. Lavery D. Towards visualizing persistent stores. Technical Report FIDE/95/122, ESPRIT Basic Research Action, Project Number 6309—$FIDE_2$, 1995.
16. Lavery D. and Cockton G. A Pilot Study of Early Usability Evaluation Methods for Software Visualisations. FIDE Technical Report FIDE/95/141, Department of Computing Science, University of Glasgow, 1995.
17. Lavery D. and Cockton G. Iterative Development of Early Usability Evaluation Methods for Software Visualisations. In Gray W.D. and Boehm-Davis D.A. (Eds) *Proceedings of the Sixth Workshop of Empirical Studies of Programmers.* Ablex Publishing, 1996, pp 275-276.
18. M. Mira da Silva. Automating type-safe RPC. In *Proceedings of the Fifth International Workshop on Research Issues on Data Engineering: Distributed Object Management (Taipei, Taiwan, 6th-7th March 1995).* IEEE Computer Society Press, 1995.
19. M. Mira da Silva. *Models of Higher-order, Type-safe, Distributed Computation over Autonomous Persistent Object Stores.* PhD thesis, University of Glasgow, 1996.
20. N. Paton, R.L. Cooper, D. England, G. al Qaimari, and A.C. Kilgour. Integrated architectures for database interface development. *IEE Proc. Comput. Digit. Tech.*, 141(2), March 1994.
21. M.F. Porter. An Algorithm for Suffix Stripping. *Program*, vol. 14(3), pp. 130-137. July 1980.
22. D.I.K. Sjøberg, M.P. Atkinson, J.C. Lopes, and P.W. Trinder. Building an integrated persistent application. In C. Beeri, A. Ohori, and D.E. Shasha, editors, *Database Programming Languages (DBPL-4),* Workshops in Computing, pages 359–375. Springer-Verlag in collaboration with the British Computer Society, 1993. Proceedings of the Fourth International Workshop on Database Programming Languages—Object Models and Languages (Manhattan, New York City, USA, 30th August–1st September 1993).
23. D.I.K. Sjøberg. *Thesaurus-Based Methodologies and Tools for Maintaining Persistent Application Systems.* PhD thesis, University of Glasgow, July 1993.
24. Sparck Jones, K. A statistical interpretation of term specificity and its application in retrieval. *Journal of Documentation*, 28, pp 11-21, 1972.
25. C.J . van Rijsbergen. *Information Retrieval* Butterworths, London, second edition 1979. (See also: http://www.dcs.gla.ac.uk/Keith/Preface.html)
26. C.A. Waite, P.C Philbrow, M.P. Atkinson, R.C. Welland, D.O. Lavery, S.D. Macneill, T. Printezis, and R.C. Cooper. Programmer's Persistent Workshop—Principles and User Guide. Technical Report FIDE/95/125, ESPRIT Basic Research Action, Project Number 6309—$FIDE_2$, 1995.
27. C.A. Waite, R.C. Welland, T. Printezis, A. Pirmohamed, P.C. Philbrow, G. Montgomery, M. Mira da Silva, S.D. Macneill, D.O. Lavery, C. Herzig, A. Froggatt, R.L. Cooper, and M.P. Atkinson. Glasgow libraries for orthogonally persistent systems—principles, organisation and contents. Technical Report FIDE/95/132, ESPRIT Basic Research Action, Project Number 6309—$FIDE_2$, 1995.
28. C.A. Waite, R.C. Welland, T. Printezis, A. Pirmohamed, P.C. Philbrow, G. Montgomery, M. Mira da Silva, S.D. Macneill, D.O. Lavery, C. Herzig, A. Froggatt, R.L. Cooper, and M.P. Atkinson. GlasgowLibraries reference manual. http://www.dcs.gla.ac.uk/fide/napier88/GlasgowLibraries.html, 1995. Department of Computing Science, University of Glasgow.

Chapter 3.1.6

Visualising Persistent Stores

Gilbert Cockton* and Darryn Lavery*

Department of Computing Science, University of Glasgow, Glasgow G12 8QQ, Scotland

Abstract. This paper summarises work to design Software Visualisations that support Napier88 programmers in understanding and using the contents of the persistent store. Two example visualisations are described. Their effectiveness in supporting their intended tasks has been assessed by studying programmers using these visualisations.

Visualisation design can borrow existing metaphors. However, successful application of a metaphor (and thus a successful visualisation) depends upon a careful analysis of the expected context of use for the visualisation.

1 Introduction

Chapter 3.1.4 described the Glasgow Persistent Workshop, designed to support Napier88 (chapter 1.1.3) programmers develop persistent application systems. This section describes Workshop tools designed to assist users to understand and to manipulate the contents of Napier88 persistent stores.

Software Visualisations [20] use graphics to promote understanding of software systems or to make software development tasks easier or more effective. Examples of software visualisations include flow charts, program dependency graphs, the use of charts and graphs to compare the relative performance of different algorithms, and the use of animation to help novices understand, and develop insights into the workings of a particular algorithm [3, 22].

Various researchers have claimed that graphical representations of data are superior to textual representations. For example Larkin and Simon [9] claim that graphics let people use simple perceptual operators. Comparing line lengths is simpler than calculating maxima. Data can also be spatially arranged to reduce search times. However, graphics are not always better than text as demonstrated in a survey by Jarvenpaa and Dickson [8] on using graphics to support decision making.

We decided to investigate using Software Visualisations to assist users to understand and to use objects from persistent stores. Persistent stores are huge collections of objects such as data, procedures, and user interfaces. These objects can be complex and richly interconnected. Techniques to assist the user to understand what is there, and how to use it are clearly required. However, existing text-based approaches have not worked well, and have suffered from various problems including speed, being difficult to read or use, and have been non-interactive.

A number of visualisations have been developed at Glasgow, for example [2, 7]. Two visualisations developed at Glasgow, which have undergone programmer studies, will now be described, followed by a summary of our findings.

---

* now at: School of Computing and Information Systems, University of Sunderland, St. Peter's Campus, St. Peter's Way, Sunderland SR6 0DD, UK.

2 Search Path Editor

The first visualisation developed was the Search Path Editor, a tool to aid Napier88 program construction. To reference an item of data or a procedure from the persistent store, the programmer must write "use" clauses to inform the Napier88 compiler about the exact type and location of the binding in the persistent store. For example, to print "hello world" on the screen, the following program must be written:

```
use theStore() with Library:env in
use Library with IO:env in
use IO with writeString:proc(string) in
begin
      writeString("hello world'n")
end
```

Fig. 1. A Small Napier88 Program

Typically a program of even minor complexity will include many bindings which may be located deep in the store. Creating these "use clauses" requires time and effort, and presents a difficulty for the unfamiliar programmer who must know the location and type of the binding.

The solution adopted was to borrow the UNIX "PATH" metaphor. A "Search Path" of Napier88 environments would be specified. Using the Search Path, a program completer would automatically generate the necessary statements to be included in the compilation of the program. The Search Path Editor (see Figure 2) is used to view and edit the Search Path.

In the left hand panel of the Search Path Editor window, the Search Path of environments is displayed, and in the right hand area the graph of the environments of the Napier88 store is displayed. The user can manipulate the Search Path by adding and removing environments from the Search Path.

Often a binding will be multiply defined in the Search Path. The user can determine which bindings are repeated by selecting the "Clashes" button. In the screenshot above, the "Clashes" window is open and the binding "menuGen" has been selected to determine that it exists in two places in the Search Path. The completer will use the first occurrence of "menuGen" it finds — in this case, the procedure "menuGen" will be used from "Tools". Finally, the user can alter the interpretation of bindings by altering the position of an environment in the Search Path by direct manipulation.

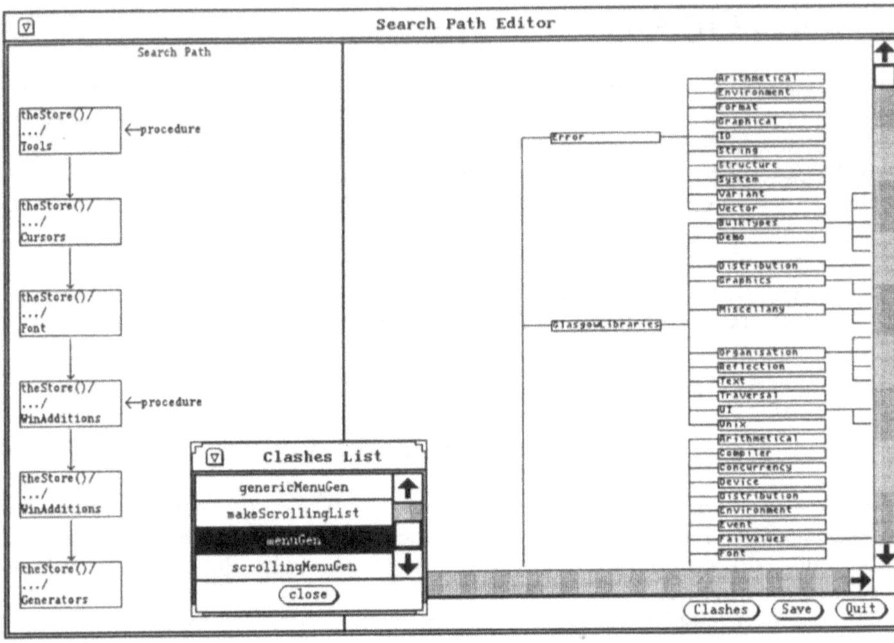

Fig. 2. The Search Path Editor

A number of methods were employed to assess the effectiveness of the evaluation for its intended use. The first method applied was a usability evaluation [13, 14]. Undergraduate students from a "Database" course with little experience of Napier88 were given a set of tasks to achieve. While performing these tasks, the users were asked to think aloud their thoughts. A video camera recorded the evaluation session. An observer recorded any problems the users encountered.

A programmer study [11] was undertaken to identify needs for new visualisations, and to assess the effectiveness of existing visualisations during long term usage. The methods employed including observing programmers working on their own projects, interviewing programmers, command logging, and analysing Napier88 and Workshop objects.

A number of problems were revealed. Users found the tool, in particular the start-up and scrolling, slow. First time users often misinterpreted various aspects of the display, for example believing the "Clashes" window to be a set of commands, or could not determine the precedence of environments in the left panel.

More serious problems with the "Search Path" model were revealed. Consider the case where the bindings "read" and "write" occur in both "C" and "D" in the Search Path. The model does not allow the binding "read" to be used from environment "C" and "write" from "D". Furthermore, there is no support for the programmer to re-order the Search Path when multiple bindings of the same name occur, and a solution exists. In summary, there is no fine control of the selection of bindings from the Search Path.

These problems did not occur during our studies because there were few repeated names in the store, but similar problems did occur with Declaration Sets (which contain type definitions), which also uses a "PATH" metaphor — see [11] for further details.

These more serious problems arose because of the unsuitability of the "PATH" metaphor. Persistent stores are not UNIX file systems, and persistent objects are not UNIX commands. Whereas, UNIX commands are relatively stable, change is the dominant activity in software development [4, 24]. Persistent objects are very likely to occur in vastly greater numbers, and multiple versions of the same library may be maintained to ensure compatibility, both increasing the possibility of name clashes.

Our experience with inappropriate metaphors is matched by the results of experiments on user interface metaphors, which "must always be considered in the light of the system functionality that they are intended to support" [1, page 193]. By choosing the visualisation before analysing the required functionality, we missed the opportunity to fully explore the programmers' real needs in persistent programming environments. Clearly, successful visualisations must be properly grounded in research into the expected context of use.

3 VIPER

Often novice Napier88 programmers lacked confidence when programming in Napier88, because they could not view the contents of the store, and thus could not confirm that their objects have been installed successfully. Using code developed for the Search Path Editor, a support visualisation, VIPER (VIsualising PERsistence), was rapidly prototyped.

Figure 3 shows an example screen shot. The left hand panel of the window displays the environments of the persistent store. Detailed contents of one environment will be displayed in the right hand panel of the window. The programmer can change the displayed environment by selecting it with the mouse. The environment will highlight and its contents will appear in the right panel — in the example below, the environment "theStore()/Library/Win/Tools" is displayed.

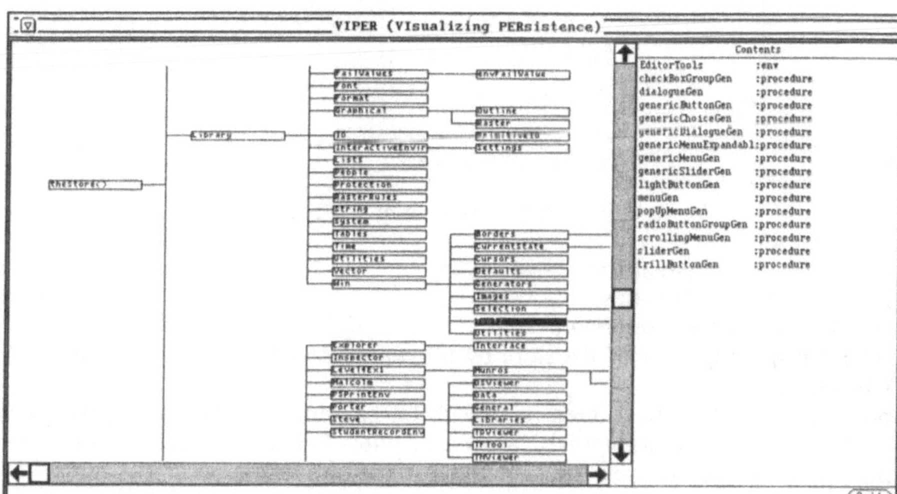

Fig. 3. VIPER

The Napier88 programming community at Glasgow gave a favourable response to the visualisation. Users of the visualisation found it useful, and novice programmers found that the view of the store helped build confidence. One Napier88 expert at Glasgow, responsible for local Napier88 support and store maintenance, used VIPER and found redundant information of which he was previously unaware.

However, a usability evaluation [13, 14] and a programmer study [11] revealed problems. For example, the visualisation, in particular the scrolling, was slow. First time users of the visualisation sometimes misinterpreted the left hand panel — they believed that all of the store was displayed, rather than just the environments. VIPER did not give enough information about each of the bindings — for example, it would indicate that a binding was a procedure, but would not describe the exact type. Searching was difficult and users often requested a search facility.

Drawing on the problems revealed and insights gained about the visualisation's use, an improved version was developed. Figure 4 shows a screen shot. As with the earlier version, the environments of the Napier88 store are displayed in the left panel, and the contents of one environment is displayed in the right panel.

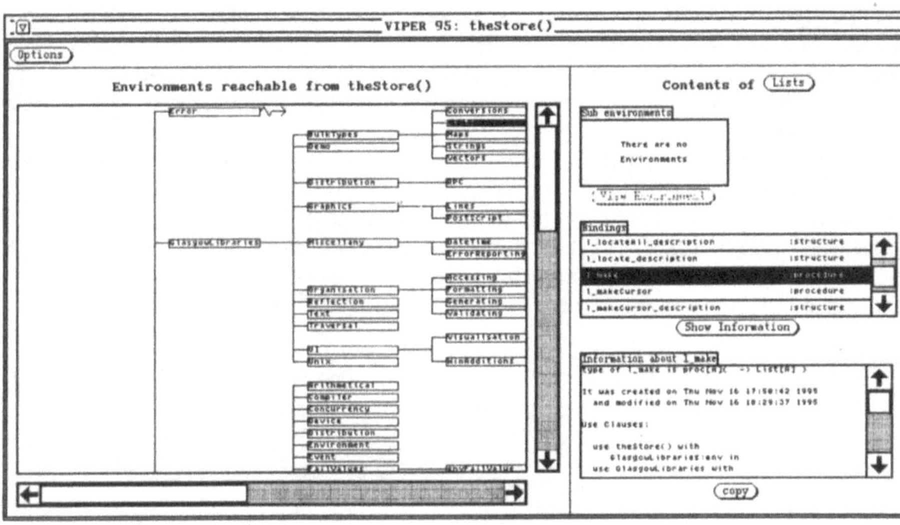

Fig. 4. A new version of VIPER

The following improvements have been made:

- providing search facilities.
- scrolling speed has been improved.
- improving navigation of the store by allowing users to use the right panel for navigation.
- presentation details have been improved, for example, the layout algorithm for the left panel has been improved, and the scrollbar handles are resized to represent the proportion of the viewport size to the size of the whole store.
- more information about the contents of the store is supplied. For example, the programmer is informed about the exact type of the binding, when it was created and modified and how to include it in a program.
- allowing programmers to focus on the parts of the store they are interested in through the use of several mechanisms. Firstly, programmers can hide or reveal

subtrees of the store. In the screen shot above, the programmer has hidden the children of "Error". Secondly, the programmer can open a view of a subtree of the store. Finally, users can choose to view only the right panel in a separate window.

The new version has been made available to the programming community at Glasgow and has been undergone a usability evaluation. Again, the new version has received a favourable response, particularly from users of the previous version .

However, the new version has problems, but apparently fewer than before. For example, the visualisation takes time to start up — this is a limitation of the underlying Napier88 system. This makes first time users uncertain what is happening, and will slow users of all skill levels. First time users often clicked or double clicked on the bindings in the right panel to obtain further information, instead of selecting the "Show Information" button.

Obtaining accurate type information about Napier88 objects is difficult. Structural type checking, as used by Napier88, offers many advantages, but unfortunately, once an object has been compiled, the name of its type is discarded. Clearly, programmers would prefer a meaningful name, rather than a detailed description of its structure, which they may not need to (or not supposed to!) be aware of.

A type name must be reverse-engineered from the structural type. However, several names could match the same type. For example, the "Win" windowing system for Napier88 has two graphical types, "Pos" (position) and "Size", both of which are structures with two integer fields "x" and "y". Although these types are structurally equivalent, they are used in different ways. Currently, it is unclear how to resolve these ambiguities.

Again, successful visualisations require grounding in the expected context of human usage. Developers of persistent object stores must consider that software developers use these stores, not just compilers and run-time systems!

4 Conclusions

Software Visualisations are interactive systems and thus require careful design of the user's conceptual model, the user's operational model and the presentation of the information.

The Search Path Editor's conceptual model was clearly inadequate — the UNIX "PATH" metaphor did not map well to the task of generating Napier88 "use clauses". However, VIPER's tree structure provided a firm starting point for visualisation.

The user's operational model concerns the methods needed to achieve tasks with a system. The Search Path Editor's Editor inappropriate metaphor makes task methods difficult. For multiply defined bindings, the programmer is given no assistance to re-order the Search Path. Furthermore, a lack of a suitable abstraction will make the generation of "use" clauses for a set of related work items repetitious. If a set of Work Items use related Search Paths, each Search Path must be manipulated independently. The Search Path Editor's lack of speed makes matters worse!

Techniques for presenting information also demand careful attention. Both the Search Path Editor and the earlier version of VIPER did not provide the user with enough cues about the contents and meanings of the symbols in each of the panels of the windows. The earlier version of VIPER did not separate groups of environments with different parents. The improved version separated these groups making it easier to search a subtree and thus decreasing search times.

Software Visualisation development should use existing HCI approaches such as contextual analysis [5, 23] for example, task analysis, user analysis and domain analysis; and usability engineering [21]. Perhaps good contextual analysis is more important than usability engineering, because a good design is no substitute for a tool which does not meet its needs. Poor contextual analysis probably caused some (if not all) of the Search Path Editor's major problems. In a more general follow-on project [10], we are developing predictive methods for Software Visualisations and techniques for their validation [6, 12-19].

Given proper attention to design inputs, we found visualisation worked well for the following cases. VIPER provided support for a wide range of fairly simple and precise tasks. The Search Path Editor tasks were more complex, requiring changes to be made to a fairly complex structure. However, the choice of the "PATH" metaphor made the tasks more complex than they needed to be.

Visualisation worked well in the presence of a suitable metaphor. VIPER used the metaphor of a tree to visualise the contents of a persistent store. The tree suggested the method of navigation and provided re-assurance to programmers. We will apply the lessons learnt developing the new version of VIPER and re-examine the underlying model and tasks involved in generating "use" clauses, and only use suitable metaphors where appropriate. One solution under consideration is to maintain the Search Path to collect a set of bindings referable in a Workshop work item or set of work items, but allow the programmer to explicitly select the interpretation of an arbitrary name. The view of the persistent store will be removed from the Search Path Editor. We will allow environments/bindings to be added from other tools such as VIPER and the Library Explorer, and investigate tool linking in the context of a persistent programming environment.

Acknowledgements. We would like to thank the Persistence and Distribution group at the University Glasgow, and the Persistence Research Group at the University of St. Andrews for their support during this research. We wish to thank those from the Glasgow community who gave up time to participate in our studies. This research was funded by ESPRIT Basic Research Action 6309 ($FIDE_2$), and by EPSRC grant no. GR/K82727.

References

1. Anderson B, Smyth M, Knott RP, Bergan M, Bergan J, Alty JL. Minimising Conceptual Baggage: Making Choices about Metaphor. In: People and Computers IX. Proceedings of BCS HCI 94, 1994, pp. 179-194
2. Ball SP. A Declaration Set Viewer for Napier88. MSc Dissertation, Department of Computing Science, University of Glasgow, 1995
3. Brown MH. Zeus: A System for Algorithm Animation and Multi-View Editing. In: Proceedings of IEEE Workshop on Visual Languages, 1991, pp. 4-9
4. Chikofsky E, Cross J. Reverse Engineering and Design Recovery. IEEE Software 1990; 7(1): 13-17
5. Cockton G. Critical Issues Discussion: Using the Human Context in Interactive Systems Development. In: Unger C and Bass L (eds), Engineering for Human-Computer Interaction, Chapman and Hall, 1995, pp. 339-347

6. Cockton G, Lavery D. Software Visualisation: Challenges for Two HCI Approaches. In: Task Centred Approaches to Interface Design: Glasgow Interactive Systems Group Research Review (GIST Technical Report G95.2), 1995, pp. 131-151
7. Herzig C. A Parametric Generator for Starfield Displays. Senior Honours Solo Project, Department of Computing Science, University of Glasgow, 1995
8. Jarvenpaa SL, Dickson GW. Graphics and Managerial Decision Making: Research Based Guidelines. Communications of the ACM 1988; 31(6): 764-774
9. Larkin JH, Simon HA. Why a Diagram is (Sometimes) Worth Ten Thousand Words. Cognitive Science 1987; 11: 65-99
10. Lavery D. The Design of Effective Software Visualizations for Persistent Programming Languages. FIDE Technical Report FIDE/95/116, University of Glasgow, 1995
11. Lavery D. A Napier88 Programmer Study. FIDE Technical Report FIDE/95/140, University of Glasgow, 1995
12. Lavery D. Specialising Design Principles and Cognitive Walkthrough for Software Visualisations (Doctorial Consortium Position Statement). In: HCI '96 Industry Day & Adjunct Proceedings, 1996, pp. 228-229
13. Lavery D, Cockton G. A Pilot Study of Early Usability Evaluation Methods for Software Visualisations. FIDE Technical Report FIDE/95/141, University of Glasgow, 1995
14. Lavery D, Cockton G. Iterative Development of Early Usability Evaluation Methods for Software Visualisations. In: Proceedings of the 6th Workshop of Empirical Studies of Programmers, 1996, pp. 275-276
15. Lavery D, Cockton G. Specialising Analytic Evaluation Methods for Software Visualisations. In: Proceedings of CHI 96 Basic Research Symposium. Available as http://www.hud.ac.uk/schools/comp+maths/private/alan/symp/, 1996
16. Lavery D, Cockton G, Atkinson M. Cognitive Dimensions: Usability Evaluation Materials. Technical Report TR-1996-17, University of Glasgow, 1996
17. Lavery D, Cockton G, Atkinson M. Heuristic Evaluation for Software Visualisation: Usability Evaluation Materials. Technical Report TR-1996-16, University of Glasgow, 1996
18. Lavery D, Cockton G, Atkinson M. Heuristic Evaluation: Usability Evaluation Materials. Technical Report TR-1996-15, University of Glasgow, 1996
19. Lavery D, Cockton G, Atkinson M. Comparison of Evaluation Methods Using Structured Usability Problem Reports. Behaviour and Information Technology 1997; 6(4): 246-266.
20. Myers BA. Taxonomies of Visual Programming and Program Visualization. Journal of Visual Languages and Computing 1990; 1(1): 97-123
21. Nielsen J, Usability Engineering. Cambridge: Academic Press, Inc., 1993
22. Stasko JT. Tango: A Framework and System for Algorithm Animation. Computer 1990; 23(9): 27-39
23. Sutcliffe A, Bass L, Cockton G, Monk A, Newman I. Report on the joint IFIP WG2.7-WG13.2 Workshop on Methods and Tools for User Interface Design. ACM SIGCHI Bulletin 1995; 27(4): 46-49
24. Zelkowitz MV. Perspectives on Software Engineering. ACM Computer Surveys 1978; 10(2): 197-216

Section 3.2

Data Modelling: Introduction and State of the Art

Richard Cooper

Dept. of Computing Science, University of Glasgow, Glasgow G12 8QQ, Scotland

1. Introduction

Data modelling is the process of creating a schema – i.e. a description of the data handled by a database application. The process uses a "data model" which is a language containing generalised constructs for the description of data structures. As such, creating an application by data modelling is akin to writing the set of type declarations in a programming language – a data model and a type system playing a similar role in application development.

Data modelling has traditionally been used as a semi-formal first step in creating an application – and, in particular, as a means of communicating requirements between customer and implementor, originally using pencil-and-paper. Eventually, graphical schema design tools began to be used as front-ends to database systems – most commercial products based on the relational model have such tools. Automatic translation techniques can then be used to generate the database automatically [1]. These exploit the intuition that when a schema has been designed, the functionality of the application can be created by instantiating generic components. The use of data modelling in this way has, so far, been largely restricted to classical database systems with their relatively simple and constrained structure.

The FIDE work has been motivated largely by the inadequacy of classical systems to manage the kinds of complex applications which now require extensive data management – Computer Aided Design, office automation, Geographic Information Systems and so on. The FIDE response has been to produce database systems which are centred around programming languages in which the structure of the data is created as a set of types. The language support systems then provide mechanisms which maintain the values of such types persistently.

The intuition behind using data modelling as an early step in creating an application still holds good when moving to a persistent programming language. However, the implementation of transformations from data models to applications becomes harder to achieve for two reasons. Firstly, the target data structures describable by the type system of the language are much more complicated than are relations – so the mapping is more difficult to achieve. Secondly, the automatic generation of code to support the management of values in those structures is much more complicated than the generation of code to manage relations.

However, the availability of a computationally complete programming language, with a modern type system including polymorphism, abstract data types and first class procedures, constitutes a significantly more powerful tool for implementing the transformation than the traditional implementation platforms for relational systems. It thus becomes feasible to integrate the data modelling phase much more closely with the application development environment – for instance a data model just becomes another application, which in a persistent system can be one or more values in the database.

Within the $FIDE_2$ project, this integration has been achieved as follows. Data modelling tools have been generated within the database system itself – by writing them in the programming language. A component of the data modelling tool can then take a schema created using the data model and automatically turn it into a skeletal application also in the programming language. The application, at this stage, consists of default behaviour, which can be extended and customised using the programming language. Information derived from use of a data model is transformed by an automatic application generator into code (both the type declarations and the accompanying program) which can be customised by a human programmer. Alternatively a rich library of database functionality can be provided which is automatically linked into the application after analysis of the schema.

The output from the automatic program generator, although capable of functioning as a complete program, is designed to be extended and amended. From this approach, another significant benefit accrues. Since the generated application has been constructed systematically from the schema, it can be made to have a clear and easily understood structure, which should support the customising activity and also later the maintenance of the software.

2. The $FIDE_2$ Contribution

Several activities have been carried out in the context of $FIDE_2$. The work at Glasgow starts from the use of the IFO data model to create schemata from which application outlines can be generated in a number of languages[2]. The work at Hamburg has two strands. Firstly, the STYLE Workbench constitutes a means for systematically constructing a customised development environment. Secondly, an experiment has shown how the extensible syntax of the Tycoon language can be used to augment the language with a textual data modelling component.

The Glasgow software (see Chapter 3.2.1) comprises a customisable graphical schema editor based on the IFO data model. The customisable aspect allows the editor to be extended to include node types more appropriate to particular languages – for instance IFO does not include a union type, although many languages do, so IFO can be extended to have union type nodes.

Once a schema has been created, an application outline can be generated in any of the languages: Napier88, O_2C, Fibonacci or Tycoon. The generated code contains four parts:

i) a description of the **data structure** – i.e. a set of type declarations corresponding to the schema;

ii) a description of the underlying **database** – i.e. a description of the data set which persists between runs of the application program;

iii) a set of **data manipulation operations** – operations to create, destroy, change, display and query the data;

iv) an overall **framework** for the application in which to embed the operations and makes them available for the user.

The code thus generated can be compiled and run directly as a very simple application or it can be used as the basis of application development through customisation by programming.

In Hamburg, the STYLE (Systematics of TYpes Language Environments) project is developing a methodology for building customised environments for data-intensive applications with different data models [Chapter 3.2.2]. It provides kernel techniques and services together with a global architecture which consists of a meta environment supporting the construction of customised workbenches. The kernel technology is based on the combination of generators and generic services. The architecture exploits a classification of services along three dimensions, a functional, an operational and a modal dimension. Workbenches are customised by applying generic tools and by incrementally and systematically extending the environment with services along the three dimensions.

The STYLE approach is prototypically verified by a customised development environment for the object-oriented data model OM1. It is realised on top of a rich persistent programming platform, the Tycoon system [Chapter 1.1.1], with bulk data management, integrity checking and user-interface management. This workbench integrates tools for object-oriented modelling and for the generation of prototype implementations of modelled applications using the Tycoon Language TL and generic services. The quality of the code generated comprises the encapsulation of objects with standard query and update methods, class extensions and integrity checking of data model constraints both inherent constraints and user defined integrity constraints.

The tools of the STYLE workbench are highly integrated and allow numerous navigation methods for moving between different views of the same design entity at different levels of abstraction (for instance, the class diagram, the class definition, the Tycoon class interface, the Tycoon class implementation and the Tycoon class user interface).

Tycoon has also been used for an experiment in using extensible grammars to generate a data modelling component [Chapter 3.2.3]. In this work a set of abstract operations which support the constructs of the model are implemented in TL and a set of syntax definitions for invoking these operations is supplied. The grammar thus specified extends TL and programs written in the extended languages execute partly by calling the operations. Using this extended language, it becomes possible to write applications abstractly using the data model and yet integrate this with other TL programs. This can have two benefits. Firstly, individual applications can have specific behaviour programmed in detail and integrated with the generic code. Secondly, different kinds of database functionality (access functions, user interfaces, and so on) can be programmed as TL libraries and be provided to multiple applications.

All three activities demonstrate that the need to make tractable the development of complex applications in persistent languages can be met by a data modelling component. Using this the programmer can create an abstract description of the application. Automatic derivation of code relieves programmers of much tedious and error prone work and yet they can develop the code generated further to meet specific requirements.

References

1. T.J. Teorey, D. Yang and J.P. Fry, "A logical Design Methodology for Relational Databases Using the Extended Entity-Relationship Model", *ACM Computing Surveys*, 18, 2, 197-222, June 1986.
2. R. Cooper and I. Tabkha, "A Semantic Framework for the Design of Data Intensive Applications in a Persistent Programming Language", *Proc. Hawaii ICSS*, January 1992.

Chapter 3.2.1

Application Development using Data Modelling

Richard Cooper

Dept. of Computing Science, University of Glasgow, Glasgow G12 8QQ, Scotland

Abstract. Data modelling is the process of creating a schema – i.e. a description of the data handled by a database application. This report describes the automatic generation of the code implementing the application from the schema. The resulting code can be used as the completed application but is more likely to be used as the basis of customisation to create the final product. This produces a number of benefits: the creation of a high-level description of the data structure which genuinely fits the application; the acceleration of application development; and the creation of a structure for the application implementation which, being regular, is easier to extend and to maintain. The code generated can be in any of four target languages – all of which are full database programming languages. The paper finishes with a discussion of how to add to this list of languages.

1 Introduction

Developing an application which requires the complex manipulation of complex persistent data is fundamentally difficult since it requires the combined use of database and programming language technology. In classical database systems, this gives rise to the "impedance mismatch' [1] between the facilities provided by the database and the programming language which is used for the application. To remove this problem, a variety of systems have been developed which more closely integrate database and programming needs. These systems, which will be called here database programming languages, include database systems which are built around the object oriented paradigm and programming languages whose values are allowed to persist between programming runs in a structured way.

Application development in such systems is significantly more complicated than database design in a relational system. It now includes:

i) the creation of a set of type or class definitions – usually described in a type system significantly more powerful (and thus more complicated to use) than the relational model;

ii) the creation of persistent repositories of values of these types;

iii) the identification of appropriate access methods for implementing these repositories;

iv) the creation of data creation, manipulation and querying operations appropriate to the intended usage of the data; and

v) the integration of this within one or more user interfaces.

This paper explores the use of data modelling to lessen the difficulty of creating applications. In essence, this is built around a graphical schema design tool and a set of generators for creating application frameworks in a number of database programming languages. The generated application will include all of parts (i) and (ii) above; rudimentary versions of part (iv); and a means of selecting between alternatives for parts (iii) and (v).

Data modelling is the process of creating a schema – i.e. a description of the data handled by a database application. The process uses a "data model" which contains generalised constructs for the description of data structures. The model may be close to the internal model of the DBMS or be more abstract and closer to real world concepts, in which case the model is called a Semantic Data Model [2]. Automatic translation techniques are then used to generate the database automatically [3].

The principal difference between creating an application by use of a programming language and by use of a data model is that in the former case the programmer has to supply all of the functionality by adding code to the type declarations, whereas using a data model much of the functionality can be added automatically. The advantage of developing the whole application in a programming language is that detailed and irregular processes can be coded in a unified language.

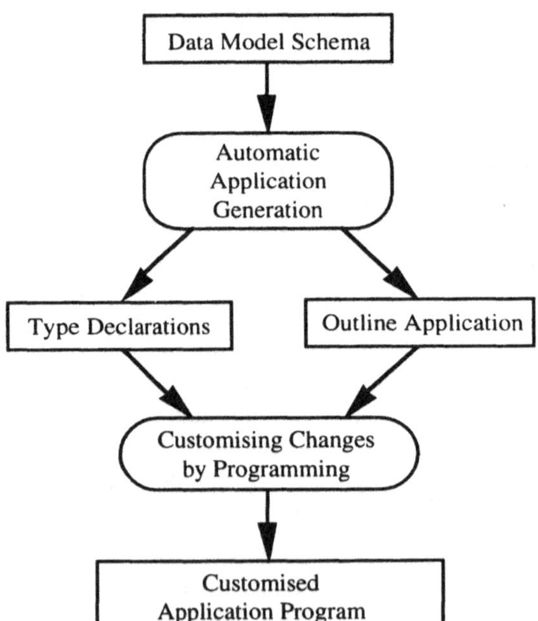

Fig. 1. Automatic Application Generation

In a full database programming language, the possibility arises of integrating the two approaches. The value in doing so is that the benefits of each approach can be combined. Thus we may have the human-oriented abstractions of a Semantic Data Model to describe the structure of the data and the machine-oriented features of the programming language to provide detail.

In the current project, this integration has been achieved as follows. A graphical data modelling tool has been developed which has a component which can then take a schema created using the data model and automatically turn it into an application in a programming language. The generated application, at this stage, consists of generic behaviour, which can be extended and customised using the programming language. Figure 1 shows the whole process of application generation. Information derived from use of a data modelling tool is transformed by an automatic application generator into code (both the type declarations and the accompanying program). This code can later be customised by a programmer.

The output from the automatic program generator, although capable of functioning as a complete program, is designed to be extended and amended. From this approach, another significant benefit accrues. Since the generated application has been constructed systematically from the schema, it can be made to have a clear and easily understood structure, which should support the customising activity and also later the maintenance of the software. One final way of viewing this approach is that it partitions the software engineering problem into discrete stages, each one which should be more tractable when taken in isolation.

The general approach described above has been implemented in terms of front ends to OODBs, both commercially and in research work [4], and to database languages [5, Chapter 3.2.2]. In this paper, a multi-language implementation is described. A graphical schema design tool is augmented with a facility to generate the application in a variety of languages. The paper will describe this implementation and the underlying analysis of an application which it supports.

2 Data Modelling and Program Construction

An application can be analysed into the five parts listed above – schema, database, access mechanisms, operations and interface. Data modelling has traditionally been used to cover the first of these, with automatic methods for generating the second. Query languages, possibly embedded, are used for the third and fourth, while the user interface is subject to *ad hoc* treatment. Database programming languages provide the ability to deal with all parts in a uniform environment, but require programming and software engineering skills to master them

Creating an application by programming shares some of the same characteristics as creating an application by data modelling. The programmer must similarly define a description of the structure of the data, but then must also add the computation which runs against this description. In most languages, the data structure is described using the type system – the type system providing an analogous set of constructs to the data model. The program is then based on the set of type declarations which form, to all intents and purposes, a schema for the application. Two main differences arise however. Firstly, the programmer must write all of the code which manipulates the data – this is not provided in any of the ways described above. The second difference arises from the first – the constructs provided by the type system are geared towards easing the expression of computation, rather than easing the modelling of data.

We thus have two technologies with offsetting advantages. Data modelling facilitates the description of data using fairly intuitive constructs, but once described, the interfaces for manipulating the data are either highly constrained or involve using an embedded query language with all of the problems that that entails. Programming, on the other hand, requires the description of data using a type system which is not particularly intuitive, but then allows manipulation of the data to be freely described. In the work presented here, an attempt is made to combine the best of both of these worlds.

Data modelling has traditionally been used to create the schema and it is not too difficult to see how the process of mapping a schema into a set of types might be automated. However, somewhat more can be done than that. A great deal of the code which makes up an application consists of repetitive programming. There will be small modules to create values of each of the types, make the values persistent, remove them from the database and so on. In effect, once the schema is known many of these can be written accurately and efficiently by an automatic process. The generation of the whole of a very regularly structured application thus becomes a possibility.

The approach, therefore, is to return to the use data modelling as a first stage of application generation. The application builder starts by creating a data model. When content with this, the modelling tool is provided with an option which generates the source code to implement the application in a programming language. The resulting code can be used either as a complete application or, more likely, as a platform for program development. The source code generated contains a default set of facilities for manipulating the data and a default user interface. To customise this, the application source code is available for modification.

The code generated contains four parts:

i) a description of the data structure – i.e. a set of type declarations corresponding to the schema;

ii) a description of the underlying database – i.e. a description of the data set which persists between runs of the application program;

iii) a set of data manipulation operations – operations to create, destroy, change, display and query the data;

iv) an overall framework for the application – i.e. an overall structure which embeds the operations and makes them available for the user – a menu hierarchy for instance.

3. A Multi-Language Data Modelling System

This section describes a program, Program Generation from a Data Model (PGDM), which is under construction. PGDM permits the capture of a data model and the subsequent creation of source code in one of four different database programming languages. The data model is based on the IFO, although PGDM permits the use of extensions of the basic IFO model appropriate for each language. Section 3 starts with a discussion of the basic IFO data model. and continues by describing the data modelling environment provided.

3.1 The IFO Data Model

The IFO data model [6] was designed to bring a common and formally defined framework to Semantic Data Modelling. It was also created to be a framework for the analysis of the semantics of updates. IFO was chosen as a basis for the present work as it provides a small but sophisticated taxonomy of types, which will be discussed with reference to the diagram given as Figure 2.

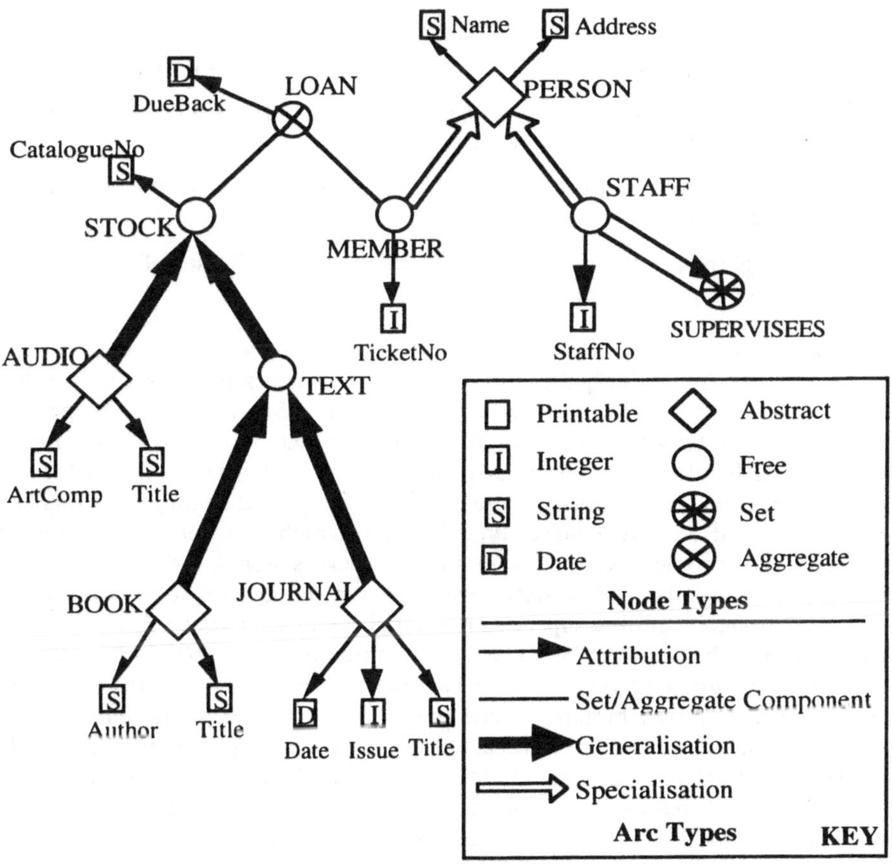

Fig. 2. An IFO Data Model

An IFO graph is a collection of nodes and connecting arcs in which there are five different kinds of node (each representing a different type of value) and four different kinds of arc (each representing a different relationship between types). The node kinds are naturally divided into atomic and complex types as follows:

There are three kinds of atomic type:

printable types are the base types of the system – integer, string and so on;

abstract types are the fundamental modelling entity types of the system, having "no decomposable underlying structure";

free types are defined in terms of other types using one of the forms of inheritance.

There are two kinds of complex or constructed type:

set types have instances which are sets of values of the same type;

aggregate types are similar to records in that their instances are constructed from a number of component values.

The four relationship kinds are:

attribution which links one node with another which is one of its properties;

part-of connects a set node with the node describing the type of its components or an aggregate node with its component nodes.;

specialisation is the relationship between a free node and a node (free or abstract) which it is sub-type of;

generalisation is the relationship between a free node and the set of nodes (free or abstract) which it generalises.

Figure 2 shows an IFO schema for a library database and illustrates the constructs described above. The principal function of the database is to record library loans which connect a library member with a stock item. Stock items take part in a generalisation hierarchy and must be either audio or text, where text items must be books or journals. Information about people stored in the database, on the other hand, takes part in a specialisation hierarchy with the type of library members being a specialisation of a more general type, person, which has another sub-type for library staff. All people have their names and addresses stored and library members also have a ticket number, while staff have their staff number recorded together with the set of other staff that they supervise (the latter being a recursive relationship) – a staff member has the set *SUPERVISEES* as an attribute and a *SUPERVISEES* set has *STAFF* as its component type. These two hierarchies have completely different semantics. The *PERSON* hierarchy permits the storage of information about people who are library members, people who are staff members and people who are neither. The *STOCK* hierarchy stores a set of stock items, which are subdivided into subsets as shown, but now the subsets completely partition the set of stock items, so that every stock item is either an audio item, a book or a journal.

The main facilities offered in PGDM are a graphical editor for this basic version of IFO together with the ability to generate code in the four languages from this basic model. However, PGDM also provides extensions to IFO which directly support the constructs in a particular language. For instance, Napier88 has a variant type constructor and the editor for IFO–Napier88 includes a union node type, which maps naturally into Napier88 variants. Figure 3 shows the way in which data model and language can interact.

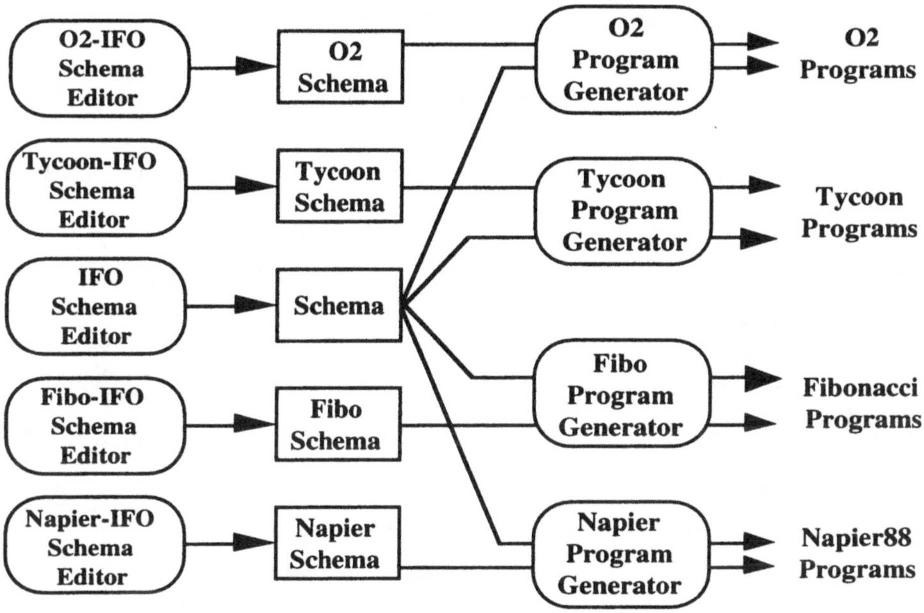

Fig. 3. Multiple Data Models and Multiple Languages

3.2 The Data Modelling Environment

The principal mode of operation of PGDM is the management of a schema in the context of a language. In fact, the user may choose to work either specifically with one of the four languages or, more generally, to work in basic IFO, in which case a program can subsequently be generated in any one of the languages. Choosing to work in the context of one the languages extends the sets of node and arc kinds to include data modelling constructs which map more directly onto the type system of the particular language. In particular, as part of the process of registering a language with PGDM, it is possible to add to the set of printable types; the set of constructed types; and the set of arcs. PGDM provides the following facilities:

- the ability to choose between the languages;
- a graphical editor for data model schemata;
- the ability to store, retrieve and remove schemata; and
- the ability to generate and store source code from a schema.

The user starts by choosing one of the languages (either one of the specific ones or a common base) and then the main interface to the system (shown as Figure 4) is brought up. In this we see an editing window on the right and a palette of operations on the left. The operations group themselves naturally into four sets:

- a set of schema operations for creating, opening, closing and saving a schema;

- a set of node and arc icons, each of which may be selected to choose which node or arc type will be inserted into the schema by use of the add operation;
- a set of editor operations for creating, deleting, editing (i.e. changing the label) and moving the nodes;
- some more general operations to gain help, switch language, generate a program and quit the system.

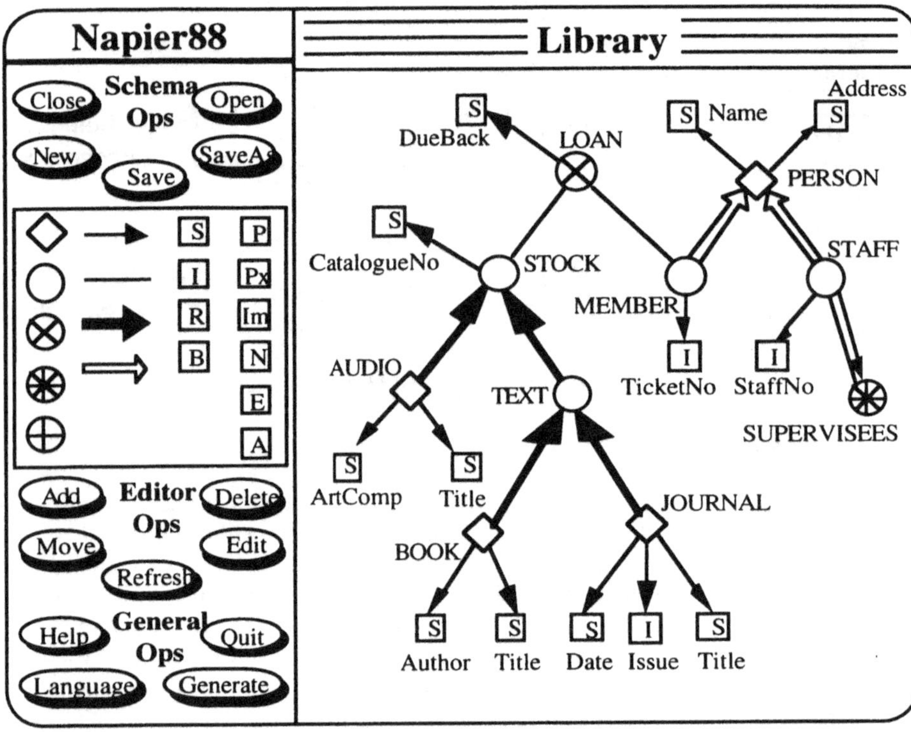

Fig. 4. The PGDM User Interface

4. Program Generation – Overview

Having generated a schema such as the above, the user may now generate an application program in the language of choice. As discussed above, the code generated from the schema comprises four parts:

- a set of type declarations
- the code to set up a database;
- data manipulation and querying operations; and
- a framework for user interaction with the program.

We will now give a flavour of how each of these is created. Each part is generated by visiting the nodes in an order which avoids forward references and creates recursive structures wherever cycles are found.

4.1 Type Declarations

The first phase is the creation of types. A type description is generated for each non-printable node in the order described above. Thus we will generate type definitions for *PERSON*, *BOOK*, *JOURNAL*, *AUDIO*, *MEMBER*, *TEXT*, *STOCK*, *LOAN*, *STAFF* and *SUPERVISOR* in that order.

4.2 Creating the Database

Creating persistent repositories for the information is less straightforward. PGDM follows the persistence by reachability paradigm [7] – i.e. certain root values will be marked as persistent and any other values to which these refer in any way are also stored. The first question is which values should constitute the persistent roots. In the library example it is probably sensible to maintain a set of values for each of the non-printable nodes. In other cases, this may create more persistent structure than is useful. Take for example an electronic mail database. If this consists principally of three types for USERs, MAILBOXes and MESSAGEs, with each USER having a MAILBOX as an attribute and each MAILBOX containing a set of MESSAGEs, then it is probably of little value to create persistent sets of all the MAILBOXes and all the MESSAGEs separately. However, as we have to take a uniform decision, we create persistent sets of all the non-printable nodes.

The second question is to decide on how to implement these persistent sets (and indeed the set nodes in the IFO diagram). Here we can either use whatever bulk type constructor is available in the language or provide an implementation of an abstract data type. In the languages being used, we find that Napier88 and Tycoon only have array types; Fibonacci has sequence types; while O_2 has sets, bags and lists. Therefore in the first three languages we use a set abstraction built on top of the type system, but in O_2 we use the built in types directly. Identifying appropriate access mechanisms for particular sets has not been attempted in the current prototype, but a method of incorporating physical design is under consideration and this will show similar integration to DDEW[8].

4.3 Creating the Data Manipulation Operations

The set of data manipulation operations, which PGDM builds, includes creation, deletion, editing, printing and querying procedures for each of the non-printable nodes. These are built in the same order as the type declarations and similarly make use of recursive value declarations where appropriate. This set of procedures ultimately rest on a set of built-in procedures for the base types. The kinds of procedures generated are illustrated for the *LOAN* class:

createNullLOAN creates a new *LOAN* value and adds it to the set of *LOANS*. The new value is created with default values for its components – in this case it will be given a null date and null values for the *STOCK* and *MEMBER* values associated with this *LOAN*. It gets the null date by calling a built-in procedure and the null *STOCK* and *MEMBER* values by calling *createNullSTOCK* and *createNullMEMBER* respectively.

createUserLOAN is similar to *createNullLOAN* except that it requests component values from the user. For each printable type there is a built-in input procedure. For each non-printable node there is installed a procedure which allows a choice from a menu or input of a new value. In this case, for the *STOCK* component, for instance, this procedure will present a menu of stock items and an alternative input new item. This option will call *createUserSTOCK*.

deleteLOAN provides menu of the *LOAN* items and when one is selected, removes it.

deleteRecursiveLOAN is similar but deletes the component values as well.

editLOAN brings up an editor for the component values of a *LOAN* value.

printLOAN displays a *LOAN* value and its components.

queryLOAN permits the input of a query on its components and returns the set of values which accord with the query conditions and displays them.

4.4 The Application Framework

The final part of the source code is the application framework in which the operations are embedded. In this respect, O_2 provides more help since it has a well-designed application framework with which to work. For the other three languages, we provide a standard interface template and a set of built-in user interaction facilities. At present these are minimal textual interfaces which are still under development, but we plan to provide graphical interfaces in the near future using such toolkits as the WIN toolkit for Napier88 [Chapter 1.1.3]. In the concluding section, we return to the possibility of permitting a choice between a wide range of application frameworks at program generation time.

5. Program Generation for Specific Languages

We now describe details of generating programs coded in each of the languages, discussing in turn the data model extensions, the types generated, the database structure and the application code produced.

5.1 Tycoon

The Tycoon system is a modern database programming environment, which includes a computationally complete, strongly typed, polymorphic and higher-order programming language, TL [Chapter 1.1.1). The type system provides arrays, tuples, variants and records orthogonally constructed ultimately out of integers, reals, booleans, strings, characters and localities. Sub-typing relationships are maintained and bounded parametric polymorphism is provided. Persistence is by reachability, but this time from any value which is in scope when the *store.stabilize* function is called.

For data modelling purposes, the following TL types are added to the list of base types: char and locality. The set of constructed types is extended to include a union node type which maps into TL variants.

Abstract, free and aggregate types map onto tuple types. Sets are modelled using an abstract data type pre-programmed in the language. The relationships *attribution* and *aggregate component* map onto fields of records. Specialisation is modelled using the *Repeat* key word indicating subtyping. Generalisation is mapped onto variant types. Recursive declarations are dealt with by the "**Rec Let** T1 **is** ... **&** T2 **is**" construction. Figure 5 shows the set of types for the library schema.

```
Let JOURNAL <:Ok = Tuple Title: String Issue: Int Date: String  end
Let BOOK <:Ok  = Tuple Author: String Title: String  end
Let AUDIO <:Ok  = Tuple ArtComp String  Title: String  end
Let TEXT  <:Ok = Tuple case Book with Book: BOOK
                       case Journal with Journal: JOURNAL end
Let STOCK <:Ok  = Tuple Catalogue: String
               case Text with Text: TEXT
               case  Audio with Audio: AUDIO end

Let PERSON <:Ok   = Tuple Name: String Address: String  end
Let MEMBER  <:Ok  = Tuple Repeat PERSON TicketNo: Int  end
Rec Let STAFF <:Ok  = Tuple Repeat PERSON
                       StaffNo: Int  Supervisees: SUPERVISEES end
and SUPERVISEES <:Ok  is set[ STAFF ]

Let LOAN <:Ok  = Tuple Stock: STOCK
                       Member: MEMBER DueBack:String  end
```

Fig. 5. The Library Schema in Tycoon Language

A set abstract data type is added to the code and for each non-printable type, a set of the instances of that type is created. These are made global and so become persistent when *store.stabilize* is called. These are named *PERSONs*, *MEMBERs* and so on – as seen for O_2C persistent sets –see Figure 6.

Procedures managing (i.e. creating, deleting, editing, printing and querying) each non-printable type are generated and a menu structure provides user access to these. These look very like their Napier88 versions – see Figure 7.

5.2. O_2C

O_2C is the object oriented version of C which is the principal programming interface to the O_2 object-oriented database system and which accords with the O_2 data model [9]. The work here can be contrasted with a similar attempt to generate O_2C from IFO [4]. O_2C describes its data in terms of both objects and values. The latter have types which are drawn from a type system which includes constructors for tuples, sets, bags and lists. These are built orthogonally ultimately out of integers, reals, characters, strings, booleans and bitstrings. Objects are members of classes which are types enhanced with the ability to define methods over members of the class and the ability to be linked to other classes by inheritance. Any object or value can be a persistent root in O2C.

O2 provides an application structure which is used by PGDM. An application in O2 is a set of (possibly parameterised) programs, from which an interface is automatically built as a menu of all of the programs available. In the Library example we might choose to include a program to create a new *PERSON*. This would be built as an O2 program which calls *createUserPERSON* and then the option "Create PERSON" would appear in the application menu.

For data modelling purposes, the following O2C types are added to the list of printable types in the PDGM user interface: bitstring and char. The set of constructed types is extended to include sequence and bag kinds which map into O2C lists and bags respectively.

The program works by creating classes for each of the abstract and free nodes. Since O2C permits forward references, there is no problem with recursion. The classes generated are similar to the Tycoon versions shown in Figure 5. Notice that the difference between the semantics of the generalisation and specialisation relationships has been lost at the type level. This is restored in the update operations provided by the insertion of code which forces generalised nodes to be partitioned by their sub-nodes.

name PERSONs: set(PERSON)
name MEMBERs: set(MEMBER)
name STAFFs: set(STAFF)
name STOCK: set(STOCK)
name AUDIOs: set(AUDIO)
name TEXTs: set(TEXT)
name BOOKs: set(BOOK)
name JOURNAL s: set(JOURNAL)
name LOANs: set(LOAN)

Fig. 6. The Library Database in O2C

Any value or object can be a root of persistence, so we have a free choice of what to make persistent. We choose to create a persistent extension for each class and create persistent roots as shown in Figure 6.

The constructed operations are embedded as methods of the classes. Each of the update operations makes checks to maintain the semantics of the schema. These are similar to the Napier88 versions shown in Figure 7. The application structure provides a simple menu of create, delete, edit, print and query operations. Within each of these, the user must choose the class to operate on and the program then uses the class methods to implement the behaviour.

5.3 Napier88

Napier88 [Chapter 1.1.3] is a strongly typed persistent programming language with a very rich type system, including constructors for records, vectors, variants and abstract data types, which are orthogonally constructed ultimately out of integers, reals, booleans, strings, pictures, pixels, images, environments or null values. Napier88 also has a dynamic type, *any*, which is the packaged union of all types, parametric polymorphism and recursive definition structures. It provides persistence by reachability from a single root attainable by calling the procedure *PS*. The root is presently implemented to return an environment (i.e. a set of name-value bindings). The persistent store is the set of values reachable from this root and this is usually structured as a hierarchy of sub-environments.

For data modelling purposes, the following Napier88 types are added to the list of base types in the PGDM user interface: pic, pixel, image, any, null and env. The set of constructed types is extended to include a union node type which maps into Napier88 variants. Figure 4 illustrates the editing window for the Napier88 language – notice that as well as the basic IFO types there are base nodes for the above set (indicated by rectangles with "P", "Px", "Im", "A", "N" and "E") and an extra complex node – a circle containing a plus indicating a union type.

The rich type system of Napier88 is sufficient to describe the structures inherent in an IFO schema. Abstract, free and aggregate types map onto record types. Sets are modelled using an abstract data type. The relationships *attribution* and *aggregate component* map onto fields of records. Specialisation is modelled using linked records, so that the instances of a sub-type have an extra field which points to an instance of the super-type. Generalisation is mapped onto variant types. Recursive declarations are dealt with by the "**rec type** T1 **is** ... **&** T2 **is**" constructions. Figure 4 shows the set of types for the library schema and is taken from an earlier and fuller report on the IFO to Napier88 mapping [5].

```
let createNullPERSON = proc( -> PERSON )
  begin
   let newPERSON = PERSON( "", "" )
   PERSONs(insert)( newPERSON )
   newPERSON
  end

let printPERSON = proc( aPERSON: PERSON )
  begin
   writeString( "name: " )
   writeString( aPERSON(name) )
   writeString( "   address: " )
   writeString( aPERSON(address) )
  end
```

Fig. 7. Some Library Operations in Napier88

The application operates in the context of the Napier88 *User* environment. A sub-environment of this has been set up called *PGDM* and below that there are environments containing the set of languages, the set of modules of the PGDM system and the set of applications which have been created using the system. Inside the *Applications* environment, there are further environments are created for each application built using the system.

The operations are coded as Napier88 procedures and these are stored in the persistent store. A very simple application framework is being built which provides a textual menu whose options are *create*, *delete*, *edit*, *print* and *query*. Each of these leads to a sub-menu of the non-printable node types. Figure 7 shows two of these.

5.4 Fibonacci

Fibonacci [Chapter 1.1.2] is a statically typed object-oriented language, but one which provides constructors for roles and associations as well as classes. The type system provides the base types: integer, real, string, boolean, null, any and none; and the constructors: tuple, union, function and sequence. It is also provides a number of constraint types, polymorphism, sub-typing, exceptions and a nested transaction mechanism. All data reachable from the global environment persists between program runs.

For data modelling purposes, the following Fibonacci types are added to the list of base types: any, null and none. The set of constructed types is extended to include a union node type which maps into Fibonacci unions and an ordered collection type which maps onto Fibonacci sequences Each of the abstract and specialised nodes is modelled using a Fibonacci role type, while generalised free types are modelled using the union types. Sets are modelled by sequences and aggregates by associations as shown.

For each role class, a set is created in the global environment as in:

let AUDIOs = **emptyClass of** AUDIO **end**;

and aggregates similarly create a set of associations:

let LOANs = **emptyAssoc of** LOAN

Fibonacci functions to create, delete, edit, print and query each role class and association are created. They are embedded in the same kind of application structure as described for Napier88 and Tycoon.

5.5 Extending the Set of Languages

PGDM is implemented in Napier88 and is designed to cope with an extensible set of languages. Each language module is built around calls to a higher order function which navigates the schema. This function is passed the schema and a number of functions one for each of the phases above. These functions are required to accept a node in the schema and to generate the appropriate string For instance, there must be a function which takes in a node, determines its kind and builds a type definition for this node. Adding a new language therefore requires:

- adding to the list of IFO node types if desired;
- providing a set of functions for generating code.

6. Conclusions and Further Work

Data modelling is often used as an initial step in programming a large data-intensive application. This is precisely what happens in current commercial data-centric software development products, but these function in the context of very restricted data models, which users find difficult to use for complex data. We extend the approach to systems which include much more powerful data abstraction facilities. This paper discusses how much of the next step can be automated – application code being automatically generated from the data model schema. Indeed, if a rigidly uniform interface style and set of operations is acceptable, the whole of the application can be generated. More typically, the source code produced can be edited to customise the application in any way desired. As such, the generator tools described should accelerate application development, since a great deal of repetitive coding is removed.

One use for this generator technology is that the application created can be thought of as a rapidly produced prototype of the desired application. The role of rapid prototyping is often restricted to providing an early check on the user interface. Here the prototype demonstrates a possible functionality for the application. Customising can then take place in the context of the observed deficiencies in the generated version.

Another advantage of the generator approach is that the generated version will have a regular structure. This has the twin benefits that the application should both be quicker to develop and to maintain. The regular structure should, for instance, be much easier for a programmer to read and traverse.

At present, the design of PGDM (Program Generation from Data Models) is complete. The schema editor and a version of all of the program generation modules exist [5; 10; 11; 12] and currently the various fragments in the process are being integrated. The versions that do exist will then require some refinement since, the implementors had a lack of familiarity with Tycoon and Fibonacci and so it is unlikely that the best job of generating applications in these languages has yet been accomplished.

Firstly, the application framework and the user interface are fixed and it would be sensible to be able to vary these systematically. Given that the operations are being provided in a uniform manner, there is no reason why it should not prove possible to set up any number of different frameworks to house the operations. As a result, the process of generating the program would require the selection of one of the available framework styles. Similarly, a menu of access methods could be added.

One requirement that is difficult to achieve with this whole approach is to integrate code customisation and data modelling changes. Figure 8 shows the problem. Supposing that having generated a program from the model, there are, on one hand, some customised changes to the code and, on the other, a change to the data model. Can the two sets of changes to the code be integrated or must the customised changes be made again? Clearly, this is a difficult problem, but one to which we will be giving some thought.

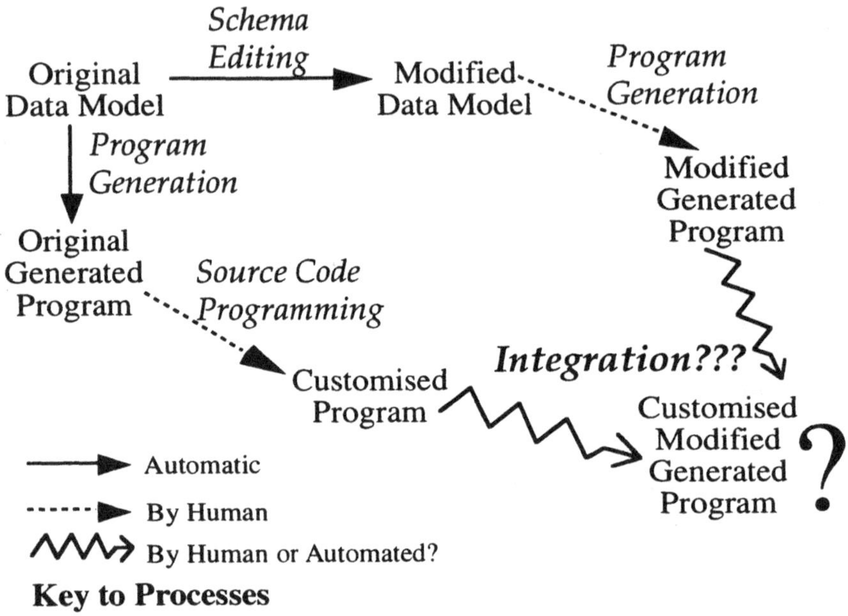

Fig. 8. Accommodating Schema and Code Customisation

Another aspect which our work only begins to approach is the role of constraints. We may divide the constraints which might be defined on the data model into two kinds. One kind are the inherent constraints implicit in the data model – for instance the acyclicity of the specialisation hierarchy. The other kind are explicit constraints which the data model could capture – for instance it would be useful to be able to assert key constraints on attributes. It has been shown how to extend IFO to capture a variety of explicit constraints [13]. If these were available in the data modelling environment, then much more of the code could be generated – particularly in a language with explicit constraint structures such as Fibonacci. In fact much of the need for a customisation phase is due to the need to insert constraint checks into the code. Such constraints are much more visible and manageable if they appear in the schema.

Process modelling tools are analogous to data modelling tools, but concentrate instead on the processes which manipulate data. Constructs for organising activities into structures such as sequences, loops and conditional or parallel branches are similar in many ways to the constructs for organising data into sets and records. Integrating a process modelling tool into our environment would have the twin benefits of producing an integrated high level description of both data structure and process, while also providing more information from which to generate an application – thus reducing the need for code customisation. This will not be accomplished within the $FIDE_2$ project.

Finally, it would be sensible to include other database facilities automatically. The application as generated is pretty raw. Given the uniform ability to generate programs, it seems possible to enhance these programs with extra facilities. One example that springs to mind is a bulk loading facility. Such a facility could take a file format and populate the application database from a file of information - see Chapter 3.3.1. This could be added to the application menu.

Acknowledgements. The work has been carried out in the context of the ESPRIT FIDE BRA 6309. As such many of the ideas were generated in discussion with our colleagues in the Hamburg group led by Joachim Schmidt, notably Ingrid Wetzel; the INRIA group led by Serge Abiteboul; the St. Andrews group led by Ron Morrison; and the University of Pisa group led by Antonio Albano. We would like to acknowledge the work on the modules of PGDM completed by Arne Hatlen, Leong Sook Meng and Poh Chee Beng. We would also like to acknowledge useful contributions to the design of PGDM by Malcolm Atkinson, Paul Philbrow, Zhenzhou Qin, Artur Serrano and Tony Printezis. We would also like to thank Sonia Berman for valuable criticism of an early draft of this chapter.

References

1. M.P. Atkinson, "Programming Languages and Databases", *Proceedings of the 4th International Conference on Very Large Data Bases*, Berlin, (ed. S.P. Yao), IEEE, 408-419, September, 1978.
2. R. Hull and R. King, "Semantic Data Modeling: Survey, Applications and Research Issues", *ACM Computing Surveys*, 19(3), 201-260, September 1987.
3. T.J. Teorey, D. Yang and J.P. Fry, "A logical Design Methodology for Relational Databases Using the Extended Entity-Relationship Model", *ACM Computing Surveys*, 18(2), 197-222, June 1986.
4. P. Poncelet, M. Teisseire, R. Cicchetti and L. Lakhal, "Towards a Formal Approach for Object Database Design", *Proc. VLDB93*, (R. Agrawal and D. Bell, eds.), 278-289, Dublin, August, 1993.
5. R. Cooper and I. Tabkha, "A Semantic Framework for the Design of Data Intensive Applications in a Persistent Programming Language", *Proc. Hawaii ICSS*, January 1992.
6. S. Abiteboul and R. Hull, "IFO: A Formal Semantic Data Model", *ACM TODS*, 12(4), 525-565, December 1987.
7. M.P. Atkinson and R. Morrison. Orthogonal persistent object systems. *VLDB Journal*, 4(3), 1995.
8. A. Rosenthal and D. Reiner, "Tools and Transformations - Rigorous and Otherwise - for Practical Database Design", *ACM TODS*, 19, 2, 167-211, June 1994.
9. O_2 Technology, "The O_2 User Manual, Version 4.2", O_2 Technology, 7 Rue de Parch de Clagny, 78035 Versailles Cedex, France, January 1993.
10. A. Hatlen, "A Graphical Data Modelling Interface for an Object Oriented Database", BSc. Project Report, University of Glasgow June 1994.
11. S.M. Leong, "A Graphical Data Modelling Interface for the Database Programming Language, Fibonacci", MSc. Project Report, University of Glasgow September 1994.
12. C.B. Poh, "A Graphical Data Modelling Interface for the Database Programming Language, Tycoon", MSc. Project Report, University of Glasgow September 1994.
13. R. L. Cooper and Z. Qin, "A Data Modelling Program With Constraint Specification and Management", in "Advanced Database Systems", P.M.D. Gray and R.J.Lucas (eds), Springer Verlag Lecture Notes in Computer Science 618, pages 192-208, July, 1992.

Chapter 3.2.2

The STYLE Workbench: Systematics of Typed Language Environments

Ingrid Wetzel[1], Florian Matthes[2], and Joachim W. Schmidt[2]

[1] Universität Hamburg, Vogt-Kölln Straße 30, D-22527 Hamburg, Germany
[2] Technical University Hamburg-Harburg, Harburger Schloßstraße 20, D-21071 Hamburg, Germany

Abstract. STYLE is a method to systematically construct a customized development environment (CDE) for a given high-level data model by exploiting and extending an existing persistent programming environment along three dimensions.

On the functional dimension, polymorphic types and higher-order functions are used to extend the system functionality with new generic services and through the integration of external tools. On the operational dimension, orthogonal persistence is provided for application and meta data related to design objects. Finally, on the modal dimension, reflective capabilities of persistent programming environments make it possible to view data as executable code and vice versa. This is used in a CDE to switch dynamically between different modes of a design object.

The STYLE approach is illustrated using a concrete CDE implemented for an object-oriented data model exploiting and extending the Tycoon persistent programming environment. This STYLE workbench provides integrated graphical and textual modelling tools, generation support and data model animation.

1 Introduction and Overview

One of the remarkable features of persistent programming languages like PS-algol [3], Napier-88 (see Chapter 1.1.3) and Tycoon (see Chapter 1.1.1) is their rich set of data structuring facilities. Languages with orthogonal persistence and a sophisticated *type system* greatly simplify the task of implementing information systems that have to work with complex, long-lived bulk data structures (see Chapter 1.4.2).

In parallel to the development of persistent programming languages, research in the area of database and conceptual models led to the development of advanced *data models* (see, e.g. [1,8,11]) some of which have been integrated into database programming languages, such as Pascal/R [20], DBPL (see Chapter 2.1.2), Galileo [2] and Fibonacci (see Chapter 1.1.2).

The STYLE[1] approach [22] described in this paper clarifies the relationship between data models and type systems. STYLE is based on the assumption that high-level data models capture important application semantics that are beyond the scope of type systems (see section 2 for a more detailed discussion). Therefore, STYLE proposes a phase-oriented design process for information systems which involves transformation tools that bridge the gap between a given semantic (conceptual) model and the logical (computational) model underlying a typed

[1] Style: Systematics of TYped Language Environments

programming language [7,23]. The requirements on these tools are described in section 3.1. Due to the continuous evolution of data models, the set of transformation tools has to be tailored to the data model at hand.

STYLE's main research contribution is a *systematic* method to construct a customized development environment (CDE) for a given high-level data model. A CDE exploits and extends an existing persistent programming environment (PPE) along three dimensions as discussed in section 3.2. On the functional dimension, polymorphic types and higher-order functions are used to extend the system functionality through the development of generic services and through the integration of external tools. On the operational dimension, orthogonal persistence is provided for application and meta data related to design objects. Finally, on the modal dimension, reflective capabilities of persistent programming environments make it possible to view data as executable code and vice versa. This is used in a CDE to switch dynamically between different modes of a design object.

In each of these three dimensions, the CDE tools are organized into four levels (kernel services, database functionality, data model support and data model usage) that exhibit different degrees of reusability. The resulting matrix architecture of a CDE is depicted in figure 1 and explained further in section 3.3.

In section 4 the STYLE approach is illustrated through a case study, the development of an integrated workbench for the high-level object-oriented data model OM1 [16] using the Tycoon system (see Chapter 2.1.4) as the underlying persistent programming environment. This CDE integrates multiple graphical and textual modelling tools, application generators and animation support which includes transactional programming and access to external servers.

2 Added Value through High-Level Data Models

This section discusses the main advantages of enriching a persistent programming environment by a high-level data model, namely:

- provision of domain-specific conceptual abstractions,
- system-enforced integrity beyond types, and
- enriched generic system functionality.

2.1 Domain-Specific Abstractions

Data models provide domain-specific abstractions that capture the essential modelling concepts required for the description of information systems. Data models emphasize the conceptual modelling of an application in terms of user concepts (e.g. classification, generalization, aggregation) instead of implementation abstractions (e.g. parameterization, modularization). These concepts are made available in a user-oriented language with a mnemonic syntax (with keywords chosen are close to natural language) that is easy to write and to understand. Many data models also specify an alternative or additional graphical representation.

Data models are a medium for the communication between software engineers and users during the modelling process and at the same time they should provide a precise specification of the system to be realized. Therefore, data models tend to blur the borderline between conceptual and computational perceptions of an information system.

2.2 System-Enforced Integrity beyond Types

Some data model concepts can be captured directly by type systems, others are beyond the scope of even the most sophisticated type systems. Nevertheless, it is possible to provide language and system support for these concepts (like exception handling, run-time integrity checking or active rules) that leads to a system-enforced integrity beyond types. The following discussion of object-oriented data modelling concepts may explain this idea which is central to the STYLE approach.

An object has structural properties described in terms of attributes. An attribute can have a complex structure and it can reference other objects. A specialized object may inherit attributes of a more generic object, possibly with restrictions on their attribute domains. Classical type systems suffice to describe and enforce such structural object properties (perhaps lacking a user-oriented presentation). The fact that an object has an immutable identity during its full lifetime is also captured easily in a typed persistent language.

A class describes objects with the same set of properties. In the context of data models, a class serves several purposes which are partially incompatible with the notion of a typed class in object-oriented programming [22]. First, a class gives a structural description of objects (*intensional aspect*). In data models a class also denotes a set of objects with the same structure (*extensional aspect*). In some data models, the identification of an object is also based on its class (*identification aspect*). Finally, a class provides generic standard methods for creating, deleting, observing and modifying objects (*dynamic aspect*).

The interaction between the intensional and the dynamic aspects of a class leads to the difficult problem of how to handle the restriction of an attribute domain when an object is specialized. A domain restriction makes perfect sense from a modelling perspective but implies a covariant method specialization which leads to well-known difficulties in static type systems for which – up to now – no satisfactory solution has been found [9].

The extensional aspect of a class also goes beyond pure static type constraints. At first glance, it appears sufficient to declare a persistent bulk type variable to store the set of complex objects that make up the extent of a class. However, plain insert and delete operations on a class extent do not enforce an extensional aspect of classes, namely that the extent of a subclass is a subset of the extent of all its superclasses. This subset constraint can be enforced easily by a programming methodology where, for example, an object inserted in a class is automatically inserted into its (transitive) superclasses. Similarly, referential integrity constraints on class extents are introduced if objects in one class reference objects in other classes. Again, the verification of such inter-class constraints is beyond the scope of type systems.

Finally, some data models permit an object to migrate between classes that are not in a subclass relationship at all and to dynamically lose attributes during its lifetime without changing its object identity. Such operations can change dynamically the type of an object which has been bound to an identifier in a scope different from the scope of the update operation (for example, in another transaction). Therefore, such operations cannot be type-checked statically, even in languages with flexible subtyping or type matching rules. However, by enforcing a programming methodology that correctly propagates a type change of an object o to all scopes that possibly reference o, global application integrity can be ensured at run-time.

2.3 Enriched Generic System Functionality

Data models traditionally provide standard generic methods for objects of any class (create, delete, update, acquire attribute, lose attribute, ...). These methods have to satisfy (at least) the model-inherent integrity constraints. As discussed in the previous subsection, the semantics of these generic methods may depend on global schema information and can therefore not be captured fully by type systems that rely on local type information only.

As described in [18], the code of such generic methods can be generated automatically based on the information provided by a data model. In a persistent programming environment, type-directed reflective programming techniques can be utilized to simplify this code generation process [22].

3 Data Modelling with STYLE

As explained so far, the STYLE approach supports a high-level data model by a customized development environment (CDE) that extends the functionality of a typed persistent programming environment.

Based on a classification of the tasks and tools in such a CDE given in section 3.1, the advantages of the STYLE approach which utilizes the PPE *itself* for the tool implementation are explained in section 3.2. Section 3.3 presents the generic matrix architecture underlying all CDEs that are built following the STYLE approach.

3.1 A Classification of Data Modelling Tools and Tasks

A CDE consists of a highly connected and smoothly integrated set of tools that automate work patterns which are typical for the design and implementation of an information system using a high-level data model. One can classify these tools based on the work patterns they support.

Modelling tools: On the data model level a CDE provides schema browsers and editors for graphical and textual modelling. Additionally, it assists in analyzing the status and the consistency of a schema through navigation tools (like class hierarchy, class association and integrity rule browsers) as well as local and global static schema checkers which are very similar to type checkers. Advanced CDEs automatically propagate local renaming and restructuring operations between different components of a large data model to ensure global schema consistency.

Generator tools: A CDE offers generators that map between different views (or modes) of a design object. On the data-model level, generators can ensure the consistency between textual and graphical schema representations. Code generators bridge the gap between data model and type system by generating type specifications enriched with procedural or declarative code to ensure the maintenance of high-level model-inherent and user-defined integrity constraints by the generic methods that insert, delete and update objects. Since the preservation of integrity constraints is central to the STYLE approach [15], the methods generated have transaction semantics with recovery functionality. Finally, generators can also be used to provide graphical or textual user interfaces that visualize typed persistent objects in a way that is consistent with the high-level data model.

Integration facilities: A CDE should integrate the modelling and generator tools described above and should provide analysis and visualization facilities for the whole design process. In particular, dependency information between design objects at different levels of abstraction should be recorded and, if possible, be exploited for automatic view and change propagation.

3.2 Specifics of the STYLE Approach

The systematic and flexible customization of development environments in STYLE exploits and expands the underlying PPE along three dimensions that should be orthogonal to each other to achieve maximum modelling and system flexibility [22].

Functional dimension: A rich language semantics including subtyping, polymorphism and higher-order functions enables the construction of libraries with generic services including type-safe wrappers for external design tool integration.

Operational dimension: Orthogonal persistence (object lifetimes being independent of the object types), distribution abstraction, multi-threading and orthogonal mobility of data, code and threads, greatly simplify the construction of CDEs.

Modal dimension: Modern persistent programming environments provide multiple, typed views onto code and data objects (concrete syntax, abstract syntax, intermediate code, executable code) and flexible bidirectional mappings between these modes as provided, for example, by extensible grammars (see Chapter 3.2.3) and reflective programming techniques [21]. This can be exploited in a design environment to realize flexible mode switches on design objects.

Each of these dimensions contributes to specific tasks in the construction of a CDE as follows.

Functional dimension for tool building: The positive consequences of using a strongly and polymorphically-typed PPE for CDE construction can be summarized as follows.

- Information system construction and design tool construction take place in the same language and system framework which facilitates code sharing and code re-use.
- The components of a CDE can be provided as an open set of typed libraries working on shared persistent data structures and not as a loosely coupled set of applications that exchange design information in an ad-hoc manner via files, command-line arguments or message queues. As sketched in figure 1, and discussed further in the next section, these libraries can be organized systematically into a matrix architecture.

Operational dimension for meta data management and analysis: Information system development is itself a data-intensive application [12] since it is necessary to store and retrieve bulk (meta) information about design objects (like graphical schemata, textual class definitions, or module interfaces) and design decisions. A design decision is an annotated relationship between design objects. For example, a design decision may relate a specification and several alternative implementations to an annotation that explains why a certain alternative was chosen.

The consequences of utilizing a PPE for CDE construction are obvious.

- Meta data of complex structure can be stored persistently without the need for complicated transformations into a canonical repository data format.
- Schema analysis and browsing tools can utilize tailored bulk data structures and high-level iteration abstractions to query meta data.
- It is possible to define declarative views on a design object that correspond to different levels of abstraction in a graphical schema or to multiple refinements of a design object.
- Change propagation can be realized by meta data analysis and updates exploiting integrity constraints defined for the meta data model.

Modal dimension for generation support: In STYLE, the graphical representation of a class, its textual description, its corresponding module and its GUI to visualize class instances are regarded as different modes of a single design object. Each mode has its own operations and tool support. Switches between different modes are implemented by parsers and generators that typically make use of the modal base services of a PPE.

A key characteristic of STYLE is the *integration* of the CDE tools as typed modules in an open persistent programming environment. This makes it possible to implement flexible cross-calls between tools for navigation purposes and to factor-out shared functionality like queries on meta data, generators or dependency tracking. A shared, strongly-typed and persistent meta data repository also contributes to a tight tool integration. Furthermore, external services can be integrated seamlessly by means of wrapper modules with strongly-typed interfaces.

3.3 The STYLE Matrix Architecture

On each of the three dimensions identified in the previous section, the CDE tools are organized into four layers (kernel services, database functionality, data model support and data model usage) that exhibit different degrees of reusability. The resulting matrix architecture of a CDE is depicted in figure 1.

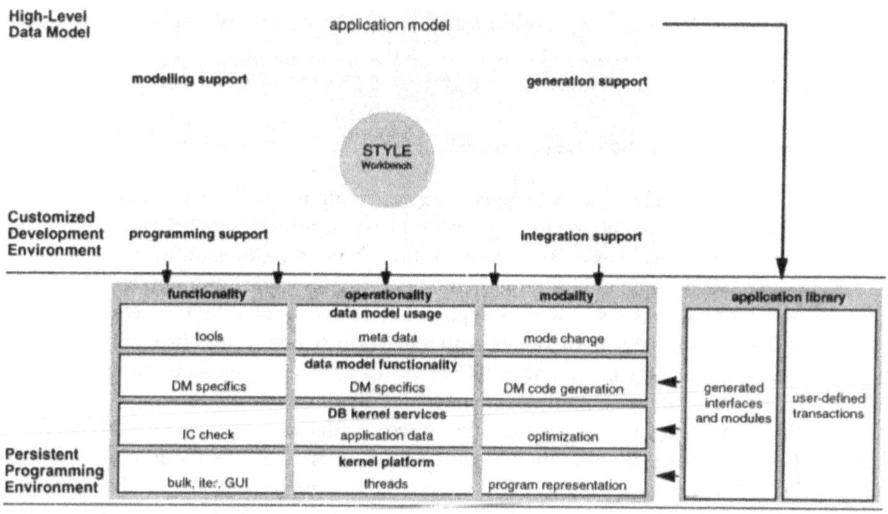

Fig. 1. The architecture of a STYLE customized development environment

The CDE is realized as a layered library of typed modules of the target persistent programming environment. The services of higher library layers are implemented based on services of lower library layers.

For example, the kernel services *bulk* and *iter* provide multiple bulk data structures (lists, sets, bags) and iteration abstractions (selection, projection, join) that are utilized by a generic integrity checking layer *IC check* that implements predicative integrity checking on multiple bulk types. These services are specialized further in the next layer to support the inherent integrity constraints of a specific data model. The topmost layer is responsible for the presentation of these services to the user.

A similar layering applies to the operational and modal dimension. Some of the modules are simply wrappers for external tools (like text editors or graph editors) and external services (like SQL databases or GUI libraries).

A typical user of a CDE environment is not aware of the fine-structure of these tools but interacts directly with an integrated STYLE workbench that provides modelling, generation, programming and integration support.

An application described in a given high-level data model is transformed with the help of the CDE tools into a self-contained but open application library in the target language TL. This library consists of generated TL interfaces and modules which exploit the type system of the target language and utilize at run-time modules of the CDE itself to provide system integrity beyond typing. This dependency between applications and the CDE is indicated by horizontal arrows from the application library to the three lower levels of the CDE library.

4 A CDE for an Object-Oriented Data Model

In this section, the STYLE approach is illustrated by the description of a specific CDE, an integrated workbench for the high-level object-oriented data model OM1 [16] using the Tycoon system (see Chapter 2.1.4) as the underlying persistent programming environment.

4.1 Overview of the OM1 Data Model

The data model OM1 is based on concepts of semantic data models [11,6] which emphasize the structural definition of objects. In addition, it provides additional constructs for formulating inter-object integrity constraints. Furthermore, OM1 is influenced by a formalization of object-oriented data models that supports both, structured values and objects [4,5,16,19]. An application schema consists of a set of type and class definitions. Values are grouped into types describing immutable sets of values with a uniform structure together with operations defined on such values. Objects are abstractions of real-world entities and have an identity. This identity is independent of the values which are used to describe objects. Object identifiers are immutable during an object's lifetime. Objects with the same structure and behaviour are grouped into classes providing mutable collections as well as abstractions of individual objects. Relationships between objects are expressed by reference attributes. The description of multiple aspects or roles of the same object is modelled by simultaneous membership of an object in more than one class and by the migration of objects between classes.

OM1 has the usual model-inherent subclass and referential integrity constraints and supports the formulation of user-defined integrity constraints.

Application-specific object behaviour is expressed in the OM1 data model using a calculus derived from formal specification languages [10,13] [17]. It is not necessary to specify standard query and update methods that satisfy the integrity constraints. Instead of this, integrity-preserving implementations for these methods are provided by the data model. Figure 2 gives an example of a textual OM1 class definition. The class *PackageTour* is part of a larger information system for travel agencies. The main classes of this application are flights, hotels and package tours (see also the nodes and arcs in the schema graph depicted in figure 3). Each package tour consists of a pair of back and forth flights together with hotel information. A user-defined integrity constraint states that the area specified for the flights has to match the area specified for the hotel.

```
Class PackageTour

Relationships

  Specialization
    isA Tour fix
  Dependencies
    deleteDependentOn Hotel with removePackageTourWithHotel,
    deleteDependentOn Flight ...

Structure

  Attributes
    key region : ▷ Region,
    key town : ▷ Town,
    hotel : ▷ Hotel,
    flights : [ forth : ▷ Flight, back : ▷ Flight ]

Constraints

  Static
    HotelFlight:
    (this.hotel.region = this.flights.forth.destAirport.region) ∧
    (this.hotel.region = this.flights.back.depAirport.region),
    (* the forth flight's destination airport and the return flight's
       departure airport must belong to the same region as the hotel *),
    ...

Methods

  Transactions
    removePackageTourWithHotel
      (packageTour : ▷ PackageTour date : Date) =
      begin
        ActualizedTour.modifyWithPackageTour(packageTour date);
        removePackageTour(packageTour)
      end
    ...

End
```

Fig. 2. A class definition in the object-oriented data model OM1

4.2 User-Oriented Modelling Tools

The actual implementation of the OM1 CDE integrates the following modelling tools, some of which are visible in figure 3.

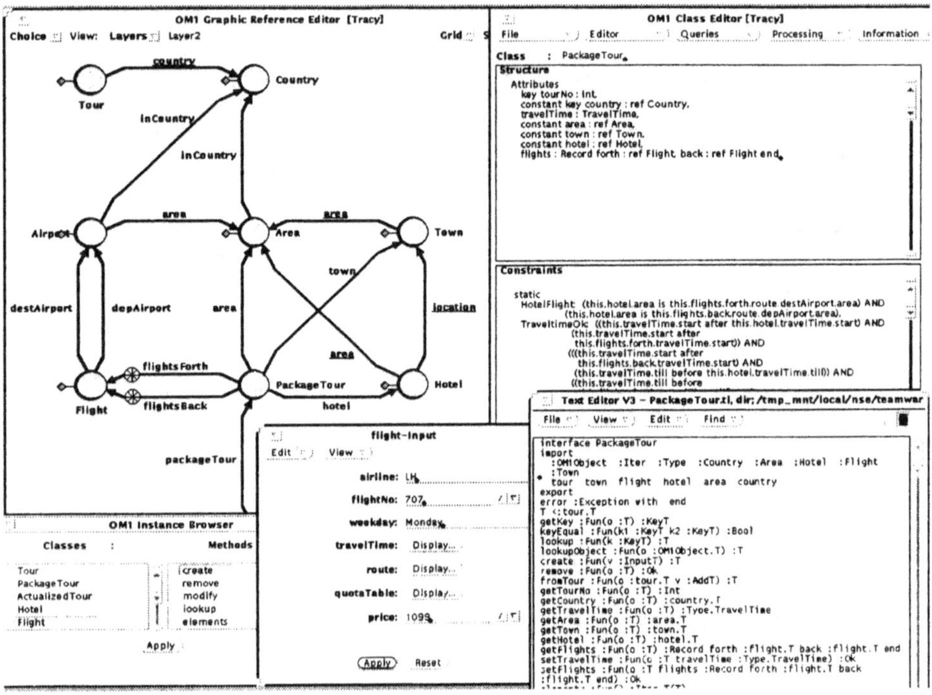

Fig. 3. Integration of components in a STYLE workbench

- A graphical schema editor is used to define class and type nodes with class reference arcs and inheritance links between classes. The editor supports views of different granularity.
- A class and type browser is used to select class and type names defined in a schema, for example, to invoke a text editor on a class.
- A textual class editor and a textual type editor are used to specify class components and type structures.
- Additional tools support the parsing, consistency checking and the generation of pretty-printed LaTeX documents for (parts of) an OM1 schema.
- A generator maps graphical OM1 class diagrams into corresponding textual OM1 class definitions.
- A toolbox provides additional local and global consistency checks and mechanisms to propagate changes in an OM1 schema (for example, class or attribute renaming). These algorithms can be invoked interactively from virtually all CDE tools.

```
interface PackageTour
import
  :OM1Object :Iter :Type :Country :Area :Hotel :Flight :Town
  tour town flight hotel area country
export
  error :Exception with end
  T <:tour.T
  ...
  getKey :Fun(o :T) :KeyT
  keyEqual :Fun(k1 :KeyT k2 :KeyT) :Bool
  lookup :Fun(k :KeyT) :T
  lookupObject :Fun(o :OM1Object.T) :T
  create :Fun(v :InputT) :T
  remove :Fun(o :T) :Ok
  fromTour :Fun(o :tour.T v :AddT) :T
  getTourNo :Fun(o :T) :Int
  getCountry :Fun(o :T) :country.T
  getTravelTime :Fun(o :T) :Type.TravelTime
  getArea :Fun(o :T) :area.T
  getTown :Fun(o :T) :town.T
  getHotel :Fun(o :T) :hotel.T
  getFlights :Fun(o :T) :Record forth :flight.T back :flight.T end
  setTravelTime :Fun(o :T travelTime :Type.TravelTime) :Ok
  setFlights :Fun(o :T flights :Record forth :flight.T back :flight.T end) :Ok
  elements :Fun() :Iter.T(T)
  classInfo :Tuple name :String end
end;
```

Fig. 4. A typed Tycoon implementation of the OM1 class *packageTour*

4.3 Application Generators

An OM1 class definition consists of structure, constraint and method specifications and is implemented by typed interfaces and modules in the Tycoon language TL (see figure 4). The TL implementation defines encapsulated objects with standard methods that satisfy the model-inherent and user-defined constraints. Access to the TL objects is only possible through the generated standard methods. User-defined class methods correspond to transactions of the information system and are built on top of the standard methods. As indicated in figure 4, the standard methods raise exceptions to signal integrity violations which can then be handled by the application code without breaking the encapsulation of the object.

The interfaces and modules created for class definitions extend the Tycoon environment with an application-specific library. The generated modules can be kept concise by utilizing pre-existing data-model-specific libraries of the CDE to factor out repeating tasks from the generated code. The provision of data-model-specific libraries is termed *situative lifting of the target language* in the STYLE approach.

The cooperation between TL code generators and the generic CDE services can be exemplified by the integrity checking task of a CDE. For a specific OM1 integrity constraint (e.g. referential integrity between two classes), preconditions and delayed conditions have to be generated for the insert and delete methods of the classes involved. Instead of hard-wiring these conditions into the method's implementation code, a generic TL library for constraint handling is utilized. It provides dynamic collections of constraints (implemented as bulk collections of function values in TL) that can be attached dynamically to methods. As a consequence, the constraint handling is fully separated from the OM1 interface and module generation process. Global OM1 constraints are transformed into boolean TL predicates which are then attached dynamically to the relevant methods.

The main benefit of this approach is *locality*. A local update of a single class definition leads to a local update of the corresponding TL class implementation and a reinitialization of the constraint database. No other method code needs to be recompiled.

4.4 Animation Support

An animation component provides a generic database browser to create, delete and update individual objects (instances of classes) and to navigate through the persistent object base following the (set-valued) associations between objects. The animation tool uses the generated application modules to guarantee the enforcement of integrity constraints specified in the data model. The type-specific visualization code is also generated automatically.

4.5 Integration with Tycoon Transaction Code

Arbitrary user transactions can be implemented on top of the generated class implementations using the algorithmically-complete persistent programming language TL. For example, a user-defined method *removeHotel* can extend the functionality of the *hotel.remove* operation by rebooking all package tours prior to the removal of a hotel. See [14] for a discussion on how generic methods and user-defined transaction code have to interact to maintain the consistency in an object base.

The language TL also provides mechanisms to enable interoperability of OM1 application code with existing (legacy) database systems like Ingres, Oracle and ObjectStore.

4.6 Application Development Using the Integrated Prototype

Figure 5 sketches the main modelling steps supported by the OM1 customized development environment. First, the structural schema information is modelled using the graphical editor.

Based on this information the structural part of the textual class definitions is generated. Interactive queries at the schema level can be utilized to detect incomplete schema information, e.g. references to undefined classes. Integrity constraints and user-defined class methods are also added at this stage using a structured-text editor. Navigation facilities to referenced and referencing classes simplify the formulation of inter-class integrity constraints.

The programming layer is automatically populated with the generated class interfaces and modules implementing the standard methods. The application programmer implements the user-defined methods on top of these interfaces. If necessary, user-defined methods can also override standard methods.

The animation component supports the validation of an OM1 model by populating a persistent object base with sample objects and by invoking standard and user-defined methods on these objects. The visualization code generated for the animation can also be reused and adapted for use after the prototype phase.

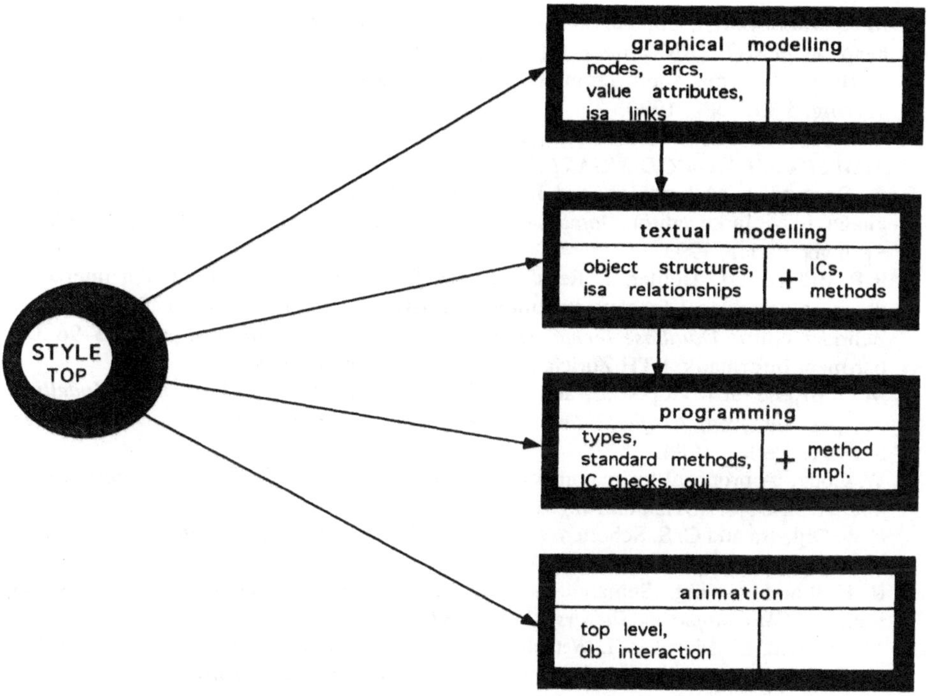

Fig. 5. Tasks and tools involved in the OM1 modelling process

5 Concluding Remarks

The customized development environment for the OM1 data model clearly demonstrates that persistent programming environments are a suitable platform for both the construction of data-intensive applications utilizing a high-level data model as well as for the construction of tightly integrated design and modelling tools.

The distinction between functional, operational and modal requirements was of great use in the organization of the STYLE tool infrastructure. It remains to be verified how much of this infrastructure can be re-used for the construction of other CDEs.

Acknowledgements. This research is supported by ESPRIT Basic Research, Project FIDE, #6309.

References

1. J.-R. Abrial. Data semantics. In J.W. Klimbie and K.L. Koffeman, editors, *Data-Base Management*. North-Holland, Amsterdam, 1974.
2. A. Albano, L. Cardelli, and Orsini R. Galileo: A strongly-typed, interactive conceptual language. *ACM Transactions on Database Systems*, 10(2):230–260, 1985.

3. M.P. Atkinson, K.J. Chisholm, and W.P. Cockshott. PS-algol: An algol with a persistent heap. *ACM SIGPLAN Notices*, 17(7), July 1981.
4. C. Beeri. A formal approach to object-oriented databases. *Data and Knowledge Engineering*, 5:352–382, 1990.
5. C. Beeri. New data models and languages – the challenge. In *Proceedings of the Eleventh ACM SIGACT-SIGMOD-SIGART Symposium on Principles of Database Systems*, 1992.
6. A. Borgida, J. Mylopoulos, and J. Schmidt. The TaxisDL software description language. In M. Jarke, editor, *Database Application Engineering with DAIDA*, pages 65–84. Springer-Verlag, 1993.
7. R.P. Brägger, A. Dudler, J. Rebsamen, and C.A. Zehnder. Gambit: An interactive database design tool for data structures, integrity constraints and transactions. In C.A. Zehnder, editor, *Database Techniques for Professional Worskstations*, pages 65–96. Department Informatik, ETH Zürich, Switzerland, September 1983.
8. M.L. Brodie, J. Mylopoulos, and J.W. Schmidt, editors. *On Conceptual Modelling, Perspectives from Artificial Intelligence, Databases, and Programming Languages*. Springer-Verlag, 1984.
9. W. Cook. A proposal for making eiffel type-safe. In *ECOOP 90 Proc. European Conference on Object Oriented Programming*, 1989.
10. E.W. Dijkstra and C. S. Scholten. *Predicate Calculus and Program Semantics*. Springer-Verlag, 1989.
11. R. Hull and R. King. Semantic database modeling: Survey, applications, and research issues. *ACM Computing Surveys*, 19(3), 1987.
12. M. Jeusfeld, M. Mertikas, I. Wetzel, Jarke. M., and J.W. Schmidt. Database application development as an object modelling activity. In *Proceedings of the Sixteenth International Conference on Very Large Databases, Brisbane, Australia*, August 1990.
13. G. Nelson. A generalization of Dijkstra's calculus. *ACM Transactions on Programming Languages and Systems*, 11(4):517–561, October 1989.
14. K.-D. Schewe. *Specification of Data-Intensive Application Systems*. PhD thesis, Technische Universität Cottbus, 1994.
15. K.-D. Schewe, J.W. Schmidt, D. Stemple, B. Thalheim, and I. Wetzel. A reflective approach to method generation in object oriented databases. Rostocker Informatik Berichte Nr. 13, Fachbereich Informatik, Universität Rostock, Germany, 1992.
16. K.-D. Schewe, J.W. Schmidt, and I. Wetzel. Identification, genericity and consistency in object-oriented databases. In J. Biskup and R. Hull, editors, *Proceedings of the International Conference on Database Theory*, volume 646 of *Lecture Notes in Computer Science*, pages 341–356. Springer-Verlag, October 1992.
17. K.-D. Schewe, J.W. Schmidt, I. Wetzel, N. Bidoit, D. Castelli, and C. Meghini. Abstract machines revisited. FIDE Technical Report Series FIDE/91/11, FIDE Project Coordinator, Department of Computing Sciences, University of Glasgow, Glasgow G128QQ, March 1991.
18. K.-D. Schewe, B. Thalheim, J.W. Schmidt, and I. Wetzel. Integrity enforcement in object-oriented databases. In U. Lipeck, editor, *Proc. 4th Int. Workshop on Foundations of Models and Languages for Data and Objects, Volkse, Germany, October 19–22*, 1992.
19. K.-D. Schewe, B. Thalheim, and I. Wetzel. Foundations of object-oriented database concepts. Informatik Fachbericht FBI-HH-B-157/92, Fachbereich Informatik, Universität Hamburg, Germany, November 1992.
20. J.W. Schmidt. Some high level language constructs for data of type relation. In *Proceedings of the ACM-SIGMOD International Conference on Management of Data, Toronto, Canada*, August 1977.

21. D. Stemple, T. Sheard, and L. Fegaras. Linguistic reflection: A bridge from programming to database languages. In *Proceedings 25th Annual Hawaii International Conference on System Sciences*, pages 46–55, 1992.
22. I. Wetzel. *Programmieren mit STYLE: Über die systematische Entwicklung von Programmierumgebungen.* PhD thesis, Fachbereich Informatik, Universität Hamburg, Germany, July 1994.
23. I. Wetzel, K.-D. Schewe, J.W. Schmidt, and A. Borgida. Specification and refinement of databases. In M. Jarke, editor, *Database Application Engineering with DAIDA*, pages 283–318. Springer-Verlag, 1993.

Chapter 3.2.3

Using Extensible Grammars for Data Modelling

Florian Matthes, Joachim W. Schmidt, and Jens Wahlen

Technical University Hamburg-Harburg, Harburger Schloßstraße 20, D-21071 Hamburg, Germany

Abstract. We present a systematic approach to the rapid implementation of high-level data models and query languages in the polymorphic higher-order programming language TL. The static semantics of data model constructs are captured by a mapping to polymorphic types and associated data constructor and selector functions. The dynamic semantics of query languages are realised by a mapping to bulk data types and iteration abstractions. Contrary to conventional approaches, these two mappings are specified by user-defined grammar extensions of the target language TL based on user-defined library code and not by separate tools in the programming environment. We give examples of this syntax-directed approach to data modelling and discuss its advantages and limitations.

1 Introduction and Motivation

To address the modelling requirements of advanced data-intensive applications, a large number of high-level data models and query languages have been proposed in the literature to overcome the limitations of existing relational, deductive or object-oriented models.

Unfortunately, the implementation of a new data model or query language for evaluation purposes turns out to be a rather complex task since it requires non-trivial language processing, software engineering and database system construction know-how. Therefore, such data model proposals lead either to ambitious long-term database system development projects (see, e.g. [17] and [16], synopsis in Chapter 2.1.2) with a very long design-implementation-evaluation cycle, or, more frequently, to closed toy implementations that lack the operational support required for experiments in a realistic setting (persistence, interfaces to production systems, user interface support).

Due to their orthogonality and their full integration of persistent data, code and meta-data management, persistent higher-order languages constitute a promising platform for the rapid implementation of high-level data models and their query languages. The static semantics of data model constructs can be captured by a mapping to polymorphic types and associated data constructor and selector functions. The dynamic semantics of query languages can be realised by a mapping to bulk data types and iteration abstractions in the persistent programming language.

The mapping itself can be achieved either by standard source-code to source-code translators (B-Tool [8] for DBPL, Sidereus [5] for Galileo) or by *reflective* code generation techniques [15] (see also Chapter 3.2.2) that exploit the fact that the target language (run-time environment) and the code generator (compile-time environment) are tightly integrated in many persistent systems and that typed persistent program representations can be utilized instead of linear source-code.

In this paper, we report on our experience using a third mapping option that exploits *extensible grammars* as developed in [9,10] and implemented in the Tycoon system (see Chapter 2.1.4) to translate systematically from declarations and statements of a high-level data model down to type and value expressions of the polymorphic Tycoon language TL (see Chapter 1.1.1).

This paper is organized as follows: We first introduce the concept and notation of extensible grammars by a simple programming language example. In section 3 we give an overview of our syntax-driven approach to data model and query language implementation. We then illustrate in section 4 this approach through a small example (SQL-style queries over multiple bulk types). Section 5 summarizes our experience gained in the Tycoon/Fibonacci add-on experiment, a larger exercise in data model implementation. The paper concludes with a comparison of our approach with generator-based techniques to data-model implementation.

2 Extensible Grammars

In this section we introduce the concept and notation of extensible grammars using a simple programming language example. We also explain how extensible grammars fit into the Tycoon system architecture (see Chapter 2.1.4).

2.1 Dynamic Syntax Extensions

The Tycoon language TL aims at minimality and orthogonality of semantic concepts which is also reflected by its syntax that provides only a small number of keywords and syntactic forms.

However, such a syntactic austerity may lead to stereotypical programming patterns in application code. As a simple example, consider a programming language that provides only a single **loop ... exit ... end** iteration construct. Other common loop structures (**while**, **repeat**, **for**) have to be expressed by systematic combinations of **loop** and **if** statements.

The idea behind extensible grammars is to provide programmers (or, more realistically speaking, application library designers) with a generic mechanism to introduce tailored syntax for the application domain at hand. The use of tailored syntactic forms often leads to more readable and understandable application code and helps to avoid accidental programming errors in repeating code patterns.

For example, the following dynamic TL syntax extension introduces a block-structured **for ... to ... do ... end** statement by a syntax-directed rewriting into a standard TL **loop** statement.

```
grammar
  value :Value |==
    "for" x=ide "=" l=value "to" h=value "do" b=bindings "end"
    hv=unique
    => value<<| begin
                  let hv = h
                  let var x = l
                  loop if x > hv then exit else b  x:=x+1 end
                end |>>
end
```

Grammar definitions can be embedded freely into TL source code and therefore have to be enclosed in a **grammar end** block. In the example above, the syntax for TL *values* is extended (indicated by the operator |==) by a new production that consists of a syntax definition preceding the arrow => and a pattern enclosed in <<| |>> that defines a *value* which is to be generated whenever the new syntax appears in the input program. The pattern utilizes pattern variables (*x, l, h, b, hv*) which are instantiated on expansion of a pattern with concrete identifiers (*x, hv*) or with complete subexpressions (*l, h, b*) as defined by the pattern variable bindings to the left of the arrow =>. For example, the loop

let *g = 40*
for *i = 1* **to** *g+7* **do** *a[i]:=g* **end**

is rewritten into the TL program

let *g = 40*
begin
  let *hv = g+7*
  let var *i = 1*
  loop if *i > hv* **then exit else** *a[i]:=g i:=i+1* **end**
end

TL grammar definitions are statically sort-checked. For example, the production *value* is checked to generate expressions of sort *Value* only. Similarly, the productions *ide* and *bindings* are guaranteed to return individual identifiers and sequences of bindings, respectively.

A syntax extension gives also a precise definition of the scoping, typing and evaluation rules for each newly defined language construct in terms of the scoping, typing and evaluation rules of the underlying base language. In the example above, the following rules apply:[1]

- The scope of the loop variable *x* is delimited by the loop body *b*. Inside *b*, a loop variable *x* hides a variable *x* in an outer scope. All other global variables are visible in the subexpressions *l, h* and *b*. The binding *hv*=**unique** ensures that on expansion, the identifier *hv* used as an auxiliary variable is chosen to be different from all other variables in the program and therefore remains invisible in all subexpressions.
- The loop variable *x* has to be of type *Int* since it appears as an argument to the integer infix function ">". This implies that the start and end expressions (*l* and *h*) also have to be of type *Int*. Assignments to the loop variable in *b* are allowed.
- The start and end expressions *l* and *h* are evaluated only once, *h* is evaluated before *l*.

Grammar extensions can be layered without restrictions, for example, a vector sum could be defined by a mapping onto a **for** loop.

In addition to the production extension operator |== used in the example above, TL provides two other operators to destructively override production definitions and to introduce new productions avoiding name clashes with existing productions.

As described in [9,10], TL's extensible grammars are superior to other syntax definition formalisms since they respect static, block-structured scoping and avoid unwanted name clashes, unlike macro definitions and preprocessor-based systems.

[1] An alternative loop semantics can be realised easily by local changes to the syntax definition.

2.2 Initial Syntax Definition

The previous subsection explained how new syntactic forms can be defined based on an existing syntax. To fully decouple the concrete syntax from the TL abstract syntax, the initial TL syntax is not hard-wired into the compiler but provided as a grammar source file. In the current version of our system, this file is compiled once for each persistent store. For example, the syntax of the **loop** and **exit** statements is defined initially as follows using the production definition operator "===":

```
grammar
  value:Value === ...
    | "loop" b=bindings "end" => mkValueLoop(b)
    | "exit" => mkValueExit()
    | ...
end
```

The notation to specify the concrete syntax and pattern-variable bindings on the left-hand side of the productions is identical to the one used for dynamic syntax extensions. The right-hand side consists of constructor applications (*mkValueLoop, mkValueExit*). At compiler definition time, the names and signatures (argument and result sorts) of all TL constructors are made available to the extensible grammar front end. These constructors correspond directly to functions in the TL compiler that create typed program representations (abstract syntax trees).

Despite its rich language model, TL provides language objects of only four different semantic domains which simplifies the orthogonal combination of these objects in the mapping process for a higher-level data model. These semantic domains correspond to the following built-in sorts used in TL grammars:

- The sort *Type* subsumes closed and parameterized type expressions like base types, structured types and higher-order type operators. The canonical type **Ok** is the supertype of all closed types and contains the canonical value **ok**.
- The sort *Value* subsumes expressions and side-effecting statements. A statement returns the canonical value **ok**. The result of an expression used in a statement context is discarded.
- *Bindings* are ordered sequences of identifier/type or identifier/value pairs. If identifiers are omitted, so-called anonymous bindings are defined. This makes it possible, for example, to represent tuple attributes, array elements and statement sequences uniformly as bindings.
- *Signatures* are ordered sequences of identifier/type or identifier/supertype pairs. Again, identifiers can be omitted. Signatures appear, for example, in functions, tuple types and module interfaces.

2.3 On the Implementation of Extensible Grammars

Extensible grammars are realised by a fully self-contained polymorphic Tycoon library implementing an extensible parser and grammar checker which are bound statically as a front-end to the TL type checker and code generator (see figure 1). Without recompilation, the very same extensible grammar package can be used for other programming languages, as demonstrated by the TooL language [11].

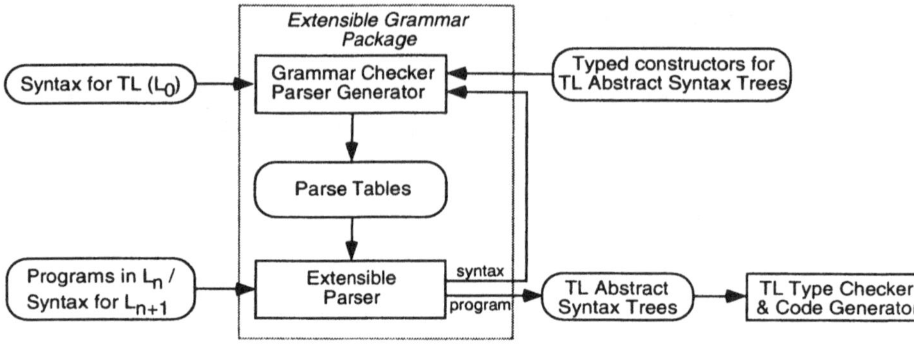

Fig. 1. Interfaces of the extensible grammar package

The grammar checker and parser generator as well as the constructors for TL abstract syntax trees are defined in TL. Input phrases accepted by the extensible parser can be either new syntax definitions which are passed on to the grammar checker and parser generator to be available for future input parsing or they can be TL abstract syntax trees that are processed further by the TL type checker and code generator.

The extensible parser is initialized with the syntax of the target language L_0 at hand (TL or TooL). Given an extensible parser for programs in a language L_n, a new extensible parser for a language L_{n+1} can be defined by specifying the context-free grammar and the rewrite rules (productions) that map L_{n+1} terms into L_n terms. This method is incremental since L_n is translated into L_{n-1} until the base target language is reached and the final (TL or TooL) abstract syntax tree is generated.

Static checks at grammar-definition time guarantee the sort-correctness of grammars (only legal syntax trees are generated during parsing), the termination of parsing for arbitrary input programs, and the absence of syntactic ambiguities. Formal proofs for these properties are given in [10]. This high degree of static correctness should be contrasted with other program transformation or reflective compilation techniques.

Extensible grammars can be implemented efficiently. In our persistent system environment, the first extensible TL parser is half as fast as the old, hand-coded standard LL(1) top-down parser. We expect the next re-implementaion of the extensible parser to outperform a handcoded parser using a simple optimization of the attribute evaluation strategy. Furthermore, the space required for the code and data of both parsers is of similar size.

3 Supporting Data Modelling with Extensible Grammars

Figure 2 sketches the generic architecture of a data model implementation in TL: Users interact with the system through data-model-specific tools like schema and data browsers. Data and schema declarations, and interactive and embedded queries are written in a data-model-specific syntax. This syntax is specified once per data model by a set of TL syntax modules (bulk syntax, query syntax, etc.). Each syntactic construct is mapped to functions and types exported from Tycoon interfaces. This mapping captures the static and dynamic semantics of

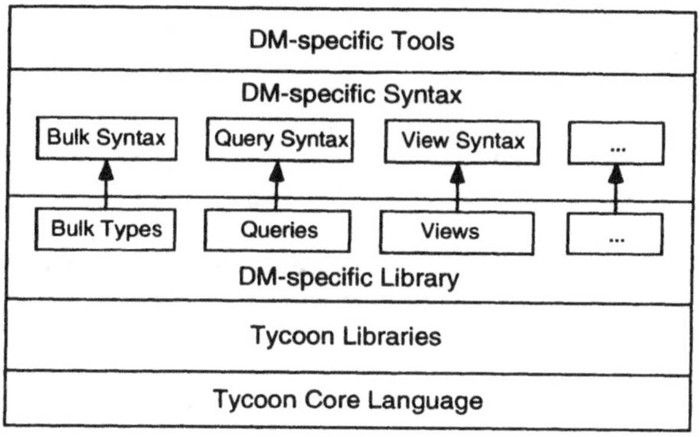

Fig. 2. A layered architecture for data model implementation in Tycoon

the data model. The data-model-specific TL interfaces in turn are based either on the existing set of TL libraries or directly on the built-in TL constructs.

The top-down methodology to implement a given data model *M* in TL can be summarized as follows:

1. Identify the semantic concepts of *M* (e.g. table, row, attribute, domain, query, view).
2. Map each concept to a newly defined or pre-existing abstract TL type or type constructor. At this stage, the implementation of the abstract types is irrelevant.
3. Identify the abstract operations available on each of the semantic objects (e.g. create a table, insert a row, execute a query, define a view, union two tables, join two tables, ...).
4. Map these abstract operations to typed TL function signatures that refer to the types identified in step 2. In order to correctly capture the static semantic constraints on the abstract operations of *M* by TL type constraints, elaborate TL type concepts (parametric polymorphism, subtype polymorphism, ad-hoc reflective polymorphism based on dynamic type inspection) can be used. The abstract types and their operations are preferably clustered into TL interfaces named after their semantic concept.
5. In parallel, develop a TL grammar definition (incrementally) that maps each syntactic construct of *M* (e.g. attribute type definition, table type definition, query, subquery, projection list, ...) into nested TL expressions that utilize the types, type operators and functions defined in the previous step. An important task of the grammar is to correctly capture *M*'s scoping rules.
   The name of a grammar production should be chosen based on the data model concept it represents. As a positive side-effect of this naming convention, later syntax error messages generated for non-well-formed data models will utilize this name and convey additional information to the data modeller (e.g. *error in tableDefinition*).
   The initial grammar should de-emphasize syntactic details of *M* (like precedence rules or alternative notations). Such detail can be added easily at a later stage. The sorts for the grammar productions (*Value*, *Type*, ...) follow immediately from the TL mapping chosen.
6. Verify the consistency of the model developed so far by compiling the grammar and by translating some examples using empty stub implementations for the TL functions

defined in step 4. That is, the static semantics of *M* (scoping and typing rules) can be checked in isolation.

7. Choose appropriate implementations for the abstract data types and polymorphic functions introduced in steps 2 and 4 to implement the dynamic semantics of *M* by TL program code. The implementation typically makes heavy use of polymorphic data structures (lists, sets, bags, dictionaries, ...) and iteration abstractions (select, map, join, ...) provided by the TL libraries.
8. Provide tools for schema browsing, data visualization, code management, data import and export, etc. Again, these tools can frequently be derived schematically from the existing, strongly-typed TL tools.

This top-down approach can also be complemented by a bottom-up composition of existing modules and grammar extensions to increase code reuse and to speed up the data model mapping process.

4 Uniform Iteration Abstraction over Bulk Types

The Tycoon libraries implement multiple bulk data types (sets, lists, relations, etc.). Each bulk data type is represented by a module that exports an abstract type operator and a set of polymorphic functions that work on bulk values of that type. Additional bulk types can be added to the Tycoon library as needed (add-on vs. built-in approach [12]; synopsis in Chapter 1.4.2). Some of these bulk types (like SQL tables) are implemented by gateways to external servers. Each bulk type has to satisfy a *bulk type algebra* (similar to [7]) to create and inspect bulk type instances in a uniform manner.

Uniform declarative access to multiple bulk data types (selection, projection, mapping, join, aggregate functions, ...) is provided by the concept of abstract iterators implemented by a separate Tycoon library module *iter*. An iterator over a homogeneous collection of values of type *E* has type *iter.T(E)*. It can be inspected and manipulated by a large number of iteration abstractions such as *iter.select*, *iter.flatten* and *iter.map* exported from the module *iter*.

Set-oriented query access to bulk data values is achieved in TL as follows. First, the bulk data is (conceptually) transformed into the common iterator type *iter.T*. Then, iterator functions are applied to this iterator which can also combine an iterator with other iterators derived from other bulk data collections. The result can then be converted explicitly into a specific bulk data structure (set, list, bag, ...).

For example, the following iterator expression joins an iteration over *Person* values (tuples with a *name* and *cityZip* attribute) with an iteration over *City* values (tuples with a *zip* and *name* attribute) based on their *cityZip* attributes returning an iteration *residences* over person name and city name pairs:

```
let residences = iter.flatten(iter.map(persons
  fun(p :Person) iter.get(
      fun(c :City) tuple p.name c.name end
      cities
      fun(c :City) p.cityZip == c.zip)))
```

The function *iter.flatten* produces a single iteration by concatenating an iteration of iterations. The function *iter.map* applies its function argument to each element of the iteration supplied as its first argument and returns the results as a new iteration. The function *iter.get* provides combined selection and projection on an iteration. The first parameter is a projection function applied to each element (*select*) of the iteration supplied as the second parameter (*from*) restricted by the predicate of the third parameter (*where*). The infix function "==" is a polymorphic test on object identity.

Clearly, it is desirable to support a more readable syntax for these declarative iterator queries. In the following, we describe how to define a SQL-style **select from where** syntax for the generalized Tycoon iteration abstractions. Other syntactic forms like *bulk comprehensions* [18] can be defined in a similar fashion. The above query can then be written more succinctly as:

```
let residences= select p.name c.name
                from persons p:Person, cities c:City
                where p.cityZip == c.zip
```

Based on the functions provided by the Tycoon *iter* module sketched above, the following small grammar extension suffices to add this SQL syntax to iterator expressions:

```
grammar
  value:Value |==
     "select" b=bindings "from"  => range(b)
  range(b:Bnds):Value ===
     v=value i=ide ":" t=type  => rangeOrPredicate(b v i t)
  rangeOrPredicate(b:Bnds v:Value i:Binder t:Type):Value ===
     "," r=range(b)  =>
          value<<| iter.flatten(iter.map(v fun(i :t) r)) |>>
  |   "where" p=value  =>
          value<<| iter.get(fun(i :t) tuple b end  v  fun(i :t) p) |>>
end
```

The expanded *value* production parses the target list (a list of bindings following the **select** keyword) and passes these bindings as parameters to the recursively defined productions *range* and *rangeOrPredicate*. A *range* specification defines an iterator *v*, a range variable *i* with local scope, and a type *t*. This information is again passed as a parameter to the production *rangeOrPredicate*. If there is just a single range iteration, the second alternative of the production *rangeOrPredicate* (starting with the keyword **where**) matches and a call to *iter.get* is generated. The first argument of this function is generated based on the structure of the target list *b*, the name of the range variable *i*, and the iteration element type *t*. The second argument is the range *v* and the third argument is the selection predicate *p*, again in the scope of the user-defined range variable *i*.

For each additional range iteration, the first alternative of the production *rangeOrPredicate* matches, and an enclosing *iter.flatten* call is generated which accumulates the results of nested iterations defined by a recursive invocation of *range*.

The reader is encouraged to verify that this syntax definition does in fact capture the scoping and typing constraints of the usual **select from where** syntax.

5 Tycoon/Fibonacci Add-On Experiment

The goal of the Tycoon/Fibonacci add-on experiment is the evaluation of the Tycoon system as an implementation platform for advanced data models. The experiment aims at a comparison of the effort required for the implementation of (a significant subset of) the Fibonacci language [2,4] (see Chapter 1.1.2) using extensible TL grammars and Tycoon's persistent system infrastructure with the effort required to implement Fibonacci from scratch using Modula-3 at Pisa University [3].

The Fibonacci TL implementation re-used Tycoon's persistent stores, code generator, interactive top level, module manager, incremental linker, and its gateways to commercial systems without change by a rather straightforward mapping of Fibonacci data and code objects onto corresponding TL persistent language objects. This fact nicely demonstrates that one of Tycoon's system design goals, the full separation of data storage, data manipulation and data presentation aspects from data modelling features has been achieved.

Another goal of the experiment is to fully capture Fibonacci's strong static type system (including objects with multiple roles [1]) by a *statically typed* mapping of data and code objects. This way, the full functionality of the Fibonacci type checker is emulated by the existing Tycoon TL type checker. In the remainder of this section we give some insight into this translation scheme at the value and type level. The development of this scheme revealed limitations of the existing TL language constructs available for the manipulation of signature lists and binding lists. The current TL primitives **Repeat** and **open** [13] (see Chapter 1.1.1) are not flexible enough to emulate the specific multiple inheritance conflict resolution strategy of Fibonacci. This deficiency could be solved by introducing a rather small (but ad-hoc) TL type checker extension matching the specific Fibonacci inheritance semantics. This extension would require approximately one week's work for a programmer who is familiar with the non-trivial TL type checker implementation. The Tycoon/Fibonacci experiment required a total of six person months by a scientist visiting our group who had no previous programming experience in persistent languages.

5.1 Module Structure and Overview

Figure 3 gives an overview of the implementation of the Fibonacci data model which was developed following the approach sketched in section 3 and involves five Tycoon interface modules and four associated grammar modules. The interfaces are implemented by modules written in statically-typed Tycoon code. A small set of record operations is implemented in type-unsafe C and is only available within type-safe programming patterns specified by the syntax-directed Fibonacci to TL mapping. C code could be avoided completely by using dynamically-typed TL code. However, this would lead to "unnecessary" additional run-time type tests (which never fail).

Table 1 gives some examples of the systematic translation from Fibonacci to TL. Some details of the translation are described below. The implementation of Fibonacci class extents, sequences and relationships (modules *FiboClass* and *FiboSeq*) is based on the Tycoon bulk libraries and utilises syntax definitions (*Class.syntax* and *Sequence.syntax*) similar to the ones described in section 4 to map Fibonacci's query language to Tycoon iterator expressions. Value-based integrity constraints on class extents were not studied in the experiment but could be realised by a mapping to an existing Tycoon add-on library (*dbenv* [14]) that provides the required base services.

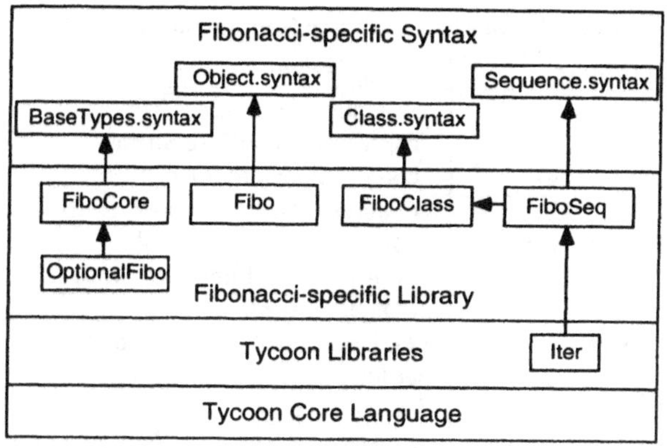

Fig. 3. Implementing the Fibonacci data model in Tycoon

5.2 Mapping of Concrete Types

The interface *FiboCore* exports the Fibonacci base types and some predefined values like booleans and functions on the base types (comparisons, arithmetics, etc.). This interface relies on the services of the interface *OptionalFibo* to ensure that the value space of each Fibonacci base type and structured type also contains the special value **unknown** (a generic null value). This value is handled explicitly by the predefined functions, for example, by raising a run-time exception *fiboCore.error* that can be caught by the programmer. The type operator *fiboCore.T(A)* defines a representation for a Fibonacci type *A* by a mapping onto a TL union type with a variant *unknown* and a variant *known* with a value *val* of type *A*. The polymorphic functions *new* and *value* construct or inspect values of type *fiboCore.T(A)*, respectively.

```
interface FiboCore export
  Let T(A <:Ok) = Tuple case unknown case known with val:A end
  error :Exception
  new(A <:Ok a:A) :T(A)
  value(A <:Ok optional:T(A)) :A  (* may raise "error" *)
  Let NoneT = Tuple case unknown end
  Let AnyT = T(Ok)
  Let StringT = T(String)
  ...
end
```

By using the Tycoon type *NoneT* to represent the Fibonacci type **None** that only contains the value **unknown** and by mapping the type **Any** (the supertype of all Fibonacci types) to type *AnyT*, the subtype hierarchy of Fibonacci is fully mapped onto the TL subtype hierarchy. In particular, this mapping preserves the subsumption principle, i.e. a value of type *A* can be substituted freely in any context where a value of a supertype of *A* is expected.

Table 1. Translation scheme from Fibonacci to TL

Fibonacci Source Code	TL Equivalent
Let Address = [name:**String** country:**String**]	**Let** Address = fiboCore.T(**Tuple** name:fiboCore.StringT country:fiboCore.StringT **end**)
let address :Address = ["Bill" unknown]	**let** address :Address = fiboCore.new(**tuple** fiboCore.new("Bill") fiboCore.noneT.unknown **end**)
Let Object = **NewObject**	**let** Object = **tuple** **Let** T = **Record** _object:fibo.Object **end** **let** to(...):**Ok** = ... **let** copy(..):T = ... **let** lateImplementationSetting(...):**Ok** = ... **let** roleExistenceTest(...):**Ok** = ... **end**
Let Person = **IsA** Object **With** name :**String** **End**	**let** Person = **tuple** **Let** T = **Record** **Repeat** Object.T name:fibo.Dispatcher(fiboCore.StringT) **end** **let** propagateToSub(...):**Ok** = ... **end**
let john = **role** Person **methods** name = "John Major" **end**	**let** john = **begin** **let rec** _object:fibo.Object = **record** **let** _oid = fibo.newOid() **let** Person = me **end** **and** me :Person = **record** **let** _object = _object **let** name = fibo.newDispatcher("name" me **fun**()fiboCore.new("John Major")) **end** **end**
john.name	john.name.late()
john!name	john.name.strict()

Using the interface *FiboCore*, the syntactic mapping of Fibonacci base types and type expressions (functions, aggregates, unions) to Tycoon type expressions as defined in the module *BaseTypes.syntax* is rather straightforward:

```
grammar
  fiboType:Type ===
    x=simpleId => type<<|x|>>
  | "Null" => type<<|fiboCore.NullT|>>
  | "Any" => type<<|fiboCore.AnyT|>>
```

```
| "String" => type<<|fiboCore.StringT|>>
| ...
| "Fun" "(" s=fiboSigs ")" ":" t=fiboType => type<<|fiboCore.T(Fun(s):t)|>>
| "[" s=fiboSigs "]" => type<<|fiboCore.T(Tuple s end)|>>
| "Choice" c=fiboCases "End" => type<<|fiboCore.T(Tuple c end)|>>
end
```

The first two rows of table 5.1 give an example of the translation of a Fibonacci type and a matching value expression into TL code.

5.3 Mapping of Object and Role Types

A key feature of Fibonacci is the support for statically-typed objects with multiple roles [2,1]. Any interaction with a Fibonacci object takes place by sending messages to a specific *role* of an object. The set of roles possessed by an object can change over time so that its behavior changes over time too. Here we do not want to go into the intricate details of the Fibonacci object model but only give a rough idea of its mapping to typed TL object representations.

A Fibonacci object is represented by a dynamically-constructed directed acyclic graph of roles that share a common object representation. Each role is a static Tycoon record that aggregates a set of named *dispatchers*, one for each message understood by a role. A Fibonacci role type is described by a Tycoon record type (a set of message signatures) and enables the static type checking of message send operations. A message dispatcher for a Fibonacci message (or attribute) of type *A* is a Tycoon tuple of type *fibo.Dispatcher(A)*:

```
Let Dispatcher(A<:Ok) = Tuple
  methodName :String
  self : Record end
  strict():A
  var late():A
end
```

The two functional components *strict* and *late* of a dispatcher realize the two forms of message dispatching supported by Fibonacci. A late binding as in *john.name* leads to the execution of the most specialized implementation of the method *name* (which depends on the run-time history of role acquisitions for the object *john*). A strict binding as in *john!name* executes the method specified statically for the current role. A dispatcher is created by a call to *fibo.newDispatcher* which provides an initial method implementation for *strict* and *late*. The function *late* is tagged as mutable with the **var** keyword since it is overridden dynamically whenever a matching dispatcher is created in a subrole. The dispatcher attributes *methodName* and *self* are utilised by the Tycoon library code that has to work uniformly on dispatchers of arbitrary roles.

The last two lines in table 5.1 show how the two forms of Fibonacci message send operations are translated into TL function calls. Once a systematic encoding of objects, roles and methods by a graph of linked TL records and function closures has been found, the translation of role type and role value expressions can be carried out in a type-safe way as indicated by examples in table 5.1.

An interesting detail is the fact that a Fibonacci role *type Person* is mapped to a Tycoon *value Person* that aggregates a type specification *Person.T* and a set of functions to work on instances of that type (*Person.copy, Person.roleExistenceTest, ...*). The aggregation of types and values into a first-class language object is a good example of the power available to data model implementors through Tycoon's higher-order type system.

The following fragments of the grammar definitions in the module *Object.syntax* (see figure 3) show that the mechanism of extensible grammars is sufficiently expressive to carry out the mappings indicated in table 5.1 and that these mappings can be written in a rather readable way.

```
grammar
  fiboValue:Value ===
     v=fiboSimpleValue => optFiboValueApp(v)
  optFiboValueApp(v:Value):Value ===
     "!" method=ide => value<<|v.method.strict()|>>
  |  "." method=ide => value<<|v.method.late()|>>
  |  (* no suffix *) => v
end
```

```
grammar
  fiboObjectValue:Value ===
     "role" roleName=ide "methods" mbnds=fiboObjectMethodBnds "end"
     => value<<| begin
                let rec _object :fibo.Object = record
                   let _oid = fibo.newOid()
                   let roleName = me
                  end
                and me :roleName.T = record
                   let _object = _object
                   mbnds
                end
                me
              end |>>
  | ...
end
```

Note that this rewriting captures the Fibonacci scoping rules, for example, the identifier *me* is bound to the "current" object in the scope of the method bindings *mbnds* by virtue of a recursive object binding in Tycoon. Similarly, the names of record attributes that should not be visible to Fibonacci programmers are made inaccessible by prefixing them with an underscore that is disallowed in the source syntax.

6 Related Work and Concluding Remarks

The work described in this paper can be seen as a contribution towards the "type alchemist's dream" [6], to express multiple data models uniformly in a sufficiently expressive type system.

The rapid implementation of a data model in the typed and persistent Tycoon framework has the following advantages compared with a system prototype implemented from scratch:

- The constructed system inherits most of Tycoon's system functionality (persistence management, garbage collection, code generation, modular compilation etc.);
- No compiler implementation know-how is needed to implement type checkers for polymorphic (higher-order) data models;
- The methodology described in section 3 supports early experimentation with newly developed data models.

Compared with source-to-source code generators and preprocessor-based systems, extensible grammars have the following advantages:

- Extensible grammars are fully integrated in the Tycoon compiler (intermediate source files are avoided, error messages refer to the original source code position, code management is simplified);
- Extensible grammars are easy to read and modify;
- Extensible grammars provide mechanisms to avoid name clashes and to invent fresh identifiers as needed.

Extensible grammars are best suited for *context-independent* local rewriting techniques. Some data model implementation techniques, e.g. the one described in [8], make heavy use of global schema information held in a central repository to drive the generation of integrity-preserving transaction code. This is not possible with the mechanism of extensible grammars since the rewrite process can only depend on the input syntax and not on schema information available at compile-time. However, as exemplified by the Tycoon/Fibonacci add-on implementation, the handling of context dependencies can often be delayed until run-time where it is possible to work on persistent meta-data generated at compile-time.

Acknowledgements. This research was supported by ESPRIT Basic Research, Project FIDE, #6309 and by a grant from the German Israeli Foundation for Research and Development (*bulk data classification*, I-183 060). Davide Berveglieri (Politecnico di Milano) contributed significantly to the Tycoon/Fibonacci experiment described in section 5. He was supported by the ESPRIT Basic Research Network of Excellence IDOMENEUS (No. #6606) and the ESPRIT Basic Research Project FIDE #6309.

References

1. A. Albano, G. Bergamini, G. Ghelli, and R. Orsini. An object data model with roles. In *Proceedings of the Nineteenth International Conference on Very Large Databases, Dublin, Ireland*, pages 39–51, 1993.
2. A. Albano, R. Bergamini, G. Ghelli, and R. Orsini. An introduction to the database programming language Fibonacci. FIDE Technical Report Series FIDE/92/64, FIDE Project Coordinator, Department of Computing Sciences, University of Glasgow, Glasgow G128QQ, 1993.
3. A. Albano, C. Brasini, M. Diotallevi, G. Ghelli, R. Orsini, and R. Rossi. A guided tour of the Fibonacci system. FIDE Technical Report Series FIDE/94/103, FIDE Project Coordinator, Department of Computing Sciences, University of Glasgow, Glasgow G128QQ, July 1994.

4. A. Albano, G. Ghelli, and R. Orsini. Fibonacci reference manual: A preliminary version. FIDE Technical Report Series FIDE/94/102, FIDE Project Coordinator, Department of Computing Sciences, University of Glasgow, Glasgow G128QQ, 1994.
5. L. Alfo, S. Coluccini, P. Corte, and D. Presenza. Manuale del sistema sidereus. Technical report, Dipartimento di Informatica, Università di Pisa, Italy, 1989.
6. M.P. Atkinson and P. Bunemann. Types and persistence in database programming languages. *ACM Computing Surveys*, 19(2), June 1987.
7. C. Beeri and P. Ta-Shma. Bulk data types, a theoretical approach. In C. Beeri, A. Ohori, and D.E. Shasha, editors, *Proceedings of the Fourth International Workshop on Database Programming Languages, Manhatten, New York*, Workshops in Computing. Springer-Verlag, February 1994.
8. A. Borgida, J. Mylopoulos, J.W. Schmidt, and I. Wetzel. Support for data-intensive applications: Conceptual design and software development. In *Proceedings of the Second International Workshop on Database Programming Languages, Portland, Oregon*, June 1989.
9. L. Cardelli, F. Matthes, and M. Abadi. Extensible grammars for language specialization. In C. Beeri, A. Ohori, and D.E. Shasha, editors, *Proceedings of the Fourth International Workshop on Database Programming Languages, Manhatten, New York*, Workshops in Computing, pages 11–31. Springer-Verlag, February 1994.
10. L. Cardelli, F. Matthes, and M. Abadi. Extensible syntax with lexical scoping. Technical Report 121, Digital Equipment Corporation, Systems Research Center, Palo Alto, California, February 1994.
11. A. Gawecki and F. Matthes. Tool: A persistent language integrating subtyping, matching and type quantification. FIDE Technical Report Series FIDE/95/135, FIDE Project Coordinator, Department of Computing Sciences, University of Glasgow, Glasgow G128QQ, 1995.
12. F. Matthes and J.W. Schmidt. Bulk types: Built-in or add-on? In *Database Programming Languages: Bulk Types and Persistent Data*. Morgan Kaufmann Publishers, September 1991.
13. F. Matthes and J.W. Schmidt. Definition of the Tycoon language TL – a preliminary report. Informatik Fachbericht FBI-HH-B-160/92, Fachbereich Informatik, Universität Hamburg, Germany, November 1992.
14. C. Niederée. Generic services for data-intensive applications: Iteration abstraction, integrity checking and recovery. Master's thesis, Fachbereich Informatik, Universität Hamburg, Germany, November 1992. (In German).
15. K.-D. Schewe, J.W. Schmidt, and I. Wetzel. Identification, genericity and consistency in object-oriented databases. In J. Biskup and R. Hull, editors, *Proceedings of the International Conference on Database Theory*, volume 646 of *Lecture Notes in Computer Science*, pages 341–356. Springer-Verlag, October 1992.
16. J.W. Schmidt and F. Matthes. The DBPL project: Advances in modular database programming. *Information Systems*, 19(2):121–140, 1994.
17. M. Stonebraker. Special issue on database prototype systems. *IEEE Transactions on Knowledge and Data Engineering*, 2(1), March 1990.
18. P. Trinder. Comprehensions, a query notation for DBPLs. In *Database Programming Languages: Bulk Types and Persistent Data*. Morgan Kaufmann Publishers, September 1991.

Section 3.3

Interoperability: Introduction and State of the Art

Florian Matthes

Technical University Hamburg-Harburg, Harburger Schloßstraße 20, D-21071 Hamburg, Germany

Today, successful application development is rarely carried out by coding application programs from scratch, instead there is a strong tendency to exploit services provided through open and modular environments already populated with prefabricated and packaged functionality and information.

In this scenario, fully integrated persistent programming environments excel through their persistence abstraction, their elaborate data modelling support and their well-organized component libraries all described in earlier chapters. However, for the construction of large-scale industrial applications, application programmers still have to utilise commerically-available system services and tools outside of the persistent programming environment, for example, to access legacy data and code. Furthermore, programmers have to be able to make persistent data and code maintained by a persistent programming environment accessible to other systems, for example, for data and system integration purposes.

The work described in this chapter applies the database and programming language technology developed in the FIDE project to improve the *interoperability* between independently developed, generic system servers. At present, each of these servers comes with its own naming, typing, binding and persistence concepts so that application developers who wish to exploit multiple services within a single application find themselves working in a quite complex and fairly unfriendly and unsafe environment. Examples for these difficulties can be found at the interfaces to file systems, SQL databases, window systems or RPC packages.

Distributed object management is viewed as a promising approach to build scalable distributed systems that are also capable of integrating legacy (database) systems by means of a unified object paradigm [6]. There are numerous proposals for specific object models like DSOM of IBM [4], DOM of GTE [6], Network Objects of Modula-3 [2] and future versions of Microsoft's OLE [7] and there are several related standardization efforts like CORBA of the OMG [3] and the OSF DCE/DME [9]. For a detailed feature analysis of these models see [8,5].

Similar to object models, the high-level type systems of the persistent languages presented in Chapters 1.1.1 to 1.1.3 provide mechanisms like type abstraction, type quantification and subtyping to write detailed specifications of external service interfaces and to classify services based on their signatures. Persistent languages go beyond object models since they also define a rich (higher-order) computational model to describe behaviour, as it is required to "glue together" services from several providers.

By re-interpreting schemas as type definitions and databases as typed variables and by treating lifetime as a type-independent property, a uniform linguistic interface for data modelling, computation and communication can be developed (see also Chapter 3.3.3). As a consequence of such an integrated view, formerly disjoint concepts such as databases, program and module libraries, files or repositories can now be treated uniformly as POSs differentiated essentially by the types of objects they contain and by the operational abstractions they provide [10]. Therefore, distributed databases, multi-databases and federated databases can be understood as restricted (particularly interesting) cases of interoperating persistent application systems.

Instead of using persistent languages to glue together services developed with incompatible technologies, one could also envision a scalable persistent architecture based on a core "low level persistent language" (LLPL) that provides a stable, secure and platform-independent basis for the construction of multi-paradigmal systems. As discussed in more detail in [1] (see Chapter 2.1.1), a major concern of this approach is to achieve high levels of longevity (data and programs have to be accessible for several 10^2 upto 10^3 years) without compromising data integrity and security through uncontrolled (non-typed) data access.

Chapters 3.3.1 and 3.3.2 show how database technology can be applied to semi-structured data stored in files and how database languages can be utilised to query and update files at a high level of abstraction. The mapping between structured database objects and linear file representations is defined by means of grammars. The results of this work in the direction of heterogeneity and data integration are applied in the O_2 *Views* system.

Chapter 3.3.3 introduces a canonical model of persistent object systems based on generalised notions of values, types, bindings and signatures to describe the issues that have to be solved to achieve a type-safe interoperation between persistent objects supported by independently-developed generic servers. The model utilised in tgar Chapter underlies the Tycoon programming language TL and the scalabe and interoperable Tycoon programming environment, both described in Chapters 1.1.1 and 2.1.4.

References

1. M.P. Atkinson. Persistent foundations for scalable multi-paradigmal systems. FIDE Technical Report Series FIDE/92/51, FIDE Project Coordinator, Department of Computing Sciences, University of Glasgow, Glasgow G128QQ, 1992.
2. A. Birell, G. Nelson, S. Owicki, and E. Wobber. Network objects. In *14th ACM Symposium on Operating System Principles*, pages 217–230, June 1993.
3. Object Management Group. The common object request broker: Architecture and specification. Document 91.12.1, Rev. 1.1, OMG, December 1991.
4. IBM Corporation, Publication No. SR28-5570. *Object-Oriented Programming using SOM and DSOM*, August 1994.

5. F. Manola and S. Heiler. A "RISC" object model for object system interoperation: Concepts and applications. Technical Report TR-0231-08-93-165, GTE laboratories Inc., Waltham, MA (USA), August 1993.
6. F. Manola, S. Heiler, D. Georgakopoulos, M. Hornick, and M. Brodie. Distributed object management. *International Journal of Intelligent and Cooperative Information Systems*, 1(1), March 1992.
7. Microsoft Corporation. *Microsoft Office Developer's Kit*, 1994.
8. J. Nicol, T. Wilkes, and F. Manola. Object orientation in heterogeneous distributed computing systems. *Special Issue on Heterogeneous Processing*, June 1993.
9. OSF. *OSF DCE Administration Guide – Core Components*. Prentice Hall, Englewood Cliffs, New Jersey, 1993.
10. J.W. Schmidt, F. Matthes, and P. Valduriez. Building persistent application systems in fully integrated data environments: Modularization, abstraction and interoperability. In *Proceedings of Euro-Arch'93 Congress*, pages 270–287. Springer-Verlag, October 1993.

Chapter 3.3.1
Querying the File

Serge Abiteboul[1], Sophie Cluet[1], and Tova Milo[2]

[1] INRIA., B.P. 105, 78153 Le Chesnay Cedex, France
[2] Department of Computer Science, Tel Aviv University, Tel Aviv, Israel

1 Introduction

Database systems are concerned with structured data. Unfortunately, data is often stored in an unstructured manner (e.g. in files) even when it does have a strong internal structure (e.g. electronic documents or programs). Unfortunately, data stored in files cannot benefit from database technology and in particular, has to rely on very primitive linguistic support. In this paper, we show how *structured files* can be queried using (high-level) database languages. In [2] (see Chapter 3.3.2) we address the problem of updates.

In actual systems, data is often stored as strings for obvious historical reasons. The problem that we are considering is thus very general. Tools based on the ideas developed here would clearly be useful in a number of fields such as software engineering (file = program) or electronic documentation (file = SGML document) and possibly in more exotic ones such as genetic engineering (file = genetic sequence).

We are interested here in files that have a strong inner structure and that we call *structured files*. Such files are typically handled using tools to manipulate files (e.g. awk, perl, emacs) or to transfer data (e.g. mailer, ftp) and tools for structured data (e.g. mosaic, framemaker, pat). In the best case, these tools know of the inner structure, e.g. SGML editors. However, they do not provide many features currently found in database systems from system oriented ones (e.g. concurrency control) to logical ones (e.g. high-level query facilities). Our aim is to propose a framework where database tools can be used to manipulate files based on the inner structure of the information they contain. In particular, we address the following issues:

- How can the implicit structure of files be described and used to define an abstract interface to the information stored in the file?
- How can this interface be used for accessing (i.e. querying)?

To this end, we introduce the notion of a *structuring schema* which consists of a grammar annotated with database programs and of a database schema. A structuring schema specifies how the data contained in a structured file should be interpreted as a database.

We can use a structuring schema to translate data from a file and load it into a database. We can also understand the structuring schema as the specification of a database view of the file. In this second case, to answer queries, one would like to avoid loading the entire file. We show that this can be achieved using (variations of) standard optimization techniques from relational databases.

The second (somewhat inverse) task is to convert data from a database to files. This is typically what is performed for instance in (database) report writers or when transmitting a part of a database between distributed databases. Some of the issues are:

- How can the translation be specified?
- What information should be recorded in the target file, in order to maintain the relationship with the original data (for further querying or updates)?

For database model, we use in the sequel the complex value model (or similarly the nested-relation model) [1]. We also consider briefly an extension with objects and there we use the O_2 model [8], although essentially any OQL [6] interface will do. For the grammar, we assume standard knowledge of context-free parsing.

The problems of extracting data from files (and encoding data onto files to a lesser extent) have been popular database topics since the early days of the field. One should notably cite the Express system in the 70's for data extraction and restructuring [12]. Our contribution obeys the same motivations since the problem clearly did not disappear over the years. We use now standard database technology tools (e.g. optimization techniques, object-orientation) to provide a modern answer to an old problem.

The paper is organised as follows. In the next section, we define structuring schemas, discuss this notion and introduce the problems that we study. Section 3 deals with queries and query optimization technique. In Section 4, we discuss the conversion of data from database to file. The last section is a conclusion.

2 Structuring Schemas

In this section, we introduce and formalize the notion of structuring schemas. We describe some basic properties of structuring schemas, and present some examples of their usage.

2.1 Informal Presentation

The problem is to connect structured strings with a database or, more precisely, to get a database representation of a structured string. The inner structure of the string can be described in a very natural way using a grammar. A first approach (that we will later abandon) requires only this description. In this case, the connection with the database is obtained in a straightforward manner by linking each non terminal of the grammar to a database type. For instance, we may associate a class A with each non terminal A. Intuitively, this means that an occurrence of A in a parse-tree will be represented by an object in class A. We call this solution *default structuring*, and illustrate it next. We then explain why it is unsatisfactory.

Example 2.1. (BibTex) Bibliography files constitute an example of semi-structured data with which many researchers are well acquainted. Consider for example a bibliography file in the BibTex format. An entry in the file is a string of the following form:

$$
\begin{aligned}
@Inproceedings\ \{\ & TLE90,\\
& author = \text{“}A.A.\ Toto\ and\ H.R.\ Lulu\text{”},\\
& title = \text{“}\textit{On Weird Dependencies}\text{”},\\
& booktitle = stoc,\\
& year = \text{“}1990\text{”},\\
& pages = \text{“}1-12\text{”}\\
& notes = \text{“}\textit{A later version of this paper ...}\text{”}\}.
\end{aligned}
$$

Consider the following partial grammatical description of a BibTex file:

$$
\begin{aligned}
\langle Ref\_Set\rangle &\rightarrow \langle Reference\rangle\ \langle Ref\_Set\rangle\\
&\quad \mid \epsilon\\
\langle Reference\rangle &\rightarrow \text{“}@Inproceedings\{\text{”}\ \#String,\\
&\quad\ \text{“}author = \text{”}\ \langle Author\_Set\rangle,\\
&\quad\ \text{“}title = \text{”}\ \#String,\\
&\quad\ \ldots \text{“}\}\text{”}
\end{aligned}
$$

Nonterminals appear between brackets (e.g. $\langle Ref\_Set\rangle$), constant tokens between double quotes (e.g. “$@Inproceeding\{$") and non-constant tokens are prefixed by the # symbol (e.g. $\#String$).

Using default structuring, the grammar corresponds to the following class definitions with standard methods (e.g. display, edit).

$$
\begin{aligned}
&\textbf{class}\ Ref\_Set &&= \textbf{tuple}(ref : Reference, refs : Ref\_Set)\\
&\textbf{class}\ Reference &&= \textbf{tuple}(key : String, authors : Aut\_Set, \ldots)
\end{aligned}
$$

The list of two references

$$
\begin{aligned}
@Inproceedings\ \{\ & TLE90,\\
& author = \text{“}A.A.\ Toto\ and\ H.R.\ Lulu\text{”},\\
& title = \text{“}\textit{On Weird Dependencies}\text{”},\\
& booktitle = stoc,\\
& year = \text{“}1990\text{”},\\
& pages = \text{“}1-12\text{”}\\
& notes = \text{“}\textit{A later version of this paper ...}\text{”}\}.\\
@Inproceedings\ \{\ & L91,\\
& author = \text{“}H.R.\ Lulu\text{”},\\
& title = \text{“}\textit{On Weird Dependencies, the Sequel}\text{”},\\
& booktitle = focs,\\
& year = \text{“}1991\text{”},\\
& pages = \text{“}120-124\text{”}\}.
\end{aligned}
$$

is then represented by an object o, where the association between objects and values is partially described below:

class name	*oid*	*value*
class Ref_Set :	o	$[ref : o_1, refs : o_2]$
	o_2	$[ref : o_3, refs : o_4]$
	o_4	$\perp$
class Reference	o_1	$[key : \text{“}TLE90\text{”}, authors : o_5, \ldots]$
	o_3	$[key : \text{“}TLE90\text{”}, authors : o_6, \ldots]$

The empty string is associated with an object with undefined value ($\perp$).

When considering a general context-free grammar, *disjunctive types* will naturally arise from non terminals defined disjunctively. When disjunction of types is not supported by the database system, it has to be simulated. There are of course a variety of means of simulating such types in particular using inheritance in the OO context. However, note that the use of a pure relational system would be very inconvenient.

The default structuring presents two major defaults. First, it clearly lacks flexibility: the resulting structure may be rather inappropriate for querying. Also, it results in the creation of too many (unnecessary) objects: e.g. in the above example o_2 and o_4 have no meaningful semantics. We would like to attach more semantics to the file, semantics that cannot be captured simply by the grammar. For instance, a perhaps more natural way to see $\langle Ref\_Set \rangle$ is as a list or a set of tuples (each representing one reference). Moreover, the choice of structure may depend on the application that is considered, but nothing in the grammar allows us to choose between these possible representations (values or objects, lists or sets).

Since this solution that is based solely on the grammar fails, we consider a second solution requiring us to explicitly state the links between the non terminals of the grammar and their database representation. This is done again in a very standard manner using an annotated grammar to which we attach a schema definition. We call the resulting couple a *structuring schema*. This solution is somewhat reminiscent of techniques used for automatic synthesis of editors for languages. They also use annotated grammars to construct editors and "unparsing" specifications to display programs. Of course, the problems studied are very different but some of the techniques they develop (e.g. incremental evaluation) seem applicable to our context. (See [9].)

A *structuring schema* consists of a schema and an annotated grammar. We first illustrate the idea informally using an example. A formal definition is presented next. The annotated grammar specifies the relationship between the grammar non terminals and their database representation. More precisely, it associates with each derivation rule $A \rightarrow A_1, \ldots, A_n$ a statement describing how a database representation of a word derived from this rule is constructed using the database representations of the subwords derived from $A_1, \ldots, A_n$.

The next example provides a possible (partial) structuring schema for a BibTex file.

Example 2.2. (BibTex continued) The schema is described first:

```
/* Non terminals type definition */
```

type $\langle Reference \rangle = \textbf{tuple}(key : string, authors : ...)$
type $\langle Ref\_Set \rangle = \textbf{set}(\textbf{tuple}(key : string, authors : ...,))$

The annotated grammar is given by:

```
/* Annotated grammar */
```

$$
\begin{array}{lll}
\langle Ref\_Set \rangle & \rightarrow \langle Reference \rangle \ \langle Ref\_Set \rangle & \{\$\$:= \{\$1\} \cup \$2\} \\
 & \mid \epsilon & \{\$\$:= \{\}\} \\
\langle Reference \rangle & \rightarrow \text{“}@Inproceedings\{\text{”} \ \#String & \\
 & \text{“}author = \text{”} \ \langle Author\_Set \rangle & \\
 & \ldots \text{“}\}\text{”} & \{\$\$:= [key : \$1, \\
 & & \quad authors : \$2 \ldots]\}
\end{array}
$$

For the action part of the rules we use a Yacc-like notation. In the example, the $$ symbol in the action part of a rule represents the data returned by this rule. A $i symbol represents the data returned by the ith nonterminal or non-constant token in the right hand-side of the rule. Tokens correspond to database basic types and their appropriated typed value is returned by the lexical analysis. All we have to know about the lexical analysis is that it returns some constant tokens (e.g. keywords in the language) or tokens that have types corresponding to the database types. The whole BibTex file is represented by a set containing one element per bibliographical reference. A reference is represented by a tuple with one attribute per BibTex field.

The schema describes the database types. One may argue that the type information can be partially or totally derived from the annotated grammar using type inference. However, the issue of type inference can be viewed in a larger context and is not the topic of the present paper. We next define structuring schemas formally.

2.2 Formal Definition

A *structuring schema* (SS for short) consists of a context-free grammar annotated with one semantic action per rule, and one type per nonterminal. We assume that the grammar is reduced. More precisely, for each grammar G that we consider and each rule in G, we assume that there is a derivation of some word in $L(G)$ that uses this rule. We now describe the types and actions that we consider in this paper.

The database types are defined by the following abstract syntax:

$$
\begin{array}{lll}
base\_type & :- \ int \mid real \mid bool \mid string & \\
\tau & :- \ base\_type \mid [A_1 : \tau_1, ... A_n : \tau_n] & \text{\% tuple type} \\
 & \mid \{\tau\} \mid \langle \tau \rangle \mid \{\!\{\tau\}\!\} & \text{\% set/list/bag type}
\end{array}
$$

A value of type int, $real$, $bool$ or $string$ is an element of the corresponding sorts. We also assume that int, $real$, $bool$ or $string$ can occur as tokens in the grammars, and that the lexical analyzer will return values of the appropriate sorts. A value of type $\{\tau\}$ is a finite set of values of type τ, and similarly for bags, lists and tuples.

To simplify, we assume that the empty collections are explicitly typed (e.g. an empty set of strings is different from an empty set of integers) and mostly ignore some aspects such as union of types, objects/classes/inheritance. We informally consider them at the end of the next section.

We next define the semantic actions that we consider in this paper. Actions are defined using functions over database types. In the following definition, some of the functions are described explicitly (e.g. set/tuple constructors). Others are only referenced as belonging to a predefined set F of typed functions. The reason for distinguishing between these two classes of functions will become clear in the sequel. At this point, we may assume that F includes addition, subtraction, division, multiplication over *int* and *real*; and the entire complex value algebra [1]. Standard issues such as type checking of actions will not be considered here.

Definition 2.1. The *actions* are terms formed as follows:

1. each $\$i$ is an action, each database constant is an action.
2. with standard type restrictions, if $a_1, ..., a_n$ are actions
   - $\{a_1, ..., a_n\}$ is an action (set construction), and similarly for lists and bags;
   - $[A_1 : a_1, ..., A_n : a_n]$ is an action (tuple construction);
   - $cons(a_1, a_2)$ is an action; it adds an element a_1 to the collection (set, list or bag) a_2;
   - $a_1 \cup a_2$ is an action (union of sets/bags, concatenation of lists);
   - $a_1 || a_2$ is an action (string concatenation);
   - $f(a_1, ..., a_n)$ for $f \in F$ is an action.

In the paper, we will mostly be concerned with $F = \emptyset$. Sometimes, we consider problems occurring from introducing some operations in F (e.g. object creation or operations with side effects).

2.3 Some Basic Properties of SS

A Structuring schema defines a mapping, denoted *parse*, from the set of strings accepted by the grammar to the set of databases of appropriate type. (This assumes that the parsing always terminates which is reasonable since the language is context-free.)

Note that there may be several parse-trees for the same file (due to ambiguities in the grammar). From a practical viewpoint, one can assume that *parse* tries the rules in some predefined order and consequently *parse* is indeed a mapping. From a theoretical view point, it is difficult to investigate properties of structuring schema taking into account the order of rules, since even very simple properties of *parse* become undecidable. For example,

Proposition 2.1. *Testing if there a successful parsing of a file (taking into account the order of rules) that uses a given rule r is undecidable.*

Proof. This can be proved by reduction from the undecidability of testing containment of context-free languages. Given two context-free grammars $G1$ and $G2$, $L(G2) \subseteq L(G1)$ iff *parse* never uses the rule $r2$ in the schema $SCH(G1, G2)$ defined below. Let S_i be the start symbol of Gi, $i = 1, 2$. $SCH(G1, G2)$ contain the rules:

$r1 : S \rightarrow S1$ { \$\$:= \$1 }
$r2 : S \rightarrow S2$ { \$\$:= \$1 }

parse will use $r2$ iff $L(G2)$ has a word w that is not in $L(G1)$.

□

We therefore concentrate on a relation that ignores the order of rules. Given a SS S, a nonterminal T, a file f and a value v, $f \leadsto_{S,T} v$, indicates that there exists a parse-tree of word f rooted at T and *yielding* the database value v.

More formally, this is defined inductively as follows. Let $f = f_1||...||f_n$ be a string, and let p a parse-tree of f with root T labelled by rule r, and subparse-trees $p_1, ..., p_n$ such that for each i, p_i is a parse-tree for f_i and has some root T_i. Let t be the action of r and let for each i, $f_i \leadsto_{S,T_i} a_i$ for some i. Then $f \leadsto t[\$i \rightarrow a_i]$, i.e. f yields the value obtained by substituting each $\$i$ by the corresponding value and evaluating the resulting expression.

When S is understood, $f \leadsto_{S,T} v$ is simply written $f \leadsto_T v$. For T_0 the start symbol, $f \leadsto_{S,T_0} v$ is sometimes written $f \leadsto_S v$. When both S is understood and the start symbol is meant, we sometimes use $f \leadsto v$. A value v s.t. $f \leadsto v$ is called the *database view* of file f.

Note that one file may have several database views (due to ambiguity of the underlying grammar). Also, several different files may have the same database view. This happens when the database image of the file does not record all the information stored in the file (i.e. the mapping involves information loss). We consider these issues in [2].

2.4 Database Interface to Files

Having a database view of a file, provides a convenient interface to the data stored in the file. Consider the BibTex example. Suppose that we want to find the title of a paper whose keyword is TLE90. This can be formulated as a database query

select r.title
from r **in** References
where r.key="TLE90"

where *References* denotes the set returned by the parsing.

For a more complex example, suppose that we want to check for each paper, whether there exists a more recent version, and add to the outdated reference a note pointing to the newer version. This can be easily formulated using a database update language and the join-like facilities built in such languages:

update r1.notes := concat(r1.notes,“ Later version appears in ”, r2.Key)
from r1 in References, r2 in References
where r1.title = r2.title **and**
r1.authors = r2.authors **and** r1.year < r2.year

Note that we use here some rather trivial criteria to detect earlier versions. Even for such simple ones, the reader familiar with sophisticated editing tools may consider how this would be specified in his/her favorite editor. For example, how would you code this as an emacs macro?

We can use the SS to parse the file and load the result into the database. In the bibText example, the database then will contain a set of tuples, one per reference. We may also use the SS to define a virtual “view” of the file. In this case, the set is not loaded into the database. In both cases, we would like to be able to query and update the references efficiently. If the data is fully loaded into a database, then the query optimization is done at the database level. One the other hand, when querying a view, we would like to avoid loading the entire file into the database, and need specific optimization techniques to achieve that. This aspect of optimization is topic of Section 3. The issue of propagating updates specified at the database level to updates on the file is considered in [2].

3 Query Optimization

Assume that we use a SS to define a virtual view of a file. A naive technique to evaluate a query on such a view is to parse the file, load all the data into the database, and then evaluate the query on the resulting database. This naive technique has a major drawback: it entails construction of the whole database, even if the the query actually uses only a small portion of the data. This is time and space consuming.

The main contribution of this section is an optimization technique to avoid constructing the entire database to answer a query. We first focus on value-based databases, and consider the issue of object-based databases separately in the second part of the section. The technique is mainly based on modifying the *action* part of the SS, (though it may also lead to duplication of some nonterminals), and uses standard query optimization techniques slightly revisited.

We start by giving an intuition of the process with a very simple example. We then present the optimization algorithm and discuss some issues and limitations that are raised.

3.1 The Technique

Consider a file containing BibTex references with the SS given above. Suppose that we want to evaluate the query:

$$\textbf{select } r.Title \quad \textbf{from } r \textbf{ in } References \quad \textbf{where } r.Key = \text{“}TLE90\text{”}.$$

The corresponding algebraic query is $\varphi(References)$ with:

$$\varphi(X) \equiv \Pi_{Title}(\sigma_{Key=\text{"}TLE90\text{"}}(X))$$

where X is a set of tuple with attributes $Key, Title$, etc.

To reduce the construction performed for evaluating the query, we "push the selection down" the grammar specification in pretty much the same way that selections are pushed down in relational algebra query optimization [14]. We leave the grammatical part of the structuring schema practically unchanged (the parser must still recognize the same file) while modifying the data construction part in an appropriate manner.

The rule used to compute the set of references is:

$$\begin{array}{llr} \langle Ref\_Set\rangle \rightarrow & \langle Reference\rangle\ \langle Ref\_Set\rangle & \{\$\$:= \{\$1\} \cup \$2\} \\ & \mid \epsilon & \{\$\$:= \{\}\}. \end{array}$$

The desired result can thus be obtained by adding a new nonterminal $\langle\varphi(Ref\_Set)\rangle$ which becomes the new start symbol and the new rule:

$$\text{(1)}\quad \begin{array}{llr} \langle\varphi(Ref\_Set)\rangle \rightarrow & \langle Reference\rangle\ \langle Ref\_Set\rangle & \{\$\$:= \varphi(\{\$1\} \cup \$2)\} \\ & \mid \epsilon & \{\$\$:= \varphi(\{\})\} \end{array}$$

A strict application of this SS would result in creating the entire set of references and then applying the query to it. To avoid that we apply some optimization, indeed a rather standard one. Observe first that

$$\text{(2)}\quad \varphi(\{\}) = \Pi_{Title}(\sigma_{Key=\text{"}TLE90\text{"}}(\{\})) \leadsto \{\}.$$

and in a slightly less standard way, we have

$$\begin{array}{c} \varphi(\{\$1\} \cup \$2) \\ \leadsto \\ \varphi(\{\$1\}) \cup \varphi(\$2) \\ \leadsto \\ \{\varphi(\$1)\} \cup \varphi(\$2) \\ \leadsto \\ \Pi_{Title}(\sigma_{Key=\text{"}TLE90\text{"}}(\{\$1\})) \cup \varphi(\$2) \\ \leadsto \\ \{\Pi_{Title}(\sigma_{Key=\text{"}TLE90\text{"}}(\$1))\} \cup \varphi(\$2). \end{array} \quad \text{(3)}$$

Part of this is rather standard, e.g. distributivity of projection w.r.t. union. Part is less so, e.g. pushing the query onto a single element ($1 is not a set but a tuple). For this, we extend the algebra to have our operations also operate on singleton elements. We obtain the new rewrite rules by viewing such an element as a singleton set. In particular, the selection on a single element is defined as follows: if it succeeds, the result is the element itself; and if it fails, the result is the single element $\perp$ (which is viewed algebraically as the empty set).

For instance, one rewrite rule that is used to obtain (3) is the following:

$$\sigma_{Cond}(\{A\}) \leadsto \{\sigma_{Cond}(A)\}$$

which is standard if A is a set and can now be accepted also for atomic values (once the selection on an atomic value is understood). The standard set of rewrite rules [4,7,10] is extended easily in this manner.

Continuing with the example, we go on pushing the query down the grammar. The query on \$1 and on \$2 in (3) is pushed down on the corresponding nonterminals. More precisely, instead of calling $\langle Ref\_Set\rangle$ and filtering its result, we use the new parser $\langle\varphi(Ref\_Set)\rangle$ that has the responsibility of applying φ. And similarly for $\langle Reference\rangle$. Thus, (3) is transformed into:

$$(4)\quad \begin{array}{ll} \langle\varphi(Ref\_Set)\rangle \rightarrow \langle\varphi(Reference)\rangle\ \langle\varphi(Ref\_Set)\rangle & \{\$\$:= \{\$1\} \cup \$2)\} \\ \qquad\qquad\qquad \mid \epsilon & \{\$\$:= \{\}\} \end{array}$$

We already have a definition for the nonterminal $\langle\varphi(Ref\_Set)\rangle$. We obtain a definition for $\langle\varphi(Reference)\rangle$ by pushing φ in the grammar rule defining $\langle Reference\rangle$ in the following way:

$$(5)\quad \begin{array}{ll} \langle\varphi(Reference)\rangle \rightarrow & \text{"@}Inproceedings\{\text{"}\ \#String \\ & \text{"}author = \text{"}\ \langle Author\_list\rangle \\ & \text{"}title = \text{"}\ \langle\#String\rangle \\ & \ldots \text{"}\}\text{"} \\ & \{\$\$:= \varphi([Key : \$1, Authors : \$2, Title : \$3\ldots])\} \end{array}$$

Observe that here again we apply φ on a single element, i.e. a reference.
We can use again a rewriting technique:

$$(6)\quad \begin{array}{c} \Pi_{Title}(\sigma_{Key=\text{"}TLE90\text{"}}([Key : \$1, Authors : \$2, Title : \$3\ldots])) \\ \rightsquigarrow \\ \Pi_{Title}([Key : \sigma_{\lambda.x(x=\text{"}TLE90\text{"})}(\$1), Title : \$3]). \end{array}$$

The selection operation has been pushed inside the tuple construction (that can be viewed as a product). We introduced a λ-expression in order to denote the element \$1 in the algebraic operation. It must be noted that, as before, we use selection on an element (here a string). If \$1 is not $TLE90$, the selection of \$1 is $\perp$, the tuple is also $\perp$ (since the standard product with an empty set is the empty set), and the value of the projection is $\perp$ as well (since the standard projection of an empty set is an empty set). Note also that part of the projection has been pushed into the tuple construction, so the tuple contains only the two attributes used by the query. The advantage of the above optimized construction is that it avoids the construction of irrelevant values.

The optimized SS for a query φ is obtained as follows:

1. add the new start symbol (φ applied to the previous start symbol) and the new rule for it.
2. apply the rewrite rules to generate alternative execution plans:
   (a) The *grammar rewriting rules* push queries down the grammar specification. In the previous example, these rules are used to obtain (1,4,5). It is applied when in a rule, each occurrence of some $\$i$ is inside some unique algebraic

query ψ (i.e. as $\psi(\$i)$). It replaces $\psi(\$i)$ by $\$i$ and replaces the corresponding parser, say $\langle A\rangle$ by $\langle\psi(A)\rangle$. If such a rule does not exist yet, it adds a rule for parsing $\langle\psi(A)\rangle$ in the obvious way.

(b) Apply algebraic *query rewriting rules* to the algebraic expressions in the action parts of the rules. In the previous example, these rules were applied to obtain (2,3,6).

The algorithm stops when no rewrite rules can be applied. In the best case (e.g. the previous example), the only values that are constructed are the ones returned by the query. In the worst case, the query remains at the root of the parse-tree and the whole database is constructed. In the rest of this section we study further certain subtle aspects of the technique, and in particular consider some limitations which introduce complexity. To conclude the section, we also extend the technique to databases with objects.

3.2 A Closer Look at the Problem

Some issues raised by the technique are summarized in the following questions:

1. The *grammar rewriting rules* generate new non terminals (e.g. $\langle\varphi(Ref\_Set)\rangle$). Can we get rid of the old nonterminals?
2. In the previous examples, the result of a view is a single set ($$ for the start symbol of the grammar). Is it possible to specify several virtual anchors with a unique grammar?
3. What are the limitations of the technique?

Getting rid of some nonterminals

The *grammar rewriting rules* introduce new nonterminals and thus new rules. Some nonterminals may become obsolete as shown by the *BibTex* example. In the example above, the annotated grammar obtained at the end of the rewriting process contains the nonterminals: $\langle Ref\_Set\rangle$, $\langle\varphi(Ref\_Set)\rangle$, $\langle Reference\rangle$, $\langle\varphi(Reference)\rangle$, etc. Considering the rules defining these non terminals, it must be noted that $\langle Ref\_Set\rangle$ and $\langle Reference\rangle$ are not reachable from the new start symbol $\langle\varphi(Ref\_Set)\rangle$, and thus, may be discarded.

Observe that, in general, the discarding of nonterminals requires a careful reachability analysis of the grammar: a nonterminal $\langle V\rangle$ may be replaced locally by $\langle\varphi(V)\rangle$ in a portion of the grammar but continue to be used in another portion.

Using Several Anchors

Consider the *BibTex* view that we defined above. One may notice that the only access the user has to the data is through the set containing all the references. This may be unsatisfactory in more complex situations. We may want to have a database view with two anchors: one is a set of references (the same as before), and one is a set of authors. Clearly, one could use a database view mechanism and define the second anchor as a view of the first one. This is clearly the correct solution from a conceptual viewpoint. However, this complicates the task of the optimizer when given a query on the set of authors. It is thus more practical to allow SSs to define more than one anchor. We show how this can be done next.

Note that, so far, the construction performed by the SS was essentially functional: at each step the parser builds new values by combining "smaller", previously built, values. This algebraic approach is the core of the optimization technique. One way to build several anchors simultaneously is to have global variables, one variable per anchor, and update them while parsing. This nonfunctional approach however will complicate significantly the optimization task. We thus propose instead the following solution.

Two anchors (say *References* and *Authors*) can be viewed as the fields of a unique tuple describing the entire database. Indeed, suppose we have a SS for each anchor, it is straightforward to construct a SS for the pair. (Some trivial simplifications are used to avoid constructing pairs with identical components.) For example, we now give a SS that constructs both a set of references ($References$) and a set of authors ($Authors$).

```
/* Annotated Grammar */
```

$$
\begin{array}{lll}
\langle BibTex\rangle & \rightarrow \langle Reference\rangle\ \langle BibTex\rangle & \\
 & & \{\$\$:= [Refs : \{\$1\} \cup \$2.Refs, \\
 & & \quad Authors : \$1.Authors \cup \$2.Authors]\} \\
 & \mid\ \epsilon & \{\$\$:= [Refs : \{\}, Authors := \{\}]\} \\
\langle Reference\rangle & \rightarrow \ldots & \\
 & \quad author\text{``}=\text{''}\ \langle Author\_Set\rangle & \\
 & \quad \ldots & \\
 & & \{\$\$:= [\ldots, Authors : \$2, \ldots]\} \\
\langle Author\_Set\rangle & \rightarrow \langle Author\rangle\text{``},\text{''}\langle Author\_Set\rangle & \\
 & & \{\$\$:= \{\$1\} \cup \$2\} \\
 & \mid\ \langle Author\rangle & \\
 & & \{\$\$:= \{\$1\}\} \\
\langle Author\rangle & \rightarrow \#String & \\
 & & \{\$\$:= \$1\}
\end{array}
$$

The set of all authors is accessible from the tuple built by the rules defining the start symbol $\langle BibTex\rangle$. Furthermore, suppose that instead of just building a set containing the authors name, we want a set of pairs with the name of the author as a first field and the set of references (s)he authored as second field. This can also be done. We shall show in Section 3.3 how this is done using objects and side effects: for each new reference, the reference is added to the references set of each of its authors. Without side effects, this entails having a more complex action for the $\langle BibTex\rangle$ nonterminal: for each reduction of the $\langle BibTex\rangle$ rule, the action constructs the set of pairs for the $\langle BibTex\rangle$ parser from the set of pairs returned by the $\langle BibTex\rangle$ sub-parser.

Limitations of the Technique

The technique seems well-fitted for simple queries. We believe that most "practical" queries will essentially involve some selection/projection returning a small amount of data. Nevertheless, we explain below how more complex queries can be treated.

Complex queries are for instance queries that also involve joins. This may mean joining data from several files and more than one SS (e.g. the list of authors cited in a LaTex file when references are stored in another BibTex file) or involving several occurrences of the same view of a file (e.g. same query when the references are stored in the same file). The problem that arises is similar to that of complex queries in any rewriting system. For instance, a join query will be rewritten so as to push selections before the joins. Once this is done, each operand of a join can be "pushed" into the SS, using the optimization algorithm described above. The resulting sets can then be joined. In the OO context, algebraic equivalences for performing this rewriting can be found in [10,11,13]. Of course, in some cases the optimization does not result in much saving and the sub-queries are such that they construct more data than is actually needed (in the worst case, the whole data corresponding to a view will have to be loaded).

However, the main reason for the limitations of the technique is that it has to deal with immutable storage, i.e. the file is accessed in a very specific way, i.e. sequential parsing. Our technique (so far) also constrains the possibilities: the query is answered by a structuring schema which does not allow side effects. As an example, consider again the BibTex example. Suppose that we want to select the reference with a certain keyword, say "AA92". Note that although the selection will be pushed to the leaves of the query tree, the optimized parser will still construct the set of authors for all references (no matter if they have the relevant keyword or not). This is because the parsing of one sub tree is independent of the parsing of other sub-trees, and thus the parser of $\langle Author\_Set \rangle$ does not know whether the reference to which this set belongs has the keyword "AA92" or not. Note that allowing parsing with side effects can lead here to more optimization: it suffices to have a global variable indicating whether this is the case, and to have the parser for set of authors construct its set only if necessary.

3.3 Dealing with objects

In this section, we consider an extension of the technique to handle objects. To allow our SSs to construct objects, we extend the set of operations used in the action part of rules and add a *new* operation that allows the (virtual) creation of objects. For instance, we can define a class *References* with associated type $tuple(Key : string, Authors : \ldots)$, and modify the BibTex SS as follows: replace the action $\$\$:= [Key : \$1, Authors : \$2 \ldots]$ in the definition of $\langle Reference \rangle$ by $\$\$:= new(References, [Key : \$1, Authors : \$2 \ldots])$. Thus, the file will be represented by set of objects of class *References* (rather than by a set of tuples).

Suppose that we want to evaluate the query

$$\begin{array}{l}\textbf{select } r\\ \textbf{from } \; r \textbf{ in } References\\ \textbf{where } r.Key = \text{"}TLE90\text{"}.\end{array}$$

This is query is very similar to one considered at the beginning of Section 3.1, except that it returns the whole object and not only the title attribute. Essentially, the same optimization technique can be applied, and will push the selection into the SS. It is important to observe that the rewriting is such that the resulting SS (that constructs the answer to the query) creates objects only for references whose keyword is $TLE90$. This is achieved using the following rewriting (we focus only on the part of the optimization involving object creation):

$$\sigma_{Key=\text{"}TLE90\text{"}}(new(References, [Key : \$1, Authors : \$2 \ldots]))$$

$$\leadsto$$

$$new(References, \sigma_{Key=\text{"}TLE\text{"}}([Key : \$1, Authors : \$2 \ldots]))$$

Observe that object creation and selection commute. The advantage of pushing down the selection into the object creation is that when the selection fails, it returns $\perp$, and then object creation also fails and returns $\perp$. So, we avoid creating unnecessary objects which results in dramatic gain in performance. Observe furthermore that, if the query should ask only for the title instead of the whole object, then the object creation would be completely absorbed (by pushing the projection) and no objects at all would be created.

The usage of objects in the above SS is rather simple and does not involve an important essence of the object-oriented model: object sharing. To conclude this section, we consider the two main issues raised by object sharing:

1. How do we avoid duplication of objects?
2. How do we handle cyclic data?

Avoiding Duplicates of Objects

As shown in [3], duplicate elimination is a crucial problem for languages allowing the creation of objects. We will see that it is also true in our context. To illustrate this, we visit again the BibTex example. Assume now that we want to represent authors by objects. For that, we may define a class of Authors (where the state of objects in the class contains a string representing the authors name).

$$\textbf{class} Authors = String$$

and annotate the rule defining the non terminal $\langle Author\rangle$ as follows:

$$\langle Author\rangle \rightarrow \#String\{\$\$:= new(Authors, \$1)\}$$

Note however that in this SS every occurrence of a name will cause the creation of a new object. Thus an author who wrote many papers will be represented by many objects; a new object will be created for each reference. What we would like to have is one object for each author name, and have all the references where this name appears pointing to the author object. We thus have to give the user the means to avoid duplicates. We do that by introducing a new primitive that we call *conditional new* ($cnew$). The usage of this new primitive is demonstrated below:

$$\langle Author \rangle \rightarrow string\{\$\$:= cnew(Author, \lambda x.\sigma_{x=\$1}, \$1)\}$$

The *conditional new* primitive requires three parameters: the name of a class, a query and a value. The query is applied to the extent of the class whose name is denoted by the first parameter. If it returns the empty set, an object is created and added to the class extent. The value (state) of the object is given by the third parameter. If the query returns a nonempty set, the "first" object of this set will be assigned to $$ (if the program is correct, there will only be one object in the returned set). In the above example the query component operates on the whole state of the object. In most practical cases the query will only compare the value of certain key attributes. (We shall see an example below).

It must be noted that this primitive requires that the system maintains the extent of the class. Note that this means having several anchors (one extent = one anchor) and that we addressed this problem in Section 3.2. If one wants to optimize queries on class extents, their members should be pushed up the grammar specification and also maintained at the root of the grammar.

Let us now consider the effect of having a conditional new on the optimization process. The problem is that now the constructions performed in non overlapping part of the tree is no longer independent. Objects created in one particular subtree p_1 may be used (tested for existence) in neighbouring subtrees $p_2, p_3, .., p_n$. Thus, even if the query we are considering is not concerned with the information generated by p_1, the construction must still be performed in order to preserve the structure generated in $p_2, p_3, .., p_n$.

One possible solution to this problem involves distinguishing a special type of class and nonterminals that we call *global*. Given a SS S, we say that a class C is *global* for S if S contains a conditional new operation for that class or any of its subclasses. We say that a nonterminal A in S is *global* if one of its rules contains creation (conditional or not) of objects in global classes or any of their subclasses. The optimization algorithm is then modified so that queries are not pushed into rules defining global literals.

Dealing with Cyclic Data

We next consider cyclic data. A more symmetric way to view references and authors is as objects with the following structure:

$$
\begin{array}{lll}
\textbf{class } Reference & = \textbf{tuple}(& key : string, \\
 & & author\_set : set(authors), \\
 & & title : String, \\
 & & \ldots \qquad) \\
\textbf{class } Author & = \textbf{tuple}(& name : String, \\
 & & refs : set(Reference) \qquad)
\end{array}
$$

This definition introduces a cycle between the references and the authors. A reference will be linked to a set of authors and an author to a set of references. In order to maintain this cyclic data, the user will have to create objects in one place, and update their state in another. This requires using update operations in the SSs. The annotated rules corresponding to the new definition of class *Authors* is as follows:

$$
\begin{array}{ll}
\langle Reference\rangle \rightarrow & \ldots \\
 & \text{“}author = \text{”}\langle Author\_Set\rangle \\
 & \ldots \\
 & \quad \{\$\$:= \mathbf{new}(References, [\ldots, Authors : \$2, \ldots]); \\
 & \quad map_{\lambda x.(x.Refs:=x.Refs \cup \{\$\$\})}(\$2)\} \\
\langle Author\rangle & \rightarrow \#String \\
 & \quad \{\$\$:= cnew(Author, \lambda x.\sigma_{x.Name=\$1}, \\
 & \qquad\qquad [name : \$1, refs : \{\}])\}
\end{array}
$$

In the rule defining $\langle Reference\rangle$, the variable \$2 denotes a set of authors. The *map* primitive is used to apply the update function to every elements of this set. The *map* statement adds the current reference to each author to the set of authors.

The fact that we have update operations, and allow the action part to contain a sequence of statements complicates the optimization process: under what conditions can a query be pushed into a rule involving updates and when pushing is allowed, how is a query pushed into a sequence of updates?

Assume, for example, that we want to evaluate $\Pi_{key}(References)$. Since the rule defining $\langle Ref\_Set\rangle$ contains only one assignment to \$\$, and no additional updates, the query can be pushed into this rule as before. After further (query) rewriting, we would like to push Π_{Key} into the rule defining $\langle Reference\rangle$. Now, having an added update after the assignment on \$\$, we have to check if this update affects the *Key* attribute. Since the update does not modify the key and is irrelevant to the query result, it can be removed from the rule, and the query can be pushed as before into the expression assigned to \$\$.

On the other hand, consider the query $\sigma_{Key=\text{“}TLE90\text{”}}(References)$. At some point of the optimization process, one wants to push the query into the rule defining $\langle Reference\rangle$. Note that this query returns the whole reference, including the $Authors$ attribute. Thus clearly we can not remove the update to the set of authors.

Furthermore, since the value of $$ is used to update the $Refs$ attribute of the authors, the query must not be pushed into the expression assigned to $$.

When objects are involved, updates to one attribute can affect the value of other attributes. This is due to object sharing. The relationship between the various assignments and updates in a rule can be very tricky. One possible simple solution is to forbid pushing queries into rules involving updates. A more lenient solution is to distinguish special cases (like the one mentioned above) where query pushing is safe, and develop rewrite rules to handle such specific cases.

4 From Databases to Files

Structuring schemas define a mapping from a file to a database. As shown in [2], this mapping can be inverted in some cases, and can be used to unparse a database and generate a file. In this case, the mapping from databases to files is not specified directly but is rather a derivative of the mapping from files to databases. The possibility of specifying the mapping directly is interesting. Indeed, the mapping from databases to files is at the core of database report generation, and taken together with the mapping from files to database it is often nowadays the main support for interoperating a database and other applications (data being exchanged via files).

We do not consider here the direct mapping from databases to files in detail. But we cannot ignore it entirely since structuring schemas that are used in practice may have been generated by inverting such mapping. Indeed, an important direction of research is the validation of the specific classes of structuring schemas (e.g. local schemas) in order to be able to generate automatically inverting mappings from databases to files.

We assume that we have structured data in a database and want to produce a string (with an associated grammar) containing some of the database information. To encode data as a string, we need (i) to specify the object or value u to encode; (ii) the encodings of its components (if any); and (iii) the encoding of u (eventually based on that of its components). This yields the following cases:

- For base types (**int, real, string**, etc.), we only need to specify the format of the encoding.
- For tuples, we have to specify the encoding of components and that of the tuple in terms of the components.
- For **collection types**, we may want to use some iteration, and for instance, the structural induction operator of [5]. The structural induction φ on a set X with parameters f, g, h is defined by:

$$\begin{aligned} \varphi(f,g,h)(\emptyset) &= f \\ \varphi(f,g,h)(\{x\} \cup X) &= h(g(x), \varphi(X)). \end{aligned}$$

  For instance, to encode a set X with members of type T, we can use: (a) a function g encoding T elements, (b) the function f returning the empty string; and (c) h defined by: for each u, v,

$$h(u,v) = concat(u,\ \text{“,”}\ , v).$$

Observe that, in this case, the resulting string depends on the order of the elements that is chosen. In that sense, the operation is non-deterministic. (This is not surprising since, in general, structural induction is non-deterministic.)

- The most interesting issue is that of encoding of objects. There are many possibilities to encode an object id, depending of the database model: logical oid's (if supported by the system), external oid (generated for the "externalization" of the object), or using a query that qualifies the object. One is also led to encode the state of the object together with some surrogate for this object. In presence of cyclic data, it is then necessary to avoid entering into loops. These choices have dramatic impact on the performance of the system and indeed even on its semantics.

Some important issues also arise:

1. The choice of the specific encoding, and consequently the structure of the resulting file, depends on the application. In some cases the resulting file should obey a fixed grammar (e.g. HTML). In other cases, the grammar may be determined by the particular database being processed. The grammar of the resulting file may also need to have a specific format (Yacc, SGML, etc.).
2. Another issue is that for large and/or complex data, one may not want to generate one large file, but rather to build several files — a *directory* with potential references between the various files.
3. Another issue is the selection of the portion of the database that is represented in the file and its consistency (avoiding dangling references).
4. The last issue is architectural. Typically, the task of generating a file may be split between three partners: (i) the database, via a view definition module that may restructure and prepare data, (ii) the report writer that generates the file, and (iii) eventually a tool that does some post processing on the file. This may be some simple stream editor (e.g. sed) or a more sophisticated tool that may involve reparsing of the file (e.g. SGML editor). The relationship and coorparation mode of these partners needs to be investigated.

5 Conclusion

We studied a general framework for queries specified logically on a database, to a file that actually stores the data (in a structured manner). We presented a technique for optimizing the queries. We also specified how data could be converted from databases to files. Another issue remains the propagation of updates to files using a database update language. This is addressed in [2].

To simplify the presentation we considered here a rather simple type system, e.g. without union types. (The impact of objects has been considered.) It would be interesting to study the impact of other modelling features (and in particular, union of types) on the technique.

Acknowledgements. We thank Eric Angel, Vassilis Christophides, Sophie Gamerman, Laurent Herr, Bernard Lang, Jean-Claude Mamou, Michel Scholl for discussions on the topic. Eric, Laurent, et Vassilis are also thanked for their implementations of part of these ideas.

References

1. S. Abiteboul and C. Beeri. On the manipulation of complex objects. Technical report, INRIA and Hebrew Univ., 1988.
2. S. Abiteboul, S. Cluet, and T. Milo. A database interface to file updates. In *Proc. ACM SIGMOD Conference*, 1995.
3. S. Abiteboul and P. Kanellakis. Identity as a query language primitive. In *Proc. SIGMOD, Portland, Oregon*, 1989.
4. C. Beeri and Y. Kornatzky. Algebraic optimization of object-oriented query languages. In *Proc. ICDT, Paris, France*, 1990.
5. V. Breazu-Tannen, P. Buneman, and S. Naqvi. Structural recursion as a query language. In *Conf. on Database Programming Languages, DBPL*, 1991.
6. R. Cattell, editor. *The Object Database Standard: ODMG 93*. Morgan Kaufmann, to appear.
7. S. Cluet and C. Delobel. A general framework for the optimization of object-oriented queries. In *ACM SIGMOD Conf. on Management of Data*, pages 383–392, 1992.
8. O. Deux et al. The story of o2. *IEEE Transaction on Knowledge and Data Engineering*, 2(1), March 1989.
9. T.W. Reps and T. Teitelboum. *The Synthesizer Generator, A system for Constructing language based editors*. Springer-Verlag, 1989.
10. G. Shaw and S. Zdonik. An object-oriented query algebra. In *Proc. DBPL, Salishan Lodge, Oregon*, 1989.
11. G.M. Shaw and S.B. Zdonik. A query algebra for object-oriented databases. In *IEEE Conference on Data Engineering*, pages 154–162, 1990.
12. N.C. Shu, B.C. Housel, R.W. Taylor, S.P. Ghosh, and V.Y. Lum. Express: a data extraction, processing, and restructuring system. *ACM Transactions on Database Systems*, 2(2), June 1977.
13. D. Straube and T. Özsu. Queries and query processing in object-oriented database systems. *ACM Trans. on Information Systems*, 8(4):387–430, 1990.
14. J.D. Ullman. *Principles of Database and Knowledge Base Systems: Volume I and II*. Computer Science Press, 1988.

Chapter 3.3.2

Updating the File*

Serge Abiteboul[1], Sophie Cluet[1], and Tova Milo[2]

[1] INRIA., B.P. 105, 78153 Le Chesnay Cedex, France
[2] Department of Computer Science, Tel Aviv University, Tel Aviv, Israel

1 Introduction

This text is a complement Chapter 3.3.1. It sketches the solution we propose for the propagation of updates specified at the database level (here a view specified using structuring schemas) to a file (here the physical storage).

Structuring schemas enable us to conveniently express updates on files using high-level database languages that work on the database view of the file. The key problem is how to propagate an update. As a first step, we propose a *naive* way of update propagation: (i) the database view of the file is materialized; (ii) the update is performed on the database; (iii) the database is "unparsed" to generate an updated file. The first two steps are rather obvious. The last one is more problematic. In [1], we present an *unparsing* technique. The problems that we meet while developing this technique are related to the well-known view update problem. The technique relies on the existence of an inverse mapping from the database to the file.

- We show that the existence of such an inverse mapping results from the use of restricted structuring schemas.
- We also show that unparsing may result in information loss. A file may be changed by a parsing-unparsing process. This is due to the fact that operators we use in the action part of the annotated grammars do not guarantee a one-to-one mapping. For instance, a set construction in an action will eliminate duplicates. We introduce a class of lossless structuring schemas.
- Finally, we show that the unparsing process may fail after a modification accepted by the database. This happens when the database satisfies the typing restriction posed by the database schema, but the database is not anymore the image of some file (according to the structured schema). We say that a structuring schema is constraint-free if this cannot occur. We show that one may decide if one element of the lossless class of structuring schemas is constraint free.

The *naive* technique presents major drawbacks. It is inefficient: it entails intense data construction and unparsing, most of which dealing with data not involved in the update. It may result in information loss: information in the file, that is not recorded in the database, may be lost in the process. A major contribution of [1] is a combination of techniques that allows us to minimize both the data construction

* This text is a synopsis of [1].

and the unparsing work. First, we show how query optimization techniques can be used to focus on the relevant portion of the database and to avoid constructing the entire database. Then we show that for a class of structuring schemas satisfying a *locality* condition, it is possible to carefully circumscribe the unparsing. This relies on the existence of a corespondance between the nodes of the database tree and the nodes of the syntax tree.

Some of the results we have are negative. They should not come as a surprise since we are dealing with complex theoretical foundations: language theory (for parsing and unparsing), and first-order logic (for database languages). However, we do present positive results for particular classes of structuring schemas. We believe that the restrictions imposed on these schemas are very acceptable in practical situations. (For instance, all "real" examples of structuring schemas that we examined are *local*.)

References

1. S. Abiteboul, S. Cluet, and T. Milo. A database interface to file updates. In *Proc. ACM SIGMOD Conference*, 1995.

Chapter 3.3.3

Lean Languages and Models: Towards an Interoperable Kernel for Persistent Object Systems*

Joachim W. Schmidt and Florian Matthes

Technical University Hamburg-Harburg, Harburger Schloßstraße 20, D-21071 Hamburg, Germany

1 Introduction

Reliable interoperation between independently developed Persistent Object Systems (POS) requires type-safe access to persistent data objects and generic services:

Persistent Object Management: It is necessary to identify, store, retrieve and manipulate objects that outlive a single program execution and that may even exist independently of the application that created them. Appropriate naming and scoping mechanisms are required to establish temporary or persistent bindings between persistent objects created independently, possibly using different tools on different machines.

Data Integrity: Type systems represent a particularly successful approach to enforce integrity constraints on data objects local to a single program. Similarly, language-independent mechanisms have to be provided for shared, persistent objects.

Generic Functions: Many functions required in a POS can be obtained by instantiating generic services. Interoperation protocols have to be capable of handling these generic functions without diminishing data integrity or duplicating code.

In this paper we seek to contribute to the answers of three interrelated questions: What are appropriate semantic models to describe POS interaction? How can these semantics be captured in a sound and concise linguistic framework? What is the impact of such lean languages and models on their supporting system architectures and their import and export interfaces?

2 Persistent Object System Model

We introduce a POS model to describe the naming, typing and binding concepts involved in Persistent Object System interoperability. The model itself is based on concepts of higher-order type systems and is sufficiently expressive to serve as a language-independent framework for program translation, generation and binding.

* This text is a synopsis of [4].

The POS model is based on the notion of *types*, *signatures*, *values* and *bindings*. Types are understood as (partial) specifications of values. Types include a set of base types, type **Any**, user-defined type variables, function types, aggregated signatures and type operator applications. Type operators denote parameterized type expressions that map types or type operators to types or type operators. Values and types can be named in bindings for identification purposes and to introduce shared or recursive structures at the value and the type level. Signatures act as (partial) specifications of static and dynamic bindings. Bindings are embedded into the syntax of values, i.e. they can be named, passed as parameters, etc. Accordingly, signatures appear in the syntax of types to describe these aggregated bindings. The exact mutual dependencies are defined in the full paper.

Interoperability aims at providing flexible and safe mechanisms to share data and programs across system boundaries. We demonstrate how the POS model captures modularization as basis for interoperability, distribution (cross-platform interoperability), persistence (interoperability over time) and bulk data abstractions as provided by the DBPL database programming environment (see Chapter 2.1.2).

Modularization DBPL programs are divided into modules with well-defined import relationships. Definition modules define signatures for type, value and location bindings defined in implementation modules. Program modules export a single, parameterless function value, the main program.

Distribution The distributed version of DBPL [1,2] adds an additional layer of type-safety to standard remote procedure call mechanisms (RPC) in federated client-server programming models. In terms of the POS model, RPC-based communication mechanisms are an implementation technology that enables the creation of function value bindings between names in a client program and function values in a server program. The POS model is also capable of giving precise signatures to the the generic client and server stub generators working themselves on signatures and bindings. The signatures of the generator functions illustrate a crucial feature of the POS model: it allows the user to capture type dependencies between the arguments and the result of a generic function.

*clientStubGenerator :*__Fun__*(Scope<:*__Sig__*() Iface<:*__Sig__*())* __Fun__*(s :ServerId) Iface*

Each application of the client stub generator to an argument of type *Iface* will return a function that returns values of type *Iface* (*parametric polymorphism*). Since the supertype specified in the generator signature (*Iface<:*__Sig__*()*) is different from the type **Any**, this form of universal type quantification is also called *bounded parametric polymorphism*. On the other hand, in contrast to classical models of polymorphism, we are assuming that the (function) value returned by the generators *depends* on its type argument.

Persistence The concept of orthogonal persistence extends the potential for interoperability along two new dimensions: sharing over time and sharing between multiple users. Bindings to persistent locations are implemented by maintaining (at compile-

and at run-time) a mapping between module-level location names and *external* locations and by having the compiler insert *save* and *load* operations at appropriate code positions for values of appropriate granularity.

Bulk Data In the process of building a POS, it is often necessary to handle large, dynamic homogeneous collections of objects (e.g. class extents). Furthermore, it is necessary to represent relationships between object collections and to perform efficient, set-oriented update and retrieval operations. DBPL provides a generic bulk types operator *Relation* and predefined polymorphic operations on values of type relation. Relations can be viewed as collections of *location* bindings (indexed by the key values defined in the relation type declaration). Consequently, it makes sense to provide element-oriented update operators and destructive iteration capabilities. Relation types provide a good example for the use of type operators and type-parameterized functions in the POS model. The built-in DBPL type environment could be represented as follows:

DBPLBuiltinEnv ≡ **Sig**(
    Relation <:**Oper**(*ElementType*<:**Any**) **Any**
    {} :**Fun**(*E* <:**Any**) *Relation*(**Any**)
    CARD :**Fun**(*E* <:**Any** *rel* :*Relation(E)*) **Int**
    :+ :**Fun**(*E* <:**Any** **var** *lhs* :*Relation(E)* *rhs* :*Relation(E)*) **Any**
    . . .)

This environment declares a type operator *Relation* that maps arbitrary types (subtypes of type **Any**) to a hidden representation type (a subtype of type **Any**). The subsequent function signatures make use of this type operator to express the type constraints on the built-in DBPL functions. For example, the standard function **CARD** takes an arbitrary type argument *E*, a relation *rel* of type *Relation(E)* and returns the cardinality of the relation, a value of type **Int**.

3 Interoperability and Genericity

The notion of interoperability applies to a more general setting in which independently developed, *generic* systems have to cooperate, i.e. to provide for inter-object interactions that handle *all* potential objects the systems may create and maintain. In the full paper we report on our experience with such generic cross-language interoperability via the DBPL/C and the DBPL/SQL gateway and outline general requirements for generic gateway implementation. We continue focusing on the underlying naming, typing and binding concepts presented in terms of the POS model.

The most primitive (but also most common) form of cross-language interoperability is achieved by having a standardized, language-independent link format that allows static bindings in a language L_{imp} to bind to values or locations defined in another language L_{exp}. In this setting, L_{imp} is able to import from L_{exp}. The next step is to define standardized, language-independent parameters passing conventions that allow argument values or argument locations defined in L_{imp} to be bound dynamically to function parameters defined in L_{exp}. If the roles of L_{imp} and L_{exp} can be interchanged, full cross-language interoperability (including "call-back" mechanisms) is supported.

Cross-language linking is an instance-base interoperability mechanism limited to individual function and data values. DBPL generalizes these concepts to provide transparent translation of families of data structures and expressions that are defined in terms of generic types and polymorphic functions. Analogous to external function bindings, DBPL supports bindings to external persistent objects in addition to internal persistent DBPL objects [3].

All DBPL statements and expressions referring to these variables are translated fully transparently into SQL update and selection expressions submitted to the database management system. These SQL expressions typically take DBPL program variables (value and location bindings) as arguments and return (set) values that are converted appropriately for further processing within DBPL.

Although the system details of the DBPL/SQL gateway are quite delicate and often require ad-hoc case analysis to achieve good system performance, this specific gateway implementation follows a more general pattern that directly reflects the model of typed programming languages in terms of types, signatures, values and bindings. In order to extend a language L_{int} by a generic gateway to an external language L_{ext} successfully (i.e. to embed L_{ext} as a sublanguage of L_{int}), the following conditions have to be met.

The *type* syntax of L_{int} must be sufficiently expressive to capture the structure of values in L_{ext}. This may require extensions to the set of base types (e.g. to handle SQL date, time and table key values) as well as extensions to the set of type constructors (e.g. to handle SQL relations, views or indices). In DBPL, the base type extensions are covered by user-defined abstract data types, while the type constructors are mapped to built-in DBPL type constructors.

There have to be tools to aid in the mapping between *signatures* in L_{int} and L_{ext}. Instead of writing a generator that maps from SQL schema information to DBPL database definitions or vice versa, we developed an interactive binding tool that automatically extracts signature information from DBPL module descriptions and the SQL data dictionary and verifies the compatibility of these separately developed descriptions.

Tool support is also required at run-time to establish value and location *bindings* from names in L_{int} to entities in L_{ext} and vice versa. If *expressions* of L_{ext} are to be generated from (a subset of) expressions in L_{int} (e.g. SQL queries based on DBPL queries), the expression syntax of L_{int} has to be sufficiently general to emulate high-level external abstractions present in L_{ext}.

Finally, there have to be means to ensure that typing assumptions in the static compilation context of L_{int} (expressed, for example, as signatures of database variables) are met by the corresponding bindings provided in L_{ext} at run-time. In the DBPL/SQL context, this limited form of dynamic type checking is achieved by having the compiler generate run-time type representations for external database variables that are checked during program startup (accessing the SQL data dictionary).

In addition to these linguistic and technical prerequisites, a smooth integration of internal and external services also requires adequate architectural support, like access to the scoping and typing phase of the compiler, support for separate compilation and persistent storage of type and signature information, or abstract program representations that support static (and possibly dynamic) program analysis and translation.

4 Towards Open Communicating Environments

In contrast to DBPL, Tycoon (see Chapters 1.1.1 and 2.1.4) takes a rather radical approach by not maintaining upward compatibility with existing programming languages and data models. Also its internal protocols for store access, program representation and linkage do not adhere to pre-existing standards. The Tycoon environment minimizes the amount of built-in system and language support by exploiting higher-order type concepts and by strictly separating the issues of data storage, data manipulation and data modeling into three distinct formalisms and system layers.

The rationale behind the design of Tycoon is to provide a lean language and system environment that provides just the kernel services and abstractions needed to define higher-level, problem-oriented "languages" and "data models". We expect such lean languages and systems, where most of the functionality of a Persistent Object System is achieved by importing external services into a conceptually sound linguistic framework, to possess a higher potential for scalability, portability and interoperability than classical "all-in-one" database systems.

Acknowledgements. This research was supported by ESPRIT Basic Research, Project FIDE, #6309.

References

1. W. Johannsen, L. Ge, W. Lamersdorf, K. Reinhard, and J.W. Schmidt. Database application support in open systems: Language support and implementation. In *Proceedings of the IEEE Fourth International Conference on Data Engineering, Los Angeles, California*, February 1988.
2. W. Johannsen, W. Lamersdorf, K. Reinhard, and J.W. Schmidt. The DURESS project: Extending databases into an open systems architecture. In *Proceedings of the First Conference on Extending Database Technology, EDBT'88*, volume 303 of *Lecture Notes in Computer Science*, pages 616–620. Springer-Verlag, 1988.
3. F. Matthes, A. Rudloff, J.W. Schmidt, and K. Subieta. A gateway from DBPL to Ingres: Modula-2, DBPL, SQL+C, Ingres. FIDE Technical Report Series FIDE/92/54, FIDE Project Coordinator, Department of Computing Sciences, University of Glasgow, Glasgow G128QQ, August 1992.
4. J.W. Schmidt and F. Matthes. Lean languages and models: Towards an interoperable kernel for persistent object systems. In *Proceedings of the IEEE International Workshop on Research Issues in Data Engineering*, pages 2–16, April 1993.

List of Contributors

FSC
www.fsc.org
MIX
Papier | Fördert gute Waldnutzung
FSC® C083411

Kolibri 360 GmbH
Ferdinand-Jühlke-Straße 7
99095 Erfurt, Deutschland
produktsicherheit@kolibri360.de